Unveiling a Better World

Deconstructing the Veracity of the American Fable

Corey David Haag

Unveiling a Better World
Deconstructing the Veracity of the American Fable

Published by Corey David Haag

Thanks to all the Free people who have dedicated themselves to sharing the light of knowledge and truth with the world.

Haag, Corey David
Unveiling a Better World
Deconstructing the Veracity of the American Fable
Cover Illustration by Idrees Nait and Eric Yan
First Edition (ISBN) 9780578293110 (ISBN) 9798218000776
1. American Mythology 2. Statism 3. Anarchism 4. Freedom 5. End the Fed 6. Liberation 7. Plandemic 8. Plutocracy 9. Modern Day Slavery 10. Civil War

Corey David Haag
contact@coreyhaag.com
www.coreyhaag.com

CONTENTS

Let us not, I beseech you, sir, deceive ourselves. Sir, we have done everything that could be done, to avert the storm which is now coming on. We have petitioned; we have remonstrated; we have supplicated; we have prostrated ourselves before the throne, and have implored its interposition to arrest the tyrannical hands of the ministry and Parliament. Our petitions have been slighted; our remonstrances have produced additional violence and insult; our supplications have been disregarded; and we have been spurned, with contempt, from the foot of the throne. In vain, after these things, may we indulge the fond hope of peace and reconciliation. There is no longer any room for hope. If we wish to be free, if we mean to preserve inviolate those inestimable privileges for which we have been so long contending if we mean not basely to abandon the noble struggle in which we have been so long engaged, and which we have pledged ourselves never to abandon until the glorious object of our contest shall be obtained, we must fight! I repeat it, sir, we must fight! An appeal to arms and to the God of Hosts is all that is left us!

They tell us, sir, that we are weak; unable to cope with so formidable an adversary. But when shall we be stronger? Will it be the next week, or the next year? Will it be when we are totally disarmed, and when a British guard shall be stationed in every house? Shall we gather strength by irresolution and inaction? Shall we acquire the means of effectual resistance, by lying supinely on our backs, and hugging the delusive phantom of hope, until our enemies shall have bound us hand and foot? Sir, we are not weak if we make a proper use of those means which the God of nature hath placed in our power. Three millions of people, armed in the holy cause of liberty, and in such a country as that which we possess, are invincible by any force which our enemy can send against us. Besides, sir, we shall not fight our battles alone. There is a just God who presides over the destinies of nations; and who will raise up friends to fight our battles for us. The battle, sir, is not to the strong alone; it is to the vigilant, the active, the brave. Besides, sir, we have no election. If we were base enough to desire it, it is now too late to retire from the contest. There is no retreat but in submission and slavery! Our chains are forged! Their clanking may be heard on the plains of Boston! The war is inevitable and let it come! I repeat it, sir, let it come.

It is in vain, sir, to extenuate the matter. Gentlemen may cry, Peace, Peace but there is no peace. The war is actually begun! The next gale that sweeps from the north will bring to our ears the clash of resounding arms! Our brethren are already in the field! Why stand we here idle? What is it that gentlemen wish? What would they have? Is life so dear, or peace so sweet, as to be purchased at the price of chains and slavery? Forbid it, Almighty God! I know not what course others may take; but as for me, give me liberty or give me death!

Patrick Henry, March 23, 1775

Opening Statements

I am authoring this book to illuminate the divisiveness of our society, and how we can come together to fight the real monster hidden in plain sight among us. I am writing this book for the silenced politician who wants to make this world a better place but is faced with the social pressure and implicit violence in divergent expression. I am writing this for the homosexual, gun carrying Muslim immigrant who is faced with acute social pressure from other Muslims and much of the general population as well as higher chances of prejudicial violence from police and the justice system. I am writing this for the gentle warrior who feels incapable of making a significant change in our corrupted world. I am writing this for the violated and incarcerated cannabis grower who has to endure prison with murderers and rapists for growing a plant. I am writing this for the police officer who sincerely wants to serve, who deals with death daily and makes the best of those experiences and being despised by much of the population he serves, continues to stay uncorrupted. I am writing this for the widowed mother who works three unfulfilling and grueling jobs to provide a modicum of wellbeing for her children. I am writing this for the college graduate with a hundred thousand dollars of debt and no job prospects. I am writing this for the 64-year-old man who prays every day for his benefits to still exist tomorrow that he worked his whole life accruing. I am writing this for the people who have been consumed by the obese and insatiable media indoctrination system. I am writing this for the seventy percent of Americans who are overweight and encouraged to be so by their local fast-food restaurant and mega-box store. I am writing this for the 7th generation family farmer who is standing on their property for the last time before they are forced to leave it because the government cited eminent domain to run an oil pipeline for Exxon Mobil. I am writing this for the father of a child who, after being diagnosed with cancer, was killed with chemotherapy so their doctor could profit off the sale of that poison. I am writing this for the orphan who is raped by the government and religious officials charged with their care. I am writing this for the people living in gated communities who have never witnessed poverty or pain, and never had to work to survive, yet firmly believe that all people who do not pull themselves up by their bootstraps are lazy. I am writing this for the Native American women who are kidnapped by sex traffickers and police all the same and very rarely looked for when they do go missing. I am writing this for the anarchists, the whistleblowers, the revolutionaries, the futurists, the radical roots, the believers, the farmers, the laborers, the truth-seekers and truth-speakers, and all the people who are waiting for the right moment. I am writing this for the nations that have been destroyed by the greed and apathy of a few men in suits. I am writing this for the human being who is forced to watch as multinational corporations and the average people decimate the environment that keeps us all alive. I am writing this for the children, who will live longer than me and be witness to a world tomorrow when I am gone, that I have the ability to make better today. I am writing this for me, and I am writing this for you.

What happened to honor and valor? Where have courage and strength of will been lost? What manner of evil has triumphed, to conquer our basic and natural dispositions? Who can yet hold firm in righteousness in a world so full of disease? Who can yet remain simple and grateful in the excessiveness and avarice of our modern society? Are we not yet ready, even after so much destruction and wasted life, after uncounted years of unnecessary divisiveness and petty disputes? Who is above reproach, and equally unadulterated to such degree that they have the right to rebuke others? Is it not an easier and more beautiful and fulfilling world, one in which we forgive ourselves, our kin, and our appointed enemies? Is it not a wiser world, one that requires no greater deeds than that which burns passionately in the hearts of each to their own? Is death really so terrible a threat to be defended against at any cost? Is friendship and family so meaningless as to be traded in for social positioning and worthless shallow interactions that leave everyone in solitary grief? Who are we as a species? What is our character? What is our future?

The design of the current models of governance, economics, and culture in the United States can be analyzed from multitudes of different perspectives, and while these perspectives can offer benefits to the system in parts, the vast majority are not inclusive of the needs and desires of the entire population. In other words, they do not offer holistic solutions to the problems that exist today. Any solution that resolves an issue for an entire population can be considered holistic. When a population is as diverse and complex as the one we encounter in the United States of America and worldwide, our solutions need to be simple and encompassing of the wellbeing of the entire group on general terms all can agree upon, while leaving the complex affairs to the localities and individuals. This means that when government attempts to answer complexity with ever larger bureaucracy, the result will be mismanagement and micromanagement. This can be seen at any level of organization.

When a business owner attempts to resolve all the issues of their business, the workload they encounter is enormous, but when that owner releases control to the ability of managers and employees to resolve issues, along a general guideline of what the business is and where it needs to go, the business will profit from being able to resolve issues in the dynamic environment they exist in. When our managers and employees are also owners of the business, and share in the success, the business becomes even more successful and profitable for everyone. If government exists, it must operate the same way as a worker owned business, such as a co-op. It must exist for the benefit of the individuals within the population, rather than at their expense and slave labor.

We are all of our government, or at least we should be. From the perspective of governments everywhere, they would say that this is the exact model in place, and that enterprising and capable individuals rise naturally to become managers of the business, while less capable remain simple employees. The difference between what I am proposing here and that perspective is that while free markets would support this process, we do not live in a free market. Our government is as much a business entity as Amazon or Bayer Pharmaceuticals are businesses. Our courts are financial institutions operating under layers of legal systems that have been built on top of one another like layers of cities built on top of one another, but while some aspects remain above ground or make up the bones or foundation of the current city, much of the old falls away. Its true nature is an extremely interwoven mesh of legal systems that has less to do practically with its written history than it does with current interpretations by whomever is in a position to dictate opinion. Much of the legal system is based on maritime laws, or the laws that exist on the ocean, which is where much of the international laws that exist today became codified. The reason I say they are financial institutions is that whatever they may be otherwise, currently, courts exist to extort funds from the population through ever increasing "laws" and codes and such, and direct those extracted funds to the federal or state government. The courts are siphons for the mining of the people's pockets in what is likely the most successful extortion racket ever produced. And the people of the nation are the chattel. The free market does not exist for cattle, and neither does it exist for the chattel. What I am proposing then, is the necessary changes in our social construction that will free the slave population and bring about a true free market and individual-centric responsible society, free from Plutocratic overlords and corporate titles used to abuse the people.

When we allow government to dictate and control the entire organization of human social design, we make it impossible to offer holistic solutions within that organism. Government is an organization of humans that endeavors to provide a more or less representative, decision-making body for the population. Representation, management, and leadership are the key aspects of what government has been created to provide. Representation is a way to increase the efficiency of producing results that benefit the population as a whole. The power included in governance is available only under the discretion of the population. The system is abused when we see a governance system that no longer represents the population as a whole, but rather selectively represents aspects of the population. When this occurs, the government is no longer a government for the entire population, but rather a government only for those it represents. This means that the population of unrepresented people no longer have a representative government, and they are subjected to designs and implemented systems that do not lend to their wellbeing.

Systems that create more centralization of power, increase the possibility of the abuse of that power. The more decentralized the power structure becomes, the more unlikely abuse of power will lead to detrimental effects upon the whole population. The point in decentralizing governance is not to eliminate human greed or abuse of power, but rather to reduce the possibility and probability that those that abuse will be able to influence the population as fundamentally or potently. The abuse of power by a monarch or other ultimate central power can be difficult to overcome, even more so a clever democratic republic with hundreds of collaborators, whereas an abuse by a figure in a position of authority in a decentralized governance system would be much more easily, and with much less harm, eradicated.

Even if we ended this conversation here, we would see the benefit in reducing the power and control of any centralized governance structure. This will not be the case here, as we will discover through delving into the benefits and costs of various systems that individual empowerment leads to the greatest wellbeing of the entire population of any organized group of people.

The main problem that can be seen, in the argument for centralized governance is the argument for voluntary slavery. It can be easy for an individual to see benefit in central governance when they are presented with the ease of living without responsibility. In effect, the people can remove their personal responsibility over the outcomes of decisions by giving the power of decision-making to another, or in this case all the people giving that power to a single organization of select individuals that presumably speak for their benefit. When the results do not meet the expectation, as in the government not making decisions that benefit the individual, the individual can easily place blame on that government, while never accepting the responsibility of their original choice to allow the small representative group to make those decisions.

Decentralization is often misinterpreted as promoting unaccountability of participants. It also suffers a perception of synonymity with deregulation, chaos, or inefficiency. Decentralization is more aptly an action of creating more accountability through the mechanism of individual responsibility. This is the responsibility of the individual to be involved in and in control of their governance system. Governance itself is not in opposition to decentralization, which supports government on the level of bottom-up power structures. This is the form of governance that empowers and is responsible to the wellbeing and quality of life of the individual. I will talk about solutions through reformation and other means later in this conversation, but I will say minimally that the entirety of the current governance model in use in the United States would need drastic and fundamental changes to produce a bottom-up model that supports the individual and the right of the individual to create their lives in their own ideal image with respect to the land and their neighbors.

The models of economics that are commonly discussed, sponsored, and supported are of the same basic misconstruction as those of government. The same basic issue is present in that, any model proposed that does not serve the entirety of the population of people the system intends to encompass, it does not actually serve that population. In today's world, with modern technological advances, it is feasible that no person on the planet must suffer from lack of food, shelter, and basic wellbeing, let alone unobstructed access to wellbeing in the way each individual requires and desires. The perception of scarcity is the singular reason for the poverty, or lack of abundance, in the world today. With this in consideration, how is it possible to overcome our current situation and bring about a holistic economy?

While I will be discussing various solutions further on, the basic principle of economics, by which I do not only mean financial economics, but rather the movement of energy from place to place, is to provide for equitable exchange to balance the needs of all participants of a system in the most profitable and efficient manner possible.

While capitalism offers a method of measuring activity through the use of currency, a medium of exchange, in a free market environment, it does not operate within a centralized and monolithic government in its pure form. A free market within a controlled and regulated governance system is oxymoronic. Thus, it is no longer a free market, and thus it is no longer capitalism.

Without government interference, capitalism becomes unregulated, and pure. In its pure form capitalism still does not support the wellbeing of all the individuals in the system, but rather supports individuals with certain characteristics that are favorable in its particular economic design. In other words, capitalism serves those who are productive in the way the society demands at any given time. When economic success or wellbeing is determined by how willing a person is to conform to the demands of the society, the benefit is obvious. It is when we look at the desire of many people to live in ways that do not conform to the demands of the majority, or accepted normality, that we see the problem. It is the people who do not desire to shape their lives around the shifting superficial demands of society that are left out in a capitalism. These are people who wish to live outside of the accepted perception and direction. With this we see that there is a lack of benefit holistically in capitalism whether we use it in conjunction with democracy or other government or in its pure form. When this is seen, we must endeavor to discover another method, or combination of methods, by which to cultivate our economic wellbeing.

The economic benefit in decentralization includes the increase in personal responsibility, in the creation of one's own wellbeing within the economic environment. While a free market may not support all the individuals within the population, when we look to maximize the value of the individual, we see that by localizing, or structuring the economics so that an individual is supported by supporting their local or direct environment, the individual is empowered to find solutions to their economic condition within populations that they are directly involved in and by which they can have an important role to play in the structuring of the systems that are used by that population. This means that individuals are empowered in their direct environment to create wellbeing for all the individuals in that environment, which would reflect upon their own wellbeing. This localization of economic incentive also benefits the population as a whole by lessening the tendency for apathy in employers, corporations, and businesses in general toward their employees, as well as the apathy that is felt from employees toward their employers. This increases incentive in the individual to work for the wellbeing of the group rather than working only for their singular benefit at the exclusion of others. The economic wellbeing of the whole population of a nation, or even the world would be directly related to the wellbeing of the local economies that make it up. The local economies would be beholden to the wellbeing of the individuals that make up their populations. By localizing the economy and eliminating the ability of large corporations and government to plunder and export those economies, we can allow for growth of wellbeing in the local populations based on their own social design. The size of these local economies would extend as far as the needs of the individuals would require. The extraneous desires of the population would be secondary and would be beholden to the will and investment of local populations.

At the same time that we are localizing the focus of economic wellbeing, we also allow local governance, if individuals choose to have such a thing, to determine regulations that can promote wellbeing in the population, while inhibiting the abuses that are common in markets where manufactured scarcity exists. Local governance means that people decide for themselves what social design is most suitable to their needs. They determine to a great degree the rules and regulations of their own society.

If we allow for the fact that scarcity exists only insomuch that markets are limited by control and design, we can see that any system designed on the limits of privately owned currency will involve scarcity and all of the detractive qualities that follow it. Manufactured scarcity is the fundamentally harmful practice of convincing populations of people that a resource or resources are limited so as to make that resource a commodity that can be sold at increasing rates as the resource becomes more and more artificially scarce.

Our technology has advanced in correlation to financial backing by private interests rather than in correlation to human needs. Sometimes these two patterns intersect, but they do not complement each other, except in the technologies that were created that enhanced the wellbeing of people and the environment. When we consider the controlled and selfishly moderated advancement of technology under the perception of scarcity, and just how easy it would be in today's world to create idyllic environments with the use of the technology available to us currently, the fact that we have not used our advancements to their optimum potential means that we have failed greatly in providing wellbeing with the current and previous economic and social models.

Rather than attempting to elevate populations to ideal situations, which would be practically impossible in current conditions, we must focus upon eliminating the practices and models that no longer serve while promoting and implementing the systems that do work in iterations that allow for the system to gradually but determinedly and without deviation from the purpose, change, to elevate the conditions of the individual and thus the entire population and the world as a whole. The sickly world we live in today can become completely renewed and revitalized within one lifetime if the systems, environments, and societies we live within are given the ability to regenerate naturally and the practices that are causing disease and destruction are put to an end.

Rather than exploitative and argumentative rhetoric regarding what is best for entire populations, one fundamental agreement must be made, which is to allow for the active testing of differing practices, and thus to allow for that which perseveres, in absence of intervention, to be the greatest form and structure. Universalizing systems and imposing them upon populations by centralized authorities is the absence of liberty and the implementation of slavery. If we make this one agreement, that different localities can implement unique economic designs based on the desires of the individuals that make up the population, we can provide a real and active experiment without limiting the freedom of the individual. By retaining basic regulations regarding abuse of power and trade at the municipal level more so than the federal or state level, we can observe the ways in which the populations create their abundance. I will continue this in more detail later, but that basic principle will be a model I will promote throughout this conversation. When we decentralize, we create more profitable interactions between the smallest and largest components of an economic design in regard to the inclusive benefit of the individual rather than the exclusive benefit of mega-monopolies and large politically supported corporations. This system of melding self-serving governments with monopolizing corporations is the essence of mercantilism and plutocracy and the single most significant reason for the revolution that formed this country, if not the truest motive for the powerful figures who commanded the revolution. We must recognize the system we have for what it is, recall our history and make the necessary changes to create a future that supports all life. When the individual prospers, so must the system that they operate within. When the system promotes holistic wellbeing, any individual's success will support the wellbeing of the entire population.

In regard to cultural designs in the US, we must look to the components of the mechanism. What we are discussing here is the value of life as is determined through the lens of wellbeing and what that means. What gives quality of life to the population, and in what ways does our current model support actual wellbeing. What can be done to produce actual wellbeing?

What makes it so foreign, strange and difficult for people, especially in this country, to do what is of greatest service to the entire population, when it is of disservice to the interests of small groups of self-identified elites, who themselves live hypocritically in regard to the very same interests or rights being given and sponsored for the entire population?

The normalizing of the corporate mentality and behavior. Apathy becomes a desired trait in business and other parts of life. Lying, stealing and cheating become symbols of the methods to success, which is then emulated. Constant and pervasive activity aimed to result in greater levels of material abundance represent achievement as follows the corporate design. Somewhere along the way, vast swathes of people forgot they were human while they became corporations.

GOVERNMENT

"We live, indeed, in a world where in actual fact the government, the constitution, the whole moral, juridical, political structure of the United States is just about the oldest, the most continuously functioning, of the great states of our world. The paradox is unavoidable: this new country is in some senses one of the oldest—older than socialist Britain, older than the Fourth French Republic, older than any soviet republic, older, incredibly, than the governments of those immemorial lands of the East, India and China." – Crane Brinton[1]

As I said before, there are multitudes of perceptions that circle the issue of how and why governments should exist. Rather than perpetuating the arguments which lead inevitably to more arguments, we must begin to practice various governance models to determine the true benefit of any of the models. Discussion leads to more discussion, while action proves or disproves the ideas proposed. This, along with the dire need for change in the current situation in the United States and the world leads me to conclude that we must take action without delay.

The most prosperous way to move forward is to allow for all the ideas available to be studied in action. This can happen in a structured way that allows for the transitions between systems to accommodate for the desires and needs of the population.

Currently in the US, we have a governance system that gives ultimate power to the federal government, while state governments and municipalities are beholden to it due to multiple factors, not the least of which is that whenever a state or municipality diverts from the will of the Federal Government, they will be threatened with removal of federal subsidies. Without the subsidies, many programs within states and municipalities would end and put political and social pressure on the politicians of those places. When we consider this process, we can understand how the federal government creates a condition of subservience in states and municipalities.

Another control system of our current governance model as used by most parts of the United States, from federally to the smallest municipalities is the way in which voting is conducted and in the way elections offer preferential or mandated choices. Regarding voting, the issues are Duopoly Parties, Factionism, Political Coalitions, the American Electoral System, winner takes all elections, and Plurality Voting amongst others. In the duopoly system we have now, the population of the United States is egregiously manipulated to conform to one of two political parties.

"When people break through the abstractions and labels they often find themselves on the same side with their opposites, especially once discussion gets down to the reality, of where people live, work, play, and raise their families. It is precisely because people want the same basic things in life, with obvious variations, that the ruling powers have driven their divide-and-rule strategies throughout history. Such tactics pit people against people over abstract dogmas or ethnicities. This enables self-interested, corporate-sponsored political parties to thrive from such destructive and distractive hostilities."
– Ralph Nadar, Breaking Through Power[2]

This is done largely by using the media to create factionism and a religious fervor amongst the voting population. Both major parties are empowered and incited toward extreme oppositional feelings and thoughts toward the other. This creates states of emotional decision-making and predetermined choices based on ones entrenched position in the cultural program that encourages shaming and shunning those who think outside of their predetermined social posture. Political Coalitions are a way in which these entrenched peoples gather to influence the political process in favor of their exclusive goals. The American Electoral System is basically a system that allows for the purchasing of votes by the small group of people who cast the meaningful votes for political positions. The Electoral College can and has ignored the will of the population in electing the less publicly favorable candidates. This means that the votes of the people are in effect meaningless except to measure the motivations of the people and their state of mind. Winner takes all elections encourage voters to cast votes based on the lesser of two evils. It means that between the two candidates who are seen as the only candidates with the possibility of winning the election, the voters will choose not based on who they think will benefit them but rather by who will harm them less. In Plurality Voting, one candidate is chosen to fill one position, which discourages third party voting, which in turn makes it difficult for third parties to access political positions and leaves minority representation absent and silent.

How can we evolve our systems and what solutions can be implemented immediately to resolve the restrictions on the individual's ability to work toward the creation their ideal governance? Firstly, it is easy to see that in a system that inhibits the will of the population to express itself fully through the process of electing representatives of their will, we will observe the decline in interest, trust, and viability of that system. With the use of media manipulation, this process of declination has been significantly slowed, but is none the less occurring. Secondly, we must account for the will of the people who genuinely and knowingly desire for the system to work exactly in the way that it is. These loyalists will fight for the continuation of the current system even when they only profit conceptually, philosophically, or socially.

Some of the things we can do immediately to produce effective results in the effort to represent the US population more adequately are reformations including Approval Voting, Proportional Representation, Ranked-Choice Voting, Multi-Member Districts, and Gerrymandering Reform.

Some of the things we can do in the effort to reduce inhibitory federal and centralized state control as it effects municipalities and individuals, are reformations that limit power, reduce the size and reach of government, and reduce income and ability of central governments to fund and defund states and municipalities. Restrictions on large government and empowerment of the smallest organization of government, which is the individual, are paramount in initiating positive transformation.

Let's talk about what the purpose of government is fundamentally. Firstly, government exists to provide for the management of a group of people organized into a unified body and to work to enhance the wellbeing of that population. Individuals are the highest aspect of governance. A well self-governed individual will empower their environment to be the same, while a poorly self-governed individual will degrade their environment the same. By offering the Individual the highest rights and order of importance in the system, a government will provide wellbeing to the entire system. When the individual is ignored, the system will eat itself from within.

Government often inherently accepts the role of protecting borders. While this can manifest in various ways, it often is seen in the creation of a state-run active military, police force and militia. Government also organizes the military against foreign threats, which may include threats that are directly confronting the boundaries of the state or are directly threatening the justified, or otherwise, interests of the state as in allied states or persons of the state who exist outside of the state borders. If a government is composed of various divisions of its whole, as in State and Federal Government, it is the duty of the encompassing agency to mediate between the divided governing bodies upon dispute, though many governments today are practicing dictation and top-down commandments instead. The most important role that a government can play for a population is in providing guidelines for the wellbeing of the population, as decided transparently and by informed consensus of the whole.

And here lies another critically important point...it's the predictability *inherent in the existence of rules, publicly known and consistently enforced, not the* content of the rules themselves, far less the *popularity of a given government, that creates the feeling of safety that allows a normative system to function. Predictability, not popularity, is the key: you*

don't need to like the police or agree with the speed limit for the road rules to make you feel safe.
– David Kilcullen[3]

The population, as Kilcullen implies, is not greatly interested in philosophical or moral correctness, but rather is informed by their day-to-day experience as to whether they feel safe and whether there are predictable circumstances that they can maneuver around and within. Rules and boundaries that have rewards and consequences, and how well those wheels are greased, determines whether a population will consent by their submission to the system provided. While this may be the condition of the population generally, it has never been the general population who have done anything significant that altered social systems or governments, but rather small groups of tireless, intelligent, willful, and uncompromising individuals. When is government ever moral, and when does the population ever truly care, so long as they have a fire in the hearth, food on the table, and modest comforts that allow the days to pass in relative ease and pleasantry?

There is no just government where government decides what is best for a population without the consent of the governed, whether a democracy or in a kingdom. It is not meant to be a relationship of slave and master, owned and owner, but rather a relationship between a representative body and its mirrored and extrapolated constituency. Today in the United States, the government is no more representative of the population than it was at its inception. In its first year, our government represented the interests of upper-class white, land-owning, tremendously wealthy men. This has changed very slightly, in its larger context, over the past 250 years due to the development of more clever ways of hiding the prejudice and the control, while making marginal changes to the fundamentally corrupt nature of the government. While I say this in harsh criticism of the structure we are still using today, we must look critically at the totality of the situation in which the constitution was written, and the amendments made to fully comprehend the nature of the progress that has been made toward a truly just government and social design. Looking at this totality we can see that, despite being in conditions in which there was often extraordinary pressures to maintain slavery and racism, or bigotry in any of its manifestations, or in which there was horrid working conditions maintained by industrial powerhouses with seemingly unbreakable political control, we have continually overcome many of these issues with sensible and powerful movements to increase the wellbeing of the population and the conditions in which we all live. We must remember these moments and continue to make appropriate movements today, to effectively create a better system for all the people.

There have been many changes in which we can see the total wellbeing of the population rise to new heights. The problem that we encounter is one based on how narrow or wide the populations perception is and how motivated the population is to increase their communal wellbeing. This must first be understood then as a problem in learning. If the population does not have the appropriate learning and thus the appropriate understanding, they will consequently not have the motivation. So, if we look through a narrow lens as in looking only at the last 250 years of government in the United States, we will be restricted to what has happened here to represent the possibility of where we might go next and what we might do. In other words, our boundaries will be set at the limit to what has been the condition in the United States. Thus, we would look at any endeavor to enhance our culture though the lens of how we have done things so far. Structurally, we would say the only way to make change is to follow the same patterns that allowed us to achieve an end to slavery and disenfranchisement. The problem with this way of looking at our government and our potential, is that we do not have a wider perception and thus a greater awareness of what is possible. With a wider perception, we might see the ways in which governments around the world have been created with greater actively and truly democratic systems and greater or lesser quality of life for their populations. We would also see the condition of our population as compared to alternate systems and a wider spectrum of possibility. We would see the ways in which our interests are not separate from the interests of the rest of the world and how the environment around the world is being affected by our decisions. We would see a longer timeframe by which to judge our position and our achievements. When looking on a timeline of 5000 years rather than 250, our supposed accomplishments seem to fade into nothingness or even appear shameful in that we have thought ourselves so great due to them. What we have done correctly or exceptionally is not often considered our great achievements by the greater population and certainly not in the school system. The organic evolution of methods of human organization is without borders and yet cannot be described without considering the ways in which different nations and groups organized themselves and how certain systems withstood the test of time and others faded into memory.

We believe ourselves to be a democracy, but we are factually not that and never have been. We believe ourselves to be free, but this has never been the case. Rather we have stated and affirmed rights that express principles of freedom that people ought to endeavor to manifest and maintain. We believe ourselves to have a high sense of morality and justice but when we look at our society with a wide lens, this simply falls asunder. We believe that we are the most evolved society on the planet, but we are far from this, unless we measure evolutionary success as how many nuclear weapons, tanks, and aircraft carriers any society creates, or by how many phones or televisions are owned. If we measure evolution as industrializing and promoting subtle violence and environmental destruction, then in fact the United States would win the Gold Medal. But since any sane person or tree knows that unnecessary violence is abhorrent and indicative of a complete lack of enlightenment, we must thus see that we have in fact been devolving our society at the same rate that we have been maintaining or increasing our actions of unnecessary violence in the world. So, to first be a witness to the truth of the failures of our government and our society is to take the first step in the right direction of making any significant change to the horrendous condition we exist in today.

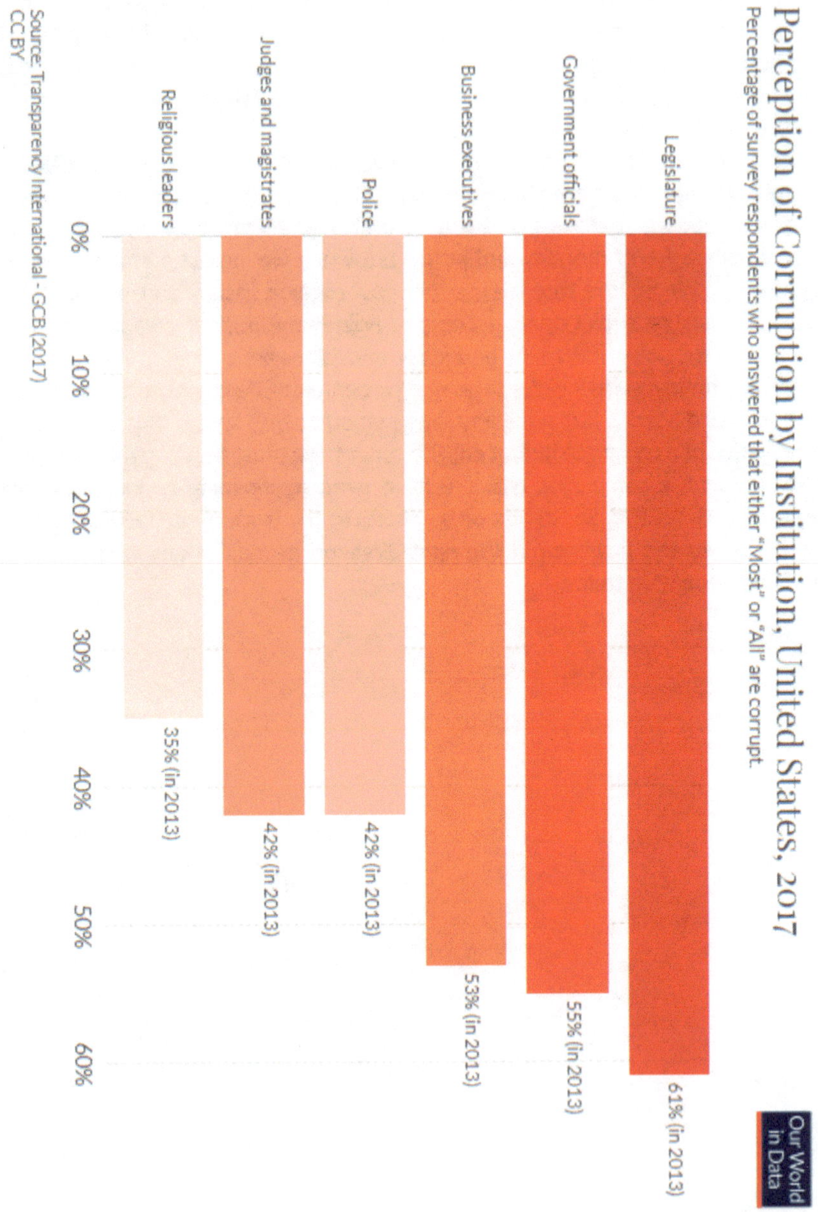

We must first recognize that we are ill before we seek a medicine. We must first become aware that we are slaves, before we can choose to liberate ourselves, for any man who accepts slavery as freedom will never attempt to be free. While it would be impossible to convince you of your own slavery by simply stating it here, it is imperative that you seek to expand your perception. It is far more difficult to perpetuate a lie when an individual takes direct action to expand their perception. This is not about imbibing information, but rather has far more to do with sitting in quiet places for extended periods of time and eliminating the constant stream of input that is tugging at your attention. It is as simple as spending fifteen minutes in meditation right away when you wake up in the morning. It is the beginning.

"Who could honestly believe that modern first-world economies could continue to borrow half their annual operating costs from their own future generations, and from foreign banks and foreign governments that were likewise borrowing from their future generations? When in history has that sweetly delusional practice ever lasted more than a few generations before cracking up? Never, that I am aware of... Our modern human folly is so easy to understand in retrospect. A gullible generation or two can be brainwashed into believing up is down, that there is no absolute wrong or right, and that the old natural laws can be abolished according to the social and political fashions of the age."
-Matthew Bracken[4]

There are some very specific governmental reformations that we need to make without delay. To discuss these, I must first describe the structure of government to a certain degree. The United States Government is the Federal Government. This is the national body of representatives that creates national laws, interprets the Constitution of the United States, and manages the daily affairs of all the agencies of the Federal Government. The nature of the Federal Government has changed and shifted over time, though we can generally see that it has been in action a Plutocracy far longer than it has been any other form of governance. On paper, The United States of America is a Federal Constitutional Republic. And while the population of the United States and all the government representatives shout about Democracy, the United States is not even close to being democratic itself. Democracy does not exist here, and none of those people shouting about it would enjoy it much if it did... well maybe the politicians would. There are three major branches of the Federal Government, which are the Executive, the Legislative and the Judicial. Each is intended to be able to inhibit the others from taking control of the entire government and thus the nation, though they are generally all in collusion together and thus we are witness to a serious deviation from the original intent.

The Executive Branch is the Branch of the President and the various divisions of his Executive Power. This Branch consists of fifteen departments, including the Departments of Justice, Energy, Defense and Transportation among others, which the President uses to maintain the daily operations of his office. The Legislative Branch is the Branch of Congress, which is composed of the Senate and the House of Representatives. Between the Senate and the House, laws are written, wars are declared, public money is raised and spent, federal officers are impeached and tried, presidential appointments are approved or denied, treaties negotiated by the executive branch are approved or denied, and investigations and oversight are conducted. The Judicial Branch is the Branch of the Supreme Court and all subordinated courts created by Congress. The Supreme Court exists to ensure that all laws and decisions made within the United States are Constitutional. There are various levels of courts both federally and in States, but the Supreme Court is the ultimate authority on the constitutionality of laws and decisions, with the exception of the authority of "We the People".

The State Governments in the United States are semi-distinct entities from the Federal Government, and they are built along the same principles and structures as the Federal Government. The main difference between the Federal Government and State Governments is the scope of power. Federal Government has the authority to veto laws, oversee national defense and foreign policy, impeach officials, impose tariffs, and enter into treaties. While these powers and more are granted to the Federal Government, the states, and the people even more importantly, are afforded legal jurisdiction by the 10th Amendment to cover all matters not specifically granted to the Federal Government.

"In fact, the description that best fits modern America is fascist... Under a fascist system, property is nominally held in private hands and the economy is officially 'free.' All appearances to the contrary, however, the economy in a fascist system is carefully controlled by the government through a labyrinth of taxes and regulation. This government control is usually exercised for the benefit of an economic elite that works to perpetuate the power of the existing political class. Other characteristics of fascist systems include a militaristic foreign policy and a police state that abuses our civil liberties. Only the willfully ignorant could deny that Americas foreign policy is militaristic, and we have already seen the myriad ways in which modern government abuses our civil liberties. A fascist system also singles out critics of the regime for harassment. From stopping scholars who are critical of America from entering the country to harassing journalists whose works displease the current administration to siccing the IRS on organizations critical of the current administration's policies, government harassment of their political critics has become increasingly common."

- Dr. Ron Paul

We need to reform our government. We, the people, are the inheritors of an imperfect but substantial agreement that was made over two centuries ago that said we are born with inherent rights, inalienable and eternal. We need to reject much of the actions that have been taken to remove those rights by clever manipulations of our society and our laws. How have these changes manifested? At the formation of the United States, when individual and unique states decided to bind their fates together to form a union for mutual benefit, there was contention over what kind of governance they would form. There were proponents for large, centralized government that would wield authority over all the individual states, and there were proponents for sovereign states that would have power in regulating themselves and perhaps sharing equitably in a small regulatory body of federal governance. This brings us to States Rights vs. Federal Rights. The Federalists, like Alexander Hamilton and John Adams, wanted to create a strong Federal Government while the Anti-Federalists, like Thomas Jefferson and Patrick Henry, wanted authority to remain with the States. Until the inclusion of the Bill of Rights, which explained the Rights of States, and gave liberties originally excluded in the Constitution, Anti-Federalists opposed the Constitution. Within the Constitution and the Bill of Rights, and among the following amendments, we can see a series of these Rights declared as inherent and explicitly expressed as Rights that cannot be denied or taken away from any person. Firstly, we have the Right to Free Speech, Religious Freedom, and Peaceful Assembly. Secondly, we have the Right to Bear Arms. These inherent Rights, expressed without ambiguity or disguise, have been violated regularly by our governments, State and Federal, and have for the most part been rejected when it suited those institutions. These are not the only violations of our people by these governments.

"Mental disorders among political leadership distort perceptions, attitudes, and actions among citizens."

- James G. Long

We need to reform our government. The historical perspective taught in our government mandated educational facilities, which more and more often resemble jails, is one that indoctrinates our youth into believing that our nation was formed because some colonists threw some tea into the ocean in protest of high taxes from a tyrant, and that the people rose up against the British forces to form a nation built upon ideals like Liberty and Justice. This is far from adequately describing a historically appropriate rendition of events. The "new world" for Europeans who thought they were pioneering untouched places is a fallacy. Immediately upon arriving to the North American continent, the Europeans encountered various tribes occupying defined lands. The lack of Christians and authorization to claim unchristian land by European monarchs gave justification to the pioneers to stake their claims on the lands already occupied. They were late to the party of global travel. The Vikings had come to this continent centuries before. The Chinese arrived in South America long ago. The Polynesians travelled great distances over the Pacific Ocean as they colonized various islands. Ancient cultural relics describing worldwide travel by many cultures have been found far from their indigenous lands. The European "pioneers" were not exploring new places, just places they themselves had not seen and commandeered. So, when the European explorers found their way onto this continent, they found it heavily populated with diverse tribes of people. The highest estimate is that 300 million people lived on the continent at that time, while the lowest estimate is around 50 million. So how did the foreigners treat the native populations? The same way they treated every other population on every other continent that they found themselves on. They began to contrive ways to conquer them, enslave them, and take their land. Immediately, a struggle ensued that lasted centuries, and resulted in the genocide, enslavement, indoctrination, and the utter decimation of culture of millions of people. This behavior was not novel in any way, as the wars between European nations and nations around the world had involved the decimation of tribes and the conquering of territory as early can be found recorded.

Since the 1400's, Europeans had increased in numbers of colonists and had reached 2.5 million in 1776. They had by that time created various colonies, with distinct and unique cultures, some ruled by representatives of England, who reported to the English crown, others ruled by Spain, France, and other European nations. These colonists developed on land they conquered, occupied, stole, or traded from the indigenous people. They did not generally confer rights to the indigenous populations, and much of their time was spent in dealing with desperate and angry native tribes. Over time, their military technology and philosophy and culture around ownership allowed them to effectively eradicate the native populations and extract the raw materials of the land and plunder the abundant environment to serve the mercantilist mandates of their parent nations. This supported the British Empire, among others, as well as the European economy. The building up of colonists over generations eventually led to strong distinctions between English people and Colonial People, though most of the population did not have animosity toward the British and most had strong family ties with people living in England.

African Slavery in the colonies did not really take hold until the 1700s, which then quickly rose to become the dominant form. Before this, the indigenous people were the main source of slavery, even being exported to the West Indies and other places as a trade commodity. In 1770, enslaved people in Georgia and South Carolina made up over 60 percent of the population, Virginia and Maryland around 50 percent, and less in the northern colonies. Four years later, and a group of wealthy, powerful, white colonial men created the Continental Congress. Two years after this, and the Declaration of Independence was written. The Constitution was then written, amended, and ratified by 1790. While several of the authors of the Constitution did expound on the virtues of ending slavery, it was rejected as a violation and prejudice of the rights and cultures of the new states. This argument came heavily from the southern states. The argument went further by declaring hypocrisy by the northerners who mostly had only just recently stopped holding slaves themselves and practiced indentured servitude. The northern economy was reliant, in part, upon cotton production in the south, and thus mutually reluctant to free slave populations. And thus, Slavery was written into our Constitution while the same document spoke of inalienable rights to liberty. Before the Three-Fifths Compromise in 1787, proposed by a liberal northern delegate, James Wilson of Pennsylvania, the southern states were on the path to ending slavery of their own accord. The economic incentive was waning. After the agreement between the wealthy representatives of the states to allow slaves to count for political representation and taxation, and disproportionate power in electing presidents, the economic incentive to maintain and even increase slavery was emplaced. In 1808, slave importation was banned, but the South simply changed tack and began breeding slaves to produce the amount of stock that would give them ample political authority.

Hypocrisy doesn't really do justice to the complete insincerity of the Three-Fifths Compromise. When we look at the effect that endorsing slavery has had on our culture, we can see that, though it may have been necessary from the point of view of the time, it has been a destructive and inhibiting force and has allowed the perpetuation and the institutionalization of classism, hatred, racism, eugenics, and segregation. This is just one example of the ways that plutocrats have used law to force the chattel, whatever their color, to produce greater economic benefit and power for select groups. This is just one example of the odious aspects of the founding of this nation. When we look at how necessity called for these things to exist due to the nature of the society at the time, we can have compassion and understanding for why the authors and legislators and the people accepted the compromises they did. What is not acceptable has been the way in which government has suppressed a population ready to go beyond the limitations of its heritage.

The founding of the United States of America was certainly a step in the right direction. It was just as certainly a launching pad that was mistaken for a bed. The population sleeps while it should be taking action to create the best possible situation for all of the people. Our knowledge and technology have evolved, though not necessarily matured, and yet the government and general sense as a people has not. This is not a small problem, but a great tragedy in the lives of the people living today and potentially the generations to come. What We the People allow is the extent to which the oppressors can operate. The government is truly a reflection of the worst aspects of the people. It is there to enforce the will of the most immoral and unjust people, who will always rise to the top in a competitive setting as they perpetually look for ways to outmaneuver their moral and just opponents by any means. With a government representative of the highest morality and justice of our people, would corporations be allowed to print our money, strip us of our constitutional and human rights, or capitalize on the destruction of our environment? Would we go to war with other countries to enforce our own ideological conclusions? I do not think that is the wish of any sane person, or any sane people. It is the work of the insane and the most depraved, who have been running and manipulating our government, and thus society, since its inception and worldwide governments for millennia.

It is not a solution to simply point fingers and shift blame on others. That is the way of the coward and the depraved. It is up to the people as a whole to accept the blame for the condition of the world. It is humanity at fault for allowing the depraved to rule and consolidate ever more power and control. The interesting thing about the relative freedoms of today compared to that of a few centuries ago, is that while most people lived in subsistence conditions, the population was balanced to the environment and that environment was relatively pristine. As the individual has gained more personal freedom to choose and own, so has the population risen out of balance to the environment, and the environment been destroyed to meet the never-ending demands of a selfish, profligate, and indifferent social paradigm. Who is to blame for the state of the world? You, your neighbor, your parents, your town, your school, and every other person and part of this thing we all share. We are all shareholders in the wellbeing of the planet and everything on her. With that said, some people and groups fill power roles within the structure of our society and use them to perpetuate harm and scarcity, while benefiting from those conditions they manifest. These people and groups are the very things that must be banished, along with the aspects of human nature they embody. The only way for the population to learn to see beyond the narrative currently pumped into them from every angle imaginable is to see the problems, and choose to actively change the conditions they live in.

> *"In a plutocracy, commercialism dominates far beyond the realm of economics and business; everything is for sale., and money is power. But in an authentic democracy, there must be commercial free zones where the power of human rights, citizenship, community, equality, and justice are free from the corrupting influence of money. Our elections and our governments should be such commercial-free zones; our environment, air, and water should never fall under the control of corporations or private owners. Children should not be*

programmed by a huckstering economy where their vulnerable consciousness becomes the target of relentless corporate marketing and advertising... The power of these ultra-rich, their attorneys, their media, and the influence their money buys constitute the core of plutocracy in the United States today... A recurrently devastating trait of the people who profit through large corporate entities is their insulation from decisive community sanctions and impunity from laws that send other less-endowed perpetrators to prison... Corporations and their bosses who enjoy the rights and privileges of the powerful simply do not bear the same risks as individuals who perpetrate similar crimes of predation or lethal neglect and abuse.

Taken all together, those being enriched are those who are advancing plutocracy over democracy, and they are bolstered by the modern, giant commercial corporation as a power-concentrating machine that seeks endless economic growth for itself by undermining, dominating, and diminishing the democratic spaces and regulatory institutions of national public interest, media, human services, and environment... they delicately call the process 'privatization' and 'deregulation'... August 2015, when the New York Times, using Federal Election Commission reports and Internal Revenue Service records, concluded that 'fewer than four hundred families are responsible for almost half the money raised in the 2016 Presidential Campaign, a concentration of political donors that is unprecedented in the modern era'. "

– Ralph Nader, Breaking Through Power[5]

We need to reform our government. Modern United States government is clearly and obviously a Plutocracy. It has been for a long time. One of the trademarks of Plutocracy is that it sees the citizens as adversaries and threats. It also views the people as a mob of chattel. This means that it views humans as a resource or commodity to be owned and utilized at the behest of the corporate owners. This is not merely a philosophical end, but a deeply ingrained, legally defined, and practically applied idea. In sovereign kingdoms or governments, the rights of rulership have been identified by necessities and understandings of the age. In corporate ownership, the chattel is seen as worth only the value it can offer to the corporation. The corporation is composed of shareholders. Shareholders are composed of other corporations and individuals, who benefit from the utilization of their owned resources. We the people are seen as those very resources that work to pay off the debts of the corporation and create positive balance sheets. The public does not own land, is not the voting population, and does not have claim to beneficiary status of the rewards of the commercial growth of its government or corporate owned suppliers of currency. The main purpose of the mob of chattel is to be used to the benefit of the shareholding entities of the Plutocracy. There has never existed in this country or any other, a true capitalism or communism. The only thing that has ever ruled is the money creating entities, resource monopolies, religious doctrine or feudal boundaries that have existed over the millennia.

Communism and socialism are both frequently contrasted with capitalism and democracy, though these can be false equivalencies depending on the usage. Capitalism refers to an economic system in which a society's means of production are held by private individuals or organizations, not the government, and where products, prices, and the distribution of goods are determined mainly by competition in a free market. As an economic system, it can be contrasted with the economic system of communism, though as we have noted, the word communism is used of both political and economic systems. Democracy refers not to an economic system but to a system of government in which supreme power is vested in the people and exercised through a system of direct or indirect representation which is decided through periodic free elections.

Capital is wealth—that is, money and goods—that's used to produce more wealth. Capitalism is practiced enthusiastically by capitalists, people who use capital to increase production and make more goods and money. Capitalism works by encouraging competition in a fair and open market. Its opposite is often said to be socialism. Where a capitalist economy encourages private actions and ownership, socialism prefers public or government ownership and control of parts of the economy. In a pure capitalist system, there would be no public schools or public parks, no government programs such as Social Security and Medicare, and maybe not even any public highways or police. In a pure socialist system, there wouldn't be any private corporations. In other words, there's just about no such thing as pure capitalism or pure socialism in the modern world.

Merriam-Webster[6]

On December 23, 1913, President Woodrow Wilson signed into law the Federal Reserve Act. This law created the Federal Reserve System, which in no uncertain terms is a private central bank using fractional reserve and credit creation banking, printing the currency of the United States, and loaning it at interest to the federal government which creates public debt, manipulating the entire social structure of the United States and the world, and operating with zero oversight by any agency or authority other than its own. This was the absolute worst event to have occurred in this nation since its inception. This action shifted the entirety of the public power and authority over the economy to the private shareholders of the Federal Reserve. At the time of its creation, the general population knew that private central banks were to be avoided at all cost, and so instead of calling it the Central Bank, the authors of this law called it the Federal Reserve, giving it a name that resembles a government agency, and thus defrauding the general population. So why would President Wilson sign this Bill into law the Day before Christmas, when most of Congress was already on holiday? Because political power in this country is bought, and money sets the stage for the political actions to take place. Three years after signing the Bill into law, Wilson said it gave all the nation over to private bankers. Even the man who made it possible declared it a debacle.

How did the Bill even get to Congress? In the early 1900's, J.P. Morgan, the wealthiest banker in the United States influenced the Copper Market at a crucial moment for the Knickerbocker Trust Company, which led to a run on their Bank, which meant that the customers of that bank all attempted to withdraw their money at the same time. This led to the Panic of 1907, which influenced Congress to become open to creating a Central Bank. The public in the late 1800's and early 1900's was vastly in favor of a public central bank, which would have been a government institution. Rather than creating this, the government instead gave control of the economy to the very people who had conspiratorially contrived to manipulate it to their personal benefit for many years, and who had followed in the footsteps of others who had the same goals but failed. Since the creation of the Federal Reserve, the United States has seen vast market manipulation at the detriment of the public, increasing wealth disparities, incredibly devastating wars, social manipulation, corporate domination of justice, media, and politics amongst other things, and ever-increasing debt to which there is no escape and payable to the shareholders of the private business that prints the money in the first place. It's a scam, and one of the most successful to ever exist. Our government has the authority and the responsibility to forcibly audit, denounce, and tear down the Federal Reserve scam. To make fractional reserve banking illegal constitutionally. To create a transparent public banking system or a government audited and accountable private banking system like Clearing Houses. The government has the authority and the responsibility to end the rape of our economy and our populations by devious and selfish people. But our government is in collusion. Our politicians have been purchased. Our representatives now represent the Federal Reserve, and the global financial institutions.

plutocracy: government by the wealthy

Ploutos was Greek for "wealth", and Plouton, or Pluto, was one of the names used for the Greek god of the underworld, where all the earth's mineral wealth was stored. So a plutocracy governs or wields power through its money. The economic growth in the U.S. in the late 19th century produced a group of enormously wealthy plutocrats. Huge companies like John D. Rockefeller's Standard Oil gained serious political power, and Rockefeller was able to influence lawmakers in states where his businesses operated.

Merriam-Webster[7]

We need to reform our government. Our election process is guaranteed by the constitution, but our right to vote is not. Our Constitution never guaranteed a Right to Vote. Over time this has been discussed in Amendments that have stated that no abridgement to voting for this or that demographic must be recognized, but there has never been a Constitutionally Affirmed Right to Vote. This means that it is not an inherent or guaranteed right that a person of this nation could not be barred from voting. "In the 1972 decision in Dunn v. Blumstein, Justice Marshall stated, 'In decision after decision, this Court has made clear that a citizen has a constitutionally protected right to participate in elections on an equal basis with other citizens in the jurisdiction.' And again, in the 1974 Richardson v. Ramirez case, Justice Rehnquist wrote: 'Because the right to vote is of the essence of a democratic society, and any restrictions on that right strike at the heart of representative government,'... voting is a 'fundamental' right." (Swisher, 2019) It would be advantageous to confirm through constitutional amendment, an affirmed right to vote, as justices change, and opinions change, but the constitution is meant to remain as a bulwark against attacks on our rights and freedoms.

We must make it possible for all people to understand and access the ballets. The DMV is a State-based organization that is used to grant identification to residents of their state. Because State Legislators can create their own rules about how people must get their ID's, this means that many people can be excluded from being able to acquire one. There must be a Constitutional Affirmed Right to Vote, so that States must find ways to make voting available to every single person who desires to vote. Though this would only be logical and practical if every person who voted was educated in civics enough to understand the structure of the government and were informed in all the matters on the table and which candidates stood for which things. Without an informed voting population, the ability to vote is no more beneficial than allowing a toddler to drive a car on the highway.

Laws regarding Drivers Licensing must be changed to reflect the social and infrastructural design of the nation. In a country that has over 4 million miles of roads and the farthest you can venture from a road is 22 miles, and in a country that allows police and the justice system to unconstitutionally erect and violently enforce limitations on the ability of the population to travel from place to place freely without the need for a license, then it is imperative that the Constitution be amended to add the Right to Travel, making the extortion of the travelling population come to an end. A license to travel is already unconstitutional and the only form of ID necessary for the individual must be a State Issued ID for Voting, given upon request by the individual. The US population is extremely ignorant as to the structure of government and the philosophies of governance. Small minded about our politics and crude in our treatment of those who think differently than we do. The United States population has an aggrandized sense of self-importance, while only making up five percent of the world population. We are far from being the most democratic or the most abundant nation, not that the two are exclusively compatible. We need to teach Civics in schools, not out of textbooks, but with philosophy and free thinking in mind. We need to teach youth the way our current government is structured and how it works. We need to teach our old people the same. We need to broadcast on Public Radio the function and structure of government and invite real conversations to the mass media domain. Our candidates for public offices must all be given equal unmolested coverage, and debates between them must be untimed, involving and focusing on public Q & A. When we subject our candidates to a minute to speak, we restrict the conversation to extremely simplified talking points and political phraseology that is used to manipulate public opinion. We need to give our candidates the control over their debates, to allow them to challenge, speak at length, and be challenged by their fellow candidates and by the public. This is a need if we are to transform into an informed democracy. We need to abolish gerrymandering, which allows dominant parties to redraw district lines and thus fuel their own interests. We need a third-party public authority to draw the lines that will not be changed by any parties or biased individuals or groups. We need to abolish the Winner-Take-All system, which supports swing-state popularity and draws candidate attention, while empowering corporate manipulation. Because each Congressional District only elects one person, if 49.9% of votes are not in favor, but 51.1% is in favor of a candidate, that candidate will win, and the 49.9% of voters will have effectively not been represented. Because it has become a precise science to manipulate voting, elections are easily maneuvered in the favor of the person who spends the most money and has the most corporate support. We must implement a Binding None-Of-The-Above option on all ballots. This is a "No Confidence" Vote showing the voter cannot in good conscience vote for any person on the ballot. If more votes exist for the NOTA option than any other candidate, the election is cancelled and a new vote with new candidates begins in a designated amount of time. By using this option, we give the public the right to refuse every person on the ballet. We need to abolish the Electoral College. This institution has voted against the popular vote many times and is a direct violation of any democratic process. It is a superfluous and outdated device of a more restrictive society. It is time to remove it from our government. We need to extend our voting timeframe from one Thursday in November to the three-day weekend at least. If polls remain open to receive voters for three full days, we will reduce the burden and stress that a single day creates. It will allow for corrections in voter rolls and registration, and it will allow for people who cannot leave work on weekdays to vote, eliminating part of the inequality imposed on those in poverty. We need to mandate same-day voter registration or eliminate registration altogether. The amount of voting fraud is so small as to be insignificant. In the 2004 Presidential Election, out of 121 million voters, voter fraud was .00002%. The number of mistakes by election officials is by factors of factors more prevalent.

> *In 2012, Pew Center on the States (Major Research Institute) found approximately 1/8 (24 million) voter registrations were invalid or inaccurate. 1.8 million dead people remain on the rolls. 3 million people had multiple registration. In 2008, 5.7 million people faced registration problems needing to be resolved before being able to vote. 3 million did not vote due to registration problems... • Election Day Voter Registration States have 10-12% higher voter turnout.*
>
> – "Electoral Dysfunction" by Victoria Bassetti[8]

We need to mandate the use of Provisional Voting. This allows for people to vote despite not being found on voting rolls at the polls. This means that people can vote, and if they are found later due to the all too regular mistakes by election officials, their vote will be counted. We need to begin active testing the use of Blockchain technology to store Voter Rolls, which can be accessed by any polling place, used by voters to check to confirm their vote was recorded accurately, and be fact checked when discrepancies are found in the counts. To encourage the best result, we can award government grants to individuals or companies to discover solutions to problems in blockchain voting technologies that make it open-source and universally publicly auditable, safer, easier, and more feasible to use this technology for large scale voting. Our government must begin proactively facilitating voter registration. Election Administrators need to affirmatively build comprehensive and accurate voter rolls. Door to Door Registration and other proactive methods of encouraging voting from the population and disseminating information on process and candidates must be developed. We must eliminate partisanship in our election officials. Nor can we have our election officials being appointed by parties. This encourages abuse, neglect, and preferential treatment between parties and among voters at polls. There needs to be created a National Register of Fixed Voting Locations, provided by States, with fixed rules regarding ballot design, machine voting, and organization of the voting process. Approval or Ranked Choice Voting must become mandated nationally. By this means, we will see many more parties and independents being elected to offices that are currently guaranteed to the duopolistic system. As to ballot design, most children could do a better job of organizing the ballet than the people who have been succeeding in disenfranchising large populations of voters. Color coding candidates, giving all candidates on ballot clear boxes and Approval or Ranked-Choice Voting numbers, and the electoral college persons named with their party affiliations on presidential ballots, would be a start to creating a reasonable ballot structure. On C-Span and Public Media, as well as at the polls, an instructional, step-by-step video, explaining the process of filling out a ballot must be provided to every person before they vote so they know exactly what they are doing. If voting machines are the future of voting, we must ensure that they are not going to make mistakes. We need machines that are not vulnerable to class breaks. This must be implemented to prevent large scale or universal hacking. At DEF CON (One of the largest hacker conferences in world) hackers hunted and exploited cyber vulnerabilities in election infrastructure in (Voting Village) including voting machines, voter registration databases, and election office networks. According to event organizers, "By the end of the conference, every piece of voting equipment in the Voting Village was effectively breached in some manner. Participants with little prior knowledge and only limited tools and resources were quite capable of undermining the confidentiality, integrity, and availability of these systems."[9]

These machines need to be of a universal design, eliminating confusion of voters, especially when over 3% of the population, about 10 million people, migrate to different states annually. End to End (E2E) Verifiable Elections must be mandated. Voters need to be assured that their choices are properly recorded, all voters must be able to verify that their vote was counted in the official results, and the public must be able to verify that the results of the election are accurate. Government sponsored or funded media reporting on elections must be non-partisan. They must state facts and thoughts and opinions from a neutral position that does not inflame rivalry and factionism. We need to put an end to the Commission on Presidential Debates. This 501c3, joint-sponsored by the Republican and Democrat Parties, excludes all third parties from the debates it hosts, and it hosts all the presidential debates. Before the CPD, the League of Women Voters hosted the presidential debates.

> *"The two parties (*Republican and Democrat*) even colluded and bankrolled, in 1987, the takeover of the presidential debates from the League of Woman Voters through a private corporation that was given a name that sounds like an unbiased non-profit or government agency- the Commission on Presidential Debates... this maneuver meant that an entity representing the narrow interests of the two political parties-not a non-partisan body open to the diverse political spectrum-would decide the rules regarding who would participate in the debates, how debates would be staged, right down to which reporters were to be invited to ask largely predictable questions before well-filtered audiences, conveyed to the voters by obedient television networks... Without viable electoral variety and competition, there is no democracy by definition; there are only coronations..."*
>
> -Ralph Nader, Breaking Through Power[10]

The Restriction of Political Campaign Intervention by Section 501(c)(3) Tax-Exempt Organizations should be enforced to bar the activity of preferential media access to any party or parties. We need to absolutely abolish PAC's, including all of their various forms. This includes Separate Segregated Funds, Nonconnected Committees, Super PAC's, Hybrid PAC's, and Leadership Pac's. These are Political Committee's organized to raise and spend money to elect and defeat candidates.

"Most PACs represent business, labor or ideological interests. PACs can give $5,000 to a candidate committee per election (primary, general or special). They can also give up to $15,000 annually to any national party committee, and $5,000 annually to any other PAC. PACs may receive up to $5,000 from any one individual, PAC or party committee per calendar year. A PAC must register with the FEC within 10 days of its formation, providing name and address for the PAC, its treasurer and any connected organizations. Affiliated PACs are treated as one donor for the purpose of contribution limits. PACs have been around since 1944, when the Congress of Industrial Organizations (CIO) formed the first one to raise money for the re-election of President Franklin D. Roosevelt. The PAC's money came from voluntary contributions from union members rather than union treasuries, so it did not violate the Smith Connally Act of 1943, which forbade unions from contributing to federal candidates. Although commonly called PACs, federal election law refers to these accounts as "separate segregated funds" because money contributed to a PAC is kept in a bank account separate from the general corporate or union treasury. Many politicians also form Leadership PACs as a way of raising money to help fund other candidates' campaigns. Since June 2008, Leadership PACs reporting electronically must list the candidate sponsoring the PAC, as per the Honest Leadership and Open Government Act of 2007. Leadership PACs are often indicative of a politician's aspirations for leadership positions in Congress or for higher office." – OpenSecrets[11]

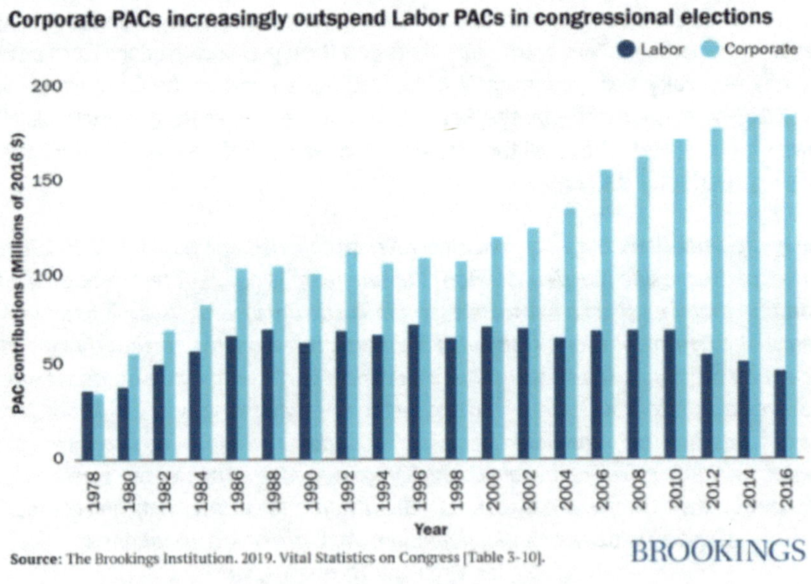

We need to reform our government. We have an enormous waste of resources, time, energy, and attention due to our election process in this country. We need to make our elections not only fair, but cost effective, transparent, unmolested by reporting bias, timely and efficient. Term limits must be changed to fit the modern political structure. Increasing term limits or decreasing wasteful practices is necessary. If politicians must dedicate enormous resources in time, money, and public attention to re-elections, they will need to be allowed longer time in their positions to adequately perform their roles. If these wasteful election practices are changed to instead reflect a system that is efficient, representative, and does not encourage corruption and manipulative personalities, we will see an increase in the amount of work that can be done in the name of creating more wellbeing in the entire population. Staff positions in Congress have oxymoronically decreased significantly over time, as our population has increased, which makes it more difficult for representatives to adequately perform their duties. We either need to allow longer terms to our elected officials, or dedicate more funds, encouragement, and incentives to long term staff positions. We need to make Congressional Staffing a career rather than a temp job. Due to the lack of incentive for staffers to stay in their roles, the amount of inexperienced, rotating staff members is huge. This leaves a significant responsibility of knowledge and experience where very little exists.

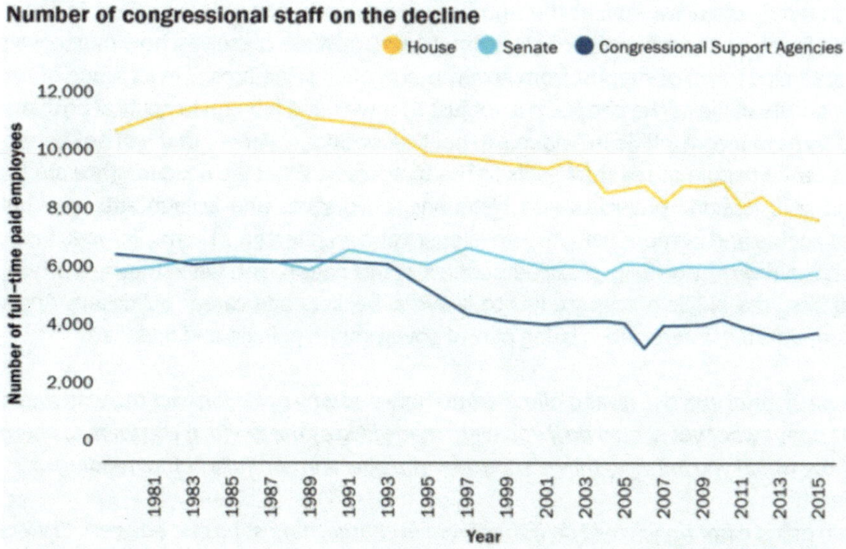

Source: The Brookings Institution. 2019. Vital Statistics on Congress [Table 5-1].

And this further leads our representatives to turn to lobbyists, biased science, and corporate agendas, as well as other private interests for information that leads to policy.

Women holding positions in Congress and other political arenas has been a desire of large portions of the population since and before the formation of the nation. As seen in the image below, there has been a slow, yet ever increasing number of women holding positions in Congress. This can tell us various things about the nature of our government. One is that it is responding to the desire of the population to accept women decisionmakers. The second requires us to remember that government need only truly represent a small percentage of the whole population to successfully perpetuate itself. If 20% of the population of any society supports the current government with their finances, their will, their obedience, and their lives, the government has everything it needs to continue to operate. The makeup of this 20% usually is police, military, political people, wealthy and successful people who have become so within the society as it is, and others who were raised with the ideological indoctrination of supporting government as a virtue. So, what this government is truly representing is a small portion of the whole population who are composed of entirely different demographics than the whole population. It is vastly more comprised of wealthy white men and women by percentage than the whole population. So, when the government allows or accepts more women into its ranks, it means that either the represented population has evolved to some degree in support of that change, or it means that enough support and demand has been produced by the whole population or some sector of it, that it would be easier to allow the change than to prevent it from occurring. When the government allows change to occur, it is not allowed fully in the way it is desired by the public. Rather it is very controlled and more likely to yet benefit the current agenda of government anyway. The system the way that it is disallows for uncorrupted people of any race, sex, or other affiliation to participate in its workings. Even an incorruptible person who somehow manages to enter the high echelons of American politics, will, if remaining incorruptible, simply be unable to operate. That is the profoundly disturbing aspect of our current situation. The system by which people organize their lives. The government that makes laws that they enforce with violent demand, is the very same system that cannot be changed simply by any individual entering into a position with a force of goodwill and benediction. Even if a group of people, let's say half of the House of Representatives were to be incorruptible, the system would still buck their efforts because the Senate would yet be an insurmountable force of opposition. With these things in mind, when we look at the number of women in congress, or sitting in Judges seats, or running for president, or any other part of government, we must ask ourselves, how much of a success is it really? Sure, it's a nice token of support from government, but it is ineffectual in its scope of real, manifest change to the quality of life of the people. It's not just that we need women in political positions, its rather that we need to have incorruptible individuals in political positions. People that will not vote on issues to the detriment of the people or sell their souls to the plutocracy. What we need in office are more master engineers and philosophers, physicists and historians, philologists and accountants, psychologists and librarians, sociologists and farmers, software developers and architects and kundalini yoga instructors. This is a glimpse at the diverse portfolio of skilled peoples in this nation, and while they are attempting to do what they do best, the public offices are left to lawyers, bankers and career politicians. And who in this world is incorruptible *and* interested in being part of government, politics, and finance?

A simple mental exercise gives a glimpse into how and why politicians act the way they do. Think about what you *would do if you were made king of the world. If you were in charge, how would you improve things? Consider the question carefully before reading on.*

When asked what they would do if they were in charge, almost no one answers, "I would just leave people alone." Instead, most people start imagining the ways in which they could use the ability to control *people as a tool for good, for the betterment of mankind. If one starts with the assumption that such control can be legitimate and righteous, the possibilities are nearly endless. One could make a healthier country by forcing people to eat more nutritious foods and exercise regularly. One could help the poor by forcing the rich to give them money. One could make people safer by forcing them to pay for a strong system of defense. One could make things more equitable, and society more compassionate, by forcing people to behave the way they should.*

Larken Rose, "The Most Dangerous Superstition"[12]

Allow me to take you on a quick tangent here. ***And who in this world is incorruptible AND interested in being part of government, politics, and finance?*** I wonder if it would be an acceptable proposition to have a somewhat mandatory service in government by a random drawing. This would of course need to have a structure that prevents those who would do intentional harm to the people from being able to participate, as well as those who would be unprepared to do so. This would include restrictions on people who have committed rape or murder or environmental destruction perhaps, and those who are underage, mentally disabled, or have important social functions elsewhere that would cause more harm than good if they were to be diverted, such as an active air force pilot. The mandatory threshold for entrance into the lottery would be to pass a test, containing questions regarding civics, political process, and perhaps those proving a measure of comprehension of philosophy, history, the scientific method, and proving the ability to reason. The test would have to be designed in a collaboration by masters in each of these different fields, and then field tested to see what it produces.

The population as a whole would be required to take the test when coming into age, and as often afterward as they desire. The lottery would draw from the pool of those who passed the test, and those who win the lottery would have the choice to not participate. This would mean the drawing would occur again for the position, until someone accepted the role. This method would certainly prove to remove much of the institutional greed and elitism in our government, and likely produce the glorious expiration of the plutocracy. It could be tiered in such a way that, of those who become local government representatives, a drawing occurs for county representatives. The pool for who gets selected for state positions comes from those who have served in county positions. The pool for national positions is composed of those who've served at the state level. And the president, the supreme court and the leaders of the house and senate could all be either elected by general vote of the population or by general vote of the people selected for government positions of any type across the nation.

I believe this would be an extremely interesting experiment that would produce plenty of beneficial changes.

Table 1-19 Women in Congress, 65th - 116th Congresses, 1917 - 2019

Congress		House		Senate		Congress		House		Senate	
		D	R	D	R			D	R	D	R
65th	(1917)		1			91st	(1969)	6	4		1
66th	(1919)					92nd	(1971)	10	3		1
67th	(1921)		2		1	93rd	(1973)	14	2	1	
68th	(1923)		1			94th	(1975)	14	5		
69th	(1925)	1	2			95th	(1977)	13	5		
70th	(1927)	2	3			96th	(1979)	11	5	1	1
71st	(1929)	4	5			97th	(1981)	10	9		2
72nd	(1931)	4	3	1		98th	(1983)	13	9		2
73rd	(1933)	4	3	1		99th	(1985)	13	9		2
74th	(1935)	4	2	2		100th	(1987)	12	11	1	1
75th	(1937)	4	1	2		101st	(1989)	14	11	1	1
76th	(1939)	4	4	1		102nd	(1991)	19	9	1	1
77th	(1941)	4	5	1		103rd	(1993)	36	12	5	1
78th	(1943)	2	6	1		104th	(1995)	31	17	5	3
79th	(1945)	6	5			105th	(1997)	35	16	6	3
80th	(1947)	3	4		1	106th	(1999)	40	16	6	3
81st	(1949)	5	4		1	107th	(2001)	41	18	10	3
82nd	(1951)	4	6		1	108th	(2003)	38	21	9	5
83rd	(1953)	5	7		1	109th	(2005)	42	23	9	5
84th	(1955)	10	7		1	110th	(2007)	50	21	11	5
85th	(1957)	9	6		1	111th	(2009)	57	17	13	4
86th	(1959)	9	8		1	112th	(2011)	52	24	12	5
87th	(1961)	11	7	1	1	113th	(2013)	56	20	16	4
88th	(1963)	6	6	1	1	114th	(2015)	62	22	14	6
89th	(1965)	7	4	1	1	115th	(2017)	62	21	16	5
90th	(1967)	5	5		1	116th	(2019)	89	13	17	8

African Americans in political positions has an interesting history. In the ten or so years after the Emancipation Proclamation "liberated" slaves in the Southern States, there was an influx of black people entering into political positions, successfully running businesses, and expanding the bounds of their social position. In the 9 years between 1869 and 1877, there were more African American people in Congress than in the next 70 years. This was due to the manufactured rivalry between poor white progressives and newly freed slaves and the creation of Jim Crow Laws.

In 1933, there was an extreme shift in position for black persons in Congress. Before this year, there was not a single African American democrat. This is because the eugenicists, the progressives, the pro-slavery, pro-Jim Crow Laws, pro-KKK, pro-segregation party was the democratic party. In 1935, the single black person in Congress was for the first time, part of the democratic party. There was not a single black Republican in the House again until 1991. In 2019, the Republican Party had all of 2 black people in their entire party. The switch from one party to another came hand in hand importantly and partly with the unification of support between poor white and poor black workers forming partnerships and unions toward mutual gain. The democratic party shifted position with Franklin D. Roosevelt, as he created what in effect socially and financially benefitted the poor, especially farmers and laborers, at least in the short term. He created systems by which these people had opportunity and flexibility to grow out of the depression and massive poverty, even if it was yet still part of the greater agenda to reduce the population to chattel in all aspects, including by seizure of small farmlands. General popularity of anti-segregation and freedom from oppressive situations only grew and unified the people more over the next half century, and arguably until now. We now have a proportionate amount of black Congress members to the population. The same can be said for Native American Representation. This is not true for women, Asians, or Latino populations.

Table 1-16 African Americans in Congress, 41st - 116th Congresses, 1869 - 2019

		House		Senate	
Congress		D	R	D	R
41st	(1869)		2		1
42nd	(1871)		5		
43rd	(1873)		7		
44th	(1875)		7		1
45th	(1877)		3		1
46th	(1879)				1
47th	(1881)		2		
48th	(1883)		2		
49th	(1885)		2		
50th	(1887)				
51st	(1889)		3		
52nd	(1891)		1		
53rd	(1893)		1		
54th	(1895)		1		
55th	(1897)		1		
56th	(1899)[a]		1		
71st	(1929)		1		
72nd	(1931)		1		
73rd	(1933)		1		
74th	(1935)	1			
75th	(1937)	1			
76th	(1939)	1			
77th	(1941)	1			
78th	(1943)	1			
79th	(1945)	2			
80th	(1947)	2			
81st	(1949)	2			
82nd	(1951)	2			
83rd	(1953)	2			
84th	(1955)	3			
85th	(1957)	3			
86th	(1959)	3			
87th	(1961)	3			
88th	(1963)	4			
89th	(1965)	5			
90th	(1967)	5			1
91st	(1969)	9			1
92nd	(1971)	13			1
93rd	(1973)	16			1
94th	(1975)	16			1
95th	(1977)	15			1
96th	(1979)	15			
97th	(1981)	17			
98th	(1983)	20			
99th	(1985)	20			
100th	(1987)	22			
101st	(1989)	23			
102nd	(1991)	25	1		
103rd	(1993)	38	1	1	
104th	(1995)	37	2	1	
105th	(1997)	36	1	1	
106th	(1999)	36	1		
107th	(2001)	35	1		
108th	(2003)	37			
109th	(2005)	40		1	
110th	(2007)	40		1	
111th[b]	(2009)	39			
112th	(2011)	40	2		
113th[c]	(2013)	41			1
114th	(2015)	42	2	1	1
115th	(2017)	45	2	2	1
116th	(2019)	52	1	2	1

The Supreme Court of the United States is the highest court of the nation. It is such a position as one would expect the highest accountability to be unburdened by and unaffiliated with corporate or political influencers. This is patently not the case. Supreme Court Term Limits and Direct Elections would assist in the necessary reform to reduce the abuse of power and the unconstitutional authority given to the Court. Without reform, major decisions are being left to the extreme bias of the Justices who represent the agendas of the duopolistic political system and corporations. Even excluding term limits and elections of justices, there are means to drastically reduce harm, such as in a standing requisite that justices must never have held roles in corporations or other organizations that have been convicted of crimes or must have been proven to have not participated in those crimes.

"...an overly ideological court, in either direction, not only distorts our politics for the worse but allows unelected, life-tenured judges to dictate policy even when no reasonable person could argue there is an "irreconcilable variance" between the decisions made by elected officials and our written Constitution."

-"Yes, it's time to reform the Supreme Court but not for the wrong reasons" by Eric J. Segall, the Kathy & Lawrence Ashe Professor of Law at Georgia State University College of Law.[13]

We need to reform our government. In 1913, the 17th Amendment was ratified, codifying the direct election of senators. Before this, Senators were elected by State Legislatures. In the original design, if a Virginian senator voted on a bill that would give subsidies to Pennsylvanian Steel Makers, he would have to answer to his State Legislature as to why he was giving away the money of the people of Virginia to some people in Pennsylvania. Direct Election eliminates people's control over what happens in Washington, through the states. The number of Senators voted upon must be relative to population size. Today, the Senate is composed largely of people unfairly voted into office. This is extremely detrimental to public representation, as it means that the vast majority of the public can be ignored as the Senate represents an extremely small portion of the population. It means that our laws, our executive appointees, and our public money are in the hands of people who do not vote for the will of the people. We must either abolish the Senate or reshape its organization.

"Even today, the majority does not rule in the Senate. The majority of States, not people, governs. Twenty-six States representing only slightly more than one-sixth of the population of the United States can block any legislation from passing. (In fact, given the Senate's filibuster rules, twenty-one States, with slightly more than 10 percent of the population, can stop all laws.) ... even in the modern era, small States still gain substantial advantages in the Senate due to their equal voting power."

– "Electoral Dysfunction" by Victoria Bassetti[14]

The Constitution declares that there must be one representative in congress per 30,000 people. This means that today, as of January 1st, 2022, we require 11,080 congressmembers to constitute a full body. Under rules of Congress, to conduct business, there is required a quorum of a majority. This means that Congress cannot conduct business, such as the passing of laws, without a full 5,540 members present. This means that any law passed, or action taken since before 1790 (date of the first census), according to the census data below, is without legal authority. Let's go back just to 2 dates though, 1929 and 1941. In 1929, the House passed the Permanent Apportionment Act which capped the number of Representatives to 435. The 1941 Apportionment Act mandated the use of the Method of Equal Proportions. In the convoluted updates to the Constitution, Article 1, Section 2 describes that both direct taxes and

Representatives are apportioned by the States respective numbers. The fact is that there has not been a single law passed within the bounds that the Constitution laid out explicitly in over 230 years. This is not surprising though as very little of the Constitution has been upheld throughout the years since it was created. Rather it has mostly been a sort of idealistic goal for most, and a minor irritation for those who crave power and control as its existence gave hope, aspiration, a sense of title and power, and a means by which to elucidate on that power, to the masses.

The number of average number of constituents pre representative is roughly 765,000. How is it that we are meant to have one representative per 30,000, but instead we have 25.5 times that number of constituents per representative? Why have we allowed this to happen? Let's look at it like this. The amount of people that can have an audience with a representative if each was given 15 minutes, and if the representative allowed audience 5 days a week for 4 hours a day, would amount to 4160 people. This workload would not be difficult as representatives are surrounded by staffers who handle the affairs that are dictated by the officeholder. But let's look at this. 4160 people is about 13% of 30,000 people. That seems a somewhat reasonable number of people who may have a genuine issue needing the assistance of their elected official. But 4160 people amounts to only .5% of 765.000 constituents. This means that far fewer people are able to meet with their representatives for any purpose. It elevates the bar on who can acquire a meeting, even for 15 minutes. It distinctly separates the people from those elected as it reduces the capacity and opportunity to post grievance or educate or make claim. The fact is that even if the representatives of today were able to receive 10 times the amount of people, which would bring the number to 5% (still far less than the original) those people would only be interacting with the representatives' staff. A single individual can only take in so much information when they are expected to be occupied with an already extremely tight operating schedule. This individual is accountable to represent the people they do not know and will never meet or even potentially meet. This creates a vast chasm between the people and the officials, the plutocrats, who are elected most often not based on popular votes anyway, but through the manipulation of the entire voting structure and system to narrow results to extremely predictable results, where beneficiaries of elections are almost universally the same corporate entities and political groups that hedge their bets on people who are competing within defined and dedicated boundaries in which resulting policy and action will be the same.

Representatives need to be in touch with the people, and today they are not even close. Social media is not the bridge, but the excuse. It makes us feel connected despite massive amounts of social and political coercion and the fact that it is a mockery of real interaction between people. The harm that social media has caused humanity is so extreme as to be one of the worst self-inflicted crimes against humanity. Our system will never work for the people until it is demanded and enforced by the people to become localized, with representatives that *only* represent 30,000 or even less, maybe even much less. The reasoning behind the capping of the House at 435 was because they had to keep the number reasonably efficient. That excuse wasn't good then, and its far worse today with the amount of connectedness that exists, the amount of technology that can encrypt, the amount of open-source Stechnology that can be put to use, and the amount of people that are now alive. We the People need to be adequately represented, and it would be much more difficult to corrupt a congress of 11,080 than of 435. 535 with the Senate. No matter what else, the Constitution stands. The illegal changes made that directly fly in the face of the Bill of Rights, like direct taxation and the capping of the House, are illegal and ought not be paid heed.

Table B. **Population Base for Apportionment and the Number of Representatives Apportioned: 1790 to 1990**

Census year	Population base[1]	Number of Representatives[2]	Ratio of apportionment population to Representative	Date of apportionment act
1990	249,022,783	435	[3]572,466	Nov. 15, 1941
1980	225,867,174	435	519,235	Nov. 15, 1941
1970	204,053,025	435	[4]469,088	Nov. 15, 1941
1960	178,559,217	435	410,481	Nov. 15, 1941
1950	149,895,183	435	344,587	Nov. 15, 1941
1940	131,006,184	435	301,164	Nov. 15, 1941
1930	122,093,455	435	280,675	June 18, 1929
1920[5]	...	435	...	...
1910	91,603,772	435	210,583	Aug. 8, 1911
1900	74,562,608	386	193,167	Jan. 16, 1901
1890	61,908,906	356	173,901	Feb. 7, 1891
1880	49,371,340	325	151,912	Feb. 25, 1882
1870	38,115,641	292	130,533	[6]Feb. 2, 1872
1860	29,550,038	241	122,614	[7]May 23, 1850
1850	21,766,691	234	93,020	[8]May 23, 1850
1840	15,908,376	223	71,338	June 25, 1842
1830	11,930,987	240	49,712	May 22, 1832
1820	8,972,396	213	42,124	Mar. 7, 1822
1810	6,584,231	181	36,377	Dec. 21, 1811
1800	4,879,820	141	34,609	Jan. 14, 1802
1790	3,615,823	105	34,436	Apr. 14, 1792
Constitution	...	65	[9]30,000	1789

[1]Excludes the population of District of Columbia; the population of the territories; prior to 1940, the number of American Indians not taxed; and, prior to 1870, two-fifths of the slave population. In 1990 and 1970, includes selected segments of Americans abroad.

[2]This figure is the actual number of Representatives apportioned at the beginning of each decade.

[3]Ratio of resident population to Representative in 1990 is 570,352.

[4]Ratio of resident population to Representative in 1970 is 465,468.

[5]No apportionment was made on the basis of the 1920 census.

[6]Amended by act of May 30, 1872.

[7]Amended by act of March 4, 1862.

[8]Amended by act of July 30, 1852.

[9]The minimum ratio of population to Representative, as stated in Article 1, Section 2 of the United States Constitution.

*www.census.gov[15]

Our President is not held to any ethical standard by law. We need to rethink this and enact an ethical standard that applies to the position of President. Whomever is in this position, must be held to an even higher standard than any other person in the nation. This is obvious and necessary. How can we not, when the president is holding the keys to the largest nuclear weapons arsenal on the planet? We must enforce these standards to ensure our nation is protected from those who might abuse their power to dominate others as has been the case with the vast majority of presidents of the United States.

We must make a priority of eliminating the influence of money in funding politicians and policies. There is a significant amount of control over the US Government being held by corporate interests and potentially other entity interests. We must end the practice of the unofficial, but substantively influential, "committee dues". These are subtly enforceable dues charged to US Congressmembers for seats on committees. This practice is not only enforced by the Major Parties, but its methods are conveyed to members in such that members are taught how to encourage, through Party designated fundraisers, receiving funds for their committee positions. We must eliminate Pork Barrel Spending, which is the practice of appropriating government spending for localized projects secured solely or primarily to bring money to a representative's district. This practice serves private interests while casting the financial burden on the entirety of the population. It is not competitively awarded and serves to prejudice the use of funds to politically favored people, particularly for the purpose of creating positive public perception within that representative's district, and thus supporting their reelection. It also incentivizes and reconfirms the federal government to continue to position itself by funding states and districts off loans and debts.
We need to RE-FORM our government if we are to avoid slavery and revolution, and these things spoken of in this book are only the beginnings. We are NOT a democracy. We are not the standard for wellbeing or freedom in the world. We need to recognize the roots of our problems and let go of the perception that we can remain free while not directly confronting that which means to enslave us, or that which has already applied the chains.

"I pledge allegiance to the flag of the United States of America..."
Why would any sane person pledge their allegiance to a piece of cotton? This inane practice has been created to manufacture loyalty to an idea, even when the idea is not what is currently manifest. Meaning, people will get all worked up about service to the flag, burning of flags, not allowing flags to touch the ground, flags being presented in particular ways, but they will pass the homeless and the suffering without a thought for how they are treated.
"...and to the republic for which it stands..."
We are not and have never been a republic. We have been so on paper, but the true nature of our government has been that of mercantilism and plutocracy. This means that people are reciting a phrase every day for large portions of their life that breeds into them some emotional and visceral attachment to an idea that is not manifest. The idea that millions of people are swearing fealty to a piece of colored cloth is the essence of insanity.
"...one nation under God..."
Though we are supposed to have freedom of religion in this country, it seems we are ignoring that particular right for the much more unpleasant privilege of declaring ourselves to be under a God. Who's God? Why are we under this God?
...with freedom and Justice for all."
When Francis Bellamy, a Christian socialist, wrote the first version of this indoctrinating propaganda, it was actually the second attempt to create a national pledge to instill loyalty to the United States in children through the educational system. The first attempt was by George Batch, the auditor of the New York Board of Education. His version went, "We give our heads and hearts to God and our country; one country, one language, one flag." The idea that we need to force children to think that their country

deserves their inherent respect is a perverse notion and is a splendid example of how we have abused and manipulated the consent of the population to be governed. The practices of indoctrination are cumulative, and the pledge of allegiance is just one of the things that have been created and perpetuated despite its rigid and obvious theme of inculcating loyalty and patriotism, without truly earning that loyalty or patriotism.

What Bellamy originally wanted, was a phrase including equality and fraternity, but he knew that those terms would not be accepted by the state superintendents of education who were opposed to equality for women and non-white races. We need to eradicate this Pledge. We need to eradicate the idea that mindless and ignorant patriotism is preferred over the government having to earn the loyalty and respect of an intelligent, informed, and free population.

The flag of the United States has changed twenty-seven times as our nation has changed. Our first flag, besides the Gadsden flag, was the Betsy Ross Flag, which contained thirteen stars and thirteen stripes representing the original colonies. Over time more stars have been added until we reached fifty states and thus fifty stars. The reason for which the flag is symbolically important to the American people, is due to the meaning that it held to those who fought to create a distinct nation and break free from the British Empire and the abuse of mercantilism. The story of the American Revolution is not as black and white as has been made to seem in nationalized schooling. It was a complex series of events with many personalities, agendas, and interests. Very few of the people in the colonies gathered together to fight the British and the vast majority of those who did join in the fight were militiamen. The support for the revolution was around 45 percent of the American Colonists. There was a considerable number of loyalists as well who fought against the revolutionaries in support of Britain. Without support from France and Spain in particular, the revolution would most likely have been unsuccessful. The revolution and subsequent separation from Britain were significant as those set a precedence for similar actions around the world by other colonies of empires.

The American Revolution was significant as well because of the ideals it codified in its manifesto, the Declaration of Independence. The idea of real ownership, private property, and the promise of increasing one's position and status. The ideas of liberty for all equally and freedom at birth, though selectively and prejudicially applied to begin with, were imparted into the ideological core of the new nation. Over time, as the ideas matured in the population, we saw the gradual inclusion of originally outcast groups into this agreement. The inclusion of these ideals in the Declaration of Independence and in the Constitution was due entirely to the adamant presentation of their merit by select individuals and not by the desire of the group as a whole. Rather, our agreements regarding these higher ideals were admitted by consensus with the understanding that not all people would actually be given these liberties. The gift that those who demanded these ideals be included gave was a gift to the future generations. It was a gift to a society ready to adopt them. We are the inheritors of this gift that was undervalued for far too long and is yet misunderstood and devalued today. It was a gift that many died for, and many more lived and fought for.

The great ignorance that lays heavy on the population today is a burden to our evolution into the future and the understanding of what we must do to make it possible. The simplest things that we so often take for granted must be examined to truly understand why our society is the way it is. Where did we come from and where are we going to? Why do we recite a pledge of allegiance or care if our national flag touches the ground? Where does our national anthem come from?

Today's national anthem is part of a poem written by Francis Scott Key during the British bombardment of Fort Henry in 1814. This poem was then applied to a British drinking song called "To Anacreon In Heaven". The song was adopted as the National Anthem in 1931, but only the first stanza. Key's poem was not truly representative of the people. The first stanza of his poem was easily adopted into a propaganda tool that many people do not truly understand. Key's full poem included pro-slavery leaning phrases which are not included in the National Anthem. On the other hand, William Billings was the author of much of the music that was sung by the revolutionaries. These were songs that were sung on the march, in the camps, and amongst the population in general. These songs represented the population at the time. The unofficial anthem of the patriots was the song, "Chester".

Chester

Let tyrants shake their iron rods,
And Slav'ry clank her galling chains.
We fear them not, we trust in God.
New England's God forever reigns.

Howe and Burgoyne and Clinton, too,
With Prescott and Cornwallis joined,
Together plot our overthrow,
In one infernal league combined.

When God inspired us for the fight,
Their ranks were broke, their lines were forced,
Their ships were shattered in our sight,
Or swiftly driven from our coast.

The foe comes on with haughty stride,
Our troops advance with martial noise;
Their vet'rans flee before our youth,
And gen'rals yield to beardless boys.

What grateful off'ring shall we bring,
What shall we render to the Lord?
Loud hallelujahs let us sing,
And praise his name on ev'ry chord!

Historically, it is never the majority of any population that makes major changes and evolves their society, but rather a minority that has a wider perception than the rest. This is what we see in the American Revolution, and it is what we see in every social uprising. The American revolutionaries were among the forefront of their society at the time, generally. We see that their willingness to take decisive action against a stronger, more structured and battle proven, and significantly more well supplied enemy in the form of a war, if necessary, could possibly have been called insane at that time. We are again in a time that demands decisive and immediate action. We are in a time of even more desperate circumstance than the people of two and half centuries ago. We have been secretly and cleverly invaded, manipulated and contorted to the will of those we fought so hard to break free of. The original flag, the Gadsden Flag, bearing the words "DON'T TREAD ON ME" beneath a coiled timber rattle snake was at one point a symbol that encouraged people to fight against tyranny by forming a coalition that supported their mutual needs. This ideology of collective empowerment has been almost entirely lost as the population of the nation today and for several generations has been inundated with propaganda that has indoctrinated them to aggress upon the rest of the world and ignorantly defend corporate dominance. While the ideology is used to entrap the docile population, those that understand the true meaning of the symbols and the language used in the founding of the nation are imprisoned, outcast, vilified and declared unpatriotic. The tables have been completely reversed. In today's United States of America, Incorporated, the society bleats various bombastic claims and ignorantly shouts about the state of the world and the condition of the nation but is completely oblivious of the conditions that led to the formation of the agreement that affirmed and guaranteed the right to opine in the first place. The right is taken for granted, and yet it is the first of our most sacred agreements written into the core of our social design. We had the affirmed freedom to speak when much of the world was openly censored. These rights were not given to all the people at the time of the agreement, because of a few self-serving plutocrats, but during the process developing from this agreement, it was the people themselves who rose to the challenge to demand the inclusion. We the people fought for and won the right to have and share our prosperity and our rights. While the population became accustomed to the inclusion of those they disagreed with, the laws came to change. It is the struggles that we encounter that allow us the knowledge that we can and must do better. We must become greater than our past. We must now look toward a future that disallows the abuse of the many by the will of the few. In 1776, the colonies took action to become sovereign and they worked together to make that possible. They chose to abandon the economic abuse of private central bankers and puppet governments. They chose to forcibly remove the control of vampirical foreign governments and private entities. They chose to make their own way into the future, and they did so despite overwhelming odds. For those people, the possibility of a brighter future was worth dying for. For those people, righteous action, truth, and freedom were not words used to bolster consumerism, but words that held sacred meaning and power. We the people are the only government that has ever existed, and when we choose, the world will become idyllic. We the people have the power, but only when we choose. Today's world is in collapse, economically, spiritually, and physically. This is the only moment we have in evolving our society and if we do nothing or perpetuate our condition we will succumb to the ultimate destruction of all life on this planet within a few generations, either by technocracy or war.

History is not black and white, just as our lives today are not. People have flaws, and in groups these flaws can often lead to consensuses and agreements that cause harm to our common wellbeing. While the flaws must surely be pointed out and understood, they must not lead us to hatred and separation. We must learn to accept the things that have happened and grow out of those understandings. It is the maturation of any society that can look upon its past and its present and forgo judgement for the much more beneficial process of understanding our faults and changing our behaviors to better ourselves and provide for the betterment of our societies as we progress into our communal future. We must learn to recognize what we have done well and what we need to work on. We must recognize the things that have caused harm, and we must change.

If slavery never existed, would we be better off? Would we know the terrible nature of the thing? Would we have the will to codify the abolition of such a thing. If terrible working conditions had not existed during the industrial revolution, would we have been able to point out the oppressors so easily? It was not the government that fought for the people when the Revolution occurred. Industrialists, bankers, and politicians create the conditions for war which the people fight either in ignorance at the call of their government, or in revolution to cast down the tyrants from their illegitimate perches. We the people are the only thing that create and change the system that we live within.

JUSTICE

Let us talk about our Justice system for a little bit. To talk about Justice, we need to understand what it is and how it developed in the United States of America. The word justice goes back to Latin *Justitia*, which means *equity* and *righteousness*. The idea of justice exists only in a society where unjust actions are taking place. In a just society, people have no need of government. Interestingly there is a feedback loop between law and justice. Where a law exists, it predisposes the absence of righteousness and equity. Where the absence of equity and righteousness exists, laws will exist. To have justice, a society must adequately apportion reward and punishment according to the principles of equity and righteousness.

This brings us to the social paradigm. If a society determines that a duel to the death between two willing participants is righteous, it will not have laws denying the act of dueling and it will consider the act a right of the people. If a society determines that healthcare is a human right, there will be laws created to prevent the restriction of that right. If a society determines that spitting in public is unrighteous, laws will be formed to prevent individuals from spitting. Inhibiting the qualities a society disapproves of while rewarding the qualities a society holds as being righteous, will create the social design, the rule of law, and the justice system. This would be true if we had a truly holistic governmental and societal organization. In a true, or direct democracy, society regulates their laws and thus their justice system. This falls apart in a supposedly democratic government that inhibits democracy. In the United States, corporate control of the monetary supply, the government, the market itself and the media, means that instead of the accurate representation of the will and social structure of the population, the laws and the justice system are actually reflective of the will and the society of just a small group of people who then exert their social design upon the rest of the population. This means that justice, or equity and righteousness, is based solely on the morality, ethics, and social condition of that group, but affects the entire population. When we look at the justice system of the United States, we see vast prejudices towards populations that are most vulnerable. This is also a feedback loop to the system that has manifested due to its representative body. The small number of people that have influenced and manufactured the social structure of today, and thus benefit from that structure, have made it in such a way that people who are disinclined to succeed in that structure are made vulnerable to the justice system, which no longer represents their paradigm and their opinions on what is just, righteous, and equitable.

We have been witness in the last 200 years to a shift in society from agrarian majority to urban industrial majority. This was not accidental, and it was not a favorable or accepted transition for the majority population. It was a controlled, intentional, and forceful shift sanctioned and executed by private banking interests, industrial interests, and proponents for centralized authoritarian government. In the first half of the 1800's, the United States was mostly composed of farmers. Over 50% of the labor in the country were farmers. In 1850, farmers owned 75 percent of the nation's wealth. By 1890, with the advancement of industrialization and migrations to urban centers, farmers percentage of US wealth dropped to 25%, a major shift and not easily disregarded. As this shift was occurring, the private owners of the industries that people were working for, were absorbing larger and larger portions of that displaced wealth. Leading up to this massive shift, was over 75 years of struggle between private bankers and industrialists and those who desired to create a truly democratic or anarchic or any other form of society. While the government did allow several times for central banks to exist, they did not allow them to exist for longer than the government needed them. I will get into this more later, but the takeaway is that while government changes apparently significantly every few years, the private interests that want to greedily absorb the world do not have to limit themselves to four years. They can operate constantly in the effort to maximize their influence and their control. The very structure and internal rules of corporations are designed to maximize their profits, control, and influence at the exclusion of any other factors. Governments have the choice.

In 1913, the efforts of these bankers and industrialists and their associates fruited. They were not only given the exclusive right over banking in the country but also were given the exclusive right to print the national currency. This handed the society over to the newly crowned social designers. The bankers and the industrialists, who more often than not were the same people or in direct collusion. Now that the economy was in the hands of this small group of people that were socially very different than nearly everyone else in the nation, it was only a matter of time until their influence would permeate through the society and alter the paradigm. The Great Depression occurred seventeen years after the Federal Reserve was founded under the promise to end recessions, or "panics", and during this devastating period for the population, these bankers and industrialists, who had exited the banks before the run on the banks occurred, purchased much of the economy from competitors who were devastated and had to sell their businesses for pennies on the dollar. Only ten years after the bank run, the country found itself on the brink of war. The United States got in later than other countries for many reasons, but primarily because the bankers were profiteering on the war. Henry Ford was supplying Nazi Germany with military vehicles, and Standard Oil was supplying petroleum to the Nazi's. These were only part of the exported goods that fueled and funded Adolf Hitler and his war and consequent genocide of the Jews, the Poles, the mentally disabled, homosexuals, and defined deviants of the Aryan ideal. While Hitler may have taken eugenics to its fullest expression, he notably said that he got his inspiration from the United States. This is because the United States had been leading the world in eugenics theory and application. Eugenics is the practice of controlled selective breeding of humans to improve upon the genetic composition of the population. The US had been conducting sterilizations of prisoners, the diagnosed mentally ill, the physically disabled, and various other "deviant" groups. It was popularized and even movies and publications were made around this concept. Who funded this ideological spread? Who funded the antisemitism in the United States? It was John Rockefeller who funded the first school of psychiatry in 1930, which was prior to this considered unscientific and not a medical practice. This school was the beginning of the formalization and acceptance of the psychiatric method. It was Henry Ford who printed and disseminated millions of copies of the Protocols of the Elders of Zion, which was a book that created a perception of Jews as being evil, diabolical, and inhuman beings. Antisemitism was manufactured in the population of the United States just as it was manufactured in Germany. This was probably why Hitler awarded Henry Ford with the highest civilian honor that the Nazi's had, the Grand Cross of the German Eagle, in 1938.

In the 1930's, to be considered a valid or competent doctor in the United States, a student would have to study in Germany, as it was considered to have the greatest schools for higher learning. The very amalgamated society of educated people between Germany and the United States was strengthened by mutualistic philosophies like eugenics and psychiatry. Of course, the populations of both nations were not the profiteers of any of these philosophies as war, mandated by the international banking structure and their loyal government servants, resulted in the deaths of millions of people who had no real interest in fighting anyone and were uninformed as to the real reasons for which they were being forced to.

After the war, the farming industry of the United States was booming. The New Deal programs had mandated a living wage for farmers. When the 60's came around, the farming industry came under attack by industrialists once again, and all protections for farmers began to be stripped from law, the farming labor slowly but consistently migrated to city centers and industrial labor jobs. From 1962 to 1996, the decrease in farmers was mitigated by New Deal programs that were still in place. In 1996, Bill Clinton removed the last vestige of protections for farmers. We were now part of the WTO and NAFTA.

Today, the agrarian culture of less than two centuries ago is nearly eradicated. We now have less than one percent of our population involved in farming, and most of the involvement comes from industrial farms. Our cities are more populated than ever and that is only increasing. Our environment is being eviscerated, our government is wholly bought and dictated to, and our population is a clear reflection of the desire of industrialists and bankers to create a disparity between themselves and the rest of the population of the world.

Shares of income growth accruing to the top 1% during economic expansions, U.S. and by region

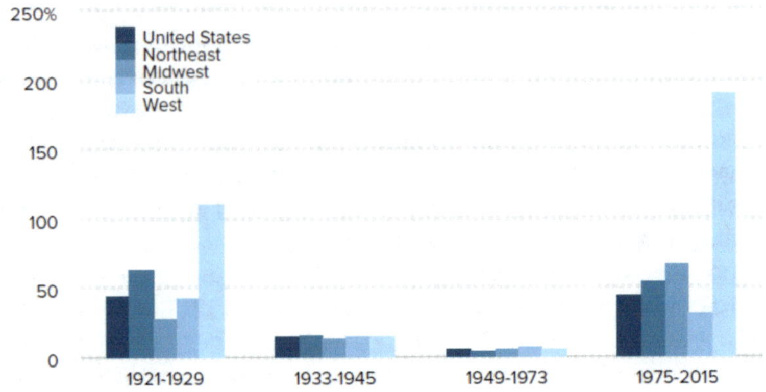

Notes: Shares greater than 100%—accruing to the top 1% in the West across the three expansions from 1921–1929 and the five expansions from 1975–2015—are the result of falling incomes for the bottom 99% in one expansion during each of these periods, specifically during the expansion from 1924 to 1926 and the expansion from 1975 to 1980. Excluding those two expansions, the fraction of growth accruing to the top 1% over the two remaining expansions from 1921 to 1929 averaged 18%, and the fraction of growth accruing to the top 1% over the four remaining expansions from 1975 to 2015 averaged 50%.

Source: Authors' analysis of state-level tax data from Sommeiller 2006 extended to 2015 using state-level data from the Internal Revenue Service SOI Tax Stats (various years), Piketty and Saez 2016, and Tcherneva 2014

Economic Policy Institute

Today our society is consumed by indifference, apathy, and the superficial shifting events of their censored media outlets. The society of today views the victory of their political party as being equal to the victory of their favorite sports team. The drive to demand their rights has been relegated to a drive to maintain the modicum of comfort they have been able to sequester for themselves. The fear of not participating in society by predetermined and acceptable standards is enough to make people commit suicide and to commit acts of mass murder. To fully comprehend the society of today we would be talking for a longer time than we have. To understand enough to see that we must take action to change this thing we have allowed to be created is another thing. To understand that our society today is not just by the standards of any honorable or honest person is the place to start from.

We need to reform our government. We need to recognize that the measure of our greatness is in the way we treat our most vulnerable people and our environment. When we imprison and are violent to our homeless, when we steal children from poverty-stricken mothers, and when we exclude and deny rights to our minority groups, we are defining ourselves as an unhealthy and unjust society. We need to make major and minor changes, but we must make them now. This is the only moment that will ever exist, and when we accept enslavement, abuse, and unrighteousness, we become responsible for the perpetuation of those very things. We need to overhaul our inhumane prison system. This begins with an audit of the Bureau of Prisons by Congress, observed by a third-party human rights organization. We need to eliminate the use of Executive Sessions of Congress on this audit. The public needs to be involved and aware of the crimes and the quality of the government. Since 1980, the prison population has tripled, and one of every nine people in prison are serving life sentences. Two out of every three people serving these life sentences are black or Latino. We need to abolish imprisonment for non-violent drug offenses, and we need to release all people from incarceration who are in this category, which amounts to 20 percent of the 2.3 million persons in the prison system today.[16] We need to abolish life sentences and replace them with 20-year maximums, with exclusions for continued violence. A review of the condition of prisoners by Certified

Health Professionals before release will determine if the persons are safe to be released. This will reduce cost of imprisonment while providing greater care to the imprisoned population.

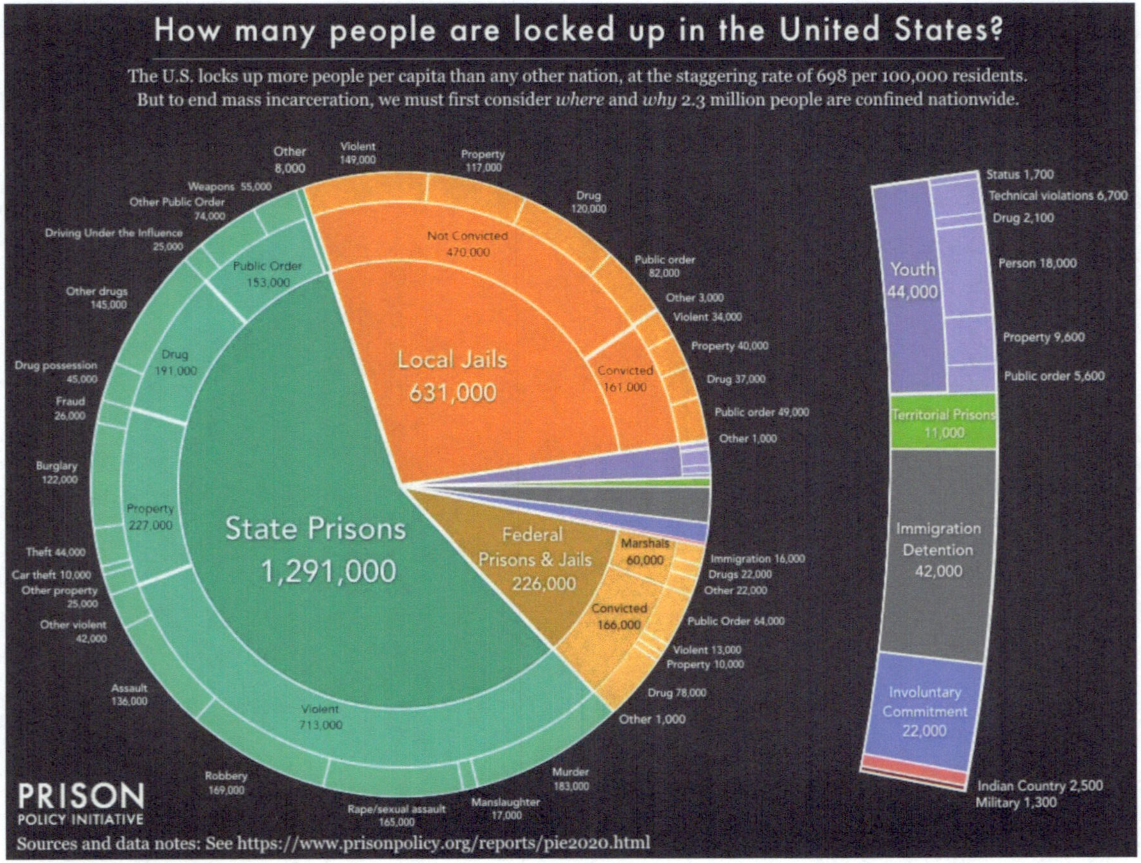
How many people are locked up in the United States?
The U.S. locks up more people per capita than any other nation, at the staggering rate of 698 per 100,000 residents.
But to end mass incarceration, we must first consider *where* and *why* 2.3 million people are confined nationwide.
State Prisons 1,291,000
Local Jails 631,000
Federal Prisons & Jails 226,000
Violent 713,000
Property 227,000
Drug 191,000
Public Order 153,000
Not Convicted 470,000
Convicted 161,000
Marshals 60,000
Convicted 166,000
Other 8,000
Weapons 55,000
Other Public Order 74,000
Driving Under the Influence 25,000
Other drugs 145,000
Drug possession 45,000
Fraud 26,000
Burglary 122,000
Theft 44,000
Car theft 10,000
Other property 25,000
Other violent 42,000
Assault 136,000
Robbery 169,000
Rape/sexual assault 165,000
Manslaughter 17,000
Murder 183,000
Violent 149,000
Property 117,000
Drug 120,000
Public order 82,000
Other 3,000
Violent 34,000
Property 40,000
Drug 37,000
Public order 49,000
Other 1,000
Immigration 16,000
Drugs 22,000
Other 22,000
Public Order 64,000
Violent 13,000
Property 10,000
Drug 78,000
Other 1,000
Youth 44,000
Status 1,700
Technical violations 6,700
Drug 2,100
Person 18,000
Property 9,600
Public order 5,600
Territorial Prisons 11,000
Immigration Detention 42,000
Involuntary Commitment 22,000
Indian Country 2,500
Military 1,300
PRISON POLICY INITIATIVE
Sources and data notes: See https://www.prisonpolicy.org/reports/pie2020.html

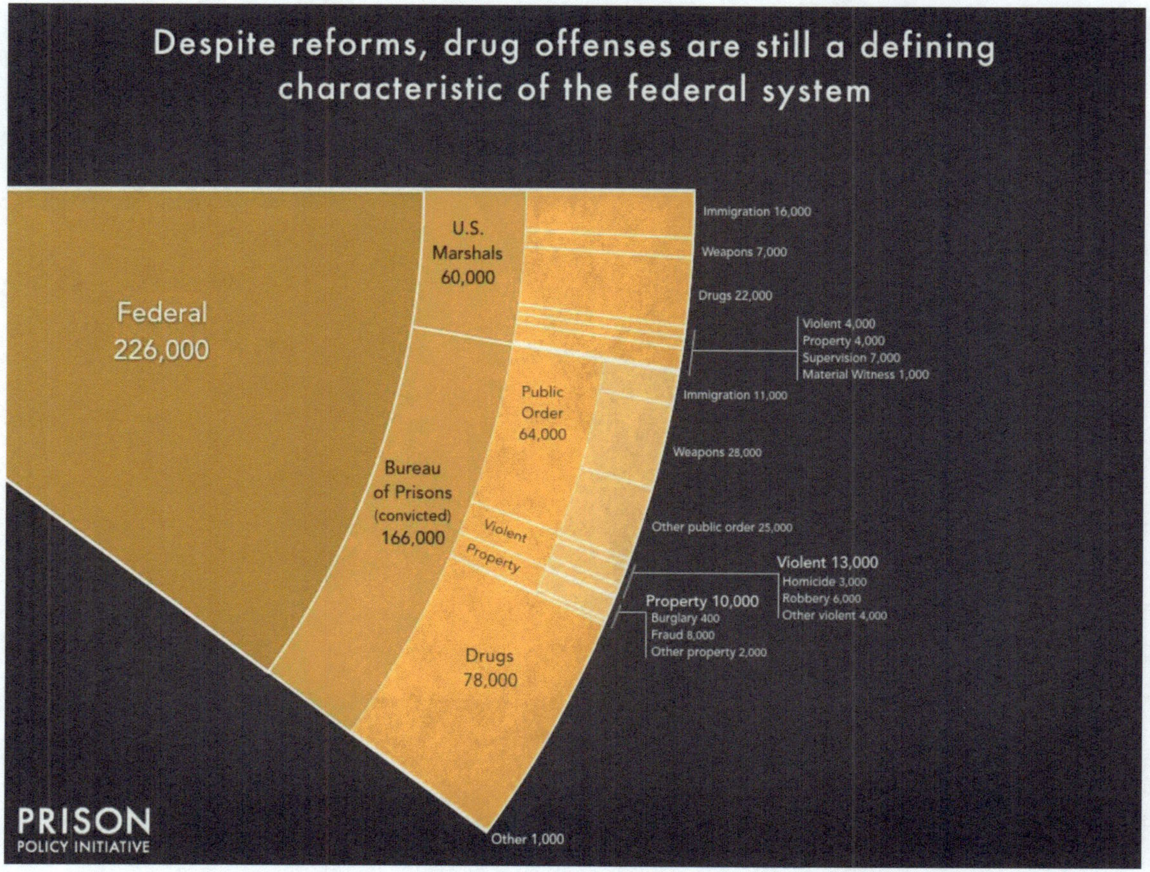
Despite reforms, drug offenses are still a defining characteristic of the federal system
Federal 226,000
U.S. Marshals 60,000
Bureau of Prisons (convicted) 166,000
Public Order 64,000
Violent
Property
Drugs 78,000
Immigration 16,000
Weapons 7,000
Drugs 22,000
Violent 4,000
Property 4,000
Supervision 7,000
Material Witness 1,000
Immigration 11,000
Weapons 28,000
Other public order 25,000
Violent 13,000
Homicide 3,000
Robbery 6,000
Other violent 4,000
Property 10,000
Burglary 400
Fraud 8,000
Other property 2,000
Other 1,000
PRISON POLICY INITIATIVE

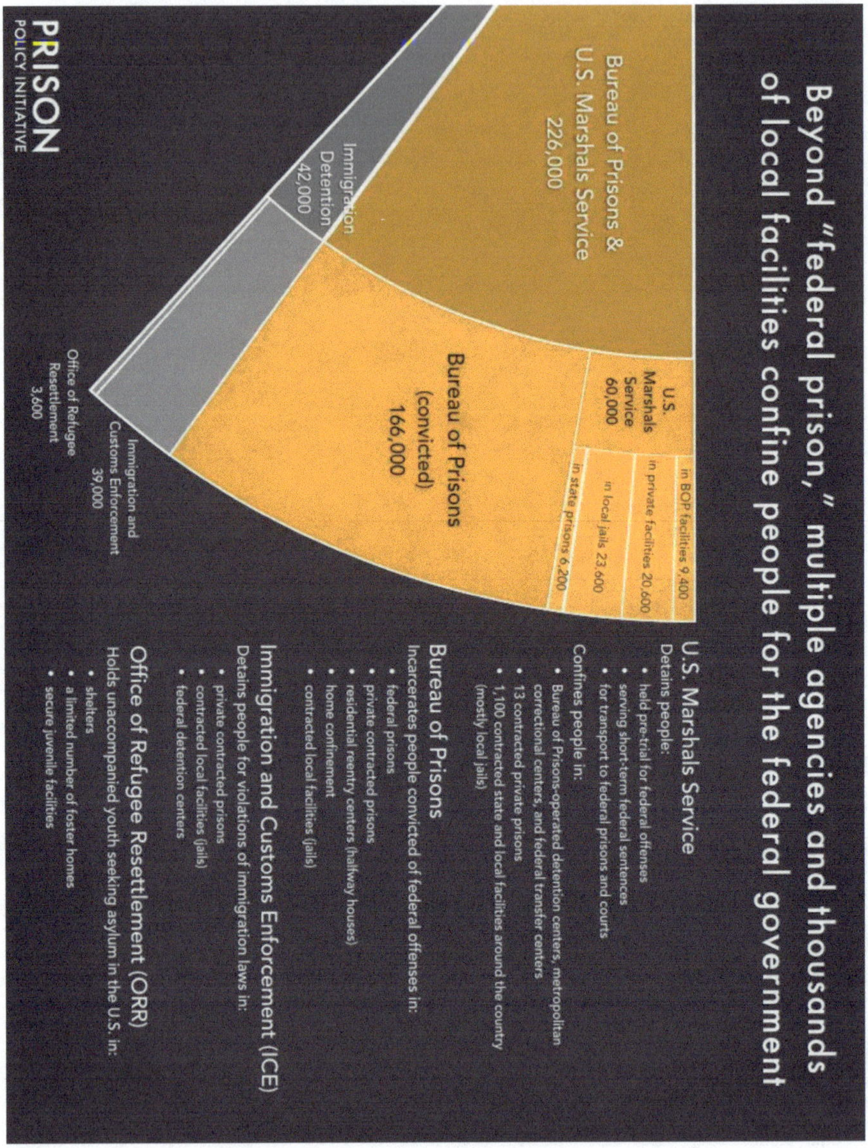

Beyond "federal prison," multiple agencies and thousands of local facilities confine people for the federal government
Bureau of Prisons & U.S. Marshals Service
226,000
Immigration Detention
42,000
U.S. Marshals Service
60,000
Bureau of Prisons (convicted)
166,000
in BOP facilities 9,400
in private facilities 20,600
in local jails 23,600
in state prisons 6,200
Immigration and Customs Enforcement
39,000
Office of Refugee Resettlement
3,600
U.S. Marshals Service
Details people:
• held pre-trial for federal offenses
• serving short-term federal sentences
• for transport to federal prisons and courts
Confines people in:
• Bureau of Prisons-operated detention centers, metropolitan correctional centers, and federal transfer centers
• 13 contracted private prisons
• 1,100 contracted state and local facilities around the country (mostly local jails)
Bureau of Prisons
Incarcerates people convicted of federal offenses in:
• federal prisons
• private contracted prisons
• residential reentry centers (halfway houses)
• home confinement
• contracted local facilities (jails)
Immigration and Customs Enforcement (ICE)
Details people for violations of immigration laws in:
• private contracted prisons
• contracted local facilities (jails)
• federal detention centers
Office of Refugee Resettlement (ORR)
Holds unaccompanied youth seeking asylum in the U.S. in:
• shelters
• a limited number of foster homes
• secure juvenile facilities
PRISON POLICY INITIATIVE

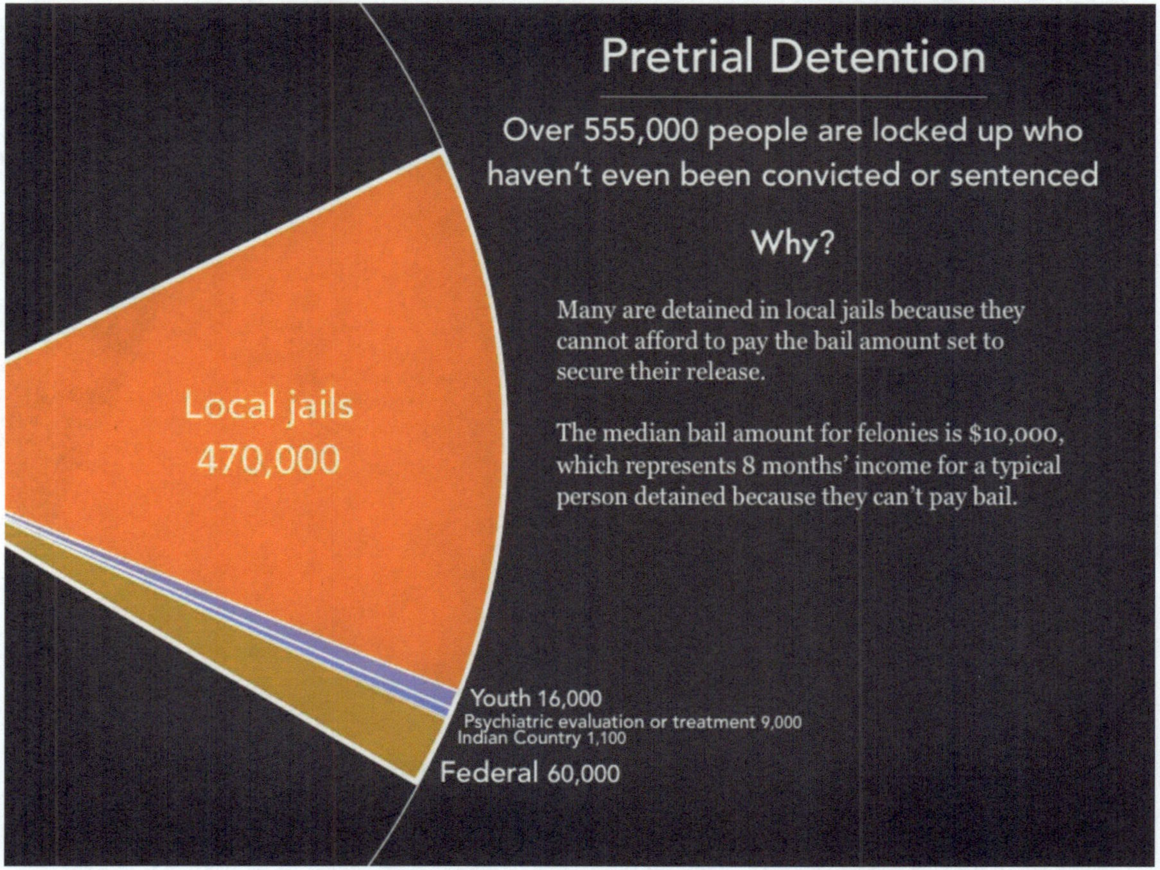

Pretrial Detention
Over 555,000 people are locked up who haven't even been convicted or sentenced
Why?
Many are detained in local jails because they cannot afford to pay the bail amount set to secure their release.
The median bail amount for felonies is $10,000, which represents 8 months' income for a typical person detained because they can't pay bail.
Local jails 470,000
Youth 16,000
Psychiatric evaluation or treatment 9,000
Indian Country 1,100
Federal 60,000

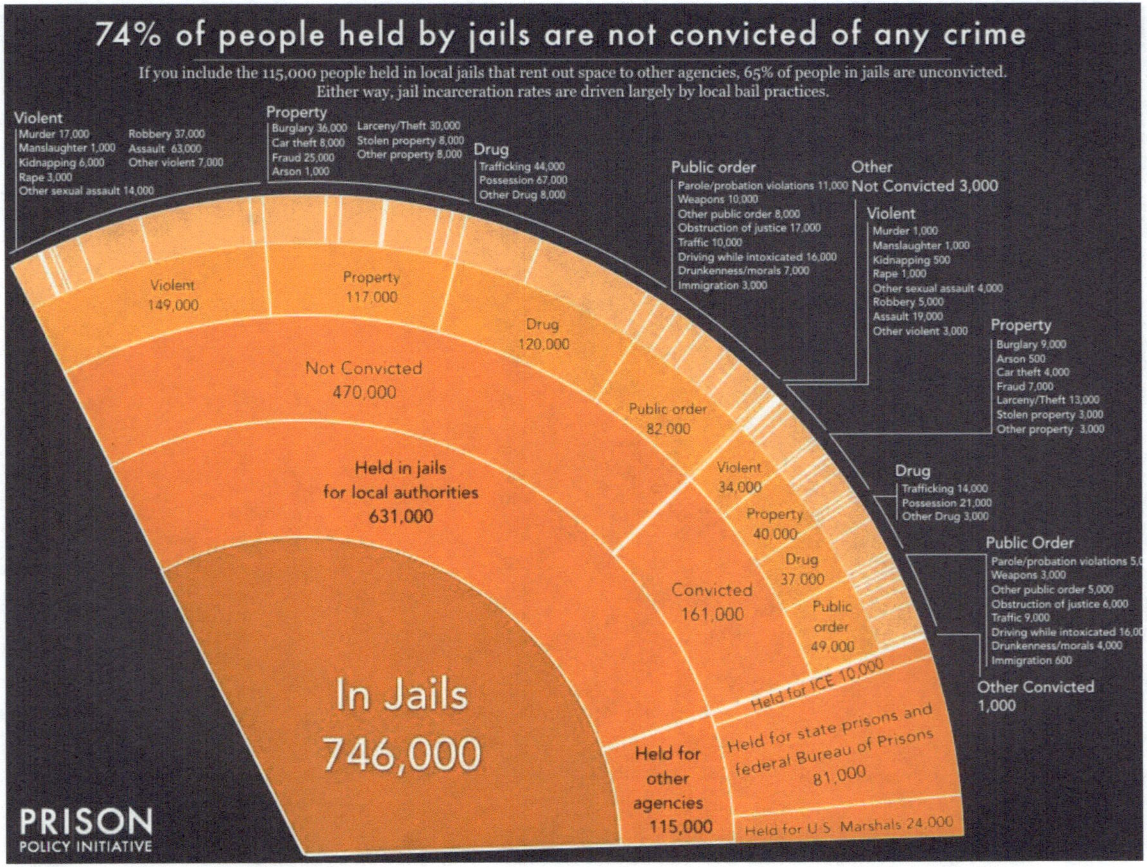
74% of people held by jails are not convicted of any crime
If you include the 115,000 people held in local jails that rent out space to other agencies, 65% of people in jails are unconvicted. Either way, jail incarceration rates are driven largely by local bail practices.
Violent
Murder 17,000
Manslaughter 1,000
Kidnapping 6,000
Rape 3,000
Other sexual assault 14,000
Robbery 37,000
Assault 63,000
Other violent 7,000
Property
Burglary 36,000
Car theft 8,000
Fraud 25,000
Arson 1,000
Larceny/Theft 30,000
Stolen property 8,000
Other property 8,000
Drug
Trafficking 44,000
Possession 67,000
Other Drug 8,000
Public order
Parole/probation violations 11,000
Weapons 10,000
Other public order 8,000
Obstruction of justice 17,000
Traffic 10,000
Driving while intoxicated 16,000
Drunkenness/morals 7,000
Immigration 3,000
Other Not Convicted 3,000
Violent
Murder 1,000
Manslaughter 1,000
Kidnapping 500
Rape 1,000
Other sexual assault 4,000
Robbery 5,000
Assault 19,000
Other violent 3,000
Property
Burglary 9,000
Arson 500
Car theft 4,000
Fraud 7,000
Larceny/Theft 13,000
Stolen property 3,000
Other property 3,000
Drug
Trafficking 14,000
Possession 21,000
Other Drug 3,000
Public Order
Parole/probation violations 5,0
Weapons 3,000
Other public order 5,000
Obstruction of justice 6,000
Traffic 9,000
Driving while intoxicated 16,0
Drunkenness/morals 4,000
Immigration 600
Other Convicted 1,000
Violent 149,000
Property 117,000
Drug 120,000
Public order 82,000
Not Convicted 470,000
Violent 34,000
Property 40,000
Drug 37,000
Public order 49,000
Convicted 161,000
Held in jails for local authorities 631,000
Held for ICE 10,000
Held for state prisons and federal Bureau of Prisons 81,000
Held for U.S. Marshals 24,000
Held for other agencies 115,000
In Jails 746,000
PRISON POLICY INITIATIVE

"The excessively lengthy incarceration of offenders—yes, even for violent crimes—is counterproductive, costly, and inhumane. Research by leading criminologists Alfred Blumstein and Kiminori Nakamura demonstrates that an 18-year-old arrested for robbery is no more likely to be arrested for this crime by the age of 26 than anyone in the general population. Thus, each successive year of incarceration after this decline sets in produces diminishing returns for public safety. No one—including the judge—can predict who those people are, or how individuals may mature over a 20-year period. For this reason, policymakers could establish a mechanism to evaluate the public-safety risk of select prisoners as they near the end of their 20-year term. A review board comprised of psychologists and other professionals could make recommendations either to a judge or a parole board regarding whether continued confinement is necessary for public safety. And in such cases, they should also propose appropriate treatment interventions designed to produce behavioral change leading to eventual release.

While some might think this is unrealistic, sentences of more than 20 years are quite rare in many democratic nations. Norway, for example, limits prison terms to no more than 21 years, followed by a period of civil confinement when deemed necessary. Even the worst mass killer in the country's history, Anders Breivik, who killed 77 people in 2011, is serving such a prison term. Contrast this to the current practice in the United States, where countless drug offenders are serving far lengthier terms."

- "A 20-Year Maximum for Prison Sentences" By Marc Mauer on Democracy: A Journal Of Ideas[17]

The number of people serving life sentences continues to grow even while serious, violent crime has been declining for the past 20 years and little public safety benefit has been demonstrated to correlate with increasingly lengthy sentences. The lifer population has nearly quintupled since 1984. One in nine people in prison is now serving a life sentence and nearly a third of lifers have been sentenced to life without parole.

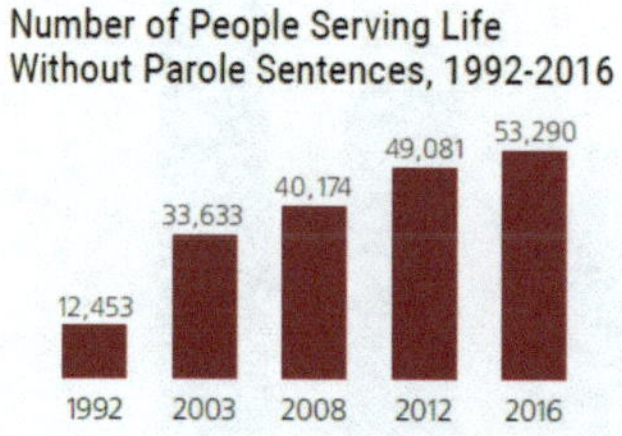

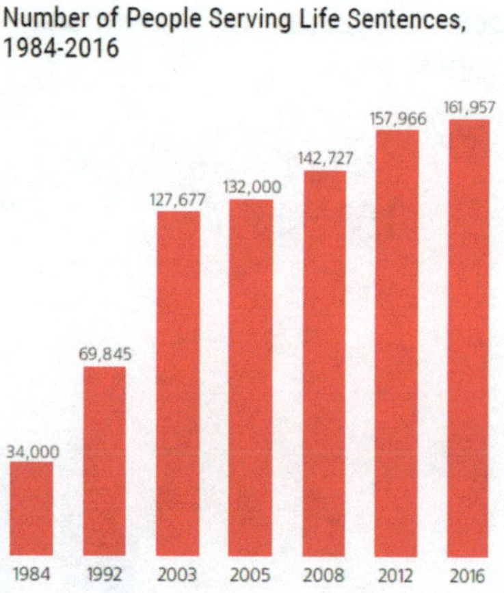

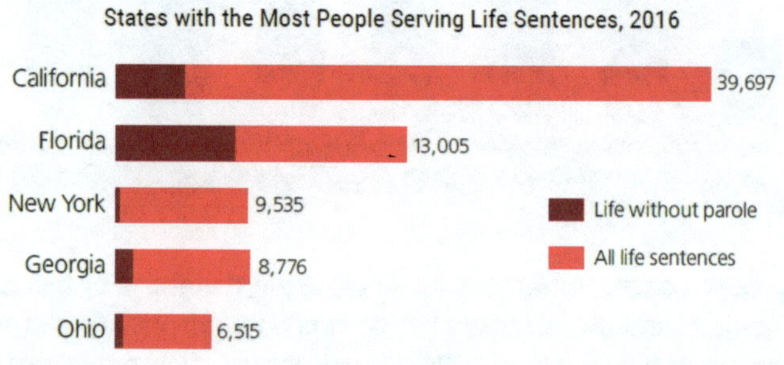

Source: Nellis, A. (2016). *Still Life: America's Increasing Use of Life and Long-Term Sentences.* Washington, DC: The Sentencing Project.

Hang 'em high! What easier, more efficient and compassionate solution exists to deal with violent criminal behavior? It is no place for the Federal or State governments to get involved in local matters, and thus it is up to local populations to collectively determine the proper correction to violent behavior. In this way, different municipalities or counties could determine what they feel is the best way to deal with violence. This allows the population to be witness to a real-time test of methods to see what works best to reduce violent acts. The death penalty is certainly more humane than forcing a person to live in a confined space surrounded at all times by extremely dangerous people who may choose to rape, murder, maim, or emotionally and psychologically torment them at any given moment. Today's prisons are training grounds for criminality, a place where novice criminals, innocent wrongly accused people, and non-violent individuals get thrown in with the truly deranged, extremely violent, professional killers, assaulters, and thieves, and are recruited into gangs and criminal cliques to survive. Would it not be more compassionate and practical in the use of resources and finances to simply hang those murderers, rapists, and child molesters? Does it not come down to the people victimized and their local customs to determine the correct punishment and thus the proper justice applied? Today, the politically correct theory and posture is that we must be non-violent to child molesters and gangbangers but come down hard on whistleblowers and gunowners. Basically, it is the idea that people who are actually violent need to be let off easy, while those people who expose the dishonest government and corporations and carry firearms to defend against those violent crazy people and their violent and crazy government ought to be punished even though they have not been violent. If, while reading this, you are thinking to yourself that hanging a rapist from the nearest tree is a terrific way of dealing with the violent people of this world, you are not alone. The death penalty serves to protect the people from violence by sending a message to the rest of the violent people and serves the pocketbook of the population by eradicating the need to pay for prisoners and prisons.

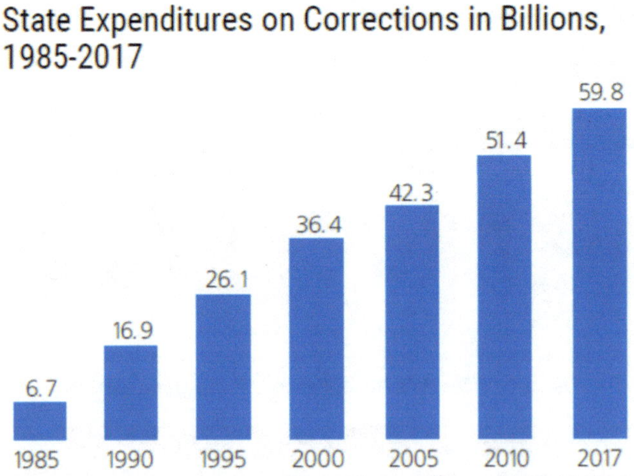

Source: National Association of State Budget Officers (1985-2017). *State Expenditure Report Series.* Washington, DC: National Association of State Budget Officers.

We need to eradicate private prisons, which exemplify yet again the abuse of the people by government and private corporate interests and the contracts between private prisons and states, where states agree to keep prisons at 90 percent or higher capacity. Private prisons use their prisoners to manufacture goods that now flood the consumer market. 100% of military helmets and much other military gear are made by inmates. Many corporations use prison labor to manufacture their outfits, like McDonald's. Minor violations leading to prison sentences, to produce goods with cheap labor. Current crime rates being lower than the last 40 years means that new and increasingly minor laws need to be, and are being, produced to supply the prisons with their required quotas, and to keep police employed

and crime rate statistics high. Debtors' prisons, which were once considered an abomination of justice in this country must be banned and made absolutely illegal and a violation of human rights. We need to eliminate Mandatory Minimum Sentences, which only act to promote the inequity and prejudice in our hypocritical society. We need to end the cash bail system which serves to prejudice yet again the population in poverty.

"The United States is one of the only countries in the world that requires cash bail for anyone who has been arrested and wants to stay out of jail while awaiting trial. The bail system discriminates against people of color and the poor, and it is in dire need of reform. Some states and cities are making progress, but much more work is needed to bring fairness to this corner of the criminal justice system.
Pretrial detainees make up more than 70 percent of the U.S. jail population — approximately 536,000 people. Many of them are only there because they can't afford bail."
"Defendants who don't have the funds to pay a bond premium are forced to await trial in jail. Pretrial detention has dramatically negative effects on the outcome of a defendant's case: those who are held pretrial are four times more likely to be sentenced to prison than defendants released prior to trial. Pretrial detainees are also likely to make hurried decisions to plead guilty to a lower charge to spend less time behind bars rather than chancing a higher charge and longer sentence at trial."
"Bail practices are frequently discriminatory, with Black and Latino men assessed higher bail amounts than white men for similar crimes by 35 and 19 percent on average, respectively."
-"How Cash Bail Works" By Adureh Onyekwere on Brennan Center For Justice[18]

Number of Sentenced People in Federal Prisons for Drug Offenses, 1980-2017

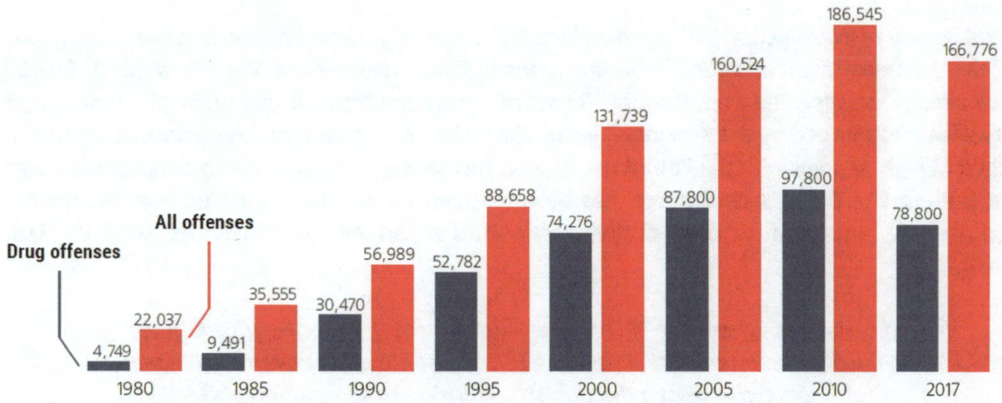

Sources: *Prisoners Series*. Washington, DC: Bureau of Justice Statistics.

We need a universal decriminalization of cannabis and fungi, as well as any other substance. It is not the substance itself that we must criminalize, but rather the action that a person might take on the substance. Cannabis has never resulted in a death but driving while smoking has. We must decriminalize all substances, but very strongly prohibit using them while taking action that can cause harm to others.

We need to universally pardon whistleblowers and provide protection to these people. The difference between whistleblowers and those who commit treason, is that whistleblowers share information about criminal activity, such as human rights or constitutional rights abuses and violations, and those committing treason are exposing sensitive information secretly for private gain to outside parties or sharing that information publicly to cause harm to the people of this nation in some way. These people who have publicly declared, or released information of, illegal activity in US Government or in Corporations must be honored and supported by the government. The penalization of these people is an obvious abuse of power by the government against those who speak out against human rights crimes by those same people. Along with all other falsely imprisoned people, we must free Leonard Peltier and provide him and those like him with exemplary service in returning them to whatever kind of life they wish to live. We must not shrug off these mistakes but serve the population with integrity and respect. The false judgements placed against this Native American leader must be overturned and this man must be released with a formal government apology, and we must identify and penalize the people who knowingly and intentionally allowed this to happen.

POLICE

We must restructure our police and law enforcement system in this country. The enormous amount of abuse that occurs in our law enforcement system is not a new event. If we look at the history of policing in this country, we can see that abuse goes back to the beginning of our nation and further.

In the states, after the United States was formed, policing was a matter of municipalities discretion in creating a position not unlike a nightguard to protect against thievery and was not a professional agency. In the northern states, merchants created private police organizations to protect their assets. These forces evolved over time into professional police forces operating out of police stations. In the southern states, professional policing developed largely from slave patrols. During the late 1800's and early 1900's the Pinkertons acted as private police/military for industrialists, and often were used to sabotage union efforts to better conditions for working people. The Pinkertons and their ilk are the ancestors of the modern professional police.

The Federal Bureau of Investigation (FBI), formed in 1908 by Pres. Theodore Roosevelt, is the investigative aspect of the U.S. Department of Justice, reporting to the U.S. Attorney General. The FBI, within its first 10 years, was already violating the Constitutional Rights of Americans through execution of wiretaps and other surveillance authorized by the Espionage Act of 1917. This type of invasion only increased with time and reached its highest point with the Patriot Act. The FBI has served to hamper real criminal activity over the years, but just like the municipal police, has been mostly used as a tool to create fear and docility among the people, and produce political dominance. It is a part of the coercive facet of the U.S. government.

"Indeed, so impressed was the FBI with the Nazi order that, as the New York Times revealed, in the decades after World War II the FBI, along with other government agencies, aggressively recruited at least a thousand Nazis, including some of Hitler's highest henchmen, brought them to America, hired them on as spies and informants, and then carried out a massive cover-up campaign to ensure that their true identities and ties to Hitler's holocaust machine would remain unknown. Moreover, anyone who dared to blow the whistle on the FBI's illicit Nazi ties found himself spied upon, intimidated, harassed, and labeled a threat to national security."

– John W. Whitehead[19]

Further militarization of the police occurred during Prohibition (1919-1933) during which organized crime took up the job of supplying alcohol to the population illegally, and for which the FBI and police took greater and greater military measures to counter that small population of publicly popular criminals, such as carrying automatic machine guns. During the Cold War, the police were given greater and greater authorization and enticement to approach the general population with suspicion and violence as it became culturally normal to suspect anyone as a spy. The government also used this as a motive to spy on everyone indiscriminately and record data on everyone to ensure "public safety" and "homeland security". The Omnibus Crime Control and Safe Streets Act of 1968 created the Law Enforcement Assistance Administration (LEAA) giving federal grants to police departments to purchase military equipment and created SWAT teams and other units. Special Weapons and Tactics (SWAT) teams were developed in the 60's to respond to riots and other more dangerous situations with militarized force, circumventing the Posse Comitatus Act of 1878. These are extremely militarized police units that are trained explicitly in military tactics, gear, and weaponry.

The war on drugs was and is an example of the use of false justification for the amplification of police militarization and violence. Mirroring the effect of the 1920's prohibition on alcohol, the extreme penalties on drug use and distribution has made possible and is accelerating the modern militarization of the police to combat the very localized and specific groups that have taken advantage of the illicit economy made available by the illegalization and restriction of the substances that large numbers of people in the society demand. Meth is a prime example of the failure of the War on Drugs, as it is a new and more detrimental, highly addictive, substance that has come to ever greater demand and prevalence throughout the United States. The exposure to it by the general population, despite the efforts of policing, advertising, and new laws and threats, has made it extremely harmful. By making the substance have a financial value to those groups that would violate laws in the first place, the government has in effect given a green light to gangs to distribute this lucrative product and to perform numerous crimes against the population while doing so. The black-market value of the substance is of huge financial reward for minimal losses to gangs. Despite ever increasing budgets, better technologies, increasingly violent and invasive policing, and restrictive laws that violate the populations Human and Constitutional Rights, the amount of illegal drug use, distribution, production, and trade is only ever increasing. The average person is the only victim, both from the pushers of truly dangerous drugs and the violence surrounding their activities, and the agents of government who every day encroach more deeply into their privacy and enact laws to restrict their behaviors and make them into carbon copy mindless statists.

MS13 and the 18th Street Gang, both originating in Los Angeles, were in effect, transplanted, when the United States deported over 32,000 Hondurans in 2012 alone. This deportation of thousands of violent criminals to Honduras made the trafficking of drugs to the United States all the easier as these gangs acted as transportation agents for the substances into Mexico and the United States in contracts with the Sinaloa Cartel. It seems that every action the police state takes to reduce the criminal enterprise produces the opposite effect. Aggressive crackdowns on gangs in Honduras by the central government led to "increasing violent activity and driving gangs underground. It turned the gangs into dark networks that were much harder to see and deal with and created prison fraternities that became training and radicalization engines for the gangs, so they were primed for action..."[20] This sounds a lot like what has already happened in the United States. The prisons in the US certainly act as training and recruitment grounds for gangs, which provide security to their members and thus can control their members to a great degree. This indoctrination of inmates into gang behavior and thinking leads to greater and pervasive criminal enterprise. The irrefutable truth... The WAR ON DRUGS IS A SCAM!

The Comprehensive Crime Control Act of 1984 created the Department of Justice Assets Forfeiture Fund, giving police departments encouragement and incentive to profiteer through civil forfeiture. This practice reinforced the cultural gap between the police and the regular population as the police were now authorized to steal property in violation of the constitution and utilize the funds from the asset seizure to purchase military weapons, equipment, and training. In 2017, the national forfeiture fund was valued at over $1.5 billion, while in 2014 alone, Americans had $5.1 billion in assets seized by police. After 1997, the 1033 Program, created by the DOD, gave police departments surplus military gear. 36% of the property transferred through the 1033 program is brand new. The Patriot Act, passed in 2001, opened wide the door wide to police abuse and disregard for constitutional rights. Everything from interrogation to warrantless searches, to invasive body scans, to direct military training and direct access to ever more dangerous and overtly militarized technology and weaponry. Today, police are armed with military-grade machine guns, APC's (Armored Personnel Carriers) and MRAP's (Mine Resistant Ambush Protected), drones, night vision, thermal imaging technology, camouflage, and much more.

The Fraternal Order of Police was hacked, and the leaked documents showed that clauses exist in police departments allowing or mandating the destruction of records of civilian complaints and department disciplinary action and investigation, indicating the further estrangement from accountability by the ever more socially detached police. Some of the commonly used tactics that police use to meet arbitrary quotas are planting evidence, fabricating evidence, fabricating reports, and perjury among other crimes against the population. The police departments that range across the country today are rife with historical and current examples of criminal enterprise within their ranks. Because police are expected to make mistakes in the conduct of their duty, the Supreme Court has given police protections from being held accountable for violating human, constitutional, and civil rights. In fact, the police rarely are held accountable for anything at all. Even if it be murder, like that of Johnny Hurley in Arvada Colorado, who had stopped a mass murder from occurring, saved police lives, and was a community leader to boot, only to be shot by a cop who is not being held accountable for the murder. So we are looking at a highly militarily advanced police force, in equipment, training, and firepower, protected from criminal charges when guilty, isolated from the public through indoctrination and social pressures from police unions and the mob mentality, trained to suspect and produce criminals and victims from the general population, and goal-oriented for higher quotas for objectives that are unjust and misaligned to the fundamental law of the land and the wellbeing of the population they are sworn and made to appear to protect and serve.

"The number of SWAT raids have grown from approximately 3,000 annually in the 1980s to around 50,000 in 2014."

Dr. Peter Kraska, Professor of Justice at Eastern Kentucky University

In a study by the ACLU, conducted between 2011 and 2012, looking at 800 deployments of SWAT teams among 20 local, state and federal police agencies, it was found that 62% of SWAT raids were conducted for drugs (not in their mission statement) and only 7% were for hostage, barricade or active shooter situations. 65% of raids resulted in forced entry through battering ram, boot, or explosive device, with the reason being cited as the presence of a weapon, while in more than half of those raids no weapon was ever found. Just under 80% of deployments of SWAT teams were to serve warrants, showing extreme exaggeration of force necessary, indicating their purpose was intimidation rather than service.[21]

Surveillance by police departments has become so invasive as to limit one's privacy to only the thoughts in one's head. That's not even including federal invasions. Corporations like Persistent Surveillance Systems (PSS), which is fundamentally a military support agency have been supplying aircraft for constant surveillance over American cities. The technology is built into the CCTV's and all the automated tracking tools used in cities, like facial recognition technology, such as Clearview AI, license plate readers, StingRays (cell-site simulators), among others. This network of data gathering technology is all linked into platforms that allow police departments to track everything that happens within a city. Microsoft created for the

NYPD a city-wide surveillance technology, the Domain Awareness System (DAS), which provides real-time alerting, investigations and analytics to the police.

Through the DAS, the NYPD watches the personal movements of the entire city. In its early days, the system ingested information from closed-circuit TV cameras, environmental sensors (to detect radiation and dangerous chemicals), and automatic license plate readers, or ALPRs. By 2010, it began adding geocoded NYPD records of complaints, arrests, 911 calls, and warrants "to give context to the sensor data." Thereafter, it added video analytics, automatic pattern recognition, predictive policing, and a mobile app for cops. By 2016, the system had ingested 2 billion license plate images from ALPR cameras (3 million reads per day, archived for five years), 15 million complaints, more than 33 billion public records, over 9,000 NYPD and privately operated camera feeds, videos from 20,000-plus body cameras, and more. To make sense of it all, analytics algorithms pick out relevant data, including for predictive policing.

– Michael Kwet[22]

Microsoft is hosting a move toward total police integration into the future absolute surveilled United States, through its Azure Government Cloud, hosting many other surveillance and militarization of the police-oriented companies. Microsoft is developing the Microsoft Advanced Patrol Platform (MAPP) which is the next generation of police patrol vehicle, made to see everything happening in its environment through its cloud connection and myriad integrated surveillance technologies. Genetec offers cloud-based CCTV and big data analytics. Aeryon Labs, part of FLIR Systems, provides the SkyRanger, a patrolling drone providing real-time video capture as it tracks above the MAPP (patrol vehicle). ReconRobotics provides remote controlled robots that can stream footage to command centers and the officer in patrol. SuperDroid Robots provides two compact remote-controlled robots to the MAPP system that can overcome difficult obstacles. Facial recognition is being provided through partnerships with companies like Generec and Veritone. The move toward the all-seeing police agencies of the United States is being guided by the motives of those in power who fear the civil unrest of a disgruntled population and the technology being made available to force submission on the population. The Internet of Things (IoT) is the future of policing as it connects all information to their analysis, from the overt, imaging from CCTV cameras, to the covert, data scraped from households through the proprietary technology in smart meters that monitors electricity use in enough detail to determine what brand of hair dryer a person uses at what time in the morning, and whether the pattern of use is consistent or intermittent. Atlanta integrated 10,600 cameras into the city and Chicago 35,000, both utilizing Microsoft and Genetec for cloud services. Many other cities are doing the same. The purchase of all this surveillance technology by the nations police departments is actually bought and paid for by the public through taxes. So it is YOU who is purchasing your own privacy invading technology and hiring those who will wield them against you, watching and manipulating you in your most vulnerable moments.

"Over the years, Microsoft has grown its business through the expansion of its cloud services, in which storage capacity, servers, and software running on servers are rented out on a metered basis. One of its offerings, Azure Government, provides dedicated data hosting in exclusively domestic cloud centers so that the data never physically leaves the host country. In the U.S., Microsoft has built several Azure Government cloud centers for use by local, state, and federal organizations. Unbeknownst to most people, Microsoft has a "Public Safety and Justice" division with staff who formerly worked in law enforcement. This is the true heart of the company's policing services, though it has operated for years away from public view. Microsoft's police surveillance services are often opaque because the

company sells little in the way of its own policing products. It instead offers an array of "general purpose" Azure cloud services, such as machine learning and predictive analytics tools like Power BI (business intelligence) and Cognitive Services, which can be used by law enforcement agencies and surveillance vendors to build their own software or solutions." – Michael Kwet[23]

"The most complete accounting to date was recently compiled by the Electronic Frontier Foundation (EFF), which combed through thousands of public records to build an "Atlas of Surveillance." The map offers the most detailed look at the wide variety of automated surveillance tools at the disposal of state and local law enforcement all across the country. Some of the numbers are eye-popping: at least 1074 jurisdictions and/or police departments use drones; 360 use facial recognition; 64 use StingRays; 24 use video analysis and/or computer vision tools (automated data analysis tools); and 26 employ predictive policing measures... 1,328 police departments have partnerships with Amazon's Ring home security camera system, giving police access--and in some cases live access--to recordings from private property without getting a warrant first... the global video surveillance market is expected to reach \$144 billion by 2027 from about \$40 billion in 2019. As the Wall Street Journal noted, the surveillance industry grew from practically "$0" in 2001 to the multibillion-dollar global market it is today. In pursuit of more data and digital eyes and ears on its citizens, the US government is among the market's biggest players: although estimates of the cost of government surveillance programs are difficult to make, in 2016 the Washington Post reported that the FBI's budget included \$600-\$800 million for its Office of Advanced Technology to develop high-tech surveillance tools, including how to break all forms of digital encryption... State, local, and national police have access to more than 20 databases that cover a person's criminal history and his or her interactions with the state (e.g., drivers licenses) to build a "pattern of life" of the targeted individual, who may or may not have committed a crime...

To get an idea of the amount of information the government has collected on Americans, take the National Crime Identification Center (NCIC), the FBI's centralized crime database. These records include such things as the content of communications such as phone calls and emails; medical diagnoses, treatments, and conditions; Internet browsings; financial transactions; physical locations; bookstore and library purchases, loans, and browsings; other store purchases and browsings; and media viewing preferences. Both local and federal law enforcement also maintain biometric databases, including those containing blood samples, fingerprints, facial recognition, and DNA samples (in addition to those maintained by police, consumer genetics databases such as GEDMatch are proving invaluable sources of information...

fusion centers serve as the link between local and federal police so that data and intelligence tools can legally flow in both directions. Although they are young, another post-9/11 creation, the government already operates 76 such centers across the country. Fusion centers receive information from a variety of sources--local, state, and federal law enforcement as well as homeland security partners and private entities--functioning as, regional focal points for gathering and sharing government and private information... Though decentralized and diffuse, fusion centers are the focal points of a growing, mass surveillance network that connects state and local police with the tools and data intelligence of the national spy agencies. Law enforcement at all levels of government share information to expand the total pool available to them with little oversight or transparency about how the data is used...

Written to tie the hands of the state, the Fourth Amendment of the US constitution protects citizens from unreasonable searches and seizures without probable cause and a warrant that lays out specifically what the police think they might find. But technology has opened the door to mass surveillance, enabling governments to build the very dragnet systems that give the government a picture of a person's "pattern of life" without a warrant or probable cause.

– Bryan McMahon[24]

The nature of warfare globally is shifting into a far more decentralized non-state event that will heavily rely on littoral megacities that can conceal the actions of non-state groups that are directly integrated into the community. This produces a internationally recognized difficulty in legal distinctions around war. Partly for this reason, police are being trained in military tactics and weapons and are being provided with the equipment that would be needed to combat these nonstate groups in the future. The war of tomorrow very likely will involve rapidly shifting environments, very often amidst overloaded city terrain with technically advanced, hyperaware, swarming enemy groups. These enemy groups would make the distinguishing of jurisdiction nearly impossible as they would be acting in terms of warfare against the nation but would be within the nation's cities and other environments, enmeshed with the population. The nature of the militarization of police is a preparation for that scenario. Despite this protection of the state, the militarization of the police is directly confrontational to the values of this nation.

Codified in our Fourth Amendment is the affirmed natural right to be free from government invasion of our homes and privacy. SWAT teams barging into homes, Smart Meters collecting data on energy use down to specific devices and times of use, and endless wiretaps are all infringements of our Constitutional Rights. Those rights that were not granted to us by the government, but rather affirmed, reiterated, and enshrined in the marrow of our society. They were protections against government abuse of the people. Today they are being ignored and the government is growing bolder and bolder in their overreach. Sure, it's a fine and expected thing for the government to respond the future war situation with arming their faithful police agents, but that will ultimately prove to be more fatal, as the population becomes ever more distrustful and disquieted and fed up with abuses. The only way to allay the situation of the future war is to reaffirm and enshrine anew the constitution and to make firearm ownership completely unrestricted. In this way, the population becomes the frontline and can provide for its own defense from these groups that will inevitably make aggressions in this country. In many ways these groups are already doing this, and they are most successful in places where the population is disarmed and helpless, and where the police are concurrently heavily militarized, with extreme surveillance systems and meshed with all sorts of federal agencies.

When we are talking about reformation, we are not attempting to relate only to history to measure our success, but also our potential future and what our potential was in the past. Especially during and following the industrial revolution we can see a significant increase in private police being used to put down civil rights and human rights movements, often expressed through Unions. These movements were the expression of the public in protest to extremely inhumane treatment. They were often broken by "strike-breakers", the private thugs paid by industrialists to put down strikes and union organizations and force the people back to work in terrible conditions. Public Police were used similarly, though with less efficiency. Today, we have about 20 percent more private police than public police, amounting to over 1.1 million private security personnel.

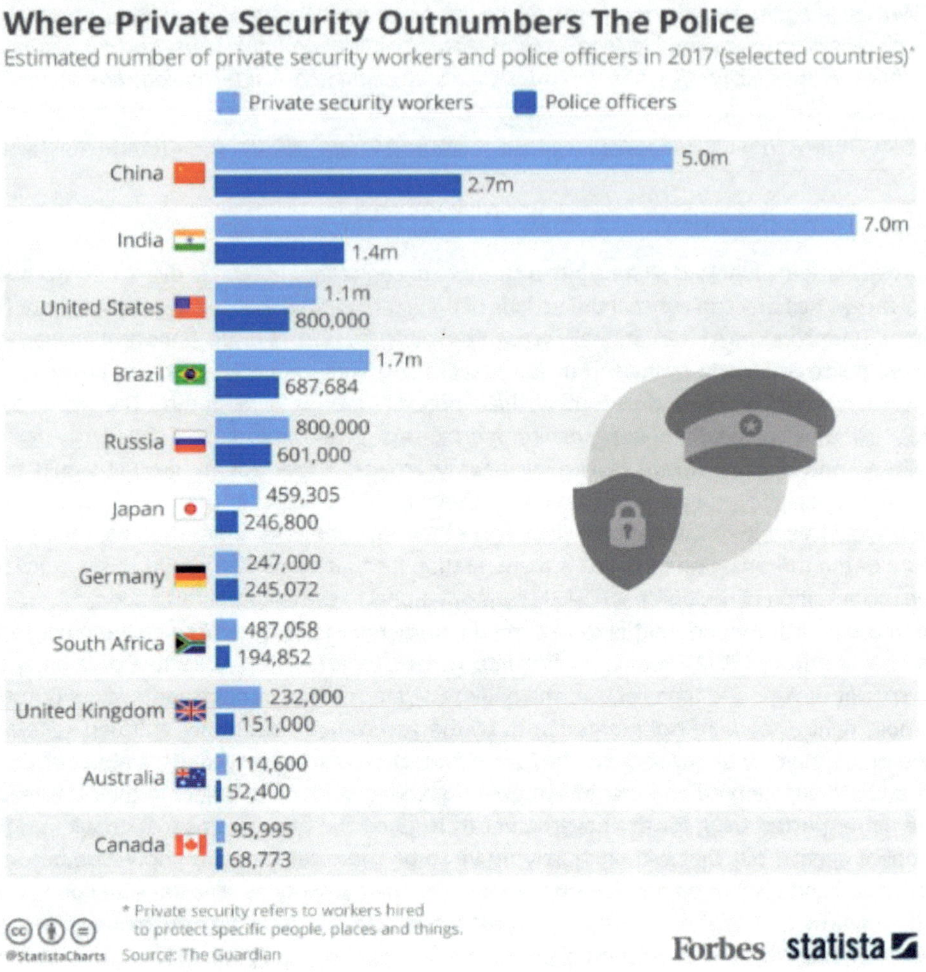

This is largely due to the success of companies like Blackwater and Securitas securing government contracts and other security agencies being incentivized to grow. We need to abolish moonlighting in any capacity as a Police Officer or alter the current system in which police can act with on-duty authority when off duty. We need to remove police authority from off duty officers working as private security because as private security officers they are bound in service to a corporation and are serving the corporate interest at that time. If they are exercising police power while serving in a private capacity, there exists an extreme conflict of interest, an easily abused distinction between service to the public and service to their employer, and an inability for the public to identify them as police officers. The authority of private security is sometimes extended to be equal to public police authority. This must be eradicated and made illegal. We must not allow private interests to police the nation at their leisure. The public needs to be free from the abuse of private, corporate interests and government. It must be free to live without the burden of private armed guards in every shopping mall and convenience store with the police authority to physically harm them or to arrest them. This must be completely eradicated.

The idea of private security is not completely wrong in any sense, only its particular expression by corporations that are monopolies and part of the plutocracy oppressing the people. Private security is far more preferable to municipal police in any case, as the record of corruption and public harm that has been done by government run policing has shown. While public officials are meant to be accountable to the constitution, todays militarized police are only accountable to the secret code of honor between their fellow officers, which allows for molesting the population in a multitude of ways. Private security hired by small communities or individuals would still be accountable to the constitution and would be held accountable in performance and outcome by the free market. This market would allow for only the most qualified individuals to be hired by communities. This private security would have no allegiance to a gang like the Fraternal Order of Police, protected by the government against the very people they are sworn to protect. If private security officers decided to assault a person on the side of the highway for not showing paperwork, they would be guilty of a crime and punished as such. If the Private security officers decided to cavity search a woman at the airport, they would likely be imprisoned. The big difference here is that private security could mean either greater oppression of the population if in the hands of the multinational corporations that influence and are part and parcel of the globalist agenda for total dominance, or greater freedoms if in the hands of the people, who choose to hire them as stewards of the common wellbeing. While police officers are shielded from accountability, private security would be held to the same standards as the people.

Police Need to be held to the highest standards. We must raise the bar on who can be police officers, and how they perform their duties. We need to demilitarize the Police and promote and create unbiased and unprejudiced education and training. The purchasing of military equipment through the Military recycling program has furthered a problem that began a long time ago. It has made it possible for the distinction between our domestic police force and our military which exists to guard against other nations and entities, to become blurred in the most visceral and apparent way. Today's police in many cities, like LA (10,000 police officers, over $2 billion in Police funding), Chicago (13,400 police officers), New York City (36,000 police officers), and others have adopted military gear, practices, and rules, all under the guise of protecting the population from great harm.[25] sThe fact is that these new methods and means are the militarization of the police of the United States. Armies within the United States, aiming their rifles and tanks at the American people. It is the opening moves of the final march toward genocide.

The police do not exist to parrot the national guard, but now are doing so. They are dressing in camouflage, using Armored Personnel Carriers, APC's, and Mine-Resistant Ambush Protected Carriers (MRAP's) that are used in war zones, and conduct militarized training. Fusion Centers now give authority and discretion to determine jurisdiction to federal agents whatever the location in the United States, and unite forces under the banner of Homeland Security, like Hitler's own Heimatland. The police of modern America are focused on finding criminals around every corner, and demanding subservience under the barrel of an Armalite rifle and tread of an APC, especially for those dreaded terrorists who don't pay taxes, or go five miles over the speed limit, or build a composting toilet in their backyard, or grow a plant some folks in suits in a big white house don't like. It's a strange world we live in where people can forget their parents' history, only to relive it, and at the time that the reliving actually occurs, they say, I remember my father told me of this once.... I never thought it could happen to me. The ignorance of the population is leading the charge forward to militarization of the police, amongst the ever-increasing deconstruction of our internal security by the fascistic central government puppeteers.

Plumhoff v. Rickard (2014) – Police using deadly force to terminate a car chase are immune from lawsuit
Navarette v. California (2014) – Police can stop cars and question drivers on anonymous tip only.
U.S. v. Westhoven – Driving too carefully, with rigid posture, taking a scenic route, and having acne are acceptable reasons for an officer to detain, search cars, and arrest people, with no other cause.
Wood v. Moss (2014) – Secret Service has "Qualified Immunity" for any actions done in the name of security.
Salinas v. Texas (2013) – Right to remain silent only exists when people actually assert the right.

Florida v. Harris (2013) – Officers may use drug-sniffing dogs on routine traffic stops to justify searches without warrant.
Maryland v. King (2013) – Without conviction of a crime, police may forcibly take an arrested persons DNA.
Hiibel v. Sixth Judicial District Court of the State of Nevada (2004) – not answering a policeman who asks for a person's name, without cause, is a crime.
Quinn v. Texas (2014) – Legal firearm ownership is justification for no knock raids, including forceful entry, on private residences.
Hedges v. Obama (2014) – President and U.S. military can arrest and indefinitely detain American citizens.
Burlison v. Springfield Public Schools (2013) – Students can be forced to endure random lockdowns and mass searches in school.
Brooks v. City of Seattle (2012) – Officers who knowingly break the law cannot be guilty of a crime.
- John Whitehead[26] (Whitehead, 2015)

In every single one of the cases above, Constitutional Rights were ignored and trampled over by the officers and by the judges who made the ruling to extend powers to police that are repugnant to the constitution. The Department of Justice tells us that we do not have to abide by these false laws though, as they are without true authority.

> *"It is a crime for one or more persons acting under color of law willfully to deprive or conspire to deprive another person of any right protected by the Constitution or laws of the United States. (18 U.S.C. §§ 241, 242). "Under color of law" means that the person doing the act is using power given to him or her by a governmental agency (local, State, or Federal). A law enforcement officer acts "under color of law" even if he or she is exceeding his or her rightful power. The types of law enforcement misconduct covered by these laws include excessive force, sexual assault, intentional false arrests, theft, or the intentional fabrication of evidence resulting in a loss of liberty to another. Enforcement of these provisions does not require that any racial, religious, or other discriminatory motive existed."* – United States Department of Justice[27]

There is an obsession with police officer safety at the expense of the population they assault, despite the fact that police officers voluntarily assume the risks of the position they undertake. They need to be made of sterner stuff, more discriminating, and better trained in how to handle and calm stressful situations. For all of the propagandizing of the peril of law enforcement, the truth is that the profession is actually far from dangerous relative to very many other professions. Logging workers, fishermen, aircraft pilots, roofers, garbage collectors, electrical power line installation/repair, truck drivers, oil and gas extraction, farmers and ranchers, and construction workers all have significantly higher casualty rates than law enforcement. Imagine that! All that stuff with the Thin Blue Line... makes you think, we ought to have a thin black line for oil workers, a thin brown line for garbage workers, and a thin yellow line for electricians. Either that, or we can end the nonsense altogether, and recognize that policing is far from a dangerous profession, excluding those officers that deal with extremely violent neighborhoods within cities, gangs like MS13, or handle violent criminals specifically. In fact, the amount of violence perpetrated by police departments and their minions is factors greater than that perpetrated against them. Between excessive violence and sexual assault, police agencies have a vast undocumented and unpunished record of abuse of the very people they are supposedly protecting. Police agencies predominantly recruit 18–21-year-old males who become desensitized to the scenes of violence and depravity they witness in the aftermath, and have no resources to turn to for real psychological and emotional support, so they lean on the veteran officers who often teach them to perform criminal acts like not reporting complaints, sexually assaulting female officers and civilians, and violating the constitutional rights of the people simply because they learned to do these things as a response to trauma, coercive power, and ample opportunity without accountability. The code of silence between law enforcement officers, makes whistleblowing socially and financially disincentivized. That code protects criminals behind badges, and threatens and blackmails inherently, those who speak out against wrongful behavior.

"...the fatality rate of on-duty patrol officers is reportedly far lower than many other professions, including construction, logging, fishing, truck driving, and even trash collection. In fact, police officers have the same rate of dying on the job as do taxi drivers."
– John Whitehead[28]

We need to create a system by which the police are held accountable by even more severity than the general population. We need to Repeal the Law Enforcement Officer Safety Act of 2004, which allows off-duty police officers to carry concealed firearms anywhere in the country. What makes police officers worthy of the "privilege" to carry concealed weapons wherever and whenever they wish across the nation while the average person cannot even access his constitutional right to carry whatever he may. We have to understand here that police are often woefully undertrained and highly ignorant of not only firearms in general, but of even their issued sidearm. The standards that police are held to around the country is extremely lax and does not provide suitable training to make these supposed "public servants" capable of handling the very thing the LEOS Act encourages them to carry even when not in uniform.

For police officers in most States, the State certification requires as low as a 25-round test, again shot at static targets. In fact, according to nationwide law enforcement estimates, an overwhelming majority of officers fire an average of less than 100 rounds per year in practice and qualification. Due to budget cuts in departments across the nation, training is the first thing to be cut. Qualification requirements have also consistently been reduced and shortened... is there any wonder why, when the FBI police-involved shooting statistics are released, they indicate officers' accuracy nationwide is 15%-20%. That means statistically about 80% of officer-fired rounds in deadly confrontations are complete misses. Many of those rounds end up injuring innocent bystanders and hostages. It's a safe bet that many officers themselves were injured due to them failing to stop a threat in time or because they could not hit the suspect(s) with effective fire."
– Varg Freeborn[29]

It is complete nonsense to believe that because someone is a cop or federal agent of some kind, or current or ex-military, that they are proficient with firearms beyond the average or even at the average for all firearms carriers and owners. There are far more average people with far more firearms experience than the average cop. The fact that police are allowed to carry their weapons beyond the boundaries set for the rest of the population is reminiscent of the patterns seen in every fascist central government that eventually massacred its least "valuable" citizens. I'll talk about that later though. The point here is that police are no more capable, and are often far less so, than the population at large to carry firearms, and any amount of granting them more freedom to do so does nothing to help our nation be a safer place, as I'm sure that Act was intended to look like it was doing. The best thing we can do to protect the lives of police and the population is to have strict and exhausting training mandated for all police and all others who swear to protect the population by the carrying of a firearm. While this is not a necessity for the private person, who may carry or not, choose to practice at leisure or do whatever they like, it most certainly becomes tantamount to willful ignorance and ineptness by the government to not demand the highest level of proficiency from those who act to protect the people and thus are the point of the spear against truly dangerous criminals who seek to murder and cause mayhem amongst peaceful people. It is tantamount to the intentional harm of the population at large to not train these potential guardians of the public to the highest level and degree.

We need to provide a national hotline that anyone can call to report police abuse (abuse by government workers), which reports and immediately contacts law enforcement officials in that jurisdiction and the FBI. This hotline can also be used to provide legal assistance through a database of attorneys that would be called upon request. This would give legal weight to an individual who otherwise does not know every aspect of the complex, corrupt and often contradictory US legal system. This would also be a tool in the effort to reduce criminal activity by the police, who are often similarly ignorant of the law. We also need a publicly accessible website by which videos of crimes by government employees can be uploaded and used as a database to record patterns and correct dysfunction in our justice system and government. We need to provide incentives for police to act in a way that supports the evolution of our society in becoming more Peaceful and well. We need to offer our police monetary incentives for exceptional behavior, and award and elevate our police based on reaching goals that include not having a single abuse of power in their record and having measurable positive public sentiment for their service. We cannot and must not measure the quality and efficacy of a police officer's promotion on number of arrests, quantity of funds derived from tickets, or their prior education. We must measure their quality on their behavior and on the public's approval.

A police officer must not be unaccountable to the public. If they refuse to answer a call for help from the public, they must be held accountable for this. There must be a direct method by which the public can force any police officer to be removed from that position, as in a hearing in which the public vote. If there is a real concern about the behavior of a police officer, it must be taken with even greater concern and public awareness than any member of the public. We need to increase funding to the police through only local voluntary contribution to increase personnel to perform stratified duties with relative pay. We do not need to train all police on all things. We need to focus on training entry level police to deal with high stress and dangerous situations, law, and human rights. They should have limited responsibility and limited authority. As the responsibility, authority, knowledge and pay all increase, we must assure that we are appropriating resources according to need. We do not need to encourage fear of police by encouraging fear tactics used by police. We must form a more appropriate police force. Police violence will decrease when the laws of the nation and states reflect sensible and honorable practices and regulations. When we are encouraging and demanding our police to enforce laws that are unconstitutional, dishonorable, and inhumane, we are at fault when violence by police permeates through our society. It is a responsibility for our police, and our military, and all officers and politicians and agents of the government to act by and defend the oaths they swear. It is not a viable defense that these agents were only acting under orders.

"the justification for acts done pursuant to orders does not exist if the order was of such that a man of ordinary sense and understanding would know it to be illegal."
-United States v. Keenan

We are similarly responsible, as a whole, for the crimes of the population which is almost always a matter of environmental, social, and economic degradation and inequity. We must respect that our police face the dangers that the general population avoids and is mostly ignorant of. We must respect our honorable officers and the fact that they are duty bound to uphold the law, under the Constitution, and we must insist on behaviors respecting human rights and dignity. We can see that violence is often a result of social conditioning and disparities. We must work to evolve our police as we evolve our laws and our society as a whole. We need to uphold and enforce the highest standards upon those granted authority to manage our nation, our cities, our laws, and our safety. We must remember that the only real authority is We the People, and nothing but our own surrender of that sacred duty has removed that authority from us.

The government is not a tool for commanding the population to live according to the will of lawmakers. It is a tool of the public to govern itself to the benefit of the entire population. This must become the reality. When government is owned by private interests, we all suffer. We need to enforce justly and equitably the uncorrupted, natural, law of the land.
Corporate executives need to be held accountable. Jail time when having presided over frauds will hold corporate executives personally accountable for their crimes. The punishment must be equal to the crime. If an executive is directly aware of a fraud or theft of one person, they must be held accountable for that equal to any theft committed by any individual. If the crime is a fraud or theft involving thousands or millions of people, they must be charged and judged appropriately. When the crimes committed involve environmental harm or destruction, the punishment must meet these crimes with the severity of the harm. The environment must be held to a standard even higher than the individual person or group of people, as it does greater harm now and into the future for all the people that live here and will live here, the ecosystem, the biosphere, and the planet.

The Constitution did not give us Rights, nor was it the people who wrote it that gave us those Rights. The Constitution simply enumerated the inherent Rights that we had simply by our existence. Maritime Admiralty Law is superseded by civil law, and only applies to informed persons who willingly contract themselves into it. Admiralty Law is a body of private international law governing the relationships between private entities which operate vessels on the oceans. It was created to govern ships docking in foreign nations for importation and exportation of products and resources. It deals with banking and merchant affairs. Upon receiving product from foreign land, the receiving nation takes custody and accounts for that custody with a certificate of berth. A certificate is “a document evidencing ownership or debt,”[30] and a “Paper establishing an ownership claim.”[31].

“Registration of births began in 1915, by the Bureau of Census, with all states adopting the practice by 1933.
Birth and marriage certificates are a form of securities called "warehouse receipts." The items included on a warehouse receipt, as descried at §7-202 of the Uniform Commercial Code, the law which governs commercial paper and transactions, which parallel a birth or marriage certificate are:
-the location of the warehouse where the goods are stored...(residence)
-the date of issue of the receipt.....("Date issued")
-the consecutive number of the receipt...(found on back or front of the certificate, usually in red numbers)
-a description of the goods or of the packages containing them...(name, sex, date of birth, etc.)
-the signature of the warehouseman, which may be made by his authorized agent...(municipal clerk or state registrar's signature)

Birth/marriage certificates now appear to at least qualify as "warehouse receipts" under the Uniform Commercial Code. Black's Law Dictionary, Seventh Edition, defines: warehouse receipt. "...A warehouse receipt, which is considered a document of title, may be a negotiable instrument and is often used for financing with inventory as security."

Since the U.S. went bankrupt in 1933, all new money has to be borrowed into existence. All states started issuing serial-numbered, certificated "warehouse receipts" for births and marriages in order to pledge us as collateral against those loans and municipal bonds taken out with the Federal Reserve's banks. The "Full faith and Credit" of the American people is said to be that which back the nation's debt. That simply means the American people's ability to labor and pay back that debt. In order to catalog its laborers, the government needed an efficient, methodical system of tracking its property to that end. Humans today are looked upon merely as resources - "human resources" that is. Governmental assignment of a dollar value to the heads of citizens began on July 14, 1862 when President Lincoln offered 6 percent interest bearing-bonds to states who freed their slaves on a "per head" basis. This practice of valuating humans (cattle?) continues today with our current system of debt-based currency reliant upon a steady stream of fresh new chattels to back it."

– David Deschesne

A Maritime Lien or "tacit hypothecation" is a maritime lien on a vessel, given to secure the claim of a creditor who provided maritime services to the vessel or who suffered an injury from the vessel's use, enforced by an action in rem (against the thing, not the person). "The term "person" means an individual, partnership, corporation, trust, association, and any other entity subject to the jurisdiction of the United States."[32]

"In 1921, the federal Sheppard-Towner Maternity Act created the birth "registration" or what we now know as the "birth certificate." It was known as the "Maternity Act" and was sold to the American people as a law that would reduce maternal and infant mortality, protect the health of mothers and infants, and for "other purposes." One of those other purposes provided for the establishment of a federal bureau designed to cooperate with state agencies in the overseeing of its operations and expenditures. What it really did was create a federal birth registry which exists today, creating "federal children." This government, under the doctrine of "Parens Patriae" now legislates for American children as if they are owned by the federal government. Through the public school enrollment process and continuing license requirements for most aspects of daily life, these children grow up to be adults indoctrinated into the process of asking for "permission" from 'big Daddy' government to do all those things necessary to carry out daily activities that exist in what is called a "free country."

Before 1921 the records of births and names of children were entered into family bibles, as were the records of marriages and deaths. These records were readily accepted by both the family and the law as "official" records. Since 1921 the American people have been registering the births and names of their children with the government of the state in which they are born, even though there is no federal law requiring it. The state tells you that registering your child's birth through the birth certificate serves as proof that he/she was born in the united States, thereby making him/her a United States Citizen. For the past several years a social security number has been mandated by the federal government to be issued at birth.

In 1933, bankruptcy was declared by President Roosevelt. The governors of the then 48 States pledged the "full faith and credit" of their states, including the citizenry, as collateral for loans of credit from the Federal Reserve System. To wit: "Full faith and credit" clause of Const. U.S. article 4. sec. 1 requires that foreign judgment be given such faith and credit as it had by law or usage of state of its origin. That foreign statutes are to have force and effect to which they are entitled in home state. And that a judgment or record shall have the same faith, credit, conclusive effect, and obligatory force in other states as it has by law or usage in the state from whence taken. Black's Law Dictionary, Fourth Edition cites omitted.

The state claims an interest in every child within its jurisdiction. The state (via CPS) will, if it deems it necessary, nullify your parental rights and appoint a guardian (trustee) over your children. The subject of every birth certificate is a child. The child is a valuable asset, which if properly trained, can contribute valuable assets provided by its labor for many years. It is presumed by those who have researched this issue, that the child itself is the asset of the trust established by the birth certificate, and the social security number is the numbering or registration of the trust, allowing for the assets of the trust to be tracked. If this information is true, your child is now owned by the state. Each one of us, including our children, are considered assets of the bankrupt UNITED STATES. We are now designated by this government as "HUMAN RESOURCES" with a new crop born every year."

– Joyce Rosenwald

"Maritime law - is a complete system of law, both public and private, substantive and procedural, national and international, with its own courts and jurisdiction, which goes back to Rhodian law of 800 B.C. and pre-dates both the civil and common laws. Its more modern origins were civilian in nature, as first seen in the Rôles of Oléron of circa 1190 A.D. Maritime law was subsequently greatly influenced and formed by the English Admiralty Court and then later by the common law itself. That maritime law is a complete legal system can be seen from its component parts. For centuries maritime law has had its own law of contract:

– contract of sale (of ships),
– contract of service (towage),
– contract of lease (chartering),
– contract of carriage (of goods by sea),
– contract of insurance (marine insurance being the precursor of insurance ashore),
– contract of agency (ship chandlers),
– contract of pledge (bottomry and respondentia),
– contract of hire (of masters and seamen),
– contract of compensation for sickness and personal injury (maintenance and cure) and
– contract of risk distribution (general average).

It is and has been a national and an international law (probably the first private international law). It also has had its own public law and public international law.

Maritime law is composed of two main parts - national maritime statutes and international maritime conventions, on the one hand, and the general maritime law (lex maritima), on the other. The general maritime law has evolved from various maritime codes, including Rhodian law (circa 800 B.C.), Roman law, the Rôles of Oléron (circa 1190), the Ordonnance de la Marine (1681), all of which were relied on in Doctors' Commons, the English Admiralty Court, and the maritime courts of Europe.

This lex maritima, part of the lex mercatoria, or "Law Merchant" as it was usually called in England, was the general law applicable in all countries of Western Europe until the fifteenth century, when the gradual emergence of nation states caused national differences to begin creeping into what had been a virtually pan-European maritime law system"

- University of Rijeka[33]

Whether or not you want to consider or believe the idea that identification systems like the certificate of birth and social security cards are part of a control system that imposes legal slavery over the recipients, the fact remains that our government and the other governments of the world are composed of people who cross the boundaries of nations, corporations, and governments regularly for employment and these interwoven connections lend to the plutocratic style of control over the population of the world. The means by which these governments coerce and control their populations should be of prime concern and no theories and no evidence should go unheeded or uninvestigated.

The similarities in the language used between international merchant law and U.S. domestic law and agencies could evince the very slavery that is outlined by Mr. Duchesne and Ms. Rosenwald, or it could simply be the evolution of terms that were adopted and molded to fit the system that they were being adopted into. In that case the argument would have to be evident in the function of the nations law. It would have to show a indisputable difference from the origin language from which the terms were adopted. There is no such thing as coincidence and everything that is can be traced, if investigated carefully enough and with enough reference material, to its reason for being, and the motive offered in the case of language adopted from international merchant law into domestic law is that the system of law was functional for the beneficiaries and regulators and those who sought to govern domestically in the US and profit from such, sought to mimic the success in a different medium and thus came about the transfer of language into the domestic laws of the United States, and thus came about what can be viewed as "legal" slavery or at the very least unethical population tracking, privacy invasion, and illegal taxation.

> *"When one considers the growing list of opinions and activities which may make a federal agent or local police officer think you're a terrorist, or sympathetic to terrorist activities—advocating states' rights, believing the state to be unnecessary or undesirable, 'conspiracy theorizing,' concern about alleged FEMA camps, opposition to war, organizing for 'economic justice,' frustration with 'mainstream ideologies.' opposition to globalization, and, ironically, ammunition stockpiling—the picture becomes that much more alarming... ...Whatever the threat to so-called security—whether it's rumored weapons of mass destruction, school shootings, alleged acts of terrorism, or a serial killer on the loose—it doesn't take much for the American people to march in lockstep with the Government's dictates, even If it means submitting to martial law, having their homes searched, and being stripped of their constitutional rights at a moment's notice."*
>
> - John W. Whitehead[34]

What is a crime? Is smoking cannabis a crime? Is speeding a crime? Is it a crime to sleep with a prostitute, or to be one? Let's investigate this a little bit. Firstly, a crime exists when there is a victim. A victim can only be a living being, not an entity, such as government itself or a corporation. What is considered alive varies amongst cultures and nations, but it includes generally, a human being, an animal in certain circumstances, and in the more liberally applied, though in my opinion correctly identified, oceans, rivers, trees, and the natural world as a whole. The ways a victim is produced include only a few categories of interaction. One may be murdered, assaulted, robbed, had their persons or property trespassed upon, or been raped. These five things constitute obvious criminal actions. These five things make up the entirety of the scope of crime. What is not a crime is that which does not produce a victim. So, is smoking cannabis a crime? No, there is no victim produced from the act of smoking cannabis. The arguments against smoking cannabis, let alone being outdated culturally at their inception, do not remove the baseline innocence of that act. The only reason why it is considered a crime today in various places is due the laws identifying it as a harmful drug. The proofs against it being such are too numerous to count and too obviously true to be argued. So, being that it does not produce a victim, and is not a crime, the fact that it is illegal is an act of overreaching by governments around the globe. It is a crime of course to hit a person while travelling in a car, as that produces a victim. If someone is travelling in a vehicle under the influence of mind-altering substances, an argument can be made that it was due to those substances that the incident occurred, though proving that is beyond the bounds of normal investigation. It could be said that the person had never used the substance before, and had a perfect record, and the correlation would indicate that it was due to the use of the substance that the incident occurred. But that would have to be viewed side by side with incidents of the same type, absent of substance use, to determine if the event occurred simply on par with the averages for that sort of incident. By indicating the number of incidents of this type by only selecting the cannabis users, the statistics would be skewed out of favor for its use. My argument is simply stating that incidents of this type may not always be correlated to the use of cannabis. Either way though, cannabis use while travelling in a vehicle results in criminal charges often.

The same argument can be used in the events that speeding was involved in vehicular incidents in which a victim was produced. Rather than speeding being the cause, it may well have been various other factors that were the actual cause. Speeding cannot be a crime, as no victim is produced simply by speeding. That sort of law is a proponent of the concept of future crime, which is the idea that something you do now *may* result in a crime in the next moment. That is an extreme injustice to the people. The difference between that and recklessly travelling in a motor vehicle is apparent. Speeding has no victim, while going the wrong way down a one way at high speed is much more likely to produce a victim. Even reckless travelling can be seen as nuisance until a victim is produced. Instead of treating it as a crime, a sheriff could easily pull over that person and ask them why they are doing what they are doing. Perhaps they were needing to get to a hospital promptly and were in a state of panic. In that scenario we see that the danger of a potential crash was real, but it had cause. At that point, the sheriff could lend assistance rather than penalize the victimless action. the point here is that we cannot lay atop the entire population enforcement of non-criminal actions. It is only at the will or lack of voice of the people that corrupt laws are created.

Is prostitution a crime? No, it cannot be a crime unless there is a victim. A religious objection to the act is not sufficient to declare it illegal. Nor is it a crime simply because some people do not agree with the practice. If a willing person chooses to engage in that practice of their own volition and free will, they have all the right in the world to ply their trade. The victims in this situation, are those women, or men, who are forced into the act by others. That action is an assault and rape of those people. The difference is vast. The free person who chooses and the kidnapped, assaulted and raped person who is forced are the difference between the absence of crime and the presence of crime.

If one is forced to go to a court for a speeding ticket, that person has then become the victim of the government, the officer, the judge, and whoever else chooses to assault them. In giving the ticket, the officer has demanded that the person give the government money and/or go to court, where they will demand that money or time in jail be served. This is called extortion and is a theft and assault upon the individual who has committed no crime. In court, the language used is not the English language, but rather legalese. Historically in China, the legal language was Mandarin, while the normal language spoken by the population was Cantonese. In France, the legal Language was French and Latin, though the population most often spoke various dialects that only partially could be recognized as French. In this way governments prevent the populations they are supposedly serving from understanding what is being said in the courts of law. In this way, the United States has separated the people from an understanding of the law. Legalese is a mixture of various languages, with updated definitions though time, culminating in the use of words to declare different things. Without Legalese the people would have better results in court, as the language would be the common language. As things stand, the population is ever hard pressed to make real and successful claims in courts, as they do not understand the language used in that space, just as they would not understand French unless they were taught to. Once the language is grasped, there is still a mountain of procedure to comprehend.

We must understand that the basis of crime lies in the ability for people to be free and safe as a collective. Crime is that word that describes an act that affects the safety and freedom of self or others. A murderer, who has never murdered, is not a murderer. A pimp that has never forced someone into prostitution and only accepted willing participants is not a criminal. A person who grows and consumes cannabis is not a criminal. These things exist to serve the freedom of the people. When they turn into crime, then they must be confronted, but not until such time, for we must not slip into a society that penalizes future crime, pre-crime, or thought crime, lest we slip into true despair.

While constitutionally we have affirmed certain Rights, we are by nature and our very existence granted Natural and Inalienable Rights. I have dedicated an entire section of this book to Human Rights vs Constitutional Rights, but I'd like to add here that if we forget the fundamental agreements that have been affirmed only through centuries of conflict and discourse and study, then we risk losing more than our lives, but the entire historical cultural evolution as well as the potentially ever greater freedoms and wellbeing of our progeny.

The Pro-Corporate, maritime Judicial system created by corporate interests is succeeding in two goals. It has obstructed access to judicial justice for ordinary people who are wrongfully injured or defrauded by corporate practices and it is making it easier for corporations to win those cases that do manage to make it all the way to the court's dockets. By doing these two things, the judiciary has prejudiced the public and has given extreme latitude to criminal corporations. We need to stop empowering pro-corporate judges. We must disallow the erection of elaborate procedural obstacles that wear down plaintiffs and their lawyers after they file suits in court against corporations. Eminent Domain must be clearly defined as not being able to be used for Plutocratic Interests. This is important specifically in the right of people to deny the theft of their land by the corporate interests controlling government.
Freedom of Contract is being completely negated through the 'compulsory arbitration' clause... the "I Agree" problem. If you make a purchase, after you sign the dotted line or click "I Agree", your right to reject whatever additional costs, penalties, or even change the terms that your vender chooses to make, is taken away by a 'unilateral modification' clause. We need to reject these changes to our rights to understand what we are signing, and to be able to negotiate our contracts.

"No government can take away your right to your day in court. But corporations can and do...there is no collective bargaining by consumers for terms on purchasing cars, mortgages, insurance, or even credit cards."
- Ralph Nadar, Breaking Though Power[35]

Organizations like WTO, NAFTA, and TPP impose their rules, which supersede the domestic laws and rules in the United States through their ability to enforce trade violation punishments. These include fines and trade restrictions. This means the US is forced to endure trading in goods that violate domestic laws in favor of the mandates of international trade organizations. This includes trading in goods made by workers in conditions that violate US law. These "treaties" get through congress, because they are called "agreements" by the President. Only 51 percent of the vote is required from the house and senate to pass agreements rather than the two-thirds required for treaties. They are sent to Congress for an up or down vote, under fast-track procedure prohibiting amendments, and restricting debate time in the house and senate. We must remove these restrictions on our control over our trade. We must define and draw our lines on what we will and what we will not accept in trade and stick by our decision to adequately influence global markets to change the behaviors that cause harm economically and in the health and wellbeing of their people and those they trade with. Our justice system is ignoring these violations to our nations authority and sovereignty.

There was never a time in this country where liberty was extended to all people. By the time women and Native Americans were able to vote, we had already sold our country to the most depraved individuals through the Federal Reserve Act, which was the beginning of the subtle enslavement of the whole population. This was tantamount to the most important and significant event in this nation's history. It was the turning point in the battle over control of the economic system. It gave the keys of the kingdom over to the people most incentivized and motivated to, and capable of, manipulating the market to create a global self-serving economy at the expense of the individual and the nations of the world. Since 1913 the rate of collapse of the environment has rapidly increased, the disparity of wealth around the world has increased, and the relative wellbeing of the world has decreased, while our technology has increased. While people are seemingly happily tapping screens all day, the rate of extinction has inflated so much that we are now experiencing a mass extinction that has been created not by natural patterns, but man-made destructive practices. Let's say that the environment was not being destroyed for private profit for a second. Would it then be okay for a small group of bankers to manipulate the world? The answer is obviously no. No, it is not okay for small groups to control big groups. Nor is it okay for big groups to control small groups. It is imperative that we do not allow this atrocity to continue to destroy our world. We must act, without a moment of delay. In 1776 a small group of people representing the interests of many more came together to sign their affirmation of, and apply their will to, the forming of a coalition separate from the private central bank controlled English empire. They did not accept the demands to bend their knees and become docile slaves, and neither must we today. The same exact entities that were being fought against in 1776 are those that have dominated not only our nation, but effectively the entire planet. It is those that privately own the central banks that supply the currency of the world. That is the fiat money in all its forms. We need to strip all power from these entities with unrelenting force and adamantine will before we are left without a shred of dignity or opportunity. We need to consolidate as humanity against the greatest threat to our planet, let alone our species, that has ever existed.

"No man is good enough to govern another man without that others consent."
-Abraham Lincoln

Foreign Policy

Foreign Policy is the aspect of government dealing with our nations interactions with other nations. How we conduct foreign policy in the United States can encourage or discourage wars and trade agreements, make friends and enemies, and determine how much of the world relates. The President of the United States takes the lead role in foreign affairs as the Chief Diplomat and has the responsibility of representing the nation's population. He is responsible for the reception of foreign ambassadors and in the negotiation of treaties. The State Department, Defense Department, and the intelligence agencies handle the workload of diplomatic work for the President. Congress has the authority and responsibility to manage the budget which plays a significant role in the way we interact with other nations. The Senate has the authority to ratify treaties with a two-thirds vote, though the President often creates foreign policy through Executive Agreements, which only require majority vote in both the House of Representatives and the Senate.

War and security go hand in hand. There is a complex array of reasons for a country or group to engage in war. If we look at the face of every war ever engaged in, we can easily point to a single event or a string of seemingly individual events that can be used to describe causality. We can say, because the World Trade Center in New York was attacked by terrorists from the middle east, we went to war with terrorists in the middle east. This is only looking at a singular event to justify engaging in a war. When we take a more intensive look into causality, we can describe more complex motivations, patterns, and layers of events that correlate together. This requires extensive research, keen insight a strong will to remain objective, and often involves wading through mountains of false evidence, manipulated stories and devious people. Having said this, we can also describe our reasons for going to war in more fundamental ways by looking at human nature and the way we respond to unpleasant situations. The people of the United States are highly indoctrinated into a competitive social design. Much of the population is deeply influenced by the idea that competition produces the greatest reward for any group. This is incorrect and has been proven to create less productive social organization and higher rates of violent inclinations. Cooperative societies provide higher quality results in production and quality of life. Our current social design is largely functioning with high levels of inappropriate fear and unnecessary stress. The classism, racism, ageism, and other classifications of separation are more a result than a cause. They exist due to the underlying themes of competition and scarcity. It is within this environment, that it is seen as an appropriate response to unnecessary violence to create more unnecessary violence. An eye for an eye. When we see the world as a dangerous place, we treat it as such. When we see the world as a place filled with people who want what we have, and want to hurt us, and want to change us, we feel we must build a wall around ourselves. Interestingly, it is the very act of building a wall that makes people pay attention to us. They begin to say, what is it that they have behind that wall. And thus, the act of building a wall creates a stronger enticement and effort for people who are looking to do harm to do so. War is an abhorrent way of responding to small threats. War and violence must be seen as the least desirous and last choice to any situation. Instead, we have empowered the government to demand the population to engage in war before there is proof of the need. The suggestion of the need has the ability to convince that the need is real, but it very rarely if ever truly is.

Economic Goals and Foreign Policy are complimentary to each other. We must formulate our economic goals around our political position in the world. Nations or regions respond in different ways to how we represent ourselves to the world. We must respond to nations in such a way that we do not conform to unjust or harmful practices to appeal to them, while maintaining relations that support the wellbeing of all involved. This is complex in its implementation, but it is simple in its motivation and in its demand for integrity. We cannot demean nations we wish to work with, and we cannot applaud nations that violate human rights or attempt to control our actions. In fact, we have done much of the opposite of this in the US. If we desire to create a better world for all, by which we cannot help but benefit from, we must begin to engage the world in a respectful, helpful, and dignified manner. We must also place greater focus on the things that are mutually important and work from there to produce stronger bonds and stronger cooperation toward universal wellbeing.

As I talk about elsewhere in this book, the idea that the US is an independent nation is almost completely wrong at this point. While there is much posturing and chest beating on the media, the real measure of our independence is economic freedom. As a nation we are beholden to the international organizations and especially to the international banking cartel. What we can or cannot import, from where, how it is done, and what must be paid in the transaction is all dictated by the WTO and other international organizations. When we talk about foreign policy at this point, we must recognize that the world has become no different in its classes of citizenry despite the increase in technology and connectedness. There are the haves and the have nots. The In-club and everyone else. And the In-club hasn't changed all too much over the centuries. Those who make decisions that have global effects are those who learned how to do their work from those who did it yesterday. When we look back at the millennia of accepted human history, we see the same characterization of the classes of society. Those who are in the club don't fret over the issues of the chattel because they are a part of the machine that keeps on rolling along. Those who are in the cold stay there and die there and the next generation or maybe ten generations on are forgotten. Are the US president and the Russian president really enemies? Do they really not have a similar aim? There are only so many presidents and other world leaders. It is a small club. It is a very small club with a relatively protected, prosperous, powerful and long life. Even smaller is the international banking cartel club. Ever smaller are the rooms at the pinnacle of the pyramid.

The opportunity has been there for all these millennia, for the people to recognize their true power and to take hold of it to create a world filled with peace and prosperity for all. International relations has become something that every person in the United States feels connected with because of the constant media, but they are not connected with the actual global events, the feelings, the textures of the socio-political, financial, and cultural weave of anything other than what they know in their present day to day. While

technology has advanced to the point that it could be used to provide true information and experiential analysis of global affairs to every person, it has been abused for the achievement of the goals of those who prefer selfish success and power over others. Foreign relations has evolved from being something that presidents do, to something that every person has a responsibility to interact with, by exposing the truth, wherever they are, of the culture they live in. For those who are well travelled, it is apparent that the world is more alike than different. People have needs and wants that generally align across religions, genders, races, regions, and languages. It is the continued separation of people through manipulation and perpetuated scarcity that increases fear, hate, and desperation to the point that gangs and terrorist cells are born. Foreign relations is the act of making relations with people globally, and encouraging peace. Your government will not do this, so it is left to the people to make sure that the world knows that We the People, are NOT Coca-Cola and we are NOT Big Brother, and we are NOT murderers invading their countries and attempting to strip them of their dignity and lives.
The United States is both a bully and a liberator, dependent on who you ask. But opinions stray from fact. The facts indicate that the United States is neither bully or liberator, but rather self-interested and willing to serve that self-interest no matter what. It can be efficiently and accurately predicted to do whatever it takes to maintain and increase its power, control, and prestige.

"As I tried to indicate, the American-led effort to deal with nuclear weapons by way of establishing a regime of non-proliferation, basically engages in a mind game that makes, tries to make, the world believe that the danger of these weapons (nuclear weapons) is not associated with the countries that possess them and have used them in the past and threatened to use them in the future, but rather the danger is with the countries that don't have the weapons. And that that is where the focus of political energy should be put. That's such a perverse conception of how to address a potentially apocalyptic threat of a bio-political nature that can imperil not only civilization but the species itself. And what I think this geopolitical realism has blocked our perception of the futility of trying to address these problems through these kinds of mechanisms, and has made us aware that only this kind of fundamental revision of human consciousness can address these kinds of problems... the most focused problem of this period in human history is the mismatch between the territoriality of political arrangements and the non-territoriality of ecology, of technology, and of the general economic arrangements in the world... The way in which world order is structured and ideologized in the modern period is such that it can't promote and protect the global interest and the human interest either at the macro levels or the micro levels... Syria in my view is emblematic of 21st century postmodern conflict, which has actors that don't fit the paradigm of international relations... it has non-state actors that are that are transnational as well as internal. It has regional actors that are engaged in a proxy war. It has global actors such as Russia and the United States that are seeking to pursue their own global ambitions in relation to these conflicts. I think (we) never had a conflict with so many complexities that are not susceptible to a positive treatment given the structures that exist."

- Richard Falk: A New Geopolitical Realism for the 21st Century, Dec 18, 2015[36]

Population growth in cities, especially due to immigration of rural populations, is creating conditions for global economic, social, and security changes and challenges. Immigration from rural areas is only increasing annually due to drought, desertification, soil salinity, war and economic demands for survival. Roughly 4 billion people live between Asia and the Pacific nations, where 13 of the world's 25 megacities are located, mostly in coastal areas. Coastal urbanization is threatened by flooding wherever it is developing. With the potential for rising ocean levels, most of the urbanization and megacities are under significant risk in the near future as coastal cities. Infectious disease becomes a far more important topic as coastal urbanization means rapid development of slum conditions as refugees, immigrants and others move to cities in substantial numbers. The lack of sanitary conditions, health standards and clean resources correlates to greater numbers of deaths and injuries due to infectious diseases like malaria. The connectedness of the global population and the ease of travel would indicate a possible rapid transmission rate for infectious diseases between urban cores and surrounding regions, as well as other urban cores and their surrounding regions. Coastal urbanization depletes fisheries and overfishing in the ocean creates shocks to the environment that have massive effects on the survivability of humans in an affected area. Coastal megacities are threatened by pollution, especially in the form of waste disposal, which is often piped into the ocean where fishing fleets work to haul in food for the population, effectively poisoning the same population. As populations grow, and expand into surrounding farmland, food must be transported further and in greater quantity, putting a strain on the land and increasing the desertification of the region. The urbanization of the human population globally creates ever greater dependency on food distribution chains that are exceedingly fragile. Water sources where cities currently draw water will be developed upon as megacities develop further and further to accommodate growing populations, forcing water to be drawn from further away and from deeper in the earth. Rivers will be depleted, soil degraded into desert, forests into shantytowns and suburbs and skyscrapers, and populations will eventually be completely reliant upon outside resources that they consume at greater rates than can be sustained by the land surrounding. The hunger and thirst, besides the political, social, and educational exclusion, makes destitute populations highly likely to form into local militarized groups that extort their neighbors and collude with political elites for personal gain. These gangs compete for territory, status, and access, leaving behind the corpses of the innocent and unlucky in their wake. As cities grow in area and population, the number of gangs will grow as well.

"But the trends are clear: more people than ever before in history will be competing for scarcer and scarcer resources in poorly governed areas that lack adequate infrastructure, and these areas will be more and more closely connected to the global system, so that local conflict will have far wider effects... population growth, urbanization, littoralization, and connectedness suggest that conflict is increasingly likely to occur in coastal cities, in underdeveloped regions of the Middle East, Africa, Latin America, and Asia, and in highly networked, connected settings."

– David Kilcullen[37]

In these developing conditions that will come to be the world of tomorrow globally, we must understand also that our methods and means of interaction as a nation, as a local community, or as an individual in foreign relations will change in some drastic ways. Cities of tomorrow will be essentially malignant overgrowth and incubi, draining the life from the earth and the populations that live outside their walls to feed their endless greed and hunger. What a wonderful thought. Not unlike the world of today but multiplied in its monstrosities and diminished in its endearing qualities. The great sprawling megacity metropolis of the future is one covering tens of thousands of square miles and composed of tens of millions of people all dependent on the ever-depleting resources of the land surrounding the metropolis. It is estimated that 70% of the global population will live in cities by 2050. The largest Megacities today are Tokyo (37 million), Delhi (30 million), Shanghai (27 million), São Paulo (22 million), Ciudad de México (22 million), Dhaka (21 million), Cairo (21 million), Beijing (20 million), Mumbai (20 million), and Osaka (19 million). The largest megacities in the US are New York (19 million) and Los Angeles (12 million)[38]

The internal conflict of megacities like Karachi will directly affect megacities in the US. The nature of the highly connected global economies alone will have vital importance as each megacity will be dependent is some way to the other megacities and their regions. The web of trade and migration of populations will make each megacity more and more interlocked by blood ties. The non-state actors that control crucial resources, regions and territories will have influence over cities and regions in other parts of the world. Those Americans who adhere to the principle of non-intervention will be absorbed into a world where everything that is happening globally affects their daily life. This will create an impetus toward interventionism. The globalization of everything includes social attitude and political power and motive. When an oppressive leader of an impoverished country chooses to withhold a necessary crop supply to wield control over their neighbor, and that neighbor demands US support or they will stop exporting a necessary crop to the US, it is clear that the US would be forced into intervening out of necessity. While this is oversimplified and the solution to the problem is far from interventionism or dependency systems, it gives an example of the condition that is currently in action and developing further every day by the efforts of international organizations that are taking ever more control from sovereign nations year after year. Governments, such as the United States, with strictly defined rules and legal boundaries, with large unwieldy bureaucracies, complex treaties and international agreements, and extremely divided populations, will be hard pressed to keep up with the changing power structure of the connected megacities and the way they influence the world.

The Economy, Private Banking, and the Federal Reserve

"Banking was conceived in iniquity and was born in sin. The Bankers own the earth. Take it away from them, but leave them the power to create deposits, and with the flick of the pen they will create enough deposits to buy it back again. However, take it away from them, and all the great fortunes like mine will disappear and they ought to disappear, for this would be a happier and better world to live in. But, if you wish to remain the slaves of Bankers and pay the cost of your own slavery, let them continue to create deposits."
- Sir Josiah Stamp,
President of the Bank of England in the 1920's, the second richest man in Britain

The nature of our economic system is one that has a long and complex history, though the complexity diminishes as patterns become more apparent. If we look only as far back as the last century, we will not understand the economy of this nation or the world. If our perception is overly broad, we will miss some of the instrumental moments that have shaped our current situation. So, the vision must be sharp and broad and take into account many centuries and millennia of events and the patterns they describe. This conversation is not intended as a history book, but to put into context various attributes concisely to present the argument and the dire need for change in our present situation. There is far too much information to provide in even a thousand books to describe what is being condensed here, and what has been condensed before into easily digestible content. It is up to the reader to become the researcher and delve into these things to discover the truth for themselves if it is not apparent to them in these words. Our system today is mostly misunderstood and the vast majority of people in this nation are consumed by and indoctrinated into thinking that the transient issues on the privately owned news channels are the major problems in the world today. This is far from the truth and yet people are suffering their ignorance while supporting those who are perpetuating both their suffering and their ignorance.

Our economic structure today could be called many things. Captive capitalism describes our controlled and manipulated market denying free and true capitalism. Plutocracy describes the way in which our society is ruled by the super wealthy, private corporate interests, and how the government is directly owned and controlled by them. These two describe the most important of the terms that can be used today to understand our economic system. We live in a Plutocratic society with a captive capitalistic economy. This is all veiled skillfully behind mountains of propaganda and oceans of legalese, but the patterns are easily discernable when one begins to recognize them and how they affect the social condition.

Since 1913, the Federal Reserve System has increasingly and exclusively commanded the printing of the national currency, the setting of interest rates, and the manufactured inflation. Before this, there were only a few other times when the government or people allowed the existence of a private central bank. Primarily these were times when the government needed lots of money very fast. The existence of these banks was synonymous with exorbitant inflation. When the government no longer needed or accepted them, they were consistently shut down. The argument over central banks is older than the nation and was contested by nations in Europe before the American Revolution. Over the centuries, the central banking model has dominated nations and set itself into a position of international economic control, able to dictate its will to various nations and create wealth or poverty within its dominion based on the agenda it alone determined and had knowledge of. The formation of the coalition opposing England and mercantilism gave the people of the colonies a chance to live outside the dominion of these economic parasites and tyrants. Even among the signers of the Declaration of Independence, though, there were proponents for central banking, like that of Alexander Hamilton. On the other end of the spectrum were those that despised central banks and understood the importance of not allowing the presence of international private banking influence and central banking practices.

"The insidious crime of secretly or surreptitiously altering the monetary laws of a State— than which no morę dastardly or fatal blow can be dealt at its liberties — is not a new one. There is a suggestion in the decree of B. C. 360, concerning the ancient iron money of Sparta, that Gylipus was not unfamiliar with this grave offence."

"Before the Discovery of America private coinage was everywhere suppressed; and the essential prerogative of Money became vested and centered in the various crowned heads who governed the states of Europe. It was not long after that great event, when avidity awoke to new life over the spoils of a plundered Continent, that attempts were renewed to snatch the prerogative of Money from the State. This time it was not the truculent noble, who impudently claimed a right that had once belonged to the Caesars and boldly exercised it in defiance of the Crown, but the sneaking billoneur, who stealthily sought to acquire it through the arts of falsehood, intrigue, and forgery. Such were the crimes of 1666, 1742, 1870, and 1873."

"In 1542 the Spaniards commenced shipping silver to China and India, from Acapulco in Mexico, by way of the Phillpines. When Potosi became prolific these shipments amounted to £200,000 a year. By this time the value of a pound weight of gold in the coinages of India had been raised to 9 pounds weight of silver; in other words, the coinage ratio between silver and gold was 9 for 1. The British East India Trading Company, formed in 1600, at once sought permission from the Crown of England to export silver to India. The policy of England had always been opposed to the melting or exportation of any portion of its Measure of Value. Penal statues, prohibiting such melting or exportation, had been enacted in 9Edw'd III., c. 1.; 2 Hen. IV., c.5; 5 Rich. II.; 17 Rich. II.; 2 Hen. VI., c. 6; 17 Edward IV; 4 Hen. VII., c. 23; and 19 Hen. VII., c. 5."

"In accordance with this policy, Queen Elizabeth refused the request of the Company... However, permission was given them to import new silver from foreign parts, which silver might be struck into coins at the Mint for their special use (after due payment of seigniorage), with further permission to annually export a limited sum of coins thus struck."

"In 1613 the Company obtained a charter with extended powers; and its numbers, wealth and influence having greatly increased, it made several attempts to enlarge its privilege of export, one of which attempts was discussed in the Star Chamber, 1639, but without success to the Company. With the downfall of Charles I., the Company was almost extinguished. Its aggressiveness and avidity had procured it many enemies, and rendered it so unpopular that in 1655, Cromwell annulled its exclusive privileges and declared the Oriental trade open to all Englishmen.

"Two years later the Company's influence with the Council of State was sufficient to induce the Protector to renew its monopoly. In 1662 Charles II. confirmed this renewal and, for a corrupt consideration, permanently established this Company of money-changers, privateers, filibusters and bullies. From that year dates a new order of men in England"

"The Estates formerly consisted of the Crown, the Church, the Lords and the Commons. To these were now added the financiers, or Billoneurs, who have since almost entirely swallowed the others. Originally the financiers consisted of 215 monopolists under the title of the East India Company: they now comprise the entire world of money- changers and bankers. This cosmopolitan band threatens the peace of mankind."

"...the Production of silver has always been, and if not disturbed by legislation would always be, far more steady than that of gold. Its gradual demonetization is therefore without any apology either in the manner of its finding or production... it has been the result of intrigues which originated and have continued to emanate from the city of London, a place in which there are neither gold nor silver mines but a plentiful accumulation of "financial" and commercial shrewdness."

"I would not have it inferred from these remarks that I prefer silver to gold for a general Measure of Value. A general or universal Measure of Value is a chimera invented by the bankers of Threadneedle Street to foist their Metallic scheme upon the world and render their city the centre of a system of cosmopolitan Barter. A national Measure of Value, consisting of silver metal ("free coinage" system), is but little better than one of gold metal. No metal, as such, can measure value with precision or equity. This is what Money alone can effect; and if there were no question of policy in the matter, I should advocate a monetary system independent of metals. But the monetary question is a practical and political one. We cannot ignore history; we cannot ignore the status quo; and as the status quo is a complex metal and paper system based upon history, law and practical politics, the most that can be done is to reform it in the interest of the government, that is to say, of the people. For the present I would advise a return to the coinage laws prior to 1873 and the retirement of bank notes, to be replaced by greenbacks. These reforms will not only benefit the great mass of our people, they will save the commercial classes from what will otherwise end in widespread bankruptcy and perhaps even more serious results. Unfortunately the commercial classes are too greedy to accept reforms that do not promise them unfair advantages."

- Alexander del Mar, "A History of Monetary Crimes" – American political economist, historian, numismatist, author, and first Director of the Bureau of Statistics at the U.S. Treasury Department[39]

To synthesize this excerpt, we can see there are a few significant points made regarding the historical markers that wade it possible for the Federal reserve to exist. Firstly, the creation of the East India Trading Company in 1600, which was composed of 215 monopolists, and their initial reward of a partial charter in 1662 to export silver. This allowed the company to deliver silver to India, exchange for gold at a 6 ounce of silver profit, and rebuy gold with the profits. This was limited only to the caps on the charter. Which makes our second point. In 1666, the company was rewarded an unlimited charter to export metals. Thirdly, del Mar, over 200 years after the fact, makes a strong statement, that "From that year (1662) dates a new order of men in England". He is making the case that from the time of Charles II onward, the state of England has been changed and controlled by "this Company of money-changers, privateers, filibusters and bullies". He is saying that central bankers overtly took control of the economy through their charters to export the gold and silver of the nation for personal profit. They created a bulwark for which the state could not return to their prior condition. He is also saying that this was the moment in which the planning of panics (economic depressions) was put into plans for the first conceivable time. Bankers were now allowed to print money and control monetary systems, rather than kings, through the coinage law in 1666.

"But their (bankers/monopolists) main argument was supplied by the East India Company, who were anxious to ship silver to India in exchange for gold, a transaction that at that time afforded a profit of cent per cent (100%). Behind this argument there was bribery of the court officials, of the king's mistress, Barbara Villiers, and even of the king (Charles II.,) himself. After several years of intrigue, the merchants finally succeeded; and in 1666 was enacted that "free" coinage law which practically altered the monetary systems of the world and laid the foundation of the Metallic theory of money. The specific effect of this law was to destroy the Royal prerogative of coinage, nullify the decision in the Mixt Moneys case and inaugurate a future series of commercial panics and disasters which down to that time were totally unknown."

"After a century of unexampled prosperity and brilliant progress in England, due... to the stimulus afforded by the influx and coinage of silver from Spanish America, the English Parliament was so stupid or criminal as to pass the East India Company's Mint Bill in 1666 and thus permit the country to be drained of its Measure of Value by a band of adventurers. Some of the disastrous consequences that ensued have been eloquently described by Macauley; but nobody thought of repealing the Act and nobody thinks of it yet; the profits of the Bank of England and other banks of issue standing in the way. It was in the midst of the first drainage of silver to the Orient, when the coins of England were clipped and sweated to two-thirds or one-half their original weight, that the American Colonies were first brought face to face with the great subject of Monetary Law. It need hardly be said that this was a subject concerning which they were profoundly ignorant.

The early trade of the Colonies had been effected by barter, but by the last quarter of the 17th century the population had grown too numerous, widespread and differentiated in occupation to render such an archaic system of exchange any longer practicable."

"So early as 1652 (October 19) the province of Massachusetts found it necessary—for it was no mere act of wantonness or of profit-seeking by the colony—to defy the Royal authority by erecting a Mint and striking Pine Tree shillings. These were to contain 662/3 gr. fine silver, the same as the actual circulating clipped shilling of England, though not the same as the theoretical or minted shilling of the Commonwealth, which should have contained about 853/4 gr. fine."

"From this moment began in America a contest between Barter and Exchange, between Capital and Blood, between the Plunder of the Seas and the Credit of the Colonies, between the Metallic product of slavery and the Fiduciary issues of a free people, that has not yet ended and that never will end until the principles which Aristotle distilled from the republics of antiquity have again asserted their vitality in the halls of legislation. These principles were revived in the Mixt Moneys case in 1604. They were affirmed by Bastiat in 1840: "Exchange is political economy; it is society itself, for it is impossible to conceive of society as existing

without exchange, or exchange without society." They were again affirmed by Destutt Trący in 1870: "Society is in fact held together by a series of exchanges." And they will be again and again affirmed until they are nailed inseparably to the Constitution of every free State in Christendom. "Exchange is a social act; money is a social mechanism; it is a public measure of value, the unit of which is not one coin, nor one note, but all the coins and notes of like currency under the law of each nation when added together; money to be equitable must be of stable volume; stability can only be secured by national authority and limitation; if you want prosperity you must trust the national government to conserve the Measure of Value; if you fear to trust the government, you may indeed preserve the size of the coin in your pocket, but you cannot secure the profits it may earn for you; and persistence in this course will force ruin upon others and probably upon yourself."

- Alexander del Mar[40]

The comparisons we can make concerning what occurred between the moneychangers of 1666 and the Federal Reserve money changers of 1913 to today are many. One thing to see here is del Mar's comment that "nobody thought of repealing the Act and nobody thinks of it yet; the profits of the Bank of England and other banks of issue standing in the way." If you replace the Bank of England with the Federal Reserve... nobody thought of repealing the Act and nobody thinks of it yet; the profits of the Federal Reserve and other banks of issue standing in the way. It's too easy. It is the most obvious things that go so often missed. The Bank of England was founded in 1694. Less than a century later, at a time when information moved slower than people today will be able to imagine, the Colonists in America rose up in Revolution. This revolution was fueled by the possibility of regaining the monetary sovereignty that England itself had lost in 1666. It did not work in the end, except to relieve the colonists of slavery to English Mercantilism and central banking, only to be caught in the midst of American Mercantilism and central banking. The Federal Reserve is simply a chapter in the success story of the ancestors of the bankers of the turn of the 20th century. The real final goal being to dominate and control global economic activity and assets. We can see it clearly though, that had the Federal Reserve not been formed, the bankers (monopolists) would have simply pushed for a central bank again in 1930 or 1950, when they were better collected, wealthier, more deeply engrossed in the political system, etc. At this point, approaching the problem of central banks legally is not a solution. The likelihood of abolishing the Federal Reserve through legal means is nearly impossible. Their methods are many and their moral and ethical limits are fictions dreamed up by their loyal slaves, the taxpaying statists.

"If we survey the entire history of money... it divides itself into five distinct periods. First, the Pontifico-royal period, which lasted from the earliest times to the epoch of the Greek republics... money was coined exclusively in the temples, and stamped with the sacred emblems of religion. Second, the Republican period, when money was controlled by the senates of Sparta, Clazomenæ, Byzantium, Athens, and Rome. Third, the Pontifico-imperial period, when the coinage was assumed by the Caesars, and so regulated by them that for thirteen centuries its essential features remained substantially unaltered. Fourth, the Kingly period, when the princes of the West, having freed themselves from the dominion of Rome, seized the coinage prerogative and exercised it independently. Fifth, the period of Private Coinage, when the goldsmiths and merchant adventurers chartered to trade with and despoil or conquer the orient, obtained control of the royal prerogative of coinage, and thus opened the door to the last of degradations, Private Coinage. This period has not yet ended."

"What has been the result (of the bankers taking over the monetary system)? From the day when the royal voluptuary resigned a prerogative which, more than any other one, pleads for the continence of kingly rule, to the present time, the commercial community has been subjected to alternate epochs of monetary contraction and expansion, in which much of what it accumulates at one period is insidiously filched from it at another... The suspensions of banks of issue therein shown involved losses to the note-holders and others amounting to more than all the gold and silver money in the world several times over. Not only this; the surrender of the prerogative of coinage has tended to estrange the Crown from the People, whose disappointment has manifested itself in many painful symptoms."

"These tremendous powers (to coin money) have been wielded with such inadequate perception of the equities and consequences they involved, with such lack of scientific of financial skill, and in so narrow and selfish a spirit, that its arbiters have repeatedly plunged the commercial world into bankruptcy, and confiscated or inequitably redistributed its accumulated earnings, either for their own benefit or else to save themselves from the effects of their own blundering."

"...(the) Mercantile system of Great Britain...encouraged the import and discouraged the export of the precious metals from England. It was evident that with money, the supplies of which were subject to the power of a distant sovereign and an apathetic ministry, the orderly development of the colonies was impossible, and hence followed those efforts to establish at first a silver coinage and afterwards a paper system of their own, which led to the contentions between them and the Crown that distinguished the latter half of the 17th and first half of the 18th century. The bitterness arising from this source was enhanced by the contraction (depression/panic) of 1750..."

"Soon after this abortive attempt to introduce private promissory notes into the circulation, the Colony of Massachusetts resolved to relieve "the scarcity of money and the want to an adequate measure of commerce" by issuing its own Bills of Credit to the modest extent of £7,000. This was done February, 1690."

-Alexander del Mar[41]

"Money exists not by nature but by law"

– Aristotle

In 1774, England passed the Stamp Act, requiring the colonies to buy paper from the Crown with silver and gold. This was done to force the colonies to relieve themselves of the silver and gold they were using to back their bills of credit and to form their coinage. The Crown intended for the Colonists to simply acquiesce.

"Among the first act of the Massachusetts and the Continental Revolutionary assemblies, was the emission of paper money and the teeth of the Royal prerogative, and this was done while yet the Colonies had no fixed determination of separating from the mother country."

-Alexander del Mar[42]

Thus did the colonies respond, by issuing paper money, as the cost of the purchasing paper from the Crown was theft of their gold and silver resources. England did not send armies to the colonies over spilled tea, or a minor whipping for tax evasion. The armies of the largest empire on earth landed in America to punish the colonists for their refusal to participate any longer in central banking, mercantilism, and their own extortion. Oddly, del Mar also comments, that the colonists were not thinking seriously of separating themselves from England, but rather they simply wanted to do what was necessary for their survival and wellbeing, that which was not being provided for by the Crown. Their need became a refusal, a refusal became a war, a war that ended in the emergence of a nation with the potential to evade the central bankers schemes. This new nation failed. It succumbed to the bankers as easily as the British had only a few generations before it.

The argument against private central banks was well understood by many people in the first half of this nation's history but this wisdom was degraded with time and extreme influences by international banking interests. At the start of the industrial revolution, the nation was mostly agrarian, and farming accounted for the vast majority of the national wealth and labor. After 160 years, we have become a nation of less than one-one hundredth agrarian labor and the ownership of the land has moved more and more away from the public and into the hands of the private super wealth. During the industrial revolution, the owners of the private industrial powerhouses used economic and government influence as well as social influence to force the public into believing they would profit more by working in terrible conditions in factories than by working as farmers. As more laborers moved to urban factories, these private owners began to build their fortunes and their influence to ever greater heights. After J.P Morgan influenced the copper market and the Knickerbocker Trust Corporation to manufacture the recession of 1907, the public clamored for the creation of a stable public central bank. They were still aware of the dangers of private interests and were vehemently opposed to the industrialists and private bankers who were considered to be villains and enemies of the public. With this understanding, the meeting held at Jekyll Island was organized, the Federal Reserve Act was written by the industrialists and bankers that arrived there, and soon after that bill was presented and passed in Congress and signed by the President, Woodrow Wilson. This all happened in the most secretive and insidious manner. Instead of calling this by its real name, they chose to give it a name that would trick the population into believing the new banking system was a government bank, which is what the population was largely clamoring for, to provide stabilization to the economy. The Federal Reserve was and is a private banking cartel owned by the private industrialist and banking families and entities that have been consolidating control over Europe and the rest of the world for centuries. In 1913, this control extended to the United States. We have been under the financial, and thus the social, control of the very private and very exclusive owners of this private bank called the Federal Reserve, for over a century. Very few people are alive today that were alive at the signing into law of the Federal Reserve. But today we can look at the patterns and we can see these institutions, even when blind to the more insidious aspects, do not work. The Federal Reserve was a promise to correct for inflation and be a guard against market volatility. It has been a force for the exact opposite. It has done absolutely nothing of any good for a single individual outside of its own organization, and when we look at the grand stage of the holistic system that we live in, they have harmed their future as much as anyone else. When this planet becomes unsuitable for human life, they may last a while in bunkers, but they will not last forever.

"Every system has groups that benefit from it, and hence have no desire to change it. There is probably no country in the world that has changed its economic, social, and political system in a significant way without a crisis. It is the crisis that convinces citizens and interest groups of the need for change... The examples of the Japanese and Asian crises illustrate how crises can be engineered to facilitate the redistribution of economic ownership, and to implement legal, structural, and political change... From 2004, under the ECB's (European Central Bank's) watch, bank credit growth in Ireland, Greece, Portugal and Spain increased by over 20% per annum, and property prices skyrocketed. When bank credit fell, property prices collapsed, developers went bankrupt, and the banking systems of Ireland, Portugal, Spain, and Greece became insolvent. The ECB could have prevented these bubbles, just as it

could have ended the ensuing banking and economic crises. But it refused to do so, until major political concessions had been made, such as the transfer of fiscal and budgeting powers from each sovereign state to the European Union... The deliberations of the ECB's decision-making bodies are secret. The mere attempt at influencing the ECB, for instance through democratic debate and discussion, is forbidden, according to the Maastricht Treaty. The ECB is an international organization, that is above and outside the laws and jurisdictions of any individual nation. Its senior staff carry diplomatic passports, and the files and documents inside the European Central Bank cannot be searched or impounded by any police force or public prosecutor... The world over, central banks hold significant, yet little understood powers. Often independent, unaccountable and obscure, central banks operate in the shadows, yet their actions affect us all. To create a public consensus for the need for structural reform by purposefully creating a recession, and then needlessly prolonging it, must constitute an abuse of power. Do citizens really want to be manipulated in such a costly and dishonest manner?"

- Princes of the Yen: Central Bank Truth Documentary[43]

I am going to discuss two different solutions that seem to compete with one another on the outset, but when linked together in an appropriate timeline and series, make it possible to access even greater rewards than either done exclusively. The first is a way of utilizing central banks to eliminate bad assets and empower banks to expand credit and thus empower the economy for real producers. The second is a way of creating real money with intrinsic value. Both of these solutions are pointless if we do not decentralize. If the power to regulate the economy, print money/currency, and dictate policy is centralized and privatized, the unavoidable result will be the destruction of the economy, the enslavement of the population, and the removal of holistic representative governance, if such a thing could exist regardless.

Central banks create money out of thin air. It's as simple as that. Three theories of banking have been in existence for at least one century. The first is the Financial Intermediation Theory. This theory says that banks act as financial intermediaries that simply lend from deposits made. The Fractional Reserve Theory says that banks lend money out of reserves. The final theory, the Credit Creation Theory says that banks create money from nothing at all.

"Economists say that banks are deposit-taking institutions that lend money. Banks don't take deposits and they don't lend money. They don't take deposits because they borrow from the public. A deposit suggests something held in custody, a bailment, and this is not what happens. Instead, the money that you lend to the bank, which they call, erroneously, a deposit, is actually their money. They own it. Its just a loan. You're a general creditor. Banks never lend money, unlike firms and non-bank financial institutions. They are in the business of purchasing securities. When you get a loan, the loan contract is a promissory note, just like the bank of England Promissory note, of course not legal tender, as you may have noticed, but the bank will purchase that security from you. That's what it does. And now it owes you money, and it creates a record of the money it owes, which we call deposits, and that's how the money supply comes about."

"So you get a loan, a £1,000 lets say. The loan contract is purchased by the bank. It increases the banks assets and the bank then records the money it owes you, which it calls slightly incorrectly, a customer deposit, because no customer has deposited this and in fact nobody has deposited this anywhere. And its not transferred anywhere inside or outside the bank. It's created out of nothing. These fictitious deposits are our money supply. So, banks are special. They create the money supply. 97% in most countries, of the money supply, out

of nothing through the process of what's called credit creation.
-Prof. Richard Werner, "Today's Source of Money Creation"[44]

The Central Banks create 3% of the real money supply. 97% of money creation occurs through bank lending. Credit Creation means that a commercial bank produces loans for customers out of nothing. The money is not taken from some other account or from prior deposits by other customers of that bank or any other. The bank literally creates money from nothing. Legally there is no such thing as a bank deposit. When you deposit money in a bank, you are actually loaning that money to the bank as a creditor. The receiving bank owns that money exclusively upon receipt, and it is no longer owned by you, even if it was yours prior to the "deposit". You aren't depositing money, rather, you are borrowing money to the bank. This money is not then lent to other customers, as banks do not participate in loaning money as intermediaries. When a bank "loans" you money, you are signing into an agreement to issue a security, or debt instrument, to the bank. The bank purchases this security from you, and thus the bank owes you money for the product that you are selling them. This is the deposit, which is a record of debt owed to you by the bank, and the fake "customer deposit" for the lender, which is you. This is the process by which the money supply is created. It means that the money comes into existence when the banks create "customer deposits", when people make issuance of debt instruments, purchased by the bank, to the commercial banks. Another way to see this is, if I have a dollar, and you the reader are the bank. I want to deposit my dollar into an account I make with you. I sign a contract with you, which says that I release ownership of my dollar upon "deposit". When I come back to take out a loan, I sign another contract with you that says that you are purchasing a security I'm issuing to you, and that you owe me a certain sum for that security. It means that we are transacting on debt. I am offering you a financial instrument, and you are purchasing that for a cost of whatever "loan" amount has been agreed to. You then create a "customer deposit" of that amount, which can be used in the real economy. You did not have that money to begin with, nor was it transferred to you. It simply appeared at the behest of the transaction of the debt instrument.

"...when banks create credit for the real economy, but its used for business investment in the creation of new goods and services, productive investment or implementation of new technologies. That creates growth without inflation and without crises... So why haven't the central planners at the central banks ensured that? Well they have in some countries but not in others... (The question is) really centralization versus decentralization. Should this decision be made by central planners or in a decentralized market-based fashion. Germany... has been very successful, its economy for 200 years, and its exports are often larger than Chinese exports, although the population is only 6 percent of the Chinese population. How is that possible? If you look at market champions... companies that are number one, two or three in terms of market share globally and hidden champions of small firms that are global market leaders, global champions... Germany has the largest number of hidden champions. Small firms that are global market leaders by far of any country. Most exports from Germany are from small firms, family-owned businesses. Well, its because of the community banks... in Germany there's 1500. It's the largest number of banks in the European Union. Big banks lend to big companies, small banks lend to small firms. Germany has lots of small banks. Decentralized decision-making that's been highly successful. 70 percent of banking are with not-for-profit community banks. We already have public money creation, in the form of local community banks... So, that's unique in the world and that's delivered high growth without the bubbles. (Central Banks) admit they've been telling porkies... and now they propose to increase their power. So central bankers belatedly admit... banks create the money supply, so let's abolish that now and also by the way, lets abolish cash... introduce digital cyber currency that central bank's issue and control and

thereby gain total control over all economic transactions, decisions... The greatest concentration of central banking power in history is really the bid they're aiming at... and of course digital accounts of dissenters could be switched off. (It would) be very difficult to even purchase necessities. This is an Orwellian dystopia of total control. The end of any freedoms. That's really what central banks are aiming at. Several central banks... have already prepared their microchip implant RFID chip to be implanted under your skin... The overarching trend of the 20th century is concentration of power in the hands of the few... We don't want to have these unaccountable central planners making decisions. We need decentralization. The solution therefore is to maintain public money in the hands of local community banks... Give local people the power in the form of local public banks and local not-for-profit community banks... We shouldn't really abolish banks. We just have to get rid of the too-big-too-fail banks, introduce a few rules; that you create credit for productive purposes, and then we can solve many of the world's problems."

-Prof. Richard Werner, "Today's Source of Money Creation"[45]

Near the conclusion of WWII, the US Dollar become the reserve currency at the UN monetary conference held in Bretton Woods, New Hampshire. 44 countries agreed to fix their currencies to the US Dollar which was tied to gold at $35 per Ounce. Countries could trade their currencies for US Dollars, which could then be exchanged for gold. Meaning all of these currencies were backed by gold. When countries exchanged for gold, the gold was stored in the US for "safekeeping". This applied to foreign countries and central banks.

Post-war spending in the US was remarkably high, especially with its war effort in Vietnam, and other countries became worried that the US didn't have enough gold to back its spending. They began exchanging for gold and demanding physical delivery of that gold to their country. To prevent this, Nixon suspended the gold convertibility system on August 15, 1971. Without the gold backing, countries ran perpetual deficits. From 1971 onward, the US has never run a surplus and has sustained only by perpetual stimulus. All currency became backed by nothing, i.e., fiat currency. Fiat is based in government promises and perpetuated through force.

"Money is a medium of exchange and the way it has evolved is that it's always something of intrinsic value, until the modern age, when the politicians say, well we don't need anything of intrinsic value anymore. All we need is political decree. We can say this is money, this piece of paper is money. Now money has a new characteristic, but underneath it all there's the same concept in place that nobody ever seems to challenge. That governments have a right to declare something of no value to be money and you must accept it. That's really the problem... it's destroying the economies of the world."

-G. Edward Griffin, Gold & Dollar: How Money Became Worthless[46]

As there is no fixed rate of value to gold, the U.S. government can spend and take out loans at its whim. It has nothing to limit its borrowing but its own moral or ethical inhibitions if it is even knowledgeable enough to understand the mechanism anyway.

Allow me to discuss the composition and other aspects of the Federal Reserve. The Federal Reserve is composed of 12 Regional Federal Reserve Banks. Each bank has its own balance sheet. And the Federal Reserve total balance sheet is the sum of the balance sheets of each of its member banks. The 12 Regional Banks aren't Government institutions, but corporations nominally "owned" by member commercial banks. Commercial banks are privately owned businesses trying to earn profits primarily by lending money to other businesses and to individuals. The FOMC (Federal Open Market Committee) is the monetary

policymaking body of the Fed system. It is composed of 12 members, including the seven members of the Board of Governors and five of the twelve Reserve Bank presidents, though all Fed bank presidents attend FOMC meetings and participate in discussion and assessment of the economy. Its meetings are held eight times annually. Meeting minutes are released immediately, though Transcripts, Exhibits, and Documentation provided to attendees prior to the meeting are only released 5 years later.
The Fed produces Reserve Dollars, which cannot mix with Bank dollars. Reserve dollars may influence and direct the creation of Bank dollars though. The two systems operate independently but the effects that they have on each other is reflective of the intent of the Federal Reserve.
Currency was not backed by treasuries until 1932. The currency was 40% backed by gold, and 60% by commercial paper (short term IOU's issued by American businesses). The 60% backing by commercial paper disappeared. Government IOU's took over (treasuries). From 1932 to 1935, it shifted to 40% gold, 60% IOU's. After this, gold was getting shipped out of the US by international bankers to such a degree that the currency could no longer backed by gold. Instead, as of 1935, currency has been backed by 100% US Treasuries. Treasuries represent the "Full Faith and Credit" of the US Government, or in real terms, "we the people". It means that every time the government takes a "loan" out from the Federal Reserve, it is the people that are indebted to the Fed, while the government operators relieve themselves of any responsibility, while ensuring their pockets are fully lined.
We have allowed the existence of the Federal Reserve and the Internal Revenue Service (IRS) to our extreme detriment. These entities have no real authority under the constitution though most of the population just acquiesces to their demands. Why is it that you need a social security card? Social Security Numbers (SSN) were first assigned in 1936, to make it possible for these two entities to track the earnings of the people, while the Social Security Administration (SSA) tracked taxes for the purpose of redistribution of funds to benefits for workers. That doesn't sound so bad, right? Well, the general pattern seen here is the increasing bureaucracy, centralization of information and power, and the forced application of a tracking number to every individual upon birth. The Federal Reserve loans currency to the federal government, with interest, while the IRS is the agency that facilitates unconstitutionally extorting direct taxes from the people, shifting wealth constantly from the people to the shareholders of the Federal Reserve.

	2019				2020				2021		
	Q1	Q2	Q3	Q4	Q1	Q2	Q3	Q4	Q1	Q2	Q3
Current receipts	**5,808.5**	**5,906.8**	**5,908.8**	**5,965.9**	**5,966.9**	**5,631.8**	**5,931.2**	**6,072.3**	**6,301.8**	**6,577.0**	**6,758.3**
Current tax receipts	3,985.2	4,062.7	4,059.7	4,110.8	4,080.6	3,815.0	4,040.9	4,149.1	4,353.5	4,565.1	4,689.8
Personal current taxes	2,169.3	2,222.8	2,205.2	2,223.2	2,241.6	2,099.0	2,181.8	2,259.8	2,412.1	2,532.5	2,623.7
Taxes on production and imports	1,504.8	1,520.9	1,547.4	1,556.3	1,577.1	1,460.5	1,544.0	1,557.0	1,580.1	1,636.3	1,654.7
Taxes on corporate income	284.4	291.7	279.6	303.9	233.3	229.3	288.5	304.0	331.9	366.9	381.2
Taxes from the rest of the world	26.6	27.4	27.5	27.4	28.6	26.1	26.6	28.3	29.4	29.3	30.3
Contributions for government social insurance	1,413.0	1,419.8	1,427.2	1,446.5	1,477.2	1,410.8	1,463.7	1,506.5	1,539.2	1,577.7	1,613.2
From persons	1,407.6	1,414.6	1,422.0	1,441.4	1,472.0	1,405.9	1,458.7	1,501.3	1,533.8	1,572.2	1,607.6
From the rest of the world[1]	5.3	5.2	5.1	5.1	5.2	4.9	5.0	5.2	5.3	5.4	5.6
Net government saving	**-1,183.6**	**-1,157.6**	**-1,231.4**	**-1,213.4**	**-1,292.5**	**-5,072.0**	**-3,582.6**	**-2,188.3**	**-4,100.6**	**-2,484.0**	**-2,051.1**
Current expenditures	**6,992.0**	**7,064.4**	**7,140.2**	**7,179.3**	**7,259.4**	**10,703.8**	**9,513.8**	**8,260.6**	**10,402.5**	**9,060.9**	**8,809.4**
Total expenditures	**7,165.6**	**7,243.4**	**7,319.8**	**7,418.4**	**7,470.8**	**10,910.4**	**9,706.2**	**8,471.9**	**10,790.8**	**9,245.7**	**8,994.2**
Net lending or net borrowing (-)	**-1,333.9**	**-1,315.5**	**-1,389.9**	**-1,430.9**	**-1,480.4**	**-5,249.6**	**-3,749.5**	**-2,374.2**	**-4,462.4**	**-2,641.4**	**-2,193.1**

* Bureau of Economic Analysis, 2021[47]
*In the national income and product accounts (NIPAs), personal current taxes include tax payments on income (including realized net capital gains and net of refunds), tax payments on personal property, and payments for personal licenses by U.S. residents.[48] (Bureau of Economic Analysis, 2010)

Debt Held by the Public under Two Policy Simulations

Percentage of GDP

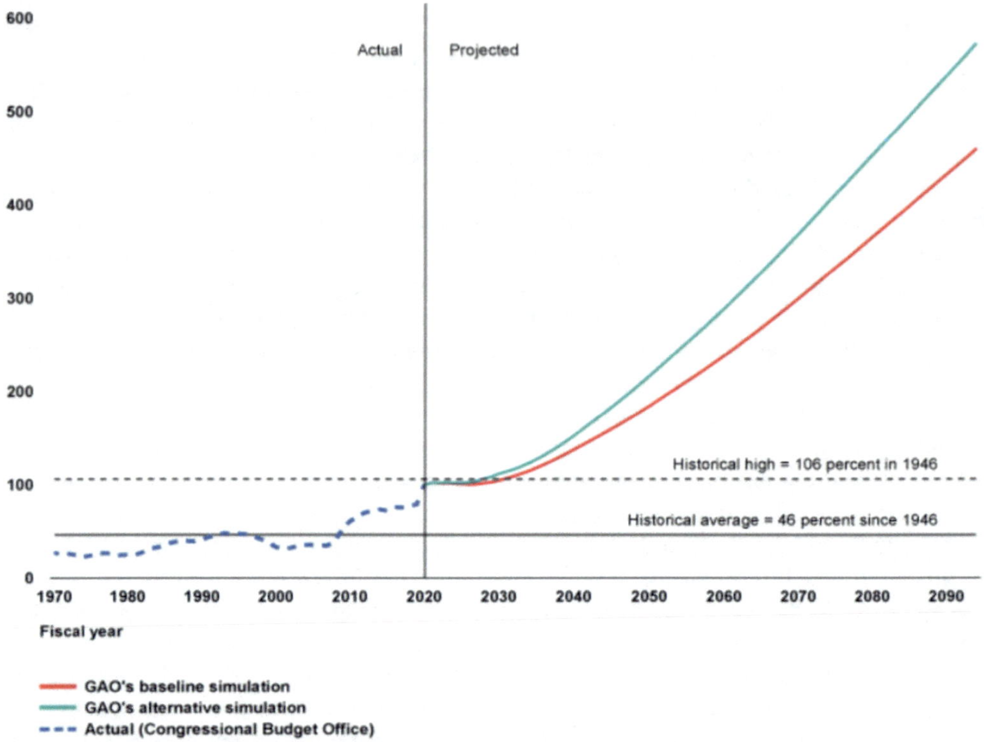

Federal Debt Held by the Public, 1900 to 2050

Percentage of Gross Domestic Product

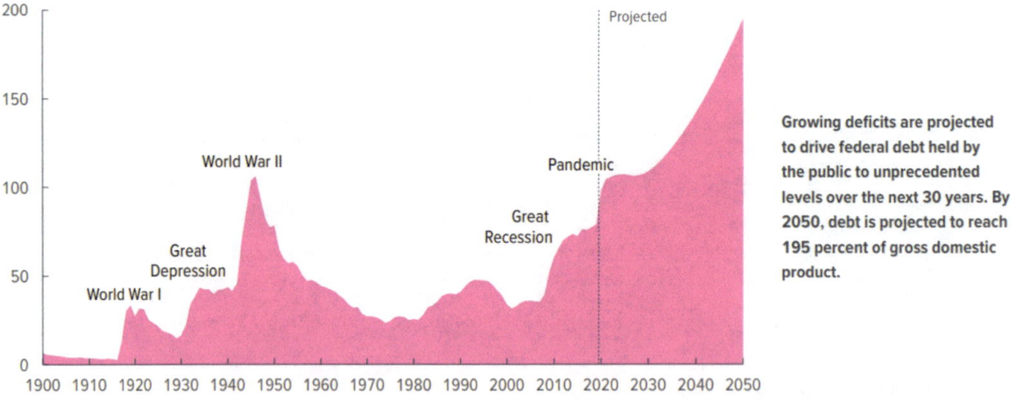

Source: Congressional Budget Office.

Before the 2008 and 2009 financial crisis, The Fed's only assets on their balance sheets were U.S. Treasuries, under one trillion T-Bills in total. The assets were treasuries (IOUs from US government (we the people) to the Fed) and the liabilities were the same amount of currency in circulation, federal reserve notes. Treasuries are IOUs plus interest, and Currency is IOUs without interest. This creates an imbalance in the balance sheet.

In 2009, the Fed began a type of quantitative easing program and took assets not issued by the Treasury onto its balance sheet. Mortgage-backed Securities. When the Fed began buying mortgage-backed securities, they were backed up by the FFC (Full Faith and Credit) of the US Government. Federal Reserve's corresponding liability to MBS was balanced by excess reserves. The Fed credited the Federal Reserve accounts of the commercial banks who had accounts at the Fed. Then the Fed began crediting accounts of entities other than commercial banks, perhaps the US Treasury and foreign central banks.

If the Fed wants to shrink the balance sheet... It goes on the market and tries to sell MBS and takes a severe loss likely. Rather than the Fed being responsible for the balance sheet losses, it is up to the US Government (i.e. you the taxpayer) to cover the loss and Treasuries are then used to fill the gap made by the Fed's liquidation of worthless assets (MBS).

This all means that fundamentally, you the taxpaying slave of the corporate government and international banking cartel must pay (through taxes) the debts (Fed loans to US government) that can never be fully paid because there isn't enough money in the world to pay the debts plus interest. In other words, you are at the bottom rung of a global ponzi scheme that has no interest in your wellbeing, only that you continue to pay taxes (otherwise known as debt collection) to an agency that is neither part of your government or any other, nor possessor of any value for which to back their currency, making it only as valuable as its use determines. If nobody used these Federal Reserve Notes, the notes would be less than worthless, they would be a massive liability to the Fed. The Fed would have no authority at all. As long as you continue to use this valueless paper and accept the responsibility of debt payments to the IRS (Federal Reserve collection agency, medium through government), then you continue to accept, support, and perpetuate the rulership and dictates of this private global cartel of "money-changers, privateers, filibusters and bullies", as del Mar rightfully and gently put it.

The reason why the stock market is going up is pretty simple: the economy is doing well, earnings are rising, and the Fed has basically said they're on hold for quite a while."
-William "Bill" Dudley, 10th president and chief executive officer of the Federal Reserve Bank of New York, Jan. 29, 2020[49]

"(Fed assets are) on hold according to Dudley... Well, heavens to Betsy! Who knew that the Fed being on hold for quite a while would mean it would take 107 years for the Fed to get the balance sheet to 4 trillion dollars, and it would take 107 years and 3 months to get the balance sheet to 7 trillion dollars... Ladies and gentlemen, it appears we have a dollar for dollar match between the most recent blast of QE (Quantitative Easing) by the Fed on the one hand, and its evil twin M2 in the real economy on the other hand. In other words, Bill Dudley is simply a straight up liar... The stock market goes into free fall on February 26th (2020) and the Fed wastes no time coming to the rescue one week later on March 4th and adds a cool 83 billion dollars to its balance sheet. Two weeks after that before any lockdown in any state in the U.S. you have on March 18th, the Fed has added already half a trillion dollars to its balance sheet. And guess what, after that the Fed packs on another 2.5 trillion dollars to its balance sheet and the market gets back up to where it was... Bill Dudley telling you that reserves don't leak out and Fed doesn't, you know, try its damnedest to pump up the stock market, that's just a straight up lie... the Fed single handedly injected 2.8 trillion dollars of bank money into the real economy... but something doesn't add up here. The last time I checked, there's 160 million stimulus checks had gone out. Even at 1200 dollars a check, which I know that it wasn't 1200 dollars a check, some people got partial checks, but even for the full amount that comes to 192 billion dollars. That's not even .2 trillion dollars.

As we saw, like I said, the Fed added 2.8 trillion dollars in M2 (Bank Money) to the economy by itself. And that's going on against the backdrop of a bunch of mainstreet businesses, millions of them, flat on their back, that are otherwise viable businesses, that are about to go bankrupt as a result of this pandemic and be picked up for pennies on the dollars... and you don't see the Fed's fingerprints all over this so-called pandemic?"

-John Titus, The Fed's Silent Takeover of the U.S.[50]

Let's consider this for a moment. The Federal Reserve has the ability to create infinite amounts of currency by clicking buttons on a keyboard. This currency can be used to purchase Treasury bonds from the U.S. Treasury, which is called a loan, and is traded bearing interest. Other nations also purchase Treasury bonds. The money from these IOU's that government is issuing, is used on paying for things within the country, and paying off past IOU's. Larger and larger "loans" must be taken out from the Fed to cover the costs of the principal and the interest, which makes it impossible for the government to EVER cover these debts. So, the Federal Reserve is creating debt within the taxpaying population, because the government is greedily and obsequiously borrowing currency from the Fed, with ever increasing losses due to ever larger loans, and ever larger liabilities. It is a circle of insanity. AND IT IS NOT BY ACCIDENT OR IGNORANCE!!! IT IS INTENTIONAL!!! One other note to an oddity. The injection of money into the economy was supposed to be in response to coronavirus. Why then did the Fed inject over half a trillion dollars into the market by March 18, 2020, when lockdowns hadn't even begun or been deigned necessary. These things do not just happen. 500 billion dollars does not just happen. It requires justification that will never come from the Fed or the government, because those who know why it was happening were the same people that attended and coordinated event 201, the economic plunge, the lockdowns, the mainstream media propaganda, the otherwise media censorship, the unscientific dictate of mask wearing, etc., etc., etc.

"The fact of the matter is that the Federal Reserve is a private institution... when the fed adds assets on to its balance sheet like it is doing now. Taking dodgy assets onto its balance sheet, you the taxpayer are on the hook when that asset valuation implodes into nothing... in the last ten to twelve years, astronomical asset valuations by private bankers at Wall Street bankers have fueled hundreds of billions of dollars in bonuses. You got none of that money. That is not your role. Your role in the Federal Reserve system is to absorb losses. You are the chump. You are the sucker. The Federal Reserve Is here to facilitate your absorption of those losses and that's going on right now as the Federal Reserve is adding bad assets onto its balance sheet, where, when the depression hits with full force, you dear taxpayer are going to eat the loss, not the Wall Street bankers who are already paid on those assets. They already got their bonuses. That money was cashed a long time ago. That's not your role."

-John Titus, Kicking People When They're Down[51]

Here is a six-step plan for the correction of our national and global economic systems. While it not overly specific, neither is it created to leave out any critical steps. The process can be quite painless economically speaking actually, but the likelihood is that, in its death throws, the beneficiaries of the current economic model would do everything and anything in their power to prevent this, including but not limited to, manipulating countries to engage in needless wars.

Step 1- Central Banks purchase non-performing assets from the commercial banks.

While central banks may not be apt to do this if they were aware of the totality of this plan, this step is not farfetched in the slightest. In 2009, the Federal Reserve purchased the bad assets that were plaguing the commercial banks in the country. Seeing as central banks are making this purchase with reserve dollars, the effect on the real money economy would be negligible, unless post-purchase manipulations occurred within the central bank to disrupt the real money economy.

Step 2- Stop issuing government bonds. Commercial banks issue loans to government, creating credit. Bank lending creates money supply.
When the bad assets have been purchased in their entirety by the central banks, the commercial banks can then, in full relief of their debts, be able to create credit, and thus, money, and inject it into the real money market through loans to the government and public. Rules would need be applied here that disallow the practice of lending for financial assets, and rather that credit is created specifically for productive businesses that would inject these loans into their production, in ways that would increase their ability to produce. This would prevent inflation as it would balance the loans with growth from the borrowing entities and thus the ability to fulfill the loans. Banks are now beholden to the lending arrangements at the core of the new agreements, which is to support local business creation, and local economy empowerment.

Step 3- Public audit of the Federal Reserve
This step is extremely important. Before we can abolish the Federal Reserve, we must have a 100% transparent audit of its books, with unbiased 3rd parties overseeing. All documentation must be released open source to the public at large, so that we may see what damages have been done and apply the correct treatment and justice in every sector.

Step 4- Abolish the Federal Reserve, illegalize private central banks, and jail the criminals
Here we follow the logical trail, that after auditing the Federal Reserve, we have confirmed the undeniable and verified proof of criminal activity by the entities and individuals who engage in central banking. It is this point in which we demand recuperations and justice. In this process, we also have discovered the criminal actors that operate through large financial institutions that have conspired with the Federal Reserve to the detriment of the people. This would include those at BlackRock, Inc. and The Vanguard Group among others. I spoke on the appropriate application of justice earlier in this book and how a fraud against a single person amounts to certain justice, and the fraud of millions would be correctly more heinous and require greater measures of correction.

Step 5- Reimplement the Gold and Silver Standard
As we no longer permit and allow the existence of private central banks, and we have become more decentralized and localized, we can now move to the revaluation of our currency, and again peg it to gold and silver. A public audit here will have to be conducted as well to determine how much gold actually exists within the United States, and how much was appropriated after the criminal organization of the Federal Reserve was relieved of their holdings. Many countries around the world, not part of the core of central banking monopoly have been acquiring 100's of tons of gold, and it will be relatively easeful to bring about a gold standard, just as it was relatively easeful for Nixon to dispose of it for nations around the world in 1971. We are now able to back our money with intrinsic value, limit government growth and power organically, and provide a historically stable medium of exchange.

Step 6- Encourage gold and silver purchases by general population
Finally, we encourage the people of nations around the world to acquire gold and silver for safekeeping and savings. These savings can be passed generationally and used in times of need to balance any unforeseen economic challenges. All may enjoy the stability and prosperity of this new decentralized economic system, where small, local banks offer more appropriate economic management.

"If banks mainly lend to companies that invest in the expansion of their equipment to produce more goods and services, you will get non-inflationary growth, and that is the growth that is also sustainable. Then you know you are not going to have a banking crisis."
- Richard Werner, On Quantitative Easing and Central Banks, 2015[52]

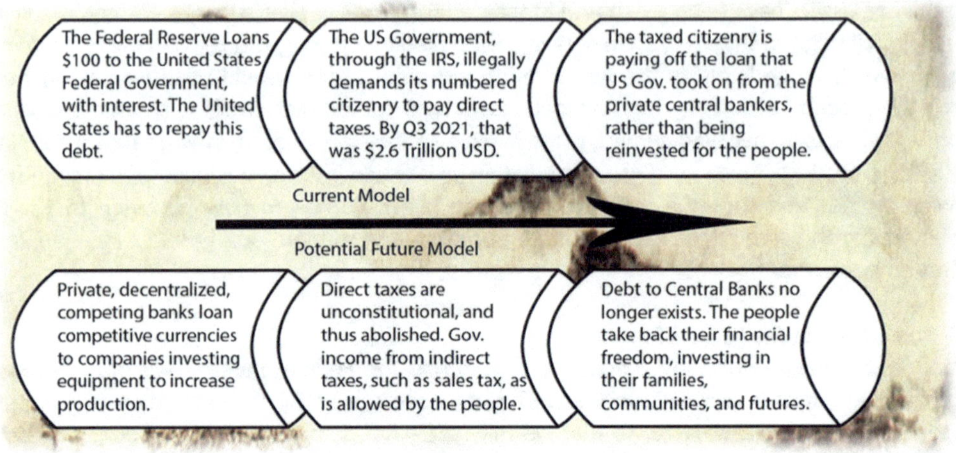

On Private Global Monopoly and Financial Dominance

The top financial institutions in the world are run by a constantly shifting (like musical chairs) pool of top tier executives and managers that are often hired based on social positioning rather than particular skill. The pool of potential hires to any of these institutions is exceedingly small, and of those that are able to be hired, the probability that there is a conflict of interest (whether recognized as such or not) and that they profit from the uncompetitive nature of the globally conglomerated interests is extremely high. Power in finance is built in the same way that power in politics is built. It is through positioning, perception, alliances, and coercion. In capitalism, businesses compete. This is fundamental to a capitalism. This includes banks, which are businesses like any other, only that, currently, their product is debt instruments like Federal Reserve Notes, mortgages, loans, lines of credit, credit cards, bonds, and debentures. The problem is that we are, of course, NOT a capitalism. One of the most evident reasons for this is the intertwined nature of the government and the global financial institutions.

Between three investment corporations, BlackRock, Inc., The Vanguard Group, and State Street Corporation the ownership portfolio includes top investment shares in GlaxoSmithKline, Pfizer, Johnson & Johnson, Moderna, Novartis, Abbott, Merck, BioNTech, Bayer Pharmaceuticals, AstraZeneca, Time Warner, Comcast, Disney and News Corp. (90% of the U.S. media landscape), The New York Times, Reuters, Google (inc. YouTube and Android), Facebook (inc. Instagram and WhatsApp), Twitter, Apple, Microsoft (inc. XBOX and Bing), Skyscanner (inc. Trip.com and Expedia), Airbnb, Amazon, eBay, Alibaba Group, BP, Shell, Exxon, Total, Glencore, BHP Billiton, Rio Tinto, China Shenhua Energy, Anglo American plc, John Deere, Cargill, Phillip Morris, R.J. Reynolds Tobacco, Ford, GM, Toyota, Volkswagen, Samsung, Dell, Philips, Sony, Mastercard, Visa, Western Union, PayPal, American Express, Viacom, JP Morgan Chase & Co., Bank Of America, Goldman Sachs, Barclays, Wells Fargo, BBVA, Vodafone, McDonalds, PepsiCo, Coca Cola, Netflix, ATT, Tesla, FedEx, American Airlines, and United Airlines. This is a small and incomplete list of the ownership portfolio of these three corporations. "BlackRock and Vanguard form a secret monopoly that own just about everything else you can think of too. In all, they have ownership in 1,600 American firms, which in 2015 had combined revenues of $9.1 trillion. Bloomberg reported that these companies will exceed $20 trillion by 2028, potentially matching or exceeding the GDP of the nation, and having monopoly ownership of nearly every industry. When you add in the third-largest global owner, State Street, their current combined ownership encompasses nearly 90% of all S&P 500 firms. Vanguard is the largest shareholder of BlackRock. Vanguard itself, on the other hand, has a unique structure that makes its ownership more difficult to discern, but many of the oldest, richest families in the world can be linked to Vanguard funds... The elite who own Vanguard apparently do not like being in the spotlight but of course they cannot hide from who is willing to dig. Reports from Oxfam and Bloomberg say that 1% of the world, together owns more money than the other 99%. Even worse, Oxfam says that 82% of all earned money in 2017 went to this 1%... In other words, these two investment companies, Vanguard and BlackRock hold a monopoly in all industries in the world and they, in turn are owned by the richest families in the world, some of whom are royalty and who have been very rich since before the Industrial Revolution." -Joseph Mercola, 2021

Gross National Income is often a more proper indicator of financial wellbeing of a group than GDP. The US GNI in 2020 was $21.3 Trillion USD ($24 Trillion USD by Sep. 30, 2021) while the entire world GNI in 2020 was $84.7 Trillion USD. This means that the United States makes up a full quarter (25%) of GNI of the entire world, despite having only 4.25% of the global population. The next two nations are China at $14.6 Trillion USD and Japan at $5.1 Trillion USD. Together, these three nations, with 1.85 billion people (23% of global population) account for 41% of the global GNI.[53]/[54]/[55]/[56] This means the shareholders of The Vanguard Group, amidst their collaborators for total monopoly, have as much wealth, that can be tracked, as the GNI of the United States, equal to 25% of the global GNI. That, my friends, is insane.

The Bill and Melinda Gates Foundation, the Open Society Foundation, and the Clinton Foundation, are all non-profit corporations that are used to avoid taxes, hide identities of those transferring funds, launder on immense scales and finance projects and people in the shadows. The Bill and Melinda Gates Foundation is the largest sponsor the World Health Organization, giving the Gates family and their collaborators immense political power at the WHO and in medical affairs globally, as national medical programs and mandates are designed by the WHO. Bill Gates himself is the son of philanthropists and eugenicists, his father, William Henry Gates II being fundamental to eugenics programs after the public collapse of this belief system following WWII.

The World Economic Forum, Bill and Melinda Gates Foundation, and Johns Hopkins Bloomberg School of Public Health organized the Event 201 on Friday, Oct 18, 2019, in New York City, which simulated a global pandemic of a novel zoonotic coronavirus that becomes transmissible between humans, and even more transmissible between people with mild symptoms. The World Economic Forum, founded by Klaus Schwab in 1971, openly confesses its ultimate goals are to bring about a centralized global governance and economy, controlled by a select group of institutions and individuals. The "Great Reset" to "Build Back Better", is a WEF program intended to bring about the vast wealth and power transfer from the people of the world to a ridiculously small group of controllers. It is succeeding.

The Board of Trustees of the WEF are:

Mukesh D. Ambani (Chairman and Managing Director, Reliance Industries); Marc Benioff (Chair and Co-Chief Executive Officer, Salesforce); Peter Brabeck-Letmathe (Vice-Chairman of the Board of Trustees, World Economic Forum); **Thomas Buberl (Chief Executive Officer, AXA); Mark Carney (United Nations Special Envoy for Climate Action and Finance, United Nations); Laurence D. Fink (Chairman and Chief Executive Officer, BlackRock)**; Chrystia Freeland (Deputy Prime Minister and Minister of Finance, Office of the Deputy Prime Minister of Canada); Orit Gadiesh (Chairman, Bain & Company); **Kristalina Georgieva (Managing Director, International Monetary Fund (IMF)); Fabiola Gianotti (Director-General, European Organization for Nuclear Research (CERN)**; Al Gore (Vice-President of the United States (1993-2001); Chairman and Co-Founder, Generation Investment Management LLP); **Herman Gref (Chief Executive Officer and Chairman of the Board, Sberbank)**; André Hoffmann (Chairman, Massellaz); Paula Ingabire

(Minister of Information Communication Technology and Innovation, Ministry of Information Communication Technology and Innovation of Rwanda); **Christine Lagarde (President, European Central Bank)**; Yo-Yo Ma (Cellist); Peter Maurer (President, International Committee of the Red Cross (ICRC)); **Luis Alberto Moreno (Managing Director, Allen & Company)**; Patrice Motsepe (Founder and Executive Chairman, African Rainbow Minerals); **Ngozi Okonjo-Iweala (Director-General, World Trade Organization (WTO))**; H.M. Queen Rania Al Abdullah of the Hashemite Kingdom of Jordan (Queen of the Hashemite Kingdom of Jordan, Office of Her Majesty Queen Rania Al Abdullah); L. Rafael Reif (President, Massachusetts Institute of Technology); **David M. Rubenstein (Co-Founder and Co-Chairman, Carlyle)**; Mark Schneider (Chief Executive Officer, Nestlé); **Klaus Schwab (Founder and Executive Chairman, World Economic Forum)**; Tharman Shanmugaratnam (Senior Minister, Government of Singapore); **Jim Hagemann Snabe (Chairman, Siemens)**; Julie Sweet (Chair and Chief Executive Officer, Accenture); Feike Sybesma (Chairman of the Supervisory Board, Royal Philips); Heizo Takenaka (Professor Emeritus, Keio University); Zhu Min (Chairman, National Institute of Financial Research).

While all of the names listed are significant, the ones in bold are noted here, as they hold particular significance as financial institutions or otherwise particularly interesting institutions, including the WTO, which primarily acts as a tool to force nations into submission to the global financial collaborators. Particularly noteworthy is Larry Fink, who's multinational investment management corporation is soon to be the largest financial entity in the world. Its total assets are greater than that of the Federal Reserve. Larry Fink created and popularized Mortgage-Backed Securities trading, which led to the 2008 economic collapse. Interestingly, he was the one who was called upon by the U.S. Government and the Federal Reserve to advise on what actions they ought to take to correct the depression. Fink's answer resulted in the government guaranteeing the commercial money-market funds, thus bailing out the largest financial institutions in the United States at the expense of the taxpayer and dishing out huge bonuses to already extremely wealthy executives, who were tremendously responsible and culpable for the economic collapse due to their dealings in dangerously high-risk assets.

> *"Along with Lew Ranieri, of Salomon Brothers, he* (Larry Fink) *would be credited with developing the multi-trillion-dollar debt-securitization market that transformed the face of finance. By 2008 this market—of mortgages, and car and credit-card loans, purchased from banks, sliced into pieces, repackaged, and sold to thousands of investors—would help bring the economy to its knees. But long before it spiraled out of control, it was considered an incredible innovation. Looking back, Fink says, 'We were able to narrow the cost of housing in America.' Recalling how "rewarding" it felt 'going to Washington to talk with Fannie Mae and Freddie Mac about mortgage opportunities,' he says, 'even in my 20s, I felt there was an enormity to what we were doing to help.'"*
>
> – Suzanne Andrews, *Vanity Fair*, 2010[57]

So, while the dark knight of the plutocracy, Larry Fink, was coordinating the wealth transfer of 2008 and beyond, the shareholders of The Vanguard Group, the owners of BlackRock, were enjoying the show and their accrescent portfolios. Here we ought to describe how a seemingly small share percentage could afford true and total ownership of a corporation. It starts with circular ownership.

> *Circular Ownership is "a particular method to structure business entity ownership. Here, two or more entities in a legal structure part-own each other, ultimately resulting in a "circular" nature to the ownership structure. Furthermore, one or more of these entities may be owned and controlled by an individual, who, on the surface, appears to hold a low or minority percentage that would not meet ownership thresholds requiring disclosure or*

due diligence investigation, when in actuality that low percentage ownership belies actual control indirectly. By setting up a circular ownership structure, companies are able to mask true ownership and control through various and sometimes complex ownership loops. Circular ownership structures may take several different forms. For example, in some structures, all direct and indirect owners are inside a singular ownership circle... The primary subject entity is both the 100% owner of its ultimate parent entity and of its parent entity, in other words, the subject owns itself. This closed-circle structure makes it impossible to identify the beneficial owners of any entities within the circle (First Diagram)... Another example of circular ownership is an open-circle structure where one or more beneficial owners are external to the ownership loop and appear to own a low percentage of shares, while in reality, these individuals may ultimately own a larger percentage of the entity. Below is a simplified example, where the sole individual in the structure ultimately owns 100% of the entities, even though it appears she only owns 3 percent. The result is that while she falls under any thresholds requiring due diligence or beneficial ownership reporting, in actuality, she is 100% the owner of all involved entities (Second Diagram)... The result of utilizing either of these circular ownership structures can be that the ultimate natural person owner(s) are masked through this complexity."

- Steele Global, *Exploring Circular Ownership in Compliance Investigations*, 2020[58]

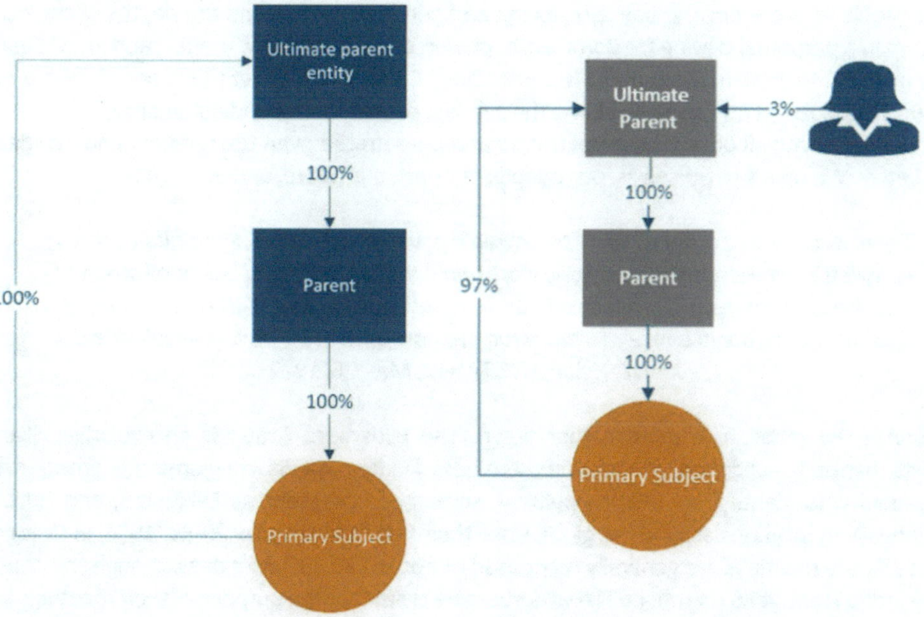

- * Steele Global, *Exploring Circular Ownership in Compliance Investigations*, 2020[59]

The exact shares owned by any entities are consistently shifting, so it is not particularly useful to pinpoint them exactly, but The Vanguard Group institutionally owned (as reported in only the top 10 holders) 12,175,676 shares at a value of $10,211,252,434 on September 29th, 2021, and in various mutual funds 8,354,989 shares valued at $14,323,663,348 reported between August 30th and September 29th, 2021. This is a total of roughly $24.5 billion invested in BlackRock, Inc., which yet amounts to a total share percentage under reporting requirements for beneficial ownership. BlackRock has similar ownership of Vanguard, and each has this same model of ownership of thousands of major corporations in every industry, making the beneficial owners of The Vanguard Group the most powerful collaborative group in the world. The model of circular ownership, intermixed with the use of trusts wrapped in foundations, wrapped in for profit corporations wrapped in trusts, and so on, makes the discovery of the beneficial owners of The Vanguard Group and other corporations, particularly challenging. "State Street Corporation is an American financial services and bank holding company...with operations worldwide. It is the second oldest continually operating United States bank... State Street is ranked 15th on the list of largest banks in the United States by assets. It is one of the largest asset management companies in the world with US$3.9 trillion under management and US$43.3 trillion under custody and administration." And who owns State Street? The same owners of Vanguard and BlackRock is who. The question that must be answered, and quickly, by the people of the United States of America and of the world, is whether all of the wealth of this world will be allowed to leave them for the acquisition of total monopolized control of the world by the small group of plutocrats, robber-barons, authoritarians, moneychangers, and psychopaths that work every day to bleed them dry of all sovereignty, resource and wellbeing.

The average person is generally a decent person who is interested in generally benign activity. They are not thinking about how to take away other peoples power or resources. They do not believe they aer better than their neighbors to the degree that they think their neighbors are subhuman. Thet are satisfied with simple lives of peace and prosperity, of challenges met and overcome, and of raising a family.
It is for this very reason, that people aren't psychopaths, that it is virtually unattainable for them to truly comprehend that our entire global species is ruled, manipulated, and controlled by psychopaths. How can we expect people who are decent, peaceful, loving and gentle to understand the depths of the diseased souls that are in a perpetual craving for dominance, power, control, territory, money, and are willing to do absolutely anything to achieve those ends. Not just Hillary Clintons hitlist, but the genocide of group after group around the globe. Who can really blame the average person for not understanding?
Well, I can. I do. I blame all of us. The perpetrators and perpetrated even the resistors and avoiders. We can all do better. We owe it to ourselves, our people, our past, our future, and our legacy.

"The real menace of our republic is the invisible government, which, like a giant octopus, spawls it's slimy length over our city, state and nation. At the head is a small group of banking houses generally referred to as 'international bankers.' This little coiterie of powerful international bankers virtually run our government for their own selfish ends."
- John F. Hylan, NYC Mayor, Mar. 26, 1922

But, of course, the rabbit hole goes further down. The Bilderberg Group is an exclusive alliance of industrialists, bankers, politicians, monopolists, business leaders, media conglomerate presidents, and military leaders who identify, sometimes publicly, sometimes privately, as Fabianists, and have been meeting annually at locations around the globe since their first meeting May 29-31, 1954, in Oosterbeek, Netherlands. These meetings are generally composed of about 120-130 attendees, though the consistent core of the group is about 80 members. The Bilderbergers claim that the purpose of their meetings is to be able to discuss opinions amongst other powerful people without having to be constrained by the media attention, giving its members the ability to speak freely about any topic. The Bilderberg Group was founded, in part, by Prince Bernhard of Holland, acting as the host and first president, and who was an officer in the Reiter SS Corp and a board member of Farben Bilder (subsidiary of I.G. Farben) which endeavored to produce and maintain a group of wealth-building leaders under the protection of Heinrich Himmler.[60]

It is difficult to re-educate people who have been brought up on nationalism to the idea of relinquishing part of their sovereignty to a supra-national body.
– Prince Bernhard

Many of the Bilderbergers are directly linked with the Nazi's, such as David Rockefeller and Allen Dulles. The BIS (Bank of International Settlements) was created to launder Nazi gold that they stole from the nations they invaded. This bank is maintained by Bilderbergers, along with all other central banking and international banking structures. Some of the most influential Bilderbergers are/were Henry Kissinger, David Rockefeller, Zbigniew Brzezinski, John Kerr, and Józef Retinger.

The Bilderbergers, in their literature, state their policy as avoidance of direct involvement in actions they agree upon. Instead, they choose to project influence onto others who then steer the project toward the outlined goal.

NATO was formed after it was agreed upon at Bilderberg that it was necessary to have an international policing system, a military, which no government could overrule, and which could act as the coercive arm of the industrialist agenda.

The Bilderbergers are not the only supra-national organization in the world, though they seem to be one of the core of the many that exist today. There is also the Round Table, the Council on Foreign Relations, the Trilateral Commission, the Club of Rome, The World Bank, the International Monetary Fund (IMF), the European Union (EU), the United Nations (UN) and the North Atlantic Treaty Organization (NATO), the World Health Organization (WHO), Organization for Economic Cooperation & Development (OECD), World Wide Fund for Nature (WWF), the World Trade Organization (WTO), the International Criminal Court (ICC), the G20, and many others. What about the agencies and institutions that support globalism despite their nationality? We have the Tavistock Institute, the Royal Institute of International Affairs (RIIA), Dartmouth Conference, the Aspen Institute for Humanistic Studies, RAND Corporation, the Atlantic Institute, the Hoover Institute, Johns Hopkins SAIS (School of Advanced International Studies), the Brookings Institution, the Hudson Institute, Institute for Policy Studies (IPS), the Institute for Social Research, the Institute for the Future, Stanford FS Institute for International Studies, Open Society Foundations, the Carnegie Endowment for International Peace, the American Enterprise Institute (AEI), and on and on and on. Looking at Treaties that dictate to the world and walk all over national and personal sovereignty, we have the "WHO Framework Convention on Tobacco Control", Feb. 27, 2005, which set precedence for global health dictation, as the first world public health treaty. We also have the Nuclear Weapons Ban Treaty (TPNW), Jan. 22, 2021, which was only signed and supported by countries that were non-nuclear anyway. Oh yes, and we have the USMCA, the United States-Mexico-Canada Agreement, which replaced NAFTA with almost no significant changes, even though President Donald Trump railed against it as a failure of American negotiation and sovereignty. Its almost like he said that because it was his job to appear opposed to the globalist agenda, while in actuality being truly opposed to the very people who are hailing him as a savior, similar to the very same hailing being done toward President Obama when he was president. The ultimate goal with these free trade agreements, is to iteratively increase the boundaries of the agreements, until the entire world is in one perpetual free trade agreement, with one administrative body, and ruled by one global charter.

RAND National Defense Research Institute focuses heavily on misinformation and manipulation of large populations, and is funded by foundations controlled by CFR, such as the Ford Foundation. It is literally focused on developing techniques to use doubletalk to confuse and inhibit the people. The Tavistock Institute was created in 1946 and was the arm of the British Round Table that dealt with developing behavioral manipulation in individuals and populations. The Tavistock programming method is used to manipulate individuals and entire populations to reduce them to imbecilic, anxious, paranoid, neurotic, and ineffectual slaves. This method includes isolating a subject, surrounding them with traitors, enemies, or simply making them believe they are surrounded, confusing them, leaving them uncertain of where they stand and what may happen, vacillate between extreme discipline and promises of good treatment, provide a constant stream of contradictory news, make the cognitive structure of their situation unfathomable, and incite a constant redirection of attention to prevent them form being able to keep up with whatever is actually occurring. Between the RAND Corporation, the Brookings Institute, the Stanford Research Institute, the Hudson Institute, the Institute for Policy Studies (IPS) and the others, the Tavistock programed-learning techniques have become standard in the US to indoctrinate the American people into an apathy toward a shift to global governance and commerce, and to inculcate "strife and unrest."

The Council on Foreign Relations was co-founded by the Marxist, Edward Mandell House, (Woodrow Wilson's chief advisor 1913-1921) who proposed private central banking, graduated income tax (16th Amendment), and wrote the draft for the League of Nations. Another founder of the CFR was Paul Warburg, the intentional banking mogul. The CFR is funded primarily by the Rockefeller Foundation, the Carnegie Foundation, and the Ford Foundation amongst others. CFR headquarters is the Harold Pratt House in New York City.

The CFR, like Bilderberg and the Trilateral Commission, has a dominant core of conspirators and planners who dictate to those in the periphery of the group, who often hold very public, very powerful positions, their roles and duties. This compartmentalization gives the core people plausible deniability and makes it nearly impossible for anyone outside of the core to discern the true goals of any action or how they truly fit into the agenda. In this way, the very few control the very many.

The Trilateral Commission, established in 1973 by David Rockefeller, is composed of the American, European, and Pacific-Asian regions. Each of its roughly 350 members serve three-year terms. It was founded to promote and work toward global government by inviting 3 major regions of globalists to interact and form policy and design the new world order. Each of these regional control centers, through the global central banking cartel, has subjected nations in their controlled regions as modern-day plantations, from which they source cheap labor, goods and services. The US has Latin America, The EU has Southeast Europe and Africa, and Japan has Southeast Asia.

"The influence of establishment insiders over our foreign policy has become a fact of life in our time. This pervasive influence runs contrary to the real long-term national security of our Nation. It is an influence which, if unchecked, could ultimately subvert our constitutional order. (In favor of the creation of a New World Order.)"

– Senator Jesse Helms, Senate Floor, Dec. 15, 1987

The public is fed the lie that parties or other political figures or entities, governments, nations, corporations, and public figures of all types, are conflicting and that these people's differences are important, carry weight, and give them choice. The fact is that this is entirely manufactured. The differences and conflicts are made to distract from the perpetually active agenda of the global government proponents and organizations. The Hegelian Dialectic describes the method used to distract, manipulate, and control societies. It is the process of problem-reaction-solution, or in other words, it is when government uses a black flag event to generate chaos, responds to the supposed "attack" with a proposal to resolve the matter if only people give it more power over them, then resolves the supposed attack, while in actuality it is simply stripping away the sovereignty of the people of the world piecemeal. The method used most often is the manufacture of a crisis (whether real or imaginary), and then using the premade and exclusive solution to that problem as an axe over the heads of the target people and nations, a threat against which those nations are then forced to accede, and which then binds otherwise uninterested nations together in common purpose, against a global threat, economic, political, terrorist, or medical in nature.

The goal is to create ever more dependency on supranational organizations, that would supersede democratic authority, especially in Congress, State and local governments. To avoid rebellion by populations, they intend/work to centralize power in Congress and decrease expectation in college education resulting in meaningful or worthwhile careers. This reduces specialized and advanced abilities in the wide population. They limit freedom of the press by imposing government restraints with claims of "unspecified unusual circumstances," reinstating the "law of libel," and "enforcing standards of professionalism." Even PBS is owned by Bilderberg/CFR corporations and members.

The Logan Act in the United States absolutely prohibits elected officials from meeting in private with private business interests to discuss public policy. This is completely ignored by the Bilderbergers and other organizations and pretty much across the board in American politics. The amalgam of politicians, bankers, military leaders, corporate powerhouses, and international supranational organizations is so knotted together that it would be impossible to separate them without needing 10 times the amount of people to fill roles. These globalists are often holding multiple positions in various sectors simultaneously, such as a military advisor to the government also being on 5 corporate boards each having nothing to do with the military, while acting as a honorary professor at a number of universities, and running a political campaign for office. In this instance, it is so very obvious the number of conflicts of interest this type of lateral involvement could create. This is the very same activity that is occurring amongst the several thousand members of the globalist effort, the core of which is maintained by an exceptionally small number of key players who operate mostly in the shadows, despite the fact that they are common names.

"The real truth of the matter is, as you and I know, that a financial element in the large centers has owned the government ever since the days of Andrew Jackson"
– Franklin D. Roosevelt, Nov. 21, 1933

These organizations members have maneuvered global politics and commerce over the last century, but the origins of the principles to which these people adhere is far older. As you will read later, monopolists have been encroaching upon the realm of finance, commerce, and politics for centuries. The transition of financial dominance from royal prerogative to bankers has been occurring at least 500 years, and in many ways for much longer. Today, we are facing the final stages of the plans of the monopolists of the world, which is total global control. It has not replaced royalty, but rather entwined with it, so that the old powers were incentivized to allow the transition. The transition from royal prerogative over money to the private banking monopoly was facilitated by the increasing abilities and freedoms given to the enterprising, money-changing, business class of society. Centuries of pressure placed on monarchs and royals led to the eventual opening of the floodgates over the last 3 to 4 centuries in which the corporation was created, private banks have flourished (some may say conquered), and the dynamics of the social construction of humanity has shifted drastically anywhere one looks globally, so that those who were slaves and serfs could become millionaires, and those who were royals could become destitute, but the monopolists would remain. The real effect of this was that those who were most ambitious, greedy, and willing to do whatever it took to achieve, crushed the rest of the world on their way. The average quality of life has risen drastically in the last 150 years due to technology and the effects of certain liberating ideals, paralleling the massive population increase. It is these money-changers, monopolists, and corporate people that are now dictating to the world. They are the new authority and became so in such a silent manner so as to not rouse the populations they were taking control of. In the end, it was a simple transaction that has been taking centuries to complete. We are in the final stages of the transition to global control by the monopolist families who have been engaged in this effort for centuries. They view it as their inheritance.

Andrew Carnegie established the Endowment for International Peace shortly before his death, which had its mission to bind together international financiers and socialists in a union to create a League of Nations to enforce global peace. The endowments board of trustees created in Marburg Plan to accommodate for this mission, which led to the formal creation of supranational governments/companies. Every major event around the globe in the last 150 years has been influenced, funded, or orchestrated directly by globalists. The Russian Bolshevik Revolution was incited, in part, by the Rockefellers, who's singular real competitor in oil globally was Russia's Tsar Nicholas II, who was modernizing and westernizing his nation.

When, after the revolution, the new leaders, Vladimir Ulyanov Lenin and Leon Trotsky, were designing the new Communist State, they parroted the desires of international monopolists by declaring their motives as to create a total state-controlled financial system, centralizing power and control and eliminating personal liberties. Trotsky even declared himself an "internationalist." John D. Rockefeller, Paul Warburg, and J.P. Morgan, amongst other conspirators, were largely responsible for the Bolshevik success, Through Wall Street banks they supplied millions of dollars in funding, gave sanctuary to Trotsky in the U.S. and Lenin in Switzerland, as well as returned them safely to Russia in 1917. President Woodrow Wilson facilitated at every opportunity the collapse of the Romanovs, and the subsequent communist power grab. His predecessor, Theodore Roosevelt, mediated the peace negotiations between Russia and Japan which resulted in Russia's loss of enormous land holdings, its Eastern and Baltic fleets, and left Russia seriously, and intentionally, weakened. This weakened Russia was just what was needed for the Bolsheviks to rouse the population to revolution and was the precursor to all the destruction and suffering that followed, including the genocidal actions of Stalin, and even opened the way for Nazi Germany.

For much of the last century, Rockefellers Chase National Bank has been funding and thus upholding, Communist Russia, not to mention funding the Nazi's and financing practically all parties of all wars to encourage ever greater crises followed by ever greater centralized control. The Rockefellers have been instrumental, though not alone by any means, in the destruction of liberty, free markets, and national sovereignty over the course of four generations, each inheriting more global control than the last.

It takes a non-static society to exceed the boundaries of its day. A static society is one that is controlled. "A growing, competitive, and free society gives new people a chance to make their fortune and replace some of those already at the top. So, legislation is promoted to restrict entrepreneurial effort and tax away capital accumulations not protected in the tax-free foundations of the Establishment insiders. Every effort is made to press a medium-sized business to the wall and allow it to be swallowed up by the Establishment giants." -Gary Allen, *None Dare Call it Conspiracy.* It is a profitable, abundantly successful, and expanding middle class that leads to revolutions. It is not the destitute that drive revolutions, but the ambitious, hopeful and successful, who see their potential as being limited by current regulations or boundaries, and have the strength in spirit, the education, and the communal integrity and trust to take action to defy them. This is why lockdowns occurred and why the plandemic was manufactured. It was to destroy the class of society that includes the hopeful, the energetic, the independent, and those that threaten the monopolist's position. It is these people that were attacked the last 3 years.

The Real ID (national ID) is a step toward the North American Union (NAU) which is the American version of the EU, with RFID chips with biometric identifiers. Also, part of this movement towards regional government is merging collective consciousness beyond national, creating a common currency, which is the Amero, and forming free trade treaties that erode and disintegrate borders and sovereignty over time. Soon, there will be no independent small business, no sovereign nationality, no real money, and no affirmed rights. Is that a world you want to live in?

"They (Globalists) have sacrificed our dreams, our independence, and our self-sufficiency at the alter of their New World Order."

– Daniel Estulin, *The True Story of The Bilderberg Group*

Monopoly of power and control is the goal. Whatever leads to that total monopoly is what will be utilized by globalists. The most successful method to their success is the tried and proven method of creating a crisis, then propagandizing their exclusive ability to resolve it. They are masters at controlling the minds of the masses. It is potentially the most funded aspect of the globalist agenda. The organization of globalists is so tightly controlled a group, that any dissent from members of its institutions can be handled by nullifying their assets and through sabotage and assassination, as well as blackmail. Blackmail today can be done completely artificially. Realistic prosthetics, voice changing technology, and compromising footage, and boom, you got a real nice piece of blackmail. Everything is dictated by an inner core and executed by a more or less willing participant globalist cadre.

Over the last century, nearly all media sources with any significant reach, and even those that don't, have been acquired by the ever-growing umbrella companies that dominate the planet. From Rupert Murdoch's, Fox network to Disney Corp., all the media is owned by one group of collaborators, who all can be identified by reading the member lists of the Bilderberg meetings, the CFR, and the Trilateral Commission. We can conclude very simply and obviously that any media on the radio and television, and most provided on major internet outlets are controlled and dictated to by this very small group of conspirators that proclaim themselves privately and publicly as the owners of the earth.

Every president and political personage express exactly what the people want to hear. That is their job. They are the masters of the stage, the orators, the image of popular strength, the holy state, the figurehead, the ornament on the hood. They are there to do the bidding of their real masters while making it appear that they are doing the exact opposite, serving the people. They are the most successful liars. While they lie, they have one other job, which is to fill as many governmental roles as possible with globalists, sign off on all globalist agendas they are presented with, and do everything in their power to extend the globalist plan for global dependency, the end of the nation-state and national identity, and the eradication of personal liberty. There are no political persons outside of the control, influence, and orchestration of the globalist organizations.

China is actively practicing what the globalists wish to achieve. A state-controlled pseudo-capitalism. Welfare reform and Regulation are methods used to concentrate state power. Today, the Chinese people live in a absolute controlled environment. They are the guinea pigs of the state, which is the only permitted god, and they are made to focus on insignificant things while they are dictated to in every way, watched at all times, and are on the path to a full technocracy. Overt social systems will soon be in place in China, that disallow even the smallest of privacies. The rest of the world is watching and are not far behind.

Globalists, following the along the ideological lines and reasonings of Brzezinski, are motivated out of a desire to control humanity within a general expectation of how humanity is organically evolving and adapting to technological advances that are fundamentally altering their experience of life. They see it as their duty to manage the affairs of humanity as they have either inherited or acquired authority, power, wealth, or influence, by which they can dictate of suggest the course humanity must take. These self-appointed and continuously reaffirmed controllers and managers of humanity are encouraged to believe and act on their belief that what they support is for the good of the world as they are consistently rewarded with supporting masses of people. It does not concern them that some die, or even if most die, because it is relatively relegated to intellectual and self-preserving consideration rather than empathetic or humanistic considerations. The globalist policies, actions, and organizations are all aimed at producing the highest benefit to that social group, and lesser degree, the members of the population that enforce and maintain their control, at the detriment of all others.

There are two names that appear time and time again when researching globalists, and these are Henry Kissinger and David Rockefeller. The influence that these two people have/had on the world in enormous. They have, for many decades, supported in any way possible, the creation of a one world government and are responsible directly for innumerable human lives lost, human suffering, societal collapses, wars, slavery and geopolitical struggles. Certainly there are a large number of other individuals involved, but rarely does anything occur that doesn't have David and Henry sitting in the background whispering in the ears of those on camera. The ties between these globalists are stronger than acknowledged, and they are yet small enough in numbers and organized enough that managing those ties and maintaining them is quite an easy task. One such tie is that Klaus Schwab's professor at Harvard happened to be Henry Kissinger. Kissinger was a mentor to Schwab. Kissinger's entire life is geared toward the bringing about a one world government/one world company. Schwab's World Economic Forum is explicitly focused on actualizing that very thing. The WEF is member funded, with costs of attendance running between $19,000 and over $600,000. Obviously, an event at those prices, with its specific theme, will be hosting only those who are tied into globalism at this point, and thus give them the opportunity advance their common agenda without political backlash. Main Goal? How to get the people to accept their own slavery, and even beg for them it?

Here is a list of a small portion of current and former participants in one to all three; Bilderberg, CFR, TC: **Henry Kissinger (Former U.S. Sec. of State & National Security Advisor, Bilderberger, CFR, and TC); David Rockefeller (Chairman, Chief Exec., Chase Manhattan Corp. Founding Bilderberger, CFR, and TC);** Alexander Haig (Former NATO Commander, Former U.S. Sec. of State); Allen Dulles (Dir. CIA, Chairman Sullivan & Cromwell LLP, CFR); Laurence "Larry" Fink (Bilderberger, Chairman and CEO of BlackRock, Director, CFR); **Zbigniew Brzezinski (Former National Security Advisor, Founder of Trilateral Commission, Member CFR and Bilderberg, Professor Johns Hopkins SAIS)**; Cyrus Vance (Former Sec, State and Former Dep. SecDef.); Paul Volcker (Fromer FED Chairman); Richard N. Haass (Bilderberger, Pres., CFR); Paul Wolfowitz (Former Pres., World Bank and Dep. SecDef and Dean of Johns Hopkins SAIS); **Peter D. Sutherland (Bilderberger, Founding Director General of WTO)**; George H.W. Bush (Former President, USA, Former Ambassador to the UN, Former Dir. CIA, Member CFR and TC and Bohemian Club); Bill Clinton (Bilderberger, Former President, USA and Governor, Arkansas, Member, TC); Hillary Clinton (Bilderberger, Former First Lady); Richard "Dick" Cheney (Former SecDef and VP, USA, Director, CFR, Member, TC, Chairman and CEO, Halliburton, and member Board of Advisors, Jewish Institute for National Security of America); Jeffrey E. Epstein (Child Sex Slavery Mogul, Member TC); Queen Beatrix of the Netherlands (Daughter of Bilderberg Founder, Prince Bernhard); Prince Bernhard of the Netherlands (Founding Bilderberger); Queen Sofia of Spain (Bilderberger); Christine Lagarde (Bilderberger, Pres. ECB); **Klaus Schwab (Steering Committee, Bilderberg, Exec. Chairman, WEF)**; Angela Merkel (Bilderberger, Chancellor, Germany); **Józef Retinger (Founder, European Movement and Bilderberg Group)**; Jose **Manuel Durão Barroso (Steering Committee, Bilderberg, Former Pres., Euro. Commission, CEO, GAVI)**; Kenneth Clark (Bilderberger, Former Chancellor of the Exchequer); Denis Healey (Founding Bilderberger, Former Chancellor of the Exchequer); **John Kerr (Steering Committee, Bilderberg, Former Ambassador to the EU, Chairman of Centre for European Reform, Exec. Committee, TC)**; Margaret Thatcher (Former PM); Tony Blair (Former PM); David Cameron (Former PM); Timothy Geithner (Bilderberger, Former Treasury Secretary, CFR and TC Member); Jared Cohen (Bilderberger, CEO, Jigsaw, TC and CFR Member); Jared Kuschner (Bilderberger, Senior Advisor to Pres.); **David H. Patreaus (Bilderberger, 4th Dir., CIA, Chairman KKR Global Institute, CFR and TC Member)**; Robert Rubin (Bilderberger, Co-chair CFR); John Hickenlooper (Bilderberger, Former Gov., Colorado); **Jaap de Hoop Scheffer (Bilderberger, Former Secretary General, NATO)**; Keith B. Alexander (Bilderberger, Commander, US Cyber Command, Dir., NSA); Philip M. Breedlove (Bilderberger, Former Supreme Allied Commander Europe); Emmanuel Macron (Pre., France); Paul Warburg (CFR); Ruth Bader Ginsberg (CFR, US Supreme Court Justice); Frank McKenna (Bilderberger, Premier, New Brunswick, Dep. Chair, TD Bank of England); **Mark Carney (Bilderberger, Gov., Bank of England); Henri de Castries (Steering Committee, Bilderberg, CEO, AXA)**; Jean-Claude Trichet (Bilderberger, Former Pres., ECB); Paul M. Achleitner (Treasurer Foundation, Bilderberg, Deutsche Bank); Ana Botin (Bilderberger, Exec. Chairman, Banco Santander); Baron Edmond de Rothschild (Bilderberger, Rothschild Family Banking); Jorma Ollila (Bilderberger, Chairman, Royal-Dutch Shell); Josef Ackerman (Bilderberger, CEO, Deutsche Bank); Werner Baumann (Bilderberger, Chairman, Bayer); Joe Kaiser (Bilderberger, CEO, Siemens); Klaus Kleinfeld (Bilderberger, CEO, Alcoa); Jurgen E. Schrempp (Bilderberger, Former CEO, DaimlerChrysler); **Peter Andreas Thiel (Steering Committee, Bilderberg, Founder PayPal and Palantir Technologies)**; **Etienne Davignon (Chairman, Steering Committee, Bilderberger, Former VP, Euro. Commission)**; Jacob Wallenberg (Bilderberger, Chairman, Investor AB, V. Chair and Treasurer, WEF, Member, TC); **Marcus Wallenberg, Jr. (Steering Committee, Bilderberg, CEO, Stockholm Enskilda Bank)**; Daniel Vasella (Bilderberger, Chairman, Novartis); Sam Altman (Bilderberger, President, Y-Combinator);

Jeff Bezos (Bilderberger, Founder and CEO, Amazon); Bill Gates (Bilderberger, Chairman, Microsoft); Louis V. Gerstner, Jr. (Bilderberger, Former CEO, IBM); Donald E. Graham (Bilderberger, CEO and Chairman, The Washington Post Company); Reid Hoffman (Bilderberger, Co-Founder and Exec. Chairman, LinkedIn); Chris Hughes (Bilderberger, Co-Founder, Facebook); Alex Carp (Bilderberger, CEO, Palantir Technologies); **Henry Kravis (Bilderberger, Co-Founder and Co-Chairman and Co-CEO, KKR)**; Satya Nadella (Bilderberger, CEO, Microsoft); Eric Schmidt (Bilderberger, Exec. Chairman, Alphabet); Peter Mansbridge (Bilderberger, Anchor of The National, CBC); Conrad Black (Bilderberger, Media conglomerate owner); Zanny Minton Beddoes (Bilderberger, Editor-in-Chief, The Economist); Richard John Micklethwait (Bilderberger, Editor-in-Chief, Bloomberg News); Charles Rose (Bilderberger, Host and Exec. Producer, Charlie Rose Talk Show); George Stephanopoulos (Bilderberger, ABC News Chief, Washington Correspondent); **Rupert Murdoch (Bilderberger, Founder, Chairman and CEO of News Corp and Fox News, Member, CFR)**.

Again, this is just the smallest of possible lists of the heavy hitters involved in Bilderberg, the Trilateral Commission, the Council on Foreign Relations amongst all the other globalist organizations.

"We shall have world government whether or not you like it—by conquest or consent."
– James Warburg (CFR founder Paul Warburg's son, and braintrust to FDR), Senate Foreign Relations Committee meeting, Feb. 17, 1950

These people's number one fear is "organized resistance". Individual liberty is their enemy. The ability for their goals for a one world government to succeed relies heavily on the orchestrated ignorance and disbelief of the general population. The goals are to eradicate national identity, centralize control, eliminate general prosperity, maintain a constant state of duress to increase apathy and decrease drive, centralize education, empower the United Nations to the degree of total world governance, creation of a conglomerated western trading bloc, Expand NATO into all corners, emplace the International Court of Justice as the sole legal system for the world, monopolize violence and illegalize production and ownership of weapons, and enforce a socialist welfare state (Presidential Decision Directive No. 25 and Department of State Publication 7277). This agenda can only be accomplished if the people remain reliant on governments for their survival needs, whether in real terms or based on fallacious propaganda. Things that would impede their mission would be the widespread use of free or high yield-low impact energy technology, a well armed and well trained general populace, local regenerative food practices, the maintenance and increase of domestic production facilities, consistent commerce between small businesses domestic and foreign, free market capitalism, competitive domestic monetary systems and competing currencies, the abandoning of any state run education systems, the dispersal of people away from cities and their integration into self-sustaining lifestyles (off-grid living), trade unions, worker owned businesses, and local community organization.

The United States of America is a dream that was dreamed by people who saw the opportunity to be free and took it with iron and blood. They stated their position and stood against the tide of pressures that was applied against them. Then they cut their bonds, and when the might of their enemy crashed upon them, they organized, called for voluntary participation, and weathered the storm upon the great principles that all men are born free. They did not sit a wait. They did not expect handouts. They gave the moment its deserved attention. These dreamers were not delusional, but rather hopeful, willful, adamantine, energized, and organized. They were guilty of sedition, treason, and were sentenced to death upon their signing of the Declaration of Independence. It is always so. Those who choose to defy the powers that be are those who are firstly and most likely to be attacked by those powers. The signers did nothing but see the problems, attempt a peaceful resolution, and when all attempts were spit on did what they had to do. There has never been a nation in recorded history that did what the Untied States did. It enshrined our inherent natural rights, which gave power to the individual to seek, earn, enjoy, profit and derive a life equal to their effort. Of course, this was something intended to work continuously upon the people if it could not all be explicitly and immediately understood.

Now, we are seeing the ignorance of the people who tear away at their own protections against those who would enslave them and make their lives a torture, an apathetic quagmire, in which all meaning turns pale, God in any form is replaced by the state in its one form, and the world is owned, and the fist tightened to the point of strangulation. The measure of the soul of humanity is in its ability to rise above these encroachments upon its ultimate liberation. We are not animals, but divine creators. We are beings with choice. Currently, collectively, We the People are choosing apocalypse. Perhaps that is what is needed, but I do not think so. I think it is simply the awareness of the horrors, which requires empathy, that makes it possible for humanity to avoid the peril. But that's just me. It is up to you what you will do.

World events do not occur by accident: They are made to happen, whether it is to do with national issues or commerce; most of them are staged and managed by those who hold the purse strings.

– Dennis Healey, former British Defense Minister

The Trilateral Commission doesn't secretly run the world. The Council on Foreign Relations does that.

– Sir Winston Lord, Pres. Council on Foreign Relations, 1978, Assistant Sec. of State, Oder of Skull and Bones Member, *Aid & Abet,* Vol. 2, No. 2, Pg. 7

On Taxation

Taxation is definitely an important facet in understanding how our system is corrupted and has subtly and overtly enslaved/indentured the population. In the mercantilist system, which was the standard in Europe in the 18th Century, the colonies of Britain were taxed without consent. This means that the colonial peoples were never allowed to vote or oppose the taxation that was imposed on them. They were the subjects of theft by a government. Some of the taxes leading up to the American Revolution, were the Molasses Act, Navigation Acts, the Sugar Act the Stamp Act, the Townsend Act and the Tea Act. The Molasses Act imposed high tariffs on molasses from the West Indies, which led to the creation of some very wealthy colonists who became smugglers, like John Hancock. The Navigation Acts forced colonists to trade only with ships built in the British Empire, whose crews had to be crewed by ¾ British Subjects. Enumerated goods, such as fur, sugar, tobacco and indigo, from the colonies could only be shipped to Britain which would then trade with other nations. The colonies were even disallowed from trading certain goods between each other. Following the Seven Year War, Britain had to pay off war debts and increased colonial taxation. It created the Sugar Act in 1764, which imposed higher tariffs on sugar imports, and which brought tax enforcers to the colonies. Kangaroo courts prosecuted people who did not pay their sugar tariffs and informers were given 1/3 of the cargo of any ship suspected of evading the import tax, leading to rivalries between colonial businesses, and made it possible for them to basically steal cargo from one another. The Stamp Act of 1765 made it a requirement to get a stamp on every paper transaction or legal document. The Continental Congress was formed as a result of this Act and resulted in the King repealing it. The Townsend Act created more import tariffs and allowed, through the Quartering Provision, British "tax collectors" and troops to stay in the homes of colonists while they audited their taxes. The 1773 Tea Act imposed higher tariffs on tea, except from the Dutch East India Trading Company. These taxes influenced the unrest in the colonies to the point that revolution followed.[61]

After the revolution, The Articles of Confederation were written, which had extremely small federal government and mostly regarded local governments free to cooperate and trade. If taxes needed to be raised, it was the purview of local governments. Central government was financed by tariffs, excise taxes,

and land sales primarily. The Constitution outlawed direct taxes including income tax. Taxes were not apportioned to states based on population.
The average tariff rate in the 1850's was 15%. The day Lincoln took office, it was raised to 32%, then 49% one year later, and remaining that high until 1913. In 1861, during the Civil War, tariffs accounted for 95% of all federal tax revenue. In 1861, the southern economy was exporting 75% of all its produced goods, making it export dependent, with higher prices to produce, lower sale prices, and was heavily disturbed because the high tariffs were of benefit exclusively to the New England and northern manufacturers whose goods were protected from competition due to these tariffs. During the Civil War, the Lincoln led government ignored the Constitution and created the first income tax, calling it excise tax, for which the average American paid about $45 annually through the Post Office. The Lincoln Administration also reinstituted the Stamp Tax, instituted the first Inheritance Tax and the Federal Income Tax, created the first Internal Revenue Bureaucracy, created 185 Tax Districts for collection, created Withholding Tax, and created numerous excise taxes that continued after the war as well. The first Income Tax was applied to anyone who made $600 annually or more, which is equivalent to about $10,000 today, at a rate of 3%.[62]
By 1880, Midwest farmers were so harassed by exorbitant tariffs that they saw as discriminatory and oppressive, they accepted and supported a 10-15% Income Tax as a better of two evils. The Revenue Act of 1894 was passed with an including Income Tax but was denied by the Supreme Court who ruled Income Tax Unconstitutional.

"When we consider that the theory of our institutions guarantees to every citizen a full benefits of all the fruits of his industry and enterprise with only such deduction for taxes as may be his share for the careful and economical maintenance of the government which protects him, it is plain to me that the exaction of more than this, is indefensible extorsion and a culpable betrayal of American justice. This wrong inflicted upon those who bear the burden of national taxation multiplies a brood of evil consequences. A public treasury becomes a horde of money needlessly withdrawn from trade and the peoples use thus crippling our nation and suspending our countries development, preventing investment in productive enterprise, creating financial disturbance and inviting schemes of public plunder."

-Grover Cleveland, Speaking on Budget Surpluses at the 3rd annual Message to Congress 1887

In the 1913 revolution, not only was a private banking cartel placed in command of the U.S. treasury, economy, and mint, but there was placed in law, and accepted by the Supreme Court, a Federal Income Tax. In response to the problem of budget surpluses from this tax, was the idea of increasing tariff rates until they strangled foreign trade altogether, inhibiting foreign goods from entering the country, and thus not taxing them, which would produce decreased revenues and surplus. In 1922, the average tariff rate was 33% and by 1930 the rate was 60%.[63]
The ultimate consequences of this Income Tax were the reinstitution of debtor's prisons, total consolidation of government, Inflation Tax, and the 17th Amendment, which created direct election of Senators. It also generated a huge amount of money that could be used to purchase votes to keep certain people in power forever and made it possible for them to fundraise anywhere, rather than focusing on the people of their own state. Federal Government is *the* major infringer upon natural rights and has the power to control the states and dictate its will, though only by the docility of the population.

"Sadly, the belief in "authority" even makes people feel obligated to assist in their own *enslavement, oppression and sometimes death. In fact, only a small percentage of the coercion of "government" is implemented by the enforcers of "authority"; most of it is*

implemented by its victims. *The ruling class merely tells people that they are required to do certain things, and most people comply without any actual enforcement taking place. As one impressive example, tens of millions of Americans, every year, fill out lengthy, confusing forms known as "tax returns," essentially extorting themselves. If the victims of the IRS agreed to pay, but only if the "government" figured out their alleged tax liabilities, the system would collapse. Every tax return is basically a signed confession, with the victim of the extortion racket not only revealing everything about his finances – essentially interrogating himself – but also even figuring out the amount that will be stolen, so the thieves do not have to."*

- Larken Rose, "The Most Dangerous Superstition"[64]

The individual is now the smallest part of government. The idea of communities supporting themselves is forgotten as communities now see the federal government doing all the work to care for the elderly, our neighbors, the ill, education of children and encroaching upon every other facet of society. Civil society has been eliminated by government intervention, and the likelihood of war only grows with centralized government growth. Rather than being used for saving and investment, money collected by Income Tax is now used for income transfer programs administered by the state. Less capitol means less productivity in the economy, meaning all of the population is poorer in the long run.

What the Income Tax supposedly does and what it actually does are two vastly different things. The common sayings by statists, such as, "I'm a taxpaying patriotic American", shows enough idiocy for any knowledgeable person to quickly walk away from such a person. They are likely ignorant enough to believe they can violate you if you disagree or try to educate them. The taxes that you pay to the IRS every year are NOT theirs to take. It is unconstitutional, inhumane, and societally compromising to have people give substantial portions of their earned incomes to a government that increases its (and thus your) debt to a private institution. Seeing as you had no hand in the creation of that agreement though, you have no contract binding you to do such a thing as to give your money away to a private or government agency. It is so totally detestable a situation that we are left in, that we must either accept that most people will continue to be slaves of the Fed and thus be feeding their greed and lust for global power and invasion of life on every level or be relegated to a corner of society that is bereft of support, censored, and marginalized in every way, whether we be economists, quantum physicists, psychologists, historians, gurus, politicians, futurists, anthropologists, civil engineers, pathologists or simply observant people. Income taxation is a key factor in the enslavement of the people of the world. The moment it is no longer fed is the moment this corrupt government will collapse, and the people have the opportunity for much better.

What the Income Tax Really Means:

"Your Earnings are not exclusively your own. We (We, the Government) have a claim on them, and our claim precedes yours. We will allow you to keep some of it because we recognize your need but not your right. But whatever we grant you for yourself is for us to decide."

- Frank Chatterough

Our economic system is not only unsustainable, but it is an outright violation of human rights and is responsible for suffering on scales that can hardly be accounted by normal standards. What is the correct justice for planetary slavery and genocide? What is the correct justice to be applied to the people who have profiteered on the deaths and suffering of millions and billions of people? It goes beyond punishment. We need to act to change this before we all perish.

"I can hire one-half of the working class to kill the other half."
– Jay Gould, American railroad developer and robber baron, 19th Century

Let us talk about what we can do today. An obvious response to the profiteering of individuals on the suffering of others is to take away their power, their money. Today, with three people owning more wealth than half of the population, we must take action to prevent these types of behaviors and the ability for markets to behave this way. We must tax the wealthy. Even if we were to tax those among the top one hundred wealthiest families at 95 percent of their wealth, they would still be wealthier than the vast majority of the population in the nation. Even taxed at 99 percent, they would be in the top one percent of wealth in the nation. This is beyond ridiculous. How did we allow this to happen when we have homeless and hungry populations? How could we allow this if there was even one hungry or homeless person on this planet? We need to evolve as a species. We need to grow, and we have no time to wait for those who have become lost in greed, corruption, and ignorance. We must bypass these ones and push forward for the benefit of all. We need to generate support for social programs and regulations that support, offer, incentivize, and empower healthy food, clean water, adequate shelter, health care, clean energy, non-harmful products and services and access to education, determined by the local population, for people as basic human rights. These programs must be built in such a way that they be used as a ladder. Each program offering education and resources on how to create firstly sustainable practices, secondly regenerative practices, and thirdly empowered and inspired evolution. We need to cultivate our system to provide an abundance of possibilities to every individual, so they may participate in the fullest with their environment in beneficial ways. Elitist, competitive economic systems serve populations that are not ready to collaborate for the highest wellbeing of the entire population. As long as government exists, is has the responsibility to act for the highest good of all the people.

When we install trust and support into the foundation of our system for all people, we encourage more trust and support. When the government acts with cooperation and responsiveness to the entire population, and endeavors to construct relationships that are non-competing, the population will also see similar changes in their lives to this new political and social attitude. Open trade is particularly important. In this I include Contract Law that does not reduce or eliminate the rights of people by secretly or otherwise manipulating the Justice System. Contract Law must be considered amongst the most important aspects of the economic structure as it determines the interactions the people have with abusive and powerful corporations and individuals. Contracts must become explicit in their meaning and content to the extent that even the least educated potential signor will understand the full context of their signing.

All financial activity of the government must be made readily and easily available to the public along with expertly designed methods of making the information digestible from the least educated to the most educated in the population. A complete report on the Earth's carrying capacity must be created, and regulations must be placed on the extraction of materials that are being depleted beyond their recovery within one lifetime. This report must also indicate the rate of use that is the maximum rate possible before there is an inability to correct the depletion within one lifetime. Economic policy must be created within the scope of this reports indication of the carrying capacity of this planet of finite resources.

We need to restructure the budget to reflect a fundamental perspective change of the nation toward internal wellbeing rather than fearmongering and security systems that inherently create stronger enemies every day, while consuming vast funding without considerable rewards for those paying for them. All of our 58 National Parks have an annual budget of 2.6 billion Dollars. That is one-fifth the cost of an aircraft carrier. We need to incentivize worker-owned businesses. We need to abolish Price Fixing in any industry. Air, water, and onshore public lands (1/3 nations territorial mass) apply to the public commons. The Federal Government is constantly pressured by mining, timber, and grazing industries to provide this land for private profit. We must enact laws that prevent the wholesale rape of the commons by corporations at the expense of the population and the environment.

Airwaves are public property (television and radio) administered by the FCC (Federal Communications Commission) which allocates space on the broadcast spectrum to licensed stations abiding by its rules and regulations. FCC has been reshaped and compelled by Congress to allocate free license renewals every 8 years to big business due to corporate lobbying. Ronald Reagan, through the FCC, rescinded the Fairness Doctrine in 1987. This practice must stop, and we must demand an equitable pricing system corporations must abide by. We must stop giving away our commons to corporations. We would not give corporations control of libraries, so why would we give them control of our airwaves. A backpay for airspace that has been used without fee would generate large funds to the public interest. Public sentiment or expectation levels need to change in order to win back social control.

If every corporation that has used airwaves had to pay the people directly for use of the airwaves, not only would corporate influence diminish in that area, but the people as a whole would be stimulated economically, benefitting the entire society. This may sound strange, but the fact is that the airwaves are the real property of the public just as much as the roads and the forests, and every other part of the commons. For a private corporation to access this in order to market their goods, share their opinions and propaganda, or anything else, they must pay the people directly for the use. Paying the government does nothing as the government is in collusion with the private corporate interests and disregards the wellbeing and the wishes of the population. Thus, it makes perfect sense that the people should be compensated fairly for the use of their property. As it is the public right, airwaves must also be accessible to the public freely, but perhaps with some sort of management system for time allotments, so as to invite the public to use their property equitably.

The Federal Communications Commission was formed on June 12, 1934, replacing the Federal Radio Commission. "The FCC helps to regulate content, award station charters, and monitor innovation to make sure that all forms of communication can co-exist. The FCC is also involved in regulating the Internet in the United States, and it has created regulations that have become the center of debate for the telecommunications industry, corporate users, and the millions of people in the United States who utilize the Internet every day."[65] The FCC is literally used as a censorship and propaganda tool and media gatekeeper.

There must be a direct payment to the people for every sale of the commons to corporations. These sales must be under the direct approval of the population, in full awareness of the nature of the purchase intent, and revocable if any terms are violated. Any harm of the commons would be considered as assault or murder under the Rights of Nature.

"According to a 1994 report by the Mineral Policy Institute, Barrick (American Barrick Resources Corporation of Canada) received 'patents' on 1,038 acres. The Mineral Policy Center explains that 'patent' as follows: 'A company that discovers a valuable mineral deposit on its claim can 'patent,' or gain fee title to, the land for a price not to exceed $5.00 per acre. Upon patent issuance, title to public lands is transferred to private ownership.' Barrick 'purchased' the 1,038 acres for $5,190 or $5 per acre. Those acres held mineral reserves valued at more than $10 billion!... Corporatization-or 'privatization,' as those who benefit from it prefer to say- is the process used to commercialize and extract profit from as much of society as possible: from public water systems, from public schools, from control of the Internet, from national parks, non-profit hospitals, and even from some fire departments. These commons are seen as lucrative resources to be tapped, no matter the local consequences, and then abandoned the moment they've been picked clean."

-Ralph Nadar, Breaking Through Power[66]

Taxation, when enforced upon an unwilling population, is mass theft. When it is created under the approval of a fully informed population it can be used to their benefit. While many people feel that direct taxes are a tool of the worst design, they do not have to be. Direct Taxation is not inherently bad. Taxation without consent and representation is bad, for when taxes are used without the direct consent of the accurately represented population you have an obvious availability for corruption and private interests and agendas to direct tax revenues to projects that do not serve the people. A direct tax is a levy on the taxpayer's individual income. This has been seen as a distinctively abhorrent way to generate revenues for a state, but this would hardly be the case in a well-run and responsive government. The fact that the government is not accurately representing the people, not accountable to its errors and failings and not efficient or even functional in the passage of legislature that provide holistic benefit to the nation shows that a direct tax is not appropriate. Indirect tax is a levy that does not come from taxpayer's income. This has historically been seen as a more appropriate method for taxing since ancient Greece. In the current situation in the United States, the wealth disparity is in manifest opposition to the wellbeing of all life. When the government implements a direct tax policy, at the publics behest, and uses these taxes to equitably shift wellbeing from a small group to the entire population, the direct tax may be considered valid. Taxation is a method by which the management of the tools and systems that benefit the entire population can be funded to adequately provide the upkeep of those tools and systems while continually evolving and advancing them. Higher taxes on wealthy individuals and large corporations can distribute wellbeing to the entire population without reducing the wellbeing of any entity. A direct tax that directly gives greater quality of life to the individual is the only direct tax that is of benefit to a people. Quality of Life is not synonymous with quantity of money, but rather access to the needs and wants of an individual to fully explore their potential in life, beginning with the fulfillment of their basic survival needs. We need to heavily reform the US Tax Code. It needs to be simplified. It needs to be accessible to the understanding of the average person, and applicable to Contract Law.

With that said, the ability for any government to maintain a righteous and equitable stance is fundamentally oxymoronic. Those who crave power do anything they can to acquire and keep it. It is not possible for government to serve the population. It is only possible when systems are made by which individuals and groups are made incapable of using their influence and ambition to overtake a population. This is only possible through systems that remove the human error at the root. This can be achieved through the advancement of smart contract technology, where individuals operate within a structure that is open source, open forum, and accessible to all. Smart contracts can be used to make a government that must operate within certain parameters. It is possible that this type of government would serve the interests of the entire population, as it would place the individual in a position of power equitably to all other individuals. It would follow that something akin to the Venus Projects design would evolve from this. It is important that we do not hinder our progress by cementing our potential to one idea. This is why I often contradict myself, so as to be open to a very many potential solutions. We must always endeavor to stay in a open and clear mind when confronting the issues before us, otherwise we will simply recycle useless or even detrimental problems in new ways. When we are free to explore the options, the availability of solutions increases, and the problems become merely transitions.

Since the Sixteenth Amendment was passed in 1913, Congress has had the right to levy direct taxes from the public. This was another insult to the people who had fought for over a century to not be taxed on their income.

"The Congress shall have power to lay and collect taxes on incomes, from whatever source derived, without apportionment among the several States, and without regard to any census or enumeration."

–16th Amendment

What has been the result of this direct tax? We have watched the creation debtors' prisons. The practice of incarcerating people who are unable to pay debts derives from Western Europe, where they would lock destitute debtors in workhouses until they had worked off their debts.

> *"Nearly two centuries ago, the United States formally abolished the incarceration of people who failed to pay off debts. Yet, recent years have witnessed the rise of modern-day debtors' prisons—the arrest and jailing of poor people for failure to pay legal debts they can never hope to afford, through criminal justice procedures that violate their most basic rights.... Ultimately, debtors' prisons are not only unfair and insensible, they are also illegal. Imprisoning someone because she cannot afford to pay court-imposed fines or fees violates the Fourteenth Amendment promises of due process and equal protection under the law."*
>
> -ACLU

Direct Federal taxation is the final nail in the coffin for Jeffersonian States Rights Tradition. The Civil War eliminated the State Right of nullification and secession and made States franchises and appendages of the Federal Government, which can and does threaten Governors with regulation and withdrawal of Federal Subsidies if they do not fall in line with Federal interests, effectively making the States beggars. After the 16th Amendment, the government became totally consolidated. In 1913, the creation of the Federal Reserve Bank came with the Government generated Inflation Tax. Direct taxes allow massive amounts of money to be generated that can be used to purchase votes to keep the same people in power forever and makes it possible for them to fundraise anywhere, rather than focusing on the people of their own state or region. Federal government is the major infringer on natural rights and has the power to control the states and dictate its will. The individual became the smallest part of government, and the idea of communities supporting themselves has been forgotten as communities see the Federal government saying it is doing all the work to care for elderly, neighbors, ill, education of children, not that they actually are. Civil society is eliminated by government intervention, and war has become more likely. Rather than being used for saving and investment, money collected by Income Tax is now used for income transfer programs administered by the state. Less capitol means less productivity in the economy, meaning the general population is poorer in the long run. With all these things in consideration, the obvious conclusion is that we must either abolish income taxes or abolish our crooked government and install something better.

Trade policy is the government's stance in how we conduct international trade. Since the United States entered into the WTO, we have largely disempowered our ability to enforce our trade policies and standards. Corporations now determine trade policy. We need a change in the focus of our interactions with the rest of the world. There is a remarkably high amount of wasteful and harmful practices that the US engages in on the world stage, often reflective of the condition and values held by the corporate and political interests that control our government. We must engage in war as the last resort in international policy. We must engage in unyielding standards in trade that do not allow harmful products and services to enter the country or influence our people. This can be done by creating a definitive stance on foreign trade ethics that focuses on immediate health and wellbeing of people and the planet and by empowering third party agencies with oversight on government operations reviewing the incoming and outgoing products. We must put the planet and the life upon her first. The World Trade Organization does not resolve international trade problems, but rather is built to encourage violent unquestioned resource extraction from vulnerable countries and decrease costs of goods in privileged nations. The WTO does not allow vulnerable nations to truly have a say in these policies, which leave them with extreme poverty conditions and do not offer them fair financial imbursements for their resources. The WTO must be abolished, and possibly a new enforceable, transparent, and equitable organization of all desirous nations must be created, in which we encourage the most endangered and suffering nations the ability to overcome their current and manufactured economic disabilities and concurrently their social issues. We must invite third party human rights observers into every part of every meeting held, and we must air all international meetings on national media. Making public these negotiations and meetings will inherently discourage nefarious agreements and will make it far easier for claims for violations and damages to be validated. The problem is that these agencies already present themselves to be working in this way. They seem to the casual observer to be beneficent while they are acting against the welfare of the population of the world.

When it comes to China, Russia, and other difficult nations or nations made to look difficult in the media, we must make an extra effort to produce agreements that support mutualistic wellbeing for the populations and disregard attempts to exploit vulnerable populations wherever they may exist. Russia is currently viewed as an invader in Ukraine, despite the fact that there are many Ukrainians who wouldn't know a war was happening if they weren't being told that, as they have full markets, cheap gas at about \$2/gal, and quiet streets. Ukraine is a corrupted nation, with direct ties to corrupt U.S. politicians. At the moment of writing this, the 101st Airborne Division is supposedly being readied to deploy to Germany and maybe Poland. This means that the U.S. is aggravating a response from Russia, despite the fact that the U.S. has no legitimate reason for getting involved in the affairs of a Russian-Ukrainian war. Who is the real aggressor? I can tell you confidently that it is never the one they are identifying as such in Rupert Murdoch's News Corp, or on any other news channel, because THEY ARE ALL CORRUPT GLOBALIST BASTARDS! So, who to believe? Who knows? Best thing is to *believe* nothing and live your life as locally beneficial as possible. Grow food, buy guns and ammo, and exchange in a locally made currency that works for the people directly involved and disregard all things coming out of your television. That's a place to start anyway.

Some resources are created or only economically feasible to be acquired within certain regions of the world. Rare Earth Metals, or Elements, are predominantly mined in China, due to their abundance there and Chinese working conditions policies, which allow people to mine and process these materials at extreme health detriments. China has control over the REE market and can dictate the value of the metals by restricting or opening the floodgates on their availability to the rest of the world. We need to create mutualistic policies, that are not dictated by any particular country. The US has conducted a combative foreign policy that creates enemies rather than partners. It creates a destructive foreign perspective. We must create sovereign and cooperative unions to produce transparent trade policies. Rare earth elements are only one of the categories of imports the US currently depends upon. We must create better diplomatic relations, better economic relations, and better ecological relations. We must also find ways to become more self-regenerative and not reliant on foreign powers for our needs, as the "One World Government" and "New World Order" proponents desire.

REE's are needed to make solar panels, which has a considerable influence on our ability to generate solar energy amongst a million other technologies. We must work with China, but simultaneously develop our own minimalistic mining operations protected by non-market funding, so as to make accessible our own REE's as protection against Chinese non-market interference in trade value. Negotiations with China amongst other nations must accommodate for the needs of the planet and wellbeing of the people first. While it is important to make contracts that increase the value of our currency and bring in various products and raw resources, we must begin every discussion with asking how the products are created, how they impacted the planet in their creation, and demand and ensure that any harmful practices be changed immediately if trade with those countries is to be conducted. With cooperation between the nations on this planet, we can reduce the damage done today and thereafter. We cannot support the theft of resources from vulnerable nations by more powerful nations. This must end firstly by providing evidence publicly, secondly by sanctioning the thieves, and thirdly by support for victims economically, militarily, and by bolstering their international demands for reparations. Even in truly capitalistic systems, there would be no economic benefit from this practice.

Cooperation between sovereign nations, which is what I propose here, is far different that cooperation mandated by international trade agreements, enforceable by supranational governmental organizations. That is centralized control. Nations that wish to cooperate can do so, and even groups of cooperative nations can cooperate with other groups, just as long as no binding world government exists that supersedes the sovereign authority of nations. Ever greater centralization is the key to global slavery. Ever greater decentralization I the key to personal liberty. We need to not only prevent the creation of world government, but eradicate the federal government, as it too is simply the expression of centralized power. Even some states today, like California, New York, Texas, and Florida are so populous that they outnumber many nations around the world. It is unsustainable to have such a large bureaucracy micromanaging such a large population. Everywhere one looks in the United States, diversity has been destroyed, and everything has become standardized, corporatized, made to be efficient rather than beautiful. No wonder there are massive populations doing anything they can to appear different, to break out the mold in any way they can imagine. It is a disease born of the eradication of personal liberty and the effort to turn all the people into mindless batteries that feed the centralized institutions. It is the attempt by millions to break out of it, though most often expressed by those millions in ignorant manner, lacking the knowledge to appropriately know where and in what method to direct their energy.

Capitalism in its purity indicates that if those nations with raw resources were free to sell their resources at their desired and fair rates, there would be greater market competition created, rather than the consolidation of all resources into the hands of only a few thieving countries, corporations, or individuals. We must not only move beyond the idea of stealing resources, but we must invest in nations that are disempowered and oppressed by international trade, to increase their internal value, and thus have strong allies in trade that increase the value of our mutual trading relationship. We must engage in a mixture of various economic models, without taking away from our sovereignty and dignity.

Currently, we are raping endangered nations and stealing their inherent wealth. We must completely and utterly change this practice to its complete opposite. We must assist and encourage these nations and protect them from the danger of international interference and violations. We must encourage our manufacturing industries through investment, industry incentives, and trade priorities. We must encourage the immigrant populations to engage in these market entrance positions, wherever automation does not exist. We must give ownership of these manufacturing industries to the people and encourage advances in our production to maximize product value, while reducing its financial burden. These things can be done. They are only inaccessible because we have not begun. By building an evolved manufacturing industry, we can begin to combat the flood of harmful products and manufacturing facilities that currently are appearing all over the planet and resulting in vast waste and environmental collapse. We must make products that are valued by their ability to reduce harm to the planet, while serving the needs and desires of the population. We must work to create friendships with Russia, China, North Korea, Iran, Venezuela, and other countries that we have had difficulties with. We must find common grounds and make trade deals that support our common wellbeing.

This is balanced by the first and primary need that all interactions with other nations serve the peoples greatest wellbeing. If we are to be the representative pillar of freedom in the world, we must not engage with nations that violate the ideals of our society. We must completely deny them in fact. It is a weak people that deserve to die, that allow trade to occur with a nation that is massacring a race within their borders, just so that batteries can be cheaper. That is the cowardice. Since China is currently doing great harm to various Christian and Muslim people within its boundaries, it would make sense to cut them off entirely. This isn't possible when we have a dependency on China for our survival needs, but that has only come about through design. Strengthen our domestic manufacturing, tear down the FED, empower competitive banking, incentivize small business loans for production, remove federal control over public education, get rid of Homeland Security and all the unconstitutional surveillance programs, protect domestic water supply against depletion and redistribution, and eradicate unemployment and food services. Overnight, this nation could be transformed and set on the path to self-sufficiency, and we would no longer be left mewling, debasing ourselves and genuflecting at the feet of supranational globalist monopolists. We need to become independent, domestically secure and powerful and abundant, before we are ready to interact with a world that would take advantage, and does take advantage, of every weakness.

> *True, Congress can tax and spend, but what the chair* (Federal Reserve Bank chairman, Jerome Powell) *doesn't seem to admit is that taxation only provides so much money, compared to spending which appears to be nearly limitless. Of course, what makes up the shortfall when spending exceeds taxation revenue, if not from debt? Considering the Fed owns $4.5 trillion of US Treasury's, of a nation with a $27 trillion debt, we should come to terms with understanding that the Fed is financing a significant portion of the US government's spending activities...*
> *The majority of people will undoubtedly be watching to see how the election is called and the looming fallout, but we must remember: the government is financed by the people and also by its central bank. The trajectory we are on is one where the Fed's balance sheet will continually increase, with a corresponding decrease in the wealth and freedom of the individual. How this fits in with the concept of a strong republic by the people and for the people is anyone's guess.*
> -Presidents Come and Go. The Fed's Power Grows, by Robert Aro, Mises Institute[67]

The single greatest action we can take in our nation and in the world today is to audit and abolish the Federal Reserve System, criminalize private central banking, imprison the bankers that have been manipulating international markets to perpetuate suffering and environmental destruction, and make all information discovered through the audit of the system directly available to the public. This would begin a process of recovery that is nearly impossible to undertake with the Federal Reserve in its current position of dominance and authority over the economy. We will have to replace the system of course, so the question arrives... what will we replace the Federal Reserve with? This is not a difficult question to answer as the Reserve has only existed for a century and civilizations have existed without it or any central bank or fractional reserve system for millennia. The five major roles of the Federal Reserve are to run the system for transferring funds between banks, to issue paper currency, to regulate commercial banks, by enforcing reserve, capital, and paperwork requirements, to function as the Lender of Last Resort, in cash creation when the system as a whole is running short, and to conduct monetary policy, such as the Federal Funds Rate (FFR) which is the interest rate at which banks borrow from one another and the expansion or contraction of money in the economy.

The Federal Reserve has numerous detrimental effects on the economy and society besides its inherent depravity as a private bank loaning money to the public at interest. It subsidizes weak banks, bails out wall street investment houses, enforces harmful restrictions on banks, conducts disruptive monetary policy, breeds corruption and is materially compromised as its board consists of its regional managers. If we eliminate the Federal Reserve today, and criminalize fractional reserve banking, and jail the bankers, we could easily implement a new banking system to support our nation as the private bankers never did nor attempted to.

We can implement an Interbank Payment System run by Clearing House Associations, organized by cooperating banks, similar to Clearing House Payments Company, but with transparent oversight and market floor regulations by government. These institutions would need to be publicly auditable upon demand. The Clearing House Associations would be owned by the participating banks, just like the CHPC is today, or even better, owned by banks owned by the local populations. The people would then reap the benefit as a whole. CHPC handles half of the daily volume today of wired payments in the United States.

Paper currency can be issued by ordinary banks as it was until the 1930's. Today, private bank notes are dominant currencies in Scotland, N. Ireland, and Hong Kong. With minimalistic government regulations for security of the financial system, private banks would be allowed to print and distribute their own currencies, which would force banks to compete for customers.

Another option would be to have a nationalized central bank, though this seems more dangerous in our current political environment due to the intertwined nature of corporate and political interests. It would be safer to decentralize to begin with, then slowly reconsider the potential of a nationalized banking system that would compete with the clearing house associations, though this option reaffirms the federal position in the public money which would again produce control and abuse over time. Clearing House regulation of banks is a highly reliable system. Standards for Membership ensure quality, and banks must qualify to participate. Member banks have to be fully capable of settling up with other member banks and balance sheets must be provided to the Clearing House as well as Clearing House auditors must be allowed to audit each member banks books on demand. Clearing House Associations will act as the Lender of Last Resort, which provides its members with a mutual insurance. The government will audit these banking systems and set guidelines like universal public access to records, money laundering monitoring, and national safety issues. By having the banks compete for the public's attention and money, they will be forced to comply with the public will, rather than manipulate it to their private shareholders benefit as the Federal Reserve does today.

We need to abolish the Federal Reserve NOW and tear down its walls and cast out its villainy. Barring this, we can at least take an action that would inherently and ultimately leave the Federal Reserve powerless to generate disparity, which is to create laws that say any private institution that issues private currency or regulates the economy must give universally equal shares of the bank to all of the population. This would mean that every single individual would be equally an owner of the bank as the chairman or any other shareholder and have equal voting rights, equal pay from bank profits, and equal responsibility for the bank in its entirety. This would make the bank unable to create disparity, for as it profits, it must distribute those profits to all the people of the population rather than a small group of private individuals. This means that whenever the government takes a loan from the Federal Reserve of a trillion dollars, when they pay back those trillion dollars with interest, the Federal Reserve must then payout to every person of the public the profit made by that loan payback, though the initial debt will never be repaid. This isn't a problem though, as the Federal Reserve is not composed of real money, rather it is composed of a parallel economy without substance, and thus can take on a negative balance sheet without harming the real money economy. Let's say its one-hundred billion dollars in profit. That's about $300 for every person. Even better than this, we might make it illegal for private banks to issue loans at interest. This would eliminate the entire purpose of a private central bank and would effectively eliminate the problem. Wouldn't it just be easier to burn the Federal Reserve down and hang the crooks inside though? How about all their cronies in government? Torches and pitchforks anyone?

> *"And to preserve their independence* (the public), *we must not let our rulers load us with perpetual debt. We must make our election between economy and liberty, or profusion and servitude. If we run into such debts, as that we must be taxed in our meat and in our drink, in our necessaries and our comforts, in our labors and our amusements, for our callings and our creeds, as the people of England are, our people, like them, must come to labor sixteen hours in the twenty-four, give the earnings of fifteen of these to the government for their debts and daily expenses; and the sixteenth being insufficient to afford us bread, we must live, as they now do, on oatmeal and potatoes; have no time to think, no means of calling the mismanagers to account; but be glad to obtain subsistence by hiring ourselves to rivet their chains on the necks of our fellow-sufferers."*
>
> — Thomas Jefferson, Letters of Thomas Jefferson

Economic democracy is the idea that public stakeholders like workers, customers, suppliers, and the public should have decision-making power rather than corporate managers and corporate shareholders. There are a very many different systems that have been developed within the idea of economic democracy. In our current economic model, we see only negative patterns for the general public and only great rewards for select groups and individuals. In an economic democracy, we would see those patterns flipped on their head. The people would be given the right to manage the means of production and would benefit from directly profiting from that production. The current captive capitalistic model has a major flaw in that it relies on economic and market managers to determine and either restrict or expand supply. In a direct economic democracy, the guesswork involved in this market management would disappear as the people and the market itself would be the determinant of the supply, and thus would create a proportionate demand. While the captive capitalistic system we have today sees the world as a dead thing that can be raped and ripped apart, a system that is managed by the people will potentially have a much more reasoned and collectively determined impact on the environment, naturally leading to less destruction as people will refuse to destroy their own land.

The evolution of the idea that our economy should serve the entire population, whether through capitalism, socialism, or any other model, is the creation of a Resource-Based Economy. This model I will speak on toward the conclusion of this book. In short, it is an economic and social model that measures the carrying capacity of the planet and makes all economic decisions about the use of those resources by looking at the needs of all the lifeforms on the planet. It brings us into a technologically advanced mutualistic relationship with the natural environment. It is the optimum way of utilizing our technology to serve all life on the planet while negating detrimental impacts to any resource or aspect of life. To work toward that social and economic design must become our goal and our motivation. We must begin by giving power to the general population to determine their lives and to organize and become responsible for their wellbeing.

Worker self-management is a system by which a workforce determines its own work processes. Elected bodies can be used, or a direct voting system through assemblies or various other methods, but all methods result in the direct will of the workers determining the work process. This modality of organizational management allows for the elimination of boss culture and thus gives greater responsibility and greater self-determinism to the workers. This allows for greater influence and power to be held by every individual in the business and thus gives them the right to dissent without fear of retribution, to fight for greater wages or ownership without abuse from an individual or group who wields ultimate power and grants them the satisfaction of being responsible for their work, their production, and their livelihood.

The current corporate worker is generally under the Taylorism model, which says that a worker needs to be given simple repetitive tasks that they will perform exclusively to participate in the production of goods. This model has been implemented to such an exacting degree, that a huge proportion of factories are enforcing timeframes that do not allow their workers to deviate by seconds from their repetitive tasks. This is humorously and very accurately portrayed in Charlie Chaplin's movie *Modern Times*, in which he is on a conveyor belt crew, turning two bolts over and over again as the manager continually increases the speed at which he must complete the task. This is the model by which corporations have used their workers, to the extreme detriment of those workers. It reduces the skill level of the workers and creates mental, emotional, and physical distress, often reducing their productivity as well as their wellbeing and their motivation. The cumulative result of Taylorism is slave workers producing goods at extreme discounts to the industrial owners and sold at premiums to the public who make survival wages or less, and thus not having the capital to spend on those very same goods they produced become indebted to the banker-industrial Plutocrats.

In 1973, minimum wage was $4.30. To match this in purchasing power today, the minimum wage would have to be $23.68. This means that while we have increased our technologies and, yes computers and cell phones have advanced and offered better services over time, the actual purchasing power has decreased by 41%-78% depending on the state. So, while some commodities have become "cheaper" over that time, the ability to take one inflation corrected dollar and purchase the same amount of goods has disappeared. This means that if inflation did not exist or occur, the dollar should be able to purchase the same amount of goods 50 years apart, excluding fluctuations in organic market demand, but this is not the case. Rather your dollars can get you 22%-59% of what it could 50 years before. The average 4-year public college in 1970 cost $405. In 2019, that same education cost $10,230.[68] That's over 25 times the cost over 50 years, during the same time that our dollar has devalued compared to cost-of-living expenses. In June 2019, the average asking rent for unfurnished homes was $1,588. The average annual electricity bill was $1,334. Annual food expenditure was $7,923.[69] In 1970, the median rent was $108.[70] In 1980, the Median rent for homes and apartments was $308[71] Rent has increased in 50 years from 13% of average family household income to over 21% of average family household income. [72]/[73] The annual cost of electricity in 1970 was equivalent to $233 in 2020 dollars., which was about $35 in 1970. This is a change of almost 600% purchasing power lost.[74] Food expenditure accounts for 9.7% of household's total disposable income, which is less than the 70's, but when we factor in the toxicity of the foods sold at cheaper prices made available by merging markets and advancements in distribution, storing, packaging and preserving, and the medical deficits that have piled up as a result, we can see that the costs are far greater as we can merge much of our medical costs into the long-term cost of purchasing and consuming large quantities of toxic substances.

This is class warfare and oppression. With worker-managed systems, Taylorism would be rapidly removed as people became aware and active in applying their authority in shaping the nature of their working environment. Today, and for several generations, the U.S. and much of the world have used Taylorism in schooling and in the workplace, leaving children indoctrinated into the system of compartmentalization, subservience and obsequiousness, and generalized testing for socioeconomic position. The decentralization of power is the key to increasing the wellbeing of the general population. Interestingly, capitalism is often confused with fascism and captive capitalism. In a purely capitalistic system, the goal is not for consumers to experience scarcity and competition, but rather businesses. The business that has to compete with its neighbor businesses will naturally be forced to provide better services, goods, and prices to the consumer. In our system today, we are forced to experience manufactured scarcity by monopolized markets owned by private individuals and extremely small groups. The inability for small local businesses to compete with the large conglomerated multinational corporations means that we have left behind us even the shadow of capitalism. We have entered into plutocracy and captive capitalism. By shifting power away from these conglomerated entities and by giving that power to the workforce and the general public, we will see capitalism reveal itself. By giving control of the markets and the means of production to the workers, we will remove the cronyism that has that has controlled our economy and our government from its origination.

Regionalization of the food supply is necessary and will be a determining factor in the future of human existence and wellbeing in years to come. Today, the globalization of the supply of food may seem to have benefitted the planet, but the real result of the agricultural boom and the planetary trade of food has been the destruction of arable land, forcibly implemented and controlled scarcity by centralized producers, distributors, and retailers and ecocide on greater scales than has ever occurred before. It has also removed the local responsibility of communities to provide for their own sustenance. It has created a widely held misunderstanding and ignorance of the methods of food production and has separated people from the earth and their heritage. As more people migrate to cities, and as more agribusiness takes control of the arable land, the less the population will understand or be responsible for the means of producing food. This means that their power to decide the methods of food production will be so minimal as to be practically non-existent. With less than one percent of the population of the U.S. farming, we see that the vastly agrarian society of a century and a half ago has dwindled and forgotten its heritage already. The regionalization of the food supply will return the power and responsibility of providing sustenance to the public and especially to the local communities that will be responsible for producing what they need and trading with other communities around them. While some amount of globalization of trade does not harm the people, the power to trade on that level must be left to the individuals who collectively, or even better, individually conduct their policies.

Along with these economic system changes, we need to remember that at the core of our contaminated society today we have a privately controlled financial empire that prints all of our currency, dictates and determines financial policy, controls interest rates, and has zero actual oversight by the public through any mechanism of government. This is the root of the disease that is manufacturing suffering and scarcity in our country and around the planet. By allowing this private banking cartel to continue is to allow the perpetuation of our decline into self-destruction. We could return our country to its highest time of financial prosperity, when we had a free banking system in which banks were forced to compete to provide the best services, goods, and prices to the public, the consumers. We can obviously alter the system to meet the demands of the modern situation, but we must not allow this heinous misconduct and mismanagement to continue. We need to force the closure of the Federal Reserve and alter our foreign policy to pressure the rest of the world to eliminate their private central banks. We need to eliminate the IMF and the World Bank along with all other central banking organizations around the world that are free from oversight and wield power beyond any nation or group of nations. When these organizations are allowed to produce and manage our currency at their own reward and at all others expense, we will see the most dreadful results as has been the case for many centuries in some places, and globally for several generations.

The origins of central banking and plutocracy go back to antiquity. The ability for a certain class to own and dictate to the other "lower classes" and to determine the value of currency or exchange of any type is not a novel one. In the recent past, one of the greatest examples, if not the greatest, of the diseased governmental and economic structures in use, is the Nazi invasion of global markets and governments. Despite the belief that Goebbels was Hitlers most important subordinate, the true mastery was with Martin Bormann. Bormann was charged with the financial success of the Nazi Empire, and he was an extremely capable weapon in that regard. Bormann was the one who masterminded the funneling of the bullion of the various European countries that the Nazis attacked, invaded, and raided, such as Poland for example, to Switzerland. That bullion amounted to vast fortunes that was, for a high fee, taken into Swiss trust accounts, and then dispersed at the discretion of the Nazis, to any country and enterprise they desired. Nearing the end of the war, Bormann called a meeting between various of his international associates, such as representatives from Bayer and Ford, as well as various other major corporations, governments, and institutions. At this meeting he told them that the Nazi Party would be entrusting them with vast sums of money to purchase majority stocks in every major corporation in the world as well as to get trusted Nazi affiliates to sit on the boards of the same major corporations. Where they could not get majority shares, they would purchase minority shares and do whatever they could to integrate into every corner of the world's financial institutions and corporations. After this meeting, just such a thing happened. The hold that the Nazi Party and its affiliates, like Prescott Bush, George W. Bush's grandfather, had on global politics and finance grew exponentially, and can be viewed now as one of the greatest scams to ever take place.

The German population was not rewarded for their loyalty to the Nazi Party, nor for their great losses they received in the war, for which they were as at fault as any population forced into war by their government. Instead, the stolen bullion, and the rewards of the market purchases made at Bormann's command went to serve only the highest Nazi officials, and the Nazi friends and affiliates globally, such as; the government of Argentina; the Rockefeller Family who had supplied necessary oil to the Nazi war effort; the Ford Motor Company who supplied more than 20% of all vehicles and vehicle parts for the Nazi war machine; IG

Farben (Bayer), who manufactured Zyklon B to kill prisoners in concentration camps and provided the Fluoride for keeping the concentration camps populations docile amongst other atrocities; Siemens; Chase National Bank; AEG; Coca-Cola; Nestle; IBM (Dehomag), who supplied technology for tracking Jews and other undesirables as well as coordinated the mechanics of the extermination of millions of people in them; Allianz Ag, which insured concentration camps against claims; The Associated Press, who printed over 10,000 propaganda pieces for the Nazis; and many, many others.

The International Monetary Fund was created under the guise of making Nazis pay for their crimes but did not affect the Nazis most responsible for the crimes, but rather the general population. The IMF is coincidentally where, every two weeks, the chairmen of the central banks globally, meet to discuss global financial policy behind closed doors. What they decide in that room at the IMF becomes our financial reality around the world. No government has greater authority today than this group and their collective ambition and will. These are the arbiters of war, slavery, and scarcity. The links that exist between every government's leadership globally for the past two centuries at least, and their actions, shows the exclusive and insidious nature of the "elitist" motives they share. Aryans were not exclusively of German interest. In fact, the eugenics programs of the United States were largely the inspiration that Hitler took for his own concentration camps.

There were Nazis all over the globe. Much of the first Nazis were psychiatrists. A sizable portion of the SS certainly were and the eugenics programs in the US were conducted by psychiatrists, especially with the Rockefeller funded School of Psychiatry founded in 1929. The point here is that no matter where on the planet, there has been a consistent theme of people controlling others through a small group of followers that are devoid of empathy and believe themselves to be superior. Today, the US society is full of this. Groups that feel superior to other groups. It would not take much to create a wave of intolerance so strong that people are willing to commit murder and atrocities against others.

Today's corporatocracy or plutocracy, is exactly the right type of organization to strip rights from the people or to simply ignore them, such as Lincoln did with our right to not be under a direct tax during the Civil War. Never have we been a democracy. Never have we been a republic. Never have we been a capitalism. Never have we been a free society. Never have we been without the oppression of unjudicial treatment from the laws created by the vipers in congress and the puppets in the white house and the corrupted judges that interpret constitutional rights. Simply look at our history, and you will see naught but abuse from a select society upon the vastly greater majority. Today, we have become a more acutely desensitized, apathetic, and ignorant population, even more susceptible to manipulation and propaganda. If the government were to truly endeavor for a genocide of the inferiors, such as the Nazis did, it would be with even greater ease, as all they have to do is say pandemic, and everyone would run to the nearest "safe zone" to get their vaccines. What an idiocracy we live in, where our histories are forgotten along with their lessons, and the future is riddled with uncertainty due to the same.

We will never be given our freedoms because we want them, nor will we be allowed to prosper when we ask for gifts from a government of any kind. The only means by which anyone has ever won or armed their freedoms, is by living as one who already has them and by being willing to die that way. We could simply ignore the government, not feed it our money, not pay it any mind, not vote for its rigged elections, and instead make for ourselves the image of life we want to live with our neighbors and local communities. It's a "pick yourself up by your bootstraps" approach that doesn't involve as much suffering as would a civil war or other demonstrations of violent opposition. Just stop giving your energy to that which does not serve you and your neighbors and your planet.

The Federal Reserve holds major influence globally, and thus by removing it from power we will influence the global financial institutions to scramble and recover. We must not allow that recovery to occur. We must create a new decentralized global economic system. Minimally, we must create a banking system that has to compete, cannot create trusts or monopolies, and cannot be a privately-owned central bank, and be barred from printing a nations currency. If we allow private banks to print their own forms of currency, through the mint, but at their expense, we will see a new revenue stream for the federal government, if such a thing is even needed, which I propose it is not, a competitive, non-exploitative banking system, and a greater economic freedom and wellbeing for the general population. We need to restructure the entire economic model that is in operation today.

DoD and DHS

The National Defense is the primary and sole responsibility of the Federal Government as laid out in the Constitution. While Congress is solely authorized to declare war, the executive office of the president is the Commander in Chief and has authority over the operations, preparations, and executions of the military and other agencies. The Department of Defense is one of thirteen executive departments that exist to execute the will and authority of the President. The Department of Defense is charged with coordinating and supervising all government functions relating to national security and the US Armed Forces. Its headquarters is in Arlington, Virginia near to Washington, D.C. It is comprised of the Departments of the Army, the Navy, and the Air Force, the National Security Agency, the Defense Intelligence Agency, the National Geospatial-Intelligence Agency, the National Reconnaissance Office, the Defense Advanced Research Projects Agency (DARPA), the Strategic Capabilities Office (SCO), the Defense Logistics Agency (DLA), the Missile Defense Agency (MDA), and the Defense Contract Management Agency (DCMA) among other agencies. The DoD was created when the military branches were consolidated into one executive branch. The atrocities committed by this department are innumerable. The very first thing that must be done is a public audit, conducted by Congress for crimes against humanity by decision makers, observed and overseen by third party human rights organizations and barring executive sessions. We need to have an immediate reduction of funding, with restructuring focused on creating highly trained personnel, advanced technology that removes human error and loss of life potential, and release of information to the public through Congressional Committee.

In 1775, the Continental Congress created the Army, the Navy, and the Marines. In the time between then and now, our military has evolved, adapting to meet the demands of the times. After the second world war, the United States became the dominant military power in the world. While many people would say that we were competing with Russia in the effort to produce a dominant force, the reality is that no nation anywhere was able to compete with the post-war United States. Russia was decimated with over twenty million deaths. They were not able to compete with the United States despite the post-war propaganda and social programming that led to the Cold War. The United States used Russia as an excuse to expand its military presence around the world, which is why today, we have the largest, most globally involved, and most advanced military in the world. While this maintains its validity today, the future of our military and our global presence looks to be changing. In WWII, we were facing a major high intensity conflict (HIC). In some ways, the Korean and Vietnam conflicts were mostly low-intensity conflicts (LIC), involving protracted guerilla warfare and less than conventional warfare and involving political, economic, and military instruments. This became the norm in US military advancement around the world. When we entered Iraq, the potential conventional warfare quickly resulted in a transition to a protracted low-intensity conflict, whereas the conflict in Afghanistan was immediately a low-intensity conflict. The result of this many decades of shaping our military to respond in low-intensity conflicts with nations that are very far from equal in military capability is that we are far from prepared for a high-intensity conflict with nations that have capable and comparable military force.

Today, while our nation faces what appears to be dramatic domestic issues, the global strategic landscape is shifting and there are many nations that are increasing their capabilities while we are demilitarizing and disarming our nation and many of our allies. While it remains improbable that any major nation will attempt a direct conflict with the United States in the near future, the likelihood that the nearly global access that the US military enjoys today will be encroached upon and will diminish. This diminishing of global military presence will result in less ability to respond to situations that develop around the globe. This inability to respond will ultimately empower nations to become more emboldened and involved in their regions with any number of motives unchecked. This could and would result in many detrimental effects on our access to trade and influence and would affect our domestic economy by creating higher prices on imported commodities and force our hand to produce more internally or become more beholden to the will of foreign nations that will likely not share similar values or concern for the welfare of our population. This is obviously not a guaranteed scenario as predictability decreases with time, but we must consider this from the lens of global interest and the probable effect that would result from a weakened military presence globally. While our presence decreases, others will take advantage of that. With this in mind, we must consider the ways in which we can negate or minimize the negative effects of a decreasing, increasing or maintained military budget, a decreasing military presence and increasingly militarily empowered competing and less-than-friendly nations.

Our military today is largely comprised of wasted resources. We need to focus on creating a streamlined, small elite standing active military force, while supplementing Reserve and National Guard forces with the former active duty personnel. We need to reduce overall costs by reducing excessive waste by implementing public accounting and fiscal management systems as oversight on spending. We need a reduction in the size of active duty military forces kept in foreign countries. By rotating Reservists and Guardsmen on Temporary Active Duty Assignments, we can reduce the cost of maintaining large permanent forces, while keeping readiness in our armed forces. We can offer Off-Duty Military personnel the option to live on bases, without pay, to work on turning open spaces into food gardens and self-sustaining systems. These soldiers would live for free on the base and build these systems in exchange. Veterans and eligible civilians can also be offered this to increase the sustainability of maintaining armed forces.

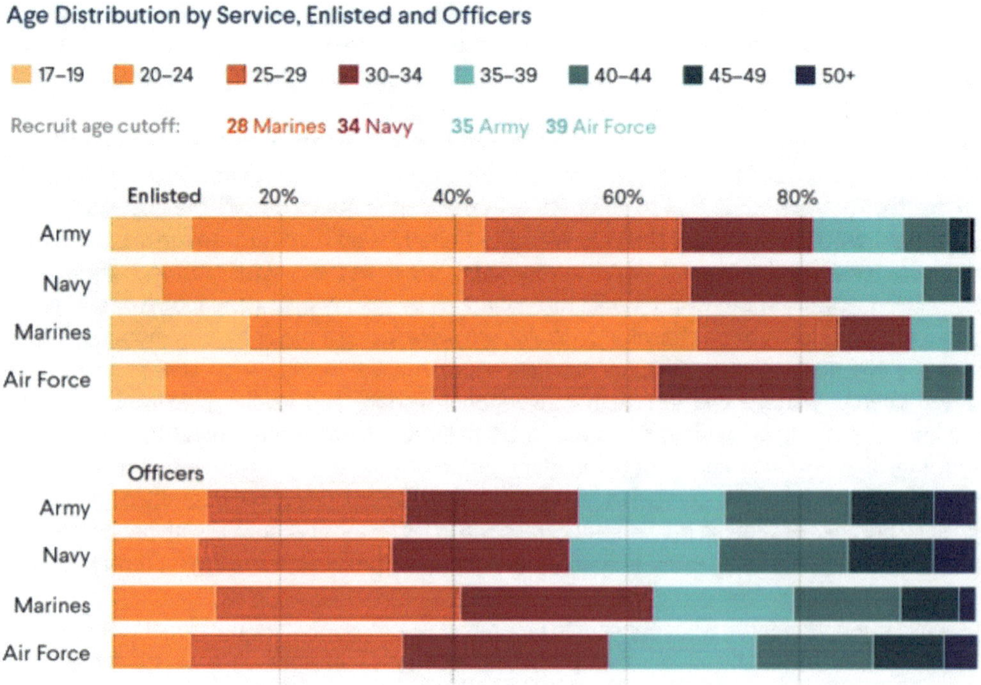

We are encountering a profoundly disturbing and serious issue within the core of our military. Americans are overweight, undereducated, and often criminally charged. To be specific, over 30 percent of the recruitable population are ineligible for service due to being overweight. 25 percent do not have a high school diploma or GED. 10 percent have criminal histories. In total, over 70 percent of 18-24 year-old potential recruits cannot continue past the recruiting station. Of the eligible potential recruits, only about 15 percent want to join the military. Of those that attempt to join, 30 percent do not pass the ASVAB (Armed Services Vocational Aptitude and Battery) or AFQT (Armed Forces Qualification Test). This leaves the total potential recruit pool in the nation at significantly under a million. And even amongst those, when they have encountered the conditions inside the military, many of them choose to leave. This is one of the biggest threats to our nation, and one that will very likely be ignored and dismissed by much of the population.

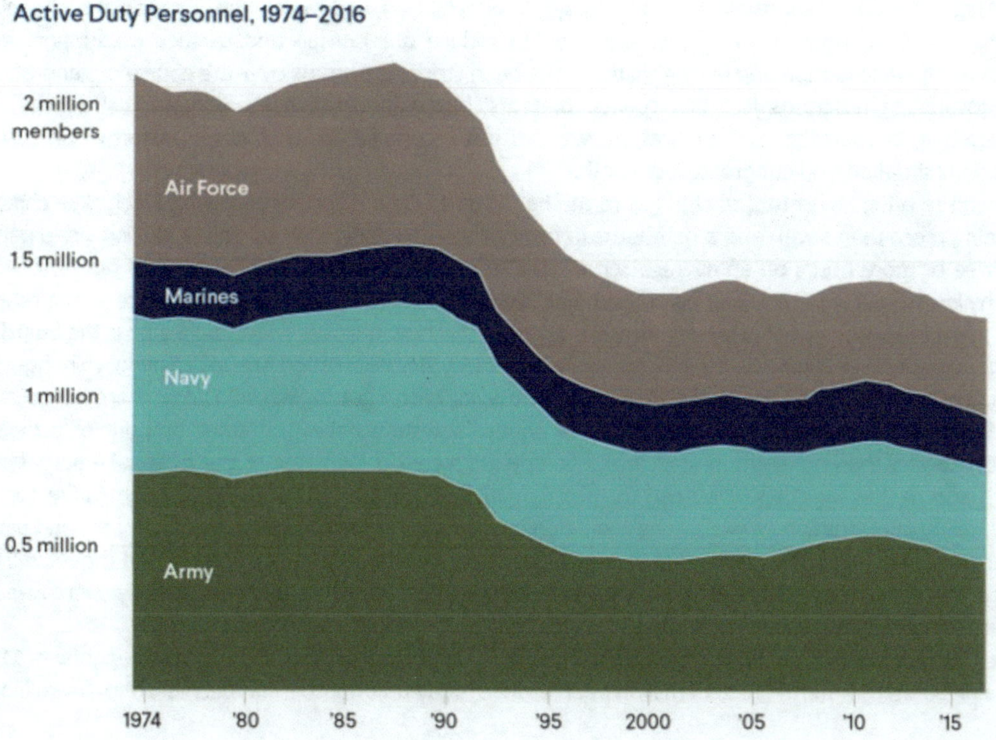

While several countries around the world are increasing their military spending and capabilities, the U.S. is faced with exceptionally large maintenance fees, seemingly endless wars and occupations, aging pilots, an unhealthy, unmotivated, and uneducated recruiting pool, and an increasingly anti-war general population among other things. As far as criminal backgrounds, we need to eliminate the barring of potential recruits due to cannabis charges. This is a backwards and unrepresentative policy that harms our recruiting and eliminates an entire major subculture of people in this nation from the recruitment pool who would potentially otherwise be incentivized to enlist. Other non-violent crimes need to be reconsidered as well, to eliminate the possibility of blocking potentially successful and sound people. Crimes like having a fake I.D., mutually agreed fighting, failure to render aid after an accident, unlawful use of a long-distance telephone calling card, and vandalism among others are ridiculous reasons to bar enlistment. While high standards must be kept, we also must understand that the applied law of today currently does not accurately portray moral or constitutional law, and the standards that are held for enlistment are not appropriate to accommodate for our need. Law abiding citizens, in a corrupt and undignified legal system, are not the ideal, but the norm. We need to consider the quality of those who are not satisfied with our national legal system and immoral and unconstitutional laws. Charismatic and strong-willed young people who get into minor legal trouble being barred from service is detrimental to our national security and our social identity.

In order to reduce the creeping threat of overwhelming levels of disease and lack of health we need to think not only of the training of individuals when they arrive for bootcamp, but of the caretaking of our national healthcare through mandatory exercise programs and health food requirements at schools. We need to provide education for our children on how to live healthy lifestyles. These programs would affect the cost of healthcare nationally and would reduce the need for more and more hospital visits for individuals. Personal responsibility must be taught to our children, and the military should not be the place for the first encounter of this virtue. We need to reduce our burden and reliance on support from government while demanding our rights that have been stripped from us over the course of generations. By encouraging programs like boy scouts, that are based in physical fitness, outdoor activity and bushcrafting, cooperation and unification, we can instill core values that can transform our current precarious situation into our greatest strength.

We need to bring about radical changes to the habits that our youth now espouses. Habits like children spending more than seven and a half hours in front of screens daily, high schoolers playing video games for three or more hours on an average school day, excessive consumption of sugar and salt far beyond healthy levels, and unnatural bolting of food that inhibits the body's natural digestive process. The ratio of time spent in sedentary behavior versus exertion no matter how minimal is over 50% across the board for the population over twelve years old. Over six years old, the population spends minimally six hours in sedentary behavior. This abnormal and unnatural behavior is only getting worse. Today, there is marketing that instructs people to do fifteen minutes of physical exertion daily. This small amount of activity is certainly better than no exertion at all, but it is far from a conclusive result to our national emergency in health and healthcare costs. We need to take definitive action to create a healthier population for the defensibility of our nation as well as the reduction in costs that are being wasted in healthcare and causal social programs. While the passage of a singular law to mandate education in health and fitness will not resolve our national problems, it is one step in a direction that we must go to successfully overcome our current social design failures.

Since 1990 the United States has drastically reduced in numbers its personnel and components. In 1990, active personnel amounted to 2.12 million people while today that number has decreased to 1.4 million.

Table 2.1
Selected U.S. Force Elements, 1990–2015

Force Element	1990	1996	2003	2010	2015
Active personnel (millions)	2.118	1.547	1.427	1.580	1.433
Army divisions (active)	18	12	10	10	10
Aircraft carriers	14	13	12	11	10
Surface combatants	206	116	106	100	105
SSNs	136	82	56	57	59
Large amphibious vessels	63	39	38	31	31
U.S. Air Force FTR/FGA	3,444	2,485	2,413	2,158	1,570
U.S. Air Force bombers	301	195	199	154	139

SOURCES: IISS, *The Military Balance*, 1991, 1996, 2003, 2010, and 2015 editions.
NOTES: FTR = air supremacy fighter aircraft, whose primary mission is air-to-air combat. FGA = ground attack fighter aircraft, whose primary mission is air-to-surface strike.

Our technology has advanced and has largely made our armed forces less reliant on large numbers of personnel. Today, much of the technology we are implementing allows for smaller amounts of people with a greater number of technical skills and higher intelligence. We are moving away, and have been for quite a while, from disposable soldiers, to indispensable, highly trained, and intelligent warfighters. This evolution makes it possible for less casualties though it has been largely developed with the current fields of operation in mind. We have been in constant war and conflict with various nations and non-state groups for almost twenty years. We have been almost constantly involved in conflicts around the world for over a century, but the current conflicts have been unceasing, giving them a different sort of operational environment. Our military has been conditioned to deal with the kind of threats faced by nations and non-state groups that are far militarily inferior and non-high intensity combatants. When we consider the fact that China, Russia, and some other nations have steadily been increasing their military funding, we can see that despite our superior military ability that exists today, without taking appropriate action, we will not be able to match the kind of threats that are currently developing. When we consider the possibility of being potentially critically outmatched in 15 years, we must consider the restructure of our military design.

We need to redesign our military to match the needs of high intensity warfare and ever increasing low-intensity situations like that which we have created in the middle east and elsewhere, while at the same time developing solutions and training for actions within the future connected megacity, where versatility and adaptability to complex, rapidly changing, politically and militarily indistinct or multi-faceted and layered hostile environments exist. High-intensity warfare is the kind that we would face if we were to go to war with Russia or China or any other modernized and capable comparable force. In these situations, we would be encountering many factors that we are less prepared for today than we would need to be to eliminate the chances of devastating results. Like I said above, there are ways to reduce many of the problems that we face today in financing our military and defensive capabilities, as well as providing for a more holistically beneficial organization of the military.

In a war with China or Russia today, there is no guarantee that we would be victorious. Some of the issues we would face are the decreasing capabilities of our own military outlined previously, as well as the fact that we are entering into a new era of warfare, which brings with it greater risks from nations that do not carry the same traditional warfare capabilities of the United States. Technology is advancing rapidly on the path of hyper-sonic precision weapons that can circle the globe and strike targets with little or no comparable defensibility. It is possible to arm small, palm-sized drones with explosives and automate them to target individuals by facial recognition and other biological signatures. These drones would kamikaze into the target and the nation or other actor sending the drone may not be able to be discovered. A nation could arm a million of these drones and deploy them against high value targets. Cyber warfare can be utilized to take down defensive systems in an enemy nation before an armed UAV attack on a target city. Offensive cyber warfare itself is most utilized by the United States, and every time the US uses its advanced viruses or other weapons, it releases that code for study to foreign nations and non-state actors. Every time the US participates offensively in cyber warfare, it gives a boost to all the actors globally who wish to advance their own cyber capabilities, which could then be used against the United States.

This kind of warfare puts the United States into a position of having to defend against nations and non-state actors employing evolved technologies that have not been prepared for or used in combat previously. While the fundamental principles of the art of war will never change, the nature of its expression has changed several times in the past and is changing on a faster scale each iteration. Today we are in a shift of the expression of warfare, and we are not leading the pack in several areas that may become critical deficiencies in a war with nations and non-state actors that are steadily and aggressively increasing their capabilities in this new era of warfare. Biotech implants like RFID chips, conductive tattoos that can store information and transmit it, and more provide an opportunity for warring agencies to use individuals' bodies as weapons. Violence requires motive and responsibility, and it often is unnecessary to achieve the result desired. The threat of harm is far more important. Militaries mostly posture through diplomacy to achieve their goals. The threat that is posed by new technologies in the hands of enemies or capable nations means that we may have to negotiate with greater risk of having to let go of large portions of our goals or even cultural identity. This is because we no longer would represent the pinnacle of global military might and presence.

Concurrently with the potential harm of new-epoch military technological advancements in the hands of our competitors, is the fact that much of the technology is available and being developed in the United States as well, on top of the traditional military might that exists to back it up. This is not the same for Russia or China, who are forced to utilize the innovative technologies to circumvent disproportions in military capability. While this does show their capacity to attack the current weak points in the armor or the US military, it does not necessarily mean that these technologies give them overall superior strategic might. Some of the limitations of our competitors are the lack of "soft power" that the US has in abundance, like the fact that most of the world has English as a first, second, or third language, while Russia and China enjoy none of that privilege and likely will not in the near future. "The things that we worry about are not the things that end up taking us down, they're the ones that we don't worry about because we don't know to worry about them."[75] – Dr. Erik Gartzke, UC San Diego.

The Virtual Theatre is a new aspect of warfare, adding another dimension to the battlefield. This is the capability for command and control centers, Predator or Reaper pilots, or even recruitment and propaganda machines to operate discretely while affecting targets anywhere on the globe. It means that a Predator or Reaper operator of the 432nd Wing of the US Air Force, reclining behind a joystick at Creech AFB, Indian Springs, Nevada, can send a precision missile at a target anywhere in the world, destroying human lives, often including ones that had nothing to do with the target. It means that command and control centers in a friendly country can directly remotely control missions against targets in other parts of the world. It means that the internet can be utilized to recruit people from anywhere around the globe to participate in actions against targets. This new dimension to warfare makes legal grey areas around the rules of war and which areas of the globe are acceptable targets as within the bounds of the theatre of war. Drone pilots who take violent military action at Creech AFB opens the door for Creech itself to be attacked by those groups being targeted. This distinction could mean that it becomes acceptable for states and non-state actors to target locations where drone operators work and live, potentially creating casualties in the general public in the vicinity of these warfighters. Since the war theatre boundaries have expanded, the threat against targets globally that are distant from the more intense location of fighting, become legally and practically more compelling targets.

The introduction of AI into the military may bring about negative results that counteract the positive. As automation and autonomy increase in use, the role of political decision-making will become more and more delegated to smaller and smaller sectors to be able to respond instantly to raid attacks while those politicians may begin to disregard their military advisors in favor of AI algorithms. Governments may lose their ability to maintain support and legitimacy of their people, while those same populations lose faith in military institutions. Wars will be much more frequent and require less to incite, as human involvement, and thus risk, increases. The military may lose its moral relation to its population of service. Machines fighting means that war will likely lose its moral prohibition. And learning machines may alter their own programs and orders as they gain greater learning. "As long as humans are responsible for directing war, for writing code, for fielding and maintaining machines, warfare is going to be an instrument of policy and the province of warriors at some degree."[76] – Dr. Frank Hoffman, National Defense University.

Major General Robert Scales, Close Combat Lethality Task Force, theorized that there are two major factors that must be considered when questioning whether we are actually seeing an evolution in warfare. These factors are: Firepower, which is composed of lethality, range, and precision and Maneuverability, which is composed of protection and speed. If technology advances these factors, then warfare will see epochal change. Between WWI and WWII, we saw the epochal change in the realm of speed with the discovery of the wireless and the combustion engine. During and after WWII, the epoch advanced with changes to lethality, range, and precision. Today, Russia's hypersonic missiles are an example of the continuation of that epochal change. "United States cannot win a war if its on the defensive. We can't risk the loss of manpower facing a peer competitor who in many ways are better than us."[77] – Robert Scales. We cannot compete but at best parity levels with Russia in the coming decades in firepower. We can use Disaggregation which means that we would need to have control of the cyber domain to aggregate forces at command quickly and disaggregate them just as quickly for offensive and defensive measures. This can only work when we control the cyber situation. Lastly, we can increase the speed variable in our military technology to bring our military to compete on the offensive. Speed increases would need to be vast to compete with the unique areas of advancements in competing nations.

Globally, urban social disorder is on rise, individual and interpersonal violence is increasing, while people are increasingly taking matters into their own hands, such as in unofficial rescue work after natural disasters and other situations. The amount of interactivity and arrangements between people, corporations, and governments in wartime may result in a shifting of power centers from where they now lie. The ability for non-state actors to take action in a warzone utilizing individuals or interacting in war environments in numerous other ways indicates a transition from traditional roles. In general, in war and combat situations, overall lethality is decreasing, and non-state conflicts (Over 1000 combatants) are increasing.[78] -Dr. Zalman, Dr. Hoffman, Dr. Gartzke, & Maj. Gen. Scales, 2018

Nations that have nuclear weapons inherently deter conventional warfare. In such, they are incentivized and motivated to utilize proxy warfare to achieve political goals. The ability for a state to hire a non-state armed group to attack an enemy in irregular warfare tactics is increased in these nuclear nations, as they will deter a conventional warfare response simply by having nuclear weapons. This creates a trend of ever-increasing amounts of unconventional actions between states, non-state groups, and even down to individuals.

"The military implications are obvious, if difficult to act upon in today's fiscal environment. There's a clear and continuing need for Marines, for amphibious units and naval supply ships, for platforms that allow operations in littoral and riverine environments, and for capabilities that enable expeditionary logistics in urbanized coastal environments. Rotary-

wing or tilt-rotor aircraft, and precise and discriminating weapons systems, will also be needed. There's also a clear need to structure ground forces so that they can rapidly aggregate or disaggregate forces and fires, enabling them to operate in a distributed, small-unit mode while still being able to concentrate quickly to mass their effect against a major target. Combat engineers, construction engineers, civil affairs units, intelligence systems that can make sense of the clutter of urban areas, pre-conflict sensing systems such as geospatial tools that allow early warning of conflict and instability, and constabulary and coast guard capabilities are also likely to be important. The ability to operate for a long period in a city without drawing heavily on that city's water, fuel, electricity, or food supply will be important as well, with very significant implications for expeditionary logistics."

– David Kilcullen[79]

The balance between endless growth of government to protect the population from foreign states and non-state actors and the fact that endless growth will inevitably lead to Orwellian dystopia, is one that will either be hammered out on a battlefield of immense complexity, or delicately threaded to form a balance between the needs of all the people. While cities in the United States are not likely to fall into the kind of struggles to be seen in Karachi or Mexico City in the very near future, the fact is that the connectivity of all major cities and their hinterlands will make it impossible to completely avoid the social and economic changes that happen in any city anywhere in the world. Building walls will no longer protect anyone. The new age of warfare will be fought far from conventional means and will involve highly trained small teams tasked to locations based on complex agendas to serve states, non-state actors, or even individuals. When civil war does erupt in the United States, it will be the states that secede and distinguish themselves as separate from the federal government that will prosper the most. Unburdened by international treaties and trade agreements, these sovereign states could commit to new agreements more suited to their populations needs and make alliances between each other to maintain military support for each other without sacrificing each states self-interest.

If you haven't noticed, Texas is *not* California, though that isn't stopping Californians from moving there and attempting to make it New California. Cities within states are *not* the state. Cities are composed of entirely different rules than the rural areas of any place. To live in a city is to become a dependent person immediately. To live in a rural location is to be forced to become independent to varying degrees. City-states could develop which would be a positive result, as they would not be able to make demands upon the surrounding lands, but rather be forced to become useful in trade with those lands. They could not expand indefinitely into the hinterlands, because they would be forced to concede to a boundary. How clear it is to anyone who has ever visited Austin, Texas, that a city can be culturally, economically, and philosophically incongruous to its surroundings. It is a disservice to people everywhere that cities and states share laws that affect each other in opposing ways.

If the United States were to fall into civil war, the real threat would not be our own government alone, but also the predatory nations and non-state actors that exist around the world that would take advantage of the disruption to attack us. What then can we do to both conquer domestic oppression by our government and protect ourselves against foreign attackers? We must consider firstly the worst-case scenario, which is that our own civil war would lead to a nation such as Russia, Iran, or China or all three and more invading and finally conquering the United States and taking it in the same fashion that the United States has taken advantage of Afghanistan, Iraq, Guatemala, and numerous other nations. That is, they would emplace a government that would act as puppet to the designs of that conquering nation. Our people, land, assets, military, and everything else being under the discretion of use of that entity. While I find this scenario extremely unlikely to ever actually occur, as states down to individuals would continue to fight any occupation successfully for quite a long time, probably outlasting any occupiers' abilities to maintain their grip, we must still look at worst case scenarios. The most likely version of any attack upon the United States is in rapid attacks upon key infrastructure that causes redistribution of assets and resources, leaving other areas open to attack, in a continual pressure that wears down the responsivity of the government. That same government would be compelled to fight on multiple fronts, both an internal war and a defensive war against highly advanced militaries and low-tech, highly tactically proficient insurgents. The threat of civil war would not only be between the federal government and the states, but also conflict between neighbor to neighbor, county to county, city to rural surrounds, racial territorialism, and lastly state to state and non-state to state.

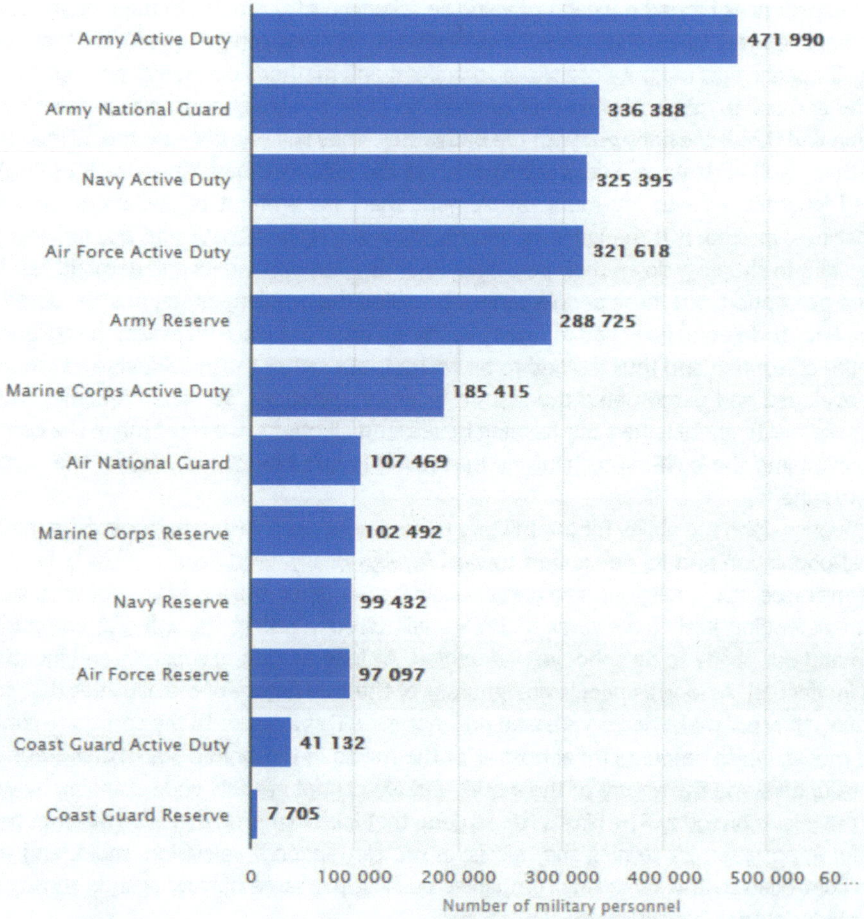

We need to implement a more socially responsible, educated, healthy and trained culture that encourages the public to join the military, become trained, and still live whatever lives they desire in civilian life. Imagine a rotating reserve force of five million people. The amount of people trained and prepared to gear up and ship out would increase our capabilities while reducing the budget required to maintain active personnel. If we reorganize the military to reflect more rotations more frequently, people could be transferred from fields of combat with efficiency and at the greater reward of the military as a whole. Our nation was founded on revolution.

The war for our liberation from an oppressive and constricting mercantilism and a tyrannical government was fought in the backyards and the streets of the revolutionary. Today, we could easily resolve many of our social problems by incentivizing the military as a technical profession and a rewarding experience that can be had while living normal lives when not active. This would serve to create a more informed and responsible gun owning population along with a higher level of personal responsibility amongst the general population. In both the military and the police, firearm education is lacking, but between the two, the military certainly provides a better education. Reservists could be trained extensively on firearms and safety and given plenty of resources and time to further their skill with their firearms. It would provide a way to inspire our younger generations to be involved, mature, and mentally and physically healthy members of our society. While many people might argue the point that the military breeds good results in society, that argument more often if not universally comes from people who have not participated in it.

In my own experiences I found a wealth of valuable takeaways from being in the military, and especially being a combat veteran. While this is true, I can easily say, as many others can as well, that I do not agree with many, if not the vast majority of policies, practices, and methods our nation and our military choose to engender and use to interact with other nations. So often people choose to take the easy way out of any situation and throw the baby out with the bathwater. They will say, because the military is involved in situations that result in death and destruction, then all the military is bad. These kinds of black and white opinionated ignorant resolves are more problematic than any amount of military action taken by any military that ever existed. It is the ignorant, dissonant, and very bombastic and opinionated people that are not hesitant in shouting down their perceived enemies and opponents and demand results to match their limited perception. But these people cannot be called the problem either. In a corrupted system like the one we have today, and have had for many years, we must not place blame on the children who grew up within the corruption and thus learned to be corrupt, but rather the individuals and groups that have devised, developed and perpetuated the system in all its limitations. So, when it comes to our military issues, just like our financial issues, our farming issues, and all others, we must make the corrections that resolve to eliminate the built-in mechanisms that result in our lack of success and the perpetuation of unnecessary suffering.

A direct influence upon the ability for our military to continually evolve and better itself is the condition of the general population and its perception toward foreign policy. While divisiveness is bred around the nation, pitting races, sexes, religions, and parties against each other, the world will not wait. Our success as a nation in defending itself from foreign threats will directly reflect the internal composition of our population and our ability to be cohesive and unified. As long as we are separate and indecisive, we are weak and ineffectual. As long as people are ignorant of the true nature of the activities that are occurring on this planet, they will make decisions based on ignorance. This leads us to the corporate controlled, self-interested media, which amounts for almost all of the media in the United States and around the world. We need to understand the nature of the world, and we cannot get this understanding by watching any media on the television today. The biases run so deep that it is oxymoronic to even attempt to gain insight into truthful information by turning the television on. Newspapers, television, radio, and much of the internet is controlled by the same few companies pushing the same narrow agenda through stringently tested psychological and behavioral manipulation.

So how do we get valid and timely information? I have found the best method to discern validity is to find independent reporters and compile information for yourself from observing the content that the people on the scene develop. Of course, many people will have bias at that level, but it is important see the conditions on the ground rather than the conditions on the privately owned set with teleprompted, indoctrinated and ignorantly emotional people that look more like manikins or cartoons than people. There are thousands of independent reporters that film on the ground all over the world. Find their content and learn what it actually looks like on the ground. Don't fight the corporate media, just ignore it. Turn off the propaganda machine by putting your attention on the factual information and the scientific approach. Give your attention to those who deserve it. We will either unite as a defensible nation or we will be divisive and divided by shallow arguments and unreal dangers fed and manufactured by intentional hysteria producing private interests. Unity breeds strength inherently.

We need to pay our military better. Private contractors who bear little to no accountability to their nation or their communities, are paid averages over six figures while the average military grunt is getting something between $20,000 and $50,000 annually and must be accountable to his nation and his community. A large number of contractors are prior military, police, or federal agents. Rather than encouraging this privatization of military force backed by government, would it not be better to incentivize career-making in the US military, combined with the transition of active-duty majority to national guard, reservist, and militia majority. An exceptionally large force could be maintained by allowing for alternating active-duty periods amongst a large population of people that have been trained and are continually being trained over the years of service that make very little interruption of their civilian life, including their education, their family life, their careers that develop their unique abilities to be even more useful soldiers. What if our military was composed of millions of people, but whom only had to be in service for one month of any year, rotating duties between them? We could pay our military service better and be fully equipped and ready at all times. Pay schedules would involve only periods of active duty, and benefits would be cumulative based on service, both temporally and by scale of risk assumed and real combat involvement.

But payment does not necessarily mean money alone. Instead, we can offer incentives that amount to great value and encourage people to join the military that otherwise would have not found interest. As the Romans did, we can offer our military personnel arable land after a certain amount of time served. We can offer free passive energy housing on bases to veterans, reservists, and even civilians who cultivate food and perform maintenance on bases, which will generate a higher level of resource fulfillment and sustainability to bases and eliminate their reliance on external sources. Multiple purposes can be satisfied by offering off-grid housing and living options on bases to veterans especially, as it will go a long way in reducing veteran suicide and homelessness. It will give meaning and purpose to veterans who are desperately seeking those things. By offering both land and on-base off-grid housing, we can incentivize much of the population to join. If we combine this with reducing our active personnel and increasing vastly our reservist personnel, we will see an increase in interest in the military. With a larger reservist force, we can have a constantly ready force, an informed and trained population, and a better managed budget.

While we pay our military subsistence wages, the bulk of personnel funding for global "war on terrorism" and other efforts is provided to mercenary groups called defense contractors. These agencies are non-state actors that provide physical and otherwise support for nations, primarily the United States, to conduct violent oppression of other nations and to promote the unjustified occupation of those same sovereign nations. These non-state, corporate actors are able to operate in the United States, against the people of the United States as easily as they can be called upon to serve U.S. interests in Iraq, Afghanistan, Yemen, Syria, Libya, or any other place they are contracted to work in. It is not irregular for an employee of a defense contractor to make 6-figure pay while soldiers make $20,000-$30,000 annually in a warzone during wartime.

Appendix A. Defense Spending: FY1950-2018

Figure A-1. DOD Spending in Historical Perspective, FY1950-FY2018

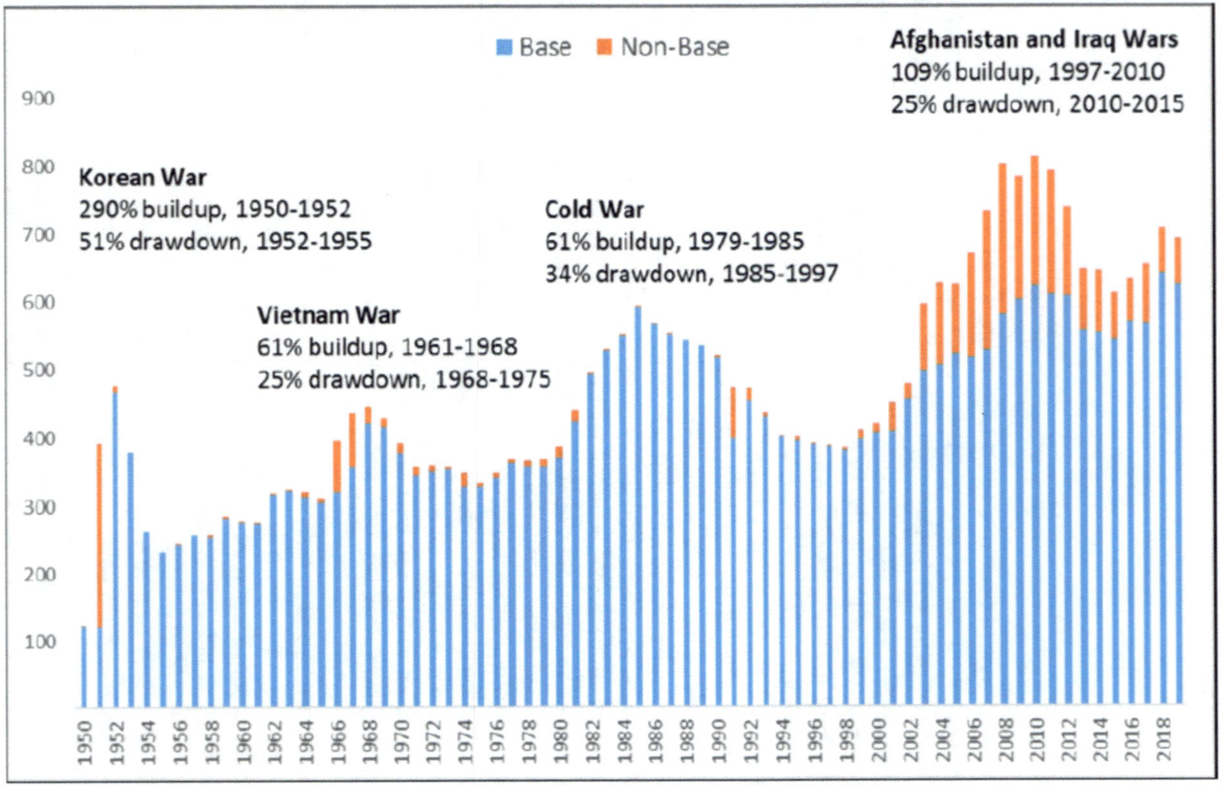

Source: Chart reproduced from CRS Report R44519, *Overseas Contingency Operations Funding: Background and Status*, by Brendan W. McGarry and Emily M. Morgenstern.

The military is potentially the most proficient money waster outside of politicians. It has almost no financial institutions and it does not have a fiduciary responsibility to keep accurate books. Enormous sums of money are lost and misused, and the public will never know where it went. Companies like Boeing, Raytheon, Lockheed Martin, Northrup Gruman, and General Dynamics are given hundreds of billions of dollars, and their CEO's make hundreds of millions of that. Bases that are no longer in service are forced to be maintained by the DoD by law since 2013. So much waste occurs, and so much could be done to enhance not only our military, but our society, if only we implemented a new structure. We need to end administrative waste, allow obsolete base closures, demand accountability by creating a public financial institution to maintain exact books, demand accountability from companies like those mentioned above, and reduce the militaries civilian workforce, unless other incentive programs like those mentioned above are created to offset direct costs. The civilian workforce can be maintained or even increased, which increases the quality of life for all people living on bases and creates better flow of military activity for higher efficiency, if we simply reorganize bases to become truly self-sustained.

The society within the military can be improved in various ways that will not only incentivize more recruitment but will enhance its performance. We can improve military society by eliminating restrictions altogether on the growing and maintaining of beards excluding in situations where the beard would interfere with necessary duties. We need to recognize what the military is there to do. It is not a video game or novel. The composition and conduct of the military has a real and direct effect upon the wellbeing of the nation. The military is the sword of the nation when needed as well as the shield. It exists to buffer violence from the general population. It exists to fight necessary wars and is composed of volunteers from amongst the population. We need to allow our military to be as advanced and flexible as it possibly can while only activating it when and where it is needed for the caretaking and wellbeing of the nation. If we consider the nature of warfare today, we must understand that the reach of violence has grown. Due to the greater reach of this violence, our military must be able to respond quickly, efficiently, and successfully to foreign threats.

The military needs to be maintained and respected. On the flip side of this, we the people, who make up the military must be ready, able, and willing to defend against tyranny and oppression from within. For many generations, we have been subjected to incremental takeovers of our society and removal of our Constitutional Rights and our human rights. Mostly this has not been hidden from the public, but rather it has been a slow encroachment in which the people have given away their rights for unsatisfied promises for greater wellbeing or security. Our military is not a tool of the government to wield for private interests, it is a tool of the public to defend themselves from real threats to their wellbeing. We need to recognize the corrupted government and deny them the authority to wield the military when that authority is abused. This knowledge and empowerment must be taught to the military, rather than blind obedience and servility despite the nature of the commander and the government. This may or may not be possible due to the fact that the military leadership is directly politically involved and thus just as likely to be corrupted as the average politician undoubtedly is.

Our military is not a separate entity from our population, but it is to a certain degree unrepresentative of the entire population. New England has a relatively low recruitment rate compared with any other part of the nation. The Southeastern states have the highest representative number of enlistees. Enlistment age individuals from Florida, Georgia and Maine are twice as likely to enlist than those from North Dakota or Utah. The vastly greater number of enlistees come from the South. This disproportionate recruitment means that the culture within the United States military is predominantly influenced by these highly represented States. Another way of looking at this is that the military is composed of people who have preference for military service as well as those that are culturally supportive of the military.

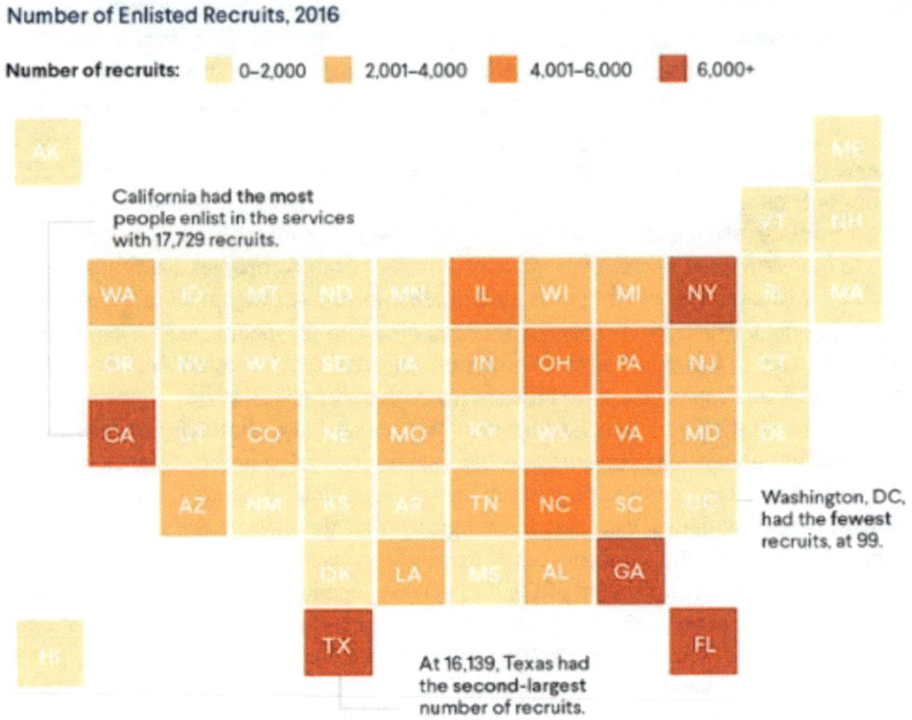

We need to increase pay and offer further incentives to make enlistment a preferable choice to a wider range of potential recruits in the population, especially amongst technically proficient sectors of the population.

We need to release the budget of all intelligence agencies in the United States. Congressional Committees need to directly monitor and audit the activities of the intelligence community. Congress specifically needs to audit the intelligence community to determine what, when, why, where, and how activities or programs have targeted the American population. Intelligence gathering on specific targets of interest that have shown patterns of risk behavior that could harm the population in some way and gathering intelligence on the entire population regardless of criminal or innocent activity, the government has no right or excuse to surveille its own population. In fact, in the United States, we have it written into the bones of our laws, the constitution, that no government interference is permittable where there is not prior reasonable evidence of criminal activity. Our government excuses itself by using legalese and interpretations built upon other interpretations of the law that eventually eradicate the bounds of their given powers. Releasing all intelligence budgets open source, including historical budgets, where regards the use of assets to target the American population, would reduce some of the harm, as the accounting of these transactions would hold those who benefitted directly from harming their own nation to account. Congress is not truly capable of being accountable to the population and is equally as corrupted as the intelligence agencies that have violated their constitutional oaths and the people of this so-called free nation where people are nearer to thought crime and future crime punishments than they can imagine. 1984 in 2026 perhaps.

Some number of violations by the intelligence agencies have been made publicly accessible by whistleblowers like Edward Snowden and many others. The public now has the proof of abuse by the government to evoke a revolution, and yet the public is mostly ignorant of the fact that Edward Snowden even exists beyond some fleeting bite-sized media coverage that discourages further investigation.

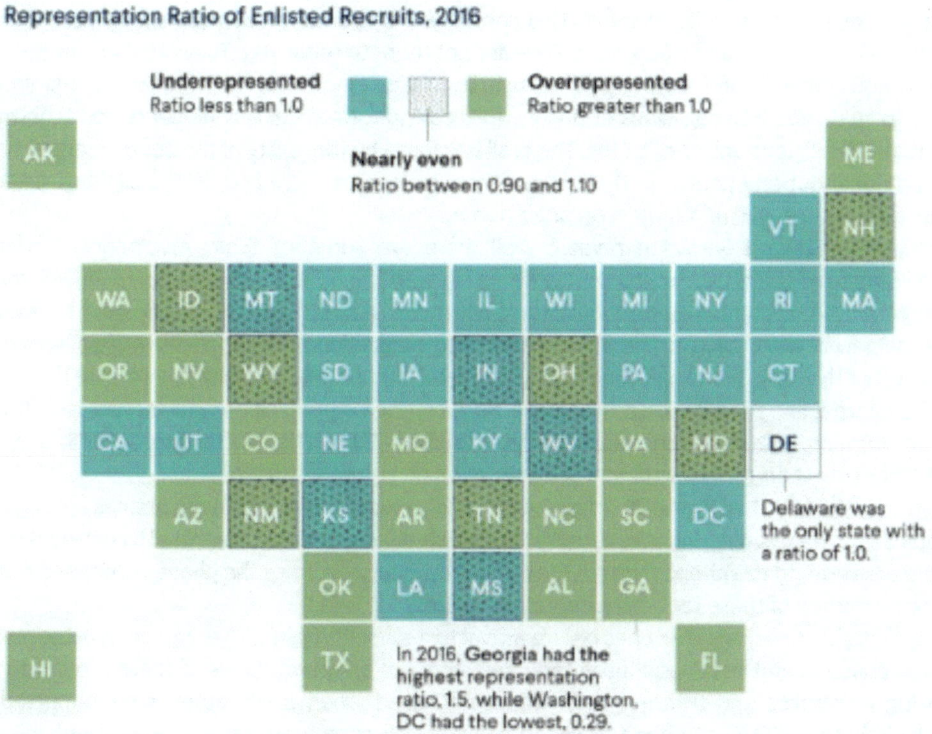

What is the balance between the public and thus the world knowing what the military and agencies of government are doing, and the protection of the people from abusive foreign entities, whether they be nations or stateless? The greatest threat to any population in all of history has been its own government. Thus, the clear order of operations ought to be for any population to guard itself from that entity, and to secure it to the greatest extent possible before moving on to the challenges posed by foreign nations and others. When the nation itself is secured internally, then the population can consider its neighbors and the threats they pose. Firstly, the population must be free from the state having the potential to cause great death and suffering to the people. Secondly, the people must have security in small cells, thus keeping diversity of responsivity alive. This means that townships and villages, and cities, and finally states maintain their sovereignty to the degree that they can defend themselves instantly from the aggressions and demands of the institution that claims greater authority. These two tenets will allow for the nation to be kept from internal genocide and other types of harm perpetrated by centralized governments.

One uncomplicated way to provide for the first tenet, taking away central governments potential, is to disregard all firearms laws entirely and affirm that the clear right to bear *any type* of arms includes those that could be used by the population to defend against missiles, tanks, UAVs, and other modern military technology and firepower. Besides solving the problem of one's own central government potentially seeking to drone strike the population, you also provide the greatest barrier to any foreign powers ability to conquer the population, as every person in your nation potentially has more firepower at their fingertip than a squad or platoon of the enemy has. I'd feel quite a bit safer if I knew my neighbor had an anti-aircraft missile launcher in his shed, but that's just me. Perhaps this wouldn't work everywhere though. I will talk later about the differences between city and rural populations and the ways in which the laws might be framed to better suit these distinct cultures.

We must remember to focus on problems in the correct order, rather than the ones that get shouted the loudest by puppets on the television. What the tell-a-vision does today, mostly, is serve the interests of the very same gatekeepers and social engineers that control the entire spread of major media coverage, even those channels that seem so indie and fresh. They are not there to serve you. They are there to direct your attention various objects and events and to use linguistic, emotional, and behavioral manipulation techniques to guide you into conscious or unconscious conclusions about world events, social norms and even spiritual and religious universal truths. This is all bolstered by the ability of the government to harness any information about any person in the United States so long as there is even the slightest use of the internet or even the use of smart meters on one's home.

What exactly did Edward Snowden reveal? Well, here are some of those revelations. Virtually all telephone companies share their customers information with the NSA. A program called PRISM, makes it possible for the NSA to compel Google, Facebook, Microsoft, Apple, and other companies to release to them user data from their servers. The Government Communications Headquarters (GCHQ), which is the British version of the NSA, teams with the NSA to tap fiber optic cables globally to intercept data flowing through the internet in a program called Tempora. Some of the companies that collaborate with Tempora are Verizon Business, British Telecommunications, Vodafone Cable, Global Crossing, Level 3, Viatel, and Interoute. They collect enormous amounts of information on all internet users.

GCHQ, and thus the NSA, has the ability to control people's phones, even while the phones are turned off. The various things they can do include, turning phones on or off remotely, listening to conversations and noise in the area around the phone through the phones microphone, track the phones position constantly, and hide the presence of these tools from detection by users.

The NSA can intercept package deliveries before arrival to a person's home. They can open these packages and observe contents and install espionage tools and software programs. Some of these tools include the ability to log keystrokes and transmit them wirelessly, even when a computer is disconnected from internet, to imitate a GSM cell phone tower to monitor cell communications, the ability to inject and monitor device data via radio waves, the ability to transmit cell phone geolocation through secret text messages, and to hack computers and provide remote access through mimicking USB and ethernet connectors. These tools allow the NSA to invade almost any type of prevention measures to protect and secure one's privacy.

The NSA collects email and contact lists from internet and smartphone users that amounts to potentially 250 million contact lists annually. The Boundless Informant (BOUNDLESSINFORMANT) is an NSA code name for a data analysis tool that tracks all metadata collected by the NSA globally and makes a heatmap of that data to indicate locations and target countries. Billions of pieces of information were being collected every month, with billions of data pieces collected in the U.S., despite the NSA declaring it did not gather data on Americans and didn't even have the capacity to do so. A project named Bullrun used a variety of hacking tools, like Brute-Force Attacks to invade encryption systems like HTTPS and SSL, which are used for online banking and purchases across the internet. This was part of the greater project to decrypt the internet entirely to prevent anyone or any entity from being able to secure and privately hold information. Even the opening of apps on your phone, like games, can provide NSA access to your personal data, like name, age, sex, email, and geolocation. Some of the worst offenders are Twitter, Google Maps, Flickr, Facebook, Instagram, and Pinterest.

Another project of the NSA, revealed by Snowden, is XKeyscore. This program is a tool that allows the NSA to search all user activity on the internet. The NSA destabilizes and bypasses encryption technologies used by private people and companies by forcing companies to install backdoors, hacking into servers and computers, and promoting weak algorithmic encryption technology use. The Tailored Access Operations (TAO) are an elite unit of hackers employed by the NSA to hack computers, infect them with malware and other types of invasions. They are the black bag team of the NSA. The NSA also has infiltrated the links connecting Google and Yahoo data centers when they could not get access legally. The NSA collects over 200 million text messages daily through Project Dishfire.

"I don't want to live in a world where everything I say, everything I do, everyone I talk to, every expression of creativity and love or friendship is recorded."
-Edward Snowden

On September 2nd, 2020, a three-judge panel of the United States Court of Appeals for the 9th Circuit ruled that "the metadata collection exceeded the scope of Congress's authorization ... which required the government to make a showing of relevance to a particular authorized investigation before collecting the records..."[80] This ruling does not indicate the actual removal of the NSA tools or the deactivation of them, but reflects the court decision to refute the legality of the tools and actions. What NSA does could be anything from the end of surveillance or a simple a process of hiding their activities deeper in the amalgams of the legal justifications they use to practice surveillance in any way on Americans and the rest of the world. Seeing as their behavior shows a fundamental pattern of conduct that aims to inspect all people in total intimacy, it is almost insane to believe they will not be progressing on the path of technological and physical invasion. The decision only reflects one aspect of the NSA collection anyway.

A couple of the agencies that work with the NSA and other government intelligence agencies are Raytheon and Booz Allen Hamilton. These agencies are the equivalent of Academi and Titan Corp, but instead of working as military contractors, they are cyber security contractors. In the end these amount to the same thing, as cyber warfare is the task at hand in regard to the hiring of Booz Allen Hamilton, Raytheon and other private agencies. It is often a cyber war on the people of any target nation, including the U.S., at the behest of the government, domestic or foreign.

I do not mean to impugn the governments of the world alone in this, but to also criticize the growing data collection that exists in private business hands that can be easily mishandled. We know that it is possible for a service to exist like google, without the need for them to have access to the personal information of its users. It is completely possible that these companies formulate their products to work for the people, anonymous to the creators of the programs. They do not do this because their business model is invasion, collection, and dissemination to the highest bidder. These mega-servers that store user data can be eliminated completely in the service to the people and have no effect on the ability of the product to serve the people. It is possible, and very probable, that an even greater threat than NSA data collection exists when that data is in the hands of these monopolist, banker-affiliate, plutocratic business moguls. How will they use this information but to influence the population of the world to conform to their will? And when we really look at this problem, can it not be seen that Google and NSA are one and the same. The Plutocracy exists, and it will operate through whatever medium presents itself to achieve its ultimate and immediate goals. Of course, we are always the hopeful, docile population, who will await the decree of our masters, the state, and its friends the monopolists, are we not?

When we know that we are being surveilled universally and that our constitutional and human rights have been circumvented and intentionally violated, what makes the public shrug it off and continue to support the system? It is an amalgam of decisions made by mostly subconsciously weighing the cost/benefit ratio of taking action against the government. It is easier to continue as if the information did not exist and that the government was not doing what it is now proven to be doing. It is easier to continue to go to work and school and perpetuate the system if it means the uncomfortable confrontation with our government and our ignorant neighbors can be avoided. It is largely indoctrinated cowardice and docility. It is the effect of the mass surveillance itself, along with other factors such as political and private industry collusion.

We need to increase funding to research and development in the creation of technologies that can reduce the possibility for wars to manifest. DARPA, among others, needs to be empowered to a great extent to produce these technologies, as they are perfectly placed for this cause. We need to focus more attention on technology that will inhibit war rather than technology that will fight one. We need technology that can serve the advancement of the population as well as create defense systems to meet the demands of security from modern threats. While some technologies and research must remain secret to the world for security reasons, much of the technologies can also be used for the public wellbeing. There must be interactions with universities, labs, and public agencies to produce these technologies for the betterment of the public and the planet. We need a reduction in arms production to match the needs of the United States alone thus ending the sale of arms to foreign countries, pending an audit by Congress observed by human rights organizations. All sales of arms must be publicly and explicitly declared, with statements from officials on the purpose and intended effect of the arms. All this can be done, but the likelihood of its success is almost zero. We have a corrupted Congress, and thus we must ask, who audits the auditors. It seems we must establish a system for ensuring the total transparency of our Congress before we can proceed with these and other programs for auditing. Again, the likelihood of success is nearly zero. Those with power are extremely unlikely to relieve themselves of it willingly.

DHS

The Department of Homeland Security, or DHS, is a cabinet department of the U.S. Federal Government with responsibilities in public security, including anti-terrorism, immigration, border security and customs, cyber-security, and disaster prevention and management, created in response to 9/11 in November 2002. Supposedly comparable to Interior or Home ministries of other countries. The DHS is the third Largest Cabinet Department after DOD and Veterans Affairs. The DHS includes the Coast Guard, Customs and Border Protection, Secret Service, TSA, and FEMA. It has over 240,000 full-time workers and a 2021 budget of $197.9 Billion.[81] Originally created to prevent terrorist attacks on US soil, the DHS has grown into the most hostile, invasive, criminal, fanatic, and unaccountable agency in the United States. The agency has purchased enough ammunition to date to wage constant war for over 20 years, with more stockpiled ammunition than that appropriated to the U.S. military. DHS trains police agencies to militarize and mesh with federal controllers.

The Federal Emergency Management Agency (FEMA), an agency within the DHS, was created in the 1970's under President Carter. It is an amalgam of the disaster relief agencies that existed prior, with the focus of prevention and response to disaster emergencies. FEMA is documented and has been verifiably building American detention/internment/concentration camps.

> *"...in 2006, it was announced that Kellogg Brown and Root, a subsidiary of Halliburton, had been awarded a $385 million contract to build American detention facilities. Although the government and Halliburton were not forthcoming about where or when these domestic detention centers would be built, they rationalized the need for them in case of 'an emergency influx of immigrants,* or to support the rapid development of new programs' *in the event of other emergencies such as 'natural disasters.'"*
>
> \- John Whitehead[82]

A database called "Main Core" contains information on over 8 million, as of 2008, Americans who are considered potentially dangerous threats to the government. Both left and right wing "extremists" are included in that list, including animal rights activists and libertarians, and military veterans returning from Iraq and Afghanistan. By now, you are likely to be on this list, especially if you are reading books like this one. Constitutional defenders, bulk food purchasers, and gun owners are prime targets on this list. DHS has funded and incentivized the surveillance network that extends across the country and is becoming ever more invasive and inescapable, scanning images for license plates and biometrically for facial recognition en masse. Stingray devices allow local police agencies, let alone the DHS and other federal agencies, to track cell phones and their users wherever they go and create track records of movement and interaction. DHS Checkpoints on roads and VIPR task forces at "soft targets" like malls and stadiums make random, forced, illegal ID checks and create a pervasive atmosphere of fear and anxiety in the public, producing chronic docility in the weak and stupid and growing disaffection in the intelligent, willful, and resilient. The strict bureaucratic and hierarchical nature of today's national police force, structured like the military, with less accountability and more murder, makes our nation and thus the world a far more dangerous place for the people of today, and more importantly for the people who will inherit the results of a police state. Just ask the Poles or Cossacks.

"The menace of a national police force, a literal standing army, vested with massive power cannot be overstated, nor can its danger be ignored. Indeed, just about every nefarious deed, tactic, or thuggish policy advanced by the government today can be traced back to the DHS, its police state mindset, and the billions of dollars it distributes to police agencies in the form of grants... Historically, the establishment of a national police force has served as a fundamental building block for every totalitarian regime that has ever wreaked havoc on humanity...the calling cards of these national police agencies remain the same: brutality, inhumanity, corruption, intolerance, rigidity, and bureaucracy—in other words, evil."

– John W. Whitehead[83]

Rex-84 was the code name for militaristic training in the 1980's, created and facilitated by the DOD and FEMA, in how to counter domestic civil unrest. 34 different federal agencies participated.

We need to conduct a universal audit by Congress to determine human rights violations and violations of citizens' rights in the US, observed by a human rights organization. This department needs to be renamed. The history of the reference to the Homeland and the purpose of the agency, reflects the Nazi Party in Germany, and a statism and nationalism which used the term in its actions violating human rights. We need to reduce the size of the agency, eliminate it altogether or reallocate the assets and focus of the agency. The three largest cabinets being those that support military action, police state activity and the people that are harmed by those things, indicate a flawed structure. We do not need more police enforcement. We do not need TSA molestation of children, or adults, at airports. Today, the TSA has the means and authority to run searches on travelers extending deep into their personal life, including prior flight itineraries, property records and other personal information. They have implemented body scanners that emit harmful radiation and take extremely intimate, detailed images of travelers.

We need to reduce these agencies to reflect the reality of the needs of the nation rather than the indoctrinated story of our situation spouted on the privately owned news channels and the bought and paid for political establishment of today. If the government is the only part of society that has the authority to abuse people and violate their constitutional and inherent rights, we the people need to remember why the second amendment exists.

There is no justification for engaging in warfare without provable provocation that threatens the safety of a population. I will speak more on interventionism later, but the act of interfering in other nations for selfish interests is a violation of the human rights of the people. Humanitarian propaganda has paved the way for the United States and other nations to invade and destroy nation after nation and bend them to their will. If we can say it was wrong for Britain to flush Chinese markets with opium to induce a crisis through addiction, which they did, we can equally say that the United States interfering in the economies, politics, and other social aspects of other nations to those nations' detriment and subjugation, is as heinous and wrong or worse as it means we are continuing to utilize these practices century after century for ill-gotten selfish gains.

"Clausewitz thought that the use of absolute war or total war would be counter to the desired political ends of a war, thus making limited war preferable to meet limited political

ends. But we've seen however that the NATO alliance has gone beyond seeking limited political ends. Vis-à-vis, its state enemies. They now seek a state's total annihilation, and they are therefore willing to use absolute war without limits to achieve that. This use of absolute war has even extended into the legal realm. One American legal academic, David Kennedy, at Harvard, said in a paper discussing hybrid warfare, that warfare has become a legal institution and that therefore the rules of war, while limiting conduct in war, also positively permit the killing of people as a function of that institution... over the centuries we've tried to place rules and limits on the methods and weapons that can be used. But the rules enshrined into various Geneva Conventions and the Nuremburg Principles governing superior responsibility are more designed for conventional war and are more difficult to apply practically in hybrid war. Hybrid war blurs the distinctions between combatants and non-combatants. For instance, an obvious example is a civilian computer operator engaged in cyber warfare or a civilian contractor working somewhere in the United States operating a drone which drops a bomb on a wedding party in Afghanistan. Is that person a combatant or a civilian? (If) he's a combatant, he's subject to... retaliation. If he's a civilian, he should be protected. What is his status?... The blurring of these lines is a justification for committing war crimes against civilians. Now NATO irregular forces, generally, are not subject to military discipline... they use Blackwater mercenaries, and other, what they call, contractors...the command structures are more fluid, enforcing discipline is very difficult, and the rules are more and more difficult to apply, and punishing them, their officers, for crimes is more difficult to prove, chase them down, and even identify them. Their chain of command is not clear and even the identity of commanders are often not known... who is responsible for their actions? Is it the corporation, is it the shareholders of the corporation, the director of the corporation, or the United States government which ordered the actions and engaged those men? This is not at all clear and not defined in the codified law. (Vague rules of warfare are) an attempt to evade the laws of war by obscuring them and totally negating them. Now we see this attempt to blur the legal lines with the use of the word, for instance, terrorism, to describe an armed attack by combatants against U.S. forces, or other approved forces. This means an act of war is redefined as a criminal act and so the combatants are not entitled to be treated as combatants but neither are they treated as ordinary criminals, they are placed outside of all legal norms and subject to arbitrary punishments and torture and execution. It also obscures the causes of the attack, the political objective of the attack and denies there is one. This clouds all analysis of events and leads to false conclusions in action. We also see this, where NATO has tried to justify its illegal actions through the use of criminal indictments issued by controlled tribunals to attack and delegitimize enemy leaders as heads of state. We saw that with Gaddafi, Milosevic, Saddam Hussein, as you've seen it against Laurent Gbagbo and others in Africa. We see it also with the phrase humanitarian interventions, creating and using false morality to justify immoral and illegal wars. We see it in the creation of the construct of the war on terror. A war on tactic, not an idea, to justify... any and all operations that are outside permitted legal actions of war. We see it expressed at Guantanamo Bay in Cuba, with the Americans redefining prisoners of war as unlawful combatants, to avoid proper treatment of prisoners of war pursuant to the Geneva Conventions... the whole purpose of international law and humanitarian law is to make sure civilians and combatants are protected and that war is eliminated and abolished... and the American attempt to try to negate international law is a crime against humanity and I think it should be regarded as such and exposed as such."

- Christopher Black: Limited and Absolute War: Clausewitz and NATO Aggression – Theory and Reality, Jan 26, 2016[84]

Terrorism is defined variably by different sources as...

a. *the systematic use of terror especially as a means of coercion* – Merriam-Webster
b. *the calculated use of violence to create a general climate of fear in a population and thereby to bring about a particular political objective* – Encyclopedia Britannica
c. *Criminal acts intended or calculated to provoke a state of terror in the general public, a group of persons or particular persons for political purposes are in any circumstance unjustifiable, whatever the considerations of a political, philosophical, ideological, racial, ethnic, religious or any other nature that may be invoked to justify them.* – U.N. General Assembly

' Terrorism' may well be the most politicized term in the political vocabulary these days. Used as a label for a certain form of political violence, it reflects, if it 'sticks', negatively on a political opponent, demonizing him and de-legitimizing his conduct. In its pejorative dimension. The fate of the term 'terrorist' is comparable to the use and abuse of other terms in political vocabulary - terms like 'racist', 'fascist' or ' imperialist'. As one author, Philip Herbst, put it,
"Carrying enormous emotional freight. terrorism is often used to define reality in order to place one's own group on a high moral plane, condemn the enemy. rally members around a cause, silence or shape policy debate, and achieve a wide variety of agendas.... Terrorist became the mantra of our time, carrying a similar negative charge as communist once did. Like that word, it tends to divide the world simplistically into those who are assigned the stigma and those who believe themselves above it. Conveying criminality, illegitimacy, and even madness, the application of terrorist shuts the door to discussion about the stigmatized group or with them. while reinforcing the righteousness of the labelers, justifying their agendas and mobilizing their responses."
- Schmid, Alex P., "The Definition of Terrorism". The Routledge Handbook of Terrorism Research. Routledge. p. 39[85]

Before September 11, 2001, the number of terrorist events worldwide were insubstantial compared to the number of events that followed. In death tolls in the last 30 years, terrorism has never produced the equivalent of suicide (>1%) or drug disorders (>.2%) or even come close, as its highest rate was .08% of global deaths in 2014.[86] The direct statistical correlation that exists between the War on Terror, instituted after 9/11, and the increase in reported global terrorism activity is undeniable and obvious to the extreme. Without a doubt, the cause of the increase in terrorism by its current definition and use, is the creation of the War on Terror and the methods by which the United States primarily chose to interact with nations around the world, with extreme prejudice towards middle eastern Islamic countries, as it had dealt before with Central American Sovereign States, like Nicaragua, Southeast Asian Countries, as in Vietnam, and Eastern European Countries, as in Kosovo, just to name a few, though the term applied was communists, fascists, or any other controlled demonizing terminology.
Even though the rise in terrorism has occurred strategically over the last 20 years, almost humorously, it has not led to significant enough loss of life to justify the incredibly massive funding that has been delegated to war and "Homeland Security". Why would the country require TSA to molest our nation's youth to prevent planes being used as missiles, when a nominally intelligent person could devise a thousand ways to blow up a building without needing a plane in the first place. The TSA hasn't prevented a

single terrorist event. What they have done extremely well is show just how docile the population of Americans is today. They have been one more slice of our constitutional and human rights cut out.

Terrorism is a joke. If we want to be afraid of something because it may, *may,* kill us, we need look no further than cardiovascular disease and cancer which amount to between 40 and 50 percent of all deaths in the US. We don't need to be at war with "terrorists", but we do need to end the chronic diseases that are running rampant through our society due to environmental manipulation and commercial greed and apathy. It does not take a brilliant mind to see the depravity of our societal norms. It only takes a small amount of courage to look at things outside of the box in which we are forced to conform.

"Terrorism" has now been around for the entire life of the world's population of people 20 and younger. The war on terror, having never reduced the threat of attacks or produced a single notable positive effect on the wellbeing of any population of people on the planet, has in fact made our world considerably more dangerous. It has allowed the corporate governments to centralize even more than they already were and to consolidate internationally to become ever more dominant in deciding the fates of individual people around the globe. Larger central government with little to no real accountability and less represented and affirmed rights of the people amounts to one thing in any timeline, and that is slavery. The inevitable fate of the population of the world, and most potently the United States, is the realization that they have never stopped being slaves. That they have been influenced and manipulated for generations beyond count, and that in that moment of insight and revelation, they realize it is too late. They have already given the rights that protected them away in exchange for the insincere and deceptive empty promises of puppets on a screen.

Or...

The population comes to realize it's been duped and rises together to build a better world.

"I am not terrified of the terrorists; i.e., I am not, myself, terrorized. Rather, I am terrified of the terrorized; terrified of the bovine masses who are so easily manipulated by terrorists, governments, and the terror-amplifying media into allowing our country to slip toward totalitarianism and total war."

– Dan Sanchez

"Considering Islamic terror killing an average of 3.2 Americans per year (45 deaths divided by 14 years) since late 2001, here are ten causes of death more worthy of their fear:

1. Television: TV might be linked to earlier deaths among those who watch more than a few hours a day, but more concretely, the devices themselves kill 176 people a year. Literally. They fall on people. That's 55 times more deaths than Islamic terror claims annually.

2. Fireworks: According to the Consumer Product Safety Commission, celebrating the 4th of July might be more deadly than Islamic terror attacks. The organization reports an average of 7.1 deaths per year — meaning Americans are more likely to blow themselves up than be eviscerated by the jihadist bombers they so fear.

3. Cows: Yes, cows. According to the CDC, cattle slay an average of 20 Americans every year. While these deaths occur mostly among farm workers, dogs kill 28 Americans per year, spiders kill seven, and venomous lizards and snakes kill six. All of these animals are still more likely to kill an American than the caliphate and other Islamic boogeymen.

4. Elevators: While the fear of dying as a result of an elevator malfunction has probably plagued many Americans at one time or another, such a worry is likely fleeting. However, if Americans are truly concerned with "common sense," a virtue Donald Trump frequently touts, they would do well to readjust their phobias. Elevators kill 27 Americans per year, according to the U.S. Bureau of Labor Statistics and the Consumer Product Safety Commission.

5. Choking: Americans will sooner perish from choking on food or other objects than from an Islamic terror attack. At least 2,500 people per year are killed by this type of asphyxiation — 781 times more than from a jihadi assault. Hot dogs are particularly menacing. Perhaps we should ban them in the same vein as Trump's proposed ban on Muslims. Then again, killing fewer cows to grind up for beef dogs might lead to an uptick in cattle-on-human violence. America is at a perilous crossroads.

6. Lightning: People often quip that one is "more likely to be struck by lightning" when they want to highlight an event's improbability. However, even as the number of deaths from lightning decreases over the long-term, it is still higher than the number of people killed by Muslim terror attacks each year. Forty-nine people per year die from being struck by lightning — more than 15 times the rate of death from Islamic extremist murders.

7. Car accidents: Though most Americans are aware of the high risk of death by car accident, this knowledge doesn't mitigate their extreme Islamophobia. The Association for Safe International Road Travel estimates about 37,000 Americans die each year in vehicular accidents, over 11,562 times the number killed by Muslim fanatics.

8. Heart Attacks: Heart attacks are one of America's leading killers, claiming 190,625 times more American lives than Islamic terror. 610,000 Americans die from heart attacks per year. Cancer kills 589,430 Americans annually, and diabetes is the main cause of death for 69,071 Americans per year. They are responsible for astronomically more fatalities than radical Islamic terror.

9. Police: According to a three-year average of American police killings logged by killedbypolice.net — a more comprehensive database than the federal government's — police killed 998 people on average per year from 2013-2015. That's roughly 312 times the average annual number of people killed by Islamic extremists since 9/11. The average number of people killed by Islamic terrorism in the last three years is 7.7 — including the recent shooting in San Bernardino — and by that parallel measure, police are still about 130 times deadlier than terrorists.

10. Prescription Painkillers: The CDC estimates that 44 people die per day from overdosing on pharmaceutical painkillers. Never mind that that number is almost 14 times the number of Americans killed by Islamic terrorism each year. Based on the CDC's figure, about 16,060 Americans die annually from painkillers — making the Big-Pharma money-makers 5,019 times more deadly than the Islamic terror that has Americans trembling whilst hiding under their blankies.

Other notable risks of death greater than an Islamic terror attack include scalding tap water, which kills 100 American per year; bad medical care, estimated to be responsible for at least 100,000 deaths in the U.S. annually; and hypothermia, which kills 1,340 Americans per year. Oh, and don't forget Christmas trees. Fires caused by Christmas trees kill roughly ten people every year. Are Christmas trees conspiring with their lights to traitorously wage war on Christians via suicidal self-combustion?

-Carey Wedler, 10 Things More Likely to Kill You Than Islamic Terror, The Anti Media, 2015

The Nazis had a name for their propaganda and mind-control operations: Weltanschauungskrieg– "world view warfare." As good students, they had learned many tricks of the trade from their American teachers, including Sigmund Freud's nephew, Edward Bernays, who had honed his propagandistic skills for the United States during World War I and had subsequently started the public relations industry in New York City, an

industry whose raison d'être from the start was to serve the interests of the elites in manipulating the public mind.
In 1941, U.S. Intelligence translated Weltanschauungskrieg as "psychological warfare," a phrase that fails to grasp the full dimensions of the growing power and penetration of U.S. propaganda, then and now. Of course, the American propaganda apparatus was just then getting started on an enterprise that has become the epitome of successful world view warfare programs, a colossal beast whose tentacles have spread to every corner of the globe and whose fabrications have nestled deep within the psyches of many hundreds of millions of Americans and people around the world. And true to form in this circle game of friends helping friends, this propaganda program was ably assisted after WW II by all the Nazis secreted into the U.S. ("Operation Paperclip") by Allen Dulles and his henchmen in the OSS and then the CIA to make sure the U.S. had operatives to carry on the Nazi legacy (see David Talbot's The Devil's Chessboard: Allen Dulles, The CIA, and The Rise of America's Secret Government, an extraordinary book that will make your skin crawl with disgust).
-Edward Curtin, Psychological Warfare: The CIA Then and Now: Old Wine in New Bottles, GlobalResearch[87]

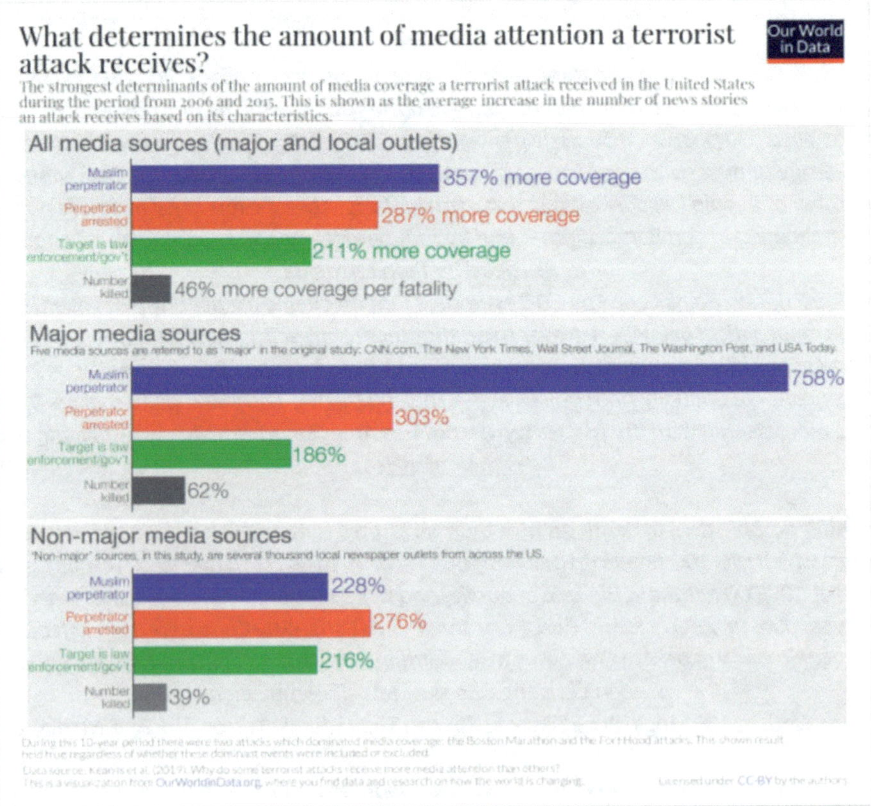

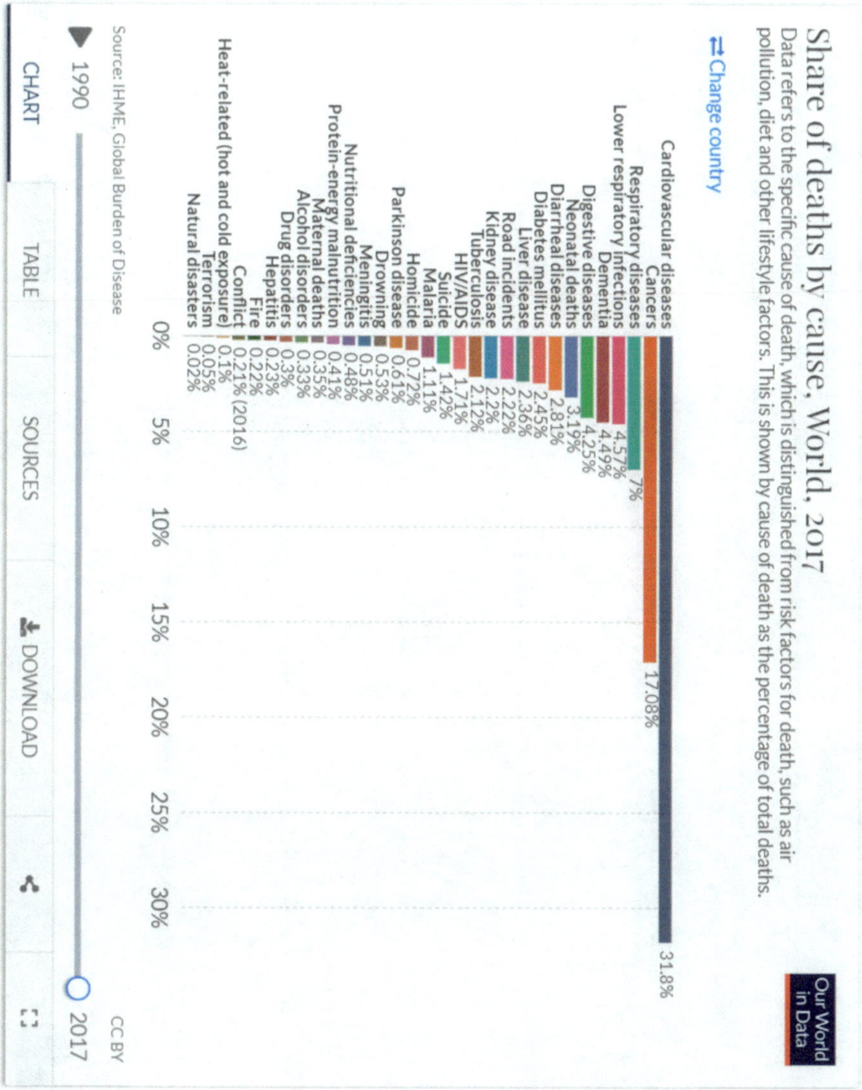
Share of deaths by cause, World, 2017
Data refers to the specific cause of death, which is distinguished from risk factors for death, such as air pollution, diet and other lifestyle factors. This is shown by cause of death as the percentage of total deaths.
Our World in Data
Change country
Cardiovascular diseases 31.8%
Cancers 17.08%
Respiratory diseases 7%
Lower respiratory infections 4.57%
Dementia 4.49%
Digestive diseases 4.25%
Neonatal deaths 3.19%
Diarrheal diseases 2.81%
Diabetes mellitus 2.45%
Liver disease 2.36%
Road incidents 2.22%
Kidney disease 2.2%
Tuberculosis 2.12%
HIV/AIDS 1.71%
Suicide 1.42%
Malaria 1.11%
Homicide 0.72%
Parkinson disease 0.61%
Drowning 0.53%
Meningitis 0.51%
Nutritional deficiencies 0.48%
Protein-energy malnutrition 0.41%
Maternal deaths 0.35%
Alcohol disorders 0.33%
Drug disorders 0.3%
Hepatitis 0.23%
Fire 0.22%
Conflict 0.21% (2016)
Heat-related (hot and cold exposure) 0.1%
Terrorism 0.05%
Natural disasters 0.02%
0%
5%
10%
15%
20%
25%
30%
Source: IHME, Global Burden of Disease
CC BY
1990
2017
CHART
TABLE
SOURCES
DOWNLOAD

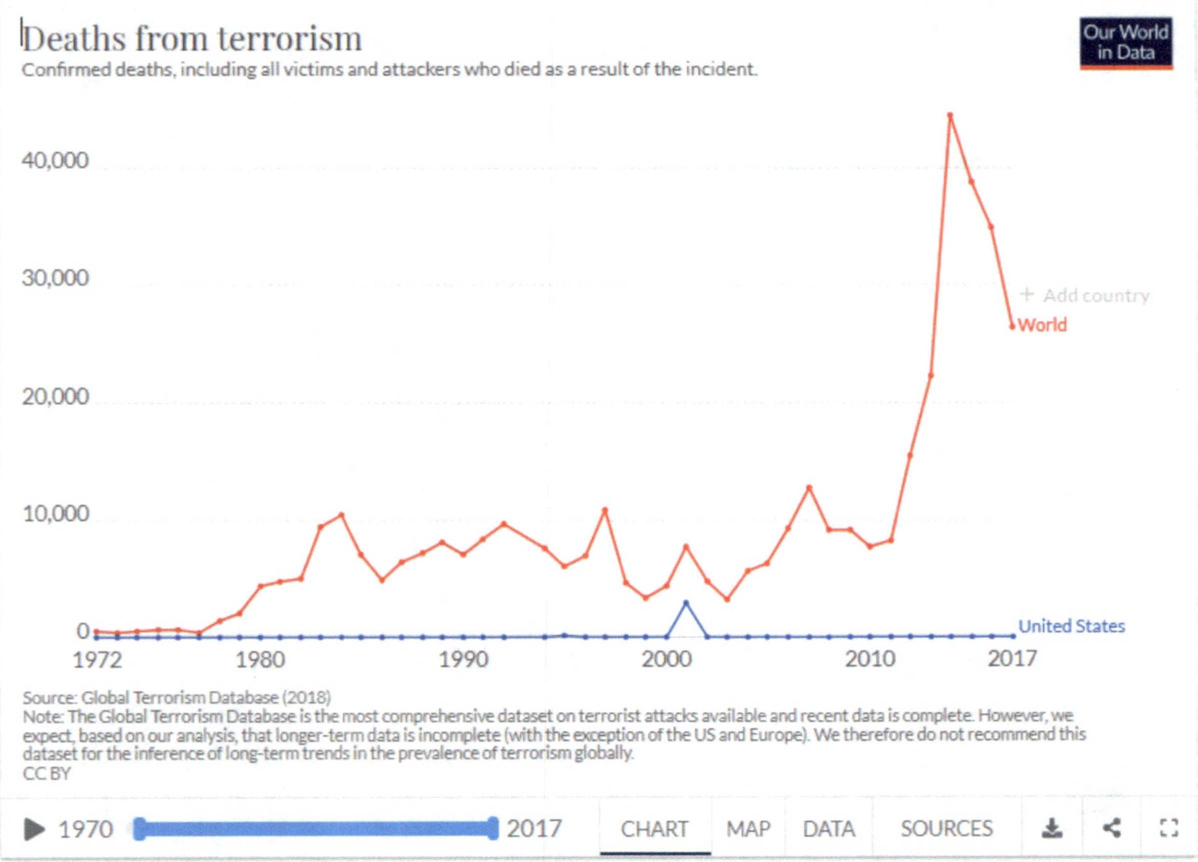
Deaths from terrorism
Confirmed deaths, including all victims and attackers who died as a result of the incident.
Our World in Data
40,000
30,000
20,000
10,000
0
1972
1980
1990
2000
2010
2017
+ Add country
World
United States
Source: Global Terrorism Database (2018)
Note: The Global Terrorism Database is the most comprehensive dataset on terrorist attacks available and recent data is complete. However, we expect, based on our analysis, that longer-term data is incomplete (with the exception of the US and Europe). We therefore do not recommend this dataset for the inference of long-term trends in the prevalence of terrorism globally.
CC BY
1970
2017
CHART
MAP
DATA
SOURCES

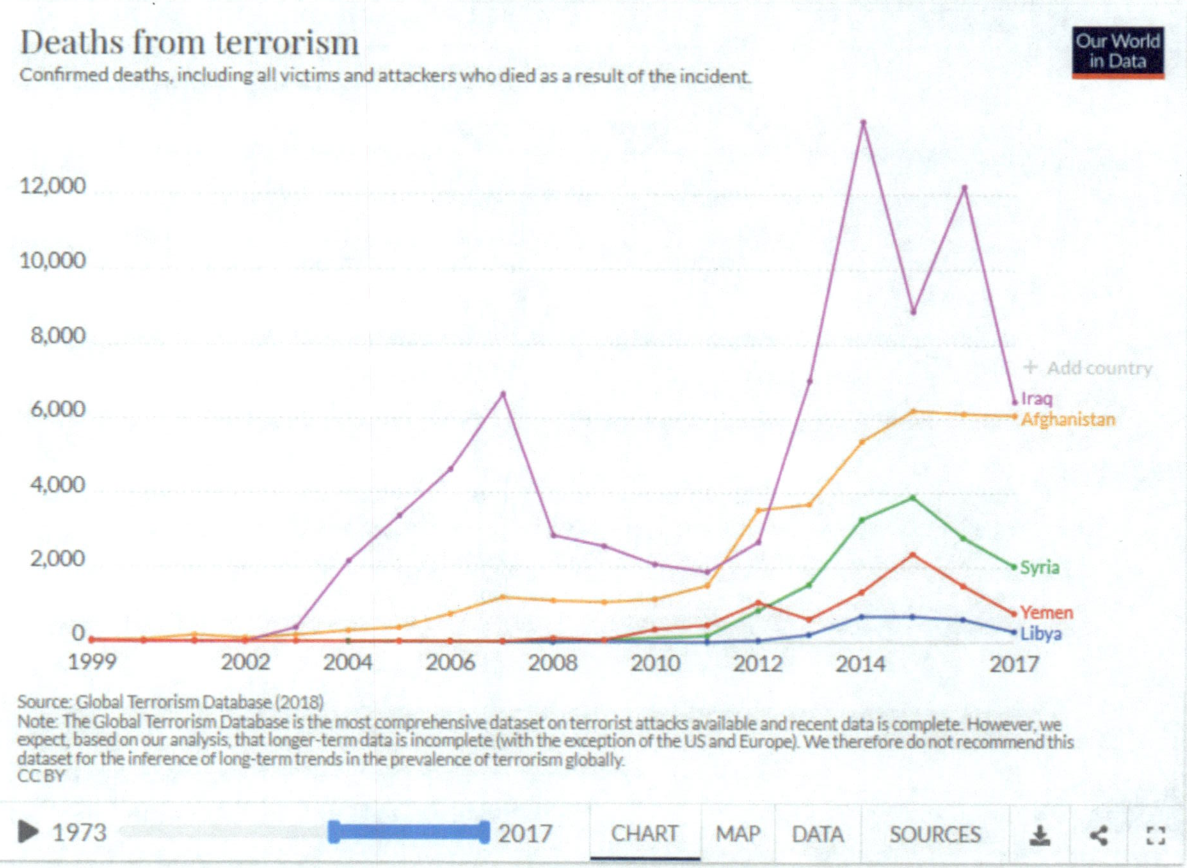
Deaths from terrorism
Confirmed deaths, including all victims and attackers who died as a result of the incident.
Our World in Data
12,000
10,000
8,000
6,000
4,000
2,000
0
1999
2002
2004
2006
2008
2010
2012
2014
2017
+ Add country
Iraq
Afghanistan
Syria
Yemen
Libya
Source: Global Terrorism Database (2018)
Note: The Global Terrorism Database is the most comprehensive dataset on terrorist attacks available and recent data is complete. However, we expect, based on our analysis, that longer-term data is incomplete (with the exception of the US and Europe). We therefore do not recommend this dataset for the inference of long-term trends in the prevalence of terrorism globally.
CC BY
1973
2017
CHART
MAP
DATA
SOURCES

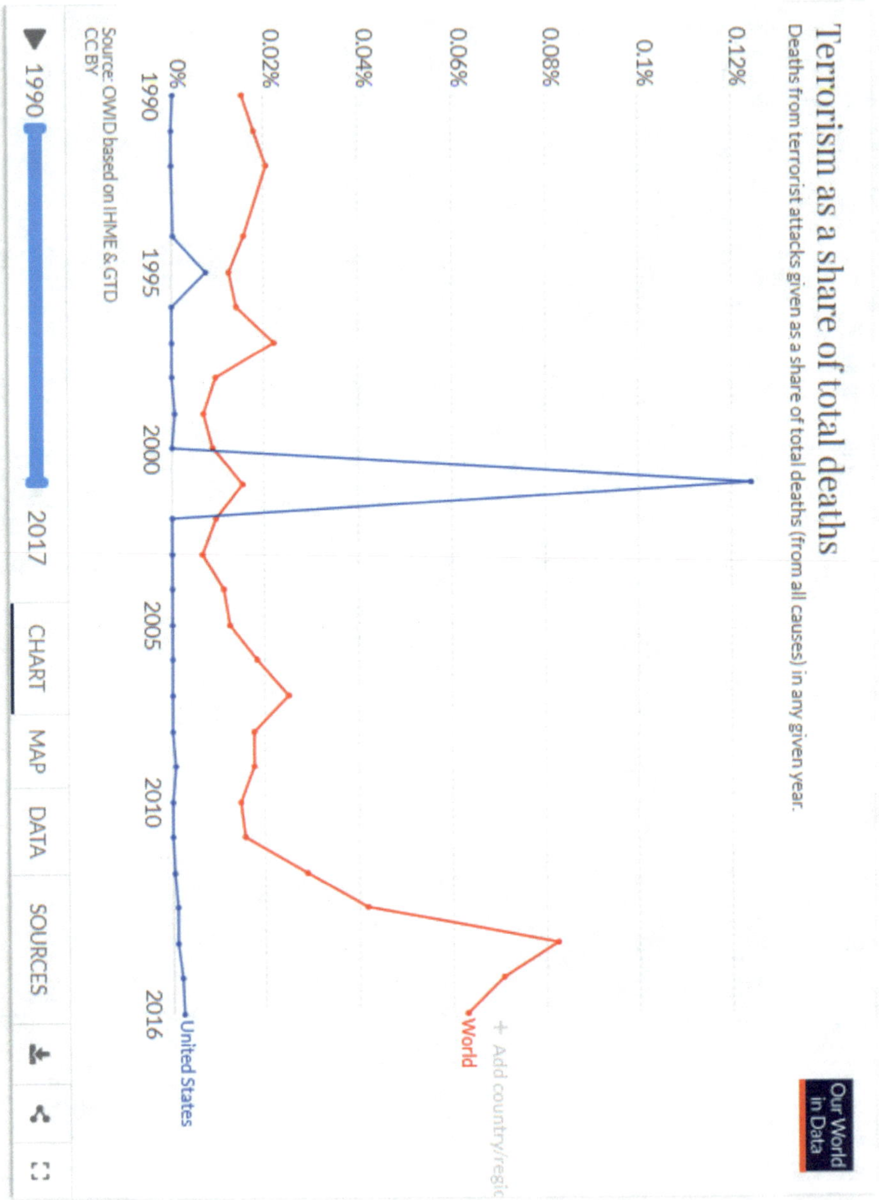
Terrorism as a share of total deaths
Deaths from terrorist attacks given as a share of total deaths (from all causes) in any given year.
Our World in Data
0.12%
0.1%
0.08%
0.06%
0.04%
0.02%
0%
1990
1995
2000
2005
2010
2016
World
United States
Source: OWID based on IHME & GTD
CC BY
1990
2017
CHART
MAP
DATA
SOURCES

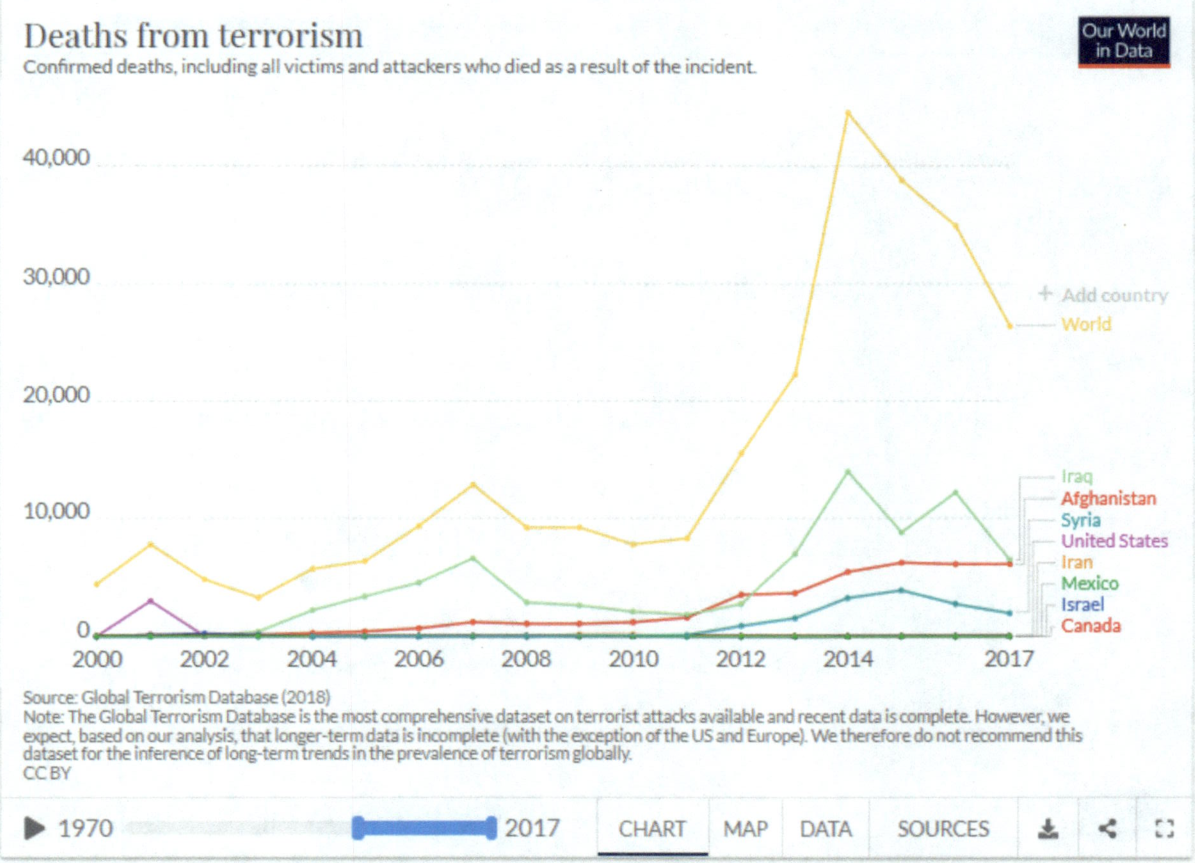
Deaths from terrorism
Confirmed deaths, including all victims and attackers who died as a result of the incident.
Our World in Data
40,000
30,000
20,000
10,000
0
2000
2002
2004
2006
2008
2010
2012
2014
2017
+ Add country
World
Iraq
Afghanistan
Syria
United States
Iran
Mexico
Israel
Canada
Source: Global Terrorism Database (2018)
Note: The Global Terrorism Database is the most comprehensive dataset on terrorist attacks available and recent data is complete. However, we expect, based on our analysis, that longer-term data is incomplete (with the exception of the US and Europe). We therefore do not recommend this dataset for the inference of long-term trends in the prevalence of terrorism globally.
CC BY
1970
2017
CHART
MAP
DATA
SOURCES

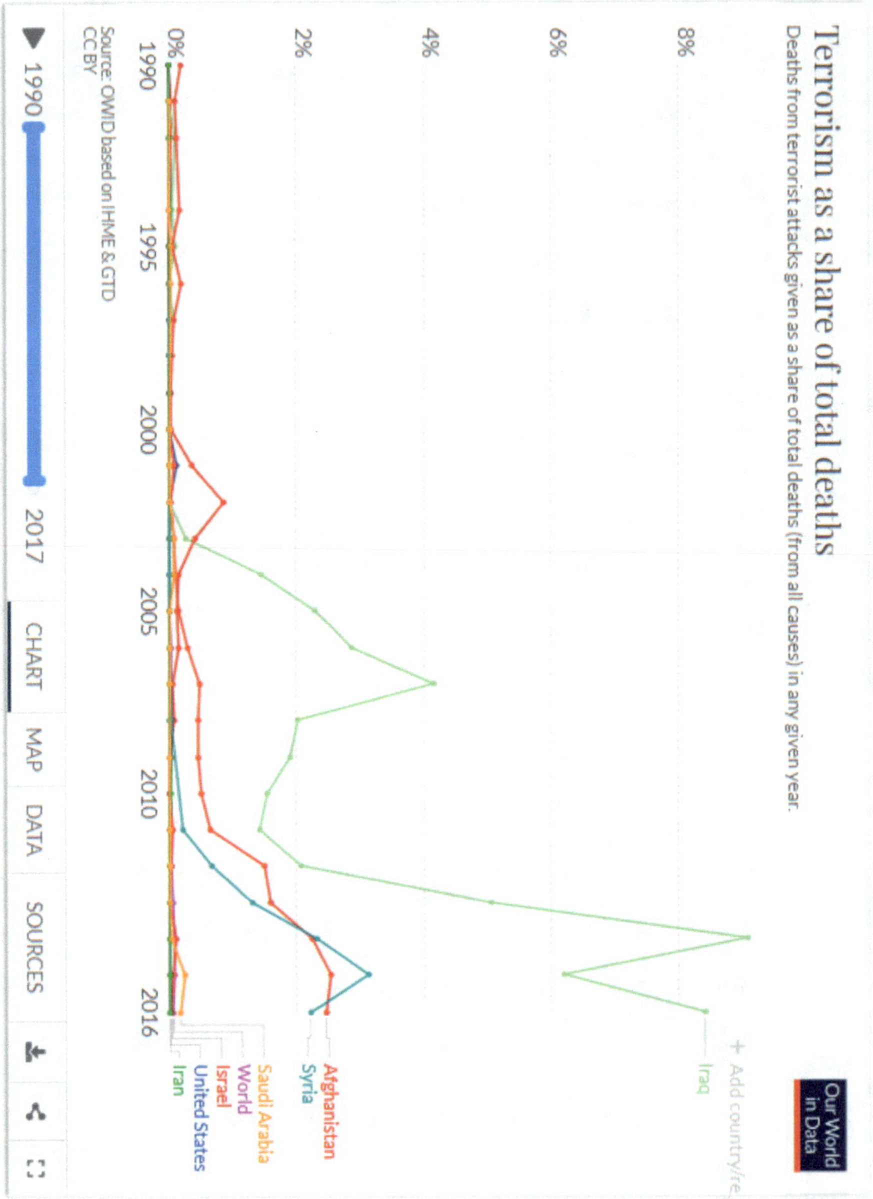

Terrorism as a share of total deaths
Deaths from terrorist attacks given as a share of total deaths (from all causes) in any given year.
Our World in Data
+ Add country/re
8%
6%
4%
2%
0%
1990
1995
2000
2005
2010
2016
Iraq
Afghanistan
Syria
Saudi Arabia
World
Israel
United States
Iran
Source: OWID based on IHME & GTD
CC BY
1990
2017
CHART
MAP
DATA
SOURCES

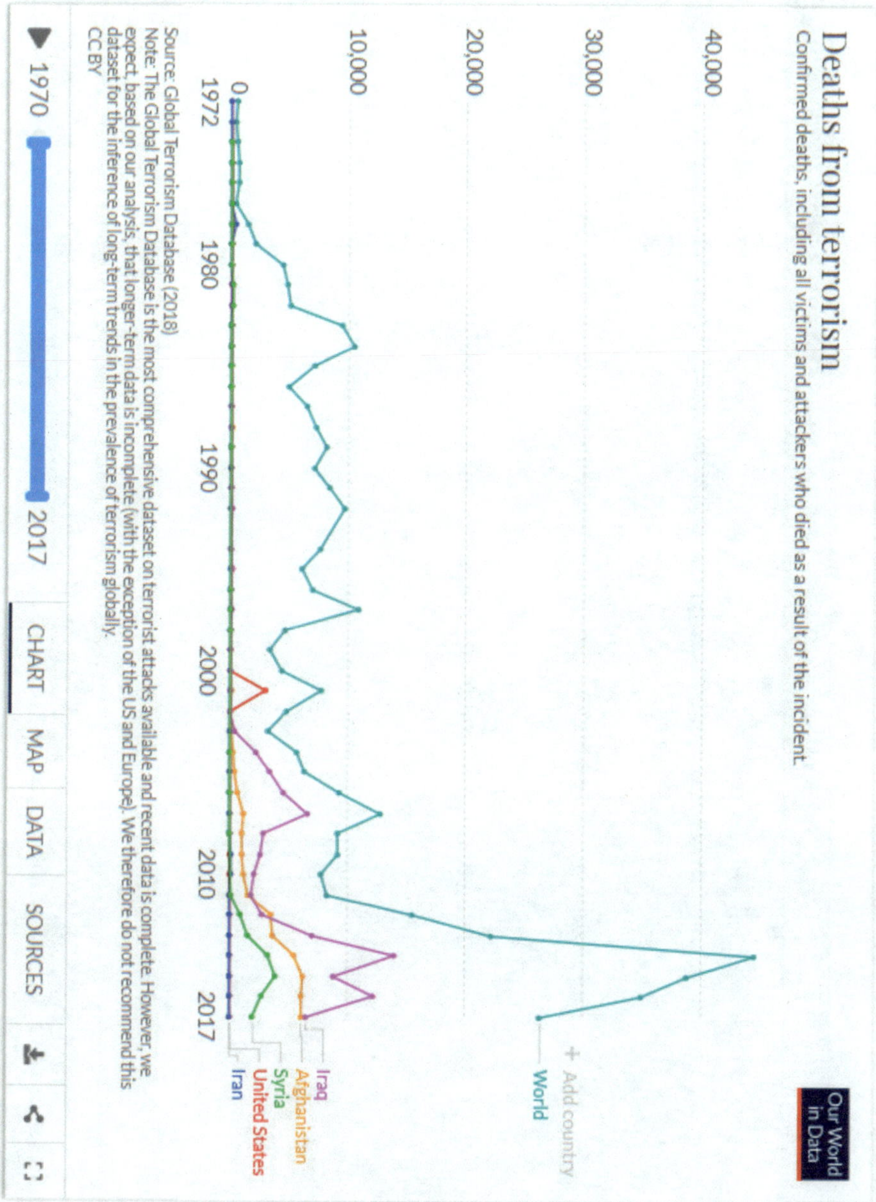
Deaths from terrorism
Confirmed deaths, including all victims and attackers who died as a result of the incident.
Our World in Data
40,000
30,000
20,000
10,000
0
1972
1980
1990
2000
2010
2017
+ Add country
World
Iraq
Afghanistan
Syria
United States
Iran
Source: Global Terrorism Database (2018)
Note: The Global Terrorism Database is the most comprehensive dataset on terrorist attacks available and recent data is complete. However, we expect, based on our analysis, that longer-term data is incomplete (with the exception of the US and Europe). We therefore do not recommend this dataset for the inference of long-term trends in the prevalence of terrorism globally.
CC BY
1970
2017
CHART
MAP
DATA
SOURCES

Number of articles cited by Factiva containing the words "terrorist attacks"

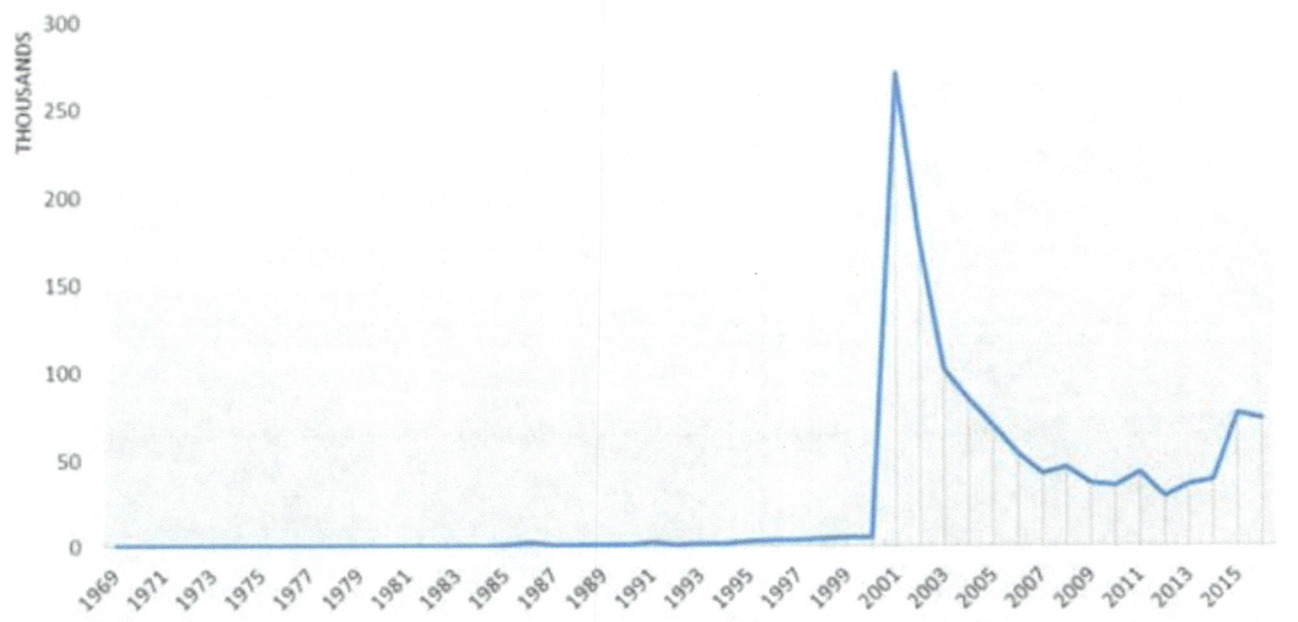

Source: Factiva. Filters: all dates, duplicates similar (exclude); search date: February 11, 2017

Does the news reflect what we die from?

Comparison of the share of deaths from 13 different causes in the US to the share of media coverage these topics get in the *New York Times* and *The Guardian* newspapers.

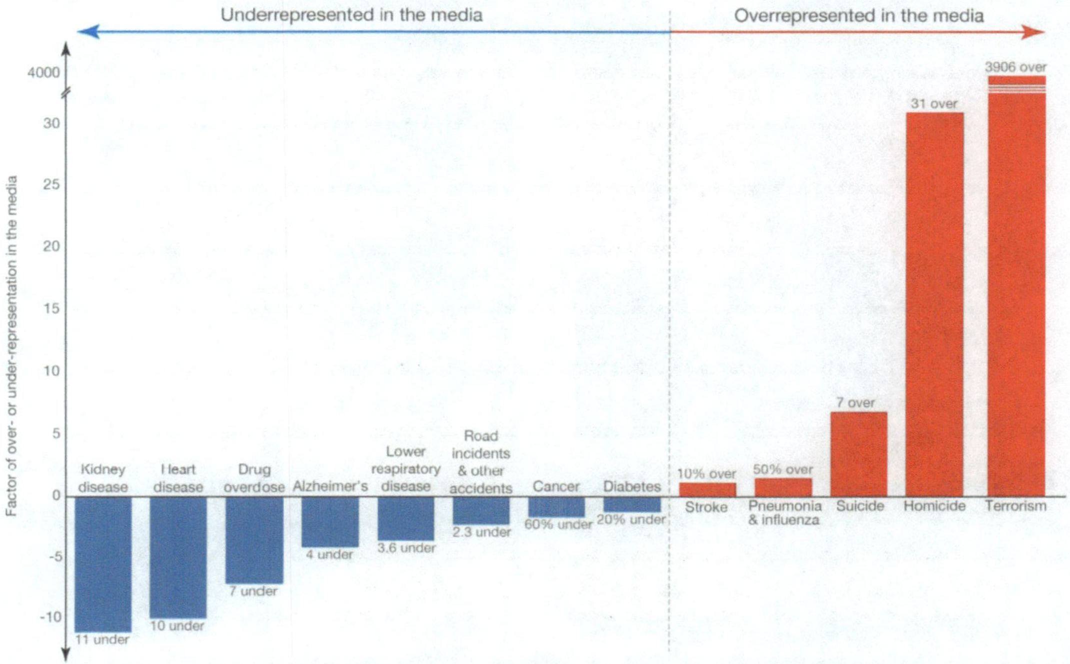

Source: Based on data from Shen et al (2018). Death: reality vs. reported. *Full data available at: https://owenshen24.github.io/charting-death*
This is calculated based on the ratio of each cause of death's proportion of total deaths (in the 13 categories) to each causes' share of media coverage. The figure shows the factor by which each cause of death in 2016 is over- or underrepresented in the media (e.g. homicides are overrepresented by a factor of 31 in the media relative to its share of deaths).
Media coverage data is measured as the annual average over the period from 1999 to 2016. The causes of death shown here account for approximately 88% of total deaths in the United States in 2016.

This is a visualization from OurWorldinData.org, where you find data and research on how the world is changing.

Causes of death in the US

What Americans die from, what they search on Google, and what the media reports on

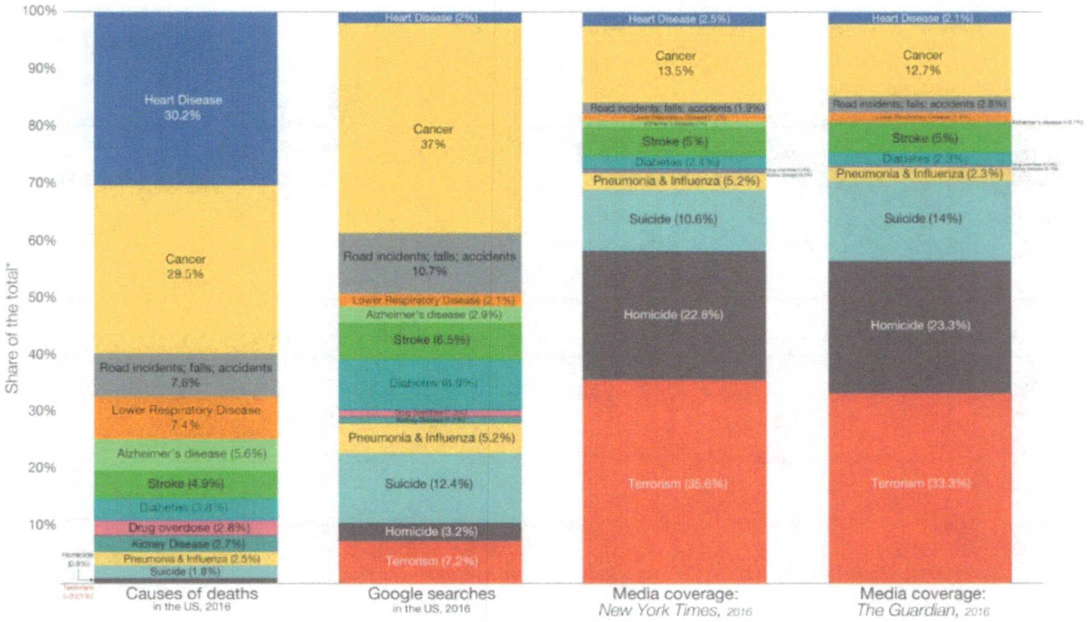

*This represents each causes's share of the top ten causes of death in the US plus homicides, drug overdoses and terrorism. Collectively these 13 causes accounted for approximately 88% of deaths in the US in 2016. Full breakdown of causes of death can be found at the CDC's WONDER public health database: https://wonder.cdc.gov/

Based on data from Shen et al (2018) – Death: reality vs. reported. *All data available at: https://owenshen24.github.io/charting-death*

All data refers to 2016.

Not all causes of death are shown: Shown is the data on the ten leading causes of death in the United States plus drug overdoses, homicides and terrorism.

All values are normalized to 100% so they represent their relative share of the top causes, rather than absolute counts (e.g. 'deaths' represents each causes' share of deaths within the 13 categories shown rather than total deaths). The causes of death shown here account for approximately 88% of total deaths in the United States in 2016.

This is a visualization from OurWorldinData.org, where you find data and research on how the world is changing.

What share of global deaths result from terrorism?
Our World in Data
In the period 1990 to 2017 the annual share of deaths from terrorism has ranged between 0.01% to 0.08% globally.
55,945,000 people died in 2017
26,000 were victims of terrorism in 2017
(terrorism accounts for 0.05% of all deaths)
Licensed under CC-BY by the authors Hannah Ritchie & Max Roser.

"On the morning of September 11th, 2001, 19 men armed with box-cutters, directed by a man on dialysis in a cave fortress half-way around the world, using a satellite phone and a laptop directed the most sophisticated penetration of the most heavily defended airspace in the world. Overpowering the passengers and the military combat trained pilots on four commercial aircraft before flying those planes wildly off-course for over an hour without being molested by a single fighter interceptor. These 19 hijackers, devout religious fundamentalists, who like to drink alcohol, snort cocaine, and live with pink haired strippers, managed to knock down three buildings with two planes in New York, while in Washington, a pilot who couldn't handle a single engine Cessna was able to fly a 757 in an 8000 ft descending 270 degree corkscrew turn to come exactly level with the ground, hitting the Pentagon in the budget analyst office where DOD staffers were working on the mystery of the 2.3 trillion dollars that defense secretary Donald Rumsfeld had announced missing from the Pentagons coffers in a press conference the day before, on September 10th, 2001. Luckily, the news anchors knew who did it within minutes... 'Osama Bin Laden'... the pundits knew within hours... 'Osama Bin Laden'... the administration within the day...'the terrorists who committed these acts and those who harbor them'... and the evidence literally fell into the FBI's lap... 'the hijackers passport was found blocks from the World Trade Center crash site, if you can believe that'... but for some reason a bunch of crazy conspiracy theorists demanded an investigation into the greatest attack on American soil in history. That investigation was 'delayed', "underfunded', 'set up to fail', a 'conflict of interest', and a cover up from start to finish. It was based on testimony extracted through torture, the records of which were destroyed. It failed to mention the existence of WTC7, ABLE DANGER, P-Tech, Cybele Edmunds, OBL and the CIA and the drills of hijacked aircraft being flown into buildings that were being simulated at the precise same time that those events were actually happening. It was lied to by the Pentagon, the CIA, the Bush Administration, and as for Bush and Cheney, well, no one knows what they told it because they testified 'In Secret', "Off The Record', Not Under Oath', and 'Behind Closed Doors.' It didn't bother to look at who funded the attacks because the question is of 'little practical significance.' Still the 9/11 Commission did brilliantly answering all of the questions the public had, except most of the victims family members questions and pin blame on all the people responsible, although no one so much as lost their job. Determining the attacks were 'failure of imagination', because 'Nobody in our government at least, and I don't think the prior government could envision flying airplanes into buildings (BUSH)...' except the Pentagon, FEMA, NORAD, and the NRO. The DIA destroyed 2.5 terabytes of data on ABLE DANGER, but that's okay because it probably wasn't important. The SEC destroyed their records on the investigation into the insider trading before the attacks, but that's okay because destroying the records of the largest investigation in SEC history is just part of routine record keeping. NIST has classified the data that they used for their model of WTC7's collapse, but that's okay, because knowing how they made their model of the collapse would 'jeopardize public safety.' The FBI has argued that all material related to their investigation of 9/11 should be kept secret from the public, but that's okay because the FBI probably has nothing to hide... Osama Bin Laden lived in a cave fortress in the hills of Afghanistan, but somehow got away. Then he was hiding out in Tora Bora, but somehow got away. Then he lived in Abbottabad for years, taunting the most comprehensive intelligence dragnet, employing the most sophisticated technology in the history of the world for a decade, releasing video after video with complete impunity and getting younger and younger as he did so, before finally being found in a daring seal team raid which wasn't recorded on video, in which he didn't resist or use his wife as a human shield and in which these crack special forces operatives panicked

and killed this unarmed man. Supposedly the best source of intelligence about those dastardly terrorists on the entire planet. Then they dumped his body in the ocean before telling anyone about it. Then a couple dozen of that teams' members died in a helicopter crash in Afghanistan... If you have any questions about this story, you are a batshit, paranoid, tin foil, dog abusing baby hater and will be reviled by everyone. If you love your country and or freedom, happiness, rainbows, rock 'n roll, puppy dogs, apple pie, and your grandma, you will never ever express doubts about any part of this story to anyone, ever. This has been a public service announcement by the friends of the FBI, CIA, NSA, DIA, SEC, MSM, White House, NIST, and the 9/11 Commission. Because ignorance is strength."
– James Corbett[88]

Governments around the world have used false flags to accomplish their goals despite their unpopularity, including the United States government, such as in the Pan Am 103 bombing, USS Cole bombing, Oklahoma City bombing and the 1993 bombing of the World Trade Center. The amount of collusion that exists between all the major financial and political persons makes it obvious to the casual observer that insurance claims on the towers set just before their controlled demolition/false flag, the witness of Israeli Special Forces celebrating a few blocks from the towers in the aftermath, the complete lack of scientific approach and investigation, the ridiculous claim that the "planes" that crashed into the Pentagon and Shanksville were vaporized but fingerprints and DNA survived, the lack of evidence to accuse Osama bin Laden or Al Qaeda or any other middle eastern person, the lack of technical capability of the supposed hijackers, the concurrent military simulations of the exact scenario that was actually occurring, the lack of public accountability by government officials including President Bush and VP Dick Cheney, and the use of fear and crises to deny human rights and constitutional rights to people around the world and people of the U.S.A., especially through the Patriot Act, the MCA (Military Commissions Act), the NDAA (National Defense Authorization Act), the AUMF (Authorization for Use of Military Force Against Terrorists (2001 – Present)), and in general every other action of the government in some way, that **THE GOVERNMENT FUCKING DID IT!** To even consider anything else after truly considering all the evidence and diving deep is to profess complete cowardice or stupidity. To willfully ignore the truth professes the same. The fallout from the population's general acceptance of the official narrative includes the accumulating deconstruction of our rights, the murder of innocent people around the world to combat the ambiguous "War on Terror", and the immense wealth transfers that have accompanied the diminishing voice, health, and intelligence of the people.

The Patriot Act expanded the definition of terrorism to include very many normal activities and gave permissions to government agencies to spy on Americans, you know, just in case there might be someone out there who didn't care for direct taxation. "Hastily passed 45 days after 9/11 in the name of national security, the Patriot Act was the first of many changes to surveillance laws that made it easier for the government to spy on ordinary Americans by expanding the authority to monitor phone and email communications, collect bank and credit reporting records, and track the activity of innocent Americans on the Internet. While most Americans think it was created to catch terrorists, the Patriot Act actually turns regular citizens into suspects."[89]

The MCA of 2006 gives the president absolute power to decide who is an enemy of our country and to imprison people indefinitely without charging them with a crime. It eliminates due process, rejects core American values, and permits coerced evidence.[90]

"The NDAA is an annual bill that lets Congress set guidelines for defense policy. Though funding for the U.S. military must be approved through appropriations bills, Congress uses the NDAA to establish defense priorities, make organizational changes to military agencies, and provide guidance on how funding should be used. In addition to the Department of Defense, the legislation also covers military-related programs run by other agencies, such as the Department of Energy's nuclear weapons programs and the Federal

Bureau of Investigation's counterintelligence activities. A relatively rare example of bipartisanship in Congress, the NDAA has been passed for 60 straight years. That consistency has also made the bill a popular vehicle for tacking on legislation that has little to do with defense." – Tom Barkley.[91] "Let's be clear: the NDAA grants the president the power to kidnap any American anywhere in the United States and hold him or her in prison forever without trial. The president's own signing statement, incredibly, confirmed that he had that power. As I have been warning since 2006: there is not a country on the planet that you can name that has ever set in place a system of torture, and of detention without trial, for an "other", supposedly external threat that did not end up using it pretty quickly on its own citizens." – Naomi Wolf[92]

The AUMF, passed 3 days after 9/11 allowed "the President to use all necessary and appropriate force against those nations, organizations, or persons he determines planned, authorized, committed, or aided the terrorist attacks that occurred on September 11, 2001, or harbored such organizations or persons, in order to prevent any future acts of international terrorism against the United States." In other words, he could point his finger at anyone, and a bomb would drop, no questions need be asked. "By 2017 it had been invoked over 30 times to justify U.S. troop deployments in over 10 countries. In 2016 President Obama pointed to the AUMF as authorization allowing him to use military force against ISIS in Syria and Iraq without additional congressional authorization. In July 2019, after the Trump administration briefed Congress on possible ties between al-Qaeda and Iran, many questioned whether or not the act could be used to authorize war against Iran 18 years after the 9/11 attacks." – Michael Boyd[93]

The amount of evidence and expert reporting on the collapse of the towers on 9/11 is so vast that it is impossible at this point to refute. The Architects and Engineers for 9/11 Truth Petition is signed by 3,529 Architects and Engineers. These are experts across many fields that have shown solidarity for the truth about 9/11 to be shared openly. The fact is that not a single building collapsed due to airplanes. The official narrative states that "...the planes hit the towers, cutting through some exterior and interior supporting structural steel columns. The fuel from the planes ignited office fires across several floors... According to official government reports, the fires weakened the structural steel framing of both twin towers, leading to sudden, progressive and total collapses... Does the official explanation make sense? Was there a comprehensive investigation that examined all of the evidence?" - Richard Gage, AIA, Founder of Architects and Engineers For 9/11 Truth[94] (Gage)

"The heat from the fire supposedly softened the steel and thereby brought the buildings down. If you have a flame at 750 degrees, you can hold that flame under a steel beam forever and you'll never reach a high enough temperature to bend steel let alone melt it. So immediately I knew, at that point, that the official explanation was dead wrong." - Robert Podolsky, M.S., Physicist/Engineer. First responders and others on site reported waves of explosions before, during and after the moment of the plane crashes. "The only way that I can see that the towers could have collapsed is that the interior columns were compromised." - Richard Humenn, P.E., Original WTC Chief Electrical Design Engineer. Multi-ton steel beams were propelled and ejected laterally away from the collapsing buildings, which could only happen if there was something to propel them, exclusively indicating explosions.

The amount of material left after the collapse was far from the total material composing the towers, indicating that somehow whole floors and major steel beams, and other material was disintegrated, pulverized, or melted. FEMA documented that steel had been melted and partially evaporated, though NIST omitted this evidence from their official report. Molten steel flowed throughout the collapse site. "So, what is this molten metal? It is direct evidence for the use of thermite."-Steven Jones, Ph.D., Physicist. Steel Melts at 2750°F and thermite reaches over 4500°F in about two seconds.

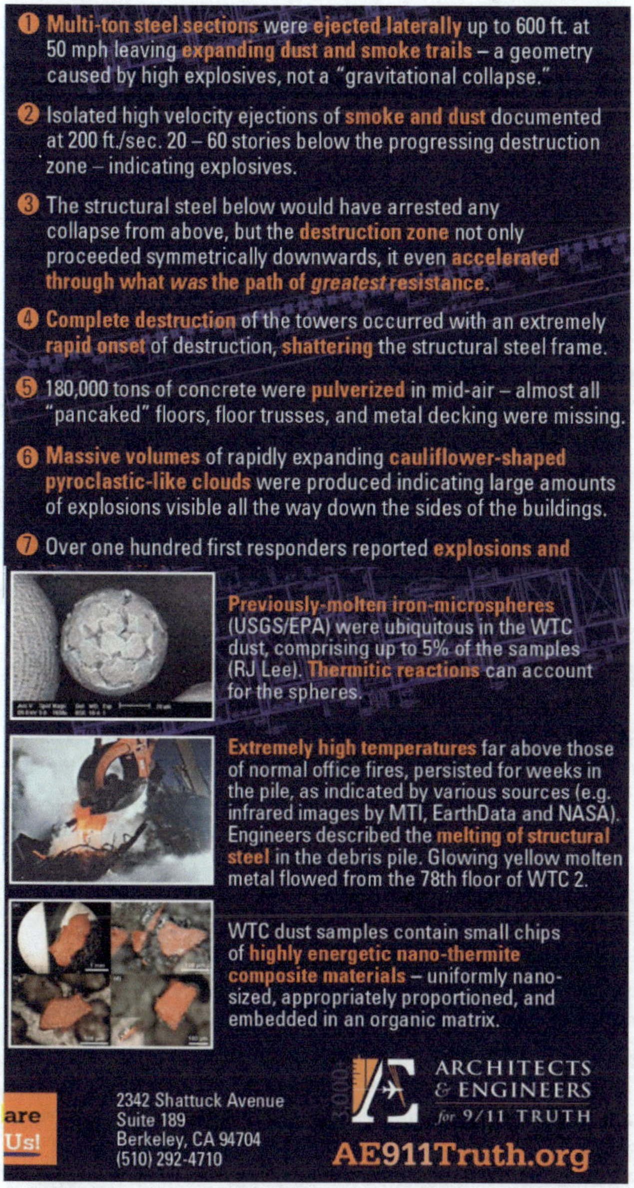

"In the dust we found what we characterize as unreacted thermitic material, in the shape of some very tiny red grey chips, and in the reaction they produce molten iron, which is the prime indication of a thermitic reaction, and such a reaction can be used to destroy steel structures. What we have found is a modern version of thermite, which we call nano-thermite, which is produced in a different way. It is not just two powders being mixed, the material is actually built from the atom scale up, we call them bottom-up procedures, which is what you do in nano technology. The ingredients are much smaller which means they're reacting faster, and they're more easily ignited." – Niels Harrit, Ph.D., X-Ray Time-Resolved, Spectroscopy Research.

But what happened to World Trade Center 7, a 47-story steel frame skyscraper, not hit by a place, but symmetrically collapsed regardless on the same day as the other WTC buildings? The official report claims the building collapsed due to normal office fires. Interestingly and notably, no building of this kind has ever collapsed due to office fires. "High rise buildings simply do not collapse due to fire. There has never been... an experience where a high rise building that was steel frame completely collapsed." – Scott Grainger P.E., Forensic Fire Protection Engineer. "The coup de Grace for me was when I found out that building 7 had collapsed later that day, and when I saw building 7 come down, to me, the fact that it looks like a perfect controlled demolition of an intact building, I mean, that's what I call a smoking gun." - Dr. Robert Bowman, Lt. Col USAF, Ret. and Former Director, Advanced Space Programs, DoD

Before any investigations could get underway, all the demolished materials were hauled out of the site and shipped out the of the country. The mobilization of the cleanup was extremely efficient and was

underway before people had even absorbed the shock. Premeditated demolitions work similarly efficient, sometimes. "400 truckloads per day of material were taken away from the world trade center site and sent to China for recycling."- Joel Miller, High-Rise Architect. Investigations into the cause of collapse were never properly done. Building 7 was collapsed through controlled demolition. That is the ONLY way.
All of the World Trade Center buildings were demolished by controlled demolitions, as evidenced by experts globally, and denied by government agencies across the board. The propaganda machine was phenomenally successful, as usual, in demonizing anyone who contradicted the official narrative, and despite many reporters and news agencies accidentally revealing precognizance of the event, such as reporting on the plane crash in the first tower before it even happened, the media blitzkrieg of terrorism news, emotional manipulation, and subtle coercion effectively hypnotized the willfully ignorant, stupid, statist, or highly impressionable population. Hate for middle easterners, fear of terrorist attack on one's church, patriotic music about putting boots up asses, because "that's the American way," all created a seemingly beautiful catharsis, while yet a highly stressful, lightshow distraction.

"Our job is to give people not what they want, but what we decide they ought to have."
– Richard Salant, Former President of CBS News

So much psychological warfare energy has been applied to this topic, that many people just can't even focus upon hearing it brought up. The emotions that have been pegged to catchphrases and keywords, such as "conspiracy theorist", have made the conversation nearly taboo in the minds of millions of Americans. I have not gone into any extreme detail here, but simply laid out some crumbs. If you have the ability to focus for more than eight seconds, the capacity to hold two opposing viewpoints at the same time without needing to define one or the other as the truth, and the skill to do independent research or the energy to learn how, please investigate this more for yourself. Once you start to genuinely look for the truth, there is no way it will be shielded from you. Sometimes it is frightening to think that such a thing could happen as one's own government killing its own people, but historically, that is what all governments are most skilled at and most notorious for. There are millions upon millions of people who all share in the liberated perspective, seeing what they simply refused to look at before. It is up to you to choose whether you will blindfold yourself or walk boldly into dark places carrying a light for others.

Private Ownership Of Earth And All Upon Her

What is fundamental to society more than anything else? Land. Without the land, there would be no us. It provides us with shelter, food, fresh naturally filtered water, and the means by which to conduct our life in all other ways. When we consider the vast importance of land, it must come naturally next to consider how to live in care of it both individually and communally. Interestingly and devastatingly, the more freedom that has been given to wider sectors of the human population, the more destruction of the natural environment has occurred. We need to investigate thoroughly the way land has been utilized and how that has gotten us, the human population into precarious environmental, political, social, and financial situations globally.
In Europe, India, and China peasants worked the earth and owned its produce, but plots were shared ownerships through families, clans, a local potentate, or a monarch.

"A disruption of this pattern is the great revolution of the last two hundred years. The idea of individual, exclusive ownership, not just what can be carried or occupied, but of the

immovable, near-eternal earth, has proved to be the most destructive and creative cultural force in written history. It has eliminated ancient civilizations wherever it has encountered them, and displaced entire peoples from their homelands, but it has also spread an undreamed-of degree of personal freedom and protected it... Biology underpins the pivotal influence that ownership of the earth exerts on human life. There are givens that remain as true for nearly seven billion of us presently living here as they were for the five hundred million people scattered across the land in 1583. The body's core temperature must remain within a degree or two of 37 degrees Celsius or 98.6 degrees Fahrenheit. To maintain this temperature, an adult must consume a minimum of 1,800 calories a day, preferably 2,450 according to the Food and Agriculture Organization of the United Nations, and closer to 4,000 calories for the sort of labor demanded of the fishermen in Saint John's harbor. That adult must also be clothed and sheltered from the burning sun and freezing rain. Except for some coastal communities, the earth's population in every era has always depended on the land for at least 85 percent of the energy that keeps it alive, and for all its clothing and shelter. This inescapable fact of life makes the challenge of caring for the nine billion inhabitants who will inhabit the earth in fifty years' time daunting. They must be fed, clothed, and housed on the produce of some forty-five million square kilometers of farmland, roughly eighteen million square miles. In optimum conditions, less than half of this area might be sufficient to produce the calories needed for survival. But the land must also produce biofuels, animal feed, minerals, timber and cotton and other clothing fibers. At the same time, the soil degrades, cities spread, climate changes, and natural disasters such as droughts and floods, earthquakes and tsunamis, whittle away spare capacity to danger levels."

– Andro Linklater[95]

Ancient cultures, from the Iban in Borneo to the Aboriginals in Australia, to the Irish, to the Wampanoag, to the Israelites, had lived in strongly egalitarian societies. Their societies were marked by inherent mythological and social connections to the land they lived and worked upon. Often, the practice of redistribution was fundamental to the equity of the society. This meant that lands would be rotated between clans and families so that all the people would share in the best and worst land. Property rights or land use rights were determined by the tribal chiefs and other leaders, but also by the community itself, in ways to most equitably distribute amongst the people what they could use. Lands equitably and highly specifically identified allowed for transitioning land use in its most beneficial amounts to every family in a tribe. Need and fairness determined land use and temporary ownership, though land was never considered owned in the sense that it is today. Rather, nature or God, offered the land, and the people distributed it amongst themselves to the highest benefit of the individuals and the collective. Communal land ownership involved all participants in a society in the lives of each individual and family within it. Everyone was involved in decisions that affected everyone. Without redistribution, only the most efficient cultivators could add to their holding and also pass them on to the next generation.

"In Europe, medieval legal structures grew out of Roman law whose goal, in the words of its sixth-century codifier, Emperor Justinian, 'is the constant and perpetual wish to render to everyone his due.' These dues were based on mutual obligation, and the best example of how this worked was always taken to be the family. Thus parents had a duty to guard their children, an obligation matched by the children's duty to obey their parents. And wife and children were subject to the authority of their husband and father, their obedience gave them inextinguishable rights to a share in his property. The same principle applied where land was concerned. Roman law held that it had to have a lord who was obliged to guard it,

as a father guarded his family, on behalf of his sovereign. In return he could expect to be obeyed by those who lived there and to enjoy their services. This was the matrix of the feudal system."
-Linklater[96]

In the 12th century, King Henry II began to use common law to undermine the power of barons manor courts, so that all people held common rights to royal justice over any permanent local manor justice. The Magna Carta, written in 1215 by 25 barons, who forced King John to sign it into law, protected freeholders of land against the royal government, by identifying absolute rights, extending common law rights to freeholders, and giving them a power beyond the King. While common law protected people from the Barons, it now protected the barons from the royal authority as well.

Property law changes in 1540 resulted in the erosion and destruction of "the core of the contractual structure of feudalism, leaving in its place a system of rights." The law of "couverture", enacted in 1542, removed the right of wives to a reasonable part of family property and forced them to transfer all property to her husband's name. This law indicated a change from the Roman law and feudal system of fairness.

The first expression of "ownership" in the New World occurred when Sir Humphrey Gilbert imposed English Law upon the lands of Saint John's Harbor, Newfoundland on Aug. 5, 1583, with Queen Elizabeth's permission. She granted him rights to any land not already occupied by "any Christian prince or people." The royal authority was seen as backed by divine grace and was the ultimate authority on who could and could not claim property. "Real estate was, literally and legally, royal estate."[97]

The first democratic act by European pilgrims to the American Continent was to distribute land to each member of the party according to the size of their family. The Mayflower carried over 102 puritans in 1620, and by 1623 the remaining 50 or 80 were dedicated to private property, conducting their affairs as was fitting to each according to their need and effort and strengths. Communal ownership resulted in the symbolic founding of the American spirit.

Native Americans held then, as they hold now, that the land cannot be owned, only used by some for some time, but that the land is impossible to be owned by an individual or group. In Judaism and Islam it is the same, that no man can own the earth, that only God has that capability. Across the ages and lands of the Earth, land ownership has been only on the authority of divine right. That is, that people, whether kings or emperors or peasants, can only manage, occupy, and "own" land on the grace and authority of the God as recognized by each unique culture.

John Winthrop published a pamphlet in 1629, in which he argued that "private ownership of the earth" was "created by human toil." He argued that the God granted natural right to earth was based on use and occupancy. Common lands, never replenished or subdued were available to enterprising individuals who would occupy and improve upon the land. Thus, private property found its divine argument and divine origin. It also stated that the natural right exercised would become a civil right.

The idea of individual ownership of plots of land developed in Europe in the 1500's, expressed in the way they built their homes. Prior to this time, peasants were generally living in communal single room shelters with little privacy or comfort. As the interest in privacy and comfort grew and became feasible for peasantry, so did the reality of individual private ownership take root. Private property instituted itself by a combination of factors, including the large influx of German silver and Spanish gold that made peasants wealthy enough to pay years of rent to landowners and build more comfort into their life. Properties went from being shared grazing lands of manors, to being boundaried, private, and compact, wherein the landowner was the sole owner to do with it as he will and reap the according reward. In exchange for the new gold and silver, and thus comfort, landowners transformed their lands from feudal systems to grazing enclosures for sheep, to sell the wool to satisfy the universally predominant wool clothing need of Europeans. Mutual obligation to the land, community centrism, became individually centric obligation to self-profit.

The Royal government of Britain attempted to prevent enclosures and trusts in the 1500's through royal proclamations, fining and imprisoning peers of the realm who disobeyed. The new landowners were highly represented and membered in the House of Commons, and thus was able to pass laws to protect their property against the royal government. The trusts that the landowners created circumvented the mandatory taxes due to the king, and thus denied nearly two-thirds of tax revenues.
In 1540, due to Thomas Cromwell's investigations, King Henry the VIII acquired by forced surrender, the lands owned by England's monasteries, that amounted to two million acres, 20 percent of cultivated farmland in England, with £150,000 worth annually. Henry the VIII sold half of this land to fund foreign wars, for £1.4 million to aristocrats wanting to enclose the land for sheep to sell wool. Concurrently the wool market crashed, and thus the aristocrats sold their new properties to "London merchants, careful farmers, government officials, even tenants on fixed rents—anyone looking for 'secure investment.'"[98]

"Altogether some seven million acres were transferred into private ownership through the enclosure orders, (passed by Parliament between 1700 and 1830) brutal testimony to the political power now wielded by landowners... the total value of enclosed land represented the transfer of about £175 million of assets from communal possession to the lawyers, merchants, and wealthy landlords who controlled Parliament."
-Linklater

"As surveyors gave shape to property, a subtle change in mortgage law allowed it to be translated into financial muscle. In its old use, a mortgage meant 'dead pledge,' signifying that a borrower automatically forfeited his land if he failed to repay the money in full on the specified date. As Sir Thomas Lyttleton, the leading legal authority of the sixteenth century, put it, 'If he [the borrower] doth not pay, then the land which is put in pledge upon condition for the payment of the money, is taken from him for ever, and so is dead to him.' The forfeiture of an entire property as a penalty for failing to repay every penny that has been borrowed naturally struck the new landowners as inequitable. In response to their growing political influence, sympathetic judges began to interpret the law so that failure to repay the debt at the required date did not totally extinguish an owner's title to the land. Instead, under the principle known as 'the equity of redemption,' the courts ruled that so long as a borrower paid off the mortgage, even years late, he could reclaim his property. Modern mortgage law grew out of this interpretation, but so too did modern finance. To regain his money, the lender now had to get a writ to foreclose, forcing the borrower to sell the land. Once the debt was paid, however, the remainder of the proceeds belonged to the former landowner. This was his equity in the land. As the new idea took hold during the seventeenth century, equity, meaning fairness, would gradually morph into equity, meaning capital."
- Linklater

"To every individual in nature is given an individual property by nature, not to be invaded or usurped by any. For every one, as he is himself, so he has a self-propriety, else could he not be himself; and of this no second may presume to deprive any of, without manifest violation and affront to the very principles of nature and of the rules of equity and justice between man and man... No man has power over my rights and liberties, and I over no man's... For by natural birth all men are equally and alike born to like propriety [property], liberty and freedom; and as we are delivered of God by the hand of nature into this world, every one with a natural, innate freedom and propriety—as it were writ in the table of every man's heart, never to be obliterated."

-Richard Overton, mid-17th century satirist

Overton extended the private property revolution argument to encompass individual human rights. By indicating that the individual was property unto himself, he made it possible for the inclusion of legal rights to parallel the progress made by those profiteering on the privatization of land and their ever-growing political influence.

From the Diggers to the Levellers, from Oliver Cromwell to Thomas Hobbes, the fight over what place private property held in society was battled. Diggers in opposition, claiming it was intended as a control mechanism of the government. Cromwell pushing for rights to be extended only to the propertied, the invested. In 1656, James Harrington put forth the idea that the Shape of government was dependent upon the manner in which land was owned. Whoever owned the most land could sustain the most soldiers, in its last resort. The progression toward democracy driven by the ever-widening distribution of power by property ownership by the commonwealth. Harrington created a blueprint for his ideal commonwealth, outlining limitations on land acquisition, rotating members of legislature, mostly every three years, and created the Rota Club to promote these ideals. His ideas on property controlling the government structure and type are still in use today.

While civil rights, created by law, could be removed by law, natural rights could never be destroyed, only temporarily obscured, or ignored. This became the fundamental driving force for our modern world. The Puritan English influenced property owners read well the texts of Harrington. On the European continent and in other parts of the world, like China, the language of power separated the governed and the government. Latin used for courts of law, while the population mostly didn't even speak a single dialect of their majority language made them always unable to represent let alone understand. Only privileged classes in these other countries could read and engage with natural law treatises at that time.

In 1682, William Petty described in Essays a functioning capitalist economy, wherein he outlined free trade principles and mechanisms. His theories had at their root two ideas: land is capital, and only labor releases its value. He put forward that, outside thoughts, conflicting with the views of the wealthy and powerful, and thus the majority population as well, and proposed and carried by ambitious outsiders, would cause competitive advantage and benefit to any economy. By treating land as capital, once labor released its value, it would create multiple benefits such as families sustained by wages, profits guaranteed for further investment, and taxes on operations financed by government. The land resale value increasing by very much when treating as capital. When so, an adequate money supply is required for its value to be realized. Too little money investments in land improvements were due to rents being two-thirds of the whole supply. Thus, credit creation through a national bank was needed. Reputable national banks could make available double the cash in its vaults through credit and adjust the flow to keep the market stable. In 1694, William Patterson founded the Bank of England, authorized to issue paper notes backed by £1.2 million invested by private investors in the bank. Petty practiced and essayed on the use of specialized labor, such as in the later 'division of labor' used by Henry Ford to produce his motor vehicles by the assembly line. To ensure that its resources were used to their full potential, Petty assumed governments would care for its citizens health and education, as only labor released value of capital. The new capitalist agriculture included larger farms and commodity farming rather than self-sufficiency farming. Petty saw property investment was bettered by the growing population, which saw increases in land values. Thus, an ever-increasing population in one place or another would see increasing property values and better the financial condition of the investors of such properties.

"In the early seventeenth century, the seven United Provinces of the Netherlands (roughly today's Belgium and Netherlands) boasted the most advanced capitalist economy in Europe, with the largest stock market, the highest per capita income, the finest houses—'In all Europe,' a contemporary English commentator Bernard de Mandeville, asserted, ' you

shall find no private buildings so sumptuously magnificent as the merchants' and other gentlemen's houses are in Amsterdam'—and a merchant fleet equal in size to those of England, France, Spain, and Portugal combined. All this was built on a dynamic trade economy based largely on fishing and the import of spices, silk, and china from the Far East. In 1602, the inner circle of bankers, traders, and guild masters in six of these cities used their political clout to create the United East India Company, in Dutch Vereenigde Oost-Indische Compagnie or VOC, by amalgamating those companies trading with the Orient and especially the spice islands of modern Indonesia. The behemoth that was set up, eight times larger than the English East India Trading Company founded in London two years earlier in 1600, transformed the financial and corporate environment. Its funding brought into existence such innovations as the public sale of shares, the concept of the joint stock company where the owners' liability for debt was limited to their shareholding, the issue of bonds backed by future earnings, a stock exchange for trading the company's shares, and a board of directors responsible to the shareholders for running the enterprise."

"The phenomenal wealth generated by the VOC—for two centuries its dividends averaged almost 20 percent—lifted the development of commercial capitalism to a new level, but the company was not designed for free enterprise. Not only did the States-General, the Netherlands federal parliament, guarantee the VOC a monopoly of trade with the east for twenty-one years, it enforced restrictions on competition to the point of forbidding any Dutch ship to enter either the Indian or the Pacific Oceans, by sailing around the Cape of Good Hope or through the Straits of Magellan at Cape Horn, without its permission. To recycle the profits from this immense monopoly, and from other smaller trading companies, Amsterdam bankers and politicians generated a range of financial and fiscal instruments, including government bonds, annuities or rentes, and debentures, that reduced the cost of government borrowing to just 4 percent. Nevertheless, the basic structure of this complex financial market was what socialist historian Eric Hobsbawm described as 'a feudal business economy.'"'

-Linklater

London's trading monopolies prevented laws from being created that would have allowed competition to challenge their market dominance. While the English were expanding private property rights, the Dutch were still operating by state run mercantilist fiefdoms. Both of these systems functioned and were successful, as they were based on the acceptance and practice of the people.

In 1732, in his *Essai sur la nature du commerce en general*, Richard Cantillon explained that mercantilism only enriched the powerful few who managed a country's financial institutions, while private property economics created dynamic and shifting free market economics that allowed prosperity to exist for the entire population.

Dr. Francois Quesnay, founder of the physiocrats, asserted that feudal restrictions, myriad taxes, and other government interference creates problems for entire nations, and that it would serve better to have one tax on profits of landowners, allow the markets to self-regulate and operate freely, and remove all government involvement in the economy.

Adam Smith, 1763, was influenced by the Scottish Enlightenment, with which sentiments such as government existed only to serve the people and to safeguard their property and right to personal liberty were fundamental. He theorized that people were motivated by the general welfare of their society and concern for others happiness. He claimed that justice was the main component that upholds a society, and without this any society would crumble in upon itself. Wealth of Nations depicts the free market as an endless balancing act to achieve an impossible equilibrium. As long as the theory that people were motivated by concern for others wellbeing, the mechanism would serve even those who were

unproductive. He fiercely criticized mercantilism and claimed that the only way to prevent it was for governments to give way to free markets, and to absolutely prevent monopolies.
"(In the mid-1800's) Both Sir Edward Coke, the preeminent spokesman for English common law, and the German jurist Samuel Pufendorf, chief exponent of a European theory of natural law, agreed that the word for monopolies was 'odious.' In Pufendorf's view, they offended 'against the law of humanity' and in Coke's 'against the liberty and freedom of all the subject and laws of the land."[99]
In 1654, Francis Yeardley purchased Carolina from natives for £200. By 1669, the Fundamental Constitution of Carolina was made to appeal to the "adventurers" of the British colonies in the West Indies including Barbados. This Constitution was built to incorporate the highly stratified societies of those colonies, including legal slavery and hierarchies based on land ownership alone. 40 percent of the territory was given to six Lords Proprietors and landgraves and caciques. The rest available at 3 pounds per acre. 50 acres qualified the owner to vote. This constitution worked, and among the newcomers was Sir John Yeamans in 1673, and who was instrumental in bringing slavery to Barbados. Another concession made to those who would move not only to Carolina, but many of the colonies, was the surveying and registration of all the lands owned to avoid deceits and lawsuits. In the mid-1670's, settlers of Carolina, became fed up with the dues to the Proprietors, religious tolerance toward Jews and Quakers, the Proprietors refusal to allow settlers to purchase pelts from the Native Americans and raid Spaniards in Florida who harbored runaway slaves.
In *Two Treatises on Government*, John Locke expounded that private property was an inevitable outcome of nature, and that land gave opportunity to express the inherent freedom of mankind. He argued that before government, people were free and lived in vast empty lands and that it was by the creative work of an individual on land that gave him right to ownership of that land. The individual who toiled to improve land, mixing his labor into it, made the land his own and thus the land itself was a part of him, and thus his own. Self-ownership had divine origin. Creation made each person Gods property, and by similar suit the cultivated earth made it owned by the cultivator. He said, "The great and chief end therefore, of Mens uniting into Commonwealths, and putting themselves under Government, is the Preservation of their Property." Democracy thus leaves sovereignty ultimately with the people. Agreements between individuals that reduce their natural liberty to preserve what is already theirs.
Taxation, within this way of thinking, without assent of the property owner of any kind was oppressive and an attack on his possessions and freedom. John Locke's Treatises describe exclusive ownership as a result of the right to own what one has created. He describes it as a matter of justice that each have the right to own their creations, and also the responsibility to be charitable. Property is guided by moral fairness rather than man-made laws, making it superior to law and government.

"If taxes are laid upon us in any shape, without our having a legal representation where they are laid, are we not reduced from the character of free subjects to the miserable state of tributary slaves?"
– Samuel Adams, 1764

The origin of private property in the 1500's in England also saw the origin of the role of private property owners taking account and seeing to the wellbeing of the "lame, impotent, poor, old, blind, and such other among them being poor and not able to work." There was in 1601 a law passed taxing landowners one percent GDP to serve this cause. The only successful way for private ownership to succeed in its goals is to be seen as fair by all the participants in the society, including the propertied and unpropertied.
On December 1, 1719, after South Carolina's provincial assembly denied the Proprietors Government, they mustered a militia and replaced the Lords Proprietors' governor with James Moore, Jr., in the first coop in the colonies. The Crown accepted this change, and with its acceptance, in 1729, the Lords

Proprietors charter was revoked, and the colony fell under direct Royal control, solidifying their status as colonists rather than tenants.

In the 1641 Irish Rebellion, between 300,000 and 600,000 people were killed in Ireland by 1661, Prior to this rebellion, two-thirds of land in Ireland was owned by Catholics, and by 1659, 90 percent was owned by Protestants. Protestants also took control of government. For over 1000 years, Ireland was under attack and servitude to its neighbors. Russian Serfs, even, and especially, in the late 18th century, were basically slaves. Landowners had wide latitude to treat them how they wished and buying and selling them was part of the culture.

China had an ancient, somewhat private property society until the Red Army Communists led by Mao Zhedong defeated the Kuomintang in 1949 and abolished private property rights. The peasantry was subjected to atrocious states of living and working, in effect, as slaves to the landlords. Mao believed the lack of increase in the wellbeing of the people was due to Feudal exploitation of the peasantry and foreign domination. The difference between the East and West private property forms, was that while the west gave personal freedom explicitly through landowning, the Chinese demanded high property taxes and that landowners be responsible for their entire families housing, work, and wellbeing. Land had to be passed equally to all sons. By 1910, the value of land evolved from production capacity to how many people it could support living upon it, matching the population explosion, about 400 million in 1910.

"The Marquis de Condorcet, a friend of Thomas Jefferson and a progressive thinker steeped in Locke's writing, declared roundly 'there is no connection between ownership of an invention and that of a field which can only be cultivated by one person.' A patent was a social arrangement created by society for its own good, and thus, 'It is not a true right, it's a privilege.'"[100] In 1710, the first copyright law was passed, guaranteeing authors ownership of their books. The reason for this law's creation was to encourage educated people to write useful books for the public wellbeing. It was not considered a right, but rather a tool to enhance the general public, and thus the nation.

Adam Smith amongst others, including those wealthy enough to afford a patent, argued that, as land improvement establishes ownership, so does the mental and manual labor of authoring a book or inventing a technology establish individual ownership as a real right. By 1806, intellectual property was the standard, as it was seen that the individual who produced something was the owner of it, same as the one who enhances a parcel of land.

By the mid-1700's and up until the mid-1900's, the society of England was formed by a free-enterprise model following the landowning model. The new society involved three classes, landlords, tenants, and laborers, similar in design to shareholders, managers, and workers, or capital, machinery, and laborers. This design created an "elite democracy, closed to all but the wealthiest or most determined." The landowners used "political dominance to loot communally owned land... and treated government posts as property that could be that could be mortgaged and inherited... it was out of Britain's highly capitalized, stalled land market that the Industrial Revolution emerged."[101]

Landowners looked for ways to utilize their land for profit, beyond the initial, such as coal mining, clay mining, and other diverse methods and means. Canals were dug to transport coal, and obligatory land purchase contracts returned capital to the investor of the canal, on top of their coal operations, and opened up a cheap, easy transport system for manufacturers and miners to reach their markets. Before large private banks, capital was held in land, rather than financial securities. A progression occurred such that enterprising individuals went from peasantry or royalty to landowning enclosure profiteers, to landowning political dominance, to landowning industrialists, to landowning bankers, with each of the transitions funded by the land itself, or its uses. The industrialists turned bankers transitioned away from the land as the "prime source of wealth and income" and began the age of financial securities.

Throughout major revolutions of the past several centuries, the pattern exists that... "Yet in all of these societies, it is the government that is in financial difficulties, not the societies themselves." While prospering, the "middle class" of merchants, lawyers, and businessmen and such become unwilling to lend money to the government or pay taxes. Rather than increasing suffering leading to revolution, it was the increasing success of these people that led them to aspire for ever greater success and thus demand the freedoms needed to achieve it. The quality of life was set higher for the entire population and thus they demanded a reformed government that would accommodate for the newly made possible aspirations. "Our revolutions, (French, American, English, Russian) then, clearly were not born in societies economically retrograde; on the contrary, they took place in societies economically progressive... the more prosperous the peasants, the more discontented.""...we look at economic life in these societies in the years preceding revolution, we note first, that they have been on the whole prosperous; second, that their governments are chronically short of money—shorter, that is, than most governments usually are; third, that certain groups feel that policies are against their particular economic interests..."[102]

The land price boom between the mid-1600's and mid-1700's sparked an incredible population increase in America, and specifically in New England, which went from 20,000 to 400,000 by 1750. After the Seven Years War, British Government believed American Colonists ought to pay taxes to assist in reducing the British national debt, as a consequence of the war was the new possession of title to use formerly French owned territory in America. This allowed land speculators, and average people, to venture into and claim land for personal use and for profit. Increasingly, colonial rule was seen as oppressive, and because taxes in the colonies were minimal, the demand from Britain for indirect taxes was unacceptable to the colonists, despite the fact that by 1776, American proprietors net worth growth was twice the rate of the British proprietors, and four out of five Americans owned their own land. In William Blackstone's Commentaries on the Laws of England, "civil immunities... (protected the individual from being) constrained to pay and aids or taxes, even for the defense of the realm or the support of government, but such as are imposed by his own consent, or that of his representatives in parliament." Seeing as the Colonists had no representatives, they were in effect being forced to either allow themselves to become slaves or rebel and become independent. "What differentiates this ideal world of our (American Intellectual) revolutionaries from the better world as conceived by more pedestrian persons is a flaming sense of immediacy of the ideal, a feeling that there is something in all men better than their present fate, and a conviction that what is, not only ought not, but need not, be."[103]

Parties or factions produce vendetta politics.

"...the alternate domination of one faction over another, sharpened by the spirit of revenge... has perpetrated the most horrid enormities."
- George Washington

James Madison believed that a large republic would be functional in a democratic system as, "Society itself will be broken into so many parts, interests, and classes of citizens, that the rights of individuals, or of the minority, will be in little danger from interested combinations of the majority." Madison argued that without a shared sense of justice in constitutional terms, providing each section of society with inviolable rights, the system would collapse. He believed every group or faction in the society needed to enjoy political equality to truly be free.

Thomas Jefferson proposed an experiment in social engineering with his suggestion that newly claimed US territory be divided into square territories that could apply to join the union after their population exceeded 20,000. Jefferson appointed Professor Jared Mansfield as surveyor-general in 1803, who created a system of Principal Meridians, north-south lines precisely marked as controls for the rest of the surveying of lands across American territories.

Ohio was the first purely American society and system. It was seeded by Americans after Independence and surveyed according to Jeffersons model of 36 square mile sections and sold privately and to land companies. By 1820, the population had exploded into 581,000, where even 20 years before it was only

45,000. These square divisions, eventually being broken up into 40-acre sections in 1832, ignored geographically important structures, like springs or hills, which made little agricultural or building sense, but made for extremely easy speculation and trading. This was the Public Lands Survey, organizing the land for use and purchase privately and by companies. Land purchasers very regularly purchased land to improve it, and then sell it to the quickly growing population, at a premium. Even simply clearing trees and breaking impacted soil doubled the value of property. The rising value of land allowed farmers to borrow from the banks, which allowed the rapid specialization in farming to include dairies, and to invest in cotton mills, bridges and other infrastructure, and even banks and insurance companies. Federal government policies created the impetus for the burgeoning free-enterprise capitalism of the early 1800's, and if not for various fundamental changes, would have been a driving force for the continued growth of individual wellbeing across the nation, after the first half of the 1800's. "...the Public Lands Survey continued to Americanize immigrants from every culture by making ownership of conquered territory available to all who wanted it." It only took 66 years for the Public Lands Survey to extend coast to coast. "What had been measured out was unmistakably a democracy, and quite clearly a republic, but its foundation was undeniably imperial."[104]

In 1816, the year it was created, the Second Bank of the United States, to control the supply of money and to pay off the last payment to European banks for the Louisiana Purchase, called in silver from its branches and state banks at the same time customers were changing paper for cash, causing a panic and land market collapse. The Monroe administration did not bail out banks, but rather cancelled debts and extended pay periods for those who had purchased private land, many on credit. This allowed individuals and companies to weather the panic and hold onto their capital and investments. This kept purchasing power and ownership in the hands of the people rather than transferring wealth from the people to the banks. This policy allows people to continue to expand their efforts and weather the storm.

"...only 384,000 of the Southern white population of 8,099,760 in 1860 actually owned slaves. And the great majority of owners held fewer than five slaves, not enough to be important economically, and socially significant only after color had come to define the difference between free and unfree." That is, 4.7 percent of Southern whites owned any number of slaves, and the great majority of those owned less than five slaves. Slaves in 1850 were valued at $1,000, making the total value of slave property four billion dollars, four times the northern manufacturing industry value. "In effect, the basis of slavery was contractual, a penalty imposed because a military or financial failure to maintain one's freedom. The manumission laws on both sides of the Atlantic gave legal status to this moral outlook by enabling owners to return slaves to their naturally free state once the slave expiated the failure, wither by paying off the debt or securing the owners forgiveness. Since all British colonies in North America began adhering to this concept of slavery as a mixture of servitude and freedom, there was initially little to distinguish between slaves and indentured servants."[105] (Linklater, 2013)

The incredible sadism that is often remembered in regard to African American slavery existed between the late 1600's up until the end of the Civil War. The transition to harsh treatment was facilitated by the change in the type of property a slave was. Rather than real estate, the laws of the south especially began to identify slaves as chattel and unmixed property, meaning slave owners had absolute rights to their slaves, to do with as they pleased.

Starting in 1691, prohibitions on racial intermixing between whites and blacks only increased along with severity of punishments associated with doing so. Laws did not prevent mixing though, as huge portions of the population were mixed race. Southern Congressmen enforced the "gag rule" in US Congress, banning speech regarding slavery. Slave codes in the South forced white people to treat slaves in only prescribed ways, regarding everything including hiring, punishments, travel, and education. The entire population was taxed to the benefit of the small group of profiteers of the slave industry. Abolition of slavery was an avoided topic as cotton served as a majority of American exports, valuing at $120 million annually. All the states shared in that economic benefit. In the end, the moral question needed to loom larger than the comfortable economic benefit.

After slavery was abolished and the war concluded, rights for blacks were enforced by Northern interference in the Reconstruction. After the 1873 economic crash, the Northern presence left and the South fell under Jim Crow laws and made land ownership, voting rights, and education nearly universally unattainable for blacks, giving Southern whites a political monopoly.

"The 1860's marked one of the great watersheds in the history of individual liberty when some forty-seven million serfs and four million slaves were set free, and the most powerful serf and slave economies in the world were destroyed." Russia's Crimean War defeat and the Union victory in the United States both led to liberation of the slaves in both societies. Between 1861, when nobility owned 80 percent of land in European Russia, and 1912, when two-thirds of that was owned by the freed serfs, more than half the Russian forests were destroyed in the production of industry to improve land for profit. The freed serfs produced ecological destruction on massive scale within 50 years of their liberation. By 1914, more than 10 million peasants had travelled to the wild east Siberia seeking and finding cheaper land more profitable than that offered in the west, in the same spirit of American pioneers travelling west. During this time, and leading up to the 1917 Bolshevik Revolution, Tsar Nicholas II attempted reforms that would have led to peasants becoming private propertied smallholders but resulted in splitting the nation into deeper factions leading to revolution, as the Tsar was unwilling to provide representation to these freed serfs. "...the majority of freed slaves, like the majority of freed serfs, were to find that without political power individual liberty was eroded swiftly as it was won."[106]

The Southern states surveyed their lands around geographical structures using the old English method of metes and bounds. This made property very hard to patent correctly and to simply measure. A very small portion of the population, at times less than 1000 people owned huge tracts of land, that by 1850 earned them nearly as much as the rest of the population. The uneven tracts and incredibly complex and corrupt surveying industry in the South led to this incredible income disparity.

Acres of land in 1800 were sold at $1.25 or $27.14 in today's dollars. Never today will a person find land this cheap. The advancement of transportation technology increased population, globalization of economics, and immigration to the unimproved vast tracks of land in Australia and North America, amongst other similar places. "The first coordinated global crash (panic/depression) came in 1873. It was also the first where measures were taken to deal with financial instability in one country—Germany's attempt to stave off inflation by tying its currency to gold rather than silver—rippled through others, destabilizing their booming, credit-swollen economies from Austria to Zanzibar. Silver-backed currencies like the dollar lost credibility, triggering runs on the banks and a rolling wave of company failures. In the United States, bankruptcies totaled $775 million in four years, including that of the great tycoon Jay Cooke. American railroads defaulted on bonds worth $790 million, 65 percent of which were held by foreign investors, setting off crashes in Europe." By the late 1870's, resources in land began to get more restricted, and thus a shift of egalitarian society based on resourceful farmers on private property, to landowners growing wealthy on rising land costs, and the poor unable to purchase any land, concentrating wealth amongst the propertied.[107]

The 1855 Limited Liability Act and 1856 Joint Stock Companies Act in Britain gave protection to investors by making them free from any liabilities greater than their investment. This opened the door for borrowing/lending to major industry around the world, at low risk, despite huge costs associated in erecting the structures of each industry. Large monopolies also utilized bonds for funding their industrial needs. Due to the vast instruments made, and the cost of shutting down, these major industries instead traded at a loss whenever panics hit. Overproduction and capital and labor waste was the result, with greater effect being an uncapitalistic wrench in the economic engine of free market economics globally. The London Stock Exchange quoted a majority of global national debt in 1872, meaning more than half of all debt globally was owed to investors in Britain. "In 1913, British financial institutions owned nine billion dollars of assets in the British Empire; six billion in Africa, Latin America, Russia, and the Far East; and $3.8 billion in the United States."[108]

"In the United States, a collection of big producers who fixed prices amongst themselves, and adjusted production accordingly was known as a trust. Most of the rest of the industrial world used the word 'cartel,' but the practice spread rapidly everywhere during the hard times after 1873, when large-scale manufacturers maximized production in order to service their debts. On razor-thin margins at best and chronic losses at worst, many were effectively owned by their banks and creditors. In order not to lose their investment, their financial backers seized at the opportunity offered by more powerful competitors, notably such industrial titans as Cornelius Vanderbilt, Andrew Carnegie, and John D. Rockefeller, to arrange price agreements, production targets, and trusts and so to be absorbed into existing webs of railroads, steel factories, and oil refineries. No one understood the new order of capitalism more clearly than J. P. Morgan, who used his influence as a banker to set up trusts in railroads, electricity generation, and steel manufacture—his creation, United States Steel, capitalized in 1901 at $1.2 billion, was the first billion-dollar industrial producer in the world, and had two thirds of the market." $1.2 billion in 1901 is equivalent to roughly $39 billion today. The ongoing production kept industrial activity at greater pace than anywhere else.[109]

Between 1870 and 1890, banks mortgaged many of the new farms being purchased, as demand for land exceeded supply, thus increasing land value over time. More and more farms shared ownership with banks. Yields increased as margins contracted, and international trade marked extreme market and political reactions to overabundances of supply, especially of cereal from American farms. Tariffs provided protections from these overabundances, especially in Germany.

Overconsumption became the theme to dispense of overproduction. Credit was given liberally to allow installment purchases of valuable home and work products. Hybrid ownership of land, housing, and home goods led to great conflicts between the people, the banks, and the government. The overabundance of industrial supply was balanced by the home goods market accelerating rapidly in the 1920's, when home goods became responsible for around 70 percent of GDP in the US. This market led to enormous increases in both materials production plants and factories and services geared toward homeowners. The push and rush to buy homes led to majority of homes and home goods to be purchased with mortgages and loans from banks, who shared ownership for the majority or all of the working life of the average American family.

"...the larger and more dynamic part of it (the American economy) was based on the construction, equipment, and servicing of the industrial home, and that in turn depended on the interest rates charged on Wall Street's bond market." Moneylenders borrowed at lower rates than they loaned, all backed by Wall Street's interest rates. "...when banks lost confidence following the (1929) stock market crash, the engine when into reverse, sucking so much credit out of the system that the human owner of the industrial home, hit by a perfect storm of unemployment, high interest rates, and foreclosure, could not buy anything at all, leaving industry with a pile of goods it could not sell."[110]

Progressives came into dominance at the turn of the century, creating antitrust legislation (Sherman Act, 1890), joining trade unions, and demanding age pensions and employment benefits. While calling for a nationalized public central bank, the industrialists cleverly created it privately under a public sounding name. Fundamentally, the private central bank, the FED, failed in its charter, to prevent panics/depressions. The elimination of debt in the FED would have restored faith to banks and allowed the economy to grow and capital to continue to be accessible by the population, but that was not the goal of the private bankers. It allowed the wealthiest groups to purchase vast assets at incredibly low cost.

The base differentiation between communism and capitalism comes down to the way the earth is owned. Private or communal ownership. General Douglas Macarthur redistributed property from landlords to the peasants who worked the land by forced reform after Japan's surrender in 1945. Six million acres, or one-third of Japan's farmland, was taken from 2.3 million landlords and sold to 4.7 million farmers. Profit maximization became the goal for landowners in Japan and was accompanied by mass exodus to urban centers to find work, which lead to an urban land market allowing borrowing on urban properties. This same process was repeated in Taiwan and South Korea, to somewhat similar effect.

Vladimir Ilyich Ulyanov "Lenin's" Bolshevik revolution dreamed of collectivizing all Russian land but was prevented from doing so by the Kulak farmers in Ukraine, over two-million counterrevolutionary farmers on the most arable land in Russia, who forced Lenin to accept private ownership. Stalin, in 1929, forced collectivization and made a death or exile campaign against the Kulaki. By 1932, over half a million families were killed or exiled. In 1936, over 90 percent of land was collective farmed, on farms averaging 6000 acres. In the 1950's, Nikita Khruschev created the Virgin Lands program which conglomerated 90 million acres of Kazak Steppe and Ural plateau into collective cultivation. Between 1928 and 1970, Russia's economy growth was second only to Japan's. It proved collective farming's potential.

Che Guevara was an Argentinian traveler to Guatemala in 1954, where he saw the coup of the democratically elected President Jacobo Arbenz. Arbenz was going to radically diverge from the United Fruit Company's oppressive social and political dominance. Thus, the CIA, under the leadership and direction of Allen Welsh Dulles, orchestrated the coup to protect United fruit Company assets and to ensure US control over Guatemala. After witnessing this, Che began his campaign to Socialize land. After 1959, when Che and Fidel Castro had taken control of Cuba, Che used the National Institute of Agrarian Reform (INRA), with Castro leading, to enforce the Socialist system of land redistribution from estates larger than 1000 acres to the peasants and owner cooperatives. Sugar plantations, tobacco farms, and cooperatives were collectivized into state farms, and private sellers had to sell at state-controlled prices to state controlled outlets. The INRA executed 20,000 people over 50 years, and in its harsh policing, led over one million Cubans to flee Cuba, over 10% of the population. The US economic blockade of Cuba made it impossible for them to sell the vast nickel resources mined in Cuba, and thus prevented modernization through industrialization, thus hamstringing the already oppressive government of Cuba and their socialist goals.

Land redistribution lost its political importance in the 1950's after Guatemala's landlords were protected and South Vietnam the same. Where North Vietnam and other communist or communist-leaning states reformed land into collective and state-run farms, the capitalists reformed by taking land from landlords and selling it to private buyers, who would work the land themselves. 1950's Latin America had 1.7 billion acres of farmland; two-thirds owned by one percent of the population. These estates were called Latifundias and haciendas. In Uruguay, at a meeting of Latin American Countries in 1961, the US called for the replacement of Latifundias for equitable land use through redistribution. Land reforms that dispersed property in the 1950's produced longer life expectancy, more stable political systems, and better education.

In China, Mao Zedong abolished private property in 1958 and forced all farms into state owned communes, responsible to create their own factories. The famine that followed resulted in 42 million or more deaths, with 5 million deaths from unreserved violence from the party members against farmers. Mao's response was, "When there is not enough to eat, people starve to death. It is better to let half of the people die so that the other half can eat their fill." Sounds a bit like Thanos, doesn't it? Only after individual family holdings were introduced did the starvation slacken and capital increased to begin industrialization. Despite language describing property rights being added to their laws in 2002 and expanded in 2007, the practical result was to expand industrial property rights and to shift land from farming communities to the ever-expanding urban centers. While more pressure is coming from farmers, the state is yet the official owner of property as rights are not declared. Urban developers continue to take farming collective lands with government support. Political power is denied to the people.

Russia's collectivization of property into state run farms, called Sovkhozi, only increased over 30 years, until nearly 40 percent were state controlled. The 4 percent of farms in the USSR that were owned privately by farming families accounted for 30 percent of national agricultural production, with markedly higher quality products. The land use model of collectivization led to systemic failure.

In the 1960's, the US policy and practice regarding land and property was based on Walt W. Rostow's theory that industrialization was the marker and precursor to modernizing states. Industrialization leading nations to becoming market economies and democratic governments. Authoritarian government was seen as crucial to facilitate the transition from pre-industrialization to industrialized to market to democracy, and thus, the US supported and forcibly and most often covertly implanted autocrats in nations around the world in the hopes that while ownership was being privatized by force, the people would industrialize, which would eventually bring about democracy.

This theory was blown apart by its universal failure to produce democratic nations from autocratic rulers, the alienation of whole populations to the US as an invasive force, and the corrupted autocracies granting privileges to cronies versus true land redistribution. It also became exceedingly obvious that capitalism could succeed and thrive absent a modern democracy.

The introduction of ammonia-rich nitrogen turned unproductive farms around the world into high-yield super-producers. Production, through testing and crossing strains, drastically increased yields as crops began to be modified to most successfully meet the needs of the people, evolving disease-resistant, nitrogen-absorbing strains. This was especially helpful to the nearly starving Indian population in the 1960's, only 20 years following their revolution and independence.

The Green Revolution of the 20th century increased production, population, profit, and supply of goods globally. It began the globalization of food production and distribution, while seating power firmly in the hands of the richest farmers, who could employ labor and capitalize land. The poor farmers were left to struggle, and the corporatizing of agriculture was fueled by the apparent success of the system. The Green Revolution created a system of agricultural control with banks and agribusiness at the top, that even the most productive farms could not overcome.

While the Green Revolution did produce solutions to problems both economic and political in the middle east, it did not resolve the moral base that was demanded socially and religiously by the Shi'ite and Sunni populations. It kept landlords profiting, increasing populations fed, and universally corrupt political, military, and business leaders powerful and wealthy. The lack of justice and the mix of ideology and religious philosophy by the numerous competing social sects, left the middle east in constant internal contrasts. The US supported autocratic leaders suppressed and violently eliminated all claims that feudal ownership models be eliminated and replaced with electoral systems. When food prices skyrocketed in 2010, the people responded with revolution, dubbed the Arab Spring, eliminating autocratic rulers in the effort to produce a moral and judicial system of ownership and government. Democracy wasn't the moral option though, as it was proven globally to produce corruption, thus not supplying the moral structure sought. Wahabi Islam was birthed from the effort to produce justice and morality.

Friederich von Hayek, student of Ludwig von Mises, who was mentored by Carl Menger, claimed that any amount of government interference or planning led to dictatorship. "Planning leads to dictatorship because dictatorship is the most effective instrument of coercion and, as such, essential if central planning on a large scale is to be possible." The Austrian Economic theory was that absolute market freedom led to corrections to all disturbances of the market. No interfering agencies would benefit the economy by their manipulations which always revolve around guesswork.

If the market is to be left to its own with no government interference, then laws of all sorts would need to be abolished as well. The absence of the corrective public representative body would mean the public itself would be the corrective, even to the extent of hanging the crooked banker or banning a corporation from operating in their town. No central agency could impose itself on the justice seeker, but only the natural corrective could apply, such as is created by those directly, individually, involved.

"Hayek did not pretend that the rewards would be equitable, but argued they were just. In a flight of genuinely innovative thinking, he explained that the very imperfections of a free marketplace made it a more efficient means of rewarding effort than a centrally planned system. Because it involved many players, each forced to adjust to local conditions of supply and demand but equipped with only fragmentary knowledge of the wider world, the market would react more quickly and appropriately to the unpredictable complexities of life than would a centrally directed structure aiming at perfect knowledge and a rational response."[111] Austrian economics does not see property as a right, nor life, liberty, and the pursuit of happiness. Hayek saw the government being charitable to the poor in that it would supply the minimum to produce food, shelter, and clothing, to preserve health. He believed a financial elite, passing wealth through inheritance would lead to the most capable being in positions of power and influence. Austrian economics sees government regulation and social programs that manipulate and redistribute within the market as feeding the unproductive parasites of society. It proposes that there is a true elite that exists by its own abilities to operate with high productivity within an absolutely free market. All who cannot are of a lower caste. Interference by government is considered an attack on property, as government can only take what was had by those who worked or inherited to have it. As long as the models available for general consideration fluctuate only between socialism, capitalism, democracy, and communism, we will be unable to have meaningful results. The container is too large to caretake the diverse, eclectic population within, leading to applied force to achieve results for the minority in any direction.

Lyndon B. Johnson's Great Society program in 1965 created Medicare and Medicaid, increasing personal taxes 75 percent and dividends 95 percent, though it never practically went above 60 percent. From 1950 to 1980, the US population grew by 50 percent. GDP increased by 3.7 percent annually from 1950 to 1973. Between 1955 and 1965, 40 million babies were born, the decade prior to the introduction of contraception. In 1945 about half of Americans rented homes, but by the 1970's two thirds owned their own home, mostly on credit and loans, and by vast majority in the suburbs by the 1980's.

In 1979, Margaret Thatcher, new Prime Minister of Britain, privatized industries across the board, following the Austrian economic model. In 1986, she deregulated the City of London's financial markets. In the same year, Ronald Reagan deregulated markets, but in tandem with monetarist models which thought inflation control by regulated monetary supply was the way to manage growth. By 2000, the home goods market became yet again, "a functional adjunct to Wall Street," which drove economic progress.

The Austrian model failed in 2008, when Lehman Brothers went bankrupt, showing that a business could be so big that it can break the market with its own failure.

> *"Once a mortgage became not just an accountancy asset with equivalent item on the debit column but a trading asset that increased the capital value of the lender, it became logical for the sales forces working for any kind of lending institution to create as much debt as possible. Even the notorious 'Ninja' loans to borrowers with 'no income, no job, and no assets' became valuable. By March 2007, the value of subprime mortgages was estimated to be $1.3 trillion. The same process converted credit default swaps, the insurance issued against such transactions going wrong, into capital assets, and the insurance on foreign exchange trades underwent the same process. So long as investment traders agreed, anything could become money... money could be degenerated just as spontaneously. As news spread of the rising default rates on risky mortgages, trade in derivative bundles dwindled, and then quite suddenly in the summer of 2008 their standing as capital assets evaporated."*
>
> *"At a stroke, the health of financial institutions that held them became poisoned. The roll call included the investment bank Bear Stearns, with eleven billion dollars in equity but almost four hundred billion in potentially worthless assets; the American International Group, the largest insurers in the world, notionally worth more than $110 billion but whose London office alone issued credit swap defaults valued at more than $440 billion; and the*

blue-blooded investment bank Lehman Brothers, broker to more than a hundred hedge funds, with equity of $639 billion but potential debts of $1.3 trillion."

"When Lehman Brothers was allowed to go bankrupt in September 2008 as Austrian economics required, the Dow Jones index dropped five hundred points, stock markets around the world fell by close to 5 percent, and more significantly, banks stopped lending to each other. The realization that money could dissolve so quickly left every financial institution haunted by the same nightmare: any bank, however vibrant it appeared to be from its visible asset sheet, might turn out to be bankrupt when the real value of its untradeable assets was revealed. The marketplace was filled with zombie banks, and it was impossible to tell the living from the living dead. Fear halted lending and brought the entire mercantile capitalist system close to gridlock."

"In every country, the rescue plan involved government intervention on a massive scale. In the United States alone, government guaranteed more than one trillion dollars in direct rescue funds, followed by trillions more in federally invented money, the so-called quantitative easing, designed to take the place of traders' invented money and persuade the banks to start lending again. The Austrian experiment had failed."

-Linklater

Without regulatory barriers, lending increased from $500 million in 1990 to $2.6 trillion in 2007, which "drove property values up, powering the phenomenal expansion of the consumer economy and creating an apparent unquenchable appetite for automobiles, toys, clothes, and furniture." Demand for home goods led to outsourcing and the creation of an urban manufacturing economy in Asia, especially China, where the people invested in American debt rather than property, as property rights were absent in China. Over 100 million peasants migrated to cities to earn incomes producing cheap consumer goods. This debt purchasing kept interest rates artificially low, mortgage lending constant, house values climbing, consumer market growing, and subprime loans increasing. When the subprime mortgage market collapsed, it brought down the new global economy with it.

The idea that democracy can only be achieved through industrialization was the motivator for a vast amount of international interference by the United States. It was the primary theory on how democracies form for decades.

"Many of the countries offered as examples (of this theory) were from eastern Europe and became democratic not because of industrialization but because they were liberated from former Soviet Union by the end of the Cold War; others, such as Spain, Portugal, and Greece, were industrialized but then became dictatorships, and only later became democratic due to persistent pressure from western European neighbors; yet more, including South Korea, Taiwan, Uruguay, and Costa Rica, arrived at modernization through the prior redistribution of land as private property, while some at least of the remaining examples, such as Romania and Pakistan, were hardly shining examples of either industrialization of democracy... (Professor Francis) Fukuyama's entire 'development' thesis (industrialization leads to stable democracy) has been blown into oblivion by a series of Freedom House maps showing an entire swath of the globe from Moscow to Beijing and Hanoi occupied by some of the world's most vibrant industrial economies operating within repressive, undemocratic regimes... Up to 1987, the influence of the United States Constitution so permeated the aspirations to democracy that Time Magazine claimed an analysis of 170 written constitutions showed all but ten to have borrowed 'substantially' from the one drawn up in Philadelphia two centuries earlier.. Among the forty-four new

democracies that were born between 1987 and 2008, there was a clear tendency to guarantee human rights above property rights... these individual rights were set in a context that stressed the importance of communal and family needs... From a searching analysis of 729 constitutions adopted by 188 countries between 1946 and 2006, it is clear that sympathy for its (the US Constitution) values tuned to antipathy during the 1980's and 1990's, the very years when the Austrian version of private property capitalism took over in the United States and Britain, and began to be exported around the world by globalization... By the twenty-first century, it had become clear that in a private property society taken over by Austrian economics full and positive freedom had become a privilege confined, as in the Austro-Hungarian empire, to the financially favored few."

- Linklater

Between the 1970's and 1990's, top earners personal tax went from 70 percent to 35 percent, and capital gains from 40 percent to 15 percent. This created a federal income shortage that led to government borrowing. National debt increased by 200 billion with Reagan and 5 trillion under George W. Bush.

"As a result, the bond market that provided the loans became a more powerful influence on government policy than the electorate. But to service the interest and eventually pay back the principal, all taxpayers, including the unborn, inescapably became liable for a burden once shouldered immediately by the wealthiest. In 1980, fortune 500 CEO incomes were 42 times that of the average worker, while in 2010, it became 300 times.

"By 2007 there were 392,220 taxpayers in the United States with gross incomes of a million dollars or more, but the aggregate income, including capital gains, of the wealthiest four hundred Americans reached almost ninety-one billion dollars every year, meaning that on average each received an annual income of $227.4 million while paying tax at a rate of only 21.5 percent. Income eventually translates into capital wealth, and in 2007 the ultrarich four hundred owned as much wealth as the 150 million poorest Americans. Slightly below these peaks, the top 1 percent of Americans owned 34 percent of the nation's wealth while the bottom 90 percent owned just 29 percent. Hayek's goal of creating an aristocracy of wealth had been achieved."

- Linklater

After 1970, markers for economic growth and social growth showed a regression from the growth seen past WWII to 1970. The economy expanded faster during the more egalitarian years before Austrian economics took hold.

"...from 1951 to 1976 when the Untied States labored under a business-deterring, high-taxation, heavily regulated regime, America launched no fewer than twenty-three of the largest companies in the world, three more than were created in the thirty-year Austrian period of low taxation, high rewards, and light regulation from 1976 to 2007. And after recording annual returns close to 10 percent from 1950 to 1970, Wall Street's returns dropped to a pallid reward of 5.58 percent for the two decades from 1988 to 2008... In eighteenth-century Britain, the landowners who spearheaded the first free-market capitalist system behaved in the same way, using their political dominance to safeguard their own interests. With the backing of the law, they looted public land, insulated their property against moneylenders, and entailed their estates to keep them in the family. And to achieve these ends, they also corrupted the parliamentary system to the breaking point so that other groups could not gain access to the political marketplace. Yet none of this was

intended, or even perceived, by a class that prided itself on its public-spirited patriotism... Justice was not just a moral good, it was, as Adam Smith had always counseled, a practical necessity. Unless most people could be persuaded to believe that the market was fair, in both politics and the economy, it must wither and fail."

- Linklater

The advent of political acceptance of Austrian Economics was limited to aspects of the philosophy. The regulatory government actions existed still, and influenced every aspect of this financial system. In fact, we can only truly say that a Frankenstein of financial philosophies and systems is all that is ever emplaced, as it is always the goal of plutocrats to utilize whatever tools are available to expand their control and wealth and to limit that access to everyone else. The Frankenstein version of Austrian economics was used brilliantly to accomplish its original goals, to shift wealth from the masses to the self-titled global financial and social managers. The disparity of wealth and wellbeing continues to grow wider and deeper every day and every moment we allow the plutocrats to control markets and the bankers to make deposits and the central banks to create fiat currency.

Intellectual property has been more and more recognized by the law since the 1970's. In 2011, it was credited with creating millions of jobs and worth 34 percent of GDP, 5 trillion dollars. "One trend, however, is unmistakable—a corporate goal to make property out of anything that has required original mental activity."[112] Until the 1970's monopolies from patents were considered to be harmful to the general public.

"A sea change occurred in the course of the 1980's and 1990's. Not only were defenses strengthened, they were extended from inventions and copyrights to cover trade secrets, distinctive designs, and trademarks. Between 1983 and 2010, the number of patents issued each year in the United States increased fourfold from 64,000 to 244,000, and in the United Kingdom from just over two thousand to more than ten thousand. Under pressure from the motion picture industry, the life of copyrights was extended from twenty-eight years after an author's death to seventy years, while other major corporate interest groups persuaded the courts that the appearance of a fast-food restaurant and the development of a surgical procedure should be judged to be a property exclusive to its creator. Any lingering belief that the public interest might be harmed by such monopolies disappeared."

"During the Uruguay round of trade agreements concluded in 1994, the World Trade Organization brought into existence the concept of TRIPS or Trade-Related Aspects of Intellectual Property Rights. Every signatory nation was required to accept as intellectual property anything deemed to be so in another country 'without discrimination as to the place of invention, the field of technology and whether products are imported or locally produced.' Only where patents endangered public order or the environment could a national government modify the agreement."

"Without public discussion, one particular kind of ownership was embodied in the TRIPS agreement and planted in the legal structure of every signatory nation of the WTO. Ignoring past concerns that monopolies constituted a restraint of trade, the TRIPS agreement asserted bluntly and fallaciously, 'intellectual property rights are private rights' that had to be protected. Varieties of communal ownership of knowledge, such as the use of the periwinkle plant in traditional folk medicines in Madagascar, were deemed ineligible for protection, while the private, exclusive property that the pharmaceuticals company Eli Lilly claimed for its research into the plant after learning of its medical properties was instantly recognized, allowing the company to develop products from it worth two hundred million

dollars worldwide. With TRIPS, the idea of private exclusive property that first appeared in relation to land in sixteenth-century England could be said to have conquered the world."

- Linklater

Digitized information and file sharing sites created on the internet defied private property rights, as anything uploaded could be copied and shared. Digitized property defied ownership by the nature of its possibly infinite stemming inventions and adaptations made to whatever was made digitally available. While patent numbers rose, research and development and profits fell.

"Research into innovation in sixty countries by Harvard's Professor Josh Lerner, covering a period of 150 years from the 1850's, showed that strengthening patents not only failed to encourage innovation, 'the impact of patent protection-enhancing shifts on applications by residents was actually negative.' Following a more detailed examination of the spread of protection since the 1980's, Lerner described its effects as an 'innovation tax.'... Every monopoly is a restraint of trade, and the more there are, the smaller the scope for new enterprises... what used to be a culture of sharing information on new discoveries has been replaced by one of secrecy for fear that a rival might patent results and so impede future development... the usefulness of any new idea had become of lesser importance than the chance of using the patent to pry damages from a rival or to knock the competition out of some potentially lucrative line of development... Monopoly, by definition, damages competitiveness, but nowhere more destructively than in the realm of ideas... The very nature of exclusive ownership rewards those who can defend it. That is the prize that drives owners to seek political influence."

- Linklater

The pattern of control is the same whatever century, nation, or society. When monopolies are allowed to exist, they seek to defend their property and wealth through political control. It is the result of unmanaged private property societies in particular. While management can be a central government, which precludes corruption, in a truly informed society, it could be managed by the free market in a decentralized, localized, and individually responsible fashion.

As the population increases, so does the value of farmland. Major purchases of land across the world have been occurring since 2008 by the wealthy and international financiers.

"Until 2008, large-scale land purchases averaged less than two million hectares, or 4.8 million acres, a year, but in 2009 alone almost 110 million acres of farmland, seventy million of them in Africa, were bought by corporate purchasers from the United States, Europe, the Middle East, and China. The area was greater than the total of agricultural land in Germany, France, Belgium, Denmark, the Netherlands, and Switzerland, combined. In Liberia, where traditional family holdings of a few acres used to be the norm, the median size of privately owned farms in 2011 leaped to almost 130,000 acres. Although Sudan's corporate holdings were smaller—a relatively modest median area of eight thousand hectares, almost twenty thousand acres, each—they amounted in total to almost four million hectares, or about one fifth of the country's cultivated land."

"In Russia, 45 percent of the cultivated area was corporately owned in 2012, with the thirty largest companies farming a total of 6.7 million hectares. The proportion was higher both in Kazakhstan at 60 percent, and in Ukraine at 55 percent, where just forty companies, many of them foreign, owned 13.5 percent of the country's farmland in 2011. In southern Brazil, the median size of corporately owned sugar plantations was thirteen thousand hectares,

and in Argentina the thirty leading agribusinesses, including Soros's, owned on average eighty thousand hectares each of cattle, wheat, and oilseed land."
"The most authoritative estimate of the amount spent–foreign landgrabbing is too sensitive a topic to be open to easy scrutiny—is that one hundred billion dollars have been invested up to 2012. Some of the money came from China, which signed about thirty agricultural cooperation treaties that gave food producing companies, such as New Hope, a giant producer of pork and poultry on an industrial scale, access to farmland in countries ranging from Kazakhstan and Mozambique to the Philippines and Queensland. Other major investors were Saudi and Middle Eastern sovereign funds, and commodity producers such as Brazil's JBS, the world's largest source of palm oil. And a growing proportion, up to fifteen billion dollars in 2012, came from institutional investors in Europe and the United States, such as the $650 million Altima One World Agriculture Fund, which boasted of it's aspiration to be 'the first Exxon Mobil of the farming sector.'"
- Linklater

International investors are buying land to be used in the same fashion as absentee landlords of feudal times. The land purchases are being done in nations lacking clear property laws and effective governments. The seeming theft of the people's land by foreign investors has created strong opposition by the people of these nations, making the investments potentially frail in the future as governments may be overthrown. Foreign land ownership will lead to uprisings and to growth of extremist organizations that will appear to defy the occupation of stolen land. Contestation over water and land rights will come to a head when populations are starving. The transfer of these rights to corporations will lead to an eventual battle between those dispossessed and those seeking profit through absentee landlording. Who will be prepared to fight this fight?

**Substantial portions of this section derive from the very informative book, "Owning the Earth" by Andro Linklater. While I do not share in all of his conclusions, I found his book to be a thorough source of perspective. I encourage all my readers to read his book if you found this section interesting.*

LABOR

Let us talk about the workers. Let us talk about the working people who make up the U.S. and how they developed into what they are today. Let us talk about the conduct of the corporation and the condition of the people who make it profitable. Let us begin with Daniel Shays, who led a revolt in Boston, Massachusetts in 1786, just 10 years after the Declaration of Independence was signed to signify the separation of a free peoples from the abuse of tyranny and mercantilism. In 1687 in Boston, one percent of the population owned twenty-five percent of wealth in the land. In 1770, that same group owned forty-four percent of the wealth. In that same timeframe, the number of people that owned no property increased from fourteen percent to twenty-nine percent. In 1786, Shays and many others, mostly veterans of the Revolution, indebted, overtaxed, facing foreclosure of homes and farms chose to petition for redress, but no help came from the state legislature. Daniel Shays had served as a captain in the Continental Army. Under his leadership, the rebels forcibly closed local courts and released imprisoned debtors from jail. Governor James Bowden retaliated with a state militia funded by wealthy merchants.

They crushed the rebellion. This was the first revolt against the new nation, but it was not the last and even during the same timeframe, many states were encountering similar situations.

In Federalist Ten, James Madison spoke on how we deal with factionism. He said that if too much power is placed in the people, or in the hands of the rich and powerful either would endanger the nation. Madison said income inequality would coincide with increasing population. He foresaw industrial capitalism and mercantilism and how it displaces the general population and eliminates true democracy. Mercantilism is *the economic theory that trade generates wealth and is stimulated by the accumulation of profitable balances, which a government should encourage by means of protectionism.* Protectionism is *the theory or practice of shielding a country's domestic industries from foreign competition by taxing imports.*

Encyclopaedia Britannica states,

> *"Mercantilism contained many interlocking principles. Precious metals, such as gold and silver, were deemed indispensable to a nation's wealth. If a nation did not possess mines or have access to them, precious metals should be obtained by trade. It was believed that trade balances must be "favourable," meaning an excess of exports over imports. Colonial possessions should serve as markets for exports and as suppliers of raw materials to the mother country. Manufacturing was forbidden in colonies, and all commerce between colony and mother country was held to be a monopoly of the mother country."*

Of course, this practice was in use in the British colonies of North America, with industries like the fur trade being economically beneficial to Britain but leaving the colonies poverty stricken, unable to bear the burden of inflation and taxes, and unable to practice free trade to their benefit. This left the population largely discontent with the situation and made revolution a consideration. The people wanted their work to produce value that they could keep and use as any sane human would want. What actually occurred was remarkably similar to what is happening today. People work very hard, to make survival or subsistence wages, while the vast majority of the value of their work is transferred to large private banks and organizations, governments, corporations, and individuals. Today, the immense credit disbursed to the people with no backing on any real money, is the only reason the poverty of our nation and most of the world is not felt as it was at the time following the revolution. The amount of cheap and accessible technology also makes the wealth disparity less perceptible. Television, video games, cars and phones create a false sense of abundance.

In 1803, Thomas Jefferson purchased the Louisiana Territory rights of treaty or conquest for fifteen million dollars. These 530 million acres were purchased to offer the colonists turned Americans the possibility of establishing themselves as independent landowning producers rather than working for others at personal expense. This land was given at the expense of the Natives, with whom the people would have to compete with or drive out to acquire the land. Jefferson was a proponent for American Republicanism and the rights of the average person rather than the disparity of aristocratic elitism, including the profiteering of private bankers, merchants, and manufacturers. He felt that people had the civic duty and responsibility to aid in the Resistance of corruption by self-proclaimed authorities like aristocrats and plutocrats. The Republican Party was created in this image but was later termed the Democratic-Republican Party as distinguished from the Republican Party of Abraham Lincoln.

Despite the efforts of Jefferson and Jeffersonian Democrats as well as other proponents of social equity and individual rights, those like Alexander Hamilton who spoke for the central banking industry and the mercantilists like Robert Morris, who funded and founded the first national banking monopoly in the United States, were able to spread their infectious influence across the political spectrum through bribery and political promises. Robert Morris's bank monopoly in 1782 was called the Bank of North America, which was directly modeled after the Bank of England. Murray Rothbard said, "An important part of the

Morris scheme was to organize and head a central bank to provide cheap credit and expanded money for himself and his allies."

Robert Morris profiteered on the Revolution and did his best to profiteer on the peacetime American population. Alexander Hamilton, who was uneducated in finance or economics became the governmental proponent for the mercantilists as the first Treasury Secretary, where he worked to institute a system of shoring up national credit and creating a national bank, including high protectionist tariffs, creation of large public debt, property taxes, and poll taxes. Not only did Hamilton support mercantilism, but also supported and argued in favor of creating an American Royalty. He wanted the nation to be run by a king, which he called a permanent president. The labor movements that gained traction in the late 19th century and the early to mid-20th century were really begun in the same moment the Federalists became active in the newly created nation. It was and is the centralizers and moneylenders who work against the welfare and wellbeing of the general population and the working population. It is the plutocrats that dictate to the population and profiteer from the sweat and suffering of the laborers. It is the Plutocrats that have controlled this country and most of the world for centuries.

During the Civil War, 625,000 soldiers died, but the wealthy had a loophole created in 1863 that allowed them to not participate in the war. The Conscription Enrollment Act allowed the rich to avoid military service for a cash payment of $300. This inequality and legal draft dodging led to draft riots, including the New York riot of 1863, ending in the deaths of over 2000 people. The wealthy and African Americans were targeted. But those that this loophole was created for were not affected. This is an example of the consistent and obvious plutocratic behavior that led to the major labor movements.

Irish immigrants were at the bottom of white society. Fierce oppression in Ireland led to vast migrations to the U.S. Unskilled Irish came desperate for work in late 19th century. Irish people were one of the first ethnic groups to form labor unions. While Irish were called white negroes in the South, they were not treated the same as slaves, which were considered valuable property and not given dangerous work. The Irish were given the most perilous jobs. African Americans were forced into conflicts with the poor white working class and were often used as strike breakers.

"You are made to hate each other because upon that hatred is rested the keystone of the arch of financial despotism which enslaves you both."

- Tom Watson, American Populist Leader, late 19th Century

At the conclusion of the Civil War, slaves were freed, and their labor and their future were opened to great change from slave-like conditions. They attempted to seize lands, build schools, and otherwise reconstruct life. There were black judges presiding over white citizens. The opportunities were there for immense changes to the social conditions. This created a terror amongst the industrialists and bankers who wanted them back working in the production of cash crops. Black Codes, new laws, were passed all over the south that prohibited and retarded any of the aspirations of the freed slaves to balance the social structure. Poor whites were similarly affected. The effort to repress the blacks and poor whites was led by a coalition of elite democrats who attempted to maintain the conditions of slavery in all but name. They were the self-proclaimed champions of the property owner against the property-less.

The US expansion and conquest of Mexico began with non-violent attempts to purchase the land, but when purchase failed, the architects of expansion orchestrated a war that allowed them to occupy various places of import such as New Mexico, Arizona, Los Angeles, and San Diego. After cessation of the war, the US acquired the Southwest with the signing of the Treaty of Guadalupe-Hidalgo in 1848, which compelled Mexico to forfeit the northern half of its country and tens of thousands of its people who lived on those lands. Shortly after, the incoming Anglo-American population was larger than the native population and set up legal regimes to displace the landowning Mexican population and the rest of the population to labor in new industrial firms such as railroads, mining, agriculture, etc. Jim Crow laws applied to Mexicans as well. By 1900, American corporations were largely in control of the Mexican economy. Mexican rulers served American corporate interests over their own people. This is not to say that the people of the now American Southwest and then the Mexican North were better off under Mexican rule. In fact, the Mexican claim on these lands was as inappropriate as the American. Truly these were the land of the native populations that had fallen under the corrupt regimes of first Mexican government, then American. Before these was the Spanish invasion of their lands, in which the populations were largely massacred, enslaved, or otherwise conquered. The people of the American Southwest were, in the long run, benefitted from the Treaty of Hidalgo, as the quality of life in the United States has been far greater than the quality of life in Mexico. The end does not justify the means though, as cruelty toward the native peoples of these lands was rampant under the Spanish, the Mexicans, and the United States. The oldest known claim to these lands can be made by the inhabitants who existed before the Spanish invasion. Even then, who was truly the original people of that place is a never-ending discourse and study, and it is better to view the progress by its result on the general wellbeing of the land and those who occupy it. Today the land suffers far more than any other moment in known history. Rivers are being drained and aquifers drilled. This is the practice of ignorant managers of the land. It was the native people who practiced co-existence and regenerative practices with the land. This is our greatest loss as humans, and life on planet earth.

Poor Americans began banding together. Massive protests began in late 19th century, at a time when 20% of American workers were under age 18. It was around this same time Metropolitan Police were created. They enforced elections by acting as private armies for political machines and acted as breakers of protests and strikes.

In 1869, The Knights of Labor was founded. This was the beginning of the union movement. The Knights opposed the wage system, calling it an insult to the divine nature of man. They accepted blacks and women. They were opposed to the aristocracy of labor, which was trade unions exclusion of members due to skill level. They excluded bankers, lawyers, liquor manufacturers, and stockholders who they labeled unproductive members of society. Their ideal was not met as they weren't functionally able to organize the substantial number of members. At their peak they were comprised of about 700,000 members. The American Federation of Labor replaced the Knights, as did other smaller, less powerful unions. In 1877, the Great Railroad Strike demonstrated the ability of ordinary workers to coalesce into a national powerful force. This was the first major uprising against the capitalist order. Entire communities participated in striking against the railroads. Several cities such as Chicago turned into general strikes, stalling the entire city. The president sent in Federal troops to put down working class insurrection. By doing so, he shifted the position of the nation from protecting the free people of the south, where the troops were stationed, to a rights repression of the working class. This was the first great protest against the captive capitalism, industrialism, and plutocracy in the U.S. The uprising was defeated but concretized the idea amongst the working class that they could fight for their rights. Workers began to further socialistic and communistic ideas. Edward Bellamy's utopian socialist novel "Looking Backward" sold over a million copies while unions were becoming more militant and sabotage becoming common practice.

In 1884, The Anarchists of Chicago argued for the creation of a free society.

> *"Establishment of a free society based upon cooperative organization of production; organization of education on a secular, scientific, and equal basis for both sexes; and equal rights for all without distinction of sex or race."*

The Haymarket Incident in 1886 was used to discredit anarchism. After a scuffle at a picket line, police shot and killed several workers outside McCormick Harvester Factory in Chicago, which was the largest factory in the country, where 1300 men worked 10 hours a day, 6 days a week, for non-subsistence wages. The mayor and chief of police routinely received bribes from the factory owner, again showing the consistent abuse of power that is the mark of plutocracies. During an organized rally at Haymarket Square to protest the violence, police charged the protesters. An unknown assailant threw a bomb at the police killing one and harming several others. The police then opened fire, killing several workers and policemen. The rally organizers were anarchists who were never linked to the bomb but were arrested and charged with conspiracy. Seven out of the eight were charged with death, and the eighth with fifteen years in prison. The trial was a farce. Prior to the arrests, States Attorney Julius Grinnell, publicly recommended to make the raids first and look up the law afterwards. The handpicked jury consisted of businessmen, their own clerks and a relative of one of the dead policemen. They were instructed that, "Anarchy is on trial...Make examples of them, hang them and...save our institutions, our society." -Julius S. Grinnell, Prosecuting Attorney.

August Spies Statement before being hanged, excerpt, "Address of August Spies", October 7, 1886:

> *"My efforts in behalf of the disinherited and disfranchised millions, my agitation in this direction, the popularization of economic teachings—in short, the education of the wage workers, is declared "a conspiracy against society." The word "society" is here wisely substituted for "the State," as represented by the Patricians of today. It has always been the opinion of the ruling classes that the people must be kept in ignorance, for they lose their servility, their modesty and their obedience to the powers that be, as their intelligence increases. The education of a black slave a quarter of a century ago was a criminal offense. Why? Because the intelligent slave would throw off his shackles at whatever cost. Why is the education of the working people of today looked upon by a certain class as an offense against the State? For the same reason! The State, however, wisely avoided this point in the prosecution of this case. From their testimony one is forced to conclude that we had, in our speeches and publications, preached nothing else but destruction and dynamite. The court has this morning stated that there is no case in history like this. I have noticed, during this trial, that the gentlemen of the legal profession are not well versed in history. In all historical cases of this kind truth had to be perverted by the priests of the established power that was nearing its end.*
>
> *We have interpreted to the people their conditions and relations in society. We have explained to them the different social phenomena and the social laws and circumstances under which they occur. We have, by way of scientific investigation, incontrovertibly proved and brought to their knowledge that the system of wages is the root of the present social iniquities—iniquities so monstrous that they cry to heaven. We have further said that the wage system, as a specific form of social development, would, by the necessity of logic, have to give way to higher forms of civilization; that the wage system must furnish the foundation for a social system of co-operation—that is, Socialism. That whether this or that theory, this or that scheme regarding future arrangements were accepted was not a matter of choice, but one of historical necessity, and that to us the tendency of progress seemed to be Anarchism—that is, a free society without kings or classes—a society of sovereigns in which liberty and economic equality of all would furnish an unshakable equilibrium as a foundation for natural order*
>
> *It is not likely that the honorable Bonfield and Grinnell can conceive of a social order not held intact by the policeman's club and pistol, nor of a free society without prisons, gallows, and State's attorneys. In such a society they probably fail to find a place for themselves. And is this the reason why Anarchism is such a "pernicious and damnable doctrine?*

Grinnell has intimated to us that Anarchism was on trial. The theory of Anarchism belongs to the realm of speculative philosophy. There was not a syllable said about Anarchism at the Haymarket meeting. At that meeting the very popular theme of reducing the hours of toil was discussed. But, "Anarchism is on trial!" foams Mr. Grinnell. If that is the case, your honor, very well; you may sentence me, for I am an Anarchist. I believe with Buckle, with Paine, Jefferson, Emerson, and Spencer, and many other great thinkers of this century, that the state of castes and classes—the state where one class dominates over and lives upon the labor of another class, and calls this order—yes, I believe that this barbaric form of social organization, with its legalized plunder and murder, is doomed to die, and make room for a free society, voluntary association, or universal brotherhood, if you like. You may pronounce the sentence upon me, honorable judge, but let the world know that in A. D. 1886, in the State of Illinois, eight men were sentenced to death, because they believed in a better future; because they had not lost their faith in the ultimate victory of liberty and justice!

You have taught the destruction of society and civilization," says the tool and agent of the Bankers' and Citizens' Association, Grinnell. That man has yet to learn what civilization is. It is the old, old argument against human progress. Read the history of Greece, of Rome; read that of Venice; look over the dark pages of the church, and follow the thorny path of science. "No change! No change! You would destroy society and civilization!" has ever been the cry of the ruling classes. They are so comfortably situated under the prevailing system that they naturally abhor and fear even the slightest change. Their privileges are as dear to them as life itself, and every change threatens these privileges. But civilization is a ladder whose steps are monuments of such changes! Without these social changes—all brought about against the will and the force of the ruling classes—there would be no civilization. As to the destruction of society which we have been accused of seeking, sounds this not like one of Aesop's fables—like the cunning of the fox? We, who have jeopardized our lives to save society from the fiend—the fiend who has grasped her by the throat; who sucks her life-blood, who devours her children—we, who would heal her bleeding wounds, who would free her from the fetters you have wrought around her; from the misery you have brought upon her—we her enemies!! Honorable judge, the demons of hell will join in the laughter this irony provokes!

Grinnell has repeatedly stated that our country is an enlightened country. The verdict fully corroborates the assertion! This verdict against us is the anathema of the wealthy classes over their despoiled victims—the vast army of wage workers and farmers. If your honor would not have these people believe this; if you would not have them believe that we have once more arrived at the Spartan Senate, the Athenian Areopagus, the Venetian Council of Ten, etc., then sentence should not be pronounced. But, if you think that by hanging us you can stamp out the labor movement—the movement from which the downtrodden millions, the millions who toil and live in want and misery, the wage slaves, expect salvation—if this is your opinion, then hang us! Here you will tread upon a spark, but here, and there, and behind you, and in front of you, and everywhere, flames will blaze up. It is a subterranean fire. You cannot put it out. The ground is on fire upon which you stand. You can't understand it. You don't believe in magical arts, as your grandfathers did, who burned witches at the stake, but you do believe in conspiracies; you believe that all these occurrences of late are the work of conspirators! You resemble the child that is looking for his picture behind the mirror. What you see, and what you try to grasp is nothing but the deceptive reflex of the stings of your bad conscience. You want to "stamp out the conspirators"—the "agitators?" Ah, stamp out every factory lord who has grown wealthy upon the unpaid labor of his employees. Stamp out every landlord who has amassed fortunes from the rent of overburdened workingmen and farmers. Stamp out every machine that is revolutionizing industry and agriculture, that intensifies the production, ruins the producer, that increases the national wealth, while the creator of all these things stands amidst them tantalized with hunger! Stamp out the railroads, the telegraph, the telephone, steam and yourselves—for everything breathes the revolutionary spirit.

You, gentlemen, are the revolutionists! You rebel against the effects of social conditions which have tossed you, by the fair hand of Fortune, into a magnificent paradise. Without inquiring, you imagine that no one else has a right in that place. You insist that you are the chosen ones, the sole proprietors. The forces that tossed you into the paradise, the industrial forces, are still at work. They are growing more active and intense from day to day. Their tendency is to elevate all mankind to the same level, to have all humanity share in the paradise you now monopolize. You, in your blindness, think you can stop the tidal wave of civilization and human emancipation by placing a few policemen, a few gatling guns, and some regiments of militia on the shore—you think you can frighten the rising waves back into the unfathomable depths, whence they have arisen, by erecting a few gallows in the perspective. You, who oppose the natural course of things, you are the real revolutionists. You and you alone are the conspirators and destructionists!

The necessity of common ownership in the means of toil will be realized, and the era of Socialism, of universal co-operation, begins. The dispossessing of the usurping classes—the socialization of these possessions—and the universal co-operation of toil, not for speculative purposes, but for the satisfaction of the demands which we make upon life; in short co-operative labor for the purpose of continuing life and of enjoying it—this in general outlines, is Socialism. This is not, however, as you might suppose, a mere 'beautifully conceived plan,' the realization of which would be well worth striving for if it could only be brought about. No; this socialization of the means of production, of the machinery of commerce, of the land and earth, etc., is not only something desirable, but has become an imperative necessity, and wherever we find in history that something has once become a necessity, there we always find that the next step was the doing away with that necessity by the supplying of the logical want."

August Spies is talking here about Socialism of the "means of toil," or in other words, in the creation of a system where those who labor within an organization are the benefactors of the success of that of that organization. It is the idea that an ironworker is on par in ownership as the factory manager and the company accountant. All the elements of the labor force making up an organization having an ownership share. Beyond this is his assertions on the evils of wages. Wages are a way of forcing a population forcing a population to accept legal slavery or indentured servitude. They are temporary, and disconnected, incentive to give labor to an organization. When all workers are beneficial owners, every person is incentivized to work and to remain in that organization as they receive a portion of the financial success of that organization. They work harder and smarter and are more loyal.

The Federation of Trade and Labor Unions was founded in 1881 and changed its name to the AFL (American Federation of Labor) in 1886. Founded by Samuel Bonkers, the AFL organized skilled craft workers such as printers, carpenters, and steel workers. Union membership increased twenty-fold between 1886 and 1905 and resulted in over 35,000 separate strikes.

At the Homestead Steel Factory in Pittsburg, one out of every eleven workers died on the job mostly due to lack of sleep. Pay disparity was vast between workers and management and new technology was deskilling workers and driving them to poverty. Steel Magnate and plutocrat, Andrew Carnegie fled to Scotland when labor actions resulted. The Pinkerton Detective Agency was hired to intimidate workers into submission. These private armies served as infiltrators of unions, watchmen, guards, strike breakers, and incited riots and served as agent provocateurs. In 1892, the Homestead Strike occurred with the Steel Workers fighting for better wages and better hours. 300 Pinkertons arrived and the strikers armed themselves to defend themselves from the Pinkertons. A shot was fired from an unknown person, and after a day of fighting, the Pinkertons were captured and eventually released. The governor sent in the National Guard to protect the strike breakers, which led to the defeat of the union. The strength of unions in general was deflated due to this, until the 1930's. 160 workers were charged with treason and murder, but no juries would convict the strikers. The entire strike committee was then arrested and charged, but also did not result in conviction.

There were comprehensive exclusionary practices toward Chinese labor, though socialists often spoke out against this. Labor unions did not want to see their work undermined and undercut by different kinds of workers. As a tactic to prevent worker organization, employers would bring in people to work side by side that were of different races, religions, and languages making it extremely hard for them to organize and protest. Over time, the labor unions did catch up and became more and more inclusive. They had to overcome their own prejudices so as to challenge their mutual enemy, the plutocracy.

In the New Orleans Strike of 1892, teamsters, scalesmen and packers united into the "triple alliance". They demanded a ten-hour workday, overtime pay and a union shop. This represented the first general strike to enlist skilled and unskilled labor, black and white, and to paralyze a city. After the governor threatened to bring in the National Guard, the strike ended. This strike symbolized a unification of workers beyond prejudice. In response, the Jim Crow laws were created to legally demand segregation between the people and thus divide the workers. In the late 19th and early 20th Centuries, the Populist and Socialist Parties and the Peoples Movement worked to promote the unification of all the people. This led to the creation of the Industrial Workers of the World.

Class war between industrialists and workers led to the highest rate of casualties from Industrialization of any nation. About thirty-five thousand deaths and one million injuries occurred in the workplace annually. Workers were mostly paid below subsistence wages, and many were paid starvation wages. In 1890, Idaho Commissioner of Labor Statistics detailed a 33-item standard budget for the American family, which eliminated any number of luxuries including transportation costs and medical assistance. The typical family, he concluded, required $549 annually to survive. Despite working an average of sixty hours weekly, 88% of Idaho laborers earned less than the required amount. During the late 19th century and early 20th century, the richest 2% owned over 1/3 of the nation's wealth, while the bottom 40% owned no wealth at all. The wealthiest 1% owned over 51% of the land while the bottom 44% owned less than 1.2%.

Metropolitan police grew apace with the labor unions. By the 1890's, the Pinkerton's had more agents than the entire standing army of the United States. During the Homestead Strike of 1892, the National Guard protected the overwhelmed Pinkertons to support the crushing of the workers' strike. Pinks were known to spread false rumors, infiltrate their targets, assassinate targets, perform false flag operations, and commit other nefarious deeds. The Molly McGuire's were a secret society of Irish immigrants active in the Anthracite coal fields of Pennsylvania during the 1870's. They were often blamed for bombings and assassinations carried out by Pinkertons and in 1877 ten Irish coal miners were hung and ten more over the next two years.

The American Railway Union organized a boycott against the Pullman Palace Car Company and workers from many cities came together in solidarity. This was the beginning of the Pullman Strike of 1894. George Pullman had a monopoly over sleeping cars for railroads. His major factory was in a company town called Pullman, in a suburb of Chicago. This meant that everyone who worked for Pullman lived in this company town, where Pullman owned the shops, the schools, the police, and all these things were dictated to by Pullmans will. In the summer of 1894, the economy went into a recession and Pullman cut wages while maintaining workers rent at the same level. The workers went on strike.

In the spring of the same year, there was a strike on the Great Northern Railroad in St. Paul, owned by James Jay Hill, who cut his workers' wages. In 1888, railroad workers developed a new type of union called industrial union, which meant all railroad workers were in one union. Eugene V. Debs, who started off as a coal shoveler, also called a fireman, created the American Railway Union in 1888. In the spring of 1894, the Great Northern Strike in Montana moved into St. Paul and all railroad workers became involved against the wage cut. The entire railway was inoperable. Another magnate, George Pillsbury, stepped in to mediate to get his flour to its destination rather than having the trains not moving and his business stalling. He negotiated to get the workers back their pay cut.

This success encouraged many more workers to get involved in the industrial union. Three months later, in Pullman, IL, the workers joined Eugene Debs union and he asked all his union members to boycott any train that had Pullman cars on it. This meant practically every train. Debs had basically called a nationwide railroad strike. This shut down the entire railroad system. Following this, Pullman sent his lawyer to a federal court in Chicago to call for an injunction on the boycott on the pretense that every car caries federal mail and thus the boycott was also targeting the mail system. The judge granted the injunction, which was the first time this happened against a strike. Twelve-thousand US Army troops were sent in to attack their own people! Riots broke out in many cities. Thirty strikers were killed, and fifty-seven wounded. Property damage was around eighty million dollars. Debs was sentenced to 16 months in prison, where he become educated in Socialism and eventually renounced capitalism and led the Socialist Party for many decades.

In 1897, in Lattimer, PA, nineteen coal miners were massacred as they ran away from company assassins. This inspired workers across the anthracite region to unionize under the United Mine Workers. Over 10,000 men joined UMWA over next 3 years. The WFM, The Western Federation of Miners was formed after the corrupt and illegal arrests of miners who were attacked by Pinkerton spies.

"The more division of labor and the application of machinery extend, the more does competition extend among the workers, the more do their wages shrink together."
– Karl Marx, "Wage, Labor and Capital"

The 13th Amendment, Section 1 states: "Neither slavery nor involuntary servitude, except as a punishment for crime whereof the party shall have been duly convicted, shall exist within the United States, or any place subject to their jurisdiction." This Amendment allowed for criminals to be leased to corporations for their labor or to be used as strikebreakers. Blacks were highly targeted in the south. Prisoners were often forced to sleep naked on bare ground without blankets and given extreme punishments for minor offenses like being whipped for slow hoeing or sorry planting. More African Americans may have died under the convict leasing system than under slavery. As unions were unable to legally be heard in their demands for the ending of this practice, in 1891, in Chattanooga, TN, coal miner's set 500 convicts free and burned down a prison.

"Civil government, so far as it is instituted for the security of property, is in reality instituted for the defense of the rich against the poor, or of those who have some property against those who have none at all."
– Adam Smith, Wealth of Nations

Thomas Jefferson had written that the American ideal was, "Life, liberty, and the pursuit of happiness". This was a variation on a previous statement by John Locke, who said, "Lives, liberties...property." The caste system in the States was built around property owners and non-property owners.

"You pompously call yourselves Republicans and Democrats. There is no Republican Party. There is no Democratic Party. There are no Republicans nor Democrats in this House. You are lick-splitters and panderers, the creatures of the Plutocracy."
– Jack London, "The Iron Heel"

The Democratic Party has its roots in slavery and Jim Crow for its first century of existence. The Peoples Party or Populist Party in early 1890's competed with the Democratic Party in South and rural Midwest, which forced both parties to adapt and change. The choice was made to amalgam the two parties. William Jennings Bryan, who had marginal popularity and credibility with the people's party, ran for election, and consequently lost. The energy of the Peoples Party was disintegrated by this melding with the Democratic Party and Democrats did not win the presidency for the next forty years.
The two-party system is built and maintained to prevent independence and to absorb and deflate any 3rd party potential. The Socialist Party in early 1900's became influential, especially in Kansas, Oklahoma, and Texas. Small Socialist Parties came together to form the Socialist Party of the United States in 1901. Eugene Debs ran many times as the Socialist Candidate. Socialism, Populism, and Reformism were causally related to the creation of anti-trust laws, the Pure Food and Drug Act, as well as eliminating child labor and corporate crimes. In 1938, the Fair Labor Standards Act created the definitive elimination of abusive child labor. The progressive movement often did not only represent equality and rights of all, but exclusionary practices like the disenfranchising of blacks or Mexicans.
Progressives also brought about many of the most horrid practices and social designs. Ethnic cleansing forced indigenous people onto reservations. The 1887 Dawes Act divided tribal lands into individual allotments to make them easier to sell. Federal Policy makers worked with churches to impose Christianity and to enforce the Civilizing Project, imposing bans on traditional cultural practices such as eating peyote and the Sun Dance. The cultural assimilation program forcibly removed native children from their parents, and making them attend abusive residential schools, where they would have their mouths washed with lye soup for speaking their native language, locked up in guard houses with only bread and water, and abused sexually and with corporal punishment. Hitler based his ideas on concentration camps and genocide largely on the experience of the Native Americans. Eugenics also had its beginnings in the United States, which was supported by many if not all of the industrialists, including Henry Ford, John D. Rockefeller, the DuPont Family and J.P. Morgan. Eugenics justified discrimination of non-whites. The Republican Party increasingly distanced itself from fighting for non-white rights. Poor whites who were often the actors in lynching blacks, were sublimating their anger against the blacks. After the disillusion of the Knights of Labor in the 1880's, most unions had become exclusive clubs. Many supported Eugenics. The Industrial Workers of the World (IWW), or Wobblies, eschewed divisions based on race, sex, creed and skill and directly competed with the AFL, which was a Eugenics supporting racist and exclusionist organization.

"Í cannot think it probable that (working people) will be permanently conceded with the condition of laboring for wages as their ultimate state. To work at the bidding and for the profit of another, without any interest in the work...is, not even when the wages are high, a satisfactory state to human beings."
-John Stuart Mill, 1948

William Dudley "Big Bill" Haywood delivered the IWW's first Speech on June 27, 1905 in Chicago:

"Fellow Workers, this is the Continental Congress of the working-class. We are here to confederate the workers of this country into a working-class movement that shall have for its purpose the emancipation of the working-class from the slave bondage of capitalism. The aims and objects of this organization shall be to put the working-class in possession of the economic power, the means of life, in control of the machinery of production and distribution, without regard to capitalist masters.

Another phrase of Haywood's was, *"I've never read Marx's Capital, but I have the marks of capital all over me."* The IWW attempted to organize all workers into one big union. It wanted to overthrow the entire wage system and create worker owned businesses. Workers of all skill levels were included as well as all races and sexes. They advocated strict non-violence. By 1910, they had even organized Mexican farm and construction workers.

"The mass of men serve the state thus, not as men mainly, but as machines, with their bodies. They are the standing army, and the militia, jailers, constables, posse comitatus, etc. In most cases there is no free exercise whatever of the judgement or of the moral sense; but they put themselves on a level with wood and earth and stones; and wooden men can perhaps be manufactured that will serve the purpose as well. Such command no more respect than men of straw or a lump of dirt. They have the same sort of worth only as horses and dogs. Yet such as these even are commonly esteemed good citizens. Others—as most legislators, politicians, lawyers, ministers, and office-holders—serve the state chiefly with their heads; and, as they rarely make any moral distinctions, they are as likely to serve the devil, without intending it, as God. A very few—as heroes, patriots, martyrs, reformers in the great sense, and men—serve the state with their consciences also, and so necessarily resist it for the most part; and they are commonly treated as enemies by it. A wise man will only be useful as a man, and will not submit to be "clay," and "stop a hole to keep the wind away," but leave that office to his dust at least: "I am too high born to be propertied, To be a second at control, Or useful serving-man and instrument To any sovereign state throughout the world." He who gives himself entirely to his fellow men appears to them useless and selfish; but he who gives himself partially to them is pronounced a benefactor and philanthropist. ***How does it become a man to behave toward the American government today? I answer, that he cannot without disgrace be associated with it. I cannot for an instant recognize that political organization as my government which is the slave's government also.***

- On the Duty of Civil Disobedience (original title: Resistance to Civil Government) by Henry David Thoreau, 1849[113]

**Substantial portions of this section derive from the extremely well-made documentary series,* Plutocracy, *by Scott Noble. I encourage all my readers to visit www.metanoia-films.org and watch his amazing work. It was enlightening for me as I am sure it will be for you. Further investigation can be had through his well cited documentaries, featuring some very bright minds, and plenty of archival footage that transports us back to the times and events that are today seemingly forgotten, though no less important to the current state of the nation and the world. Thank you, Scott Noble, for all the magnificent work that you do.*[114]

Medicine, Health and Food

"Sunshine, fresh air, wholesome nutrition, exercise, rest and the hygienic mode of living are far more effectual than all the subsequent medication in existence."
Oral Hygiene, vol. 1, no. 1, January 1911, pp. 183-184[115]

A quick note on this section of this book. I am quite the believer in not attempting to rephrase things that have been elucidated perfectly already. I could attempt to paraphrase or to synopsize to the extent that only my words are presented, but my preference is the exact opposite in this case. I have left this section largely to quotes by those who have the experience, credibility, practical knowledge, and the rhetorical capacity for expressing in detail to the layperson the material they have to share. Much of this section is left then to original quotes. I hope you will enjoy reading through them as much as I have enjoyed collecting them for your contemplation.

Very simply, the pharmaceutical industry is the enemy of any sane human being. This oxymoronic industry claims to bring health through "medicine" yet we observe increasing disease due directly to the practice of selling toxins to the people at exorbitant rates. This abusive evil monopoly has many names, like Bayer and Merck, that exist on the death and suffering of its misled customers. We cannot say that it is only a small cabal of twisted minds and souls that have perpetuated this business, because the society has accepted this nonsense and abused themselves willfully in exchange for temporary superficial rewards. That isn't to say that those responsible are off the hook. These people ought to be hung from a short rope. What else would serve for those that would poison the entirety of their own species. Let's say that even one percent of the products produced by the pharmaceutical industry are of benefit greater than natural remedies, there are several reformations that must occur, if we do not just tear the whole malicious empire down.

There must be price regulations to disallow Big Pharma to profiteer on the population. This will not work to heal the society we live in but will act as a band-aid unless there is a parallel effort to eliminate the Federal Reserve and the political and societal corruption. An open-source index must be created with major countries around world to determine justified prices on necessary medicines such as epinephrine. Drug reimportation will allow distributors of prescription drugs to purchase them from elsewhere in the world and charge the lower priced drugs in the US. We must abolish price fixing by Big Pharma, if we aren't just going to destroy the industry altogether.

A problem that remains, despite every proposed solution, is the fact that our money is not actually money. It is currency. It is fiat. It is privately owned. We do not own our means of valuing our trade and our labor and our time. So long as this fundamentally disastrous system continues, nothing else will have long lasting and real effect, besides a complete revolt by the people, which would inevitably eliminate the cancerous central bank anyway. Besides this, a government large enough to mandate what care ought to be offered to over 300,000,000 human beings is a government that needs to end.

"...(I was) a medical doctor with 19 years of experience... When I pointed out the connection between vaccines and worsening or new-onset kidney failure to a couple of open-minded colleagues, they understood, started taking vaccine histories, and saw what was happening. Yet they remained silent. Most doctors continue to practice with comfortable indifference. Some see the errors, damage, and limits to their practices, but still walk lockstep with the herd and protect the brotherhood.
I don't know what it will take to get these doctors to resist the dictates who rule over them. I've had far more success reasoning with parents and intelligent people who are not attached to traditions that are damaging, unscientific, and not even supported by our own medical literature."
-Suzanne Humphries[116]

Vaccinations are an abomination of medicine and science and are in no way to be considered a medicine. The idea of vaccinating people to prevent a disease that they currently do not have by injecting them with a concoction of various similar diseases and toxins is simply idiotic. Vaccinations have not prevented **ANY** disease but have caused egregious harm to humankind at the private and exclusive benefit of a few individuals invested in the stated goals of the eugenics movement. It is simply untrue that vaccination cured people of disease historically. At the same time that vaccines were being introduced as a solution, environmental and educational advancements in sanitation and disease prevention were being made.
Between 1870 and 1924, the number of municipal waterworks increased from 244 to 9,850. Before this, people in cities often were drinking their own sewage. The lack of sanitary water in urban conditions led to waterborne illnesses and exacerbations of preconditions. Tenants would often have to share a water closet or outdoor privy, which led to various overcrowding and sanitation problems. The first plunger type water closet appeared in 1875. Before this, people relied on chamber pots and open windows and backyards for disposal. In the 1870's, knowledge of drainage and venting procedures for toilets became available, preventing sewer gases from backing up into the home. The number of private toilets went from 10% before 1920 to 60% in 1940.
Before the introduction of the motor vehicle, horses were used as transport intracity and by rural farmers. The manure that was left on a daily basis in cities was vast and needed large numbers of workers to clean the streets of their waste. This obviously left plenty of opportunity for diseases to flourish.

> *Anyone who at all questions the safety or efficacy of vaccines is labelled as spreading false claims and misinformation. The population has been fooled into thinking that the crafty influence of Pharma stops at the door of vaccines and instead that people speaking out about problems with vaccines are the villains... I've discovered there's a ton of evidence that vaccines cannot be considered universally safe and effective. Just one quick example, the neurotoxicity of aluminum in injectable vaccines hyperactivates the immune system in fetuses and also in the first few years of life. That in turn results in brain and immune system injuries and also autoimmune diseases. This is well documented... Vaccines are huge money makers for Pharma. They're the top sellers for many of them. It took me two seconds to find this Financial Times article documenting operating margins of 25-30% for vaccine manufacturers and billions and billions in profits for the big four vaccine makers; Pfizer, GlaxoSmith Kline, Merck, and Sanofi... We pay for them. And we also pay for the public health for these education sessions.*
>
> -Rosemary Frei, MSC Molecular Biology, University of Calgary, Medical Journalist and Researcher[117]

The first vaccine was developed in response to smallpox, and was created by Edward Jenner, who, in 1798, claimed that vaccination with cowpox was a lifelong protection against smallpox. "Smallpox, Orthopox Variola, was an infectious viral entity that served up febrile illness and painful, oozing skin lesions (pox) to its victims." It was utterly eradicated by 1949 in the United States, 1980 worldwide. Jenner's conclusion that cowpox vaccination protected people from smallpox was derived from the result of only one test case, in which he "took disease matter that he believed to be cowpox from lesions on the hands of a dairymaid... and vaccinated James (Phipps, 8) with it." Later Jenner exposed the boy to smallpox, and when he did not contract it, Jenner claimed his cowpox vaccination a success. Preexisting immunity was not part of this experiment and despite having only a solitary case, Jenner spread his cowpox vaccination as a solution. Over the following years the medical community embraced Jenners' vaccine, vaccinating around 100,000 people by 1801, despite numerous proofs of ineffectuality. Jenner's claim of lifelong immunity was replaced over time with ever decreasing immunity timelines, sometimes even limited to 6 months. "Doctors and surgeons were paid well to perform vaccination and embraced it as a new form of income."[118] Of course, it is always easier to support something that may have harmful effects on patients, when you can sleep in a nicer house in a nicer neighborhood, and care for your family in ever nicer ways.

"Because using pox material directly from cows was initially disagreeable to people, Jenner developed "humanized cowpox vaccine... Even modern smallpox vaccines do not usually contain cowpox or smallpox virus but a human/animal hybrid agent that never existed in nature until the era of vaccination. It has been cultivated over time by passing pox material back and forth between animals and humans. Now vaccinia can infect wild animals such as water buffalo, as well as humans."
-Bystrianyk & Humphries, 2015[119]

"In 1840, as doctors and citizens realized that vaccination was not what is was promised to be, vaccine refusals increased. Governments passed various laws to force people to be vaccinated. Vaccination was made compulsory in England in 1853, with stricter laws passed in 1867."
- Bystrianyk & Humphries, 2015[120]

"...in 1855 Massachusetts took the most advanced stand ever taken by any of the states and enacted a law which required parents or guardians to cause the vaccination of all children before they were two years old, and forbade the admission of all children to the public schools of any child who had not been duly vaccinated. The selectmen of towns, mayors and aldermen of cities were to "enforce the vaccination of all the inhabitants" and to require re-vaccination whenever they judged the public health to require it; all employees of manufacturing companies, all inmates of almshouses, reform schools, lunatic asylums, and other places where the poor and sick are received, or houses of correction, jails, prisons, of all institutions supported wholly or partly by the state were to furnish the means of vaccination to such persons as were unable to pay."
Susan Wade Peabody, "Historical Study of Legislation Regarding Public Health in the State of New York and Massachusetts," The Journal of Infectious Diseases, suppl. no. 4, February 1909, pp.55-51.[121]

"Bavaria [Germany] in 1871 of 30,742 cases 29,429 were in vaccinated persons, or 95.7 per cent, and 1313 in the unvaccinated, or 4.3 per cent. In some of the small local outbreaks of recent years the victims have been nearly all vaccinated (e.g., at Bromley [England] in 1881, a total of 43 cases, including sixteen confluent, all vaccinated).
Encyclopaedia Britannica, vol. 24, Philadelphia, 1890, p. 29[122]

"Every recruit that enters the French army is vaccinated. During the Franco-Prussian war there were twenty-three thousand four hundred and sixty-nine cases of small-pox in that army. The London Lancet of July 15, 1871, said: Of nine thousand three hundred and ninety-two small-pox patients in London hospitals, six thousand eight hundred and fifty-four had been vaccinated. Seventeen and one-half per cent of those attacked died. In the whole country more than one hundred and twenty-two thousand vaccinated persons have suffered from small-pox... Official returns from Germany show that between 1870 and 1885 one million vaccinated persons died from small-pox.
G.W. Harman, MD, "A Physician's Argument Against the Efficacy of Virus Inoculation," Medical Brief: A Monthly Journal of Scientific Medicine and Surgery, vol. 28, no. 1, 1900, p. 84[123]

"Among the great number of little epidemics which produced the 18,110 deaths mentioned, I will only note the following: Badolato, with a population of 3,800, had 1,200 cases of smallpox; Guardavalle had 2,300 cases with a population of 3,500; St. Caterina del Jonio had 1,200 cases (population 2,700); Capistrano had 450 cases (population 2,500). All these villages are in Calabria. In Sardinia the little village of Laerru had 150 cases of small-pox in one month (population, 800); Perfugas, too, in one month had 541 cases (population, 1400); Ottana had 79 deaths from small-pox (population, 1000), and the deaths were 51 at Lei (population, 414). In Sicily 440 deaths were registered at Noto (population, 18,100), 200 at Ferla (population, 4,500), 570 at Sortino (population, 9,000), 135 at San Cono (population, 1600), and 2,100 deaths at Vittoria (population, 2,600)! Can you cite anything worse before the invention of vaccination? And, the population of these villages is perfectly vaccinated, as I

have proved already, not only, but obtained from the local authorities a declaration that vaccination has been performed twice a year in the most satisfactory manner for many years past.
Charles Ruata, MD, "Vaccination in Italy," The New York Medical Journal, July 22, 1899, pp. 188-189[124]

"From 1885 to 1892, there were more than 25,000,000 recorded vaccinations and revaccinations, yet smallpox epidemics still wreaked havoc upon the Japanese."
- Bystrianyk & Humphries, 2015[125]

"...the official records show that during the seven years mentioned [1885-1892] they had 156,175 cases of smallpox and 39,979 deaths. By a compulsory law, every infant in Japan had to be vaccinated within the first year of its birth and in case it did not take the first time, three additional vaccinations had to follow within the year, and every year to seven years after. In the event of an outbreak of smallpox the Japanese authorities rigidly enforced general vaccination. Now in spite of these precautions the official records show that from 1892 to 1897, Japan had 142,032 cases of smallpox and 39,536 deaths. Another act passed in 1896 made repetition of vaccination every five years compulsory on every subject regardless of station; yet in the very next year, 1897, they had 41,946 cases of smallpox and 12,276 deaths—a mortality rate of 32 per cent, nearly twice that from smallpox previous to the vaccination period."
Simon L. Katzoff, MD, "The Compulsory Vaccination Crime," Machinists' Monthly Journal, vol. 32, no. 3, March 1920, p. 261[126]

"Numerous well-documented incidents of vaccine contamination have occurred. Even today, a contaminant cannot be screened for unless the scientists suspect it is there, have designed a specific test, and perform the test adequately. Occult infections (infections first recognized by secondary manifestations) are known to exist inside various vaccines in present times. The SV-40 virus was a known contaminant of polio vaccines grown on monkey kidney cells up through the 1980s. As long as animals and animal cells are used for vaccine manufacture, the potential for infection will exist. There is no proposed end to the use of animals in vaccine production."
- Bystrianyk & Humphries, 2015[127]

The city of Leicester, England protested and won freedom from forced vaccinations in 1885. Despite prophesies of doom from the medical community, the population of Leicester suffered far less than well vaccinated cities. After 1885, only 11 to 12 percent of births were vaccinated. When the 1893 smallpox outbreak occurred, Leicester had 32 times less deaths than the well vaccinated Flintshire, England. 144 per million vs Flints 3,614 per million. In the 1891-94 smallpox outbreak, vaccinated Birmingham had 63 cases and 5 deaths per 10,000 while Leicester had 19 cases and 1 death per 10,000. By the 1903-4 outbreak, Leicester death rate had dropped to 1-2 per 100,000.

"...in Leicester during the 62 years since infant vaccination was abandoned there have been only 53 deaths from smallpox, and in the past 40 years only two deaths. Moreover, the experience in Leicester is now confirmed, and strongly confirmed, by that of the whole country. Vaccination has been steadily declining ever since the "conscience clause" was introduced, until now nearly two-thirds of the children born are not vaccinated. Yet smallpox mortality has also declined until now quite negligible. In the fourteen years 1933-1946 there were only 28 deaths in a population of some 40 million, and among those 28 there was not a single death of an infant under 1 year of age."
C. Killick Millard, MD, DSc, "The End of Compulsory Vaccination," British Medical Journal, December 18, 1948, p. 1074[128]

When an epidemic appeared in Yugoslavia in 1972, the Yugoslavian Federal Epidemiologic Commission vaccinated 18 million citizens despite knowing that vaccinations were ineffective. Even the WHO acknowledged the ineffective nature of vaccines and implemented the Leicester Method. The vaccines were touted, but the Leicester Method was the true cure.

"By the mid-1800s and into the 1900s, governmental support for vaccination as the only means of controlling smallpox was firmly entrenched... despite a parent's belief that a vaccine had caused a child's injury or death and despite dissenting medical opinions, governments and courts were unified in their decree that vaccination had to be enforced. Fines, seizure of property, and imprisonment were instituted to compel the population into compliance of the law based on the dominant medical paradigm. Punishments were carried out for not vaccinating."
- Bystrianyk & Humphries, 2015[129]

"In order to stamp out smallpox, which is semi-epidemic here, the Board of Health started compulsory vaccination to-day. The work was begun in East Boston, where 125 surgeons, each accompanied by a policeman, made a house-to-house canvass, vaccinating all who had not been recently inoculated. Those who refused to allow the operating will be hauled into court.
"Fighting Smallpox in Boston, 125 Surgeons, Accompanied by Policemen, Vaccinated 15,000 Persons Yesterday," New York Times, January 27, 1902.[130]

Beginning in the mid 1800's health boards and public health commissioners and city planners and governments began to consider health rather than economy alone. They began moving toxic industries like slaughterhouses, meatpacking plants, glue factories, tanneries, and others outside of cities, improving public health. After the turn of the century, in 1913, chlorination had come into use so prolifically, practically all waterborne diseases were eradicated, including typhoid, cholera, and dysentery, with increasing positive results thereafter. Pasteurization became mandatory in the early 1900's, which is the process of heating milk to 140°F for 30 minutes, destroying tuberculosis, typhoid fever, and diphtheria, amongst many other organisms. Infant mortality due to unsterile bottles were mitigated by ever superior sterilization methods.

"In the United States, the big transformation in personal hygiene started after cities instituted "water works," which piped filtered water directly into the home from a central distribution system. By 1890, 1.4% of the urban population was so served by water works; by 1910, this number had increased to more than 25%. As water became available, sinks, bathtubs, showers, and indoor toilets were installed. The sale of soap and washing machines increased in a parallel fashion. The personal hygiene transformation was on the way, fueled by aesthetics, social pressures, commercial advertising, and even theologic incentives ("Cleanliness is next to Godliness").
Velv W. Greene, PhD, MPH, "Personal Hygiene and Life Expectancy Improvements Since 1850: Historic and Epidemiologic Associations," American Journal of Infection Control, August 2001, p. 205[131]

"Medicine in general, and vaccines even more so, contributed very little to this phenomenal transformation. Regardless, the medical paradigm became the dominant belief, generally displacing all other vastly important human innovations... Scarlet fever... was a far bigger killer than smallpox, whooping cough, measles, and diphtheria... During the Sanitation Revolution from the mid-1800s and into the early 1900s, scarlet fever deaths plummeted. The death rate declined by 100 percent by the mid-1900s. Even by the early 1900s, anyone who became ill with scarlet fever had a 95 percent decreased mortality risk compared to the antecedent century. It is noteworthy that the terror of scarlet fever became a distant memory—Long before antibiotics were available to treat it... nothing was eradicated. Something altered the susceptibility of humans to scarlet fever bacterial toxin. Even today, the organism innocently colonizes 15-20 percent of school children and remains ever present. By the time a vaccine arrived on the scene for whooping cough, the death rate had declined by more than 99 percent... (In England) deaths from whooping cough has declined by more than 90 percent prior to the introduction of a vaccine in the mid-1940s. Deaths from measles had declined by more than 98 percent before the introduction of a vaccine in 1963... it is highly probable that... an even earlier decline had already begun before the United States began to chart its national statistics. In fact, the introduction of diphtheria antitoxin in 1895 preceded a large spike in diphtheria mortality...The rise in deaths was

approximately 10 to 15 times higher than it had been for the previous 57 years (1838-1895) and continued for 5 more years (1896-1901). From 1900 to 1943, deaths from diarrhea declined from 143.7 to 9.4 per 100,000—a 93.5 percent decrease. This mortality decline occurred before any antibiotics were in use and probably had little, if anything, to do with vaccination."

- Bystrianyk & Humphries, 2015[132]

"Diphtheria can be cured in man by the administration of massive frequent doses of hexuronic acid (vitamin C) given intravenously and/or intramuscularly. To the synthetic drug, by mouth, there is little response, even when 1000 to 2000 mg. is used every two hours. This cure in diphtheria is brought about in half the time required to remove the membrane and give negative smears by antitoxin... During an epidemic [of measles] vitamin C was used prophylactically and all those who received as much as 1000 mg. every six hours, by vein or muscle, were protected from the virus."

F. R. Klenner, "The Treatment of Poliomyelitis and Other Virus Diseases with Vitamin C," Southern Medicine and Surgery, vol. 111, no. 7, July 1949, p. 209-214[133]

"Fully 675,000 Americans died in the Spanish flu pandemic of 1918-19, a relatively small fraction of the estimated global mortality toll of 20 million to 50 million, which far exceeded fatalities caused by World War I. The precise cause of the pandemic was never determined, the study of viruses being in its infancy at the time. It was not until 1933 that the influenza A virus was isolated and not until 1944 that the first influenza vaccine was introduced. The "Spanish" nickname for the pandemic came about because wartime censors limited reporting to preserve public morale, and the wartime neutrality of Spain meant that much of the influenza news came from that country, leading to the belief that Spain had been the origin of the event. Leaving aside the 1918-19 flu pandemic, the conquest of infectious diseases proceeded gradually over the first half of the twentieth century. The McKinlays compare the timing of the decline in mortality from each infectious disease with the introduction of the medical intervention designed to treat that ailment---for instance, penicillin and other vaccines. Their finding is striking: that most of the decline in mortality from the major diseases, particularly tuberculosis and influenza, had already occurred before the introduction of the medical intervention. Their conclusion is that "3.5 percent probably represents a reasonable upper-limit estimate of the total contribution of medical measures to the decline in mortality in the United States since 1900. Edward Meeker agrees with the McKinlays that the main drivers of the decline in the death rate, which for him begins around 1885, were the tamping of infectious diseases. Meeker rejects as causes either improvements in medical practice of genetic changes in the virulence of disease organisms. Instead, his searchlight beams in on the crucial improvements in public health, such as the urban sanitation infrastructure, largely consisting of filtered central water supplies and sanitary sewers... Meeker provides data on the sharp decline in the incidence of typhus in twenty American cities after a filtered water supply was introduced. The importance of pure water was not a new idea: "From time immemorial the human race had recognized that, if health was to be maintained, such bodily wastes as urine and feces must be kept rigidly separated from food and water."

- Gordon, p. 215[134]

"In general, medical measures (both chemotherapeutic and prophylactic) appear to have contributed little to the overall decline in mortality in the United States since about 1900—having in many instances been introduced several decades after a marked decline had already set in and having no detectable influence in most instances... it is estimated that at most 3.5 percent of the total decline in mortality since 1900 could be ascribed to medical measures for the diseases considered here."

- John B. McKinlay and Sonja M. McKinlay, "The Questionable Contribution of Medical Measures to the Decline of Mortality in the United States in the Twentieth Century," The Milbank Memorial Fund Quarterly, Health and Society, vol. 55, no. 3, summer 1977, p. 425.[135]

The story of the vaccine doesn't end with its falseness as a medicine, but by seeing this, it allows us to begin to discover the reason why it's been allowed to continue to exist despite its apparent ineffectuality. Who benefits from the manufacture, sale, and use of vaccines? Pfizers top selling product in 2015 was "Prevnar", a vaccine that generated $6,500,000,000 in sales to them in that year alone, which was three times more than Viagra which Pfizer also produces.
Other environmental, technological, and social changes were occurring in the turn of the 20th century as well, such as the invention of window screens in the 1870's to prevent insects from communicating diseases into the home.

Infant life expectancy increased between 1870 and 1940. 60 y/o life expectancy increased after 1940. Life expectancy at birth in 1900 was 46 for white rural males, and 39.1 for urban white males. "Urbanization moved people from lower to higher mortality regimes, exacting a price for the increased economic opportunity of the city." - Pope, p. 294[136] "In 1900, nearly 18 percent of males born in the United States died before their first birthday; today, cumulative mortality does not reach 18 percent until age 62." - Murphy and Topel, p. 871[137]."During the pre-1940 era, improvements in medical care by doctors and hospitals played a relatively small role in the decline of mortality rates and the accompanying increases in life expectancy at birth. Higgs concludes that 'changes in medical practice during the period 1870-1920 could at best, have contributed only negligibly to the decline in the rural crude death rate.' Gordon, p. 213[138] "The first conclusion is that more than 37 percent of deaths in 1900 were caused by infectious diseases, but in 1955, this had declined to less than 5 percent and to only 2 percent by 2009. In contrast, over the same period, the percentage of deaths caused by three chronic conditions (heart disease, strokes, and cancer) increased from 7 percent to 60 percent. The second conclusion is that almost all of the decline in the infectious mortality rate had been achieved by 1955, which is before the share in GDP of medical care spending began its inexorable rise from 4 percent in the mid-1950s to 17 percent by 2010. A central question... is whether the chief causes of the decline in mortality before 1940 had anything to do with drugs, doctors, and hospitals---and if not, what set of factors caused the decline." - Gordon, p. 214[139]
"Earth was scarred by mining pits and railway tracks; airways fouled and darkened by factory soot; water was polluted by industrial wastes that ran unchecked down eroded mountains once covered by forests. Americans became imperialists within their own nation." - Hart (1950, p.157). The percentage of urban households supplied with filtered water increased from .3 percent in 1880 to 42 percent by 1925, to 93 percent in 1940. Between 1890 and 1900, due to the waterworks that were being built across the nation, 80 percent of the decline in total mortality is accounted for by diarrheal disease, typhoid, tuberculosis, and diphtheria. "These authors (Cutler and Miller) estimate that clean water filtration... systems explain half of the overall reduction in mortality between 1900 and 1936, as well as 75 percent of the decline in infant mortality and 67 percent of the decline in child mortality." Gordon, p. 218[140], Cutler and Miller, p. 2[141]
"Another aspect of late nineteenth-century environment was air pollution... New York City was not immune from the observation that, 'no dumping ground, no sewer, no vault contains more filth or in greater variety than does the air in certain parts of New York City during the long season of drought. No barrier can shut it out, no social distinction can save us from it; no domestic cleanliness, no private sanitary measures can substitute a pure atmosphere for a foul one.'" Bettman, pp.2, 10, 14[142]

"Food spoilage and adulteration was not an ancient problem suddenly addressed after 1890, but rather a new problem created by industrialization itself. Before 1870, when Americans mainly lived on farms and in small towns, much of the food was either grown at home or purchased from neighbors.

Each household could take steps to protect itself from spoilage and contamination. But as America urbanized, more of the food was produced in factories and shipped long distances in a world in which mechanical refrigeration had not yet been invented. Avarice and greed by food manufacturers combined with new chemical processes that could accomplish the adulteration and disguise the results with coloring agents. Consumers were helpless, for most food items were subject to adulteration. Only by purchasing alternative brands, tasting them, and observing the results could consumers begin to make an informed choice, because so few unadulterated products were available. About milk adulteration, a cynic once remarked "a water shortage would put the milkman out of business... all [dealers] required was a water pump to boost two quarts of milk to a gallon... to improve the color of milk from diseased cattle they frequently added molasses, chalk, or plaster of Paris." The dangers posed by market-purchased milk were significant because of adulteration with polluted water. "As late as 1900 the nation's milk supply was seriously contaminated with tuberculosis, typhoid, scarlet fever, diphtheria, and streptococcal germs."

- Gordon, p. 220[143], Bettman, p. 114[144], Ewbank and Preston, p. 121[145]

"The quality of food sold at the corner and the butchers' shops in this neighborhood deserves a more extended notice than it can receive here. A casual examination shows much of it to be unfit for human sustenance. Unwholesome meat, particularly slunk veal [flesh from the fetus of a calf, found during the slaughter of its mother], is constantly vended and consumed. Piles of pickled herrings are exposed to the air till the mass approaches a condition of putridity.; and this slimy food, with wilted and decayed vegetables, sausages not above suspicion, and horrible pies, composed of stale and unripe fruits, whose digestion no human stomach can accomplish, all find ready purchasers. These decaying animals and vegetable remains are daily entombed in the protuberant stomachs of thousands of children, whose pallid, expressionless faces and shrunken limbs are the familiar attributes of childhood in these localities."

– Citizens Association of New York, "Report of the Council of Hygiene and Public Health of the Citizens Association of New York, 1865[146]

"Infectious diseases were a constant terror during the 1800s. With increasingly dense populations, wars, and abject poverty, diseases of all varieties exacted a horrendous toll. The poverty-stricken masses carried the brunt of the relentless assaults of these diseases, yet no class was spared. Periodic epidemics and pandemics swept across the globe, wreaking havoc and killing millions, rivaling the horrors of war. Abysmal sanitation, hygiene, nutrition, and working and living conditions, combined with a sense of utter hopelessness, laid the foundation for the devastation. Sanitation was not a new concept. In the time of the Old Testament, there were clear-cut biblical rules laid out governing the management and disposal of dangerous human waste and rubbish outside the cities and away from water sources. Greece and Rome also perfected well-regulated public health systems. During the Dark Ages, these ideas simply dropped out of the collective memory in many areas of the world.

In the United Kingdom, as a result of the Enclosures Act that pushed people off common land and the Industrial Revolution, dispossessed people suddenly massed into cities. People lived waist deep in their own midden heaps in overcrowded hovels, drinking filthy polluted water and eating terrible food. These living conditions were the single common factor that led to rampant disease epidemics... The gastrointestinal tract is known to contain around 70 percent of a person's immunity. With insults to a healthy digestive system from toxins, infections, and parasites in water and food, it is easy to see how myriad diseases were able to take hold... People threw their garbage out onto the city streets, where it was consumed by scavenging pigs, dogs, and rats... The filth in New York City streets had amassed to a depth of two to three feet in the winter."

- Bystrianyk & Humphries, 2015[147]

Life before modern convenience was not easy. It was a toil that involved all the members of a family. It required all to work for the benefit of others in the family to survive. Children would begin working at what we consider to be far too young today, because life expectancy was often under 30 years. What a great deal we take for granted today, while just 5 generations ago our ancestors globally lived without telephones, electricity, refrigerators, cars, and even simply clean homes to sleep, eat, and relax in.

> "For millions, entire lives-albeit often very short ones- were passed in new industrial cities of dreadful night with an all too typical socio-pathology: foul housing, often in flooded cellars, gross overcrowding, atmospheric and water-supply pollution, overflowing cesspools, contaminated pumps, poverty, hunger, fatigue, and abjection everywhere. Such conditions, comparable to today's Third World shanty town or refugee camps, bred rampant sickness of every kind. Appalling neo-natal, infant and child mortality accompanied the abomination of child labour in mines and factories; life expectations were exceedingly low-often under twenty years among the working classes- and everywhere sickness precipitated family breakdown, pauperization, and social crisis... Twenty percent of pauperism was due to fever, and the blame fell on overcrowding, negligent waste disposal, dirty water and bad diet. Poverty could not be abolished, but poverty due to preventable disease could be: The primary and most important measures, and at the same time the most practicable, and within the recognized province of administration, are drainage, the removal of all refuse from habitations, streets and roads, and the improvement of the supplies of water."
>
> Roy Porter, The Greatest Benefit to Mankind, Harper Collins, New York, 1997, p. 399-411[148]

It was an abysmal situation for populations globally. Medical progress was leading the way toward the cliffs that we now walk along the edge of. The practice of reductionistic medical science was potentially more detrimental to the health of humanity than even the most genocidal campaigns of Mao and Stalin and the rest of the maniacs that have ever wielded great power and influence. It was and is more detrimental than the diseases it attempts to categorize, replicate, and cut or burn out. Puerperal Fever is an infection affecting mothers immediately after birth.

> *"Severe pain, pelvic abscesses, sepsis, high fever, and agonizing death were brought about by an ascending infection introduced by the contaminated hands of doctors and unsterile medical instruments... wherever conventional midwifery was abandoned and taken over by the new male midwives known as obstetricians and medical students, puerperal fever followed... Doctors often went from touching infected corpses in the cadaver dissection lab, to the maternity ward, where they examined women and delivered babies without handwashing."*
>
> \- Bystrianyk & Humphries, 2015[149]

> *"Instead of an emphasis on hygiene, nutrition, and appropriate vitamin supplementation, immune system support, and natural remedies, the emphasis is always on costly antibiotics, vaccinations, and other medical procedures. These choices have not been without consequences, as they fight the germs instead of supporting the life force. The host cannot rid its surroundings of microorganisms and, in fact, may be best served by cultivating the beneficial ones as they are actually part of the host's defense."*
>
> \- Bystrianyk & Humphries, 2015[150]

> *"The prevailing view of interactions between complex, multicellular hosts and the microbes that surround them is skewed by a historical focus on pathogens. But in our rapidly accelerating exploration of the microbial world around us, there may be advantages to taking the broader view of immunity to pathogens as one aspect of a microbiome management system that regulates interactions with intimately associated microbiota, the great majority of which may be beneficial."*
>
> \- Eric T. Harvill, Cultivating Our 'Frenemies': Viewing Immunity as Microbiome Management," Journal of the American Society for Microbiology, vol. 4, no. 2, March 26, 2013, pp. 1-3.[151]

> *"Live virus vaccines against paralytic poliomyelitis, for example, may in each instance produce the disease it is intended to prevent; the live virus vaccines against measles and mumps may produce such side effects as encephalitis. Both of these problems are due to the inherent difficulty of controlling live viruses in vivo [once they are placed in a live person]."*

- Jonas and Darrell Salk, Science, March 4, 1977[152]

"Despite many well-documented historical problems, polio and smallpox vaccines serve as the anchor for vaccination faith today... The term poliomyelitis is a description of spinal pathology. The meaning of the word comes from Greek Polios (gray), muelos (marrow), it is (inflammation), and denotes inflammation of the gray matter of the spinal cord... Poliomyelitis can occur in the brainstem and the spinal cord... incidence was very low when compared to that of other infectious diseases. Polio has... been portrayed as a vicious crippler... Those who still embody a fear of polio may argue that it was a monster because it crippled people, especially children. But it was later revealed, after a vaccine was lauded for the eradication of polio, that much of the crippling was related to factors other than poliovirus, and those factors could not possibly have been affected by any vaccine."

- Bystrianyk & Humphries, 2015[153]

Throughout the mid-1900's, native tribes were evaluated in Brazil and Australia, untouched by the modern world, and often not having lived with white people. They were conclusively absent of problems from any diseases such as poliomyelitis, scarlet fever, measles, etc. while they did carry the same infecting agents in their blood. They simply did not have a mortality rate at all from these diseases, and when they did experience illness from them, it was extremely mild.

"The white man's diet of refined and processed foods with the resulting lack of vitamins, the environmental and agricultural poisons, and specific invasive medical procedures all contributed to the rise in susceptibility of people living in industrialized parts of the world. But by the time those connections were made, disease-causing food was well ingrained in the modern palate. Medical advances were met with gratitude even though many of them were dangerous and overused. Refined sugar, white flour, alcohol, tobacco, tonsillectomies, vaccines, antibiotics, DDT, and arsenic had become financial golden calves that led humanity blindly down a spiral of disease and misery."

- Bystrianyk & Humphries, 2015[154]

Misdiagnosis of polio in patients greatly increases and distorts the picture of polio danger in the population. Before 1958, large proportions of patients diagnosed with polio actually had a number of other diseases, such as lead poisoning, arsenic toxicity, transverse myelitis, hand, foot, and mouth disease, spinal meningitis, acute flaccid paralysis, enteroviral encephalopathy, and Reye's syndrome to name some. No polio vaccine would have worked to cure these problems. So, of the small proportion of cases that were true polio cases, which were on a natural decline, how many were actually benefitted, if at all, by the highly dangerous Salk or Sabin vaccine. Modern researchers even have concluded that FDR actually had Guillain-Barre syndrome.

"The pictographic and cinematic images of polio that were used to rally the public toward vaccine development and acceptance dropped away after the vaccine campaign began. The public gratefully embraced the vaccine that was believed to have removed the frightful disease. To maintain public belief in the vaccine, especially in light of several serious instances of vaccine-induced paralytic polio, the images of polio in the new, highly vaccinated population had to be deleted. Optimism regarding the vaccine prevailed. The March of Dimes campaigns that were once designed to impact human fear and emotion transitioned into what we see today as advertising for "working together for stronger, healthier babies"—funding vaccines for infants and pregnant mothers."

- Bystrianyk & Humphries, 2015[155]

Splinting and casting paralyzed limbs, being the improper treatment of polio around the world before Sister Elizabeth Kenny's method was accepted and practiced, led to limb dysfunction with or without virus presence. Immobilization led to flaccidity and paralysis with or without intact motor and sensory nerve pathways. It was the treatment that was the paralyzing agent. It took Sister Kenny 30 years to influence the mainstream medical community enough to force admittance of their incorrect treatment of polio and to accept that physical therapy, massage and vigorous exercise, were the correct treatment.

"Approximately 33,000 people are afflicted by transverse myelitis in the United States, with 1400 new cases per year... This is but one disease that would have been called polio in the years leading up to 1954... "The paralysis that the world witnessed in the first part of the 20th century was largely from toxins in the environment like DDT, lead, and arsenic. Those toxins seriously disrupt mucosal immunity, allowing a previously benign virus to bypass the innate immune system and cause paralysis and other clinical symptoms. Where those chemicals are still used today, you will see reports of paralysis, which used to be called polio, but authorities now call it "acute flaccid paralysis" ... toxicity cases would have been diagnosed as polio and treated as such, often with a crippling outcome. It is not surprising that Dr. Fred Klenner was able to cure 60 out of 60 cases (100 percent) of polio (including bulbar polio) with the detoxifying agent, vitamin C, given in high intravenous doses."

- Bystrianyk & Humphries, 2015[156]

"Transverse myelitis also may occur as a complication of syphilis, measles, Lyme disease, and vaccinations."

Transverse Myelitis Fact Sheet, National Institutes of Health
(National Institute of Health)

DDT and refined sugar were used in abundance and in conjunction led to severe toxicity and damage to the bowel and systemic immune system. This damage made the otherwise innocent virus quite deadly and painful. Dr. Klenner and all others who supported and gave proofs for the efficacy of vitamin C treatment success were ignored, despite extensive publishing and detailed analysis of cases that almost always resulted in curing polio entirely in all cases.

India and China still use DDT and still battle polio. Symptoms of DDT include anterior horn spinal cord damage, respiratory paralysis, muscle spasm, and weakness, which are still being used to diagnose polio in India. Indian children get vaccinated 15 times or more with live vaccine by the age of five. Acute Flaccid Paralysis correlates directly to vaccinations for polio in India. In Bihar and Uttar Pradesh, AFP rates are 25-35 fold higher than international norms. This AFP comes directly due to the vaccine virus that is being pumped recklessly into the population. Children often getting 30 plus rounds by the time they are five years old. WHO's and GAVI's (Global Alliance for Vaccines and Immunization) solution is to encourage and pressure for more vaccination. Because obviously they have the best interests of themselves in mind. In the 1940's, people were told in the U.S. that social hygiene was the cause of polio, but in India today, they are told it is due to poor social hygiene. How the truth changes. Arsenic was considered safe and used in everything from dyes, to tobacco, to paper, and wallpaper and was used as a spray for fruits and vegetables. Therapeutic injections, approved by the AMA, contained arsenic in the medicine. Arsenic toxification led to symptoms resembling polio and which would often be misdiagnosed and treated for as such, resulting in incredible harm.

"...arsenic, even in a few hours after its ingestion, may cause acute central myelitis or acute poliomyelitis."

Ralph R. Scobey, MD, "The Poison Cause of Poliomyelitis and Obstructions to Its Investigation," *Arch Pediatr*, vol. 69, April 1952, pp. 172-193

"Healthy tonsils were removed by surqeons for various financially rewarding but scientifically unsound reasons. Fifty to 80 percent of middle-class and upper-class children in the United States were needlessly subjected to tonsillectomies in the polio epidemic era. Anderson showed in his large group from a 1943 epidemic in Utah that poliomyelitis was more than 2.5 times more prevalent in tonsillectomized children than age-matched non-tonsillectomized children. The incidence of bulbar

poliomyelitis was 16 times higher in tonsillectomized children than in the general child population. Forty-six percent of the bulbar polio cases had been proceeded by recent tonsillectomy."
- Bystrianyk & Humphries, 2015 *p. 260*[157]

"Nowhere else in polio's history was there more panic than during New York City's 1916 epidemic. Dr. H. V. Wyatt published a document in 2011 discussing the possibility that a highly virulent laboratory engineered strain of poliovirus "escaped" from the Rockefeller laboratories, causing the largest epidemic of polio in U.S. history. Just what exactly could have escaped from the lab is unknown... The epidemic was unique in that the virus was highly destructive to the nervous system, much like the Rockefeller labs cultivated "MV" strain."
- Bystrianyk & Humphries, 2015[158]

"It is a remarkable coincidence that a unique neurotropic strain of the poliovirus was developed a few miles from an epidemic caused by a uniquely pathogenic strain of the virus. A few blocks from the Rockefeller Institute...the 3rd Avenue elevated line linked... at 3rd Street and 5th Avenue where the first case lived."
H. V. Wyatt, "The 1916 New York City Epidemic of Poliomyelitis: Where Did the Virus Come From?" *The Open Vaccine Journal*, vol. 4, 2011, pp. 13-17.

DARPA funded Dr. Eckhard Wimmer and others to generate an infectious virus in laboratory settings in absence of a natural viral template. Does this not sound familiar? Why do we give so much credit to the trustworthiness of government when it comes to life and death matters but commonly associate the government, politicians, lawyers, bankers, and monopolists with despicable greed and shamelessness. The government does not deserve our trust anymore than the corporations producing vaccines.

"Our experiment has thus overthrown one axiom in biology—namely, that the proliferation of cells or, for that matter, viruses depends on the physical presence of a functional genome to instruct the replication process. It was believed that without parental genomes, no daughter cells or progeny viruses would arise. We have broken this fundamental law of biology by reducing poliovirus to a chemical entity, which can be synthesized on the basis of information stored in the public domain... Just like a common chemical, poliovirus has been synthesized in the test tube."
E. Wimmer, "The Test-Tube Synthesis of a Chemical Called Poliovirus: The Simple Synthesis of a Virus Has Far-Reaching Societal Implications," special issue, European Molecular Biology Organization Report, vol. 7, July 20, 2006, pp. S3-S9
(Wimmer, 2006)

"Dr. Wimmer also reports that neurovirulence can be manipulated readily in synthetic polioviruses, though he presumes that this capability will be used for attenuation rather than for raising more virulent species. Either one is equally possible."
- Bystrianyk & Humphries, 2015[159]

"From its peak in the 1800's, whooping cough deaths had declined by more than 99 percent before a vaccine was in widespread use. In 1985, the Institute of Medicine report estimated there were 17,994,600 whole-cell vaccine doses administered, resulting in "7,197,840 cases of minor reactions, 10,283, convulsions, 164 cases of encephalitis, and 58 cases of chronic disability... caused two to four deaths per year." They chose to recommend the switch to the acellular, DTap, containing inactivated pertussis toxin "and one or more other bacterial components... In regard to whooping cough, "who is providing better hard immunity in the face of bacterial exposure? Vaccinated individuals who presume they are immune, yet remain asymptomatically colonized for 42 days spreading bacteria? Unvaccinated kids who get infected and remain colonized for 38 days? Or the naturally convalesced who are not able to be colonized and therefore do not spread bacteria at all upon re-exposure? Better still: natural convalescence makes for decades longer, solid immunity than vaccination... Before the vaccination era, naturally acquired disease usually provided comprehensive long-term immunity because natural immunity involves a more broad-spectrum response to the entirety of the bacteria and their toxins. Remember that being immune to any degree does not stop the bacteria from flying around and entering the airway. When a naturally immune person reencounters whooping cough bacteria, the body will efficiently respond and clear them from the system. This is not necessarily true of vaccinated people."

- Bystrianyk & Humphries, 2015[160]

"The concept of original antigenic sin (OAS) was coined by Dr. Thomas Francis, who became well known during the Salk vaccine era when he oversaw and interpreted the results of the largest (and most controversial) vaccine trial in history. He explained the phenomenon of OAS using natural influenza virus as an example. First, let's define how the body responds to natural infection. When a person gets an infectious disease for the first time, the body's immune system uses its innate powers, which mostly involve cellular immunity. In the process, it prepares for the future. The next time that same infectious agent comes around, the body will use its memory of the first experience so that it can react faster. But after a vaccine, when the natural microorganism comes along later, the body will act according to how it was programmed by the vaccination—and that is what is meant by original antigenic sin... The reason immunologists and vaccine scientists don't talk about original antigenic sin is because if they had to explain to the public just what it means in principle and in practical fact, they'd have to explain that vaccination breaches a fundamental immunological tenet. They would have to admit that whooping cough vaccine immunity is vastly inferior and that vaccine immunity has immunological unintended consequences in the future. As an aside, OAS was also a factor in morbidity of the influenza vaccinated when H1N1 infection arrived... Far from being eliminated as a disease, whooping cough is endemic in highly vaccinated populations. It is important to understand that the pertussis vaccine can only prevent serious infection in some vaccinated people, but it will never prevent carriage and spread in anyone, vaccinated or not. Because of original antigenic sin, the vaccinated will be unable to clear the bacteria as efficiently and, thus, are more likely to be vectors for the disease."

- Bystrianyk & Humphries, 2015[161]

B. Pertussis bacteria secrete adenylate cyclase toxin (ACT) after attaching to cells in the bronchi, which acts as an invisibility cloak to shield itself from the immune system for a couple of weeks, by acting as an anti-inflammatory and antiphagocytic. "The naturally convalesced have 17 times the amount of antibody to ACT than DTap recipients and more than 9 times than DTP vaccinated..." Those who have recovered naturally from pertussis have high levels of ACT immunity, and thus have protection against parapertussis as well, while vaccinated persons do not, as the vaccine does not contain ACT, and thus the immune systems of the vaccinated do not have to overcome and develop memory of that toxin.

"There's still another problem with pertussis vaccines, and that is that the vaccines themselves are now a source of false-positive pertussis PCR tests. How do you think this complicates the doctor's task, and how is it affecting humanity overall, given the rampant and unnecessary use of antibiotics for all cases that test positive?"

- Bystrianyk & Humphries, 2015[162]

"... at least 80% of the total decline in mortality, since records began to be kept in the United Kingdom in 1860, occurred before any vaccine or antimicrobial drugs were available and 90% or more before there was any national vaccine programme."

- Gordon T. Stewart, "Whooping Cough in Relation to Other Childhood Infections in 1977-9 in the United Kingdom," Journal of Epidemiology and Community Health, vol. 35, 1981, p. 144.[163]

"...We can't even be sure how to tell when the immune system's not working right, let alone why not, because we don't have good metrics of what a healthy human immune system looks like. Despite billions spent on immune stimulants in supermarkets and drugstores last year, we don't know what—if anything—those really do, or what "immune stimulant" even means."

- B. Goldman, "The Bodyguard: Tapping the Immune System's Secrets," Stanford Medicine, Summer 2011.[164]

"If more people understood that the incidence of whooping cough has increased with increasing vaccines, bacterial Resistance is emerging, and there is a nontoxic treatment available, surely vaccine uptake would decline further. Since early diagnosis and treatment with antibiotics is not sufficiently effective, a reevaluation of the necessity of the entire medical approach is warranted. But that won't happen until the "delicate fabric" of interlaced pharmaceutical companies, government, and academia becomes torn."

"Throughout the 1800's measles epidemics occurred about every two years in the United States and England. During these epidemics, some hospital wards overflowed with children, up to 20 percent of whom died. However, by the 1960's, the deaths had dropped to extremely low numbers in both England and the United States. In England, the percent decline from its peak level reached an astonishing 99.96 percent by the time the vaccine was introduced in 1968... Many think that antibiotics were responsible for the vast decline in mortality. For measles, scarlet fever, typhoid, whooping cough, and diphtheria, the overall downward trend in mortality was unaffected by the introduction of penicillin, which was not mass produced until 1944... When the measles vaccine was licensed in 1963, the measles death rate in Massachusetts had reached zero. Similarly, in Washington State, as in other locations throughout the Western world, the measles death rate had been steadily trending toward zero for years. By 1963 Washington State had a measles death rate of 0.3 per 100,000... New England had only 5 deaths attributed to measles. Deaths from asthma were 56 times greater, accidents 935 times greater, motor vehicle accidents 323 times greater, other accidents 612 times greater, and heart disease 9,560 times greater... Child mortality due to measles is 200 to 400 times greater in malnourished children in less developed countries than those in developed ones. In addition, measles brings about consumption of nutrients in marginally nourished children, so they will also do worse if not supplemented during infection. As nutrition improves, complications from measles diminish."

"The reason that vaccines are not done in "pulse" fashion to interrupt transmission is that if they were administered on specific days, any damage from vaccination would become blindingly obvious to both parents and authorities. It is much more difficult to make any connection between vaccine and reactions when they are given to individuals, spread out over the whole year, as per the childhood, age-based schedule, or the gradual administering of flu shots over several months. Pulse days eliminate the ability of the authorities to claim coincidence due to "background incidence."

- Bystrianyk & Humphries, 2015[165]

"During a class-action case in Australia over Merck's heart-attack and stroke-inducing drug, Vioxx, it was revealed that a "doctor hit list" circulated within the ranks of the hierarchy. This list contained names of the doctors who spoke out against the drug using labels such as "neutralize," "neutralized," and "discredit." During the testimony, Julian Burnside, QC, acting for the plaintiff, read one email from a Merck employee that said, "We may need to seek them out and destroy them where they live."

- Milanda Rout, "Vioxx Maker Merck and Co Drew Up Doctor Hit List," April 1, 2009, www.theaustralian.com.au/news/drug-company-drew-up-doctor-hit-list/story-e6frg6n6-1225693586492[166]

In the 1960's it was discovered that antibody production is not the definitive marker of immunity. This occurred when "individuals with a deficit in antibody production, called agamma-globulinemia, recovered from measles just as well as normal antibody producers." This occurred even with children with congenital agamma-globulinemia, who could make no antibodies whatsoever. Innate immunity is the reason most people recover entirely from acute infections.

"This involves a part of the immune system that requires no memory or previous exposure and does not involve preformed specific antibodies. Instead, it involves the activation of white blood cells,

including macrophages, natural killer cells, and antigen-specific T lymphocytes, as well as the release of various cytokines (immune system proteins) in response to a foreign invader. This aspect of immunity is present regardless of vaccination and is highly dependent on essential nutrients. When cellular immunity is impaired—for instance, in leukemia—measles is disastrous. The pro-vaccine argue that the reason to vaccinate all healthy people is to protect those at highest risk. Huge amounts of money are spent figuring out why so many vaccinated remain susceptible to infection and why the same people who are susceptible to disease complications don't respond to the vaccine. The appearance of one case of measles in the highest vaccinated populations always promotes widespread fearmongering by public health officials because they know the fragility of vaccine immunity."

- Bystrianyk & Humphries, 2015[167]

(ADE) Antibody Dependent Enhancement occurs when an anti-body makes a person more susceptible to disease. Inactivated measles vaccines resulted in abnormal immune response by only programming recipients to manufacture antibodies to one of the two virus surface proteins, making them more vulnerable.

"Vaccine efficacy could depend on enhancement of the immune response for those with weak immune responses, but enhanced responses could be detrimental in those who naturally generate strong immune responses... rather than being a static or stable characteristic, the ability of an Ab (antibody) to mediate protection is likely to be dynamic, changing as a function of time, the host response, available host receptors and inflammatory mediators, and the state of the microbe in the host... Considering that the immune response to pathogenic microbes includes Abs to many Ags (antigens) differing in the predominant isotype and amount, one can easily envision unfathomable complexity that becomes even more daunting if one considers host genetic variation. Clearly, defining protective efficacy of an Ab molecule in a predictive fashion is currently beyond the state of immunological science and may not be possible with current reductionistic approaches to scientific problems."

- A.Casadevall et al., "A Reappraisal of Humoral Immunity Based on Mechanisms of Antibody Mediated Protection Against Intracellular Pathogens," Advances in Immunology, vol. 91, 2006, pp. 1-44.[168]

Post 1968, only just over half the child population had been vaccinated against measles, but over half of all measles cases were still in the fully vaccinated population. Measles incidence plummeted despite vaccination status. The vaccine itself was an admitted failure, ineffective against measles. Only 2.5-7 percent of suspected measles cases are correct diagnoses, which leaves us with the question; how many misdiagnoses occurred, skewing statistics before our modern techniques and technologies were available?

"Breastfeeding infants borrow the mothers innate immune system and memory immunity that was acquired through her previous natural infection... infants are fed vitamin A through breastmilk... breastmilk carries a host of viral-neutralizing agents other than immune globulins, which is why fewer breastfed infants get measles than non-breastfed infants. Breastmilk immunoprotective properties involve more than just antibodies. Colostrum contains viable T lymphocytes that impart immunity to the newborn. The T cells in mammary glands are predominantly activated... enter the infants intestine, pass through to infant lymph nodes, and are used by that infant to resist disease. This type of immunity... is only present in breastfed infants... Breast milk contains stem cells, myoepithelial progenitors, immune cells, interferon, and cytokines. A vast array of "new" immune cells are being added to the list every year. There is ample evidence that breast milk has an immunomodulating effect via interferon and Th1 cell response to measles that formula does not have."

- Bystrianyk & Humphries, 2015[169]

Mothers exclusively breast fed until the mid-1800's, from which time formulas became available. By the 1940's only 25 percent of infants were breastfed. That number has steadily increased to over 75 percent today. Vaccinated mother's breastmilk contains lower levels of virus specific immunity compared to naturally immune mothers... Breastfed infants of vaccinated mothers have nearly three times the risk of measles infection than those of naturally immune mothers.

"Vitamin A stops the measles virus from rapidly multiplying inside cells by up-regulating the innate immune system in uninfected cells which helps to prevent the virus from infecting new cells... low vitamin A correlates with... increased morbidity and mortality... Vitamin A is a well-proven intervention for reduction of mortality, concomitant infections, and hospital stay... protects the retinas and the uninfected cells."

- Bystrianyk & Humphries, 2015[170]

Dietary nutrient deficiency leads to higher rates of unfavorable outcomes after exposure to infectious diseases. High quantities of vitamin A and C and B as well as other nutrients results in far less problems. Malnutrition is a primary cause of high mortality rates along with consumption of toxic substances that claim to be food.

"Nutrient levels may seem lacking today, but during the 1800's when disease mortality was more than 9 times higher, nutrient levels were far worse. Back then, people were dying of scurvy, and today we are simply having illness that doctors don't connect to focal or subclinical scurvy. Overall, society is much better nourished than 200 years ago. Nutrient deficiency is known to have a direct effect on the virulence of microorganisms. This means that a nutrient-deficient neighbor can actually influence your health... What we have now is a population of increasingly unhealthy children—with rates of many chronic disorders increasing dramatically. Vaccination, for many, is a matter of swapping one set of possible risks for another set of probable risks, which are said to be "coincident.""

"Scarcity of food and periodic famines have historically resulted in deadly malnutrition . Vitamin deficiency is a common consequence of starvation that can lead to scurvy, pellagra, beriberi, anemia, and other nutrient-deficiency illnesses. Because vitamins have a strong impact on the immune system, people who are deficient can become susceptible to all types of infections. Poor housing, deplorable and extremely stressful working conditions, and other negative consequences of poverty, combined with malnutrition, opened the door for a wide variety of infectious diseases."

- Bystrianyk & Humphries, 2015[171]

"...there were half a million fewer human beings in Ireland between 1831 and 1841 than there had been between 1821 and 1831. Commissioners of Poor-law Inquiry, in 1835, report that 2,300,000 of the agricultural population are in a state approaching starvation."

- "The State of Ireland," The Spectator, vol. 19, 1846, pp.174-175[172]

"...the notorious Great Famine in which perhaps two million people died, some from starvation, but far more from typhus and other epidemics consequent upon malnutrition and social collapse."

- Roy Porter, The Greatest Benefit to Mankind, Harper Collins, New York, 1997, p. 398[173]

"Scurvy is a disease that results from a deficiency of dietary vitamin C, which is essential for the formation of healthy collagen. Collagen is the protein that forms connective tissue in the skin, bones, and blood vessels and also gives support to internal organs. In scurvy, the body is not able to generate adequate collagen or extracellular matrix proteins that serve as mortar holding cells together. As a result, the body literally comes unglued and falls apart... the first symptoms of scurvy are apathy and weakness, and they soon die from exhaustion. Vitamin C has numerous functions in the body. Probably the most important action involves the part of Vitamin C called ascorbic acid, which is essential for normal mitochondrial metabolism. Ascorbic acid is protective against reactive oxygen species (free radical damage) in the mitochondria and keeps the mitochondria healthy. Ascorbic acid is also necessary for transport of one of three types of substrates used for fuel. Proteins, sugars, and fats are used for energy production to generate ATP, which is the main energy source for the majority of cellular functions of the body. Without ATP, cell energy flatlines, and critical cell functions stop. That fats cannot get through the mitochondrial membrane without ascorbic acid because an essential molecule called carnitine, which shuttles the fat inside the mitochondria, is dependent upon ascorbic

acid for its generation. The biosynthesis of carnitine requires ascorbic acid as a cofactor for two separate hydroxylation steps. Therefore, if there is scurvy, core metabolism shuts down, resulting in profound fatigue and fatty acid buildup elsewhere. This type of functional fatty acid deficiency manifests in the form of neurological disorders, cardiac disease, and muscle weakness. The fatigue marks the beginning of a breakdown of the body. Without normal mitochondrial function, the immune system breaks down as do all the systems that maintain bone and flesh structure. The result is obvious—death."

"Rickets is a softening of bones in children caused by a deficiency of Vitamin D, magnesium, phosphorus, and calcium. This disease can lead to fractures and deformities. Few people are aware that vitamin C is also very important for healthy bone mineralization and for bone formation."

"By 1900 deaths from scurvy were rare and steadily decreased. Simultaneously, death from infectious diseases also drastically declined. This is because immune cells are highly dependent on a component of vitamin C called ascorbic acid. Today we know that vitamin C is vital to several components of the human immune system, including white blood cells. About 50-70 percent of all white blood cells are neutrophils, the primary immune cell type that utilizes vitamin C... vitamin C is also used by granulocytes, or polymorphonuclear leukocytes, (PMNs). PMNs are white blood cells that contain a segmented lobular nucleus; they can be further classified into eosinophil, basophil, or neutrophil. Innate immunity is the part of cellular immunity that requires no memory of previous infection."

"Vitamin C's benefit during infection has much to do with the neutralization of bacterial and viral toxins and with the supply of ascorbic acid to white blood cells... But there is another more direct effect on bacteria. Today, scientists are validating the antimicrobial effect of vitamin C on certain bacterial infections. The effect involves oxidative killing via the Fenton reaction, with vitamin C essentially acting as an antibiotic. "

- Bystrianyk & Humphries, 2015[174]

Vitamin C has been used to affect positively and cure poliomyelitis, encephalitis, herpes zoster, pertussis, virus pneumonia, and pretty much all other infectious diseases. In 1949, Dr. Fred R. Klenner cured many shingles cases with high doses of vitamin C injections and fruit drinks, all within a few days. He also was curing measles, as white blood counts increased, mobilizing the immune system against the infection.

"There are hundreds of examples in the field of medicine where fundamentally flawed ideas have gained public support and were kept alive by belief momentum. Eugenics, numerous psychiatric diagnoses, harmful drugs like thalidomide, fever reducers, diethylstilbestrol, bloodletting, and unbalanced hormone replacement are several examples of faulty ideas that have historically attained a level of scientific and societal legitimacy. Not only have these strange types of beliefs been accepted, but in the midst of their unquestioned superiority, better ideas were overlooked. In the hope of preventing disease, vaccination took hold as the only way to combat smallpox. The original belief was that vaccination was a safe way to acquire lifelong immunity. This turned out to be untrue, and thus had to be redressed as a "temporary way of making smallpox milder." Even though revaccinations were required yearly for some people, even though there was great success using isolation and disinfection after abandoning vaccination in Leicester, and even though there were large numbers of vaccination-related deaths and vaccine failures, devotion to vaccination by the medical profession became firmly established... If a remedy couldn't be patented or given the AMA seal of acceptance, it generally would not have ranked in the public or medical eye."

- Bystrianyk & Humphries, 2015[175]

Cinnamon has been used to treat and cure people of various infectious diseases, such as diphtheria, cholera, typhoid, influenza, malaria, measles, and others. It contains vitamins A and C, as well as zinc, potassium, magnesium, and manganese. It is an antioxidant. Garlic and onion have been recorded as preventatives to smallpox, tuberculosis, lupus, and whooping cough. Echinacea has been used on and proven to affect a positive recovery from smallpox, flu, colds, anthrax, and sepsis. Jicama has been used to cure pneumonia and typhus. Fresh juiced vegetables have been used to cure tuberculosis. Lycopene in tomatoes is anti-bacterial. Apple cider vinegar has been used to treat and cure high cholesterol, sore throats, sinus infections, and even smallpox. It is a disinfectant, alkalizes the body, aids in digestion with numerous enzymes, is antiscorbutic, and contains prebiotics. Cod liver oil has been used to treat and cure tuberculosis and puerperal fever. Colloidal silver has been used to treat and cure influenza.

"Modern science is confirming what has been known for hundreds of years—garlic is effective in helping the body fight infections. A 2003 study examined the use of orally ingested garlic against Methicillin-resistant Staphylococcus Aureus (MRSA), which is now a common and deadly pathogen that is resistant to many conventional antibiotics. They concluded that garlic "inhibited the growth of and killed MRSA...in dose -dependent manner.""
- *STUDY REFERENCED:* Shyh-ming Tsao, Cheng-chin Hsu, and Mei-chin Yin, "Garlic Extract and Two Daily Diallyl Sulphides Inhibit Methicillin-Resistant Staphylococcus Aureus Infection in BALB/Ca Mice," Journal of Antimicrobial Chemotherapy, October 2003, p. 979.[176]/[177]

"Pulmonary Tuberculosis is a disease of malnutrition. The plan of treatment is based upon what is universally accepted as the most rational method for the relief of the disease, viz: fresh air and sunlight in abundance, good food, plenty of sleep, regulated exercise, care of sputum and attention to the small things of daily life which are known to influence nutrition favorably... The coming of the patients to the dispensary twice a day gives the opportunity to educate them how best to live according to their means. They come ostensibly only to drink emulsion and vegetable juice..."
- John F. Russell, MD, Report of Fifty-Five Apparent Cures of Pulmonary Tuberculosis Occurring in Working People Who Were Treated at a Dispensary Without Interruption to Their Work, New York, February 1906, p. 9.[178]

"Dr. Max Gerson was another pioneer doctor who, in the 1930s to 1950s, used fruit and vegetable juices, a carefully selected vegetarian diet, and vitamin and mineral therapy to heal tuberculosis, type 2 diabetes, heart disease, kidney failure, cancer, and other chronic conditions. His legacy lives on today through his daughter Charlotte in San Diego California's Gerson Institute. The Gerson Therapy activates the body's extraordinary ability to heal itself through an organic, vegetarian diet, raw juices, coffee enemas, and natural supplements."

"People are led to believe that because the world is a dangerous place, only governments and large institutions can provide protection because they are bigger and more knowledgeable than small communities. Rules and restrictions are put in place. Those who believe this lose trust in their own capability and thus surrender thinking and decision making to others. Doctors are no exception to this phenomenon. Medical practitioners cede their independent thinking to texts, advisory panels, and traditions which vary depending on political influences of the times. In medical school, doctors are taught to view the human body as a random mistake-ridden vessel that has to be forced into submission with surgery, antibiotics, antihypertensives, antihistamines, anti-inflammatories, and other medical interventions. the natural extension of this paradigm over the last 100 years has been for the medical profession to condition human beings not to trust anyone but certified medical doctors to fix these defective aberrations of creation... Ideology and myth had displaced verified historical documentation. The history of the phenomenally successful non-vaccinating experience in Leicester, the documented vaccine-related diseases and deaths, the 1872 smallpox pandemic, the fact that smallpox had shifted to a mild disease in spite of declining vaccination rates, the spreading of foot-and-mouth disease via vaccines, and the amazingly successful use of apple cider vinegar against smallpox were all trampled under the heels of conventional medicine's growing dominance. The new literature that was distributed (after 1922) to the public and doctors was predominantly mythology about "Jenner's great discovery." From here, the idea of dangerous germs and lifesaving vaccines came to dominate medical and societal thinking. Vaccination was successfully implanted into the minds of the masses as the most effective means to prevent disease. Next came diphtheria antitoxin in 1895, and then diphtheria vaccination starting in 1920."

"Opposition to vaccination was and still is deemed to be only from those who don't understand science and, because of their foolhardy resistance, can bring on more disease and death... Smallpox vaccination's virtually unchallenged belief momentum has existed for so many decades that it is rarely contemplated, let alone challenged. Most history books that make mention of Edward Jenner's discovery quickly conclude, without any or with only scant evidence, that it was only of enormous benefit. Some mention in more detail the anti-vaccine movement, but it is always cast in the light that foolish, uneducated protestors were in dangerous opposition to settled science."

"To date, despite the existence of thousands of never-vaccinated children, there has not been a "completely vaccinated" versus "never vaccinated" study to compare the difference between the short-and-long-term health of both groups. Nobody—not even the most educated immunologists—understands or can describe the complete cascade of events that occurs after injecting a vaccine. If physicians realized how little is known today about the immune system and vaccines, they would be duty bound to tell patients that there are no accurate scientific answers. Because the whole truth isn't told, adults are the only line of defense for themselves. Until the minds of pediatricians are emancipated, parents will remain the best line of defense for their children. The reality... is that vaccinology, as portrayed to the public today, amounts to writing religion on the back of ignorance."

- Bystrianyk & Humphries, 2015[179]

Iatrogenic damage is the third leading cause of death in the United States. From unnecessary surgeries to medication errors, to nosocomial infections to adverse effects of medications, hospitals are responsible for more deaths than any amount of infectious disease. We obviously live in a time in much of the world, including the United States, in which we do not have to worry whether there is fecal matter in our drinking water. We may have a concern over the fluoride, which is collected from the scrubbers at the top of the stacks at aluminum factories, then pumped into our municipal waters. But fecal matter, not so much. We do not have to concern ourselves with cholera or typhoid, because we live in a cleaner, more sanitary condition, absent the hovels of the 1800's, and absent the unrestricted presence of rats and cockroaches. We have seen the evidence for over 200 years of the inefficacy of vaccines. We have seen the complete disintegration of the old medical ideas that germs are there to harm us. When we look at the evidence and make our lives the experiment, those of us who choose to live a holistic lifestyle, with bodily, mental, emotional, and spiritual wellness at the epicenter of our attention, there is no coronavirus epidemic. For us, there is government manipulation and extortion for the publicly stated agendas of social controllers to come to fruition. There is, perhaps, some number of deaths from the flu occurring, as they will, but the toll that this year's (seasonal flu) is taking is NOT serious enough to warrant the closing of even one west Texas desert town of 20 people or one inner city bus station. Let's see it from the historically accurate, evidentiary, and simple perspective that reduces not the problem, but simplifies the solution. The problem may be complex, but the solution is so extremely simple. Do not pay/give/release attention into the hands, minds, or machinations of those who claim power over you. The moment you do this, they can no longer dictate and pollute your life. It is your firm conviction to self-determinism and self-responsibility that will prevent your mind from being toxified by the real virus, which is the thought that you need a ruler or entity to govern your life.

Coronavirus:
any of a family (Coronaviridae) of large single-stranded RNA viruses that have a lipid envelope studded with club-shaped spike proteins, infect birds and many mammals including humans, and include the causative agents of MERS, SARS, and COVID-19[180]

Covid-19:
a mild to severe respiratory illness that is caused by a coronavirus (Severe acute respiratory syndrome coronavirus 2 of the genus Betacoronavirus), is transmitted chiefly by contact with infectious material (such as respiratory droplets) or with objects or surfaces contaminated by the causative virus, and is characterized especially by fever, cough, and shortness of breath and may progress to pneumonia and respiratory failure.[181]

Let's rundown the key points of the plandemic, shall we. Vaccine immunity for covid is waning rapidly over time as all vaccines do. Masks do not stop the spread of viruses, as has been testified to by "America's Doctor", Anthony Fauci, before he became the mask evangelist. NIH and NAIAD and CDC and WHO and every other conceivable health agency on the planet has identified, sometimes overtly, other times through omission, that natural immunity is resulting in greater resistance to this infectious disease and that masks, social (6 foot) distancing, and hospitalization do not result in avoiding or healing from this disease.

Vaccine Mandates are outside of the police powers of the Federal Government, not that this fact will prevent those with power from wielding it to the fullest for private gain at the expense of the people's liberties and wellbeing. Covid Case Numbers are manipulated through WHO medical policies, such as the financial incentives and hospital mandates that artificially increase the number of actual casualties.

Dr. Robert Malone very publicly revealed on the Joe Rogan Experience, that natural immunity is 26 or 27-fold more effective in protecting a person from covid than the vaccines. He said that hospitals receive $3000 for every recorded covid case, and hospital administrators are financially incentivized to record covid cases, covid treatments, and covid deaths. One of the extremely irresponsible, illegal, and reprehensible actions of Big Pharma, collaborative government and financiers and beneficiaries is the complete and utter lack of long-term peer-reviewed publicly accessible studies. The mRNA Genetic Vaccines and DNA Virus Administered Vaccines all have symptoms of affecting menstrual cycles in women, clotting, brain fog, and other things. The common variable between the three is Spike Protein, which is probably causing the problem with all these people. The likelihood of getting Omicron is greater after vaccination and greater even after every following vaccination.

Despite all of this, Dr. Malone tells us, the State is deciding that oppressive police state tactics are the way forward, invading the family and the home, and inhibiting our children who need to see faces to be able to adequately learn how to be functional people. Masks have literally reduced the average IQ amongst our youngest generation by several points, though on the bittersweet positive side, they have shown us the amount of low IQ, docile, manipulatable, statist, and willfully ignorant people there are all around us.

"Forcing children as young as five-years-old to effectively become human shields, assuming vaccine-injury-risk despite having statistically zero risk of COVID-19 to those who are healthy, just so adults with comorbidities can feel safer — what kind of a society does that? At no time in history have we put children in harm's way to protect adults. Stripping risk/benefit discretion from parents with a novel vaccine for children, which, if healthy, are at statistically greater risk of the seasonal flu than Covid-19. Illogical, unscientific, top-down, one-size-fits-all carte blanche mandates for healthy children that directly contradict the current body of evidence and data."

– The Unity Project

Scientists often do not make direct statements, unlike laypeople, because the nature of scientific method requires maintaining an open mind, and to accept that any answer to a question is but a *current answer* which is likely to change as greater knowledge and answers become available. Also, any answer has its diametric opposite conclusions and competing theories. Rather than declaring all of those wrong, the scientist will only put forth the data, analysis, and abstract of any study. This way of speaking often eludes the layperson, who is highly likely to have formed their worldview by a series of highly acute decisions and have less flexibility of thought to consider various points of view concurrently while living effectively in their busy lives.

In his book, "The Real Anthony Fauci," Robert Kennedy expounds on the fallacies of the pandemic and spectacularly lays out the facts. What he does wrong, is focus upon Anthony Fauci, making him and a couple collaborators the key target for criticism. This will be an extremely popular approach, as by identifying one or two names, he makes it quite simple for people to adjust the enemy from covid to Fauci. A single-pointed bad guy that can be attacked and punished, as the punching bag for the people to beat away their fear, shame, hate and guilt. The other big wrong, is his use of the duopoly to support his position. Being a democrat has nothing to do with the truths in his book. Quite the opposite is the truth actually. It is the state itself that is at fault, which is both parties of the duopoly and all the health organizations and all the corporations that pull the strings. Democrat or republican or statist of any type, you are wrong.

Fauci is not the epicenter of control or planning for the plandemic. If anything, he is the front man. Gates is a financial beneficiary, mediator, and promoter. The beneficiaries of the plandemic, include the over 400 newly made billionaires since the lockdowns, and more so the fund managers that dictate corporate goals and positions. The organizations like the World Economic Forum and the Trilateral Commission are the hubs around which the planners and benefactors publicly circle. Follow the money people. Who benefits? While I still encourage all to read "The Real Anthony Fauci", here are a few bullet points from that book that I found extremely insightful, interesting, and important.

1. While the U.S. population accounts for only 4% of the world population, we suffered 14.5% of total recorded covid deaths.
2. The amounts of death due to suicide, depression, stress, overdoses, and alcoholism far exceed covid deaths.
3. 1.9 year decline in life expectancy in U.S. between 2018 and 2020, 8 times greater than comparable countries.
4. Lockdown impact on supply chains and food production forced millions of people globally into starvation and malnutrition, especially children.
5. Deferred medical treatments for non-covid illnesses created vast increases in deaths globally.
6. 41% of black owned business went bankrupt and 8 million Americans fell below the poverty line
7. American children have lost 7 IQ points since 2000.
8. Over 99.9% of people were protected by their immune system against covid-19. The extreme majority did not know they even had covid.
9. Natural immunity provides lifelong protection against the virus, and its various mutations.
10. "Masks increased social isolation and fostered divisions and fractionalization, thereby impeding organized political resistance."
11. "Medicare paid hospitals $39,000 per ventilator when treating covid-19 and only $13,000 for garden variety respiratory infections."
12. "At the outset of the pandemic, Dr. Fauci used wildly inaccurate modeling that overestimated U.S. deaths by 525%. Scammer and pandemic fabricator Neil Ferguson of Imperial College London was their author, with funding from the Bill and Melinda Gates Foundation of $148.8 million. Dr. Fauci used this model as justification for his lockdowns."
13. Early treatment was completely censored, despite the 100% treatable nature of covid-19 through early treatment methods, such as oral Vitamin A, C and D and iodine, intravenous hydrogen peroxide and Vitamin C, intramuscular ozone, and nebulized hydrogen peroxide and

Lugol's iodine. Vitamin D, Vitamin C, Ivermectin with Zinc or Quercetin, Hydroxychloroquine with Zinc or Quercetin all safely treat Covid-19.

"Ellison, Gates, and the other members of this government industry collaboration used the lockdown to accelerate construction of their 5G network of satellites, antennae, biometric facial recognition, and track and trace infrastructure that they and their government and intelligence agency partners can use to mine and monetize our data, further suppress dissent, to compel obedience to arbitrary dictates, and to manage the rage that comes as Americans finally wake up to the fact that this outlaw gang has stolen our democracy, our civil rights, our country, and our way of life, while we huddled in orchestrated fear from a flu-like virus. With fears of covid generously stoked, the dramatic and steady erosion of constitutional rights, and fomenting of a global coup d'état against democracy, the demolition of our economy, the obliteration of a million small businesses, the collapsing of the middle class, the evisceration of our bill of rights, the tidal wave of surveillance capitalism, and the rising biosecurity state, and the stunning shifts in wealth and power going to a burgeoning oligarchy of high-tech silicon valley robber barons, seemed to a dazed and uncritical America, like it might be a reasonable price to pay for safety." – Robert F. Kennedy, 2021[182]

Public health officials worry that acknowledging natural immunity will lead people to deliberately try to get infected with Covid rather than getting vaccinated... Public health officials worry that establishing whether a potential vaccine recipient has already had Covid is too inefficient and cumbersome: officials downplay anything that might slow the efficiency of vaccination campaigns or complicate the simplistic "needle in every arm" public messaging... Public health officials worry that acknowledging natural immunity will amount to admitting the failure of their prior policies, which were implemented to slow or halt the spread of the virus. The two most basic numbers in immunology are incidence and prevalence: the former designates the rate of new cases over a given period of time, whereas the latter designates the rate of overall cases for a given period of time. Once the CDC acknowledges natural immunity, the obvious question is then about prevalence: how many Americans have already been infected with Covid since the pandemic began? That 20 months into the pandemic we don't have an answer to this most basic question is astonishing, since it could easily be answered by randomly sampled population-based T-cell testing, or antibody testing sampled sequentially in a cohort every few months. If the CDC got back to epidemiological basics and finally did these essential studies, most scientists estimate that somewhere between 50% and 60% of the population will turn out to have natural immunity, including many who were vaccinated (which artificially elevates estimates of vaccine efficacy, by the way). In the mind of officials who never want to admit that they may have been wrong, this will suggest that—despite draconian lockdowns, social distancing, masking, scrubbing of surfaces, etc.—the virus nevertheless did what viruses do: over half of Americans got infected anyways. Self-interested public health agencies will see this as bad news. (The silver lining is that, of this huge number of people who have been infected with Covid, 99.8% will have survived, including 99.9996% of those under 50.)
– Aaron Kheriaty, MD[183]

Chance of Surviving Covid-19 By Age and Sex

AGE	FEMALE No Underlying Conditions	FEMALE One or Greater Underlying Conditions	MALE No Underlying Conditions	MALE One or Greater Underlying Conditions
0-9	99.99996	99.9639	99.99996	99.9603
10-19	99.99996	99.9639	99.99996	99.9603
20-29	99.9998	99.9466	99.9997	99.9037
30-39	99.9991	99.8636	99.9986	99.79
40-49	99.998	99.8153	99.9965	99.6943
50-59	99.9888	99.3647	99.9815	99.2135
60-69	99.9562	98.7605	99.8895	97.9992
70-79	99.8251	97.6094	99.5245	95.6517
80+	98.9087	92.8152	96.3318	79.9154

"Predicted COVID-19 Fatality Rates Based on Age, Sex, Comorbidities, and Health System Capacity, Stockholm University"**, June 2020**

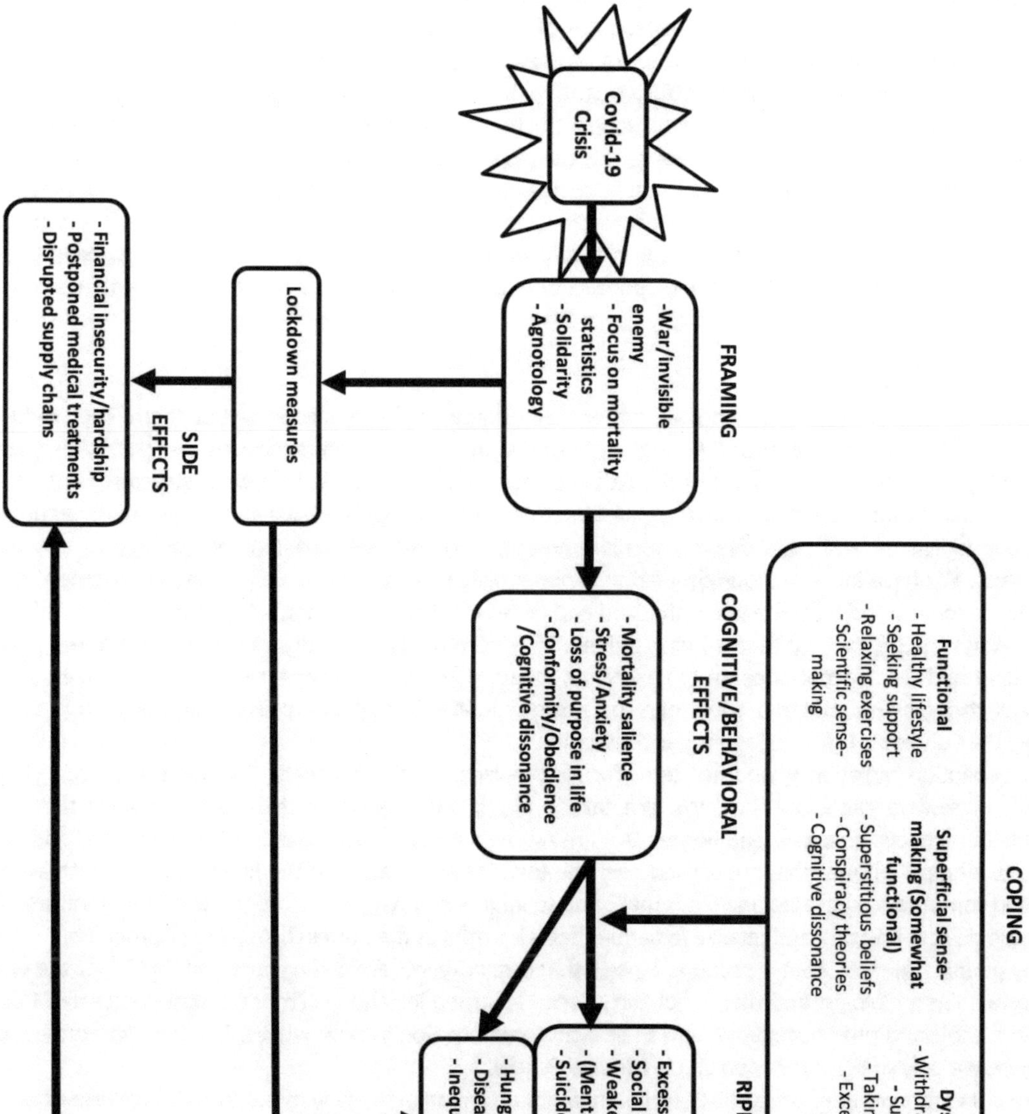

*Michaéla C. Schippers, Department of Technology and Operations Management, Rotterdam School of Management, Erasmus University Rotterdam, Rotterdam, Netherlands, *For the Greater Good? The Devastating Ripple Effects of the Covid-19 Crisis*[184]

As Schippers describes in her article, the amount of harm being forced upon the population of the world from lockdowns is extreme and generationally injurious. The psychological effects alone are causing and will cause more severe societal degradation through suicide, mental illness, and emotional ineptness. The decreasing IQ's, the increase in blind acceptance of government authority, and the fracturing of society into pathologically divisive factions are some examples of the state of today. The not so funny—funny thing about all this, is that responsibility ought to be on the vaccine makers, the government, and corporations that benefit from lockdowns to bear the burden of proof that what they are doing is explicitly harmless and for the benefit of the people. It is the opposite though, as the mainstream public shouts at their neighbors for not getting vaccines that have no long term or even short-term studies, for not wearing masks that are proven to be ineffective against viruses, and not locking down after going to a restaurant even though the chance of dying from it is nearly zero for the average person. The tables have been turned on the population to bear the responsibility of providing burden of proof that these things *cause* harm. What the Fuck? Incipient idiocracy.

EMR

Here we are. Diminished by our choices, rather than empowered and encouraged by them. The world is listening to the voices of a million tyrants, oppressors, thieves, murderers, slavers, and pedophiles, but forgetting to listen to the wise call of the Elders of our species. We have built giant structures but have grown small amongst them. We have created intelligent technology but have lost deeper understanding and our individual and collective moral discernment, and thus we use that technology to oppress ourselves. We have increased our population exponentially in a short time, only to see enslavement and apathy become standardized and emphasized and dis-ease to become a normality. With this in mind, we can discuss the technology that is being utilized by governments and industries and which is the most prevalent and sinister tool of control in existence today. "One of the newest, most pervasive stressors is now electropollution radiation. Medical researchers estimate that 90% of all illness and disease is stress related." - Center for Disease Control and Prevention

Electropollution radiation is another term for Non-Ionizing Electro-Magnetic Radiation. We are talking about microwave radiation here. We are talking about the cell phone towers and panels that are populating schools, hospitals, and homes. We are talking about microwave ovens and televisions and Wi-Fi boxes and cell phones that are carried near the testicles and placed on the head and Bluetooth in the ear and computers on the lap and iPads marketed to infants and baby monitors and even refrigerators. All of these devices transmit and receive radiation that is harmful to the human being and all other life.

Many people now say... that is pseudoscience... that is quackery.... I'm an engineer and that is not the way it works... I'm a biologist and that is not the science I learned in school... I'm a medical doctor and I can name a thousand pharmaceuticals and their symptoms but don't know what a healthy diet consists of because we only spent one day on diet in Medical School.

There is a vast number of concerns that can draw our attention in the way of modern-day disease-causing agents, but none of them top the potential harm that microwave radiation poses. This is largely due to its chronic pervasive presence, its propagandized benignity, and the massive funding of its continued growth. The censorship and denial of whistleblowers, technical experts, and peer reviewed scientific studies is as skillfully done as it is done regarding vaccines, GMOs, and the war on terrorism.

Electro-Magnetic Radiation (EMR, EM, "light") is a self-sustaining energy with electric and magnetic field components, with EM waves propagating through a vacuum at the speed of light (2.998 x 108 m/s), "waves that are propagated by simultaneous periodic variations of electric and magnetic field intensity".[185] The EM spectrum consists of radio waves, microwaves, and infrared waves as non-ionizing radiation, and ultraviolet waves, x-rays, and gamma rays as ionizing radiation. "A frequency of one Hz means one wave is generated each second, one kHz means 1,000 waves are generated per second, and one GHz corresponds to one billion per second."[186] Microwave Radiation is a form of electro-magnetic radiation with a wavelength between one millimeter (.1 cm) and one meter (100 cm) and frequency between 300 MHz and 300 GHz. The human heart frequency is 2 Hz.

> *"Think of the emectromagnetic radiation spectrum as a guitar string stretched over eight frets. Play the lowest note and you get radio waves, play the highest one and you get gamma rays. On a guitar, different vibrational patterns in the string will give off distinct sounds in the form of notes — our perception of them varies, but they're all basically the same thing set on different intensity settings. Similarly, different oscillation patterns of magnetic and electrical fields will generate various kinds of EMR. We perceive them as completely different (some we can't directly sense at all,) but they're all basically the same phenomena on different intensities."* - Alexandru Micu[187]

Ionizing radiation has enough photonic energy to break chemical bonds like covalent bonds, while non-ionizing radiation does not. This means that ionizing radiation slices through genetic material like a hot knife through butter. Industry funded scientists and their biased studies indicate that microwaves are harmless based primarily on this fact. The truth takes more contemplation, consideration and study of the effects of chronic exposure over decades. Whether its 5G, 4G, cellular towers, microwave ovens, baby monitors, radar, Bluetooth, wifi, smart tv's and smart meters, airport scanners or a thousand other sources, the danger is relatively the same. "(Microwaves) need a direct line of sight to the receiver, as microwaves don't bend (diffract) around hills or mountains, they don't reflect back from the ionosphere, or follow the planet's curvature as surface waves. But they pack more of a punch than radio waves and can pierce through some of the things that radio can't — like thick clouds or dust — due to their higher frequency."[188]

> *"...electromagnetic radiation stands apart from the rest of EM phenomena in that they are 'far-field' effects. These waves aren't limited to interacting with close-by objects, unlike the electrostatic effect, for example. Once generated, the waves can also hurtle through space (they 'radiate,' where the term 'radiation' comes from) without any more input from the charges that generated them. So these waves will keep going until they run out of energy — either because they hit some particles they can interact with, or because they simply fizzle out."* – Alexandru Micu[189]

The human body like all biological life is a self-regulating, self-healing organism. A single use of a microwave emitting device like a cell phone, or short-term close proximity to a Wi-Fi router, while having an effect on the body, would not be nearly enough to cause serious illness. The same exposure to gamma or x-rays could cause not only illness but death. The difference between these types of radiation exposure can be expressed through a simple equation, with time, or rate of exposure, and potency of exposure equal to the rate of declining health. This means that although microwaves are far less damaging in the short term, the chronic exposure to a vast array of microwave emissions from cellular towers, Wi-Fi and Bluetooth, smart meters, etc. affect the body in a similarly destructive way. Rather than breaking covalent bonds, chronic microwave exposure increases colloidal osmotic pressure of the blood plasma causing blood cells to stick together in chains called rouleaux formations. The small capillaries that run through the deep tissues of the body are capable of allowing passage of only a single blood cell, and while cells are in rouleaux formations, the deep tissues are not receiving H_2O, oxygen, from the red blood cells and relieving CO_2, carbon dioxide, which then builds up and results in a toxic stew in the body. This process and the resultant stagnation in the body is a precursor to cancer and as the CDC has stated, "90% of all illness and disease". This is one of the effects of microwave radiation exposure and when it is present chronically, the body is far less oxygenated than it needs to be; it acidifies, calcifies, and behaves in the same way as it would under the effects of immunocompromising diseases of diverse types. Over time the body's defenses are worn down and it is incapable of warding off diseases that would otherwise have not had significant effect if any effect at all.

In the presence of these information carrying waves (man-made microwaves), which do not occur and never have occurred in nature, the cells in the body quickly respond by sending a message through microtubules to all the surrounding cells, informing them that they are under attack and telling them to protect themselves. The cells then proceed to close down active transport channels internally, hardening cellular membranes, making it impossible for nutrients to enter into the cell and waste product to exit the cell. The lack of nutrient intake by the cells makes them energy deficient, leading to the inability to communicate through microtubules, which require a significant amount of energy. Rapid intercellular communication is thus shut off, eliminating cellular communication, and making tissues and organs unable to operate efficiently. In the waste product built up within the cells, are free radicals, which migrate to the mitochondria, compromising the respiration of the cell and decreasing overall energy even further. Messenger RNA informs the DNA in the nucleus and the mitochondria in the cell of the hardened cell membrane, resulting in highly reactive unbounded mRNA and DNA in the cell, attracting the free radicals, which disrupt the process of information transfer from mRNA to DNA, resulting in micronuclei. Micronuclei are mRNA and DNA that function efficiently enough to form a membrane around themselves. At this point the free radicals have disrupted the mitochondria to the extent that the mitochondria inform the rest of the cell that it cannot properly function any longer and is going to die. This triggers apoptosis, which is cellular suicide, so as to make room for a new cell. The cell bursts open and releases waste and micronuclei into the interstitial fluid between cells. Normally, globulins would consume these pieces, eliminating them, but because the intercellular communication has been shut down, the micronuclei proliferate within the interstitial fluid, leading to tumors. Symptoms are different depending on the age, environment, and other factors in the life of the individual, resulting in autism, ADHD, Parkinson's, Alzheimer's, or any number of other conditions. The disruption of intercellular communication leads to a host of disease. If the cell undergoes mitosis after the production of the genetic material in response to the perceived attack and the stress response, the daughter cells will carry that damage, and all the following cells. This is the mechanism for autism and so many other diseases as well.[190]

Medical doctors are not educated in chronic disease. Within specialized medical education, there is sometimes study within the specific fields being taught about chronic diseases, but even then, the education is limited and reductionist rather than holistic. Very many people are willing to surrender the decision-making about their health to their doctors, just as they surrender to politicians to determine war, and bankers to determine financial worth. The problem with this is that doctors are not universally infallible, omnipotent, or even scientific. They are reflective of their educations, their experiences, and their moral, ethical, and spiritual attitude. Considering that doctors have to compete for position, adhere to hospital mandates, and are often doctors simply because of the social position and financial success that profession offers, it is not far outside the bounds of probability that your doctor has a series of higher guiding principles than optimizing your health. This goes for a very many other professions as well, where education is given through textbook and the lectures of others who themselves have been indoctrinated into a narrative or specific line of thinking about a topic.

In the last 40 years, there have been well over 6000 peer reviewed studies that show harm from EMR. More and more countries, especially in Europe, are increasing restrictions on the marketing, use in schools and public places, and distribution of devices that emit EMR. Switzerland and France in particular have restricted use of Wi-Fi and cell phones, especially with children, preferring to use the faster and more secure optic fiber LAN connection. "Cells in the body react to EMFs as potentially harmful, just like to other environmental toxins including heavy metals and toxic chemicals. The DNA in living cells recognizes electromagnetic fields at very low levels of exposure and produces a biochemical stress response." -Dr. Reba Goodman, PhD, Columbia University. It's quite interesting to me that the authorities at the World

Health Organization choose to surround themselves with LAN fiber optic connections while supporting the 5G revolution everywhere else.
So, imagine you are sitting, streaming videos for 15 or so minutes with your laptop on your lap. Sure, it's only 15 minutes. There can't possibly be harm in that... Well, it turns out that even just being near to the Wi-Fi connected laptop is harmful. Having it on your lap is more like microwaving your testicles in a microwave oven. By the way, your microwave oven isn't so great either. In actuality, you are denaturing your food, and altering the molecular makeup of the thing you are ingesting. In essence, when you have completed your microwaving, you are not eating food at all anymore, but something that looks like food. On the molecular and cellular level, you are eating a waste product. Back to the testicles. In the last 20 years, testicular cancer has increased by 50% -Safe Wireless Initiative. What else has happened in the last 20 years? Cell phones in pockets and laptops with Wi-Fi perhaps? Sperm count decreases and the motility of sperm also decreases as mutations in mitochondria are prevalent in men who wear cell phones on a belt, in a pocket, or anywhere near the groin.

"A new report reveals that sperm counts among men in Western countries, including men in North America, Australia, New Zealand and Europe, have dropped substantially over the years. According to study authors, in less than 40 years, collective sperm count among this group of men has declined more than 50%."
– Alexandra Sifferlin, TIME[191]

Power density of the microwave radiation allowed in the US, also called the SAR rating, is 10,000,000 $\mu W/m^2$. This is an extremely high specific absorption rate, highest in the world actually, on par with only one other nation, India. There is no regulating body for telecom industry, and they are the largest lobbying entity on the planet. Politicians are in the pocket of telecom just as much as big pharma and the military-industrial complex.
The push for 5G is spreading far and wide, despite the voices of opposition, the peer reviewed studies, the logic of the simple observer. 5G is often described as being in the millimeter waveband but is actually simply the most extreme end of the microwave band. 5G operates between 1mm and 10mm. 5G does not have the range of 4G because the power density is far higher, meaning the wavelengths are much closer, meaning penetration of objects like tissue and bone is far greater. The chronic exposure to greater power density of the same man-made information carrying waves is only going to speed up the diseases we are already seeing multiplying in our population. Of course, the diseases we are seeing are not solely the result of microwave radiation, but are rather the combination of exposure to toxic substances from chemicals sprayed on lawns to prevent weeds, GMO's that are composed of a small fraction of the nutrition available in the real, organic food, heavy metals, like barium, sprayed from planes to manipulate weather and mercury in flu vaccines, and a million other examples of the environmental disease causing agents that have been part of our lives for generations. We are only getting worse. The disease will only increase on this path we are walking, and no one has the ability to avoid exposure. Those who choose to generate these poisons and those who allow them to do so, are making it impossible to avoid exposure, even in the most remote parts of the globe. There is no escape except in changing the planetary course... and of course, that starts with me and you!
What else? In the corporation that is the United States of America there are around 320,000,000 people. National Cancer Institute statistical reports of 2015 say that the probability of dying from cancer in USA is 20.7% and probability of developing cancer is 39.7%. Around 2/3 of people who have cancer survive 5 years. There are no NCI stats for those who survive 10 years or more. So, around 124,000,000 people in USA will be diagnosed with cancer in their lifetime, and 38,000,000 of them will die within 5 years. These numbers are unprecedented. When did cancer become such a dominant factor in the lives of people? The past 30 years, while we've been increasing our non-ionizing radiation technology. And now, we are

marketing and designing them for infants. Cribs and playpens with tablets... This is torture and this is genocide.

If I have your attention, let me just say... research this on your own. Be unbiased and look at the research and who's funding it. Is it the telecommunications Industry, largest lobbying group in the world, or the privately funded study of notable scholars and scientists, conducted openly and peer reviewed? Follow the money. Who owns the agency drafting the articles you are reading? See the larger picture. If you don't want to do the research for yourself, just don't believe anything. Make experience your guide. Try leaving your technology for a week and see how you feel. Get a necklace of Raw Elite Shungite from Russia and wear it. More than anything else. Limit in any way use of wireless technology. Bring back LAN fiber optic connections, which are faster and more reliable anyway.

Obesity and Chronic Illness in the United States are beyond bad. These issues are so problematic to our wellbeing that we are seeing incredibly detrimental effects now and in projections of our future. We are not simply unhealthy as a nation; we are incredibly ignorant of our lack of health. Current statistical rates of obesity and chronic disease in the US are shocking and are more dangerous to our population than any war, virus, or anything else besides maybe total genocide. In the US, CDC statistics show that between 1999 and 2017, people with cancer (18+) has increased from 4.9% to 7.1%; (65+) has increased from 15.2% to 19.3%. Between 1999 and 2016, people with diabetes (20+) has increased from 10.8% to 13.9%. Between 1999 and 2016, obesity (20+) has increased from 30.5% to 38.9%; (12-19) has increased from 16% to 20.6%. Between 1988 and 2016, people overweight or obese (20+) has increased from 56% to 70.9%; Grade 3 Obesity (BMI ≥ 40) has increased from 2.9% to 7.7%. Between 2000 and 2017, Personal Healthcare Expenditures have increased from $1.2 Trillion to $3 Trillion; Per capita it increased from $4,119 to $9,106.

The National Cancer Institute statistics report that approximately 39.5% of men and women will be diagnosed with cancer at some point during their lifetimes (based on 2015–2017 data). The rate of new cases of cancer (cancer incidence) is 442.4 per 100,000 men and women per year (based on 2013–2017 cases). The cancer death rate (cancer mortality) is 158.3 per 100,000 men and women per year (based on 2013–2017 deaths). This means that about 36% of diagnosed people are going to perish from cancer. These numbers reflect that, of the 325 million people in the United States, 128 million will be diagnosed with cancer in their lifetime and of these, 46 million will perish from this disease. These numbers will obviously change over time but are projected to disfavor more survivability and less disease as has been the theme for many years now. The annual estimate for new cases of cancer in the United States in 2020 is about 1.8 million, with the rate of death being almost one in three.[192]

Is it not obvious that we have a serious communal problem here? Drastic measures need to be taken to improve upon the health of the population, and these measures do not involve pharmaceutical companies that are legally bound to provide profits for their shareholders first and foremost, and health to their clients last. What business today wants to lose money and clients? Certainly, it is quite easy to see that the Pharma companies would financially suffer if they were to actually increase the health of the population. They do not profit from healthy people, so why would they work to make people healthy.

Instead of putting our trust in companies that care not for us, we need social change on massive scale. The end to fast food and faster pill popping. The sedentary lifestyle must become a thing of the past and we must endeavor to produce a social norm of physical activity. Children must get off their phones and back to the fast-disappearing woods to scuffle and build forts. The lack of health we are seeing today, including the outrageous cancer numbers is directly correlated to the lack of activities that promote our wellbeing and the inclusion of activities that are extremely detrimental to our health. We must remember to work our bodies and avoid constant sitting and lounging and screen use. 175 years ago, and prior, farm work was the primary source of physical exertion for much of the population. Today, we can implement this again and bring back our food sovereignty and our physical health in one action.

Food

You are what you eat. Everybody has heard this, but how many people truly understand just how real this is? How many people realize how food goes from being an ear of corn, or a steak, or an apple to being a human upon consumption? The mechanism is quite long and exceedingly simple. Food is that which is consumable that provides the appropriate nutrition and material to allow for the body to replenish itself of the energy needed to do everything it needs to continue to function. So, we can say that something is not food which does not provide the appropriate material and nutrients to do the same.

The quick and easy breakdown of the way food goes from being something you eat, to something that is your body, goes like this. An apple falls off a tree. You pick it up and take a bite. You masticate that piece of apple while releasing saliva from your six salivary glands, turning starchy food matter into sugars in the first stage of digestive action. The apple is chewed until it is liquified and is swallowed unconsciously and soon enough the apple has disappeared from the mouth into the gullet, the esophagus, and further into the stomach. The stomach then processes that food by moving in a churning, rocking motion, and releasing bitter gastric juices that act as a solvent upon the nitrogenous portions of the food and glucose portions in the second stage of the digestive process. The food matter then moves into the small intestines as grayish, pasty chyme through the pyloric orifice on the bottom right side of the stomach, coming into immediate contact with bile produced by the liver and stored in the gall bladder. Bile aids the pancreatic juices in preparing fats for absorption and preventing decomposition and putrefaction, while neutralizing gastric juices. Little Hairs called villi absorb nutrients and pass them into the system through the small intestine walls. The chyme moves along the small intestine until it has been absorbed to fullest extent of the body's capability, at which point it leaves the small intestine and enters the colon, or large intestine, which absorbs water, converting the liquid into a stool. From the rectum the material not taken up by the body is then released as feces.

If any part of the digestive process does not function properly, it affects the function of all the others and the health of the person. One of the most detrimental things a person can do, and one that is done most regularly by huge portions of the population, is bolting food. This is the act of taking a bite and swallowing large chunks of the food matter, without properly masticating and insalivating the food. Food must be chewed and insalivated consciously and, done properly, will simply appear to disappear from the mouth as the partially liquified food matter is swallowed automatically at the correct moment. Hunger does not exist in the stomach and is not represented by a growling stomach. Only craving exists in the stomach, while hunger is represented by salivation. This is why one may be presented with various food products and be indifferent, but when hunger is present will salivate and be drawn to the items that are particularly satisfying. The evolutionary development of this situation has allowed for, especially in modern times, the disregard of salivation as food is readily accessible at any time, and thus is eaten at intervals disproportionate to true hunger, but in accordance with sensory cravings. This in large part, hand in hand with increasing processed sugar consumption and marketing, has led to the epidemic of obesity and health problems in the United States and globally.

It is exceedingly important to understand how food becomes the body, and how that food can influence the way the body operates on many distinct levels. By understanding this mechanism, we can also understand how the way in which food is produced must be viewed with extreme prejudice. We must be discriminative of what we eat and knowledgeable about where food comes from, who profits from producing it, and how it came to be part of a person's diet.

Large monocropped lands destroy the natural diversity of the land. We need to implement permaculture practices that allow for water retention, diversity of species, inclusion of animal life including grazing animals, and we need to implement these things on a massive scale through education and incentivization for all farmers and through the regulation of the large industrialized and monopolizing farming businesses.

This needs to happen immediately to prevent a large-scale deficit in food production that will force the US population to import their basic survival needs, which is the current trend.
The food industry, especially in the US, is overburdened with disease-causing materials that are called food, but which are actually considered by the body to be waste products or even deadly products. The vast range of ailments caused by the ingestion of these products includes all types of disease due to the fact that the body is built by the ingredients in the food we ingest. When the body does not have enough of what it needs, it becomes deficient and stressed. When there is too much of a harmful product for the body to combat there is also stress. This stress is often expressed in the blood pressure, which then affects all of the tissues and functions of the body. This is a very simplified perspective of the way food impacts our health and our lives. The basic principle here is to eat that which has the most beneficial qualities and avoid like the plague those things that offer little to no real benefit and are even detrimental to the body.
Monopolization and corporate influence and control over agriculture, food distribution, and direct sale outlets to the population makes it nearly impossible for local farmers, small business distributors, and local outlets to compete. This has a major influence on small to medium sized farmers, who are unable to sustain their farms when market prices are driven down below their profit margin.

"Most Americans have no idea that the chicken they eat is raised by a farm family that makes an average of $15,000 a year---that is, if none of their backbreaking labor is counted. Contrast this with the amount of profit made by KFC or a company like Tyson Foods. According to Mike Weaver, a contract grower who is the president of the Contract Poultry Growers Association of the Virginias, when a consumer buys 'a twelve-piece bucket of chicken at KFC or other chains, it costs around $26.99 [price depends on store location] or thereabouts. Of that $26.99, the integrator [poultry company] receives around $3 to $5 depending on the price of chicken when it was bought. KFC gets around $21, and the grower who spent at least six weeks raising that chicken gets 25 cents!'"
-Wenonah Hauter, Foodopoly[193]

Today, under one million farms produce the bulk of food produced in the United States, and farmers compose less than one percent of the population. In 1935, 54 percent of the population lived on 6.8 million farms, and just a hundred years before that, only a very small percentage of the population lived anywhere but farms or worked on farms. Between 1860 and early 1900, farmers in the country's labor pool dropped from 58% to 38%. In 1850 farmers owned 75% of US wealth, but by 1890 this dropped to 25%. Between 1950 and 1970, the farm population declined by more than half. Since the 1950's, each decade of farmers has faced lower crop prices, more borrowed capital, larger debt, higher land prices, and weaker safety nets.
One out of six farms were lost to bankruptcy, foreclosure, or delinquent-tax sales between 1930 and 1935. FDR feared a socialist revolution from the coalition of farmers, unemployed and labor unions, and thus created his New Deal programs. Industrialists feared a progressive egalitarian society, and they took measures to prevent this as in red-baiting, jailing dissenters, disinformation campaigns, and creating groups like the Committee for Economic Development or CED.

"(Nestle) sells bottled water as the healthy alternative to tap water (controlling) approximately 32 percent of bottled water sold in the United States...owns seven out of the ten leading brands of bottled water in the United States... bottled water is so poorly regulated in the United States that consumers have no way of knowing what contamination lurks within... In October 2008, the Environmental Working Group released a report that found mixtures of thirty-eight different pollutants, including bacteria, fertilizer, Tylenol, and industrial chemicals, in ten popular U.S. bottled water brands."

-Wenonah Hauter, Foodopoly[194]

By 1972, Earl Butz, Nixon's Secretary of Agriculture successfully removed 25 million acres from a New Deal set-aside program to boost grain production, leaving only 7.4 million acres in 1973. He told farmers to plant more and expand their operations as far as possible. The 1973 Farm Bill reduced parity for crops to 50% or less. By 1978, only 19% of farms were producing 78% of all crops. Between 1966 and 1977 farm debt increased by 400%. The 1977 American Agriculture Movement began in Springfield, Colorado. Farmers across the nation drove tractors to Pueblo and demanded the Secretary of Agriculture take action to preserve family farms. By January 1978, 50,000 farmers rallied in DC. And again, in January 1979 famers gathered in Tractors in the capital blocking streets.

Overproduction, dropping crop prices and farm debt increases continued through the 80's. Overseas grain demand never manifested as Earl Butz prophesied, and farmers lost homes and land to foreclosures. The land boom crashed, reducing the value of farm property. Cheap grain allowed for the expansion of factory farms, and food processors and grain traders had record profits from cheap commodities that received a taxpayer subsidy.

The North American Farm Alliance (NAFA) was formed in 1982 when over 50 farm, labor and community organizations gathered in Des Moines, Iowa organized by Merle Hansen. They gathered to demand parity prices. Clinton signed the North American Free Trade Agreement (NAFTA) in 1993, and it was passed in 1994. According to Economic Policy Institute, NAFTA has been responsible for 700,000 US job losses and two million Mexican farmers forced off their land due to incapability to compete with US corn. Clinton then fast-tracked US entry into the WTO in 1994. Countries in the WTO yield their authority to determine if agriculture programs, food safety rules, environmental regulations, and worker safety laws are illegal trade barriers. The WTO promotes commerce at the expense of all else and as final arbiter of trade disputes, it almost always votes in favor of corporate interests.

In 1995, the WTO (replaced "GATT" or Global Agreement on Tariffs and Trade) Treaty, including the Agreement on Agriculture, was created under the guise of removing trade barriers and increasing competitiveness, while what it actually did was allow the largest food companies and grain traders to source crops where they could be obtained at lowest cost. In 1996, the Freedom to Farm Bill was passed. This phased out all government intervention in commodity markets, eliminated programs that prevented overproduction, and dismantled policies that maintained fair prices, abandoning farmers to compete with corporate powerhouses manipulating the market.

CSA's must be supported and endorsed by local to federal government. Regulations and greater taxes on large agriculture and distributor corporations, while subsidies to small to medium size family and small business farms will reintroduce profitability to the dynamic farming the country needs to adequately supply the range of food in demand by the US population. At the moment we are on a path of destruction. Our farming industry needs to revert from monocropped monopolized, soil-killing industrial farming, to local, organic, water-retaining, cooperative farming. If this doesn't happen, we will see rapidly increasing desertification and reliance on foreign food imports. We are already close to national subservience.

With over 70% of the US population overweight, we must seriously begin to reform our nutrition standards. The immense and deadly amount of sugar that is added to our so-called food is outrageous and a direct cause of much of the diseases that exist. There are ways to regulate this. We must create and enforce limits to many ingredients added to our food by declaring the ingredients as harmful and illegal in specified amounts. We must abolish ingredients like artificial colors such as Yellow #5 and Bixin, Sodium Nitrate, Excitotoxins like Aspartame and MSG, BHA and BHT, rBGH and rBST, High Fructose Corn Syrup, Propylene Glycol Alginate (E405), Propyl Gallate, Azodicarbonamide, Polysorbate 60, Enriched Flour, Mercury, Sulfites, Potassium Bromate, Butane, Sodium Benzoate, Carrageenan, Olestra, Camauba Wax, Magnesium Sulphate, Chlorine Dioxide, Aluminum, Saccharin, Acesulfame Potassium, Bleached Starch, Arsenic, Partially Hydrogenated Oil, and many others. A large part of the reason we have these toxic substances in our food is due to the government subsidizing the industries and companies that create these harmful ingredients. We need to demand a change and enforce a change by refusing to subsidize any industry that creates and implements these toxins. We must force the corporations that are poisoning the population to change their behaviors. The easiest way to do this would be to impose such immense fines upon violations of health by using these toxins that it becomes financially untenable to continue to use them. Instead of taxing the population like a sugar tax, we need to tax the corporations who abuse their positions. We need to reduce these corporation's ability to create toxic products. Another solution would be to create a list of products like that above and mandate all products on this list require a skull and bones toxic and dangerous label on the food.

To benefit the Farming Industry, we need to enforce our nations antitrust laws, including the Sherman Antitrust Act, Clayton Antitrust Act and Packers and Stockyards Act. We need to stop mega mergers occurring throughout the food and agricultural sector, particularly in the seed sector where the "Big Six" seed and agrichemical firms are consolidating into the Big Three. We need to enact comprehensive pricing reform in the dairy industry and expose corporations' price manipulation on the Chicago Mercantile Exchange. We must institute supply management programs to stop the overproduction of milk. We need to reissue and finalize the USDA Farmer Fair Practice Rules to increase market transparency, establish fair contracts and protect the First Amendment rights of livestock and poultry growers. We need to reform federal checkoff programs that tax cattle ranchers, hog producers, dairy farmers, and other farmers on their goods in order to fund marketing campaigns that tend to benefit corporate agribusiness. We must reinstate Country of Origin Labeling (COOL) and other programs that increase transparency in the food system and allow eaters to support American farmers and ranchers. We need to preserve local control laws and defend the rights of local communities to stop the creation or expansion of factory farms that threaten their air, water, soil, and quality of life. And we need to advance food sovereignty and limit the role corporations can play in writing our trade deals.[195]

We need to promote cooperative ownership of many small farms, which will allow them to pool their abilities and profits. Non-Corporate mutual ownership in which decisions are made by consensus would accommodate for locally prescribed best practices. Cooperative ownership of grazing animals can make it possible for neighboring farms to remove fences and allow the grazers to organically and instinctively graze and thus fertilize where it is most needed.

If we allow trade organizations to dictate what we must import and export, we are no longer a sovereign state, let alone a sovereign people. The corporate governance machine is called plutocracy, and it exists globally, managed, and dictated to by the global central banking cartel. This is apparent to even the most limited amount of research. We must end the constant barrage of unlawful, unrighteous, and unjustified actions, laws, and systems that are upheld and enforced by our current self-appointed and self-interested plutocrats.

Definitive changes that can be made today include:

> *Eradicating the HPO. HPO or "Harvest Price Option", is the process of insuring farms not only traditional crop insurance, which protects farmers from catastrophic losses, but offers price boosts to those who can afford higher premiums to buy an HPO policy. Traditional crop insurance pays farmers when the price at harvest is less than projected prices at planting, but HPO policies guarantee that farmers will be paid either the projected price at planting time, or the market price at harvest, whichever is higher. HPO Increases payouts to large corporate farms paid by the Federal Government, and thus the pocket of the average person. When loss occurs, that is insurance also paid out by the taxpayer. This policy supports the desertification of our arable lands monopolization of farming industry by large profiteering corporations.

*WFRP (Whole-Farm Revenue Protection), needs to be the predominant insurance product in the agriculture industry, and a platform on which to build even better insurance policies. This Insurance Product offers revenue guarantee for all commodities on a single farm with up to $8.5 million in insured revenue, encouraging diversification and those producing crops, livestock, specialty crops, organic or those marketing to direct markets.
*Crop insurance has greatly increased farmland prices. Both Small Farm owners and Farmland Renters are hurt by this. Overall business costs increase and reduce profitability for the farmer. Farmland appraisals have increased by 8.5% per year between 2006 and 2015.
*Food Freedom can be implemented for local food producers to encourage local markets to invest in their own food sustainability. Although this would remove federal government oversight, one way to keep farms honest is to have a way for local governments to enforce protections for consumers like farms falsely representing products. Any person who claims a farm is falsely representing a product, the local government can investigate and penalize the farm.
*We need to incentivize or demand that large corporate farms parcel their lands. We must make a cap on farmland ownership by any corporation or conglomerate of corporations. We must make it impossible for large corporations to pressure small and midsize farm owners to sell their lands to them. We must encourage corporations rather to focus on minority percentage ownership and responsibility in many farms. This can still be profitable to corporations but will force them to serve the will of the small-midsize farmers. Large farms can be owned by individuals, but the lands must be 50% owned by the farm workers. In this way, individuals that wield large influence and power cannot bury the industry through selling out there farms for greed. 2011- 1,000+ acre farms accounted for 5.6% of all farms. 2.2% of all farms are 2,000+ acres.
*The agricultural definition of farms needs to change. Currently, the Small farm number is vastly incorrect, as any land that is of a certain size that can produce $1,000 in profit is considered a farm, even when no farming is being done at all. As commodity prices increase, as in 2005, the number of small farms increases, as smaller lands can earn greater revenues. We need to adjust these definitions that are extremely disproportionate in describing our farmlands. This also affects federal funding for agriculture, which is divvied up between states based partially on numbers of farms. This means we are inappropriately funding different states. We need to develop a way to accurately measure what lands are actually being used for farming and which are not, and the size of the farms.
*The seed market needs to be regulated to prevent large corporations from monopolizing. Between 1995 and 2014, soybean and corn seed cost spiked by 351% and 321% respectively, far greater than the market price farmers received for their products, creating tighter margins for farmers. GMO seed contamination needs to be made a severely punishable corporate offense. The contamination by GMO products often creates dramatic economic losses for farmers, including organic certification and premium losses. We need greater antitrust enforcement in the seed industry. We need increased funding to be provided to public plant and animal breeding, which will develop local and regional seeds and breeds. Farmers need access to a large and dynamic range of affordable seeds and the right to save seeds.
*GMO's
a. GMO agriculture has created superbugs and superweeds that cannot be combated with traditional farming practices. We need to completely ban glyphosate and criminalize its use. We also need to hold accountable the corporate executives and the scientists and all others implicit in the products distribution, that have profiteered on this destructive, disease creating doomsday device.
b. "Between 1996 and 2011, U.S. herbicide use grew by 527 million pounds, mostly from glyphosate. There are now at least 14 species of glyphosate-resistant weeds throughout the

country, and almost double that number worldwide. This very scenario was forewarned in a 2010 report from the National Academy of Sciences, which cautioned that the overuse of glyphosate would render it useless. There are similar reports of bollworm Resistance to the Bt toxin in GMO cotton. Herbicides, including glyphosate, can also increase plant diseases by altering plants' ability to absorb nutrients and reduce soil health by killing microbes. These chemical-dependent strategies, peddled by major chemical and biotech companies, will keep farmers dependent on increasingly toxic pesticides in a race that nature always wins.

c. We must illegalize the patenting of genetic codes and seeds. "Farmers who buy GMO seeds must pay licensing fees and sign contracts that dictate how they can grow the crop – and even allow seed companies to inspect their farms. GMO seeds are expensive, and farmers must buy them each year or else be liable for patent infringement. And while contamination can happen through no fault of their own, farmers have been sued for "seed piracy" when unauthorized GMO crops show up in their fields. Patents make independent research on GMOs difficult. Farmers must sign agreements that prohibit them from giving seeds to researchers or carrying out their own research. Meanwhile, researchers cannot conduct studies on GMOs without a license from the seed company, allowing companies to restrict the nature of research on their seeds."

On the 2018 Farm Bill:

What this Bill did Wrong:

1. Since 2013, American farmers and ranchers have had a 50% drop in net farm income. "Unconscionable: Boondoggle for the big guys: The 2018 Farm Bill widens loopholes for wealthy mega-farms to exploit commodity and crop insurance subsidies, allowing nieces, nephews, and cousins who may have never worked on the farm to receive taxpayer-funded subsidies. This will continue to drive consolidation in the farm sector, allowing the biggest farms to keep growing and gobble up smaller and midsized operations that are so critical to the wellbeing of rural communities." The 2018 Farm Bill actually worked against the interests of food security now and into the future by allowing more consolidation by corporations. We must illegalize this activity now.
2. The 2018 Farm Bill fails to provide additional mandatory funding for the USDA Farm to School Grant Program and does not provide for the regulatory flexibility that would allow school food authorities to procure local and regional food and farm products.
3. This bill reduces mandatory funding for the Community Food Projects grant program by $4 million and does not provide mandatory funding for the Food Safety Outreach Program.
4. Hand outs for factory farms: While this bill decreases livestock set-asides within EQIP that were being funneled to the factory farm industry, it does not remove these loopholes entirely and does not include any of the much-needed reforms that would limit taxpayer dollars being used to subsidize factory farms.
5. No cuts: The fact that there were no cuts in overall funding in the Conservation Title is a huge win, since the first House version of the bill slashed these programs and removed the CSP altogether. That said, this bill failed to restore $6 billion in cuts to the title made in the 2014 Farm Bill and set us up for a challenging future because...
6. Borrowing from the future: You may have to read the fine print to realize that this Farm Bill establishes cuts over the long-term for CSP past the year 2023, amounting to over $5 billion in advance cuts to the CSP and EQIP for the next farm bill.
7. Research shortfalls: This farm bill did not include important research priorities on climate change and provided no baseline funding for plant breeding research.
8. Set asides: This bill maintains, but fails to increase, allocated dollars set aside for socially disadvantaged and beginning farmers in major conservation programs (CSP and EQIP).

9. No money, more problems: The bill removes mandatory funding for the Rural Microentrepreneur Assistance Program, an important program for farmers and ranchers of all kinds. It also does not provide mandatory funding for Individual Development Accounts (IDAs), which are important for beginning farmers.

What this Bill did right:

1. LAMP (Local Agriculture Market Program) which contained the Value-Added Producer Grant (VAPG) program and Farmers Market and Local Food Promotion Program (FMLFPP).
2. It created the "Office of Urban Agriculture and Innovative Forms of Production", which focuses on creating urban and suburban funded programs for increasing and bettering urban agriculture.
3. It reauthorizes the Food Insecurity Nutrition Incentives Program and renamed it the Gus Schumacher Nutrition Incentive Program. The program will receive $250 million over 5 years and includes a produce prescription program.
4. The bill extends funding for the Supplemental Nutrition Assistance Program (SNAP, formerly called 'food stamps') without the rigid and bureaucratic work requirements initially placed in the House version of the bill. Those provisions would have deepened hunger and poverty for vulnerable Americans, including children and families. The bill also instructs USDA to allow farmers markets to operate an individual EBT device for accepting SNAP benefits at more than one location.
5. Organic: There are important improvements for certified organic growers in this farm bill, such as increases in the Organic Initiative payment cap within the Environmental Quality Incentives Program (EQIP), a new organic allocation within the Conservation Stewardship Program (CSP) – the largest federal conservation program— and $5 million in mandatory funding for the collection of organic production data. The bill also increases funding for the Organic Agriculture Research and Extension Initiative (OREI) to $50 million a year in permanent funding by 2023, with a total of $395 million in funding over ten years. Finally, the bill included $24 million in mandatory funding for National Organic Certification Cost Share from 2019-2023, although this was far less than advocates had requested.
6. Soil Health: The bill increases payments for cover crops, crop rotations and advanced grazing management within the CSP, and authorizes payment for comprehensive conservation planning. The bill also includes new research priorities around soil health.
7. Seeds for the future: This bill authorizes a National Genetics Resources Program, adopts a National Strategic Germplasm and Cultivar Collection Assessment and Utilization Plan, and makes other important policy around public, locally- and regionally-adapted seed varieties that can help farmers navigate a changing climate.
8. FOTO: The final farm bill combines the Beginning Farmer and Rancher Development Program (BFRDP) and Outreach and Assistance for Socially Disadvantaged and Veteran Farmers and Ranchers Program (also known as "Section 2501") into the new Farming Opportunities Training and Outreach (FOTO) program. The improved program has permanent funding of $50 million annually, shared equally between the two programs.
9. Fairer Safety Net: Throughout the Farm Bill, there are important improvements to programs in the farm safety net that make sure farmers of color are not left behind. For example, the bill mandates that there is a report every 3 years on Underserved Producers with recommendations for improving participation in insurance programs. And it includes equitable relief for producers who received incorrect servicing by the USDA when applying for direct loans.
10. Fairness for Heirs Property. Heirs' property refers to land that passed down to multiple descendants without the presence of a will or estate plan. It leaves the heirs without clear title to the land, which prevents farmers who are part of an heirs' property to receive FSA loans. This bill ensures that these farmers, often African-American farmers and farmers of color operating on land with

undivided interests, can finally access USDA programs that enable them to protect the soil and water, and continue to operate viable farms that feed their communities.

11. Historically Black Colleges and Universities: The bill includes $40 million in mandatory funding for scholarships for the 1890 land-grant institutions – agricultural colleges created primarily to serve African American students who could not access to higher education due to segregation.
12. Legalizes Industrial Hemp by removing it from the controlled substances list and allowing tribes, states, and territories to establish regulatory structures within their boundaries that allow farmers and ranchers to produce a high-value cash crop while retaining federal farm program benefits that were previously not allowed.

* This info ("Definitive Changes that can be implemented today" and "On the 2018 Farm Bill") was provided by www.farmaid.org. Thank you www.farmaid.org for the work you are doing to preserve the land, the genetics, the Rights, and the Truth.[196]

That being said, there are some aspects of this concise report on the 2018 Farm Bill that must be pointed out. Any time you ask for the government to make any changes, you are empowering that entity and authorizing their authority. When we beg for our rights from the government, we are justifying their decision to act positively or negatively toward our request. The only time the government will *ever* act in favor of the people's wellbeing is when the people demand it with iron in their hand and on their hip. We must not bequeath our power to the morals, ethics, and designs of those who crave power, and thus ambitiously chase it to political position. We must rather make unshakable demands backed by our iron and our iron will. Death before dishonor is not just a silly phrase, but a way of life. We *must* remember our spine and our ability to defend our position. Our land is being destroyed and stolen by the slowly encroaching slavery system that wraps and integrates itself into every aspect of society when the people do not stay strong in their highest values. We cannot entrust our future and our children's lives and safety to the plutocrats. It is time to occupy and defend our lands and refuse to accept the toxic, demonic, and forceful influence of the agents of destruction, least of all entities like the United States Federal Government and Bayer/Monsanto. We must remember our roots and rights to caretake this earth and to produce and flourish.

6 Crops dominate: Corn, Wheat, Soybeans, Cotton, Rice, and Peanuts. These 6 crops receive more than 90% of the farm bills subsidies. Large farms boosted their incomes by $13 Billion because of Redundancies within the Bill… Bill's Complexity is its major downfall.

-newrepublic.com[197]

What we must consider, despite the effects of the Farm Bill and other tools and programs created and utilized by government, is the fact that government has no real authority other than what the people allow it. When we beg for scraps from a plutocracy, and await their graciousness, we end up waiting forever while ever more rights and freedoms are scraped away. The best way to approach our farming problems in this country is to stop waiting for the tyrants to approve of the obvious, but rather take what is ours as is our inherent claim by our every existence. The land is not owned by the government, but rather it is caretaken by the people who live upon it. We need to practice radical permaculture and aggressive ecological restoration. We need to begin farming the land in a way that defies the oppression of tyrants. The way we approach this topic is only second in importance perhaps to the way we approach our right to bear arms. We need the ability to defend what is ours, and we need to respect the land, each other, and our responsibility to care for both of those things. When the people rise up, peaceful and ready and armed, stop paying taxes, begin permaculture farming on their land, and conduct markets to mutual benefit, the people will have denied the oppressors of three of their most powerful tools. Those tools are the disarming of the people, the dependency on government for sustenance, and the ability to steal money from the people to fund their underhanded and evil agendas. Let's bring back the local family farm, guarded by the community against oppression, and fueled by the economic benefits deserved.

Economic and social impact of family farms — and their loss

"Accompanied by an ever-increasing disparity between dwindling income and soaring expenses, fewer and fewer members of the current generation are willing to commit their lives — alongside work days that tally to 12 or more hours each day — to a family farm. As a result, the American Farmland Trust estimates an acre of U.S. farmland goes into development every two minutes. Farmers are often retiring without a younger family member willing to assume farm management responsibilities, thus removing multi-generation ranches and farms from production. Statistics show that less than a third of farms have a designated successor in the family."

"When corporations produce our seeds, process our meat and milk, and serve as our grocery retailers, they dominate our food system and have enormous power to control markets and pricing, They also influence food and agricultural regulations. Sure, some say that large agribusiness is efficient and offers the capacity to produce huge quantities of cheap food. However, many hidden costs of large agribusiness result in unintended consequences, including declining rural economies, loss of farmer livelihoods, environmental damage, and weakened overall public health. What are the costs when we lose small family farms?

Purity of product is diminished: You can nearly always count on the milk from local farmers to be, well, local. Giant agribusinesses merge contain the milk of hundreds of cows. Purity is also lost when there are more steps between you and your food's source, as those steps increase the more chances for contamination. Food grown in distant locations has the potential for food safety issues at harvesting, washing, shipping, and distribution.

Local control wanes: When you see your local farmers at the market, it's because they're involved in most of the farm's production processes. When giant agribusinesses move into local areas, they also take part in the distribution, processing, storage, and retail of farm products, removing local control. When family farms stay under local control, they tend to have autonomy, protect the natural resources more, and contribute to multiple social classes. The World Health Organization worries, in particular, about what they label "an unfair transfer of valuable land and water resources from the poor to the wealthy."

Subsidies hurt: Small family farms don't produce cheaply in large quantities, store over long periods, or ship easily. So, when subsidies keep prices artificially low on the world market due to surpluses and chronic overproduction, local, smaller family farms can't complete. As a result, their land is often swallowed by larger conglomerate farms. All of these subsidies ensure that farm incomes are much higher than the incomes of most Americans. Farm programs are welfare for the well-to-do, and they induce overproduction, inflate land prices, and harm the environment.

Loss of family stability: A significant indicator of a healthy society is the stability of the family unit. As small family farms vanish, so, too, do infrastructures that lead to healthy communities. An agricultural lifestyle presents wonderful conditions for children due to the variety of stimuli, allowing them to channel energy into animal care, egg collection, vegetable growing, and harvesting. For adults, farm life provides time to think, a healthy diet, and a built-in workout routine.

Jobs move away from rural areas: Small family farms provide jobs for a community. When they disappear, many jobs evaporate with them. Research has shown that family farms provide multiple economic benefits for their communities, as they employ more people per acre than large, industrialized farms and are more likely to purchase inputs locally, keeping more money in their local economies. Studies have shown that small, locally owned farms have a multiplier effect: for every dollar the farm spends, a percentage remains in the local economy, contributing to the economic health of the community.

Economic instability: Areas having more small farms have lower poverty and unemployment rates, higher average household incomes, and greater socioeconomic stability. When small family farms disappear, main streets become less active, fewer retail businesses can survive, and less money is spent in the community. While it seems counterintuitive, large agribusinesses are associated with lower incomes, more poverty. and economic inequality.

Environmental benefits: When family farms are passed down, generation to generation, location-specific knowledge is passed along, too. Small family farms have fewer acres to manage, so farmers are in tune with subtleties of their area's specific soil types, climate, and pest populations. The land of a small family farm allows the production and rotation of diverse crops in systems integrated with other ecosystems on the farm. As a result, these farms are often quite biodiverse. By contrast, large farms tend to restrict production to one or two crops, reducing biodiversity. The industrial methods used by large farms also adversely affect soil and water quality and increase global warming emissions.

Creating systems that support small family farms

Many consumers today are interested in healthy eating and want to know how their food is produced and by whom. Consumers are often willing to pay more for local food from family farms. This has led to the rapid growth of farmers markets, community supported agriculture (CSA) programs, local grocery stores, and "farm-to-fork" programs at restaurants, schools, and other institutions.

In today's society, more people have come to realize the importance of small family farm agriculture could regain great prominence. Increasing sustainable food production results from concerned consumers making informed, responsible choices. By purchasing sustainable foods from your local farmer or grocery store, you support the farmers who are raising food responsibly and actively encourage the growth of a more sustainable food system. Wherever possible, instead of giving your money to industrial agriculture, give it to a sustainable farmer.

There's also another way to stabilize small family farms. Large-scale food buyers such as supermarkets and hospitals should purchase their fruits and vegetables from local farmers. In doing so, they would create a market niche and provide communities a much-needed self-sustaining economic boost. Yes, there are many challenges to be overcome when larger businesses depend on local farms, including opportunity costs for transitioning farmers, the difficulties of adopting new methods and different equipment, and lack of access to capital or crop insurance. State and federal governments can help by offering financial incentives to help beginning and transitioning farmers grow the foods institutional and intermediate buyers want. They can provide research and technical assistance to help farmers adopt midsize, diversified farming systems. They can invest in infrastructure and coordination to get healthy food from farm to market."

-Carolyn Fortuna[198]

TECHNOLOGY

The supposed origins of man that are taught today involve our gradual advancement from barbaric nomadic tribes to farming communities, to cities, and thus to major civilizations and finally to planetary society. This narrative has an incredible number of holes in it from ancient, advanced cultures predating the "barbaric nomads" and exhibiting extraordinary technological proficiency beyond our current capabilities to evidence of humans existing millions of years ago in the same physical proportions of today's human. These evidentiary differences to the narrative are dismissed without due consideration only because they do not fit the popular and profitable narrative. Instead of investigating these major differences in the history of human evolution and thus technical capacity, I will only speak generally on our capabilities through time and give more specific reasoning behind our recent history, our present and our potential future.

We have, in the past millennia advanced our technological understanding and capacity to include written language, agriculture, animal husbandry, metalworking, plumbing, sailing, weaving, printing and various other things. In the past two centuries, we have witnessed an exponential increase in technological capacity and creation. This includes electricity, A/C, central heating, motor vehicles, municipal water systems, medical treatments and hygienic practices, refrigerators, airplanes, rockets, radio, satellites, microchips, computers, internet, lasers, microwave technology, and much more.

The most important of these advancements as far as increasing the quality of life of the individual and the collective, were discovered between 1850 and 1950. After 1950, the speed and importance of the advancements began to decline, but yet we can still see their importance none the less. The world we live in today is ignorant of the world of 1850 and before. For the average person today, to be thrust back into the world of 1850 would be terrifying and miserable. The amount of work needed to produce the level of comfort people have today would be enormous and in some cases impossible.
We must give the appreciation and recognition due to these advancements that make our lives easier today. Similarly, we must give these advancements the critique that they also deserve. Mostly, our technology has moved apace not to the demands of the population or even to our capacity, but to the manipulations and agendas of the industrialists who have mandated policies that continue today, such as planned obsolescence and Taylorism and classism and planned scarcity.

> *"We live in a world where our social system is old, our language is old, the way we acquire goods and services is outdated, our cities are detrimental to our health, chaotic and a tremendous waste of resource, and most of all our politics and values no longer serve us... If technology does not liberate all people for the pursuit of higher aspirations in human achievement, then all its technical potential will be meaningless."*
> - Jacque Fresco

And thus, we must take an altogether different view of our previous achievements and look to what could be today and tomorrow, vs what could be through the systems of oppression that have been perpetuated up until today.

Planned Obsolescence:

The practice of making or designing something... in such a way that it will only be usable for a short time so that people will have to buy another one.[199]

...describes a strategy of deliberately ensuring that the current version of a given product will become out of date or useless within a known time period. This proactive move guarantees that consumers will seek replacements in the future, thus bolstering demand. Obsolescence can be achieved through introducing a superior replacement model, or by intentionally designing a product to cease proper function within a specific window. In either case, consumers will theoretically favor next generational products over the old ones.[200]

Some technologies have been created that do not serve to benefit humanity, but rather directly influence populations to their detriment. Much of this technology has been implemented publicly, and some has not. But with a little bit of investigation, we can discover the existing technologies and their applications, as well as infer their most likely uses. When government is allowed to surveille the population even after it has been made public that it is happening in the most invasive ways, it is not hard to see that the population itself is the culprit in allowing these technologies to continue to be used to their disadvantage.

United States Patent 6,506,148 Loos January 14, 2003
Nervous system manipulation by electromagnetic fields from monitors
"It is therefore possible to manipulate the nervous system of a subject by pulsing images displayed on a nearby computer monitor or TV set. For the latter, the image pulsing may be imbedded in the program material, or it may be over-laid by modulating a video stream."

http://patft.uspto.gov/netacgi/nph-Parser?Sect1=PTO1&Sect2=HITOFF&d=PALL&p=1&u=%2Fnetahtml%2FPTO%2Fsrchnum.htm&r=1&f=G&l=50&s1=6506148.PN.&OS=PN%2F6506148&RS=PN%2F6506148

USP # 3,951,134 (April 20, 1976), Apparatus & Method for Remotely Monitoring & Altering Brain Waves
Abstract: Apparatus for and method of sensing brain waves at a position remote from a subject whereby electromagnetic signals of different frequencies are simultaneously transmitted to the brain of the subject in which the signals interfere with one another to yield a waveform which is modulated by the subject's brain waves. The interference waveform ... is re-transmitted by the brain to a receiver where it is demodulated and amplified. The demodulated waveform also can be used to produce a compensating signal which is transmitted back to the brain to effect a desired change in electrical activity therein.
Note: This patent is dated 1976. How much progress has been made since then?

USP # 5,159,703 (Oct. 27, 1992), Silent Subliminal Presentation System
Abstract: A silent communications system in which nonaural carriers, in the very low or very high audio frequency range or in the adjacent ultrasonic frequency spectrum, are amplitude or frequency modulated with the desired intelligence and propagated acoustically or vibrationally, for inducement into the brain.

USP # 5,017,143 (May 21, 1991), Method and Apparatus for Producing Subliminal Images
Abstract: A method and apparatus to produce more effective visual subliminal communications. Graphic and/or text images, presented for durations of less than a video frame, at organized rhythmic intervals, the rhythmic intervals in-tended to affect user receptivity, moods or behavior.

USP # 6,052,336 (April 18, 2000), Apparatus and Method of Broadcasting Audible Sound Using Ultrasonic Sound as a Carrier
Abstract: An ultrasonic sound source broadcasts an ultrasonic signal which is amplitude and/or frequency modulated with an information input signal originating from an information input source. The modulated signal, which may be amplified, is then broadcast via a projector unit, whereupon an individual or group of individuals located in the broadcast region detect the audible sound.

USP # 5,539,705 (July 23, 1996), Ultrasonic Speech Translator and Communications System
Abstract: A wireless communication system, undetectable by radio-frequency methods, for converting audio signals, including human voice, to electronic signals in the ultrasonic frequency range, transmitting the ultrasonic signal by way of acoustic pressure waves across a carrier medium, including gases, liquids and solids, and reconverting the ultrasonic acoustic pressure waves back to the original audio signal. This invention was made with government support under Contract DE-AC05-840R21400, awarded by the US Department of Energy to Martin Marietta Energy Systems, Inc.

USP # 7,629,918 (Dec. 8, 2009), Multifunctional radio frequency directed energy system
Abstract: An RFDE system includes an RFDE transmitter and at least one RFDE antenna. The RFDE transmitter and antenna direct high power electro-magnetic energy towards a target sufficient to cause high energy damage or disruption of the target. The RFDE system further includes a targeting system for locating the target. The targeting system includes a radar transmitter and at least one radar antenna for transmitting and receiving electromagnetic energy to locate the target.
Note: Under the background section of this patent, it is stated, "Radio frequency directed energy (RFDE) systems are known in the art for directing high power RF, microwave and/or millimeter wave electromagnetic energy to destroy or disrupt a target. Although RFDE systems typically serve as military weapons, RFDE systems need not be limited to weapon systems. For example, RFDE ... may be used for non-military purposes such as destroying or disrupting foreign objects, contaminants, undesirable atmospheric conditions, or other types of targets."

USP # 6,488,617 (Dec. 3, 2002), Method and Device for Producing a Desired Brain State
Abstract: A method and device for the production of a desired brain state in an individual contain means for monitoring and analyzing the brain state while a set of one or more magnets produce fields that alter this state. A computational system alters various parameters of the magnetic fields in order to close the gap between the actual and desired brain state. This feedback process operates continuously until the gap is minimized and/or removed.

USP # 6,239,705 (May 29, 2001), Intra-Oral Electronic Tracking Device
Abstract: An improved stealthy, non-surgical, biocompatible electronic tracking device is provided in which a housing is placed intraorally. The housing contains microcircuitry. The microcircuitry comprises a receiver, a passive mode to active mode activator, a signal decoder for determining positional fix, a transmitter, an antenna, and a power supply. Upon receiving a coded activating signal, the positional fix signal decoder is energized, determining a positional fix. The transmitter subsequently transmits through the antenna a homing signal to be received by a remote locator.

USP # 6,091,994 (July 18, 2000), Pulsative Manipulation of Nervous Systems
Abstract: Method and apparatus for manipulating the nervous system by im-parting subliminal pulsative cooling to the subject's skin at a frequency that is suitable for the excitation of a sensory resonance. At present, two major sensory resonances are known, with frequencies near 1/2 Hz and 2.4 Hz. The 1/2 Hz sensory resonance causes relaxation, sleepiness, ptosis of the eyelids, a tonic smile, a "knot" in the stomach, or sexual excitement, depending on the precise frequency used. The 2.4 Hz resonance causes the slowing of certain cortical activities.

USP # 5,507,291 (April 16, 1996), Method and an Associated Apparatus for Re-motely Determining Information as to Person's Emotional State
Abstract: In a method for remotely determining information relating to a per-son's emotional state, a waveform energy having a predetermined frequency and a predetermined intensity is generated and wirelessly transmitted towards a remotely located subject. Waveform energy emitted from the subject is detect-ed and automatically analyzed to derive information relating to the individual's emotional state.

USP # 4,877,027 (Oct. 31, 1989), Hearing System
Abstract: Sound is induced in the head of a person by radiating the head with microwaves in the range of 100 megahertz to 10,000 megahertz that are modulated with a particular waveform. The waveform consists of frequency modulated bursts. Each burst is made up of 10 to 20 uniformly spaced pulses grouped tightly together. The burst width is between 500 nanoseconds and 100 micro-seconds. The bursts are frequency modulated by the audio input to create the sensation of hearing in the person whose head is irradiated.

SILENT SOUND SPREAD SPECTRUM
The mind-altering mechanism is based on a subliminal carrier technology: the Silent Sound Spread Spectrum (SSSS), sometimes called "S-quad" or "Squad". It was developed by Dr Oliver Lowery of Norcross, Georgia, and is described in US Patent #5,159,703, "Silent Subliminal Presentation System", dated October 27, 1992. The abstract for the patent reads:
"A silent communications system in which nonaural carriers, in the very low or very high audio-frequency range or in the adjacent ultrasonic frequency spectrum are amplitude- or frequency-modulated with the desired intelligence and propagated acoustically or vibrationally, for inducement into the brain, typically through the use of loudspeakers, earphones, or piezoelectric transducers. The modulated carriers may be transmitted directly in real time or may be conveniently recorded and stored on mechanical, magnetic, or optical media for delayed or repeated transmission to the listener."
According to literature by Silent Sounds, Inc., it is now possible, using super-computers, to analyze human emotional EEG patterns and replicate them, then store these "emotion signature clusters" on another computer and, at will, "silently induce and change the emotional state in a human being".
Silent Sounds, Inc. states that it is interested only in positive emotions, but the military is not so limited. That this is a US Department of Defense project is obvious.
Edward Tilton, President of Silent Sounds, Inc., says this about S-quad in a letter dated December 13, 1996:
"All schematics, however, have been classified by the US Government and we are not allowed to reveal the exact details... ... we make tapes and CDs for the German Government, even the former Soviet Union countries! All with the per-mission of the US State Department, of course... The system was used through-out Operation Desert Storm (Iraq) quite successfully."
The graphic illustration, "Induced Alpha to Theta Biofeedback Cluster Movement", which accompanies the literature, is labelled #AB 116-394-95 UNCLAS-SIFIED" and is an output from "the world's most versatile and most sensitive electroencephalograph (EEG) machine". It has a gain capability of 200,000, as compared to other EEG machines in use which have gain capability of approximately 50,000. It is software-driven by the "fastest of computers" using a noise-nulling technology similar to that used by nuclear submarines for detecting small objects underwater at extreme range.

The purpose of all this high technology is to plot and display a moving cluster of periodic brainwave signals. The illustration shows an EEG display from a single individual, taken of left and right hemispheres simultaneously. The readout from the two sides of the brain appear to be quite different, but in fact are the same (discounting normal left right brain variations).

HAARP (High Frequency Active Auroral Research Program)
Dr. Bernard Eastlund is the scientist whose name is most associated with the creation and development of the HAARP project. His revealing website provides reliable information on his involvement with the project. A 1987 patent issued to Dr. Eastlund is titled "Method and apparatus for altering a region in the earth's atmosphere, ionosphere, and/or magnetosphere." https://patents.justia.com/patent/4686605. In this patent, which sets the stage for HAARP, Dr. Eastlund makes a number of fascinating statements which clearly contradict the claim that it is only being used for research and not for military purposes or such purposes as weather control. Here are a few of key statements taken verbatim from the patent:

1. "[The] temperature of the ionosphere has been raised by hundreds of degrees in these experiments."
2. "A means and method is provided to cause interference with or even total disruption of communications over a very large portion of the earth. This invention could be employed to disrupt not only land based communications, both civilian and military, but also airborne communications and sea communications. This would have significant military implications."
3. "It is possible ... to take advantage of one or more such beams to carry out a communications network even though the rest of the world's communications are disrupted."
4. "[It] can be used to an advantage for positive communication and eavesdropping purposes."
5. "Exceedingly large amounts of power can be very efficiently produced and trans-mitted."
6. "This invention has a phenomenal variety of ... potential future developments. Large regions of the atmosphere could be lifted to an unexpectedly high altitude so that missiles encounter unexpected and unplanned drag forces with resultant destruction or deflection. Weather modification is possible by, for example, altering upper atmosphere wind patterns or altering solar absorption patterns by constructing one or more plumes of atmospheric particles which will act as a lens or focusing device. Ozone, nitrogen, etc. concentrations in the atmosphere could be artificially increased. Electromagnetic pulse defenses are also possible. The earth's magnetic field could be decreased or disrupted at appropriate altitudes to modify or eliminate the magnetic field."

Let's explore the world of tomorrow. Not the tomorrow of 50 years in the future. Not even 20 years into the future. Not 10. But the world of the day after you read these words. It's a world explicitly or implicitly economically controlled by global central banks who dictate to tyrannical governments that manage their respective territories and subjects. Constitutional Rights exist in name only. Freedom of speech exists only when your speech is reflecting the will and interests of the authorities. The Right to not be searched or have yourself or your property seized is gone, and soldiers and other government agents can infiltrate your home at any time and occupy it. The commons no longer are the commons but the exclusive property of the private government. Any acts of opposition in word or action are seen as sedition and is a capital offense. Firearm ownership is banned completely. Anyone who possesses a firearm can be imprisoned indefinitely or executed. Hunting is allowed only through the government leasing weapons out to authorized hunters, who must return the firearms. The internet exists, but only government approved channels are accessible. Any attempt to speak in opposition to the government results in total censorship and imprisonment. Vaccinations are mandatory and more are demanded year by year. Refusal results in fines, property seizure, imprisonment and forced vaccination. RFID implanted chips are mandated for all citizens, from the time of birth, as a preventative measure against criminality and pandemics.

In this world of oppression, it would seem like people would rise up and refuse. They would protest and riot and rebel. Well, the tomorrow that is nearly today includes not just the ambitions of bankers and plutocrats to dominate, but it also includes the technological discoveries that make their domination a real threat, feasible and incipient. These technologies include those patents mentioned above and all the threats they bring. They also include even greater dangers.

Today, it is possible for a 17-year-old boy in a military installation in the side of a nondescript mountainside to control a warfighting drone, equipped with any number of incredibly powerful weapons, with his thoughts alone. This same kid in the bunker, or maybe a spymaster at the CIA, can control people or animals, from anywhere in the world, who have been implanted with the appropriate sensory influencing technology in their brain, or simply wearing the appropriate cap. Unknowingly, a person can be passed secret information through bacteria, from someone who bumps into them at the airport. This information is encoded into the genetic material in the bacteria, and cannot be tracked by anyone, except the person who knows where to look. Augmented humans, with the abilities like heartbeat detection behind walls, clear night vision, or the ability to see RF can be used to the will of their masters, whether that be that same spymaster or the local police, so they may ensure you are abiding by the curfews and other dictates of government.[201]

DREADD's (Designer Receptors Exclusively Activated by Designer Drugs), can be remotely controlled when the brain is exposed to the right signal. Meaning a "designer" cell can be injected into a body, that responds to specific signals, and then performs a specific task. This means, a person can be injected with a substance, say a vaccine, and the vaccine contains hundreds of thousands of these designer cells in dormancy, until the moment that some outside signal activates them to do some task. That task could be any number of horrendous things. And what better way to ensure that all these cells will be activated then to place 5G in every city, every rural town, and even direct it toward Earth from space, as is being constructed now.

"Once you know that the technology is there to edit, splice, and program a cell, and the technology currently exists to administer it to somebody, and have it go park anywhere you program it to go park, proliferate and do its function. You can have things activated in other people's brains."

"Between CRISPR, the storage capacity, and programming cells, the new way to hide information is gonna be in DNA."

"If you wash an area of the brain, called the hippocampus; its an area of the brain that's crucial for forming short memories, spatial memories, and then facilitating the transfer from a short term memory to something that's more permanent and stable over time... you could train the mice to run the maze, document the number of trials and errors, and then flood their hippocampus, or expose it to this (PKMzeta and ZIP) and the memory would be completely gone. Meaning that when the rats or the mice had to learn it over again, it was the same number of learning trials. Now, there's no trace of the memory left... if you wanted to poke your own hippocampus, you'd have to stick your finger through your eye... sounds impossible to get to... not if you program a cell to go there. So if you decide you wanted to program something that would selectively release PKMzeta after your meeting with someone, they probably would have no memory of it."

- Dr. Charles Morgan, West Point Talk, MWI BH 454, Apr. 2018[202]

Now our 17-year-old drone operator can have all recollection of his murders erased from his mind by that clever spymaster. All it would require is the spymaster demand the soldier to be vaccinated, which he could not refuse, and in that vaccination a dormant cell would travel to the hippocampus as it was programed to do and await instruction. After each successful assassination, or perhaps after every briefing of who was going to be attacked, the little cell or cells, would simply expose the soldier's hippocampus to PKMzeta, and his memory would be washed of any knowledge of his activity just moments before.

Or another scenario might be, that several people are injected with these cells, and are forced to place bombs at schools and hospitals else their families be tortured and murdered... so they do. And after they have done these jobs, the government agents erase their memories, and the happy individuals go back to their families none the wiser. The bombs are detonated, its called a domestic terrorist attack, and the cameras caught the images of those people who planted the bombs. It just so happens that they were all part of the NRA or were disaffected schoolkids or maybe they were Muslims or Venezuelans. Whatever they were, the false flag attack will never be traced to the criminals, because they can now wipe memories. Isn't that fantastic!

What happens when 100 million people get vaccinated for a fake pandemic, and thus are injected with various cells that do various things, like erase memories, alter emotions and thoughts, allow for their bodies to be controlled from afar, or simply create unstoppable illnesses, that eventually kill them all? Perhaps it influences them to start a civil war that leads to more consolidation of global power by the central banking world governance. Any number of scenarios could exist here, but the fundamental problem here is the fact that whatever is done at this point, it is probably too late to stop these things from happening. The best we can do would be to begin fighting it immediately. But that is surely not going to happen in a docile, fearful, comfortable society such as in the United States.

Technology is not something to despise or avoid. I do not wish for anyone to be left with the impression that technology is the error. To be absolutely clear, it is the user, the motive for use, and the use of technology that reveals its virtue or malevolence. This is the same for the use of a fork, a gun, an airplane, EMF, rockets, and genetic modification. All are tools, technology that has the potential to do a large number of things. We must ask ourselves, sincerely, whether the technology of today is being used to the benefit of life on our planet. The honest answer for any sensible person is no, it is not.

While people of every class, race, sex, and location are beset by destructive behaviors enhanced by technology, there are the technologies that have an inherent quality that would serve to benefit life, and some that when used for the benefit of life are amazing and wonderful enrichments of human capability. The printing press, the airplane, the radio, the internet, fusion-based power plants, 3D printers, bionic limbs, supercomputers, lasers, solar glass, graphene, plant-based plastics, and so much more. These things provide for the creation of utopic life for all beings on the planet. It is interesting that almost nothing has come from their discovery. That may seem a drastic statement, but when one considers the possibility that airplanes provoke, the current status of flight becomes an object of scorn for the human capacity. While humanity as a whole has drastically increased its level of possible wellbeing in the last few centuries, the technology that would liberate us in a way that would bring about an evolutionary jump into utopia remains unused for that purpose. But that does not mean we need to suffer the faults of yesterday. We instead can learn from the past, utilize the tools available to us today, to build a better future for our children tomorrow.

We must always remember that the highest technology of all is our mind. We are the authors of our individual and communal experience on planet earth. Our physical bodies are linked in infinite intimacy to the environment and the entirety of existence. The roots refer to our origin. This origin lies not in separation, but in common. We are more in common than our egos will often allow us to recognize. Humanity breathes out what the trees breathe in and vice versa. The technology we are born with and into will never be surpassed by anything humanity will ever do. No amount of tinkering will alter natures original infinite design. But we can destroy ourselves and the environment and all around us. The question we must all ask is whether we want to be alive, breathing deep the clean air that fills our lungs with life and drinking water that nourishes our bodies, or do we want to destroy the natural for the sanitized and controlled, the living death, the technocratic dystopia, the treeless, waterless, lifeless desert that only humanity can produce?

TRANSPORTATION

Transportation in the United States has developed largely in the last 60 years into what it is today. Before the 1950's, the U.S. was composed mostly of unpaved roads. An advanced road was considered a gravel road and only the most major roads were paved. The Federal-Aid Highway Act, signed by D.D. Eisenhower, created the National Interstate System with $25 Billion, resulting in 41,000 miles of highway. Today there is around 46,000 miles of interstate highway, 90 percent being paid for by the Federal Government and 10 percent paid for by the States. By the late 1960's, rail travel virtually disappeared, and the U.S. became auto dependent. This was facilitated in large by the streetcar company buyouts and corruption by General Motors, Firestone Tire, and Standard Oil, amongst others that stood to directly profit from replacing rails with private motor vehicles. Streetcars had been dismantled before the end of 10 years after the FAHA was passed. While almost every industrial country in the world is modernizing its public transportation to match modern technological capability, and many have been doing so for several decades, the United States remains locked in auto-dependence and an outdated underused railroad system.

Before 1850, walking cities were predominant as transportation was slow and meant employers and employees, wealthy and poor, lived within a few miles of each other around a central working hub. Between 1850 and 1950, intercity transport evolved from walking and horse riding to horse omnibuses, to horse-drawn street cars, to cable cars, to electrified streetcars, to rapid transit elevated and subway structures and motor vehicles. In 1833, omnibuses were introduced to New York City, which was a horse-drawn carriage. By 1850, many cities had adopted this, but the omnibus was inefficient and caused major rutting on the mostly dirt roads in cities. Rides were exceedingly expensive, up to 12 cents per ride when most working men made only a dollar a day. After 1850, commuter railroads gave rich and upper middle class an escape from the city, creating suburbs and changing cities from circular to star shaped following the rails that radiated away from the city. An interesting note here is that the evolution of cities will be bringing the chaos of the jutting suburbs and the dense-pack urban center back into the circular shape. I will discuss this in the last part of this book more.

Horse-drawn railways took over inner city travel in the 1850's, which reduced friction, allowed less animals to pull more passengers, and reduced fares to 5 cents while doubling speed of travel to 6 mph. Road destruction was greatly minimized, though still 7000 horse carcasses were needed removed from the tracks annually in Chicago alone, and between their dead bodies and the thousands of tons of manure and urine they left on the roads, cities were ripe with potential transmission of disease.

Cable cars moved by steam boilers powering the pulling of cables through grooves under the street, came to replace the horse-drawn carriages and railways, beginning in the 1870's. By 1906, cable cars were no longer in use anywhere. Trolly cars took over inner city transport from the 1880's to 1930. The continual increase in ease of travel and relative low cost contributed to city congestion, leading to the creation of skyscrapers and centralized malls. Elevated tracks began being implemented in the 1870's and in Boston in 1897, the first underground system opened.

Nominal fixed fares imposed on transport companies bankrupted most of them. Price controls imposed by government helped influence a shift from public transport to automobiles. This government support of the automobile industry was the golden ticket for industrialists like Henry Ford, who began producing the Ford Model T in 1908, 22 years after Karl Benz developed the first horseless carriage in Germany. While Mercedes vehicles cost over $12,000, and the average annual income was $1000, the Model T was sold for less than $1000. It was a 22HP, 1200 lb. vehicle able to traverse muddy terrain making it a success amongst rural farmers, who were then able to travel to larger cities easier to make cheaper purchases than at the country stores, Trading Posts, and other rural and thus non-bargaining and expensive stores, like banks, general stores, local schoolhouses, which resulted in their closures.

When the U.S. Post Office introduced Rural Free Delivery in 1899, and Rural Parcel Delivery in 1913, the government was given the rural farming communities support and encouragement to build roads to allow rural mail delivery. The Federal Road Aid Act of 1916 began Federal support of road construction. Before this, there was about two million miles of road in the U.S. mostly composed simply of dirt tracks. The universal route numbering system seen today was introduced in 1926. The 1940's highway system resembles very closely the Interstate system of today.

Automobiles were bought primarily on consumer credit and by 1926, 75% of auto purchases were financed "on time". By 1923, a new Model T cost 11% of average total family income. Government policy was favorable to the automobile and encouraged development to suit its needs, like highways, while forcing urban transit and interurban electric railways to fend for themselves as private businesses. Early roads were built on bonds, whose interest was paid by local property taxes, so the public was incentivized toward the automobile regardless of preference or efficiency. As suburbs developed, gone went the street vender and the neighborhood store.

Today, high speed rails are in use across Europe and Asia. By adopting these same models, we can do the exact same or even better by building upon their proven technologies. Offering trains that have faster transit times will reduce the amount of traffic and thus pollution especially in congested growth corridors in major metros in the nation. Cost of riding trains could be built on the cost of travel in cars with credits for reducing pollution and congestion. The rail system would divert potentially as much as 90% of air traffic on routes 3-4 hours long. This would be devastating to air travel business but would be fiscally beneficial to the entire population in cost, efficiency, and effectiveness. The cost of building High Speed Railways in the US is $20-$200 million per mile. This is mostly due to the dynamic landscape that covers much of the country, and the vast amount of regulation from government. Despite this, several privately funded projects are underway in various parts of the country, including a rail system connecting Portland with Seattle and Vancouver, one connecting Houston and Dallas, and one connecting Miami to Orlando. These need to be examples of the will of the people, and the government needs to act to create these public systems for the wellbeing and advancement of the nation into the modern world. In a 2015 TechnoMetrica Survey, 63% of Americans said they would use a high-speed rail system if it was available, while 71% of 18–44-year-olds would use it if available. Some perks to the creation of a high-speed rail system are that toll roads, many which are foreign owned or simply filling the coffers of corrupt government, would receive far less funding. With states running out of space for roadway travel, rails would minimize the need to continue endlessly paving the earth. The rail system would drastically reduce emissions that would otherwise only be escalating with increasing population density. Amtrak is currently the only rail transport system utilized in the US, though it is far inferior to rail systems in comparative nations. Amtrak is a for-profit company whose main shareholder is the federal government. The proven benefits are so obvious that to not build a dedicated rail system similar to that of China for instance, whose trains travel over 200mph, is the epitome of irresponsibility and stupidity.

On a level that all individuals must interact with, we must enact policies to rapidly phase out pollutants created by our travel industry amongst other industries. Even more successful than policy would be economic incentives for people to phase out of harmful emissions. We must abolish speed limits on Interstate Highways, excluding areas where the there is a real danger due to high-speed travel, such as on mountain roads that have tight curves. Opening "No Limit" roads, we can enhance travel times in various locations around the country. Vehicles are made to move faster and safer than 30 years ago, but speed limits need updating as well. This will also eliminate the practice of handing out tickets to travelers based on arbitrary and extortionary laws on speed of travel. This would not eliminate hazardous driving tickets (so long as police exist), as these can be due to a very many factors and can have serious harmful effects. The federal government must mandate enforcement agencies of all kinds to respect the right to travel of the population. The right to travel is guaranteed to all with no identification necessary whatsoever. The privilege of a State Driver's License is for commercial purposes only and can only apply to those who are driving commercially. Even this practice needs to be eliminated, but to the extent that people have a

constitutional and human right to travel, we must eliminate the practice of police harassment and deviancy.
Municipalities must offer or allow free zero emissions seasonal appropriate vehicles, like enclosed electric assisted bicycles for their populations to utilize. This is a phasing out process of petroleum vehicles in dense urban centers, and a phasing in for zero emissions vehicles. These vehicles already exist and are readily available in various forms. The phasing process can take as much as 10 years and will make it illegal to drive a petroleum burning vehicle in city limits at the end of 10 years. This offers plenty of time for people to trade in their petroleum vehicles for the appropriate vehicles. Large cities must ban the sale of petroleum burning vehicles in densely populated areas and encourage and incentivize dealerships with the appropriate alternatives to open. It is not that petroleum itself is harmful, but that it is the way in which we use it that causes harm, and due to the vast array of harmful effects of the use of petroleum we must change the materials we use.
The autonomy of a car is something that Americans love. The ability to hop in and be in control of your life and go where you please. This freedom is an example of the American way. The problem is that the entire transportation industry is built on the consumerist economy, American gluttony, and the fact that alternatives are not encouraged to exist. The psyche of the nation, and much of the world, is so tied to the use of automobiles, that it would seem impossible to very many people to forego their use. The alternatives to cars are numerous. Walking, as obese America needs, bicycling, and electric assist bicycling and other small devices can be used by everyone, especially urban areas to travel rapidly from place to place. Bullet trains can be built across the nation, carrying people and goods in a constant flow.
Let's take a step back for second though, and ask ourselves... *Why the fuck would anyone want to live in a city, let alone a megacity, surrounded by nothing but concrete, struggling humans, cockroaches and rats, and endless lines of cars in front of you while you are trying to get to the market to pick up some groceries that had to be brought into the city from 50-100 miles away because the city can't grow its own food and has to rely on the ever-diminishing land around it?* I could go on, but my point is made. Why is it that 70% of the globally population will soon be living in cities? Why is it that these cities continue to grow horizontally, consuming lands that are necessary for sustaining life, and converting them into condominiums? What is calling all the lost souls into the planet's tumors? I'll leave it to you to answer those questions. Instead, I'll just remind you that in this case, whatever the answers are, the juice is absolutely ***NOT*** worth the squeeze. Where destruction hits first is where it has primed its victims. The supply chain alone to keep food and medicine on the shelves in cities is so fragile that even the slightest hiccup could cause massive harm.
Okay, so we got a lot of roads, real nice ones too. It took a very short period of time to build these roads we roll around on today. I predict it'll take a vastly shorter timeframe to build the infrastructure of tomorrow. Subterranean bullet trains that pass through every city over 100,000 population in the US, never causing harm to the ecosystem on the surface or around them. Hydrogen powered helicopter taxis in urban environments. Hovercraft travelling safely above roadways. Autonomous electro-magnetic inner-city trains that detach and attach in sections to deliver and pick up passengers and cargo, never requiring the rest of the train cars to stop or even slow down. Jacque Fresco's model of the city is a prime example of engineering at its most logical and efficient. Why are we not progressing forward into the actualization of these dreams? BECAUSE YOUR GOVERNMENT AND THE CORPORATIONS AND BANKS THAT RUN IT DO NOT CARE FOR YOUR WELLBEING! The private companies and individuals that are attempting to bring about life changing advancements in technology are hampered by these entities and are not likely to change things fast enough or bring about life altering tech at all. Is that why Elon Musk is building rockets? Because the planet is lost to the bankers, and now he is looking to leave this place with whoever will come? Or are his rockets for the bankers, who need a place to go when they have sucked all the life out of the planet?

Perhaps the greatest gift the average people have is their feet. Like Bob Marley said, "My feet is my only carriage and so I've got to push on through." When nothing else works, use your feet. We are only 170 years older a world from a time when people primarily walked within cities, even for miles. The people of today are so comfortable in their air-conditioned cars and houses, that when the air conditioning fails, they suffer immensely, while the person who has never used air conditioning has no problem. The fat salesman's car fails, and they have to walk some miles for help, and they suffer immensely, while the agile biker simply takes a pleasant walk. The Coca-Cola drinking, Newport smoking, anti-depressant taking, 30 year old boy lives at his parents' house because having to do any amount of work is an assault upon him, while the 8 year old Indian boy in Calcutta wakes up at 3 to travel across the city by foot to his fruit stand, which he uncovers and moves a mile through the city to his dedicated spot, works selling fruit for subsistence wages until evening, when he hauls back the fruit stand, covers it up, and runs back to his one room home packed with 20 family members. Who do you think will survive when the lights go off?

Yes, it is important to advance our transportation technologies, but it is even more important to recognize the illness produced by personal life choices, and to alter those to fit a healthier and more productive lifestyle. How far can you walk in an hour? What if you walk to work instead of drive? Bike to the weekly fruit market. Take the new bullet train to the next city over, and if there is no bullet train, start demanding one.

Travelling in a city and traveling rurally cannot be more unlike to each other in their needs. In cities, auto travel makes little sense but to get stuck multiple times throughout the day. In rural areas, the sensible way to travel is by car, often even 4-wheel drive truck. The rules that logically apply in cities do not in rural areas and vice versa. Cities have taxis, trains, subways, distances short enough to walk and bike, and other conveniences. Rural areas do not have these same expediencies. Rather, the use of a car or truck is often a necessity for survival. This is the reason that the Model-T was successful. Because rural farmers could utilize the car to travel more efficiently to and from distant cities. While the argument could be for the use of horses, it is impractical today, as endless crossing roads make it dangerous in many ways to travel by horse long distances. So, the car continues to be useful and necessary for rural people. But these cars do not have to be petroleum fueled. They could be powered through combinations of alternative energy production, though I will not support outright the modern electric cars being produced. In fact, I have a great appreciation for petroleum and all that it has given to humanity's development.

ENERGY

Our ability to convert primary energy into electrical energy has rapidly evolved and increased in diversity over the last few hundred years. The first commercial application of an energy source in the United States was coal in 1748 near Richmond, Virginia. Wind was used in the 1850's in the American West while wood was used in 1860 as the standard for energy. Oil came into use in 1859 near Titusville, Pennsylvania. Electricity began to be used in 1880 in San Francisco, California, and hydropower in the same year in Grand Rapids, Michigan; Ethanol began being used in 1826. Geothermal energy was first used commercially in 1904 in Italy. Natural Gas began in 1816 in Baltimore, Maryland. Nuclear energy was first used in 1955 in Arco, Idaho, and Photovoltaic energy in the same year. Solar thermal energy began in 1973 in Delaware.

In 1839, Robert Anderson of Scotland built the first electric car. Between the 1940s and 1960s, the United States saw the rapid growth of natural gas markets. Today, the U.S. interstate pipeline network, laid end-to-end, would stretch almost 12 times around the earth. In 1990, the capacity to generate electricity from biomass (not including municipal solid waste) reached 6 gigawatts. Of 190 biomass-fired, electricity-generating facilities, 184 were non-utility generators, mostly wood and paper. In 2008, Idaho's first commercial geothermal power plant began operating. In 2019, U.S. wind energy production exceeded

100,000 megawatts. Wind turbine fields have become common sights in many places throughout the country.

"Global energy consumption is increasing and is expected to rise by 41% over the period to 2035 – compared to a 52% rise over the last twenty years and 30% rise over the last decade. Ninety five per cent of the growth in demand is expected to come from the emerging economies, while energy use in the advanced economies of North America, Europe and Asia as a group is expected to grow only very slowly – and begin to decline in the later years of the forecast period."[203]

- Dr. James G. Speight, Handbook of Gasification Technology; Science, Process, and Applications[204]

We need to encourage ever increasing investments in renewable energy sources. This encouragement follows hand in hand with divestments of non-renewables and dangerous energy sources like hydraulically fractured gas and oil. Prioritizing the importance of research and development in renewable resources will bring ever increasing benefits from ever evolving systems and technologies. We must utilize military research and development to provide options in new energy models to the public. This is a project that will benefit the military as much as the public. Increasingly stringent policies regarding the building, operating, and transporting of any non-renewable forms of energy will reduce their capacity to hold or gain new funding. We need to ban petroleum pipelines entirely the same as fracking wells. Both pipelines and wells break, leak and damage the environment almost assuredly in every pipeline and well.

"...the blind rush to frack Oklahoma dry of its fossil fuels has ushered in waves of earthquakes so frequent and severe... The state now suffers through, on average, at least 2 earthquakes per day, some of which have measured at magnitudes of 4.7 and 4.8. Oklahoma endured 907 earthquakes in 2015, a 50 percent increase from 2014...the profit-driven stampede to frack the fuel out of the ground continues at full throttle."

– Ralph Nadar, Breaking Through Power[205]

There has been no truly safe way to rid nuclear waste. Nuclear facilities need to be upgraded. Safety and security can be secured by providing grants publicly to anyone who can produce cost efficient methods to utilize nuclear energy and rid nuclear waste in a safe and useful manner. Concurrently as we divest and abolish non-renewable energy, we must match and exceed the loss in energy with renewable energy production. New job training must be made available for retraining non-renewable industry workers into renewable energy workers.

A huge toll on our energy production is the act of keeping our lights on at night. If we eliminate the practice of illuminating every storefront and parking lot at night amongst other sources of night lighting, we will greatly reduce our drain on the available energy which would lower costs and provide more for purposes that can greatly benefit humanity. Besides its obvious financial and social benefits, turning our lights off at night would provide a huge portion of our population a perspective they rarely encounter... the night sky. In places of extreme night illumination, such as in major cities, the light pollution is so great as to block out all but the brightest stars. This is hugely detrimental to the human psyche and health. Our bodies and minds require respite from bright light to access the recuperative and regenerative effects of sleep. When we ignore this need, we choose to proliferate a disease more detrimental than any virus or cancer. We must remove the light screen that has been placed over our night sky, and return to the natural patterns of physiological, psychological, and biological wellbeing. When we do this, we will see great benefit to all aspects of our lives. Excessive lighting at night increases greenhouse emissions, increases our energy dependence, and negatively influences our psyche. In the US, around 15 million tons of CO_2 are emitted each year to power outdoor residential lighting. This would require planting 600 million trees annually to offset. This night lighting costs more than $3 billion USD annually. Around 35% of light is wasted in this way. Shielded outdoor light fixtures will help to reduce light emitted into the sky. Turning off all lighting in offices, homes, storefronts, and other completely unnecessary locations will reduce the harm and waste.

In 2018, US primary energy consumption was about 101.3 quadrillion Btu. 88.5% of Total Btu's were distributed between Non-renewables: Petroleum (36%), Natural Gas (31%), Coal (13%), and Nuclear Electric Power (8%).

11.5% of Total Btu's were distributed between Renewables (following percentages out of Renewables Total only): Hydroelectric (23%), Wood (20%), Biofuels (20%), Biomass Waste (4%), Wind (22%), Solar (8%), Geothermal (2%).

U.S. energy consumption by source and sector, 2018

(Quadrillion Btu)

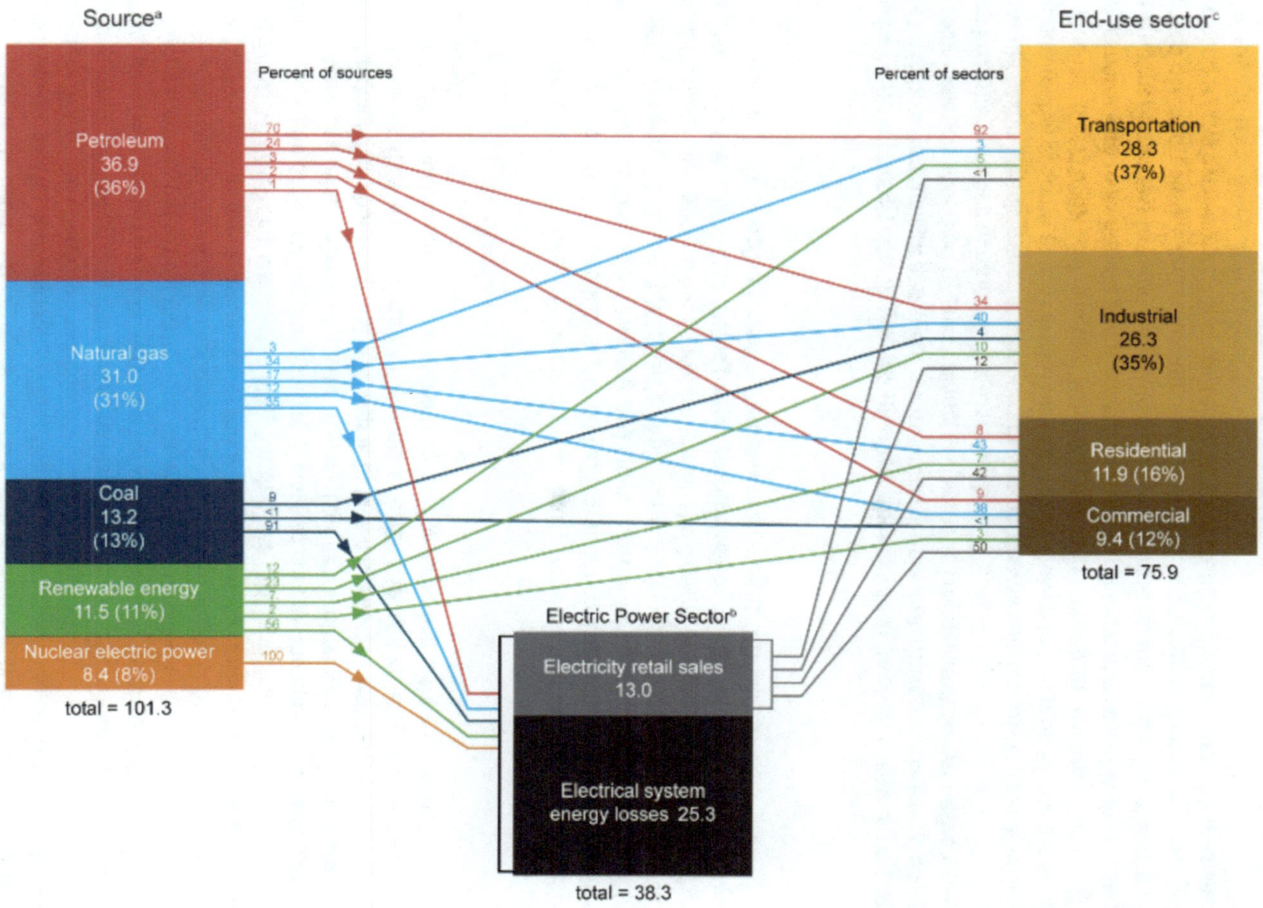

GASIFICATION

Coal:
"In many countries these data are much higher; for example Poland relies on coal for approximately 94% of the electricity production; South Africa relies on coal for approximately 92% of the electricity production; China relies on coal for approximately 77% of the electricity production; and Australia relies on coal for approximately 76% of the electricity production."
"Total recoverable reserves of coal around the world are estimated at 891,531 million tons – the United States has sufficient coal reserves to last (at current rates of consumption) in excess of 250 years.[206] Even though coal deposits are distributed widely throughout the world, deposits in three countries account for approximately 57% of the world recoverable coal reserves, viz., United States (27%), Russian Federation (18%), and China (13%) and another six countries account for 30% of the total reserves and they are Australia (9%), India (7%), Ukraine (4%), Kazakhstan (4%), South Africa (3%), and Japan (3%)."
"...gasification thus offers one of the cleanest and versatile ways to convert the energy contained in coal into electricity, hydrogen, and other sources of power. Turning coal into synthesis gas isn't a new concept, in fact the basic technology dates back to pre-World War II. In fact, a gasification unit can process virtually all the residua and wastes that are produced in refineries leading to enhanced yields of high-value products (and hence their competitiveness in the market) by deeper upgrading of their crude oil."
-Dr. James G. Speight[207]

Oil Shale:
"The United States has vast known oil shale resources that could translate into as much as 2.2 trillion barrels of known oil-in-place. Oil shale deposits in the United States are concentrated mainly in the Green River Formation in the states of Colorado, Wyoming and Utah, account for nearly three-quarters of this potential (Lee, 1990; Scouten, 1990; Lee, 1991; Bartis et al., 2005; Andrews, 2006; Speight, 2008; 2012). Because of the abundance and geographic concentration of the known resource, oil shale has been recognized as a potentially valuable United States energy resource since as early as 1859, the same year Colonel Drake completed his first oil well in Titusville, Pennsylvania (Speight, 2014a)."
-Dr. James G. Speight[208]

Biomass:
"Biomass is produced by a photosynthetic process (photosynthesis) which involves chemical reactions occurring on the Earth between sunlight and green plants within the plants in the form of chemical energy. In the process, solar energy is absorbed by green plants and some microorganisms to synthesize organic compounds from low energy carbon dioxide (CO2) and water (H2O)."
"The general formula of the organic material produced during photosynthesis process is (CH2O) which is mainly carbohydrate material. Some of the simple carbohydrates involved in this process are the simple carbohydrates glucose (C6H12O6) and sucrose (C12H22O11) and constitute biomass, which is a renewable energy source due to its natural and repeated occurrence in the environment in the presence of sunlight. The amount of biomass that can be grown certainly depends on the availability of sunlight to drive the conversion of carbon dioxide and water into carbohydrates. In addition to limitations of sunlight, there is a limit placed by the availability of appropriate land, temperature, climate and nutrients namely nitrogen, phosphorus and trace minerals in the soil."
"Biomass resources are many and varied, including (i) forest and mill residues, (ii) agricultural crops and waste, (iii) wood and wood waste, (iv) animal waste\s, (v) livestock operation residues, (vi) aquatic plants, (vii) fast-growing trees and plants, (viii) municipal waste, and (ix) and industrial waste."
-Dr. James G. Speight[209]

Solid Waste:
"Energy generation utilizing biomass and municipal solid wastes (MSW) are also promising in regions where landfill space is very limited."
"Waste may be municipal solid waste (MSW) which had minimal presorting, or refuse-derived fuel (RDF) with significant pretreatment, usually mechanical screening and shredding. Other more specific waste sources (excluding hazardous waste) and possibly including crude oil coke may provide niche opportunities for co-utilization (Brigwater, 2003; Arena, 2012; Basu, 2013; Speight, 2013, 2014b). The traditional waste-to-energy plant, based on mass-burn combustion on an inclined grate, has a low public acceptability despite the very low emissions achieved over the last decade with modern flue gas clean-up equipment. This has led to difficulty in obtaining planning permissions to construct needed new waste to energy plants. After much debate, various governments have allowed options for advanced waste conversion technologies (gasification, pyrolysis and anaerobic digestion), but will only give credit to the proportion of electricity generated from non-fossil waste."
"Biomass technologies present attractive options for mitigating many of the environmental challenges of manure wastes. The most common biomass technologies for animal manures are combustion, anaerobic digestion, and composting. Moisture content of the manure and the amount of contaminants, such as bedding, determine which technology is most appropriate."
"Urban wastes include municipal solid waste that is generated by household and commercial activities and liquid waste or sewage. Most municipal solid waste is currently disposed of in landfill sites. However, the disposal of this waste is a growing problem worldwide. Much of the waste could be used for energy production though incineration and processes. Japan currently incinerates more than 80% of the available municipal solid waste. It is also possible to use the methane produced in landfill sites for energy production."
-Dr. James G. Speight[210]

Gasification:
"Gasification is a process that converts organic (carbonaceous) feedstocks into carbon monoxide, carbon dioxide and hydrogen by reacting the feedstock at high temperatures (>700°C, 1290°F), without combustion, with a controlled amount of oxygen and/or steam (Luque and Speight, 2015). The resulting gas mixture (synthesis gas, syngas) is itself a fuel. The power derived from carbonaceous feedstocks and gasification followed by the combustion of the product gas(es) is considered to be a source of renewable energy if derived gaseous products are generated from a source (e.g., biomass) other than a fossil fuel."
"The advantage of gasification is the use of synthesis gas (syngas) is potentially more efficient as compared to direct combustion of the original fuel because it can be (i) combusted at higher temperatures, (ii) used in fuel cells, (iii) used to produce methanol and hydrogen, and (iv) converted via the Fischer-Tropsch process into a range of synthesis liquid fuels suitable for use gasoline engines or diesel engines. The gasification process can also utilize carbonaceous feedstocks which would otherwise have been disposed of (e.g., biodegradable waste)."
"Use of waste materials as co-gasification feedstocks may attract significant disposal credits. Cleaner biomass materials are renewable fuels and may attract premium prices for the electricity generated. Availability of sufficient fuel locally for an economic plant size is often a major issue, as is the reliability of the fuel supply. Use of more-predictably available coal alongside these fuels overcomes some of these difficulties and risks. Coal could be regarded as the flywheel which keeps the plant running when the fuels producing the better revenue streams are not available in sufficient quantities."
"... gasification to produce synthesis gas can proceed from any carbonaceous material, including biomass. Inorganic components of the feedstock, such as metals and minerals, are trapped in an inert and environmentally safe form as char, which may have use as a fertilizer. Biomass gasification is therefore one

of the most technically and economically convincing energy possibilities for a potentially carbon neutral economy."

"Gasification is a technology which (along with other processes) ... makes possible for the refineries to attain a zero residue target, contrary to all conversion technologies (such as thermal cracking, catalytic cracking, cooking, deasphalting, and hydroprocessing) which can reduce the volume of the resid. In addition, the flexibility of gasification permits to handle any kind of refinery residue, including crude oil coke, tank bottoms and refinery sludges and make available a range of value added products, electricity, steam, hydrogen and various chemicals based on synthesis gas chemistry (such as ammonia, methanol, ammonia, acetic acid, and formaldehyde."

"Thus, gasification is an appealing process for the utilization of relatively inexpensive feedstocks that might otherwise be declared as waste and sent to a landfill (where the production of methane – a so-called greenhouse gas – will be produced) or combusted which may not (depending upon the feedstock) be energy efficient. Overall, use of a gasification technology (Furimsky, 1999; Higman, and Van der Burgt, 2008; Wolff and Vliegenthart,
2011; Khosravi and Khadse, 2013; Speight, 2013a, 2014b; Luque and Speight, 2015) with the necessary gas cleanup options can have a smaller environmental footprint and lesser effect on the environment than landfill operations or combustion of the waste. In fact, there are strong indications that gasification is a technically viable option for the waste conversion, including residual waste from separate collection of municipal solid waste. The process can meet existing emission limits and can have a significant effect on the reduction of landfill disposal using known gasification technologies (Arena, 2012; Speight, 2014b; Luque and Speight, 2015) or thermal plasma (Fabry et al., 2013)."

-Dr. James G. Speight[211]

Let's discuss how power plants work and how electricity becomes available in one's home through the grid. Firstly, there are several different fuels, such as those listed above. Coal, petroleum, natural gas, uranium, biomass, flowing water, wind, and solar radiation are all primary energies. These are converted in power plants (power stations) into electrical energy that is supplied to the grid. One large power plant can produce 2 gigawatts (2,000,000,000 watts) of electricity, supplying a couple hundred thousand homes, and equivalent to about 1000 modern wind turbines working constantly. One kg of coal or liter of oil contains close to 30MJ of energy.

Simple cycle (thermal) Power plants (utilizing steam turbines) release this energy as heat by burning the fuel in a furnace. This heat is run through pipes filled with cold water, which boils and turns to steam. The steam flows into a turbine at extremely high pressure and temperature turning the turbine and leaves at as low pressure and temperature as possible through a condenser, to be recycled after cooling. An axle links the spinning turbine to a generator, which uses the kinetic energy of the turbine to produce electricity, which is sent to a step-up transformer by cable. Pylons carry cables out from the power plant to their destination hubs, where a step-down transformer converts the electricity to a lower voltage safe for domestic use. Cables carry this electricity into homes on the grid, where outlets are available for connecting appliances.

Power Plants using gas turbines burn a steady stream of gas to drive the somewhat different turbine design. Combined designs utilize gas turbines in a first stage and steam turbines in a second stage, called a combined cycle. The combined heat and power (CHP or cogeneration) design passes waste gases through a heat exchanger to heat water. This design can be used in small-scale power production, in units the size of car engines. Nuclear power plants are similar to the simple cycle, but smash atoms rather than burn fuel. Hydroelectric power plants funnel water into a water turbine, which turns an axle connected to a generator, producing electricity. Pumped storage power plants shift water back and forth between two lakes of different altitude, turning the turbine at each passing.

Every power plant has an immediate step-up transformer that increases the voltage from around 14,000 volts to anywhere from 44,000-750,000 volts to minimize power loss along the cables. Low voltage results in greater power loss. Pylons carry the cables to substations with step-down transformers to supply residential areas. Control centers monitor the network of stations to determine the amount of energy consumption and peg that with a constant matched supply.

CHP (combined heat and power) plants have the potential to replace large centralized, wasteful power plants. They are relatively extremely small, discrete, and can power individual buildings. They can be fueled by biomass or waste making them renewable. This also provides for a security issue for the nation as decentralized power means that an enemy could not destroy the power supply to large areas as easily.

City living demands ever more comforts and amenities. The ability for cities to alter their energy use patterns is clearly there, but it is very unlikely that city dwellers will change their behaviors. The off-grid rural life entails a much more natural and fulfilling way of living and using energy. Solar panels, windmills, small river turbines, wood stoves, passive heating and cooling, and relatively minimalistic lifestyles provide for all the energy needs and more that a person requires. Groups of houses surrounding an energy hub within a very short distance, as is likely to be the case in urban environments could provide for all the needs of a group of city dwellers. Instead of building more and more grandiose housing in urban environments, these housing groups could be made minimalistically, not requiring as much power to maintain HVAC systems for large empty spaces or appliances in every home that could otherwise be accessed in a shared or common space that connects the group of houses. Each house could contain a bedroom for each occupant, a living room, and a bathroom. The communal area that connects each of the houses could hold the major appliances, that would be accessible to every household. This would include kitchen appliances, washers, and dryers, and could even contain maker spaces like woodshops. Only small appliances would be used in each of the houses. This system would encourage community sharing and activity, creating healthier people and spaces within urban environments. It would significantly reduce energy consumption as well, as it would reduce the distance cables would need to run, the amount of energy needed from large power plants, and the space occupied on the land that disallows energy production and food production equitably. Again, we can reference Jacque Fresco's *The Venus Project* to see into these kinds of systems.

ENVIRONMENT

Our environment is degrading due to human activity. This statement cannot be argued. It can be passionately shouted down, but no amount of shouting can change the fact that human activity is decimating the natural world. There is a direct and undeniable connection between all things in the universe. Looking at the condition of the planet we live on, we can see how many of the things humans have done in modern history have created extreme detriments to our environment which has as a result caused enormous suffering and extreme danger to the human population, and all other life on the planet. We have witnessed the wholesale destruction of our natural world. We are creating vast cities and metropolis's that eliminate the ability for the natural ecosystem to operate. We are making animal migrations dwindle or die off. We are destroying biodiverse lands and waterways that are crucial to the flora and fauna and the human population. There is no excuse for this destruction and the perpetrators are the same organizations that have captured the economic management of our planet. It is the same organizations that pollute, incentivize wars and manufacture scarcity. We do not need to look at the destruction in a panic, as this does not resolve our situation. We need to look at our current state of existence on this planet with awareness, a calm assurance of what needs to happen, and an unwavering truth in the face of unending manipulations of information by those that are profiting from this cancerous activity. The real actions that need to be taken to serve our environment are the same actions that need to be taken to serve our holistic economic wellbeing. The very first step must be to eradicate fractional reserve banking. We must absolutely destroy the Federal Reserve. We must as a nation come together to eliminate this greatest threat. We must serve the world by fighting by whatever means the private central banking cartel that operates in most countries on this planet and dictates policy to our governments and prints our currency and determines its value and where it is spent. After this, we can begin to reform our systems to serve the environment and reduce and overturn the negative impacts we have had on it. We can only look at the resolution of our environmental concerns when we have eliminated the global machine that is built upon the practice of enslaving the people and destroying the environment. The environment is mostly self-correcting, and when we have stopped the practices of destruction, we need but only support the natural tendency of the ecological system to bring back clean water and clean air. Pollution can cease to exist when polluting agents are no longer supported by international trade deals authorized by the tyrannical plutocracy.

The vast majority of our bodies and the earth we live on is composed of water. The water is the most obvious example of the interconnectedness of all life here. Without water, a human would not live for more than a few days on average. Without rivers the land would be desert. Without fresh water, there would be no arable soil. Without rain, there would be no trees. Without water, life ceases on this planet. When we consider that the amount of fresh water available on this planet is finite, and that we are reducing the cyclical actions that replenish that supply of one of the most fundamental resources for our survival, we must begin to see the absolute insanity of our actions. We must begin to see that even our inaction to prevent this behavior is suicidal. Natural water cycles are being disrupted by human machinations. There are massive blockages and redistributions of the natural waterways which are causing desertification in vast proportions. Dams are causing destruction of the environment to allow for more human occupation, and rather than take serious consideration of stopping this practice, globally it is ramping up, with ever larger dams stopping up ever larger water flows. We must ensure that waterways follow their natural course to provide for the appropriate distribution across the land. We must stop the practice of piping water from abundant regions to drought regions or for the sale of water between one region to another. This practice reduces the adequate supply of water to their appropriate regions. To correct drought, we must invest in practices that have been proven to work, often called "Greening the Desert". This is not a new concept. This is an incredibly old concept that is mostly ignored or simply not practiced in favor of disastrous manipulations of natural environments for corporate greed. With modern technology, we could prevent the desertification our of lands quite a lot more easily and efficiently than what was available in the past. What right does Aquafina, Nestle, or Fiji have to drain our freshwater commons, bottle it in poisonous and polluting plastics, and sell it back to us. Water is not a tradeable commodity! It is the commons, owned and caretaken by all living beings that reside here. This behavior, which is marked by a complete lack of transparency, dignity, or honor, is mirrored in almost all the actions of the corporate methodology, whatever the name of the particular corporation may be. What right do humans have to destroy the waters and lands of this planet! What right do humans have to drill into the deep aquifers to remove ancient waters that support the structure of the lands we all share! There is no right, and yet our species is silent and culpable to these thefts.

Since the advent of industrial agriculture, we have witnessed enormous harm perpetrated upon the land and water as a direct result. Large monocropped lands destroy the natural diversity of the land. It makes it nearly impossible for the natural habitat to be present and thus the natural wildlife, which includes large amounts of migratory wildlife. Migratory wildlife needs to be reintroduced to the stagnant and destructive monocropped industrial farmlands. By allowing the natural migratory pathways to redevelop, there will be an overall and systemic benefit that will be observable in short periods of time as ecosystems begin to work in their intended natural and holistic way. We must abolish destructive practices in regard to our soil. We must stop the use of all technology, chemicals, and farming techniques that deplete the quality of the soil. This must be done immediately before any further harm can come to the material from which our life sprouts. This was apparent and well known to the agrarian society we were a hundred and fifty years ago, but when the government began to industrialize farming for its own profit and dominance, and the population of farmers began to reduce in number, the knowledge was forgotten to the population and the means by which food appeared in the box stores was less important than the price of those foods they once grew. We need to eliminate Agritech dominance of our farming practices and criminalize the destructive seed manipulation taking place by Bayer and Monsanto among other things I will get into later. Wildlife bridges over highways and roads need to be built to prevent the large-scale deaths of wildlife, and even more importantly allow wildlife to migrate on their natural pathways freely and safely without endangering themselves or travelling humans. These bridges do not impede human activity on roadways, and they will reduce the horrible impact roads have had on the natural migrations of animal life on the planet. While the convenience of our highway system has been a boon to industrial progress, urbanization, corporate distribution and military action, the roadways are invasive to the natural paths of life on the land, whether those be wildlife, plant life, or waterways. We must mitigate these negative effects by introducing more solutions like wildlife bridges.

However you choose to view "climate change" and "global warming" politically, the fact is that ice is melting, releasing fresh water into the oceans, changing the chemistry of the already polluted and misused oceans. The oceans are likely to rise severely in one generation and the ability to maintain coastal cities will likely diminish. This will lead to inland migrations, burdening the arable land and water sources and extending cities into megacities. The marine life and thus all life will be affected in ways that we cannot foresee. The increase in planetary temperatures may lead to further degradation of soil reducing arable land to desert. The concern should not be the political perspective, but the real challenges that we may be faced with in the not too far future. Potential global catastrophe ought to be enough to pull humanity together, but seeing how we've been going so far, I'm not sure that will be the case.

Fire mitigation practices are often more harmful to the environment than helpful. A century ago, the rate and expanse of forest fires were far higher and larger than currently. Forests often require burns to crack open their cones, or to clear space for new growth, or any number of reasons. It is not for the forests sake that we control and limit burns but for humans who have colonized deeper and deeper into forests and who do not wish to lose their homes and their lives. Just another example of humans interfering with the natural rhythms and systems that keep life on the planet thriving to support their infestation, dominance and occupation of space whatever the cost. When will people learn?

Our environment is not limited to the larger area, but also the domicile, the property, the community, the village, town, or city, and all the external conditions that exist within one's direct location. Within these environments, we have to consider laws other social influences that influence behavior and technologies that are used to facilitate for chosen lifestyles.

Building Codes and regulation limit the freedom of the people when they are imposed on the individual. In small business, if there is any regulation at all, there must be more regulation than on the individual, as the business involves a wider population. Large corporations must be the most heavily regulated as they are positioned to do the most harm or good. The preferable model would be to leave factors to the free market regarding business, as, disregarding any other reasons, regulationary power in the hands of any government or authority leads to collusion, fraud, extortion, coercion, and theft. This is apparent today, with governments globally colluding so deeply with international mega-corporations as to be identified as a global plutocracy. When we regulate an individual's ability to care for their own basic needs, we are not supporting the population as a whole. When we regulate large businesses, in such ways that we eliminate the possibility for abuse of the population, we are supporting the entire population. Those who wield power must be the most evolved of our species. Anything other than this and we are placing the power to do harm in the hands of those who will, whether they realize this or not. When we empower individuals to succeed, we empower the base components of our society to function to the benefit of all. Much of the building codes that exist are exclusionary of alternative ways of living and prejudicial toward the poor and destitute.

The existence of building codes implies an intelligent authority on the topic, but building codes are influenced by corporate agendas and political positioning. A public forum by which all experts and laypeople could collaborate to achieve the best results in a location, would seem to be a more appropriate approach to building codes for the unique locations in which some standards could be useful. I do not advocate for no standards. I do advocate for local populations deciding what those standards are. The blind acceptance of mandates and systems produced by international governmental organizations is not local or appropriate. With that said, when it comes to standardized systems used for the prevention of collapse from earthquakes or tornadoes, I see a huge benefit in the ability to source the best solutions for the protection of one's domicile. This could also be done within the free market. Businesses would compete to offer the most proficient systems at the most affordable price. This would also encourage the building and thus active testing of alternative systems. Rainwater catchment, composting, solar, wave and wind power generation, and permaculture farming can be done in urban areas just as must as in rural areas. We can utilize the vast array of technological advancements available to us today to create a mass producible, highly affordable, adaptable, and integrative building system that can structurally set up in a matter of hours. Understand that this is *very* possible today technologically, but *very* impossible today politically and for the monopolists. It is far more lucrative to make people purchase shit they don't need, including exorbitantly expensive houses.

Composting Toilets must be sponsored and endorsed and even subsidized by government to be used by the population. If we begin to practice greater care of our waste in this way, we will see that it is not waste at all, but fertilizer. It is the food for our food. There are practices that have been in existence since the beginning of farming, in which humans used their own feces to grow their own food. This practice is only made infeasible when the population is eating inorganic, toxic foods. Since much of our food is petroleum based and contains many waste ingredients that would not create beneficial fertilizer, this composting practice must also come with the endorsement of truly organic food products.

How about a government grant for anyone who can design a composting system that can be mass produced at low cost and installed in residential bathrooms, with minimal maintenance, easy to use, that produces viable compost for backyard, rooftop, or community gardens. How about utilizing compost to heat houses, which is a proven way to do so?

There are tested and proven methods for restructuring our standardized construction industry. We can easily implement new models by looking to organizations that have dedicated themselves to proving the viability of new systems, like One Community Global. This organization has compiled and still works to increase their content to show the many ways we can redesign our system today. A few easy methods that are proven to increase the wellbeing of the population is simply to build circular cities, create public food forests and randomly planted gardens, and decrease roads. Testing these designs can be done following in the designs of The Venus Project and other similar projects that have laid the groundwork for our regenerative future.

The materials we use in the construction industry are very often outdated and toxic. New materials like Aircrete, hempcrete, and hemp and other plant-based plastics are proven to exceed the quality of the current standardized materials. In the case of Aircrete, the cost is so minimal, houses could be built for pennies on the dollar. Aircrete can be created with simple, cheap, and easily accessible components and has a structural capability far exceeding current materials. We can implement these materials on a universal scale immediately. As far as hemp-based materials, we can subsidize and call for investment into the hemp industry to support the creation of the facilities and factories to produce hempcrete and plastic, not to mention thousands of other products currently dominated by the petroleum industry that funds the very same plutocrats that are destroying our world.

Universal Housing is not a debatable option in the modern world. We can implement universal housing by immediately funding and creating cost effective housing and community structures that allow community members to manage their own resources in hyper-local food production, cooperative business, and social design. Allowing people the right to be responsible for their living conditions, while providing the means for their access to the cost effective materials, and the deregulation of their community structures, will result in the complete eradication of needless hunger, homelessness, and destitution.

EDUCATION

"Our schools are, in a sense, factories, in which the raw products (children) are to be shaped and fashioned into products to meet the various demands of life. The specifications for manufacturing come from the demands of twentieth-century civilization, and it is the business of the school to build its pupils according to the specifications laid down."

- Ellwood Cubberley, 1920

The education system, as all other facets of this society, has been corrupted and centrally controlled for more than 150 years, or just after the Civil War, when we became a far more centralized nation, rather than a union of states. The practice of placing social position and opportunity through mandatory standard testing is a despicable and unacceptable form of identifying the capacity of any individual. Testing can be done to determine understanding but must not be used to place individuals in pass or fail systems. The federal government involvement in education must be removed. Any government involvement in education will lead to indoctrination inherently by the nature of the system. It must not enforce education standards or material taught. The local populations must be allowed to educate their youth without interference from political agendas and censorship, and even then, must accept the choice of individuals to not participate in any sort of organized schooling.

"We live with a myth that compulsory, universal education was established to produce a well-educated populace. Propaganda! Bulloney! Long before government schools were built, the U.S. had a literacy rate of more than 90 percent, and a population well-versed in history, civics, literature, philosophy and mathematics. Government schools were, from their inception, designed primarily to keep the children of "the masses" docile (and keep them out of the workplace — a huge national issue at the time compulsory school attendance laws were passed). America's compulsory education system was the brainchild of U.S. educators who had visited Prussia's highly regimented schools. These edu-controllers had admired the Prussian system's obedient, robot-like students and its philosophy that the state was the true parent of every child...You will discover for yourself that today's shocking rates of illiteracy, lack of historic knowledge, and sheeplike belief that people exist to serve the state aren't the result of a system that has failed. They are the result of a system that has succeeded beyond its founders' wildest hopes. The system cannot be fixed. It already works."

– Claire Wolfe[212]

Education does not require fees. What does require fees is educators, as long as people continue to value things with money. Local communities themselves can equitably take on the cost of schooling, without mandate from government. Students can be required within their schooling, if they choose to participate, to maintain their schools and to partake in their upkeep. To reduce costs of higher education, we must incentivize evolved and creative forms of educating the people. One solution that is easily able to be implemented immediately is remote learning. In regard to classes that do not require in-person activity, as in a chemistry lab, we can easily create certifiable online learning more accessible and prominent in the education system. Online learning is easily able to be kept affordable and accessible by leaving the whole matter to the free market. People who have the means to educate can offer their services to the people, who may choose to participate in their teachings or not. They pay their educators independently without the need for middlemen, such as schools. I do not think this is the best option in moving forward as there is a far greater benefit to learning in person than remotely, but it is unreasonable to disallow education to people simply because they cannot finance their way through a ridiculously overpriced system or because they are not able or willing to move to a different location to learn.

The importance of in-person learning cannot be overstated. For all of human history up until modern times, humans have learned through the master and apprentice model. A young person would find a willing master of a craft and apprentice themselves, giving their labor in return for room, board, and an education. Once that student was sufficiently, educated, say at around 20 years old, they would leave the masters house to open their own business. This model would still work today, but even more successfully. The education could be filmed and distributed for free, provided remotely, or even provided to several apprentices as is done often in modern day construction work. Perhaps this is the evolution of video streaming services and certification through that medium.

Student paced learning should be used rather than mandated timeframes. If a student can learn all the material in a course in a week and verifiably prove that learning, and another student takes a year, each should be considered perfectly acceptable, and both should be given favorable passing of the course when they are able to show these proofs. Who is it that determines a passing grade? Is it necessary to have an institution doing this? What about private companies that hire based upon an apprenticeship rather than what they read on paper? Is it not more reasonable for a demolitions expert to work directly with new and untested individuals, no matter what it says on a piece of paper signed by a stranger? The master-apprentice model allows for much of the necessary education in any subject, and renders schooling unnecessary by itself.

Educators must be evaluated by their communities and their students. Students must be able to choose their educators just as an apprentice chooses their master. Educators are servants of the youth and new generations and as such must be accepted by the youth itself. It only takes about 100 hours to transmit reading, writing and arithmetic to a willing audience. An unwilling audience, who are forced to endure imprisonment and wicked treatment, it may never be transmitted fully. In 1850, a 5th grade math textbook would be comparable to college level textbook today. [213]

> *"...I began to wonder, reluctantly, whether it was possible that being in school itself was what was dumbing them down. Was it possible I had not been hired not to enlarge children's power, but to diminish it? That seemed crazy on the face of it, but slowly I began to realize that the bells and the confinement, the crazy sequences, the age-segregation, the lack of privacy, the constant surveillance, and all the rest of the national curriculum of schooling were designed exactly as if someone had set out to prevent children from learning how to think and act, to coax them into addiction and dependent behavior... Over the years, I have come to see that whatever I thought I was doing as a teacher, most of what I actually was doing was teaching an invisible curriculum that reinforced the myths of the school institution and those of an economy based on caste."*
>
> -John Taylor Gatto, Dumbing Us Down[214]

The schoolteacher's job, in Gatto's analysis is to inculcate confusion, class position, indifference, emotional dependency, intellectual dependency, provisional self-esteem, and acceptance of constant surveillance.

The confusion comes from the incoherence of the daily sequence of activity and its constant deluge of fragmented and prejudicial facts and theories. Class position is the act of organizing students according to numerical values that relate directly and indirectly to their socioeconomic status. It is the reinforcement of "staying in your place." Indifference is taught by the use of bells to announce transitions between the fragmented education sequence. This means that nothing of importance is ever able to be digested by the students, and rather what they are learning is to be receptive to the ringing mandate of the order giver. The bells mean that what is being learned is less important than the inescapable demand to never find fruition or to become enthralled, as it is not allowed to disregard the bell or to not be attentive to the next class filled with another amalgam of information to be absorbed and regurgitated upon command.

Emotional dependency is generated by the removal of rights and privileges that must be granted and permitted by the authorities in the school, and by making students reliant on the good will of teachers to exercise even the smallest of their natural rights, such as to use a bathroom or exercise free speech. Anything that a student wishes to do must be granted by the authority, and if they refuse, the student must comply or be punished, creating a servile population, whose emotional state depends directly upon the will of the authority. Intellectual dependency is formed by the choosing and enforcing of subjects to be learned, and in what light they are taught by the authorities. The *successful* students are the ones who obey the mandates and do as they are told, reading their textbooks on the scheduled timeframe and regurgitating the information on standardized tests. It is the good student who waits for an authority to tell them what to think and do. It is the bad student who refuses to accept the official narrative in the material being taught.

The entire economy of today is built upon the rapid acceptance of information from declared experts, and it is as soon to fall in upon itself when people begin to think and act independently. Provisional self-esteem is indoctrinated into the people though constant judgement and evaluation by the authorized experts. Grades are used to determine self-worth and to also declare to parents and peers how much value they have, whether they should be mocked, punished, rewarded, or praised. It is the current social credit score by which all students are bound to a fate prescribed by an ever-changing retinue of strangers with little critical thinking skills and mandates to indoctrinate. Constant surveillance is the fact, and its acceptance by students is the key to its existence. By enforcing constant surveillance at schools, and at home though homework and parent-teacher conferencing...

> *"Rich or poor, school children who face the twenty-first century cannot concentrate on anything for very long; they have a poor sense of time past and time to come. They are mistrustful of intimacy like the children of divorce they really are (for we have divorced them from significant parental attention); they hate solitude, are cruel, materialistic, dependent, passive, violent, timid in the face of the unexpected, addicted to distraction... a combination of television and the stresses peculiar to two-income or single-parent families has swallowed up most of what used to be family time as well. Our kids have no time left to grow up fully human and only thin-soil wastelands to do it in... School is a twelve-year jail sentence where bad habits are the only curriculum truly learned... Our nation ranks at the bottom of nineteen industrial nations in reading, writing, and arithmetic. At the very bottom! The world's narcotic economy is based upon our consumption of this commodity... and schools are an important sales outlet. Our teenage suicide rate is the highest in the world, and suicidal kids are rich kids for the most part, not the poor. In Manhattan, seventy percent of all new marriages last less than five years. So something is wrong for sure... children and old people are penned up and locked away... and without children and old people mixing in daily life, a community has no future and no past... We live in networks, not communities, and everyone I know is lonely because of that... It's just impossible for education and schooling ever to be the same thing. Schools were designed by Horace Mann*

and by Sears and Harper of the University of Chicago and by Thorndyke of Columbia Teachers College and by some other men to be instruments for the scientific management of a mass population. Schools are intended to produce, through the application of formulas, formulaic human beings whose behavior can be predicted and controlled... Two Institutions at present control our children's lives: television and schooling, in that order. Both of these reduce the real world of wisdom, fortitude, temperance, and justice to a never-ending, nonstop abstraction. In centuries past, the time of childhood and adolescence would have been occupied in real work, real charity, real adventures, and the realistic search for mentors who might teach you what you really wanted to learn. A great deal of time was spent in community pursuits, practicing affection, meeting and studying every level of the community, learning how to make a home, and dozens of other tasks necessary to becoming a whole man or woman." – John Taylor Gatto[215]

Solutions to the schooling system include allowing children the time to self-study, solitude, and intensive problem-solving in situations that require individual investigation and contemplation. We must give children the means to discover self-responsibility and to understand the meaning and importance of communal service, apprenticeship, and family.

Considered esoteric today, the learning or education model of the trivium and quadrivium prevailed for many centuries to attain higher understanding of the universe and the self. The Trivium is composed of Grammar, Logic, and Rhetoric. This is the fundamental structure of learning that all people must hope to master. This is the construction of language, communication, and conceptualization. When one has successfully acquired a decent comprehension of the Trivium, they may begin learning the Quadrivium, composed of arithmetic, music, geometry, and astronomy. Through the learning of these 'liberal arts', the individual grows in understanding of the nature, the self, the cosmos, perspective, and opens their mind to philosophy and deep conceptions, let alone informing on any number of professional crafts and enhancing our technologies.

Sacred geometry as it is called by many today, is the geometrical associations that form the root, and all its extrapolations, of existence. It shows up as the visual component of our existence. Everything in nature has a sacred geometrical form leading back to root geometrical shapes, the Platonic solids. These Platonic solids are the tetrahedron (4 sides), the hexahedron or cube (6 sides), the octahedron (8 sides), the dodecahedron (12 sides) and the icosahedron (20 sides). These shapes define our dimension of experience. All of the four quadrivium studies are the study of the same patterns represented in different ways of experience and in how they manifest. Arithmetic is numerical, and results in equations and algorithms and functions. Music is auditory in experience, but in the study of music, the form and design of music, or sound intentionally organized, is of the same pattern as the fundamental structures found in the study of all of these arts. Astronomy is the study of the way the objects within the cosmos are oriented to each other and how they move and function and influence. Again, this study results in the same base structure, which is, in my opinion, most readily absorbed through the use of the study of geometry, or shape. The ease by which one can grasp the knowledge with geometry, which literally translates to the practice of measuring the earth, is fantastic, allowing for novitiates to ascertain truths that otherwise are more difficult to ascertain. Then again, there are so many sources to drink in this knowledge since the advent of the internet, that it has become quite simple to educate oneself. The information at least is available.

In the structure of space and time, we can see the same forms repeated, just as in the way the stars emanate light, EM fields propagate, and even how the human body is proportioned. These forms are represented in ancient architecture, art, theology, and civil engineering. The greatest structures, the most moving artwork and sculpture, and the power centers of the world are all based in sacred geometry. From the pyramids of Giza to Machu Picchu to underwater cities off the coast of Japan, the amount of architecture that is built according to exacting measurements that align to the cosmos, the perspective and ratios of the Earth, and perfect mathematical equilibrium, leaves little doubt that it was done intentionally and with skills and technologies that far surpass our current abilities. We cannot reproduce these pyramids, or the other megalithic structures around the globe, even with all the money in the world poured into doing so. There is not a device in the world that lift the megalithic stones that form the foundations of the pyramids of Giza. So, then we are also confirmed in one other thing... that the Egyptians of 4500 years ago did NOT build them. Those people were technologically incapable to a much greater degree than we are today, literally relying on hand tools such as hammers and chisels and man power in the form of slaves. It is an absolute impossibility that the people we identify as Egyptians of 4500 years ago built those structures. You are allowed to disagree of course, just like you are allowed to think that WTC 7 collapsed in perfect demolition form from a small office fire, making it the first metal frame building to have ever done so. But I have the right to then steer clear of you as I have found it far healthier to avoid people that decrease my intelligence. The Egyptians did not build the pyramids, and the Incans did not build the megalithic part of Machu Picchu, which would have been a spectacular achievement anyway seeing as they were only around for 150 years.

Much of this information has been encoded and embraced by religions around the world. In fact, they intertwine fundamentally more often than not. Jesus being the same mythological character as Krishna and Horus. The symbolism, astrology, and mythology that interlaces to form the current perspective of religions worldwide is founded upon the arcane, but once obvious, nature of the foundational forms that manifest reality as we experience it. The Christian cross and the Bible, the Islamic Kaaba, the Jewish star and Hebrew language, the Buddhist eight-spoke wheel, the Tao Te Ching structure, the Egyptian book of the dead, and the Sanskrit language, all have their roots in esoteric symbolism and sacred geometry. They are all examples of the extrapolative natural design that exists throughout the universe. We experience life through the forms of sacred geometry, and we are witness to these forms in the innumerable expressions that bleed out of the infinite potential of existence.

Even space itself has shape, dimension, and perspective, as has been identified quite clearly by physicist and researcher, Nassim Haramein. He has concluded that space, or the renormalized vacuum density is 10^{93}gm/cm^3, 39 orders of magnitude greater than the observable universe, which has 10^{55}gm/cm^3 (one cm cube of vacuum mass-energy). Atoms are made of 99.99999% space.

> *"This is nothing new; most ancient civilizations believed in an all-prevailing soup of energy embedded within the fabric of space, and later many of the world's great thinkers, including such scientists as Albert Einstein, Nicolas Tesla, Buckminster Fuller and Walter Russell, believed in an all-prevailing energy at the base of the fabric of space. The premise of this research is simple; space is not empty, it is full! It is full of an energy that creates atomic structures themselves — reality. It is a sea of electromagnetic flux we call the zero point energy, which has been demonstrated beyond a shadow of a doubt, since its mechanical effects have now been measured in laboratories, and the cosmological constant was added to the vacuum at the universal scale to accommodate for the observed acceleration of expansion.*
>
> *In simple terms, reality is not unlike the phase transition that water undergoes when its molecules change into ice. This thermodynamic effect is the result of a transfer of energy or information from one state to another. In this case water can be represented as atomic structure and ice as the energy of the vacuum structure. Now we can identify both sides of the equation--one being a wave form (water or liquid) and the other being geometric (solid) as it gets cooler.*
>
> *This research identifies the geometric relationship between space and the phase experienced by matter as related to [or illustrated by] the water/ice example. The*

relationship is geometrically communicated as a fractal tetrahedral array circumscribed by a sphere where the vector lines of forces generated by the geometric array is the structure of space itself, and the sphere is the waveform resulting from the fluctuation of space, that we observe as atoms. The geometric relationship to the waveform is non-linear, since it is fractal with spheres—from infinitely big to infinitely small—embedded within each other in all directions, thus creating the experience of reality. For instance, you can imagine in mechanical terms, that the electron spins are embedded in the rotation of the earth, embedded in the rotation of our solar system, embedded in the galactic arm, embedded in our galactic disk, embedded in our cluster, embedded in our superclusters, embedded in our Universe which duplicates fractally to infinity thus, more accurately denoted as our Multiverse. The structure resolution is described by the orbital's relationship to infinity, from infinitely big to infinitely small.

Now, picture yourself as one of these boundaries between the infinitely large and the infinitely small. The transfer of information, or energy, going across the boundaries is reciprocal in both directions. For example, the energy dispensed during the day by your body in terms of thermodynamics is reciprocal to the information gathered by your senses feeding your consciousness. The vector directions are at a 180 phase from each other or, in other words, in opposite directions, whereby the energy dispensed by your body is from the boundary outside of yourself and the information gathering is from the boundary inside of yourself, i.e. Consciousness or self-awareness. The standing waveform generated by the opposite phases is the boundary we call reality. The information transfer across the boundary is a function of the 64 codons generating the amino acids of the double helix of the DNA structure. The combinations of codons that seem to be inactive (only 20 out of 64 codons generate the DNA amino acids) are interacting geometrically with the fractal dimensions of space to transfer the information across the boundary, resulting in what is popularly known as the auric field.

To give you an idea of the amount of information transfer related to only the actual 20 codons, if you were to extend a DNA packet found at the center of a cell so it unraveled like a tight string and you were to hold end to end all of the strands that are found in one human body alone, it would take a jet plane traveling at 1,000 mph approximately 24,000 years to fly to the end of that DNA.

Now why is it that most human beings will often utter the statement that it is impossible to imagine infinity when their own existence is part of the infinite boundary generated by the fractal geometry of space? The reason is simple—the tendency is to attempt to visualize the Multiverse in the external, infinitely large vector direction. However, visualization is a function of consciousness, thereby from the boundary inward, which is a vector direction towards the infinitely small. Auspiciously, most Masters that have walked this earth have tried to educate the public about the importance of turning our senses inward, which translates in many different cultures as either prayer or meditation. Expressed geometrically or mathematically as nonlinear fractal mathematics, or expressed philosophically as levels of consciousness, the importance of taking the time to sit in contemplation becomes self-evident. As a result of this practice one can experience the true nature of their existence and their place in the infinity of the Multiverse."

– Nassim Haramein, The Geometry of Space[216]

Haramein has greatly advanced the access to understanding of ancient wisdom by melding modern science with esotericism. He has been able to identify the vector equilibrium, a 64-grid tetrahedron, or 8 connected star tetrahedrons, Merkabah's, which themselves are made of 8 tetrahedrons, as the structure

of the vacuum. There are a large number of scientists and researchers who are conducting experiments and producing theories that utilize sacred geometry to describe existence. They are often times more accurate in their results than that of 'traditional', also called outdated and unscientific, science.
Our ability to understand the universe is greatly enhanced when we employ the Trivium and the Quadrivium. Our ability to engage in other narrower fields of study is greatly improved with the foundation stones of these 7 studies.
From ancient nameless societies to religious institutions, to templars, freemasons, and governments, all the way up to today, the knowledge has been passed down, often in secret, of the sacred knowledge of the design of the universe. The education has been limited to those who sought it, because it is those who seek that are prepared to learn. Today, that knowledge is available to all who seek, and it is readily available to those who are willing to learn. The occupied minds of the modern world might seem relatively similar to the occupied minds of the preceding centuries to those who were initiated into the secret knowledge, but it is up to the people of today to prove their worth by refocusing their attentions and attenuating their energies to the enlightened frequencies that advance humanity into its evolution. It is the tragedy, a bitter end to a potential glory, of humanity that concludes our story at self-destruction.
Even without this knowledge, and often in lieu of it, the people of this world can become enlightened. It is not through study that enlightenment occurs, but rather in the deeper unfoldings that arise as knowledge shows its limits and wisdom instead comes to take its place. It is in the silent listening, the burbling, rippling song of the stream, the slow descent of the leaf as it twists in the wind, reaching to regenerate the soil, the birds that have been singing their languages for uncounted risings and declines of empires, surviving cataclysm after cataclysm. It is the deep breath and the contented sigh. When the only sound one hears whether in the middle of a crowded and busy marketplace, or on the summit of a mountain on a deathly calm day, is one's self, that is the moment of realization. Have you felt an unlimited joy while standing in line for your morning coffee, or a profound and unrelenting peace in the solitude of a stroll through the woods alone? Has the sunshine penetrated the layers of your armer and shown you the divine gift that is the light and warmth of our glorious sun? If you cannot hold the image of a rose in your mind for as long you care to, your education is incomplete. A PhD is not the measure of success, but a blip on the radar to one's own understanding of the self and the universe. I've met wise and holy men who lived in dumpsters and vicious villains who ran charities, courageous explorers who lived in jungles and weak swaggering imbeciles who ran governments. The place you are starting from has nothing to do with arriving, except to satisfy your current need for a logical series of events. It is the wisest of us all, who are free from the timeline, the narrative, and the mechanism and walk freely though the earthly plane.
Education is but the content by which we define until we define no longer and are free.

Albrecht Dürer
Melencolia I, 1514

IMMIGRATION

We are a nation of immigrants and subjected peoples. The United States is both a nation of immigrants and a nation of slaves. The only real demographics of the US is the native people and immigrants, though if we go back far enough, we will see that we are all migrants upon the earth, and any territorialism is built in ignorance. We have a population mostly comprised of European immigrants. The current minorities are comprised of the descendants of slaves, conquered native peoples and modern immigrants, mostly Latin Americans and Asian Americans. The historical perspective of why people immigrated to this country is of people seeking economic opportunity, migrating away from disastrous economic and societal situations in their home countries and people travelling to novel places in a pioneering spirit as well as indentured servants and slaves to mercantilism. The United States has an unequivocal record of persecution, of both non-white and white people, both born and native to this land, and immigrant populations.

The determination of race or classification based on being white is ridiculous in itself. White has no bearing in region, religion, culture, language, or governance model. Some Arabs are white, and as different as they come from the Scots or the Russians. Let's classify based on real terms. I happen to have ancestors of Irish, English, Scottish, Blackfoot, and other Scandinavian parts. Am I white? Am I American because I was born here? Is that my race? Am I Irish because that's dominant in my heritage? What about a Mexican immigrant? Are they Mexican? American? What if their ancestors were a mix of Spanish conquistador and native slave? Are they Spanish then? What about the Irish immigrants to Mexico during the Mexican American war? They mixed with the Mexican population and now there are red haired, blue and green eyed Mexicans. The classifications that we make today are based on ignorant views.

There is also a clear record of gradual perception changes as society has evolved. If we look at the benefits of immigrant populations, there is an overwhelming degree of economic and social reward from their inclusion into a welcoming society. Even under the burden of a hostile society, immigrants create enormous economic and social benefit as they add themselves to the workforce and society in ways that are usually held to be less desirable positions to the society. Also, large quantities of skilled workers and intellectuals have immigrated to the United States even as their social group was persecuted and subject to classism, segregation, and unjust bias. This indicates that even during harsh conditions, these migrating populations, including skilled and unskilled people, found greater benefit in living and working in the US than their former countries and regions. Immigrants form the very core of the amalgam that makes the US a powerful and successful nation in the contexts of the modern and plutocratic perception of success. Even without that perception, immigrants have created this nation.

For Slavic immigrants, along with many Irish and Italians, coming to this country in the 19th century proved to be a corrupted endeavor, as for many of them, it was indentured servitude in coal mines starting at 12 or 13 and living in company towns, where conditions were often worse than the conditions provided to African American slaves, and on par with conditions provided to natives on reservations or when they were used as slave labor in the mines for three centuries prior.

The United States must measure its capacity to receive immigrant's not by ideological bias, but by economic and safety analysis. It must be understood what the nature of the immigrant population is, but not to the extent of subjecting incoming populations to unjust searches or human rights violations. Simply asking what their profession is and where they are coming from is enough to determine statistically how they are fitting into the society. The requirement exists to know whether we are allowing dangerous people and organizations to enter freely into the country. Here we can ask, would you allow MS-13 gang members into your home to share a meal, after which they might rape your daughter and wife and kill you. Or what about a suicide bomber, though the danger of such a thing was only really solidified after the creation of the war on terror, which increased "terrorism" globally by factors.

Other questions of course will be asked, but they are for other purposes, like asking and checking if a person has a disease that requires them to be quarantined for a time. This is what was done for immigrants over a century ago, and it is not an imposing practice today, that exceeds the bounds of necessity. What are they composed of? What is their level of need and what is their ability to reinforce the social and economic structure of the nation? This analysis can provide us with an understanding of how to incentivize certain activities and roles for these immigrants to fill. There is also the measure of moral and ethical responsibility to those that come to the country in need of refuge against crimes against humanity in their origin countries. Primarily, we understand that the United States is in a fabricated critical internal situation that is easily creating stress and worry about the future of our national condition. With events like the coronavirus international shutdown, we can see how the people and local governments of today respond to stressful situations. We can see that it hasn't changed in the history of authoritarian societies. We can see that the public perception can be shaped by any message displayed by authority figures. We can see that the society of today isn't much more advanced from the Jim Crow era. This needs to change for less divisive and more inclusive methods of operating our society. We need to accept our planets immigrating populations with grace and with intelligent and wise application of guidance. Our current government cannot do this. But perhaps if the people are strong, we can change that. It is also completely possible to do these things at local levels in the absence of federal government, such as allowing the local governments to operate their own policing and military border protections. Federal government is the most egregious squanderer of resources imaginable. They are thieves and plutocrats. They are not necessary to hold a strong border and a firm policy of acceptance or denial of immigrants. Currently, the problem in our immigration policy is that we are not seeing the influx of immigrants to rural farming positions, but rather to dense cities. These cities become leeches and the worst criminal sectors of the nation. We need to bring back small farming and migrant farm work in a big way. With this resurgence of small farm labor jobs, immigrant populations can be more useful to the nation rather than becoming dependents of state charity programs that further indebt the nation to global central banking institutions. The average farmer is 59 years old and lacking successors. We need to allow for immigration to funnel people into these places to support the small and midsize farms.

There are foreign impediments to emigration which influence immigration to the United States. Some nations on this planet do not allow their populations to emigrate. Others, like Mexico, encourage their populations to emigrate to the United States as Cuba once did. The release of the enterprising criminal aspects of their society into the United States reduces, theoretically, the burden on the Mexican Government, though they are all in collusion anyway. Releasing the burden of caring for emigrating populations reduces the financial burden on home nations, and thus produces a shift of burden to the destination countries. This is a detriment to global human wellbeing. While populations must not enter into war except in grave need, there are many ways we can influence the nations of the world to become more accepting of the migratory nature of life and of humans, without sacrificing security and safety. We must encourage global migratory behavior while enforcing our borders to the extent that is needed and no more. We must treat immigrants with dignity and not harm them or disgrace them. For a brighter future and a graceful evolution, we must learn to adapt with the natural patterns of life, and that begins with ending the wars and the violence that creates these substantial numbers of destitute homeless people and nations.

The most efficient method that could implemented to ensure that immigrant populations are integrating peacefully into the American population, especially if the nation is accepting vast numbers of immigrants and refugees, as is likely and projected in the coming decades, is to accept only those people who come to the United States by applying for entrance. The reason this is efficient, is because it will reduce the financial and social burden of finding, imprisoning, and deporting violent criminals after they have integrated into the population. One reason this is inefficient is that while it allows strong restrictions on entrance, preventing criminals to some degree, it also reduces the amount of diaspora populations that can be accessed to gain information and support to infiltrate nations and groups intending to control populations through the interconnecting global megacities.

Another method would be to simply remove all the illegal restrictions on ownership of firearms of all kinds and have local populations police themselves. I doubt MS-13 would be super interested in living in a place where it was encouraged to use one's tools and talent to eradicate those who would commit needless harm. In the end, it won't be walls or border patrol, or municipal police, or open-door policies, or all the fuzzy warm greetings in the world that will prevent dangerous immigrant populations from taking advantage of comfortable Americans, but rather it will be the iron in the average Americans hand that will ultimately decide the fate of the society that has been built here so far. The world is becoming megacity-centric, diasporic, and filled with an ever-increasing number of politically and militarily involved non-state groups that will come to eventually dominate heavily populated cities due to their ability to decentralize and evolve to match rapidly changing environments. If the US is to avoid becoming fractured in this manner, it will be because our right to bear arms has been fully reaffirmed and local groups of Americans have reasserted their right to defend their persons, families, and territory. Collaborative groups of local people can prevent violent immigrants far more efficiently through decentralized self-organization, technologically advanced systems for monitoring, reporting, and communicating, and because they are highly motivated to do so.

Those immigrants who enter into American society in peace and add to our communal wellbeing must not be looked at as anything but a positive result of encouraging immigration. In fact, the US ought to seek out the farmers and other skilled populations globally and encourage their entrance into the nation. By recruiting the people we need from the global pool, we can fill niche sectors that are being left in the dust by the current populations moving toward ever more easeful existence. Perhaps the influx of farmers from other regions of the world would produce a society here where it is not uncommon for the average rural farm household to hire live-in service-oriented individuals, as they become self-sustained and profitable. This would be most beneficial if the system was profitable to immigrants not through only financial gain, but through the practice of partitioning and proffering parcels of the land to the immigrant farmers after a certain amount of time working the farm. This would make the migrant aspire to dedicate to the wellbeing and success of the farm which they, in part, own.

The guarantee of a future is not possible, but a reasonable predictability of potential outcomes is very possible. By offering a feasible outcome of higher quality of life to any population, they will undoubtedly strive to achieve it. Producing this would not be difficult, at least not nearly as difficult as attempting to shut borders with walls or prevent violence by letting in anybody with a belly button. It is better to empower local communities with all they need to secure themselves, then leave them to it. Allow the immigrants who are skilled in the ways we need to enter and incentivize their commitment to practicing that skill within this society. Great benefit will follow.

Science, Religion, Spirituality And Operant Conditioning

The scientific community is held captive by gatekeepers just as media is in the world today. The accepted and maintained narrative of our universe and everything in it has been manufactured by political manipulation and control. The current narrative that ss still taught in schools despite the fact that it has been repeatedly and definitively debunked is that we are limited by the sum of our genetics and that our history of civilization began less than 15000 years ago. These narratives and more are pushed onto the people from birth. These are absolutely incorrect.

Experiments and research that challenge the status quo are ignored or never conducted due to the inability to get funding and published in reputable scientific journals. Rather than the scientific community presenting unbiased work as they would like to appear to be doing, the gatekeepers actively marginalize those who refute the narrative that is currently most profitable. Today's most profitable science is that which is funded by corporations and government with the intent to maintain their dominance over political control, technological advancement, economic control, and the general level of knowledge and understanding in the population of our history, our current situation, and our communal future. There is an enormous body of evidence that politics, economics, and all other facets of society are controlled by gatekeepers in their respective ways. Due to the fact that a plethora of notable people have spoken out about the corruption within the scientific community it takes only a small amount of investigation to discover the truth. A current popular social construct is the denial of the legitimacy of science. This is the reactionary behavior that we see in many other areas of society when some wrongdoing is perceived. Instead of an intelligent correction of the problem, groupthink takes over, usually in the form of a polarizing and generalizing of the issue. It is not that science itself is misleading, but rather, as usual, it is the fact that an elitist profiteering model has been created within the community, and the sponsors of that elitist model are the same that have consolidated the global media, the food production, distribution, and engineering, the medical, and finance, and every other aspect of social influence. The very same people who have generated enormous wealth at the expense of others, have paid their way into owning and influencing the most fundamental aspects of society.

Science:
1.*the state of knowing: knowledge as distinguished from ignorance or misunderstanding*[217]

*mid-14c., "what is known, knowledge (of something) acquired by study; information;" also "assurance of knowledge, certitude, certainty," from Old French science "knowledge, learning, application; corpus of human knowledge" (12c.), from Latin scientia "knowledge, a knowing; expertness," from sciens (genitive scientis) "intelligent, skilled," present participle of scire "to know," probably originally "to separate one thing from another, to distinguish," related to scindere "to cut, divide," from PIE root *skei- "to cut, split" (source also of Greek skhizein "to split, rend, cleave," Gothic skaidan, Old English sceadan "to divide, separate").*[218]

Textbooks today are written as if they are the final say on what is true and false in the world. The vast majority of our knowledge is not as concrete as the average textbook makes it seem. You ask experts in any field, and, if they are being honest, they will tell you that we know nothing. Today, textbooks on elementary science do not accommodate for the proven changes to our scientific knowledge about the functions of the universe such as what is provided through quantum mechanics. Why is it that textbooks are not keeping up? And why do they claim ultimate knowledge? It is glaringly obvious that control of information is a primary method for the plutocrats and social engineers to maintain control.
While there are certainly many "alternative" theories and narratives to what is presented in most scientific journals and in textbooks, there are those that carry weight and those that don't. It is not for me or any other person to declare which is correct or not, but only to present or point to the totality of the information unlike what the gatekeepers do. Up until the invasion of the Prussian education model, the learning method that presided was the trivium. Grammar, Logic, and Rhetoric. That is, to learn the structure of language, the ability to formulate concepts and ideas through language, and the ability to communicate those ideas. This is done through investigation of life, rather than the imposition of facts and the rote memorization of them. A person who investigates many different views, increases their understanding of the world, whereas the person who only copies what is written as fact in textbooks is programmed to regurgitate that information perpetually. It is the difference between knowing how to use the faculties of the mind and intellect to derive understanding, versus the ability to store information for regurgitation later. Our global society today is indoctrinated in the ways of the latter, and thus we see the relatively fast degeneration of the human species and the world we interact with.

> *"First, not even the 'exact' sciences like astronomy or physics are exact in the sense of 'absolute' or 'infallible.' Their firmest laws or uniformities are to be regarded as tentative. They may be upset at any time by further work. But at any given moment they are not to be tampered with unless they prove unreliable in relation to observed facts... Science makes no attempt to study or describe reality—certainly not ultimate reality. Science is not even concerned with truth... Science is based, not on faith, but on skepticism, on a skepticism that will not even worry itself over its status in the universe. And so the scientist works on serenely, undisturbed by the philosopher's final thrust... the scientist by no means confines himself to 'the facts and nothing but the facts.'... Actually the scientist cannot work without a conceptual scheme: and though the relation between facts and conceptual schemes is not by any means clear, it is at least clear that a conceptual scheme involves something besides facts, involves, indeed, a working mind... The scientist's own hopes and fears, his own*

standards of what he would like to have prevail on this earth must be kept as far as possible out of his work, and especially out of his observations of, or dealing with, facts." – Crane Brinton[219]

Those who have developed the ability to think, have in parallel established skills in varying degrees to hold varying viewpoints concurrently without feeling distressed over not coming to a definitive conclusion. It is an evident sign of wisdom that multiple ideas can be entertained until new insights develop further understanding and clarity over a topic. Those who do not have this ability have likely been taught and programmed to believe in authority blindly. The authority of the textbook, the professor's aid that wrote it, the educator who directs them to read it, the administrator that defends it, the government that mandates it, and the peers that quote it. These authorities are most often unqualified to be moral or educational authorities, for the very simple reason that they learned within the Prussian model and thus have themselves been indoctrinated into believing what they are told, until they hold positions of power or prestige, or which are financially rewarding that are threatened by any narrative other than the one they supported throughout their careers. Propaganda exists within language itself. Reporting on something, the language used describes the speaker more so than the object. Everyone is selling each other as they are attempting to confirm for themselves their worldview. It is a hierarchical system with extraordinarily little to do with learning, and more to do with molding our worlds youth into predetermined roles.

A scientific approach to life, which should be fundamental to our education process, means to make hypotheses, test them, and if successful, provide the results to the world so that anyone may test the results and either disprove or prove the outcome. If enough proofs are completed and challenges overcome, the hypothesis may become a theory. That theory only remains so long as it holds true. If a competing, opposing, or diverging result is discovered, the theory changes to accommodate. In this way, our communal knowledge grows and adapts over time to the highest understanding of the universe that we occupy. In what way does our education system reflect this? In what way does our scientific community reflect this? In what way does our society reflect this? I would argue that extraordinarily little science is applied to the world we live in because the fundamental structure of scientific exploration is not applied. Where science is applied, the methods of distribution of the knowledge are censored by the gatekeepers. All knowledge is subject to the thought police manipulating it to match the mainstream narrative.

Scientific journals have editors that are influenced by the plutocracy and by such, even if they are decent people with no ill will toward humanity, will censor the studies and other information printed in their journal to protect themselves from the backlash of those who could do them severe harm. On the other hand, some journals are run overtly by those who profiteer from the censorship. Some people who have succeeded to a certain degree at circumventing much of the censorship of their explorations, experiments, and conclusions are people like Graham Hancock, Michael Cremo, and Nassim Haramein. These three alone are responsible for discovering and uncovering censored historical evidence for non-mainstream narratives of human history, revealing truths around ancient civilizations and structures like the Great Pyramids that point to highly advanced technological societies, and discovering mathematical proofs identifying the structure of space. There is so much more to these people and these topics, but you will have to discover for yourself what they are by investigating these people and their work yourself.

The separation of spirituality and science can only be maintained by those who have no real understanding of either. Science is the study of existence to gain understanding, and spirituality is the direct experience of existence. The scientist performs experiments out of curiosity, while the spiritual person does everything possible to become ever more aware of life at its root. They are not oppositional fields. They are complementary. Religion on the other hand can be either destructive or constructive toward spiritual goals. Religions are often mandated systems of living imposed upon large groups of people who have connected their personal identity to the ideology or system sufficiently to be beholden to it. Religion can also be a pattern of behavior chosen and dedicated to by an individual to achieve a certain spiritual goal. A catholic person could be so out of heritage, while a gnostic could be so out of personal choice. Whatever the reason for participating in any particular religion, the goal is to achieve a spiritual end, if done so sincerely in the ideology of the religion. Thus, we can say that a spiritual person could use the tool of religion to create patterns in their life that help to focus their minds, cleanse their bodies, or do any number of other services, in a scientific and experiential approach toward their goal.

There is a serious and outrageous fanaticism that accompanies almost any grandiose ideologically guided community. This fanaticism is represented by Soviets and Nazi's, statists and KKK members, Buddhists and Christians, Semites and otherwise. Once a group identity is hardened around an ideological core, it becomes aggressively defensive of that core in an obvious and understandable effort to stay alive. The death of one's identity is as dangerous to the ideologically calcified as the death of their physical self. The grander the ideology, and the more ingrained in their social structure, the more strongly the devotees will defend it.

The Abrahamic religions are all founded upon much older religions and stories. Jesus being quite important in all three, is but the symbolic representation of the same thing that Horus in Egypt, Mithra in Persia, Attis, Dionysus and Hercules in Greece, and Krishna of India represented far earlier. The exact details of the lives amongst these characters are often ubiquitous, including the virgin birth on December 25th with eastern star, their crucifixion and resurrection, miracle working, 12 disciples, and having similar titles like "King of Kings." Nearly all of the stories, rituals, and holidays practiced in the Abrahamic religions can be traced to the Egyptians, including Moses' God given laws, which came transcribed directly from Spell 125 in the Egyptian Book of the Dead. The mythological and astrological origin of the Abrahamic religions are so obvious and apparent that it would be logical and scientific for the people of the world to shed the literal interpretation of the of the religious scripts. Instead, when confronted with the facts and historical origins, the believers more often than not, choose to entrench themselves further in their beliefs. This is a very understandable response, as these people are often generationally indoctrinated into their beliefs, and even when this is not the case, the identity that is created around the ideological core gives security to these individuals that would be extremely uncomfortable to shed. Often, it is more willful ignorance than anything else. Besides this, there is a significant social reward for maintaining one's religious appearance, whether in adherence to Islamic prayer ritual or Catholic ceremonial communal prostrations. The Abrahamic religions are not alone in this phenomenon, but it is spread across the globe and infiltrates every part of social design, whether it appears in the form of statism, monotheism, polytheism, capitalism, or socialism. The solidified core in the identity structure of the individual and the group is so seemingly comfortable, secure, and empowering that it would seem to be in opposition to their safety and wellbeing to refute it for any reason.

Post-Modernism:

postmodernism, also spelled post-modernism, in Western philosophy, a late 20th-century movement characterized by broad skepticism, subjectivism, or relativism; a general suspicion of reason; and an acute sensitivity to the role of ideology in asserting and maintaining political and economic power.

Postmodernism is largely a reaction against the intellectual assumptions and values of the modern period in the history of Western philosophy (roughly, the 17th through the 19th century). Indeed, many of the doctrines characteristically associated with postmodernism can fairly be described as the straightforward denial of general philosophical viewpoints that were taken for granted during the 18th-century Enlightenment, though they were not unique to that period.[220]

Post-Modernism is recognized by its ridiculous notion that logic, reason, science, and Truth do not lead to advancement of the human race. It relies on an infinitely undefined notion of life because words and language itself is simply a reference to the language or word itself, not to a distinct thing in the physical world. Since we have no language to agree upon anything anymore, there is no reason to discuss a logic that cannot be formed. And if we cannot logically conclude concepts between us, there is no ability to theorize about our objective reality. Because there is no objective Truth, nothing common can exist between people.

Social Conditioning:
"Social conditioning refers to training people to think and act in a certain way by using positive and negative reinforcement by society. It starts at birth, and there are several factors that promote social conditioning. Social conditioning is the process by which people of a certain society are trained to think, believe, feel, want, and react in a way that is approved by the society or the groups within it." - TheMindFool[221]

Conditioning:
"conditioning, in physiology, a behavioral process whereby a response becomes more frequent or more predictable in a given environment as a result of reinforcement, with reinforcement typically being a stimulus or reward for a desired response. Early in the 20th century, through the study of reflexes, physiologists in Russia, England, and the United States developed the procedures, observations, and definitions of conditioning. After the 1920s, psychologists turned their research to the nature and prerequisites of conditioning. Stimulus-response (S-R) theories are central to the principles of conditioning. They are based on the assumption that human behaviour is learned. One of the early contributors to the field, American psychologist Edward L. Thorndike, postulated the Law of Effect, which stated that those behavioral responses (R) that were most closely followed by a satisfactory result were most likely to become established patterns and to reoccur in response to the same stimulus (S). This basic S-R scheme is referred to as unmediated. When an individual organism (O) affects the stimuli in any way—for example, by thinking about a response—the response is considered mediated. The S-O-R theories of behaviour are often drawn to explain social interaction between individuals or groups."[222]

It is a relatively uncomplicated process to shape or condition society when one controls education, the media, and every other major influencing mechanism. What we have today is a refined plutocracy, made up of gatekeepers to information. These gatekeepers are influencing the population by conditioning certain behaviors in the same way that Pavlov conditioned his dogs. Positive stimulus for desired behaviors, negative result for undesirable behaviors. i.e., Operant Conditioning.

Identity Politics:
Politics in which groups of people having a particular racial, religious, ethnic, social, or cultural identity tend to promote their own specific interests or concerns without regard to the interests or concerns of any larger political group.[223]

> *"Identity politics is primarily an outgrowth of the black nationalist, Black Power, and women's liberation movements and has since come to dominate the public square. It combines a focus on race, sex, sexual orientation, gender identity, and other identitarian categories with a politics of victimization. The cornerstone of the identitarian worldview is the claim that America, contrary to its egalitarian professions of faith, is at its core a supremacist regime that oppresses certain groups. Ultimately, identity politics should be rejected not because it demands justice for those who have been unjustly treated, but because it poses a threat to republican self-government by corroding patriotic ties, fostering*

hatred, promoting cultural separatism, and demanding special treatment rather than equality under the law." – David Azerrad[224]

Fundamentally, the distinctions that make us unique are either to be honored or they are to be used as tools to divide and conquer us. The plutocrats don't care what race or sex you are. They care that you stay in line like the cattle you are. Raised on their farm, fed their food, taught how to behave the way they want, and fully obeisant. Those who separate us by pointing to petty differences like skin color or sex are the very agents of the controllers and gatekeepers. We can understand the difference between recognizing our differences and honoring them and recognizing our differences and victimizing ourselves or others based on those things.

Political Correctness:
conforming to a belief that language and practices which could offend political sensibilities (as in matters of sex or race) should be eliminated.[225]

Patriarchy:
1. a family, group, or government controlled by a man or a group of men
2. social organization marked by the supremacy of the father in the clan or family, the legal dependence of wives and children, and the reckoning of descent and inheritance in the male line

1560s, "ecclesiastical province under a patriarch; church government by patriarchs," from Latinized form of Greek patriarkhia, from patriarkhēs "male chief or head of a family" (see patriarch). Meaning "system of society or government by fathers or elder males of the community" is recorded from 1630s.[226]

"Rights and privileges spread as the social and economic conditions make their manifestation possible, to some degree... and I'm not suggestion that men haven't oppressed women and that women haven't oppressed men... we've been at each other's throats in many ways throughout the entire course of human history. Men at the throats of men. Men at the throats of women. Women at the throats of men. Women at the throats of women. Parents at the throats of children... theres no shortage of contentiousness and tyranny that characterizes human history. In 1895, the average person in the western world lived on less than a dollar a day, in today's money. Way below the current UN standards for poverty. Life was very hard. There was no reliable birth control. You can't underestimate the radical consequences of reliable birth control. That opened up the world to women. And it's not just birth control, it's a whole variety of technological transformations. And also, an increase in the safety of the street and a hundred contributing factors that have opened up the world to the freedom of women. But a huge part of that was the collective striving of men and women to free themselves from the absolute tyranny of hand-to-mouth existence. A woman was sexual mature back at that time around 15 or 16, very likely to be married soon after that, partly because sex outside of marriage was so unbelievably dangerous. Very high probability of pregnancy. And then of death in childbirth. And then death of children. And then continual pregnancy. Women weren't the same even biologically speaking. The birth control pill is a biological revolution. It took a long time to extend the full coterie of rights to people... Most men in eastern Europe for example were serfs until the late 1800's. Fundamentally slaves. It's not as if the common person has had the right to vote for any substantial amount of time. In some countries for a couple of hundred years and that's all. We're clamoring out of the great darkness of biological history and creating a culture where people have enough freedom to exercise what would optimally be their full

set of rights. And to say that that didn't happen in the past primarily because of the patriarchal dominion of men is, I think, an escape from full confrontation with the absolute dreadful horror of biological history. It's a wish that all of the things about life that are deeply troublesome and terrible are the consequence of the errors made by those who control the social structure... it would be really something if they had that much power... your tyrannical patriarchy is a relatively ineffective force in the face of the absolute depredations of mother nature. It's not as if 150 years ago all men were free and all women were enslaved. The truth of the matter is 150 years ago virtually everyone was enslaved." –
Jordan Peterson[227]

The majority of the population of the United States, to varying degrees, is in collusion with the very government that oppresses them. This is not unique to this country or this era. For a government to exist, a population needs to allow it to exist. There are no slaves who are enslaved by anyone but their own disunion and inaction. It is amongst this statist, self-enslaved population that we see the passionate duopolistic party loyalties and infighting. Those who believe that government has some greater authority than their own or their chosen community fall under one of two categories; those who want a mommy state and those who want a daddy state.
Whatever form the indoctrination has manifested, the result is nearly the same. Both parties in the duopoly, and the desire for a parent government make for an incompetent and impotent population. The social degradation that comes from releasing self-responsibility and accumulating reliance on a parent government is immensely greater than any war or pandemic. When people are taught to rely on a parent state for protection, health, sustenance, and all other survival needs, the people themselves lose the ability to care for themselves. Rather than having to be responsible for their own lives, they can become slaves to the system in exchange for a constant supply of money, which they can use to purchase those things they need. When the government is no longer able, or chooses not to supply what the population needs, the people will not know how to care for and organize themselves. The recognition of this ignorance pushes the population to even greater levels of reliance on the system and greater depths of loyalty, even if it goes utterly against logic and their survival.

"Since the 1980's, society at large has bolted frantically from one panic to the next. Fear of crime reduced us to wrecks, but before long we were also howling about deadly diseases, drug abusers, online pedophiles, avian flu, teens gone wild, mad cows, anthrax, immigrants, environmental collapse, and—let us not forget—terrorists."
– Julie Hanus[228]

The fearful American is now the normal and average American. The image goes from Captain America and resilient communities to a masked, sexually confused, obese, recluse, who shouts in YouTube comments about people needing to social distance and demanding guns be melted down except for those in the hands of the government who sends him his weekly check because he has destroyed his health. What a great nation we are! What glory and honor! The society of our grandparents is not the one of today. The nation that survived the second world war would today be the nation that begs for mercy before firing a bullet. Those that have the guns and the general populations authority to use them are the agents of government that would just as likely shoot them given the order from a superior as look at them. This is a weak nation. It has become weak only recently. And we must remember, as Michael Hopf said, "Hard times create strong men, strong men create good times, good times create weak men, and weak men create hard times". Though I would change this a bit to... Hard times create resilient men, resilient men make strong communities, strong communities make good times, good times make docile communities, docile communities make strong central governments, strong central governments make genocidal times... hang on, that can't be right. How about we just accept the fact that when the population becomes apathetic to the machinations of the megalomaniacs, that population is killed. Stalin, Hitler, Mao, Pol Pot, Tsar Alexander II, Talaat Pasha, Theoneste Bagosora, Qianlong Emperor, Yahya Khan, Ante Pavelić, Idi Amin, Omar al-Bashir, George H.W. Bush, Suharto, Said Barre, Saddam Hussein, Lothar von Trotha, Efraín Ríos Montt, Min Aung Hlaing, Xi Jinping, Zhang Xianzhong, Abdul Hamid II. Do we need to investigate any more examples of genocidal freaks, leading governments whose agents massacre their own people, their neighbors, and anyone else?

It is psychologically probable that a person would choose to follow and respect the strongest person or group. This following of those perceived to be strong is the method that many people prefer in their efforts to survive and to reap greater benefit for themselves and their direct family and community. The indoctrination of a population to identify themselves deeply with religious institutions, political parties, countries, social codes of conduct, and any number of other conditions like skin color or socioeconomic position allow for those in positions of control to increase and maintain that control to their reward. It is the breaking down of these identities that allows a population to overcome its disunity and become whole.

Human Rights and Constitutional Rights

The Constitution of the United States of America is the supreme law of the United States. Empowered with the sovereign authority of the people by the framers and the consent of the legislatures of the states, it is the source of all government powers, and also provides important limitations on the government that protect the fundamental rights of United States citizens.

-Whitehouse.gov[229]

Human Rights:

rights (such as freedom from unlawful imprisonment, torture, and execution) regarded as belonging fundamentally to all persons.[230]

The difference between a human or natural right and a constitutional right, is that natural rights are afforded to all people by existence itself, whereas a constitutional right is only able to affirm or restrict the natural rights. A constitution has no authority except to identify what natural rights are not present and to reaffirm them as important to a group or society of humans. When we have to assert rights, it means that those very things are apparently lacking. We no longer need a constitution when the natural law of life is being adhered to by all people. A human right can be anything that is natural to human life. A law created by a particular society is made to produce a certain characteristic amongst the population that is seen as important or fundamental to cooperative society. Whether it truly is fundamental is dependent upon the intentions of the people who are writing the law. Usually, laws are not written with the consent or involvement of the general population, but by a select group of elitist individuals who perceive themselves as authorities that can dictate to the general population. This is the case with the constitution of the United States. The constitution was written by individuals who cleverly bypassed the wishes of their respective states and created a centralized federal government with enormous powers and limited oversight. The amendments to the constitution were made as afterthoughts, which represented the interests and wills of those who were less influential in the original construction of the constitution. These amendments were codifying rights that negated some of the more tyrannical aspects of the original constitution. The Declaration of Independence was an announcement of the intent and action of separation from the British. The constitution and its amendments were the construction of the new nations' supreme law of the land. The natural, or human, rights are the true law of the land, and are placed in the backseat to the constitution in this country. Today, and for most of this nation's history, even the constitution is placed in the backseat to unjust and prejudicial "laws" that misrepresent the will and interests of the people, to support the elitists who have claimed authority without earning it from the people or by following natural law.

Here is a select list of amendments to the constitution, that is the supreme law of the land, and are the superior to any unjust laws created post ratification.

First Amendment

Congress shall make no law respecting an establishment of religion, or prohibiting the free exercise thereof; or abridging the freedom of speech, or of the press; or the right of the people peaceably to assemble, and to petition the Government for a redress of grievances.

**Government violations of this include, but are not limited to, free speech zones, censorship, banning peaceful gatherings of people for any reason, and banning strikes by workers, and arresting protestors.*

Second Amendment

A well regulated Militia, being necessary to the security of a free State, the right of the people to keep and bear Arms, shall not be infringed.

**Government violations of this include, but are not limited to, barring citizens from owning firearms or any other form of arms, taxing arms purchases or ownership, licensing firearms or their owners, inhibiting the free organization of militias, allowing or creating gun-free cities, and restricting types of bullets or firearms allowed to be owned and carried. It also includes the act of refusing the right to defend against militarized police who enter homes illegally or mistakenly.*

Third Amendment

No Soldier shall, in time of peace be quartered in any house, without the consent of the Owner, nor in time of war, but in a manner to be prescribed by law.

**As militarized police are breaking into homes of the population for minor offenses, often falsely accused, this amendment is becoming more and more denied every passing day.*

Fourth Amendment

The right of the people to be secure in their persons, houses, papers, and effects, against unreasonable searches and seizures, shall not be violated, and no Warrants shall issue, but upon probable cause, supported by Oath or affirmation, and particularly describing the place to be searched, and the persons or things to be seized.

**Government violations of this include, but are not limited to, demanding drivers licensing to travel in a vehicle, or any other form of licensing for use of the commons or a persons property, surveillance of the population or individuals within the population without provable and verified cause for, and production of, warrant, and arrests for lack of licensure. Police conducting raids on* *homes and road-side strip searches, while the TSA forces their hands upon our children and spouses or their microwave technology scans to see through our bodies is extreme examples of the complete evisceration of this amendment. Even clearer, is the fact that the NSA and other intelligence agencies access our phone calls, emails, internet activity, medical records, and personal daily activity through smart meter energy recordings, data storage of all internet activity and other devious means.*

Fifth Amendment

No person shall be held to answer for a capital, or otherwise infamous crime, unless on a presentment or indictment of a Grand Jury, except in cases arising in the land or naval forces, or in the Militia, when in actual service in time of War or public danger; nor shall any person be subject for the same offence to be twice put in jeopardy of life or limb; nor shall be compelled in any criminal case to be a witness against himself, nor be deprived of life, liberty, or property, without due process of law; nor shall private property be taken for public use, without just compensation.

**The NDAA allows the government to arrest people indefinitely, without due process. This is a direct violation of the worst kind and completely defies this amendment. Eminent Domain often defies this amendment, such as when the government forced it upon farmers so that Exxon Mobil could run their oil pipeline without interference.*

Sixth Amendment

In all criminal prosecutions, the accused shall enjoy the right to a speedy and public trial, by an impartial jury of the State and district wherein the crime shall have been committed, which district shall have been previously ascertained by law, and to be informed of the nature and cause of the accusation; to be confronted with the witnesses against him; to have compulsory process for obtaining witnesses in his favor, and to have the Assistance of Counsel for his defence.

**Again, the NDAA has demolished this, as it has bypassed due process entirely. It is now recognized as legal by the federal government to kill citizens with drones without any court proceedings or specified offenses.*

Seventh Amendment

In Suits at common law, where the value in controversy shall exceed twenty dollars, the right of trial by jury shall be preserved, and no fact tried by a jury, shall be otherwise re-examined in any Court of the United States, than according to the rules of the common law.

**Trial by jury is very often denied to people. Considering the fact that the vast majority of self defense cases are settled by plea bargain, and the fact that there are financial, time, and learning requirements involved in jury trials means that it is out of the means for most of the population.*

Eighth Amendment

Excessive bail shall not be required, nor excessive fines imposed, nor cruel and unusual punishments inflicted.

**Government violations of this include, but are not limited to, inequitable bail requirements that prejudice the poor and thus provide injustice through financial access. What is determined cruel* *and unusual is determined, under Supreme Court rulings, by the evolving government, which currently considers drone bombing, poisoning, and imprisoning without cause, its own citizens.*

Ninth Amendment
The enumeration in the Constitution, of certain rights, shall not be construed to deny or disparage others retained by the people.

**This protects people's Rights that have not been affirmed in the Bill of Rights. It is all the things that can be considered a Right by an individual or group despite not being enumerated here. A million Rights have been violated and the power that should have been retained by the people has been transferred to the States and the federal government.*

Tenth Amendment
The powers not delegated to the United States by the Constitution, nor prohibited by it to the States, are reserved to the States respectively, or to the people.

**Through bill after bill and executive order after executive order, the federal government has stripped and subverted the powers of the state governments and the people. This amendment does not exclusively give rights to the states to dictate to the people, as may people believe it to. It says any powers not specifically given to the federal government will be either reserved to the States OR TO THE PEOPLE. That means we the people retain the power, as we form what is the State and what power it has or does not have. We are not to be dictated to by some foreign body, but to dictate our will to the public servants who serve us in government. The people have the Right to overturn their government when these amendments, even one of them, are not being adhered to by the governments. Today, every single one of our fundamental agreements and laws of the land are being denied, subverted, altered to fit a fascistic governing body, and disregarded and sidestepped. It is past the time of starting a revolution. It is time to tear down the damning evil tower by releasing our service to it and building a new world based on reaffirmations of our inherent human rights and our Constitutional Rights. A new system, that leaves people free to build their own governments is needed, from the local level upward.*

Eleventh Amendment
The Judicial power of the United States shall not be construed to extend to any suit in law or equity, commenced or prosecuted against one of the United States by Citizens of another State, or by Citizens or Subjects of any Foreign State.

Thirteenth Amendment
Section 1
Neither slavery nor involuntary servitude, except as a punishment for crime whereof the party shall have been duly convicted, shall exist within the United States, or any place subject to their jurisdiction.

**This amendment was used to enforce cruel treatment to prisoners leased to industrialist agendas in the early 1900's. But the question is, are prisoners yet enforced or coerced today to serve industrialist agendas? Yes, prisoners produce materials used by major corporations like McDonald's and even produce the Kevlar helmets used by the United States military.*

Section 2

Congress shall have power to enforce this article by appropriate legislation.

Fourteenth Amendment
Section 1
All persons born or naturalized in the United States, and subject to the jurisdiction thereof, are citizens of the United States and of the State wherein they reside. No State shall make or enforce any law which shall abridge the privileges or immunities of citizens of the United States; nor shall any State deprive any person of life, liberty, or property, without due process of law; nor deny to any person within its jurisdiction the equal protection of the laws.

Section 2
Representatives shall be apportioned among the several States according to their respective numbers, counting the whole number of persons in each State, excluding Indians not taxed. But when the right to vote at any election for the choice of electors for President and Vice-President of the United States, Representatives in Congress, the Executive and Judicial officers of a State, or the members of the Legislature thereof, is denied to any of the male inhabitants of such State, being twenty-one years of age, and citizens of the United States, or in any way abridged, except for participation in rebellion, or other crime, the basis of representation therein shall be reduced in the proportion which the number of such male citizens shall bear to the whole number of male citizens twenty-one years of age in such State.

Section 3
No Person shall be a Senator or Representative in Congress, or elector of President and Vice-President, or hold any office, civil or military, under the United States, or under any State, who, having previously taken an oath, as a member of Congress, or as an officer of the United States, or as a member of any State legislature, or as an executive or judicial officer of any State, to support the Constitution of the United States, shall have engaged in insurrection or rebellion against the same, or given aid or comfort to the enemies thereof. But Congress may by a vote of two-thirds of each House, remove such disability.

Section 4
The validity of the public debt of the United States, authorized by law, including debts incurred for payment of pensions and bounties for services in suppressing insurrection or rebellion, shall not be questioned. But neither the United States nor any State shall assume or pay any debt or obligation incurred in aid of insurrection or rebellion against the United States, or any claim for the loss or emancipation of any slave; but all such debts, obligations and claims shall be held illegal and void.

Section 5
The Congress shall have the power to enforce, by appropriate legislation, the provisions of this article.

Fifteenth Amendment
Section 1
The right of citizens of the United States to vote shall not be denied or abridged by the United States or by any State on account of race, color, or previous condition of servitude–

Section 2

The Congress shall have the power to enforce this article by appropriate legislation.

Sixteenth Amendment
The Congress shall have power to lay and collect taxes on incomes, from whatever source derived, without apportionment among the several States, and without regard to any census or enumeration.

**In this instance, the amendment itself is a violation of the constitution. In violation of the 4th amendment, this amendment states that government can steal money (property) from the people. Interestingly, because the privately owned money is printed at the behest of a privately owned company, The Federal Reserve, the money is not actually the property of the individual. It is owned by others and is loaned to the public at interest. This money is then taxed directly due to this amendment, which violates the 4th amendment and ensnares the people in a plutocratic scam.*

Seventeenth Amendment
The Senate of the United States shall be composed of two Senators from each State, elected by the people thereof, for six years; and each Senator shall have one vote. The electors in each State shall have the qualifications requisite for electors of the most numerous branch of the State legislatures.

When vacancies happen in the representation of any State in the Senate, the executive authority of such State shall issue writs of election to fill such vacancies: Provided, That the legislature of any State may empower the executive thereof to make temporary appointments until the people fill the vacancies by election as the legislature may direct.

This amendment shall not be so construed as to affect the election or term of any Senator chosen before it becomes valid as part of the Constitution.

Women's Rights, Roles, and Response-Abilities

Women's Rights is not a topic that exclusively affects women. Women are the vessel by which all human life exists. Of course, men have their role in this, but it is the female aspect of our species that carries and nurtures our race. When we limit the rights of the woman, we corrupt the wellbeing of all life on the planet. We must not tell any person what they can or cannot do with their body. When we do this, we provoke the response of the commanded to reject and rebel. There is no justifiable reason for a man or woman to command a woman to live by their standards. There is no reason for this to be done to men either. We must remove the idea that we are separate. Men and Women are fundamentally responsible and dependent to each other. Instead of imposing laws to determine what is right for a woman, we must remove laws that currently exist that determine what a woman can or must do with her body and mind.
The Right to equitable pay. Is it a right truly that people must be paid equally? Of course, it is not. One person cannot do the same quality of work as another. That is why the better carpenter or baker, or tailor is paid more by the client. What is potentially a Right, is equitable pay. This means you should be paid appropriately for the quality of work done. Considering that much of the American population works at jobs that require an extremely low level of skill like fast food industry jobs or cashiering, we can apply equity to these people by providing an equal pay to these types of entry level or transient jobs. When it

comes to professions that require unique and unusual skills like that which is required to be a mechanic or a surgeon, we can apply an equitable pay model that pays the worker according to their skill level amongst other factors. This means that a woman who is working at a more tedious job like masonry and tiling, and who does not perform at the same level as the man ought not be paid the same amount. In that same vein, the man who works as an architect, and does not perform at the same ability as the woman ought not be paid equal to her. This is less about sex than it is about the equity of pay to the most appropriately earned. Pay based on sex is just another dogmatic event in the consciousness of humanity and does not reflect appropriate distributions of money for work done. If we take out factors of race and sex, we can look at the resulting work, the produce of each workers efforts and the employer may choose the most skilled in that position. It is very destructive to believe that payment of any type is a right in the end. If you were to apply for a position at a company only to find out they would only pay a dollar a day, would you be interested working there? Obviously not. The market will naturally force employers to pay their employees relative to the market averages and then adjust from there, while the worker will continually be vying for positions with higher pay. It is not a right to be paid. It is certainly a right to have the freedom to pursue one's ideal profession, but equality of outcome is never something that can be forced if you want to have a prosperous society. Instead, governments and people must respect the autonomy of others and be active in their pursuit of their own goals. No amount of giving people something that someone else has will correct anything.

The right of any person to control their body is paramount in the liberation of all people from slavery. When we come to the point of whether a woman should have the right to abortion, we must take into account the reason for her pregnancy. If a woman is raped and becomes pregnant, it must be her choice as to whether to keep the child. There is more harm to come from an unhealthy living environment than an abortion. If an unborn child is extremely ill before birth, to the extent that there is not the capacity to provide for their needs, then there is potentially more harm in not aborting. Religious considerations cannot influence this decision as individuals cannot impose faith on others. On the other hand, if a woman with the capacity to care for a child who is yet unborn, and who is healthy, and there has not occurred any outside force, as in rape, then we must consider the act as one of needless violence. There are an endless number of unique situations that must be considered in these situations, and it would be more beneficial to have locally and socially run programs created and managed by their own members that can support women in making these choices, than to involve government, courts, law enforcement and other blunt forces to these issues. Outside personal beliefs cannot interfere in these choices. Only the society in which an individual chooses to participate in can have a say here. It is the individual's choice to live by a social code. Easily men may disregard the needs of women, as much as women can do the same with men. Instead of viewing these situations from the perspective of right and wrong, we must learn to view them in the context of what is right and wrong to the individual. These can be very fragile lines, and thus they must be empowered by universal human rights or common agreements that leave the decisions to the individual and their chosen social structure. This, like so many issues does not have a shoe to fit all sizes. Humility in the face of diversity must become a fundamental principle in the social structure. Women, and men, must be empowered by a government that stays out of their way unless it is asked for by the individual. Government must not be a dictatorial entity that steals and tramples upon individual human or constitutional rights. There must be a universally accepted practice of honoring others in their right to decide what society and what lifestyle they will lead. We must become respectful as a people of the rights of the individual, whatever their race, sex, or any other distinction.

One thing to seriously consider is the extreme apathy and irresponsibility that pervades a society where people feel they must demand the normalization of abortions for any reason at any stage of pregnancy. There are many who want to extend abortion to the point that a full grown and birthed child is allowed to be aborted. This is disgusting and shows the complete degeneration of healthy human beings and healthy humanity. My contention is that it is the responsibility of every capable person to raise a child after having consensual sexual relations. If raising a child is not possible, adoption is always available and can be done with considerable consideration of the potential adopters. Even a child born of rape can be put up for adoption, so why is it that abortion is such a demanded approach to this issue? Why are we so fucking rotten? We certainly need to rise above and find the holy, the virtuous, and the righteousness that have been distorted. The soul of humanity is at risk, let alone physical liberty.

One of the most prominent figures of the early feminist movement was Marie Stopes, founder of the first birth control centre in the UK in 1921, Stopes was a fervent believer in eugenics and was opposed to contraception and abortion, preferring the avoidance of conception altogether. Marie Stopes founded the Society for Constructive Birth Control and Racial Progress as well as the magazine Birth Control News promoting a eugenic agenda. Stopes wrote in 1920, "I would legislate compulsory sterilization of the insane, feeble minded... revolutionaries... half castes". Stopes sent love poetry to Hitler for the 'German youth' at the height of his campaigns, and wrote passionately on the theme of 'racial purity'... In the context of a global ideology centred around population control, a woman's freedom over her own body forms the most dangerous part of her rights, for the woman – in constant need of supervision and guidance in the public sphere, freedom over her body awards her agency over the right to decide future generations, and thus the future of society. This is why the roots of our current thinking are in such deep need of consideration and analysis, for we must understand what is so threatening to the established order in giving women the freedom to have complete control over their bodies... To this day there is very little real notion of female ownership over her body, marital rape was legal just over 20 years ago in the UK. The woman's body has never been hers. Invasive, often painful reproductive choices were offered to women long before sexual choices were, making it patently clear that progress was never intended to benefit women, rather the greater good of society and science through the medium of the female body. Only now are we beginning to see the ground shift in the conversation surrounding women's sexuality and therefore actual freedoms for the woman inside her own body. However reproductive freedoms are still at stake, forced sterilisation is in practice to this day in the US and the UK, and the fact that phenomenal amounts of money and resources are being pumped into genetic research whilst people live in appalling conditions in one of the richest countries in the world implies that not very much has changed at the root of our thinking. And this should concern women... Provided arguments surrounding superior genetics remain, women will not be granted social freedoms over their bodies, it is anathema to the concept. Within this structural vision of gender it is impossible for a woman to be viewed for anything more than her body, as life giving is the central function to her existence, her body becomes central to her social identity. The focus on population control rather than on individual bodies gives future value to the female body which cannot be left to the disposal of the woman alone. This process ensures the parallel demonisation and fetishisation of female sexuaity and what is considered feminine, and will continue to justify the necessity of unequal treatment. By placing science as the ultimate regulator of human society we are abdicating responsibility as to the healthy functioning of our societies; where we should be looking to develop infrastructure to care for our people we are instead looking for techniques and narratives that justify the ethnic and social cleansing of our populations. This process takes place through the woman and as such the woman is agent as well as victim of oppression, dangerous in absolutely every sense.

-Mena, Eugenics and Feminism[231]

Part of the eugenics movement in the early 1900's included the forced sterilization of women who were considered unsuitable to bear children by various qualities including criminal history, mental illness, feeblemindedness, immigrant status, marital status, race, and even being "prone to hysteria". While women were not the exclusive recipients of forced sterilization, they were certainly the more prominent victims.

"It is better for all the world if instead of waiting to execute degenerate offspring for crime or let them

Popular Science magazine, 1923.

starve for their imbecility, society can prevent those who are manifestly unfit from continuing their kind. The principle that sustains compulsory vaccination is broad enough to cover cutting the fallopian tubes."

- Henry E. Sigerist, Civilization and Disease, Cornell University Press, New York, 1943, p. 105[232]

"Eugenicists used compulsory vaccination as the precedent for their argument on sterilization to "protect" the public. They believed vaccination protected individuals and the public from disease and eugenical sterilization protected society from "racial degeneracy."

- Bystrianyk & Humphries, 2015[233]

A woman's right to choose how she uses her body extends to all things that do not inflict harm on others. Included in that is the right to work voluntarily in the sex trade. Whether an individual or even a group chooses to view sex work as morally or ethically wrong, does not mean that it is inherently wrong. Nor does it give that individual or group authority over a person's choice to participate in that trade. This does more so affect women, as the trade is more often held by females. The significant issues that must be dealt with in the sex trade is not the validity of the trade itself, but of the conduct of those who abuse it at others expense. Such is the case with involuntary sex trade, uncompromising managers, "pimps", and the manipulation of youth or adults to participate in it against their free will, or the populations youth involvement in it in any way. If the government has any role at all, that role is to prevent the abuse of persons in the trade. Socially, the shaming of those who practice this trade is something that, while may not be kind, is not within the purview of the government to do anything about. Society itself will determine its communal values. What government can do right away is to eliminate all regulations regarding the practice of sex trading for adults and release from the prison system any people who were unjustly placed there.

Traditionalism of the male and female roles within society have been shifting over the last 150 years. With more of the labor force moving from heavy manual labor to less physically demanding jobs, amongst other factors, the number of women in the workplace has increased dramatically. While some hail this as a success and push for ever more blending of traditional roles, very many female voices are drowned out who call for the maintaining of, if not all, many traditional domestic roles. While this may not seem an especially prominent issue at first glance, it becomes increasingly more significant the more we look into it. There is an inherent quality to being born male or female, or hermaphroditic. The deep psychological structures that exist in the human being that compose our means of relating to one another are not easily bypassed in the course of a few generations. Women who wish to participate domestically and socially in a more traditional format must have the means to do so, and to not be shamed for doing so due to the conditioning of the population. It is not the wish of every woman to be involved in the workforce or to participate in the military. It should be well accepted that a woman's choice to participate in society primarily as a mother and caretaker of the home is not a reflection of lack of ambition or connection to current times, but a conscious and valid decision made by a free person wishing to enjoy life as they choose.

Along with the traditionalism of roles comes the fact that male roles have been and are changing as well. While this does not mean anything bad on the surface, it does imply that the male aspect of our society is not fulfilling the roles that it held in the past. Some of the things that are being left behind are strong-willed leaders representing the alpha males of our society. Rather than this part of our society being exchanged with an applicable replacement, it is simply leaving a gap. That gap is being felt and will continue to be felt until we have corrected the displacement. The role of alpha males is not to dominate and force their will upon the world and others, but simply to be able to command their life and be adamantine pillars of guidance and support for their families and communities. With this not present, the community structure itself is not truly whole and is left with gaping cracks. We must remember and honor the strong male presence in our society and forgoe the polar opposite of denying their quality and importance. When one of the sexes suffers, both parts of our living duality suffer.

The Rights of children are inherently linked with women's rights and human rights. Where do we begin to offer or recognize the Rights of children? At what point in a flower's life do we consider a seeds value? At what point can we look and see an absence of life or an absence of the process of birth? In all humans and all life, the perpetual and necessary act of evolution through mitosis or birth or however a species progresses through time, is occurring and motivating. We must review our minds and become more sincere and less dogmatic or close-minded or superficial in our perspective of this process of life. Religion and biased science cannot remove the simple fact that there is no point at which the life of a child can be declared, or if we were to identify one, it would obviously be the moment a sperm cell and an egg unite and begin developing the new cells that are unique to the new life. There can be no disagreeing with this, but from here we can begin to look at the situation of women's rights and children's rights with a right view.

The child born of rape into a life of destitution and disease is a life of suffering that may well have been prevented by a woman's right to choose. A child disallowed to enter into the world because of social stigmas and pressures on a woman, or due to the financial stress of bearing children in today's captive economy is a life that could have been lived beautifully. There is no such thing as equality beyond life or existence itself. What we need is a clear understanding of equity. Someone may require a diet of meat and another of fruit only. They are not equal, but they are equitable. What one person needs is different from another. If we can understand this, we can understand how it can be compassion for the child that drives a woman to abort, while it can be lack of compassion to end a life unnecessarily. Of certainty, it is no place of organized religion, social dogma, or any state to dictate to any human what they may do with their body. But it is important for the whole community to also understand the rights of the child. Regardless of circumstances of conception, if a woman chooses to birth a child into the world, there are several things we must look at very seriously as violations of our most vulnerable populations and as evil in the fact that the perpetration of these things has been made socially normal and even supported when no real need is ever elucidated beyond some rhetoric on a pamphlet at the hospital.

The rights of children include the right to a healthy birth, in which they are born in a healthy environment absent of EMF, absent of overly bright light, as well as absent of other stressors like too many people, too much noise, and parental stress from financial burdens or unwanted medical procedures. A healthy birth includes a mother feeling relaxed, Peaceful, Loved, and amongst their family and friends if desired. The birthing chamber should be dimly lit by natural light only, which is better for the child's eyes. The room must not be overcrowded or burdened with unfamiliar people. The sounds must be soothing and calming for the mother as well as the child. Financial or situational stressors involved in giving birth are unnecessary and the cost of birthing in hospitals is egregious and contemptable, as well as prejudicial toward poor populations. Despite the social normality of hospital birthing, it is healthier for the mother and child to have home births, or at the least have a birth at a birthing center run by midwives. It is surely dependent on many factors, and sometimes a hospital cannot be avoided, but even there, a mother can make some key decisions to enhance their child's birth and entrance into the world. Do not allow anyone to poison the birthing experience with drugs. This will inhibit your experience and ability and drug your child. It is a direct attack upon the natural ways of human life. We must pass through the birth canal into the world in full clarity. Do not let anyone cut the umbilical cord for at least an hour after the birth of your child. After the child is born the blood still passes between mother and child through the cord, and supplies needed blood and with it chemicals, information, and a longer, safer, and more comforting connection with the mother. The umbilical can even be left untouched for several days and will simply fall off when ready. At minimum though, one hour is necessary. Do not vaccinate the children! Do not allow anyone to inject your new fragile child, for whom you are bonded with deeply in this life, with any substance you are not infinitely confident of. Truly, an injection of any kind is unnecessary. A healthy, strong baby, and even a small unhealthy baby, need but their mothers' milk and to be held to be vital. If a hospital visit is necessary, leave as quickly as possible and do not allow anyone to walk away with your child.

Children must be protected against violations. How we treat our most vulnerable populations is a direct reflection of the soul and character of humanity. The amount of child sex trafficking globally would and ought to frighten, sicken, and anger the people enough to do something about it. On the surface, which is where most Americans live and die, the American Safe Families Act (ASFA), is there to protect children and families. The reality is much, much more sinister. Child Protective Service, by whatever name your state calls it, is a private for-profit agency. Every child in CPS, including every potential child in CPS< is worth $3.3 million. If CPS adopts them out, they get a $40,000 bonus. Each CPS agent has a monthly quota, that, if met, earns them a financial bonus. That quota is in regard to how many children they can engage in the system. This is so immoral and unjust, and so very clarifying as to why the law is making it easier and easier for children to be stolen from healthy and happy homes. There are 800,000 children trafficked in the United States every year. 86% of these come from these agencies. Wake up and smell the pedophiles. They are numerous, and they are powerful in groups. Who out there has lit their torch? Picked up their pitchfork? Cocktails? Well, we are not all the victims, much of the population is just as culpable. If you find this despicable to your core, as I do, then gather with like minds. Take your children out of these literally God-forsaken schools, gather with like minds, and teach them at home, with others you trust, and form your own education system. That is the first step. Don't let CPS even know you exist, prevent the opportunity for them to come to where you live, and protect your children with your life. They deserve it. Otherwise, you may never see them again, while they live a life of extreme suffering.

"The average age of child victims is 12-14 years old; with children we have rescued as young as 03 Years of age. A child is sold for sex approximately 20-30 times per day. This is the fastest growing and second largest criminal enterprise in the world generating over $150.2 billion illegal profits a year $99 billion comes from sexual exploitation. Human tracking has surpassed the illegal sale of arms & it's expected to surpass the sale of drugs in the next years. In 2018, over half, 51.6% of the criminal human tracking cases active in the US were sex tracking cases involving only children... The estimates of how many people are in human trafficking are unclear. They project the number is between 20 and 40 million people. This is due to the fact that tracking these illegal practices is very difficult. In addition less than a half a percent of cases get reported or identified."[234] These statistics account for the trafficking we know about. The real amount of trafficking may be far higher. The amount of child pornography and sexual misconduct toward children domestically increases these numbers dramatically. The amount of abuse that is laid upon the most innocent and susceptible of our species is cause for outrage. Instead, it goes most often ignored or unknown or even casually passed over. What kind of a person can harm a child like this? Well, I'd say it's the type of person who lives next door to you likely. "The prevalence of child sexual abuse is difficult to determine because it is often not reported; experts agree that the incidence is far greater than what is reported to authorities. CSA is also not uniformly defined, so statistics may vary. Statistics below represent some of the research done on child sexual abuse. The U.S. Department of Health and Human Services' Children's Bureau report *Child Maltreatment 2010* found that 9.2% of victimized children were sexually assaulted (page 24). Studies by David Finkelhor, Director of the Crimes Against Children Research Center, show that:

- 1 in 5 girls and 1 in 20 boys is a victim of child sexual abuse;
- Self-report studies show that 20% of adult females and 5-10% of adult males recall a childhood sexual assault or sexual abuse incident;
- During a one-year period in the U.S., 16% of youth ages 14 to 17 had been sexually victimized;
- Over the course of their lifetime, 28% of U.S. youth ages 14 to 17 had been sexually victimized;
- Children are most vulnerable to CSA between the ages of 7 and 13.

According to a 2003 National Institute of Justice report, 3 out of 4 adolescents who have been sexually assaulted were victimized by someone they knew well (page 5). A Bureau of Justice Statistics report shows 1.6 % (sixteen out of one thousand) of children between the ages of 12-17 were victims of rape/sexual assault (page 18)."[235]

If you are thinking, WHAT THE FUCK!, you are right. This seems to me unacceptable and represents the extreme depravity of our society. 150 years ago, when humans lived only to 35 often and were matured far faster than the people of today, it made certain amount of sense to have marriage and childbearing at

16 or 17, and at times as young as 14, but we must account for the fact that we live longer lives, experience a longer maturation period, and have social structures emplaced that allow the innocence of youth to extend into older ages. The freedom of women to be promiscuous without risk of impregnation has, along with domestic technological advancement, given a wide array of potential experiences that was nearly universally out of reach before. This has been accompanied by an enormous amount of social decline as the bedrock of strong female presence in homes has degraded and the social norm has become the irresponsible sexuality. This irresponsibility on the parts of women, men, and adults in generally regarding children is contributing heavily to a culture of increasing acceptability of the abuse of children rather than the opposite. This is disgusting and almost irretrievably demoralizing for a person like myself. It shows the absence of the wholesome and holy, the righteous and clean, the innocent and humble. Sexual assault upon a child is one of the most criminal acts against nature and the species. It is the theft of innocence. If you can't get behind hanging these pedophiles, *what the hell* can you stand for? I am not talking about sexual relations between lovers who happen to be an 18 year old boy and a 16 year old girl. I am talking about the 30 or 40 year old man and the 12 year old boy or girl. This topic cannot be bypassed. This must be contemplated upon by the people and we must take into consideration our heritage and our future and what we want that to look like. The way we are going now, it is bleak indeed.

Don't think the government is the solution either. The government "services" are just as culpable more often than not in the perpetuation of sex trafficking and child abuse. Police sexually assaulting their victims, foster care providing a pool of abusers for children who are often stolen from their parents for reasons of not obeying unrighteous government dictates. The list of government officials and others who raped children with Epstein never came out did it? I wonder who has the power to keep that information from coming out? Never think that what you find despicable and evil is out of the reach and use of those who crave power. It is that very craving that leads to the theft of innocence through sexual assault of the most pure, our children. What are you going to do about this? Hopefully, you will at least consider this. Heal yourself if you are one of these abusers and

teach those around you whatever you may be about the rights of children. We are the sum of our parts, and you cannot avoid these things as we all live on this one planet. We all have to cooperate to survive here. We are all one. Now let's bring back hanging and duels so we can clear the weeds out.

We must remember that all life is operating together to form the reality we all experience. Women are no more separate from men, then a child is separate from its mother. Nor is the family separate from their environment in any way. Every individual is responsible for the communal situation we exist in. When individuals accept this and take the reins on their responsibility, we will see that women's rights were only important so long that people begged a tyrannical plutocratic government for their inherent rights, when they could have just lived in their rights and completely disregarded that abusive, oppressive, manipulative, and self-serving institution.

The current social dogma that is borne and perpetuated by Hollywood, government, universities, and schools, and to varying degrees the general society, is the idea that women are the victims of male oppression and toxic masculinity. The truth is that the more this false narrative is accepted by women and men, the more confusion, ignorance, and violence will exist within our society.

> *"The average man has been fed a steady diet of silly narratives his entire life, such as: "Women are oppressed," "The patriarchy is evil," "Masculinity is toxic," "All men are rapists," "Women are victims," and "Women get paid less than men for the same work." In actuality, none of these narratives bear any close resemblance to the facts. This outrage is manufactured by a "female first" primary social order, with it originating from a toxic version of feminism that is no longer about equality. But rather, female dominance and male submission. When you pay attention, you will notice an ongoing narrative that*

dismisses the plight of men, and even somehow makes women the victim of male disposability."

-Richard Cooper, The Unplugged Alpha[236]

What is it that earns men more money on average than women? It is the fact that men are far more likely to work in dangerous jobs that pay more, travel further to earn more, and accept riskier positions. Women are far more likely to choose to have children and leave long term jobs to spend more time raising their children. Having even a 10-year hiatus from work leaves a major dent in competitiveness in earnings with men who have been increasing their skills throughout those years.

"...throughout history, men have always been disposable, while women were valued and protected... To put that dynamic into perspective today, it's one of the reasons why women have a far easier time getting over a breakup than men do. Women, as a function of adaptation, need to be able to adapt quickly and move from man-to-man easily. It's part of a woman's hypergamous nature to always seek the best male that she could get. Warring tribe wins? Then the men in that tribe now become her best option for survival. Men have always been disposable protectors. Women have always selected the best men for survival. Even if that meant becoming a war bride to a conquering army that killed off, or enslaved, their family.

-Richard Cooper, The Unplugged Alpha[237]

43 percent of children live in fatherless homes in the US. 90 percent of runaways are from fatherless homes. 63 percent of youth suicides happen in fatherless homes. Teen girls without a father are seven times more likely to have teenage pregnancies. Women initiate more than 70 percent of divorces or break-ups. The vast majority of sexual violations occur between non-blood close family members, such as when a single mother remarries. So, when we look at these numbers and are able to understand the importance of fathers in the household, or life, of their children, and the fact that women are the initiators of the vast majority of separations, we can see that single parentage is oft more present due to the woman's decision than that of the man. The more sexual partners, the earlier in life, the more likelihood a woman will divorce after five years of marriage. "a virgin has 5% chance of divorce after five years of marriage... two previous partners has a 30% chance of divorce... 10 partners... 35% chance of divorce."[238] Divorce thus has direct correlations not only to female sexual history, but to fatherless homes.

"Boys raised in a single-mother household have disproportionately higher crime rates and mental health issues. 73% of adolescent murderers grew up without a father. 85% of adolescents with behavioral issues originate from fatherless homes, while 85% of youths in prisons grew up in fatherless homes... I couldn't find one news article about how boys like Nikolas (Cruz, high-school shooter) need a father growing up. Or, how 26 of the last 27 school shooters came from fatherless homes. Toxic masculinity isn't the problem – a lack of masculinity is."

-Richard Cooper, The Unplugged Alpha[239]

Marriage is sacred, the formal bonding of sexes in societies that allows for structure in communities for the care and upbringing of children, the organization of clans, and the distinguishing of various spaces for use by different families and groups. Concurrently, the act of marriage is potentially one of the most detrimental social designs in the world. Today's marriages are averaged at 8 years before the parties are divorced. Not only does this show the complete disregard for vows, but a disregard for the effort it takes to maintain positive relations, as well as the inability for the general population to make long-lasting positive choices. Almost 50 percent of marriages end in divorce. I do not support the idea of only single parents raising children, but I do support communities raising children. Large families and strong local communities are the best foundation for children. At the same time, marriage is unnecessary and only required by social conditioning. The ability for two people to collaborate positively in the raising of a child without binding themselves to marriage relieves the pressures associated with marriage and allows for a matured form of social relations. People who wish to be together because they enjoy each other's company for however long they desire is not inhibited by removing marriage from the equation. The ability to maintain positive relations after a separation of parents is extremely important for the child and even better is the ability of the parents to continue to share the parental duties and even work to live in a coordinated way to share the burdens and rewards of child raising. The ownership of our intimate partners through marriage or other attachments is fundamentally destructive. Rather, we need to understand that raising a child is a responsibility and a gift. Having an intimate relationship is the same, and it must reflect the honest and clear agreements made between the individuals. Today, we have the means to prevent most unintended pregnancies, with condoms and other methods of prevention. This has allowed for the rise of female promiscuity without the accompanying threat of pregnancy. It is important to realize the effect that this has had on our society and its fundamental principles and its structure.

"Feminism preaches radically leftist political views that fight for unlimited free abortion, elevate single mothers on a pedestal, and claim that masculinity is "Toxic." Feminists hate it when the state imposes limits on abortion and tries to force them to be mothers. However, they more than happily use State family law to force men to be fathers. Feminism teaches women to vote for the welfare state, massive government handouts, huge tax rates on top income earners, and social programs that widely benefit a female primary social order. A feminist will never appreciate you or value you as a man. Feminism teaches women to be victims, and anyone with a victim mindset can't find happiness. Today's version of feminism is so toxic that it is anti-femininity. It encourages women to hate men, while simultaneously encouraging them to behave like men and that they should ditch the notion of motherhood to prioritize their careers. Feminism doesn't seek to make women better, or more feminine. Feminism seeks to make woman into terrible versions of men."

-Richard Cooper, The Unplugged Alpha[240]

What I call the biological imperative is that which guides men and women to behave along evolved and fundamentally integrated parameters of interaction. This biological imperative is the feminine drive to produce offspring when there is environmental abundance that would naturally serve the offspring in its efforts to survive. Women are far less likely to produce offspring or have the urge to do so in a scarce environment with little opportunity for offspring to survive. Interestingly it is the poverty stricken of the world that produce more offspring. This is not in opposition to the biological imperative, but rather is a notable example of it in action. The poverty stricken utilize the larger family to produce more income and to create a larger pool from which to draw resources, and to increase the familial generational success. Those who are not concerned about security and scarcity have less than 3 and often no children, as they are less in need of the structure and resource acquisition. The feminine drive to produce offspring today is skewed drastically due to a false sense of abundance and security provided by credit and the fiat currency of the FED and the promises of the religious entity called the United States government. This security is temporary, but the feminine drive to produce offspring is satisfied in the current forecast of clear skies ahead being signaled by those driving the chattel toward the cliff.

The male biological imperative is quite simply to plant his seed far and wide. It is the drive to increase himself and to deliver as wide a net of insemination as possible in one life. However, that may strike you, the fact is that men are limited in their biological imperative by the feminine biological imperative, not to mention the social constructs that people choose to live within. It is the feminine that rules sex, it is the masculine that rules the relationship. The feminine biological imperative structures the way the mating ritual and timing must be adhered to for the benefit of the species. It is the male biological imperative that provides the fertilization and attempts to do so with as much gusto and efficiency as possible. Men are serving the species by being present in the vicinity of a vagina at the very moment the feminine biological imperative calls for fertilization of an egg. Everything after that moment has to do with being guided by the masculine structure and empowered by the abundant feminine energy.

I think it's time we accept the fact that we are orgiastic, carnal, and barbaric (from the perspective of respectable societal notions of modern "civilized" people) and relieve ourselves of the guilt and shame that has been indoctrinated like a thorn deeply into the psyche of humanity globally and has everything to do with control and very little to do with righteous behavior for the sake of one god or another. We can eat with forks and fuck like bonobos, or stick our face in a bowl like a dog and make love in missionary, but would you rather be conditioned to be a slave to doubts, fears, shames, confusions and guilts that don't even originate in your own experiences but in a religious doctrine hundreds or thousands of years old, or would you prefer a liberated experience of life that allows you to explore your most carnal urges with sophistication and clarity and sincerity. Each to their own, and as Sadhguru says, why should it matter to anyone what someone else does in the bedroom or the bathroom. Just remember that you are the one who must be responsible to yourself, and your everlasting soul.

It is more than a simple desire for equity that makes for true justice for all people, but a necessity for our species to evolve and become greater than our collective past. There can be no functional society based on the idea that everyone gets the same amount of anything, for some people require more or less of any given thing. The greatest efforts must be placed upon the recognition of how disparity is formed, the eradication of life-threatening disparity, and the cultivation of practices that promote abundance and equity for all people. We must remember that individuals are responsible for their lives, and despite any environmental factors, it is ultimately an individual who decides to bear great challenges to be free, or to wither under unjust systems. Today's world is at its greatest time of peace in recorded history, with more equity for individuals across the entire species. While that is true, much of the population is devoted to and emotionally invested in detrimental actions for the sake of "equality" that only create more separation, fear, and hate in the world. We must work together, not against each other. This message is an eternal Truth and needs no examples to defend it. All those who work to divide people are in opposition to enhancing the quality of life of our species. Let our male and female union become whole again. Let it become holy again. Let it be natural again.

Firearm Ownership

"Firearms stand next to the constitution itself. They are the American people's liberty teeth and keystone under independence. To ensure peace, security, and happiness, the rifle and pistol are equally indispensable. The very atmosphere of firearms everywhere restrains evil interference – they deserve a place of honor with all that is good."

-George Washington

There are three steps concerning firearms historically appreciable to genocide committed by government. The first is firearms registration. The second is disarmament through law and police power. The third is the corralling or otherwise distinguishing target unarmed populations.

In 1911, the Turkish government banned ownership or manufacture of firearms without their approval. From 1915 to 1917, the Turkish government massacred 1,150,000 disarmed Armenians. In 1918, the Bolsheviks in the Soviet Union passed a firearms and ammunition registration law. Within three months, the government revoked registration certificates and banned ownership of firearms. By 1929, the population was totally disarmed. Over 50,000,000, a modest estimate, people died as a result of being unable to defend themselves from their government. All firearms were confiscated in Germany in 1919. In 1928, a permitting system was created allowing firearms manufacture, sale purchase and ownership. This created lists in the government of all people owning firearms in Germany. These lists made it exceedingly simple for the Nazi government to disarm the populations and individuals they discriminated against, such as the Jews. In 1938, the government banned all private ownership of firearms. Exempted from this ban, were police, military, SA, and SS. Over 15,000,000 people were slaughtered due directly to their inability to defend themselves after accepting and complying with disarmament. In 1957, the Chinese government banned manufacture, sale, purchase, and ownership of firearms. As many as 80,000,000 people were butchered after their firearms were stolen by their government. In 1970, the Ugandan government passed a law requiring government licensure to purchase or possess firearms. Government officials in each district were authorized to deny or cancel licenses without reason. Starting in 1971, the Ugandan military and secret police, amounting to 28,000 people, killed 300,000 disarmed Ugandans, and maintained their oppression on 13 million others. In 1938, in Cambodia, the Royal order forced gun control on the population. That law remained in effect even after the Cambodian independence. After 1970, the Khmer Rouge took power, and began massacring the disarmed population. The total killed was around 2,500,000 people.[241]

"...when a citizen reaches the point where Resistance appears better than continued oppression, when fear of the government no longer outweighs the determination to throw off the shackles, the spark of revolution is struck. Whether the spark dies out, or instead starts a flame, depends on other circumstances."

-Joseph P. Martino[242]

"The actual trigger for the War of Independence was the British attempt to prevent war by disarming the Americans. After first confiscating all the privately held guns in Boston, and confiscating all the gunpowder stored in Boston's powderhouses, the British attempted to seize guns, cannon and powder in the rural areas around Boston. The troops sent to do this met with initial success, easily defeating the militia forces they encountered. However, the British attempt to make an orderly withdrawal to Boston turned into disaster, as they had to fight almost every foot of the way. The Americans laid siege to Boston... fortified Breeds and Bunker hills... Each attack (by the British) was beaten off until the Americans ran out of ammunition."[243] In the next 7 years of war, out of all British deaths and casualties, an eighth of all officer deaths and a sixth of wounds occurred at Bunker Hill.

"Every survivor of every genocide says the same thing: when they come to take your guns, shoot them!... If you give up your arms, you are placing your entire trust in the permanent future benevolence of the U.S. government. This trust is invariably fatal: ask the American Indians about those sacred treaties that they were guaranteed forever."

-Matthew Bracken, The Bracken Collection[244]

Gun ownership isn't limited to the moral compass of a government but must rest in the discriminatory powers of the individual. Of course, there are people that much of society would not want to have a firearm, but it is those people that will acquire firearms regardless of legal barriers. They would not be stopped by a law, so who in the end is being registered and barred from owning a firearm? It happens to be the very people who are the warrior-citizens that guard against these violent and dangerous aggressors. The ability to acquire firearms illegally is not difficult for criminals, but the ability to get a legal firearm for a person who wishes to be able to defend themselves or likes to shoot at ranges and competitions for sport, and those who collect, is limited by a stringent background check called the "National Instant Criminal Background Check System" or "NICS". Through NICS, even the smallest legal discrepancies can deny you from "legally" exercising your constitutional right to carry arms. But gangs don't get their weapons by passing NICS. They get their firearms through the black market. So, it doesn't seem too smart to force registration and restrictions on the population when the criminals are able to acquire firearms despite the laws.

Even if there are those who pass NICS and still commit crimes, would you really want to be unarmed in a nation where only those people who are intent upon the misuse of firearms are the ones to have them? It is not reasonable or intelligent to claim that government agents, such as police, should be the only ones armed, and that they are there to protect you. By the time police arrive to the scene, the person who used a firearm against you has disappeared into the night. In fact, you were probably dead before you could pick up the phone. So now it's up to your neighbors, who may or may not have heard the altercation. Would you trust the police to be there on the scene the moment the bad guy crossed your doorway into your home? Would you be so imbecilic as to leave yourself and your family indefensible? There is no argument against firearm ownership that can hold water against this obvious and unchanging fact. That it is the RIGHT of the person to bear arms for their own purposes, especially to defend themselves from harm and to secure their home, their family, and their society from harm. If the population is armed to the teeth, the bad guys are not going to find it very easy to get away with murder and theft and so on. Every day, this is proven true, as armed, and responsible people around the country use firearms to protect themselves and others from harm.

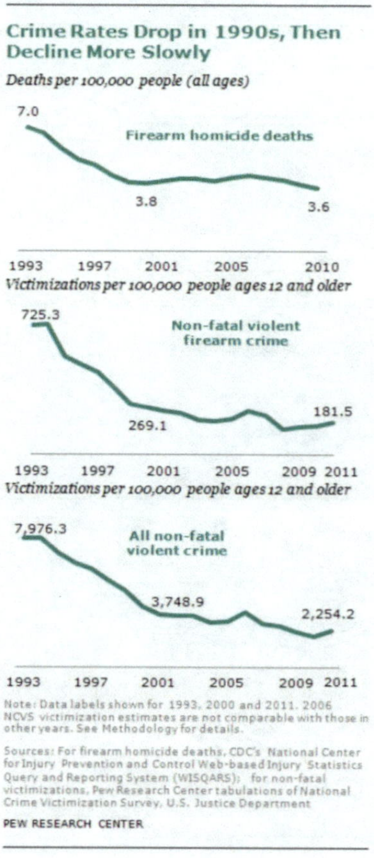

"No slave shall keep any arms whatever, nor pass, unless with written orders from his master or employer, or in his company, with arms from one place to another. Arms in possession of a slave contrary to this prohibition shall be forfeited to him who will seize them."

-A Bill Concerning Slaves, Virginia Assembly, 1779

If you find yourself thinking that the world would be great if nobody owned guns, remember that just because you would wish it so, does not mean that others would also. While you may want guns to be abolished, others will not agree to that, and they would now be the only ones to have guns. Who are those people? They are government agents, criminals, and freedom loving people who refuse to follow unjust and stupid laws. But while they all have the means to defend themselves, or in the government agent and the criminal's case, to commit violence on others with impunity, it is you the unarmed and defenseless lamb that will be left to the grace of the wolves. Also remember that to a wolf, a lamb looks like food and nothing else. A defenseless population looks like chattel to government, and soft targets to criminals.

"In 2020, the annual gun death rate was 12.2 deaths per 100,000 people. Yet, in 1974, we had a gun death rate of 16.3 per 100,000 people. Someone want to explain to me how we have a gun violence epidemic when we've seen the largest number of gun purchases in history over the last two years, but our annual gun death rate in 2020 is substantially lower than it was in the 1970's? Ill tell you how. Because the phrase epidemic of gun violence is horseshit. It's an emotional ploy to get you to believe that the gun violence is so bad, we must resort to extreme measures to make it go down... 30-40,000 people die from gun deaths every year. And every year, 60-65 percent of those deaths are from suicides and nearly 80 percent of gun homicides are due to drug and gang violence. We have over 400 million guns in this country with over 300 million people with less than one percent of the population being murdered by someone with a gun. That is not an epidemic. In 2021, the U.S. didn't even rank in the top 10 countries for firearm related homicides and we have more in the hands of citizens than any other country in the world. I don't want anyone to die, whether it be from a gun, a knife, a car, or hand, or feet, but I also don't want to be left defenseless because people keep voting to give up our rights for a false sense of safety, or in some feeble attempt to assuage their social justice warrior guilt brought on by politicians who manipulate people's emotions."

-Colion Noir

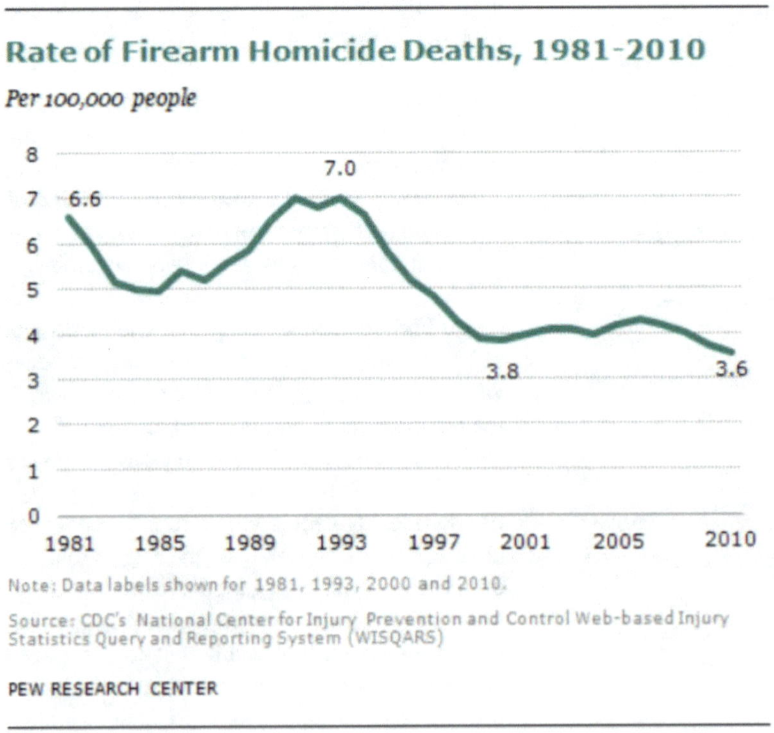

U.S. gun death rates varied widely by state in 2017

Age-adjusted gun death rate per 100,000 people, by state

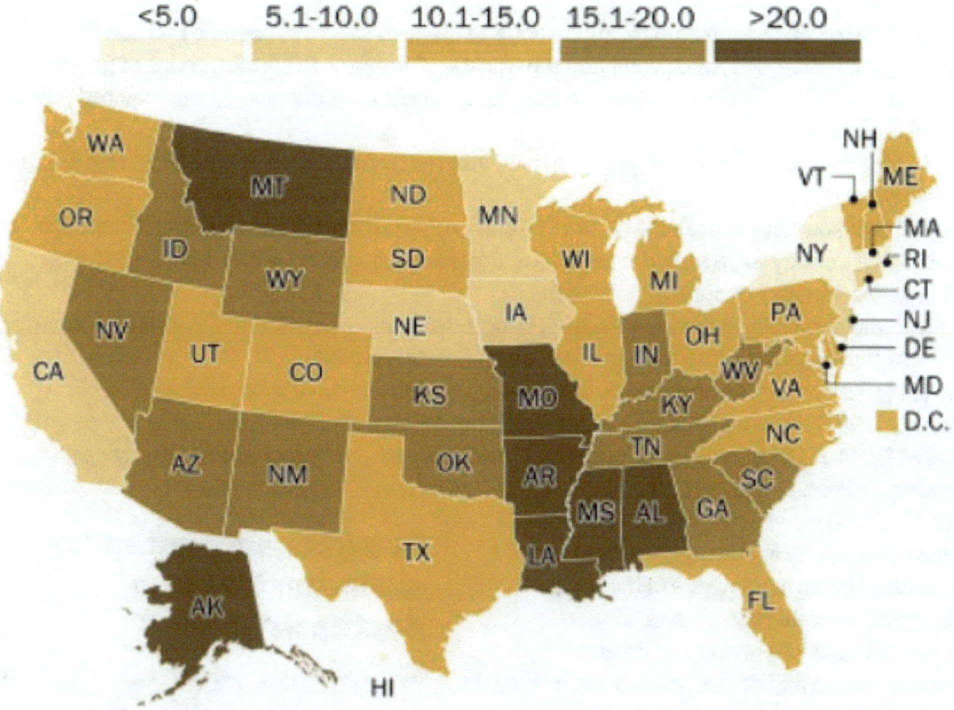

Note: Includes suicides, murders and deaths that were unintentional, involved law enforcement or had undetermined circumstances.
Source: Centers for Disease Control and Prevention.

PEW RESEARCH CENTER

Looking at this point in particular, that we had more gun deaths in 1974 than we did in 2020, we can see that all of the firearm restricting laws have not had a correlating effect on the amount of firearm related deaths. A full list of federal firearms laws include the National Firearms Act of 1934, the Federal Firearms Act of 1938, the Omnibus Crime Control and Safe Streets Act of 1968, the Gun Control Act of 1968, the Firearm Owners Protection Act of 1986, the Undetectable Firearms

Act of 1988, the Gun-Free School Zones Act of 1990, the Brady Handgun Violence Prevention Act of 1993, the Federal Assault Weapons Ban of (1994-2004), the Law Enforcement Officers Safety Act of 2004, and the Protection of Lawful Commerce in Arms Act of 2005.

- NFA (1934) made firearms manufacture and transfer taxable and forced registration of Title II weapons.
- FFA (1938) forced manufacturers, importers, and firearms sellers to become licensed (Federal Firearms License or FFL) and prohibited the transfer of firearms to certain groups of people.
- Omnibus... (1968) prohibited interstate transfer of handguns and made 21 the required age to purchase a handgun.
- GCA (1968) regulated interstate commerce in firearms by prohibiting private interstate firearms transfers.
- FOPA (1986) partially repealed GCA of 1968 and prohibited the sale of automatic firearms to civilians when they were manufactured after the laws passage, as well as required ATF approval of firearms transfers of automatic firearms.
- UFA (1988) criminalized the manufacture, import, sale, shipment, delivery, possession, transfer, or receipt of firearms with less than 3.7 ounces of metal content.
- GFSZA (1990) prohibited individuals from possessing a firearm in a school zone.
- Brady... (1993) required background checks on the purchasers of firearms.
- FAWB (1994-2004) banned semi-autos that looked like assault weapons and large capacity feeding devices. Expired in 2004.
- LEOSA (2004) granted former and current law enforcement officers the right to carry a concealed firearm anywhere in the USA, regardless of state or local laws.
- Protection... (2005) prevented firearms manufacturers and dealers from being held liable for the actions of the purchasers of their products.

Suicides accounted for six-in-ten U.S. gun deaths in 2017

% of U.S. gun deaths, by type

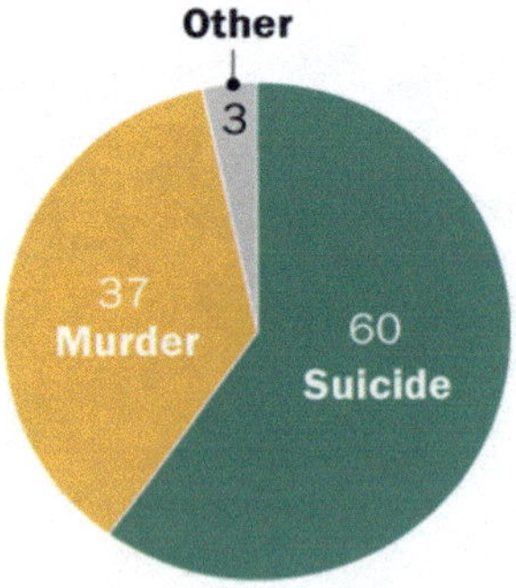

Note: "Other" includes gun deaths that were unintentional, involved law enforcement or had undetermined circumstances.
Source: Centers for Disease Control and Prevention.

PEW RESEARCH CENTER

As we can see from this information, the background checks did not decrease the amount of firearms related deaths. Nor did the semi-auto ban, nor the fact that LEO's can carry concealed anywhere in the country. Interesting. What the Brady Law *did* do, was make private purchasers have to beg their government to allow them to act upon their constitutional Right to bear arms. The argument is often made that the government does not stop people from owning a firearm, it just regulates it so it doesn't get into the hands of criminals, which is preposterous and stupid. The regulation of firearms, which results in the denial of Rights, affects the non-criminal population, rather than the criminals, who would never think to go through a federal background check to purchase a firearm they are going to be committing illegal acts with. The exception here is the examples of shootings happening in public places in which the murderer plans to commit suicide. In this case, a background check may not stop him from purchasing a firearm, which indicates a further failure of the background check system.

Let's consider the fact that much of the felonies that have been committed by individuals has been related to growing cannabis or selling cannabis, both of which are harmless actions, that are treated like they were violent criminals. In fact, many people who have committed murder and rape, have received less punishment than a person who has grown a field of cannabis. Today the cannabis laws are changing, but there are a significant population of people who have felonies from this and many other victimless "offenses" that will never be able to purchase a firearm from a dealer because they are forced to undergo an unconstitutional background check.

"The constitution shall never be construed to prevent the people of the United States, who are peaceable citizens, from keeping their own arms."
- Samuel Adams, Mass. Ratifying Convention 1788

When does the Right to bear arms become the privilege to carry open or concealed, or have a certain number of bullets stored in your private home, or have an Armalite Rifle or a Glock, or have a thousand firearms or a single short barrel shotgun? It is certainly not the Right of the government to infringe upon my ability to defend myself from them or any other entity or person who wields power and has shown little regard for my freedom and my wellbeing in the past. The government has never done anything for me that would engender my respect or love. The people of this society have been the movers and shakers that have led to our successes and our failures. It is the broken backs of miners that have given us our immense energy, and the factory line workers that have given us automotive excellence, and the scientists that have given us satellite imagery, and the hunters and outdoorsmen that have given us many of our environmental protections against corporate abuse, and the hippies in the 60's that gave us free love, and the authors that have given us ever increasing knowledge, and the investigative reporters who have given us insight into the actual happenings within our government and its corporate co-conspirators.

Today, there are over 300 federal gun laws, and over 20,000 state gun laws. If 40,000 people died this year from some gun related event, which is the high end of the average that is toted today, that would amount to all of .01% of the population. Of the 40,000, about 30,000 are suicides, over 1500 are law enforcement shootings, and around 9000 are murders. So, if we discount the suicides, the amount of gun deaths in this country, using that 40,000 high average, is actually about .0025. About a quarter of all these murders occur in Chicago, Baltimore, Detroit, and Washington D.C. which all contain large populations of poverty-stricken people in particular areas, where gangs run rampant, who are the perpetrators of the vast majority of gun violence and violence by any other type.

There were about 2.8 million deaths in the US in 2019. That is 869.7 deaths per 100,000 people. Firearm related deaths account for 1 in 70 of those deaths. Murders accounted for 1 in 280 of those deaths. Interestingly, there is a direct divergence between homicides and suicides when correlated to age. Between 12 and 21, there is a steep increase in gun violence, but from 21 onward, the use of guns for homicide falls almost equally as rapidly, but suicides see an increase as age increases. At its highest, where the actor is 21, homicides account for 11 per 100,000 deaths, but that number falls to 4 per 100,000 at the age of 44. Suicides increase from 0 per 100,000 at age 6 to 14 per 100,000 at around 80 years of age.[245]

This shows, regarding firearms, that suicide rates are more relative to higher age groups, while homicides are relative to, mostly, those in their early 20's. As most of these homicides are occurring in inner cities and are a result of extreme poverty that results in more gang activity, we can see that it is not a gun violence issue that we are facing, but rather a socio-economic issue, that is affecting the people who are most subjected to manipulated scarcity and apathy by their plutocratic government. The suicides are more likely to occur, on the other hand, in rural settings, and affect the rural white male population the most. While some may call this a mental health issue, I would call it by the same name as the problem in inner cities,

which is a socio-economic problem. They are problems that are being approached in different ways by separate social groups. "At ages 20-29 in 2012, the firearm homicide rate for black males was at least five times higher than that for Hispanic males and at least 20 times that for white males... At ages 85 and older, the firearm suicide rate for White males was 3.2 times that for Hispanic males and 5.0 times that for Black Males... Beginning at ages 60-64, more than 90% of deaths... occur among white males."[246]
Alabama, Mississippi, and Louisiana have the most homicides per 100,000 people, but Montana, Alaska, and Idaho have the largest number of suicides. In Wintemute's summary of the cited report above, he says that suicides are increasing, which is focused in white rural males, but homicides are actually decreasing, which is focused in urban black males. In his final point, he mentions that the United States has low rates of assaultive violence though high rates of mortality and suicide when compared with other industrialized nations.
The problem with comparisons made between the United States and other nations is that our Right to bear arms was affirmed in the most fundamental laws of the nation at its founding. This Right was affirmed because the authors of the constitution agreed that it is ultimately the people that are authorized to and righteous in determining the nature of their government, and due to the fact that governments are often tyrannical and oppressive or become so through attrition, it is the solemn and sacred duty of the people to remain well provisioned and armed to be able to demand and apply force upon the government to change it to serve the people. In this endeavor, it is the people who are most appropriately the bearers of firearms and the means of manufacture of such. It is the people themselves who ought to determine what is correct for their own defense *and* what is correct for their practice, sport, and collecting hobbies. It is not the government that can determine to what degree we can exercise our Right, but only to uphold the Rights that we have against tyrants. The government itself is the tyrant, the plutocratic, over-fed, power-crazed and inappropriate force the lowers nooses around innocent heads.

"The most foolish mistake we could possibly make would be to allow the subject races to possess arms. History shows that all conquerors who have allowed their subject races to carry arms have prepared their own downfall by so doing."
-Adolf Hitler

We have a massive psychological operation in play currently to disarm the population of the United States, starting with registering and itemizing firearms owners and their possessions, and resulting in forced gun buy-backs and bans, which ultimately takes the power from the people. Hospital errors are causing 7 times the amount of death in this country than firearms, but nobody is screaming at hospitals on CNN and FOX, demanding the government take absolute measures to stop this from happening. Vehicular accidents aren't resulting in the demand from anyone that cars be banned, even though they cause more death than firearms. Nobody is freaking out about the obesity that has grown extraordinarily, and its causes such as Coca-Cola and McDonalds. Where is the outrage over the fact that our military was used to murder millions of people in Iraq and elsewhere in the last 20 years? Where is the social uproar over the smart meters and microwave technology that is proven to cause cancer, and the fact that 50% of the population of the United States will get cancer in their lifetimes?
We need to educate the population on what is really at stake, because the plutocrat owned media certainly isn't going to do it. The government isn't going to serve the population. The banks aren't going to fund social programs that actually work for those people who need the credit the most. The people in the inner cities won't break their patterns until the way forward isn't fogged by government tight ropes. The rural men who see their farms going to ruin under the automated tractors of big agriculture corporations and see their traditional values being decimated by politically correct dictators aren't going to free themselves from depression until they see some solidarity and real progress. So, get your shit together people, and recognize who the real enemy is.

"...for decades we had lived inside an increasingly delicate techno-bubble, floating ever higher on digital money created from thin air, and we believed it was all as permanent as the pyramids!... I considered it a massive conceit by modern man to denigrate as backward the long-lasting civilizations that had flourished before electricity, electronic gadgets, wireless devices, and computers. Earlier generations had built great cathedrals, universities, and defensible walled cities on the surplus bounty of the nearby lands and the manual labor of the local folk. Buildings that have stood through the centuries, monuments to the past. Modern man built illusions of wealth instead. In the end, the glittering high-definition wall screens were just dream merchants, presenting the convincing chimera of a perpetual cornucopia."

-Matthew Bracken, The Bracken Collection[247]

"What we are witnessing today is nothing short of a war against the American citizenry waged by a run-away government hyped up on its own power... For those who can read the writing on the wall, it's all starting to make sense: the military drills carried out in major American cities, the VIPR inspections at train depots and bus stations, the SWAT team raids on unsuspecting homeowners, the Black Hawk helicopters patrolling American skies, the massive ammunition purchases by various federal agencies such as the Department of Homeland Security, the Department of Education, the IRS, and the Social Security Administration, the overcriminalization, the growth in private prisons, and the endless surveillance. Viewed in conjunction with the government's increasing use of involuntary commitment laws to declare individuals mentally ill and lock them up in psychiatric wards for extended periods of time, the National Defense Authorization Act's (NDAA) provision allowing the military to lock up "detainees"—that is, American citizens—who might be deemed extremists or terrorists (the government likes to use these words interchangeably) for criticizing the government only codifies this unraveling of our constitutional framework. The building blocks are already in place for such an eventuality: the surveillance networks, fusion centers, and government contractors already monitor what is being said by whom; government databases track who poses a potential threat to the government's power; the militarized police, working in conjunction with federal agencies, coordinate with the federal government when it's time to round up the troublemakers; the courts sanction the government's methods, no matter how unlawful; and the detention facilities, whether private prisons or FEMA internment camps, lock up the troublemakers. Throw in the profit-driven corporate incentive to jail Americans in private prisons, as well as the criminalizing of such relatively innocent activities as holding Bible studies in one's home or sharing unpasteurized goat cheese with members of one's community, and it becomes clear that 'we the people' have become enemies of the state. Thus, it's no longer a question of whether *the government will lock up Americans for First Amendment activity but* when. *(It's particularly telling that the government's lawyers, when pressed in federal court for an assurance that those exercising their First Amendment rights in order to criticize the government would* not *be targeted under the NDAA, refused to provide one.)...*
...If government officials can fine and arrest you for growing vegetables in your front yard, installing solar panels on your roof, and raising chickens in your backyard, you're no longer the owner of your property. If school officials can punish your children for what they do or say while at home or in your care, your children are not your own—they are the property of the state. If government agents can invade your home, break down your doors, kill your dog, damage your furnishings, and terrorize your family, your property is no longer private

and secure—it belongs to the government. Likewise, if police can forcefully draw your blood, strip search you, and probe you intimately, your body is no longer your own, either."
– John Whitehead[248]

THEORY AND METHODOLOGY BEHIND A POSSIBLE MILITARISTIC TAKEOVER OF THE NATION

People today idolize the idea of dystopic realities. From zombies to pandemics to nuclear war. The idea grips many people, though in different ways. Some people fear it while others crave it. Some may say, it is only those who have seen war, who have truly known its horrors, are those who are prudent enough to avoid it at all costs. I do not think this is correct. There are many who thrive in the conditions that exist in the chaos of war. They are the minority though. Most people will avoid the actuality of war, even if it means that the result of their avoidance leads to that very thing. We are now being set up for the civil unrest and war. When everyone, or sizable portions, are fully reliant for survival on government welfare checks they forget how to take care of themselves. They become children of the state. As the government indebts itself further and further, it snares the people into that debt. The country will eventually be unable to maintain the current financial system. The government financial "solution" will be a new digital currency, in which all people will be overtly owned by the plutocracy. This is just one example of the potential trials that are currently in the works in the United States and globally.

"Single acts of tyranny may be ascribed to the accidental opinion of a day; but a series of oppressions, begun at a distinguished period, and pursued unalterably through every change of ministers, too plainly prove a deliberate systematical plan of reducing us to slavery."
– Thomas Jefferson

"When in the course of human events, it becomes necessary for one people to dissolve the political bands which have connected them with another, and to assume, among the powers of the earth, the separate and equal station to which the laws of nature and of nature's God entitle them, a decent respect to the opinions of mankind requires that they should declare the causes which impel them to the separation.
We hold these truths to be self-evident, that all men are created equal, that they are endowed by their Creator with certain unalienable rights, that among these are life, liberty, and the pursuit of happiness. That, to secure these rights, governments are instituted among men, deriving their just powers from the consent of the governed. That, whenever any form of government becomes destructive of these ends, it is the right of the people to alter or to abolish it, and to institute new government, laying its foundation on such principles, and organizing its powers in such form, as to them shall seem most likely to effect their safety and happiness.
Prudence, indeed, will dictate that governments long established should not be changed for light and transient causes; and, accordingly, all experience has shown, that mankind are more disposed to suffer, while evils are sufferable that to right themselves by abolishing the forms to which they are accustomed.
But, when a long train of abuses and usurpations, pursuing invariably that same object, evinces a design to reduce them under absolute despotism, it is their right, it is their duty, to throw off such government, and to provide new guards for their future security. Such has been the patient sufferance of these colonies.; and such is now the necessity which constrains them to alter their former systems of government. The

history of the present King of Great Britain is a history of repeated injuries and usurpations, all having in direct object the establishment of an absolute tyranny over these states. To prove this, let facts be submitted to a candid world."
He has refused his assent to laws the most wholesome and necessary for the public good.
He has forbidden his governors to pass laws of immediate and pressing importance, unless suspended in their operation till his assent should be obtained; and when so suspended, he has utterly neglected to attend to them.
He has refused to pass other laws for the accommodation of large districts of people, unless those people would relinquish the right of representation in the legislature; a right inestimable to them and formidable to tyrants only.
He has called together legislative bodies at places unusual, uncomfortable, and distant from the depository of their public records, for the sole purpose of fatiguing them into compliance with his measures.
He has dissolved representative houses repeatedly, for opposing, with manly firmness, his invasions on the rights of the people.
He has refused for a long time, after such dissolutions, to cause others to be elected; whereby the legislative powers, incapable of annihilation, have returned to the people at large for their exercise; the state remaining in the meantime exposed to all the dangers of invasion from without, and convulsions within.
He has endeavored to prevent the population of these states; for that purpose obstructing the laws for naturalization of foreigners; refusing to pass others to encourage their migrations hither, and raising the conditions of new appropriations of lands.
He has obstructed the administration of justice, by refusing his assent to laws for establishing judiciary powers.
He has made judges dependent on his will alone, for the tenure of their offices, and the amount and payment of their salaries.
He has erected a multitude of new offices, and sent hither swarms of officers to harass our people, and eat out their substance.
He has kept among us, in times of peace, standing armies, without the consent of our legislatures.
He has affected to render the military independent of and superior to the civil power.
He has combined with others to subject us to a jurisdiction foreign to our constitution, and unacknowledged by our laws; giving his assent to their acts of pretended legislation:
For quartering large bodies of armed troops among us;
For protecting them, by a mock trial, from punishment for any murders which they should commit on the inhabitants of these states;
For cutting off our trade with all parts of the world;
For imposing taxes on us without our consent;
For depriving us, in many cases, of the benefits of trial by jury;
For transporting us beyond seas to be tried for pretended offenses;
For abolishing the free system of English laws in a neighboring province, establishing therein an arbitrary government, and enlarging its boundaries, so as to render it at once an example and fit instrument for introducing the same absolute rule into these colonies;
For taking away our charters, abolishing our most valuable laws, and altering fundamentally the forms of our governments;
For suspending our own legislatures, and declaring themselves invested with power to legislate for us in all cases whatsoever.
He has abdicated government here, by declaring us out of his protection, and waging war against us.

He has plundered our seas, ravaged our coasts, burnt our towns, and destroyed the lives of our people.
He is at this time transporting large armies of foreign mercenaries to complete the works of death, desolation, and tyranny, already begun with circumstances of cruelty and perfidy scarcely paralleled in the most barbarous ages, and totally unworthy the head of a civilized nation.
He has constrained our fellow citizens, taken captive on the high seas, to bear arms against their country, to become the executioners of their friends and brethren, or to fall themselves by their hands.
He has excited domestic insurrections amongst us, and has endeavored to bring on the inhabitants of our frontiers, the merciless Indian savages, whose known rule of warfare is an undistinguished destruction of all ages, sexes, and conditions.
In every stage of these oppressions, we have petitioned for redress, in the most humble terms. Our repeated petitions have been answered only by repeated injury. A prince, whose character is thus marked by every act which may define a tyrant, is unfit to be the ruler of a free people.
Nor have we been wanting in attentions to our British brethren. We have warned them from time to time of attempts by their legislature to extend an unwarrantable jurisdiction over us. We have reminded them of the circumstances of our emigration and settlement here. We have appealed to their native justice and magnanimity, and we have conjured them by the ties of our common kindred, to disavow these usurpations, which would inevitably interrupt our connections and correspondence. They too have been deaf to the voice of justice and of consanguinity. We must, therefore, acquiesce in the necessity, which denounces our separation, and hold them, as we hold the rest of mankind, enemies in war, in peace friends.
We, therefore, the representatives of the United States of America, in General Congress assembled, appealing to the Supreme Judge of the world for the rectitude of our intentions, do, in the name, and by authority of the good people of these colonies, solemnly publish and declare, that these United Colonies are, and of right ought to be free and independent states; that they are absolved from all allegiance to the British Crown, and that all political connection between them and the state of Great Britain is and ought to be totally dissolved; and that, as free and independent states, they have full power to levy war, conclude peace, contract alliances, establish commerce, and to do all other acts and things which independent states may of right do. And for the support of this declaration, with a firm reliance on the protection of Divine Providence, we mutually pledge to each other our lives, our fortunes, and our sacred honor.

If we but change the names out, we can see much of this applies directly today. I will give a representative example of how closely our reasons for violent separation from Britain in the 18th century has direct and obvious links to the reasoning for separating, or preferably dissolving, the United States of today.

When in the course of human events, it becomes necessary for one people to dissolve the political bands which have connected them with another, and to assume, among the powers of the earth, the separate and equal station to which the laws of nature and of nature's God entitle them, a decent respect to the opinions of mankind requires that they should declare the causes which impel them to the separation.
We hold these truths to be self-evident, that all men are created equal, that they are endowed by their Creator with certain unalienable rights, that among these are life, liberty, and the pursuit of happiness. That, to secure these rights, governments are instituted among men, deriving their just powers from the consent of the governed. That, whenever any form of government becomes destructive of these ends, it is the right of the people to

alter or to abolish it, and to institute new government, laying its foundation on such principles, and organizing its powers in such form, as to them shall seem most likely to effect their safety and happiness.

Prudence, indeed, will dictate that governments long established should not be changed for light and transient causes; and, accordingly, all experience has shown, that mankind are more disposed to suffer, while evils are sufferable that to right themselves by abolishing the forms to which they are accustomed.

But, when a long train of abuses and usurpations, pursuing invariably that same object, evinces a design to reduce them under absolute despotism, it is their right, it is their duty, to throw off such government, and to provide new guards for their future security. Such has been the patient sufferance of these people.; and such is now the necessity which constrains them to alter their former systems of government. The history of the present United States of America is a history of repeated injuries and usurpations, all having in direct object the establishment of an absolute tyranny over these people. To prove this, let facts be submitted to a candid world.

It has refused its assent to laws the most wholesome and necessary for the public good.

It has erected a multitude of offices, and sent hither swarms of officers to harass our people, and eat out their substance.

It has combined with others to subject us to a jurisdiction foreign to our constitution, and unacknowledged by our laws; giving its assent to their acts of pretended legislation:

For favoring police, political, corporate and military criminality;

For protecting them, by a mock trial, from punishment for any murders and thefts which they should commit on the inhabitants of these states or other states in the name of the people;

For imposing taxes on us without our consent and in direct opposition and abhorrence to the Constitution;

For ignoring our rights, violating our most valuable laws, and altering fundamentally the forms of our governments;

It has excited domestic terrorism, and class warfare through contrived social distinctions, to serve its own plutocratic goals and to make itself ever more powerful and the population ever more servile and dependent.

It has incited and planned numerous unjust wars, that have caused suffering and death around the world, and created a detrimental perception of the people of these states.

In every stage of these oppressions, we have petitioned for redress, in the most humble terms. Our repeated petitions have been answered only by repeated injury. A government, whose character is thus marked by every act which may define a tyrant, is unfit to be the ruler of a free people.

We, therefore, the free people of our own domain, appealing to the Supreme Judge of the world for the rectitude of our intentions, do, in the name, and by our own authority, solemnly publish and declare, that this land is, and of right ought to be free and independent states of the type and under the discretion of local populations; that they are absolved from all allegiance to the United States of America, and that all political connection between them and the state of the United States of America is and ought to be totally dissolved; and that, as free and independent people, they have full power to levy war, conclude peace, contract alliances, establish commerce, and to do all other acts and things which independent people may of right do. And for the support of this declaration, with a firm reliance on the protection of Divine Providence, we mutually pledge to each other our lives, our fortunes, and our sacred honor.

It is upon this land that we make our homes. It upon these lands that our children will build theirs. What kind of lives do we want for our children? Do we wish upon them slavery and injustice? Do we harbor such self-loathing that we are willing to doom our progeny? Why then do we abase ourselves with obsequiousness to a tyrannical, plutocratic, horde of highway robbers and thugs. You can't make a tumor beautiful by dressing it in a suit, so why would we think such imbecilic notions about our offensive and corrupt political and economic leaders? There is no crime more heinous than a leader who cares not for his followers and uses them for personal gain. It is what leads all societies to their eventual doom, unless those societies learn to overcome their limitations and become adaptive, involved, courageous and inquisitive. There is no crime more effectual than that of a person allowing their freedoms to be taken from them and their society.

We, the people, are responsible for our fates. And we, the people, will be responsible for our slavery and death, and that of our children's, at the hands of the most insane of our species, if we do nothing to stop this slow death march we are on. Where are the men? Where is the manhood of this nation and this world? Are we so docile that when that greedy tax collector extorts us, we give up our money, our courage, and our testament to personal freedom? Are we no more than the chattel these vampires think we are? It is up to you, reader, to determine your own value and worth and to face life either as a free human or as livestock.

I am here to give a little understanding, hope, and recognition to our collective suffering as well as to provide solutions that are feasible by all people who have breath. You are not alone. You have a tribe, a family, and a means to make a better world for all of us by working together.

"It does not take a majority to prevail, but rather an irate, tireless minority keen on setting brushfires of freedom in the minds of men."

-Samuel Adams

WHATS NEEDED FOR A REVOLUTION TO BE SUCCESSFUL

The most crucial factor in the success or failure of a revolution, is the perception of legitimacy by the population. The second most crucial factor is whether the Resistance is truthful. If the population sees the Resistance forces as liars and illegitimate rebels, the revolution will not succeed even if it defeats the government militaristically. It will then have to contend with a population highly likely to rebel and defy it. Other nations must also recognize the Resistance forces as legitimate, else it will have no means to interact internationally. A revolution built upon even a single pervasive and tangible truth will gain more by holding to that truth than having any number of arms to fight the government. The population that empathizes and supports the Resistance forces is the population ready for the transition beyond its current state.

"The first steps in revolution are by no means always clear to the revolutionists themselves, and the transition from agitation to action is rarely a sudden and definite thing... By and large, successful revolutionists do not often subscribe to Jefferson's desire to see a revolution every twenty years or so; rather, they endeavor to create a myth of their own revolution, which becomes the last one necessary... Indeed, one of the distinguishing marks of a revolution is this: that in revolutionary times the idealist at last gets a chance to try and realize his ideals. "

– Crane Brinton[249]

Revolution is the combined result of the proper environment and the firebrand. There are those who, when they wake up in the morning, only see what is in store for them that day. Others wake and are immediately aware of the potential of the entirety of humanity and are discontent to sit around and await the day when others see that same potential. Limited in expressing that potential by the limitations of the those who haven't yet seen it, they often become intellectuals, writing books and painting scenes showing the ideal. The population needs to be ready for radical change, but the radical planners and revolutionaries need to be very active in preparing and planning and inciting. Government inability, whatever other reason, to use adequate coercive power to put down populous uprisings leads to revolutions. Revolutionaries can only succeed if they have recruited or neutralized much of the military and police force. Generally, revolution leaders during the preparation or build-up period are successful moderates. When violent revolution breaks out, leaders are composed of those who are radical, failures or at least at-odds with the previous order. They are most often in their 30's and 40's.
Revolutions are composed of people from every walk of life in a society. It is not composed of simply the downtrodden but is more often composed of the average person and the successful. After successful revolution, moderates generally assume power, creating a division between the moderates and radicals that results in the radicals forcefully and finally assuming power. Moderates cannot fight wars, as they cannot muster powerful central command, rally popular support, and produce loyalty.

> *"The moderates, then, do not really believe in the big words they have to use. They do not really believe a heavenly perfection is suddenly coming to men on earth. They are all for compromise, common sense, toleration, comfort. In a normal society, these desires are part of their strength and give them their hold over their fellows, who share at least their desire for comfort... Their fewness is indeed one of the great sources of the extremists' strength. Great numbers are almost as unwieldy in politics as on the battlefield. In the politics of revolutions what counts is the ability to move swiftly, to make clear and final decisions, to push through to a goal without regard for injured human dispositions... You cannot in large numbers maintain the fever of fanaticism long enough to secure the ultimate victory. The masses do not make revolutions... all were achieved by small, disciplined, principled, fanatical bodies."*
>
> \- Crane Brinton[250]

To make a successful revolution, the Resistance forces must refuse to attack and endeavor not to create hardship for those they claim to be freeing from the tyranny of the government. The Resistance must maintain a moral high ground and refuse to cause harm to the population regardless of the actions of the government. By doing this, the Resistance not only will build support for the cause but will also engender the good will of those people who originally oppose the premise of the revolution. Do not lie to the population. Give a clear representation of expectations and possibilities. In outlining these, it will be useful to identify the extreme end of the suffering and hardship Resistance would create. By doing this, every minor success builds a positive feedback loop, that supports the efforts of the Resistance to gain the support of those who are originally opposed to, or ignorant of, the intent of the Resistance.
Technical difficulties begin with the consideration of the demographics of the population in question. In the United States, by 2030, one in five Americans will be over the age of 65. Over 50 million foreign-born people will live in the United States by 2030. By 2040, the amount of people born in the United States will make up almost half of the number of foreign-born migrants in terms of new population. Population growth will decrease significantly over the coming decades due to the aging population, falling fertility rates, and lower rates of net international migration. The shift from native born Americans to immigrant population, includes a shift in values and worldview, that very easily could produce a vastly different

country than what is seen today. Revolutions are formed around youth uprisings. The United States is quickly entering a period where those over 65 will outnumber the youth, for the first time historically.[251]
The amount of dependent elderly will shift financial wellbeing of the nation and will have an effect on national financial health as the voting population will be represented by those who are highly likely to demand ever increasing funding into social programs to support them in their old age. The youth of the nation will be forced to work in debt to support the aged population and will have less children, meaning less GDP produced in the long run by those born in the nation. The influence of this population will decrease as the shift in majority brings migrants into political and financial dominance. The concurrent urbanization and littoralization will produce greater burdens upon the environment and enfold the nation into global politics in fractured, complex, and often unmanageable ways, as the interactions between major cities become extremely intimate and dependent.
This major shift in worldview, values, age, heritage, fiscal responsibility, political importance, and global connectivity and dependency will create various difficulties that cannot be adequately predicted in their outcome, but we can say generally that the trend leads to extreme hardship and struggle for the youth population in the US. If the US survives these changes, it still has one more battle to wage, which is external threats by competitive nations and non-state actors. With diminishing youth, and highly dependent elderly populations, the amount of military capable and actively participating people will be severely curtailed. This means threats from outside the US will become increasingly tangible and deadly. This is likely to aggravate the relatively dormant civil unrest in the US and produce some form of Resistance. Whether or not this projection fruits, the need to understand the nature of revolution and what it entails is of vital importance, especially in a nation that codified Resistance to tyranny through revolution in its most sacred and fundamental agreements.

Strategy, Tactics and Execution

Strategy is the overarching plan to be executed to achieve a specific goal or set of goals. Tactics is the science of disposal and maneuver of assets to achieve the goal or goals defined in a strategy. Execution is putting into action strategy and tactics.
The strategy involved in a revolution in the United States would include removal of political power from those currently wielding it, potentially a change in type of government and structure, and the rebuilding of any infrastructure that was affected by conflict. The ultimate goal being to make better the conditions of the people, the strategy would include using combat techniques that reduce the number of casualties produced in the general population and truth propaganda, gaining the trust and support of more people in the population. The strategy would include taking control of key nodes, like military command centers, political centers like state capitol buildings, law enforcement hubs, such as Fusion Centers, and resource hubs, such as petroleum manufacturing facilities and power plants. In the changing global environment, where 70% of the population will be living in highly connected urban centers, often coastal, the expression of strategy in conflict will alter as well. More and more activity will be focused on controlling these key areas of commerce and flow of human migrations. The ability to source funding from anywhere in the world, through nearly invisible exchanges, makes the economics of revolution a great deal easier than in the past. As seen in the Arab Spring, the evolution of strategy and tactics will move very fast as each side or part learns and reacts to what the other is doing. The key then is to find the most successful strategy that accommodates for this rapid adaptation. The ability for the Resistance to utilize global volunteer resources, to decentralize command and expeditiously mobilize without warning, and to meld with the general populace gives them great advantages over any government. The strategy would include all these and more factors.
While there would likely be a single revolutionary group that makes up the majority of the movement, it is extremely probable that innumerable splinter groups would form with competing agendas. As long as every group, or a majority of them, is working toward the same fundamental goal, infighting could be kept

to minimums. This goal may be as simple as the dissolving of the Federal Reserve. States may have many differences, but if that one goal is the focus of the revolution, they would likely stay focused, cooperative, and coordinated throughout the effort.

The Resistance must garner international support from both the governments and the general populations of foreign nations. The United States would not exist if it were not for the support that was given to the revolutionaries during the American Revolution from France. It was the French military support that made it possible to force the British surrender and eventually their acceptance of the sovereignty of the new nation. Dual Sovereignty occurs when two governments exist within one state. One is the old regime, and one is the revolutionary government. Rather than revolutionists simply take over or cast aside the old regime and set up a new government, they must actually create an entirely successful and efficient government in parallel to the old regime, gradually recruiting enough of the population to become the new legal government. In today's world, that legality must be recognized by international bodies to avoid interference from global coalitions. The Resistance forces must create ties with foreign nations to support their interests and claim. This support could mean the difference between international legitimacy and being seen as terrorists or violent rebels. Having strong legal representation, within the current government, will help to show that the attempt for legal means of having needs and demands met is the foremost option in the minds of the Resistance. It will also help to navigate the waters when the government begins to use excessive measures to exterminate the Resistance and will aid negotiations to be had with foreign governments and entities about the Resistance's international status.

Inefficiencies in the new government create problems for the population, often coinciding with the new government's attempts to control every aspect of life in the nation to bring about a cooling off of revolutionary fervor. Preventing this is especially important, such that the new regime must be capable of managing affairs of governance rapidly or be faced with increasing disloyalty and unpopularity and perhaps uprising. The government must also allow as best as possible the free market to correct for the economic and social disturbance, setting general guidelines, and stepping back out of the individual lives of the people.

Another key aspect to successfully resisting tyranny, is at the very beginning of the militarization against the government, it is extremely important for the Resistance to occupy and operate within government buildings and to take on the responsibilities that were prior the domain of the oppressors. This includes, nearly equal in importance, capitol buildings and offices, police stations and military bases, energy production and distribution centers, news stations and other media outlets, and transportation centers such as airports, subway stations, and major highway corridors. It may even be a promising idea to destroy the capitol buildings so as to prevent their use by the government. In this way, you can force them to have to operate on the run and thus make it easier to illegitimatize them. Nothing should be done unless it moves forward the ultimate goals, which rely predominantly on gaining and maintaining the perception of legitimacy. As long as the Resistance can acquire this and maintain it, the government has no chance of succeeding, as it would preclude the support of the population.

The Resistance forces must acquire resources to succeed. These resources include everything from military gear to printing equipment to finances. The overt and covert aspects to the Resistance will require different resources and different means by which they go about using resources they have to achieve the ultimate goal. The covert, or militarized, aspect of the revolution will need supplies for their volunteer fighters, including clothing, rain gear, footwear, water purification tools, sleeping gear, tents, cooking gear and rations, maps and compasses, medical gear, hygienic gear, cutting tools, digging tools, radios, flashlights, and load-bearing equipment. They will also need a constant supply of arms and ammunition. The very minimum to this includes; for rifles, Winchester .308 (7.62 x 51 mm NATO), .223 Remington (5.56 x 45 mm NATO), Russian 7.62 x 39 mm, .50 BMG; for pistols, 9 mm, .40 Smith and Wesson, .45 ACP, .38, and .357 magnum ammunition, and firearms that correspond to these calibers as they are the most popular and available globally. They will need firearm maintenance and cleaning supplies, optics, and night vision. The forces must also be given field manuals describing how to operate their firearms, treat injuries in the field, how to fight in different conditions, and other necessary knowledge to engage in combat and other skills. The overt Resistance, including public figures and supporters in the general population who are not directly involved in fighting, will need resources that help them to spread the message and news of the successes of the Resistance forces, and to show the world the actions of the government, and to counter the propaganda the government will be spewing through mainstream media. The governments desperation to stop a spreading Resistance effort will lead them to commit atrocities against the population, and it is extremely important for the Resistance to show these things to the population to prevent the government from claiming these events as rebel terrorist activities.

The militarized aspect of the revolution will need to occupy or erect headquartering facilities, hospitals, training camps, explosives manufacturing facilities, and arms and ammunition facilities as well as major and minor weapons storage facilities and caches. It is essential that the Resistance plan to manufacture its own resources over the long term, even if it is possible to retrieve resources initially from raids upon armories, government hospitals, police stations, gun shops, and arms and explosives manufacturers amongst other places. Distinct types of camps need to be constructed and utilized, for concealment and disguise. Concealment camps are those that prevent observation of their activities through physical means of obstruction. This could be netting which blends with the area around it concealing a tunnel entrance or canopy trees above a temporary camp. These camps will be needed for the militarized aspect of the Resistance. Caves and Tunnels are included in Concealed camps. Modern technology in the form of Ground Penetrating Radar (GPR) allows the government to see underground structures and shapes. This means tunnels need to be dug only under dense natural cover and manmade above ground structures that make it harder to see under the ground. Disguised camps are those that are in plain view but appear to be nothing out of the ordinary. It needs to be legitimate in every way when observed by neighbors, customers, or government forces. While Concealed camps are usually remote and defensible, disguised camps are most often in an area occupied by other people, from a small village to a city of millions, and is indefensible.

It is exceedingly vital to the success of the revolution to create a positive impression of the Resistance effort and its goals. One of the ways to do this is to always be, and be seen, working for the wellbeing of the general population, whether they are supporting the Resistance or not. The Resistance must distribute manuals to the population of how to defend from police and military threats, and how to approach Resistance forces or to create their own Resistance force. There are many who would join a revolution that simply are afraid or ignorant, and by informing them how to proceed can allay their fears and ignorance and make them ready recruits. These manuals should also inform the population as to how to go about creating their own Resistance hub if they are not interested or are incapable of joining a larger or already existing hub. The decentralized forces of the Resistance will be harder to defeat or even infiltrate the more they are built on the actions of individuals or small groups that have no contact with other Resistance forces. As long as the ultimate goal is well defined and all the forces are actively working toward them, the general effect will produce positive results.

It is important for the covert forces to establish command centers. These will be more important regarding larger forces and will make it possible for some amount of centralized planning and organization to exist. It will be difficult to establish long term command centers until a significant momentum has been built and regions are under the control of the Resistance, through which the government would be forced to attack several layers of defense before being able to attack the command centers directly. Command centers must be considered carefully and can be tunneled, concealed in city buildings, or even comprised of several locations in which the center moves from one to another randomly, but which still has access to all of its necessary outlets.

The overt and covert aspects of the Resistance must become acutely aware of the other members of their units and be wary of new recruits to the degree that they can spot infiltrators, assassins, and spy's. Any form of counterfeiting must have methods of discovering and identifying. This is especially important for revolutionaries, as they are always facing an established and highly successful institution that has the resources and the manpower to engage in infiltration and sabotage. There are many ways to prevent infiltrators from accessing information, locations, and persons that are critical and this should be studied by all Resistance forces. At the same time, every member of the Resistance must have the adequate counterfeit paperwork to travel and operate within the state.

Safe houses must be identified for everything from creating an underground railroad for targeted people, those that wish to escape from the government, and for the families of the fighters. These safe houses must be able to store resources, host meetings, secure information, and report on events happening locally and to whatever greater extent they can. Safe houses are maintained by people who are overtly involved in the Resistance effort, which means they are not directly involved in any other aspect of the Resistance. They are innocuous in the eyes of the government and can withstand scrutiny if government agents choose to inspect them. They are key to the success of a revolution.

The Resistance must have clandestine communication systems, by which they are able to conference and communicate without the government knowing who was conveying and what was being conveyed. There are many ways to secure information, and all members of the Resistance should be made aware of information security and given private security codes by which they can be identified in their communications. In this way, any corrupted link can be identified and corrected. Some ways to conceal communications at least initially and moderately is to use disposable cell phones, and to use them only once before disposing, or to utilize an internet-based communications system on a specifically designated phone with false personal information used in its setup. This could be Signal or Telegram for example, though there are more and better services available out there, with less ease of function and widespread sector of use. Dead and Live drops may be utilized to pass information back and forth covertly. A dead drop is leaving messages in a mutually agreed upon location and indicating through subtle signs that a message is ready for pickup. This could be a note left under a bench, with a chalk mark left on the ground next to the bench. A live drop is the utilization of an innocuous person to hold the message for the receiver and pass it to the receiver on their arrival. This requires a high degree of trust in the person operating as the live drop. Email can be utilized through services like Proton Mail, with encrypts emails, and TOR which anonymizes activity over the internet. Modern encryption technology has advanced so far as to be able to implant messages and even video content into living cells. This may be a bit overkill for the Resistance force of today, but for tomorrow... who knows. To ensure security of ones electronic documents and files, the program WinZip can be used to encrypt everything, thus protecting the Resistance to some degree if sensitive laptops or other devices are captured.

Fundraising is a necessity for the Resistance. This can happen through many means but must always be untraceable to the Resistance unless the funding is part of the Resistance propaganda. Foreign nations, multinational organizations, corporations, groups and individuals can all be funding the Revolution, and in fact must for the Resistance to be successful. To encourage this fundraising, the overt arm of the Resistance must make every effort to get the information about what the Resistance is doing and why they are doing it out to the world. This is difficult in a censored world. Some means of distributing information according to ease and access are YouTube, Google, Facebook. These are the most accessible avenues to begin spreading information and directing people to locations on the internet or in person where they can learn more and get involved. As these outlets become more and more censored and the revolution more and more covert, the transition to places like Discord, Telegram, and Hive must take place. Through these freedom-oriented channels, the Resistance can become more aggressive in their recruitment, calls to action, and spreading of information.

As the oppressive government is prone to do, it will eventually start cracking down more and more fiercely against anyone associated with the Resistance, meaning people will need to begin utilizing even more secure methods of disseminating information. Several methods exist, including mass producing video and audio files that can be disseminated widely and shared over and over again through encrypted email, or passed from person to person, or even played on public speakers by the Resistance. The Resistance can make every effort to capture audio and video footage of the government committing atrocities that they most certainly will in their attempt to crush the Resistance. The creation of songs, political artwork, and jokes that ridicule the government can be remarkably effective to both garner support for the Resistance and to identify the problems with the government. Even mobile pirate radio can be used to spread information as well. The ability of the government to triangulate radio signals will mean that operators will never be able to stay in one place for too long and will likely be highly effective as long as the operators are constantly mobile and concealed from means of tracking. The overt Resistance can utilize marches and public protest events to spread information as well, for as long as the government will tolerate them. The audiences that need to be reached vary, and thus the messages and content that is put to these groups must be made specific to the audience. The general public, the state police and military, the government officials, foreign public, foreign officials, and the Resistance forces. Each of these groups requires different information. It is the duty of the Resistance to provide Truth to the world about its motives and reasoning. If this Truth resonates strongly enough, it will alter the course of the world, if not it will be smothered regardless of military efforts.

"...Mises Memo for Summer 2002: '[I]n so many ways, the state is a fiction. It has no existence apart from the people's willingness to believe it and give it life with their money and obedience. It was 12 years ago that the immense and seemingly permanent apparatus of the Soviet world empire wasted away like Oz's wicked witch of the west. Why? Because willingness to believe had been withdrawn.' That is a key point. The object of any Resistance movement is, ultimately, to cause people to quit believing in the existence of, and giving support to, the existing state... The people must start looking at the state as 'them,' and the Resistance movement as 'us.'"

-Martino, Resistance To Tyranny[252]

No government that ever existed allowed itself to end without struggle. It is the nature of government to ensure its longevity and growth just like any corporation. The methods that governments use to prevent their demise are gentle and political when the population is empowered, aware, and armed. When the population is weak, ignorant, and disarmed, the government has no need to remain tactful, and resorts to ever increasing oppressive systems of control. Modern theaters of war include a combination of physical locations and virtual ones. Volunteers assisting in revolutions from foreign nations become part of the virtual theater of war, just like UAV pilots bombing children at weddings in Yemen while sipping coffee at their desk in New York. This means that what a civilian noncombatant is, and a military combatant is, are beginning to mix. This means any person could be a target if they violate some arbitrary government rule, allowing the government to justify their murder. At the onset, or even before, of a Resistance movement, the government will justify repressive measures by creating an atmosphere of crisis. They will call for martial law to prevent the incipient revolution. They will even create real crises if the illegitimate ones fail. All of this to prevent the population from presenting a real threat to them by rising militaristically.

"Propaganda is another way of creating an apparent crisis. Whatever the cause at issue, the government can use propaganda... to lead people to think in abstractions rather than in concrete terms. Once the people's thinking is directed to abstractions, to "the whole crisis," then extreme measures are easy to justify. (Note that a "war on crime," a "war on drugs," or a "war on terror," are all "wars" against abstract nouns, not against specific individuals, institutions or nations.) Creation of crisis is a very effective way for the government to justify its oppression. It's "necessary," it's "for the public good," and of course it's "just a temporary

measure, until the crisis is over." But the people who decide when the crisis is over are the very people who gain power from the belief that a crisis exists. They will be very reluctant to give up that power. In the United States for instance, a "state of emergency" was declared on March 9th, 1933. It has never been rescinded (Senate Report 93-549). On the contrary, it has been re-declared by every president since then, through WWII, the Cold War, and the "New World Order." Americans have lived under a continuously renewed "state of emergency" since the Great Depression."

-Martino, Resistance to Tyranny[253]

The government may also allow the spread of criminal activity so as to create enough fear in the population that they accept the governments promises to eradicate the crime if they are granted extraordinary powers. This can be seen happening during the United States "war of terror", where they incited the rise of "terrorist" criminal activity, then promised to fight it on behalf of freedom, even while grinding our Rights into the dirt and blasting the national anthem. The same thing is occurring now in the spread of mass murders like school shootings. By denying our Rights, the government has set itself as the enemy, despite its constant supplication that it is doing so for our good. Another tactic government may employ is releasing violent criminals from prisons in areas of Resistance, to frighten the population and to show in the media what follows as being Resistance backed.

Other responses to Resistance forces will include, licensure and permit revocation, false arrests, the rounding up of large numbers of people to "check their papers" and investigate them for "sedition", isolating areas of cities or rural regions, to prevent the population from coming and going freely, and replacement of the currency to remove the Resistances financial capacity. This is already in the works now. The coronavirus plandemic manufacturers are now in phase two or even three of their malicious takeover of the world, which is a change in currency. The United States is working on the transition to a fully digitalized currency, in which they will have complete control over its value, over the way it is spent by the population, and will have the means to monitor users, confiscate funds, deny use of funds, and track account holders. It is the ultimate control model for the dictators of the world.

The government will not only apply heavy pressure on the Resistance through military aggression, but also, and perhaps even more effectively, through infiltration and psychological operations. Infiltration will always be a danger to the Resistance, as it will be susceptible to information insecurity in ways that the government would not have to contend with. The government will have loyalists, dedicated spies, and turncoats at its behest. The government will use fake Resistance groups to destabilize the revolution and false claims of government informants to create paranoia amongst the Resistance forces. One of the main tactics the government will use is the elimination of Resistance leaders, through their assassination, making them turn against the Resistance through threats and violence, and by defaming them, which may be even more harmful to the Resistance than their death.

"...the Communists in the Soviet Union never killed any "people". Instead, they killed kulaks, capitalists, wreckers, saboteurs, enemies of the people, counter-revolutionaries, and similar "extremists." Likewise the Nazis never killed Jewish "people." Instead they killed maggots, menaces to society, scum, parasites, bacilli, etc. By first marginalizing the people they wanted to destroy, these governments were able to get away with their murders."

-Martino, Resistance To Tyranny[254]

The government will use every trick in the book to marginalize, demoralize, demonize, and defame the Resistance. Even now the US government supports and encourages racial disparities, classism, and the demonization of undesirables. The moment there is a militarized Resistance, the amount of effort the government devotes to this task will exponentially increase. In the early 1900's, Henry Ford, a supporter of eugenics and racial cleansing, printed millions of copies of the book, "The Protocols of the Elders of Zion," which outlined a secret Jewish organization and their methods and plans for world domination. This book turned the spark of anti-Semitism into the flame of racial cleansing, which took practical root in the United States, and was carried out to its inevitable end in Germany with the holocaust. It is quite easy for governments to create hatred for sects of the population, especially when they exert their influence in media and other outlets for social conditioning.

"Josef Stalin was referred to by his Bolshevik comrades as "Comrade Filecard." He didn't need high technology to control a population of millions. A typewriter, pen and ink system, if pervasive enough ("Your papers please") can be fully effective in denying people movement, food, medical care, education, and jobs. A computerized system can be even more effective, especially if the computerized ID card is used for a driver's license, voter registration, medical care, financial transactions, and other activities... The attempt to establish some form of national ID card, particularly a computerized one, is in itself sufficient reason to oppose a government."

-Martino, Resistance To Tyranny[255]

Not only national IDs, but state ID's as well, are satisfactory cause for rebellion. Both reflect centralized government. Seeing as many of the states in the US have larger populations than many nations around the world, (California, Texas, Florida, and New York accounting for 110 million people) it makes sense to look at them as central governments just as reprehensible as the federal government, due to sheer size alone. Having a State ID is cause enough for overturning the state governments, even though most people will not agree, because they cannot see beyond the comforts of the mommy and daddy state, sending out welfare checks while demanding to always know where you are and what you are up to... *for your own safety*, of course. You want to drive? Need a license. Want to hunt? Need a license. Want a gun? Need a license. Want to fish? Need a license. Want to smoke cannabis? Need a license. Want to build a home? Need a license. Want to start a business? Need a license. Want to get married? Need a license. Want to protest peacefully? Need a permit. Want to broadcast over the radio? Need a license. Want to sell alcohol? Need a license. Because without a license, your central government would not be able to share in your successes, track your every move, and restrain your liberties. And wouldn't that be a shame.

WHAT A GOVERNMENT NEEDS TO DO TO PREVENT RESISTANCE SUCCESS

- Synchronization, coordination, and organization of their forces
- Moral/Ethical High ground by maintaining professionalism and least loss of life in operations
- Legitimacy and International Credibility
- Information and Media Control
- "Do not create more enemies than you eliminate with your action"
- Police and military presence
- Decentralized authority and decision-making
- Unity of comprehensive effort by collaboration of US and other forces
- Unity of command between coalition forces (one of the most difficult issues to resolve)
- Acquire consistent clear and reliable intelligence easily disseminated throughout their forces
- Maintenance and promotion of Loyalist Auxiliaries while upholding perception of Righteousness

Thus we are talking here of competition among organized, armed groups seeking to control populations through normative systems—a construct that applies equally well to insurgency and crime, to state and nonstate actors, and indeed to the actions of states and those of governments. Within the behavioral space bounded by its rule set, an actor can apply a spectrum of means ranging from persuasion through administration to coercion. At the persuasive end of this spectrum are arguments and inducements to support the dominant rule set. These include propaganda, political and ideological mobilization, social pressure, and identity manipulation. But as we've seen, often the most persuasive element is the feeling of security, predictability, order and cohesion... that comes with adherence to a dominant actor's norms. In the middle of the spectrum, administrative tools—justice systems, mediation and dispute resolution mechanisms, essential services, social and economic institutions—make it easier for people to follow the rules, and give them tangible benefits for doing so. At the coercive end of the spectrum are punishments that impose costs on people who break the rules. These include punitive violence—up to and including death—as well as expropriation (fines, penalties, or seizure of assets), expulsion and exile, or imprisonment...

...a government is a political organization that has successfully outcompeted its rivals across the full coercion-persuasion spectrum, allowing it to establish an uncontested normative system over a given population or territory. The coercive end of the spectrum is critical, because its supports and enables the rest of the system: the persuasive and administrative parts of a normative system work...only because they rest on the ultimate sanction of force, which a dominant actor can apply against those who break its rules.

– David Kilcullen[256]

The United States government is attempting currently, as a body, to remove the second amendment from the people. This is because the single greatest fear and threat to governments everywhere is civil unrest. When the people no longer support or accept the authority of a government, the government will become ever more afraid and build stronger police and domestic military operations, increase spying on its own citizens, registering them, and removing their ability to defend themselves. As I have detailed earlier in this book, the United States government is doing all of those things. The single most important thing to any government, and this one is no different, is the ability to use force to subdue the population when they become restive, or worse, revolutionary. Those who accept the authority of the state will uphold it. Those who do not will, at some point, change it, replace it, or extinguish it.

Those who are loyal to the state and remain so in the course of a Resistance effort are likely to remain integrated amongst the population, doing what they can to inhibit the Resistance from succeeding. Some loyalists may simply report abnormal activity that they suspect, while others may form their own militias to supplement the state military to crush the Resistance militaristically. These loyalists will be composed of an array of personalities and motivations, including those who are ignorant to any real information, glued to television news, and unable to do anything but think what the government tells them to. Others will be considered by themselves and other loyalists as patriots for defending the nation against the rebels, though they will likely be people who have limited ability to think beyond the reach of the indoctrination they underwent in the military or otherwise government agency that they work for. Others will be people who are simply eager to vent their aggression upon others and seeing an opportunity for sanctioned violence by their government will become engaged in fighting the Resistance.

Statists are those who have become so twisted that they treat the state as a religious entity and leader. These people are completely lost when it comes time for Resistance to militarize, as they will not be easily approached and will act upon the orders and mandates of the government without any personal moral or ethical adjustment. These people are some of the most confused and lost people, and it is nearly impossible for them to see beyond their prejudices. They will die and kill for their government.

Loyalist forces will form the military auxiliaries and will likely be even more damaging to the Resistance than the regular forces. Their ability to infiltrate, assassinate, and sabotage will be greater as well as their ability to operate in intelligence actions. They are the neighbors, the businesses, and the organizations next door. They are the ones who are like a minefield that must be navigated while recruiting Resistance forces. They are the people within the population that will likely continue to oppose the Resistance even after the government collapses, thus prolonging the conflict. They are the most dangerous part of the enemy forces, mostly because of the delicacy of the Rules of Engagement and Rules of Escalation (ROE) that mut be applied to them by the Resistance to both maintain the moral high ground and to prevent the legitimizing of the Loyalist efforts. The moral and individualized judicial treatment of Loyalists will also assist in the effort to convert them to the Resistance. With this said, it is extremely important to let the general population know that any collaboration with the state is acceptance of the fact that they are actively engaged in warfare against the Resistance, and thus will be targeted. It must be made exceedingly clear that this behavior will not be tolerated. It is important, especially in the beginning stages of the militarized Resistance effort to ingrain this in the minds of the population, so that loyalism is disincentivized.

The Resistance will likely need to begin its covert operations with the attitude of guerilla warfare. It will need to focus on raids and deceptions to achieve gains and prevent losses. The key mission is to gather more assets and influence greater sectors of the population while psychologically and physically impairing the agents of the state from being able to attack or defend from their position. Rapid deployment and even more rapidly disappearing afterward, for night operations, communications disrupting, key facility and asset sabotage and acquisition, and assassination of key personnel are the initial strongpoints of the Resistance warfare strategy. They will utilize ambushes, snipers, and every other means of disrupting the state's forces while reducing potential harm and capture of Resistance forces.

"The right of a nation to kill a tyrant in case of necessity can be no more doubted than to hang a robber, or kill a flea."

– John Adams

Assassination is an incredibly useful tool to disempower and create disfunction within the state. While the idea of attacking the icon or figurehead of the state, like a tyrant or president, easily comes to mind, the more functional and practical use of assassination is against the functionaries of the state and the middle to upper-level officers. Clerks, tax agents, inspectors, and other mainly office workers are good targets to generate disfunction within the enemy. The people that do rare, specialized, and difficult to replicate tasks are the most beneficial targets to the Resistance. One such role may be pilots of military fixed wing crafts. There are only so many pilots, and a large number of them being targeting by sniper teams would definitely make a dent in the ability of the state to deploy adequate force in the short term, having to train new pilots extensively. Assassinating the functionaries produces a more long-term goal, which is to produce an uneasiness within the ranks of those who are unlikely to be loyalists at heart but rather simply doing a job for pay, who become less than satisfied with that pay as their ranks are targeted. This will have an effect of hampering the military efforts overall, as the functionaries are there to make sure all the gears are greased, and without them things start to fall apart. It should be a primary goal to convert these targets into Resistance operatives and to shift into the conversation of assassination only after this has been given consideration.

Sabotage should be used only secondly to acquisition of assets or facilities or targets. If a tank cannot be acquired and used against the state, it can then be boobytrapped to cause maximum damage to the enemy and destroy it as an asset at the same time. If a weapons manufacturer will not supply arms to the Resistance, then it is an extremely viable target for sabotage, to prevent its arms reaching the state. On the other hand, if the arms manufacturer will increase production without informing the government and supply the Resistance, it may be worth allowing them to continue to produce weapons for the state as long as they are also supplying the Resistance. If a road cannot be secured for the Resistance, and it is being utilized for the passage of the state military and police, it becomes a prime target for sabotage. Improvised Explosive Devices take on two roles here, as they can both be triggered by passing troops and create enough damage in the road to make it impassable.

Resistance fighters should always look to maximize any action and produce as many immediate and long-term benefits as possible from any single action. One of the most important targets for sabotage is any systems of surveillance and tracking the government has access to. While it may prove to be of benefit to acquire these assets, it will more likely prove to be of such great detriment and time consumption to the Resistance to hold and operate these systems, that it would be better to initially destroy them entirely. These include surveillance and GPS satellite stations, which eliminate much of the threat of drones and other aircraft, and equipment like GPR (Ground Penetrating Radar) which eliminates the ability of the government to see underground for tunnels, mines, or other Resistance activity. Facilities for data storage like the NSA facility in Utah are prime targets, and once destroyed will give more leeway for Resistance actions to be public. Rather than sabotage of media outlets, it is key that the Resistance take control and hold control of these outlets. Information sabotage is very important as well, such as altering reports, creating false data on quantities of items, personnel, and enemies, and taking down websites entirely through DDOS or other methods.

LIST OF RESISTANCE HUMAN TARGETS

- Politicians (Local to Federal)
- Military and Police Command (Middle to high-level)
- Law Enforcement of all types
- Government Department Leadership
- Government Functionaries
- Corporate Executives supported the government
- Loyalists holding large assets or controlling government Auxiliary forces
- Quartermasters in both Military and Police
- Federal Reserve Executives and Chairmen
- Leadership at the CIA/NSA/DIA/DARPA, National Geospatial-Intelligence Agency/National Reconnaissance Office, the Strategic Capabilities Office (SCO), the Defense Logistics Agency (DLA), the Missile Defense Agency (MDA), and the Defense Contract Management Agency (DCMA)

LIST OF RESISTANCE NON-HUMAN TARGETS

- Power Plants
- Military Installations
- Police Stations
- Government Buildings, such as capitol buildings
- Federal Law Enforcement Facilities
- Satellite installations for GPS, Communications, and other government functions (Including corporate installations)
- News television stations
- Google, YouTube, etc. HQ Centers and other government media outlets
- Petroleum processing plants and holding tanks and facilities
- Political Meeting places
- Corporate Buildings that empower the government

∫ Arms Manufacturers
∫ Airports, Train Stations, Subway Stations, Seaports, and Border Crossings
∫ Factories of all types, but especially those capable of being converted for munitions, electronic equipment, armored vehicles production, aircraft, etc.

Intelligence activities are essential for the Resistance. From surveilling a target prior to an action to providing false information to spies in a counter-intelligence actions. The act of deception will be the primary defense of the Resistance while intelligence gathering will provide the means for the Resistance to keep steps ahead of the state.

"Power concedes nothing without a demand. It never did, and it never will. Find out just what the people will submit to and you have found out the exact amount of injustice and wrong which will be imposed upon them; and these will continue till they have resisted with either words or blows, or by both. The limits of tyrants are prescribed by the endurance of those whom they suppress."
– Frederick Douglas

Tactical education and standards need to be ingrained into every covert Resistance fighter. The ability to operate alone in hostile territory, to utilize SERE (Survival, Evasion, Resistance, Escape), to maintain control of occupied structures or territories, to work as a team regardless of who the other individuals are, and the means to know friend from foe are some of the things every fighter must know by heart. The way in which different cells come together into one large fighting force without need for a micromanaging central control or even control at all, will be determined by standards. This is a key ingredient to combating a conventional military. The ability to assemble and disperse in the blink of an eye. To come together from the mist and vanish into the crowd. An example of this is in the use of capped number cells. If a cell is composed of a maximum of 8 individuals, if any of those people are captured by the enemy, they can only inform on the other seven, and not on any others, if information is controlled properly. When a major movement is happening, the cells come together and form up organically based on standards that every individual and cell knows by heart. Commands would be given globally, as in sent to every individual or every cell for maneuvers that demanded rapid large conglomeration of forces. Commands would be delivered through cryptographic dead and live drops, or other means, when time was available. Scalable, standardized, and efficient tactics allow for rapid training of recruits and incredibly effective execution of actions.

Somalian army tactics included a "Mounted Swarm" method of approach upon a target by utilizing technicals (trucks with large caliber automatic guns mounted and seating space) in an extended line (each vehicle within visual range of the one next to it). When a cell (technical and crew) was engaged, the cells to the right and left would organically move toward the gunfire in flanking maneuvers of the enemy, with ever increasing reinforcements until the enemy was forced to retreat or was destroyed. The 6 or 7 individuals riding in the technicals would dismount and move in on the enemy on the front flanks of the technical, creating an ever-widening encirclement of the target and creating more targets that the enemy needed to engage to defeat the attack. In cities, the tactic changed very little, but was yet as effective. The cells would move on parallel streets, resetting their extended line at each cross street.

In this way, an entire attack force could be marshalled with independent cells having never been organized or documented into a larger force at all. The need for cells to be self-sufficient means that the Resistance would have to coordinate supplies for as many cells as possible through caches and other means, without ever having direct contact between different cells or command groups. Having all educational materials available to recruits on media such as flash drives, cds, or encrypted websites and other means, would make the learning process move more efficiently than waiting for recruits to come to a location to learn in person. The physical training recruits would need would be conducted by their cells or by rapidly organized, mobile training sites, depending on the local and total condition of the Resistance, at least in the beginning. As the Resistance takes control of more sites and resources, less evasive and secretive training grounds can begin to be utilized, along with increasingly conventional military organization to begin securing greater long-term positions.

The overt aspect of the Resistance would need to be consistently marching, protesting, or otherwise acting within the legal and practical boundaries to maintain their status as noncombatants while drawing attention away from the covert actions, creating smokescreens, and building momentum for the Resistance to achieve its ultimate goals. The consistent and heavily populated protests will make it easier for the covert arm of the Resistance to achieve goals militarily. Both arms of the Resistance need to operate together. When the government decides to shut down the internet, these arms need to be prepared to coordinate with makeshift two-way radios and mesh networks. When the government begins shooting into marching crowds, the militarized arm needs to be prepared to engage and protect the noncombatants. When the Resistance fighters need a safe house, the overt arm needs to be prepared to shield them within the very system being fought.

POTENITAL OPERATIONAL ORDER

1. Local populations take control of their local governments first, then aggregate to take control of the successively larger governments.
2. Resistance forces must capture, occupy and defend specific high value resources and assets to prevent a total collapse of society or the collapse of necessary infrastructure, though balanced with the ability of the US government to use those resources against the Resistance. In that case, sabotage must be used.
3. After the takeover of a government, the Resistance must erect a replacement organization to maintain control and not be confronted on two fronts. These new "governments" duty is primarily to disable and disband the "laws" and agents of the United States government. It is also responsible to assist the local populations to erect new agreements that will be used as their new social contract. All these new agreements must be built on the principles of freedom through some basic ideological understandings and a few fundamentally agreed upon rights that the Resistance as a whole is motivated by.
4. As communities are liberated, they must begin to recruit the forces to maintain their control from the enemy state, allowing the main Resistance forces to move the mission forward and onward toward the Central Government.
5. Once the Central government is removed from power and an interim structure is emplaced, the work to shape the new nation or nations begins. The Resistance needs to have in place a plan and a structure for this moment. It must include conceptual and philosophical alignment with the stated mission and a practical application plan.

POTENTIAL OUTLINE OF GOALS OR AGREEMENTS

A collection of sovereign states or city states that make fundamental agreements and affirmations that bind them in common purpose, but that leave them far more room to serve their populations as they will. What are those potential fundamental agreements?

1. Reaffirm the constitution, amended to meet the populations needs today, such as eradicating a federal government, and returning it to a union/partnership between states.
2. A central forum replaces the federal government, in which every state has ambassadors, and all activity is live streamed to all states. This forum discusses everything but does not make decisions for states. It can only record decisions individual states make, as in what interactions they choose to have with neighboring states and provide a common ground for ambassadors from every state to gather.

3. A centralized military force will exist, composed of 25% of available troops from every entity in the union. The troops rotate in and out of this service. Mostly this service exists to prevent aggression from external nations and from internal states conflicting. By sharing the military, it creates a force that can intervene on the behalf of the union, but that is not owned or controlled by any centralized government. Rather the states give the military its authority to exist, and the people control the states by migrating where their interests are served best within the union, thus altering the structure of the union through the free market. Nuclear weapons will continue to exist and the power to launch will rest with the individual states.
4. The States can choose to trade as they will with who they will.
5. No private central banks allowed to exist anywhere.

These thoughts might not be incredibly detailed here, but they aren't supposed to be. No single individual will have all the answers or determine what is to be. The formation of what comes next will be highly dynamic with many issues and concerns and will require intensive efforts to resolve. The roots and fundamentals are what we are discussing here. What *needs* to change I discuss at greater length in this book. Where we go next can be a very many things, but it *must* be something better than where we are today. The best options I can see are the elimination of anything that extorts the population for private gain, the creation of cooperative structures between sovereign states formed by willing populations, and the affirmation of nature's rights that identify rivers, mountains, and ecosystems of all kinds as having greater rights even than human rights.

"Legitimacy, the acceptance of an authority by a society... is essential to understanding the political variable in an insurgency. Who a population accepts as legitimate is dependent on the norms and values within that particular population. Legitimacy can change as a society evolves and groups or individuals change their conceptualization of who they are and what authority they accept. Sometimes large changes, such as the American War of Independence or the unification of Germany in 1871, create a change in group identity and accepted authority. Sometimes group identity changes by slow evolution, as is the case with the European Union. However, at the core, who a group accepts as providing legitimate authority to govern their actions is that group's legitimate authority... Most populations are controlled through a combination of consent and coercion... Low legitimacy may breed contempt on the part of the population and may require extensive prodding and incentives by the government to secure compliance of the population; high legitimacy... requires less effort by the government to ensure compliance. An illegitimate government's only method of controlling its population is coercion, which can be resource intensive."
"Even if a population does not see... a government as legitimate, control can be established effectively by coercion. Many states... have used domestic intelligence apparatus or other means to control every aspect of their populations. Illegitimate governments often use distrust and divisions within a population to effectively control a society... In many autocratic regimes, various groups within the population have a vested interest in continuing the current government, even if it is repressive. Legitimacy must be seen from the different perspectives of the different groups within a society."

"The legal use of population control measures, including curfews, movement restrictions, travel permits, registration cards, and biometric census may assist in identifying the insurgents and protecting the population."

"The commitment and motivation of a... nation to defeat an insurgency is an important motivation. Governments with more than one of the following traits have tended to lose historically... "

- *"Government sponsors or protects unpopular economic and social arrangements or cultural institutions."*
- *"Government is involved in corrupt and arbitrary personalistic rule.*
- *"Government operates as a kleptocracy."*
- *"Government is controlled by elites with perverse incentives to continue conflict."*
- *"Government is economically dependent on external actors."*

"In many autocratic societies, intelligence agencies provide an essential means of control over a society."

-FM 3-24/MCWP 3-33.5[257]

Our Evolution and Moving Forward

So far, we have mostly discussed the ways in which our society has formed and the ways in which we can act to reform it or replace it for the greatest benefit to all the population. Now we must articulate the dream. The utopian potential that *is* possible but seemingly improbable under our current dogmatisms and the authoritarian stranglehold on almost all aspects of life on this planet. It is only in recognizing that we are diseased or ill can we begin to appropriately apply the correct medicine. It is only when we have become witness to the corruption of the natural human and holistic life and patterns of existence can we truly apprehend the necessity of drastic and definitive change to our society. The time is now! The moment has arrived! We must be the ones to create a better world for our children to inherit.

Contrary to what nearly everyone has been taught to believe, "government" is not necessary for civilization. It is not conducive to civilization. It is, in fact, the antithesis of civilization. It is not cooperation, or working together, or voluntary interaction. It is not peaceful coexistence. It is coercion.; it is violence. It is animalistic aggression, cloaked by pseudo-religious, cult-like rituals which are designs to make appear legitimate and righteous. It is brute thuggery, disguised as consent and organization. It is the enslavement of mankind, the subjugation of free will, and the destruction of morality, masquerading as "civilization" and "society." The problem is not just that "authority" can be used for evil; the problem is that, at its most basic essence, it is evil. In everything it does, it defeats the free will of human beings, controlling them through coercion and fear. It supersedes and destroys moral consciences, replacing them with unthinking blind obedience. It cannot be used for good, any more than a bomb can be used to heal a body. It is always aggression, always the enemy of peace, always the enemy of justice. The moment it ceases to be an attacker, it ceases to fit the definition of "government." It is, by its very nature, a murderer and a thief, the enemy of mankind, a poison to humanity. As dominator and controller, ruler and oppressor, it can be nothing else.

-Larken Rose, "The Most Dangerous Superstition"[258]

What the ideal means to each is as diverse a subject as any, but I am sure we can agree on some essential principles to begin with. We want to have our basic individual needs met. We want the same for others. We want to exist in vibrant and bountiful environments with lots of opportunity and some healthy challenges. We want to explore passions and experience the fullness of life in our infinitely varying ways. It is my adamantine conviction that these things are available to us as a planetary community as soon as we dissolve the disease of authoritarianism and systemic centralized control.

How we get from where we are to a place that exemplifies these principles is something I will elucidate upon here. The path forward into a new epoch is not necessarily as dramatic as the biblical rendition would make it seem. While there certainly are monsters in the world, they are not seven-headed demons, but have taken the form of corporations, governments, and other self-designated god entities in that they refuse to perish like normal living beings and have increased their power and control to nearly all the corners of the planet. The end of the last age is at hand, and we are here ushering in our new collective experience. The entities that have dominated during the last age will perish, and a novel system will be implemented in its place, bringing humanity ever closer to its natural state of existence... anarchy. We do not need to fight the system. We do not need to protest for our rights. We need only to remove our attention from these controlling entities and give our energy to new systems and holistic alternatives.

While it may seem at first like an impossible feat, the disposal of current governments and corporations is not all that difficult a task. The difficulty exists only in people choosing to do so and being informed enough to put into practice the methods by which this can be done. The first step and the last step are the same. Stop feeding the system with your attention. Do not vote. Do not pay taxes. Do not fight unjust and unnecessary wars. Do not join the police. Do not become a politician. Do not buy from McDonalds, Taco Bell, or other poisonous waste factories posing as restaurants. Do not buy from Walmart or other box stores. In this way, with enough people participating, the system would collapse upon itself. No force necessary. Elimination of all harmful corporations through a massive boycott is possible, and when we deliver fatal economic blows to the system, it incentivizes changes to occur more quickly than any other way. The government agents will have no power to enforce corrupt and insane policy when they have no money with which to operate.

Tearing down the FED and making it illegal or infeasible for the central banking cartel to rebuild a central bank or fractional reserve system is fundamental to this change in epoch. But it does not end there. As Sir Stamp said, if you allow the bankers to make deposits, they will simply rebuild their banking structure over time. Thus, we need to not only remove the physical structures and the current model of banking, but completely irradicate the practice of valuing mediums of exchange that serve no other purpose. There are various ways of going about doing this, but the simplest and clearest option is to eradicate money itself and become a Resource Based Economy. A shorter step would be to have local banks print money that competes in free market and extends credit to truly productive businesses, owned by the local people, and built upon a blockchain to ensure proper practices through systems that leave no room for fraud and other results of greed. To remove the bankers' ability to make deposits, we must identify the individuals who have profiteered off the suffering of the people and strip them of all assets. We then would keep account of all others who attempt to repeat this. This means that bankers would have no ability to make deposits or influence the markets.

An RBE system does not measure value by means of gold or paper held by individuals, but rather determines the total carrying capacity of the planet and offers the resources equitably based on the needs of all life on the planet, which also redirects our human population forward to a state of equanimity and balance with our natural environment. A RBE like that proposed in Jacque Frescos' "*The Venus Project*" illuminates the benefits and the absence of detriments to the creation of this type of system. It is not a matter of waiting for the general population to be ready, but rather having those who are aware of how to create this type of system being allowed by the population to lead the way forward. Allowing the open sourcing of all public information, the revitalizing and renaturalizing of the commons, the deconstruction of cancerous cities, and the building of cities that meld with and benefit the environment. It is not so far away as people may imagine when hearing about it or reading these words. It is in fact so close that the current power structure does everything it possibly can to bar the population from experiencing it and learning its true value.

Of course, in an RBE, just like in any system, something like a managerial section of the population still exists, but it is far from the models that currently hold sway over the planetary community. Rather than an oppressive system of dominance and control, a RBE system promotes and demands through its very existence the open sourcing and communal models of governance. It promotes solutions thinking and progress though cooperation. No longer would war serve to enhance an economy, but rather the most cooperative parts of society would be the most successful. The federal government of the United States and the state governments need to be dissolved to even begin this process of moving forward to a better way. The only time something even slightly resembling a central government need exist is during times of war, and the only time war is called for is when the people are directly aggressed upon and choose to work together to eliminate the threat. In that time, it would be a central authority chosen by the people to address the threat and supported by the cooperating collectives, but it would not involve a dominating authority that can remove rights from the people of the sovereign states. It would be limited to its mission of defense.

The structure of our planetary community is shifting, and we have the choice while we are here to decide what kind of world we want it to be. I choose to work to create a human society worthy of this planet's great beauty and bounty. We can begin doing that by teaching our children how to think rather than filling their minds with the textbooks and mandatory content that never leave room for creative thought. Today, there are many models that have been created to "unschool" our children and give them the means to create for themselves the world they want to live in. Unschooling is what you are doing when you question what has been told to you by the indoctrinators. It is what you are doing when you open your mind to new possibilities. It is what you are doing when you learn to think rather than be filled with information. Unschooling is a method of teaching that allows the student to lead based on their own interests rather than by indoctrination and forced curriculum. The learning follows the natural pace of the child.

We must bring about a master/apprentice model again, which teaches our children not only to actively investigate various aspects of adult life, but also encourages learning skills that will serve them and their community from a young age, instilling a sense of responsibility and capability. We must empower our children by giving them choices and challenges from an early age that they must live with. They are not helpless nor are they property of older people, whether they be parents or government agents or corporate shareholders. They are the future. We must treat them with dignity and respect and allow them the room to determine for themselves the life they will lead. If we can learn this and practice this, we will see the world change fundamentally in one generation. An ideal world includes adults listening to the wisdom of youth.

The legal system in place today is more than flawed. It is a despicable and decrepit. Today's "Laws" are composed of contradiction to natural and human law. The manipulation of natural law to suit the desires of power-hungry robber barons has created an immoral, unethical, and unjust legal system, which has bled into the mind and soul of the nation and consequently assured its own destruction.

We can create a better system today. We have the means and urgent necessity to implement holistic systems that support all humanity and all life. We need a system that reflects the greatest potential of the human condition. On the path of justice, we can first consider the natural hierarchy of life itself. We can start with our universe, which has fathered our galaxy, and from our galaxy comes our solar system, and from our sun and all its planets comes the perfect planet that we find ourselves on. This is a natural hierarchy. Without the galaxy, our sun would not be here. Without our sun we would not be here. On our planet the environment is our existence. The trees, the rivers, the oceans, and the atmosphere. All of these we must see as our first responsibility to care for and protect.

Moving forward, we must draft agreements that explicitly prevent the harm of our environment. We must acknowledge that a river is inherently more important than a single tree or a single human, as it is the source of life for multitudes. They are higher on the scale of natural hierarchy and thus require greater protections. But these protections, while coming first in order of necessity, are no different than those given to every life on the planet otherwise. Harm of another must be eradicated as an acceptable practice. We cannot expect to dredge sand from the bottom of our rivers to make concrete forever. We must understand that by doing this we are destroying ourselves and that river that provides us with life.

The river and the tree and the human must have the right to life and protection from harm as the highest agreement and value of our society. In this way we create a structure that actually supports life on this planet rather than relegating it to the bottom of our to do list. It would be common agreements that are understood by all to be fundamentally responsible for maintaining health and wellbeing for all life. There is no need for centrally mandated police or judges to enforce and oppress people. The people themselves can organize to protect what is needing protection. And a knowledgeable, mature, and well-armed population is a greater threat to violence than a mafia like the government and their stooges, the police.

In a Resource Based Economy all goods and services are available to all people without the need for means of exchange such as money, credits, barter or any other means. For this to be achieved all resources must be declared as the common heritage of all Earth's inhabitants. Equipped with the latest scientific and technological marvels mankind could reach extremely high productivity levels and create abundance of resources.

Our present culture is driven by technically incompetent politicians, scarcity-oriented economics and a system of obsolete values. In order for us to make the transition to this new, more humane society, a quantum leap in both thought and action is required. Experience tells us that human behavior can be modified, either towards constructive or destructive activity. This is our plan – directing technology and resources toward problem solving for the benefit for all people and the planet, and updating our value system to correspond with the principles of this new direction. This, combined with education on how to relate to one another in a much more meaningful way, could considerably reduce both mental and physical stress and leave us free to explore and develop our abilities. As we outgrow the need for professions such as lawyers, bankers, insurance agents, marketing and advertising personnel, salespersons, and stockbrokers, a considerable amount of waste of human ingenuity will be eliminated. Considerable amounts of energy would also be saved by eliminating the duplication of competitive products such as tools, eating utensils, pots, pans and vacuum cleaners. Only a few of the highest quality products would be needed to serve the entire population instead of hundreds of different manufacturing plants with paperwork and personnel turning out similar products. The problems we are faced with today cannot be solved politically or financially because they are highly technical in nature. There may not even be enough money available to pay for the required changes, but there are more than enough resources. This is why The Venus Project advocates a transition from a monetary-based society to the eventual realization of a global resource-based economy.

The Venus Project is an organization that proposes a feasible plan of action for social change, one that works towards a peaceful and sustainable global civilization. It outlines an alternative to strive toward where human rights are no longer paper proclamations but a way of life.

-The Venus Project[259]

We must begin implementing the principles and designs produced by The Venus Project, which we can easily do by redistributing funds from the Military Industrial Complex, Political Corruption, the Subsidization of Corporations, and by ending the Fed and producing funds though publicly owned banks, whether federally, state or cooperatively owned, and private banks in the free market as I outlined earlier, and providing the total to the research, production, and testing of The Venus Project designs, which will culminate in an evolved quality of living for all people.

One Community Global is a 100% volunteer non-profit NGO that is dedicated to the collaboration of professionals and experts in fields relating to advanced and evolved social designs and technologies to develop self-replicating solutions. We need to fund and directly support the project in its current methodology while expanding it and implementing the principles concurrently with The Venus Project designs. These must be immediately and strongly empowered so as to create a future that supports not just our survival but our abundant flourishing evolution. We must begin to look at our planet as ourselves, our neighbors as our relatives, our society as a reflection of our capacity to cooperate for our communal wellbeing.

> *"Our vision is to usher in a new age of cooperation, collaboration, and sustainability. We do this by demonstrating what's possible, open sourcing and free-sharing the blueprints, and making modular or total duplication easy enough, affordable enough, and attractive enough so that positive and sustainable world-change will spread on its own."*
> – One Community Global

By integrating the practices and models described by organizations like the Venus Project and One Community Global into our system, we can begin to extricate the toxic waste material that has been growing in the consciousness of the human being. We can begin to heal the disease, bring positive, beneficial, holistic, and practical solutions to bear upon the problems of today. Let us waste no more of our lives on those politicians, governments, corporations, banks, and other institutions of death and suffering, that have not earned them in the slightest. In fact, let us return to our own responsibility as masters of our domain. Let us think local first and work with those close to us in confident uplifting work toward our greatest communal wellbeing. That becomes simple when the learning and the tools to act are known to us. The uncensored internet and global connectivity allow for all people to interact with the totality of human knowledge and learning and for dispersed interactivity between individuals to produce solutions to local problems anywhere. Free the internet everywhere!

We the People are the only thing that has ever mattered, and We the People are the only thing that ever will. Blockchain technologies, global instant communications, ultra-light yet ultra-strong and durable materials like Aircrete, self-organizing communities, sanitation education and integration, local organic farming, and 3D printing among an immense number of other things, are available today. We are not victims of overlords, but of our own inactions. Local communities, RISE UP! Farm your lawns, eat organic, build a wind turbine and get a solar system, reduce consumption, learn to cook for yourself and store food in cellars, create a community watch and fire the municipal police, and build a dome Aircrete home instead of that unnatural, multistoried, inefficient, stick home that you will be paying off for the rest of your life. Bring technology into your locality and utilize it to create what you need locally, forgoing the internet to source things your neighbor can produce. Create community funds that support the most beneficial projects to make your local community more resilient and regenerative. This is only a dream until we all do this together.

Rebellion and Revolution, or Rebellion and Evolution

We have discussed specific reforms that can transform the systems within the government that we have today. We have discussed the history of our nation from perspectives less commonly acknowledged. We have looked at future potentials that speak to everything from minimalistic needs to prevent our self-destruction to idealistic results that all benefit from. We have spoken about economies, governments, and societies. We have discussed so far, the means to produce peaceful evolution of our planet to the benefit our species and all others. We have dedicated some time to provide discourse into less pleasant means of releasing the people of this planet from the shackles of debt slavery and manufactured scarcity. We have discussed the means by which, when all else fails, the people must rise up like lions, and take possession of their rightful inheritance, the free life upon their mother Gaia. We must speak on this absent hesitation, fear, timidity, or rashness. For we are the people, and we hold the power within our own choices. We must choose to do what is necessary at the appropriate moments. And the only moment we will ever know is NOW!

A revolt is the act of a population rising up and overturning (overthrowing, casting out, replacing) their government. Usually what will occur when the old government is thrown down, is that a new terribly similar government will come to exist. This is the effect of a revolution. Revolving around a theme, and never benefitting from the toil. We must come to know a better way. If we must rise as a people to cast down the corrupt government, ought we not do so with a plan to make a better system that serves all people? Rather than a political motive, we must have as our mission a better world for all life. We must not revolve around social designs that have been perpetuated for millennia. We must design a system by which the individual can never be subjugated again. We must recognize that many systems exist today that support that goal and we must implement them.

While there have been definitive and unquestionably serious problems in the construction of society from colonial america to the modern situation we must not identify the people of this land only by those things. We must look to the moments when humanity broke through economic or power-consolidating interests. There has existed in this society of intermingling races, religions, and paradigms, a constant voice, sometimes whispering truths to keep them alive and other times reaching into the core of the culture and illuminating that which was hidden. We can look at those who have lived and died to further the cause for universal peace, harmony, and planetary wellbeing. There have been mostly limited successes involving the implementation of social redesign to benefit all people. The reason for this has the been the immense opposition that has existed to prevent that very thing. When we are confronted by a consistent, willful, meticulously organized, empowered, clever, carefully planned and multi-generationally transmitted and enforced theory and application of social domination, it becomes very understandable that we have not succeeded in eradicating scarcity, unnecessary suffering and social conflicts that result in war..

When we consider how far we have come as a society in generating more understanding, peace, and equity for all people, we can see that there have been very meaningful strides that have brought us out of comparative darkness and ignorance. As we back away from this comparison, and look at the greater possibility, our scale becomes the absolute deprivation of all quality of life on one end and on the other end the complete fulfilment of the ideal social design that benefits all beings and life. On this scale we can see that little has changed in the last several millennia. Technology has increased and the people of the world have spread themselves into every corner with increasing populations. The way people spend their days has shifted through time. There has been slavery, religious wars and genocide, and many other atrocities of human design. There have also been uncountable righteous actions. Through all of this, there have been extraordinarily little social designs if any implemented that fully adopted the inherent rights of all people to be free of all types of unnecessary abuse.

While any sane human being understands that it is not righteous to murder or steal, uncounted souls have perished in war and have participated in the pillaging that accompanies it. What has made this possible? It is the domination and manipulation of populations that have created this possibility. To consolidate any group of people to commit to war, that group must be convinced of their own danger or perverted mentally to believe that any violence is okay as long as it is sanctioned by an authority figure. We must accept that people are not inherently good or evil but are flexible and impressionable. The more impressions put upon an individual who has not learned to think, the more they will behave just as a computer program behaves; as it was programmed to. It is systems that must change. It is the environmental factors that determine the general direction and conduct of a society. When those factors include authoritarian or plutocratic systems of government, the people are directly confronted with their own slavery, whether they are aware of this or not.

During the Revolutionary War, only a small portion of the population chose to rise up against the tyranny and mercantilist economy. Despite their small numbers and lack in leadership and equipment, they succeeded in forming a new country out of the claimed territories of a tyrannical government with huge resources and generational military leaders. These people were patriots. They were courageous enough to fight a larger opponent in territory that was hostile even before the tyrants' armies landed. The population today I challenge to even turn off their televisions for a week straight. How about a day? Those people who can not only stop inundating themselves with the institutional indoctrination, in media and schools and everywhere else, but also take active steps to do the real courageous work in forming a new reality for all of us. That work today involves learning how to defend one's family and community. It takes knowing how to grow food in your backyard. It takes forming community systems to replace state systems. It takes not paying taxes to a vampirical and anti-human tax agency, i.e., the IRS. It takes not voting or giving any attention whatsoever to the plutocracy or any other central government. By doing this as even a small group, we will find ourselves naturally forming and living within a new nation that actually represents our values.

The patriot is not the one who blindly defends the structure of oppression, but the individual who courageously stands against or simply walks away from that structure. They are the patriot, the righteous warrior, the peaceful changemaker. Peaceful until they bring violence to us that is. And if you ask any true patriot or warrior for humanity today, they will tell you of the violence that is already burdening the people of the world. A patriot investigates wrongdoing indefatigably, demanding their rights as given by nature or God, and supports their neighbor and community with their sweat, blood, and virtue. The blind follower of mandates of any kind is not a patriot but a slave. Never allowing your iron to leave your hip and never allowing your chin to fall or spine to bend in the face of oppression and villainy. Never tucking tail, turning a yellow belly, or running away from the danger. A patriot stands firm in the convictions by which their society is constructed. A true American patriot is the constitution defender, the community defender, the bastion of strength and the knight that rides into battle even when outnumbered a thousand to one. If you are a public servant, you swore to serve the people and the constitution. Don't fucking lie to us, because We the People are the majesty of humanity and when you fuck with us you wake the lion, and all the weight of the cosmos will come crashing down upon you. There is no escape from the consequence of your actions. And while the people may sleep for a while, they will not stay asleep for too long. You will reap your reward.

The great terror of our time is not some person or agency 3000 miles away, but it is within our homes, our neighborhoods, and our states. It is the same terror that has crept into the councils of all timid, disunited, and ignorant people. It is the terror that has slithered deliberately into the minds and hearts of all but the most intelligent and stout people. It is the cause of the creation of central banks, tyrannies, scarcity, war, and the general suffering of the people of the world for recorded history.

When people are comfortable, they are willing to give up freedom to secure their comfort. The more comfortable you can make people (as a government or corporation) the more freedoms they are willing to part with. What happens when you are completely dependent upon the good will and resources of your government? What happens when that government is composed of criminals and highway robbers? What happens when they not only have convinced you that you can live without working, while they send you check after check of debt-based currency, but that you are safer if you have no means to personally protect yourself from harm, and are only a decent person if you give them a "monopoly on violence?" The basic tradeoff here is your freedom to choose, to defend yourself, to raise your children, to conduct your own health, to determine what the government should do or not do, to do meaningful work, to be free of institutional theft through direct taxes, to war with other nations, to have fair trials, to support or overturn laws, to travel freely, for the comforts related to having things given to you, such as housing, unemployment, mindless jobs, food stamps, with which you can continue living in modicum comfort without any effort on your part other than the effort it took to sign up for your own slavery. The cowardice and lackadaisical behavior make those who still bear the responsibility of freedom not able to even look upon this despicable population for threat of infection. Such a danger is more sinister and objectionable than death.

It is the lack of two basic and fundamental agreements that have created all of this. The first is the agreement between people that they will not force upon others their beliefs or opinions. Without this agreement, people everywhere can have reason to escalate discourse into war. If religion never became evangelical, and it was considered a fundamental crime to attempt to force others to convert to your religion, would we not have reduced warring by half at least?

The second agreement is that all people, of all races, sexes, ages, and whatever other means of sectioning the population, have the inherent and unchallengeable right to exist by their own choices. What this means, is that a person born in a nation does not have to become chattel or feel patriotism or indebtedness to their nation. This means that individuals can choose to operate their lives as they see fit.

Let us now invite those who feel called to stand against or walk out of the system to do so. In every manner, in your own way, by any means that are suited to your situation. Take yourself out of the system. Join your brothers and sisters in the Resistance, the Renaissance, the Evolution!

Infinite Blessings to ALL of you, my Family!

NOTES

NOTES

NOTES

NOTES

NOTES

NOTES

REFERENCES

A. Casadevall et al. (2006). A Reappraisal of Humoral Immunity Based on Mechanisms of Antibody Mediated Protection Against Intracellular Pathogens. *Advances in Immunology, 91*, 1-44.

Aaron Kheriaty, M. (2021, Oct 23). *Why the CDC Ignores Natural Immunity.* Retrieved from aaronkheriaty: https://aaronkheriaty.substack.com/p/why-the-cdc-ignores-natural-immunity

ACLU. (2014). *War Comes Home: The Excessive Militarization of American Policing.* New York: ACLU. Retrieved from https://www.aclu.org/sites/default/files/assets/jus14-warcomeshome-report-web-rel1.pdf

ACLU. (2022, January 13). *ACLU.* Retrieved from SURVEILLANCE UNDER THE PATRIOT ACT: https://www.aclu.org/issues/national-security/privacy-and-surveillance/surveillance-under-patriot-act

ACLU. (2022, January 13). *FACT SHEET: MILITARY COMMISSIONS ACT.* Retrieved from ACLU: https://www.aclu.org/other/fact-sheet-military-commissions-act

Andrews, S. (2010, April). *LARRY FINK'S $12 TRILLION SHADOW.* Retrieved from Vanity Fair: https://www.vanityfair.com/news/2010/04/fink-201004

Aro, R. (2020, 11 13). *Presidents Come and Go. The Fed's Power Grows.*

Azerrad, D. (2019, 1 23). The Promises and Perils of Identity Politics.

Barkley, T. (2021, February 24). *National Defense Authorization Act (NDAA).* Retrieved from Investopedia: https://www.investopedia.com/national-defense-authorization-act-5113289

Barron's Dictionary of Banking Terms. (n.d.). *Barron's Dictionary of Banking Terms.* Retrieved from Barron's Dictionary of Banking Terms .

Bassetti, V. (n.d.). *Electoral Dysfunction.*

Bettmann, O. L. (1974). *The Good Old Days: They Were Terrible!* New York: Random House.

Black, C. (2016, January 26). Limited and Absolute War: Clausewitz and NATO Aggression – Theory and Reality.

Board, N. C. (n.d.).

Boyd, M. (2021, September 11). *Constitutional cases resulting from the 9/11 attacks.* Retrieved from Constitution Center : https://constitutioncenter.org/interactive-constitution/blog/constitutional-cases-resulting-from-the-9-11-attacks

BP. (2019). *BP Statistical Review of World Energy.* London: BP PLC. Retrieved from https://www.bp.com/content/dam/bp/business-sites/en/global/corporate/pdfs/energy-economics/

Bracken, M. (2019). *The Bracken COllection, Essays and Short Fiction 2010 to 2019.* Orange Park: Steelcutter Publishing Inc.

Brinton, C. (1952). *The Anatomy of Revolution.* Vintage Books, Inc. .

Britannica.com. (n.d.). *Britannica.com.* Retrieved from Britannica.com: https://www.britannica.com/topic/postmodernism-philosophy

Britannica.com. (n.d.). *Britannica.com.* Retrieved from Britannica.com: https://www.britannica.com/science/conditioning

Bureau of Economic Analysis . (2021, December 22). *National Income and Product Accounts.* Retrieved from bea: https://apps.bea.gov/iTable/iTable.cfm?reqid=19&step=3&isuri=1&1921=survey&1903=86

Bureau of Economic Analysis. (2010, May 27). *What is included in personal current taxes?* Retrieved from bea: https://www.bea.gov/help/faq/550#:~:text=In%20the%20national%20income%20and%20product%20accounts%20%28NIPAs%29%2C,are%20shown%20in%20NIPA%20tables%203.4%20and%203.4U.

Bureau of the Census, Department of Commerce. (1971, May 20). *Median Family Income Up in 1970 Report Number P60-78.* Bureau of the Census. Retrieved from United States Census Bureau Web Site: www.census.gov/library/pubications/1971/demo

Bystrianyk, R., & Humphries, S. (2015). *Dissolving Illusions: Disease, Vaccines, and the Forgotten History.*

Carlo, D. G. (n.d.). Dangers of the Wireless Cell Phone, Wi-Fi and EMF Age.

Citizens Association of New York. (1865). *Report of the Council of Hygiene and Public Health of the Citizens' Association of New York.*

Cooper, R. (2020). *The Unplugged Alpha .* Whitby: Richard Cooper.

Corbett, J. (n.d.). 911 in 4 min and 56 seconds.

Cornell Law School. (2022, 1 5). *Legal Information Institute*. Retrieved from Legal Information Institute: https://www.law.cornell.edu/uscode/text/16/2432

Curtin, E. (n.d.). Psychological Warfare: The CIA Then and Now: Old Wine in New Bottles. *GlobalResearch*.

DiLorenzo, T. J. (2017). The Corrupt Origins of Central Banking in America. Mises Institute.

Dr. Zalman, A., Dr. Hoffman, F., Dr. Gartzke, E., & Maj. Gen. Scales, R. (2018, November). "Of Bits, Bots, or Battalions? What 'Next-Generation Warfare Looks Like'". (B. Dr. Anders, Interviewer) Modern Warfare Institute at West Point.

Dudley, W. (2020, January 29). Former NY Fed President . (Bloomberg, Interviewer)

Encyclopaedia Britannica. (1890). *Encyclopaedia Britannica* (Vol. 24). Philadelphia.

Eric J. Segall, t. K. (n.d.). *Yes, it's time to reform the Supreme Court but not for the wrong reasons.*

etymonline. (n.d.). *etymonline*. Retrieved from etymonline: https://www.etymonline.com/word/science

Etymonline. (n.d.). *Etymonline*. Retrieved from Etymonline: https://www.etymonline.com/word/patriarchy

Ewbank, D. C., & Preston, S. H. (1990). *Personal Health Behavior and the Decline in Infant and Child Mortality: The United States 1900-1930.* Canberra: Australian National University.

Falk, R. (2015, December 18). A New Geopolitical Realism for the 21st Century.

farmaid.org. (n.d.). *FarmAid*. Retrieved from FarmAid: www.farmaid.org

Fortuna, C. (n.d.). Economic and social impact of family farms — and their loss.

Freeborn, V. (2018). *Violence Of Mind: Training and Preparation for Extreme Violence* . (L. Bechtel, Ed.) Varg Freeborn.

Frei, R. (n.d.). Rosemary Frei, MSC Molecular Biology, University of Calgary, Medical Journalist and Researcher.

Gage, R. (n.d.). Architects and Engineers For 9/11 Truth.

Gatto, J. T. (1992). *Dumbing Us Down: The Hidden Curriculum of Compulsory Schooling.* New Society Publishers.

Goldman, B. (Summer 2011). "The Bodyguard: Tapping the Immune System's Secrets," . *Stanford Medicine*.

Gordon, R. J. (2016). *THE RISE AND FALL OF AMERICAN GROWTH.* Princeton, New Jersey, USA: Princeton University Press.

Griffin, G. E. (2012, August 18). Gold & Dollar: How Money Became Worthless . (T. Delmastro, Interviewer)

Hannah Ritchie, J. H. (2013). "Terrorism". OurWorldInData.org. Retrieved from https://ourworldindata.org/terrorism

Hanus, J. (2009, Jan-Feb). Overcoming Fear Culture and Fear Itself. *Utne*.

Harmon, G. W. (1900). A Physician's Argument Against the Efficacy of Virus Innoculation. *Medical Brief: A Monthly Journal of Scientific Medicine and Surgery, 28*(1), 84.

Harvill, E. T. (2013, March 26). Cultivating Our 'Frenemies': Viewing Immunity as Microbiome Management. *Journal of the American Society for Microbiology, 4*(2), 1-3.

Hauter, W. (2012). *Foodopoly.* New York City: The New Press.

in2013dollars. (2020). *in2013dollars*. Retrieved from in2013dollars web site: www.in2013dollars.com/Electricity/price-inflation/1970

Katzoff, S. L. (1920, March). The Comulsory Vaccination Crime. *Machinists' Monthly Journal, 32*(3), 261.

Kenton, W. (2019, 6 4). *Investopedia*. Retrieved from Investopedia: www.investopedia.com/terms/p/planned_obsolescence.asp

Kilcullen, D. (2013). *Out Of The Mountains: The Coming Age Of The Urban Geurilla.* New York, New York, USA: Oxford University Press.

Klenner, F. R. (1949, July). The Treatment of Poliomyelitis and Other Virus Diseases with Vitamin C. *Southern Medicine and Surgery, 111*(7), 209-214.

Kwet, M. (2020, July 14). THE MICROSOFT POLICE STATE: MASS SURVEILLANCE, FACIAL RECOGNITION, AND THE AZURE CLOUD. *The Intercept*. Retrieved from https://theintercept.com/2020/07/14/microsoft-police-state-mass-surveillance-facial-recognition/

Lee, S. (1990). *Oil Shale Technology.* Boca Raton: CRC Press .

Lee, S. (1991). *Shale Oil Technology.* Boca Raton: CRC Press.

Linklater, A. (2013). *OWNING THE EARTH.* New York, USA: Bloomsbury.

Mar, A. d. (1895). *A History of Monetary Systems.*

Mar, A. d. (1899). *A History of Monetary Crimes.*

Mar, A. d. (1899). *The History of Money in America.*

Martino, J. P. (2010). *Resistance to Tyranny* . Joseph P. Martino.

Mauer, M. (n.d.). A 20-Year Maximum for Prison Sentences. *Democracy: A Journal Of Ideas*.

McKinlay, J. B., & McKinlay, S. M. (summer 1977). The Questionable Contribution of Medical Measures to the Decline of Mortality in the United States in the Twentieth Century. *The Milbank Memorial Fund Quarterly, Health and Society, vol. 55*(no. 3).

McMahon, B. (2020, Oct 3). How the Police Use AI to Track and Identify You. *The Gradient*. Retrieved from https://thegradient.pub/how-the-police-use-ai-to-track-and-identify-you/

Mena. (n.d.). Eugenics and Feminism. Retrieved from www.dangerouswomenproject.org

Merriam-Webster. (2020, 11 23). *Merriam-Webster Capitalism*. Retrieved from Merriam-Webster: https://www.merriam-webster.com/dictionary/capitalism

Merriam-Webster. (2020, 11 23). *Merriam-Webster Plutocracy*. Retrieved from Merriam-Webster: https://www.merriam-webster.com/dictionary/plutocracy

Merriam-Webster. (2022, 1 5). *Merriam-Webster Certificate*. Retrieved from Merriam-Webster: https://www.merriam-webster.com/dictionary/certificate

Merriam-Webster. (2022, February 20). *Merriam-Webster Coronavirus*. Retrieved from Merriam-Webster: https://www.merriam-webster.com/dictionary/coronavirus

Merriam-Webster. (2022, February 20). *Merriam-Webster Covid-19*. Retrieved from Merriam-Webster: https://www.merriam-webster.com/dictionary/COVID-19

Merriam-Webster. (2022, Feb 01). *Merriam-Webster Electromagnetic Wave*. Retrieved from Merriam-Webster: https://www.merriam-webster.com/dictionary/electromagnetic%20wave

Merriam-Webster. (n.d.). *Merriam-Webster*. Retrieved from Merriam-Webster: www.merriam-webster.com/dictionary

Merriam-Webster. (n.d.). *Merriam-Webster*. Retrieved from Merriam-Webster: https://www.merriam-webster.com/dictionary/science

Merriam-Webster. (n.d.). *Merriam-Webster Human Rights*. Retrieved from Merriam-Webster: https://www.merriam-webster.com/dictionary/human%20rights

Merriam-Webster. (n.d.). *Merriam-Webster Politically Correct*. Retrieved from Merriam-Webster: https://www.merriam-webster.com/dictionary/politically%20correct

Merriam-Webster.com. (n.d.). *Merriam-Webster.com*. Retrieved from Merriam-Webster.com: https://www.merriam-webster.com/dictionary/identity%20politics

Micu, A. (2021, January 28). The different types of electromagnetic radiation. *ZME SCIENCE*.

Millard, C. K. (1948, December 18). The End of Compulsory Vaccination. *British Medical Journal*, 1074.

Miller, D. M. (2005, February). The Role of Public Health Improvements in Health Advances: The Twentieth Century United States. *Demography, 1*, pp. 1-22.

Mitel. (2022, January 21). *The History of the Federal Communications Commission.* Retrieved from mitel: https://www.mitel.com/articles/history-federal-communications-commission-fcc

Morgan, D. C. (2018, April). MWI BH 454 VIOS Work Order #2018000987. USA.

Muphy, K. M., & Topel, R. H. (2006, October). The Value of Health and Longevity. *Journal of Political Economy, 114*(5), 871-904.

Nader, R. (n.d.). *Breaking Through Power.*

National Cancer Institute. (2020, Sep 25). *National Cancer Institute*. Retrieved from National Cancer Institute: https://www.cancer.gov/about-cancer/understanding/statistics

National Institute of Health. (n.d.). *Transverse Myelitis Fact Sheet.* Retrieved from www.ninds.nih.gov/disorders/transversemyelitis/detail_transversemyelitis.htm

New York Times. (1902, January 27). Fighting Smallpox in Boston, 125 Surgeons, Accompanied by Policemen, Vaccinated 15,000 Persons Yesterday. *New York Times.*

New York Times Archives. (1973, April 8). *The New York Times.* Retrieved from The New York TImes Web Site: www.nytimes.com/1973/04/08/archives/108-a-month-rent-was-median-in-1970

newrepublic.com. (n.d.). *New Republic*. Retrieved from New Republic.

Noble, S. (Director). (2015). *Plutocracy* [Motion Picture]. Retrieved from www.metanoia-films.org

Noble, S. (Director). (2015). *Plutocracy* [Motion Picture].

Onyekwere, A. (n.d.). *How Cash Bail Works.* Brennan Center For Justice.

opensecrets.org. (n.d.). *opensecrets.org*. Retrieved from opensecrets.org: www.opensecrets.org

Oral Hygiene. (1911). Oral Hygiene. *Oral Hygiene, 1*(1), 183-184.

Oswald, M. (Director). (2014). *Princes of the Yen: Central Bank Truth Documentary* [Motion Picture].

Peabody, S. W. (1909). Historical Study of Legislation Regarding Public Health in the State of New York. *The Journal of Infectious Diseases*(suppl. no. 4), 55-51.

Peterson, J. (2019, 3 5). Jordan Peterson on the idea of a 'Tyrannical Patriarchy'.

Pope, C. L. (1992). Adult Mortality in America before 1900: A View From Family HIstories. *Strategic Factors in Nineteenth Century American Economic Growth: A Volume to Honor Robert W. Fogel*, 267-296. Chicago, IL, USA: University of Chicago Press.

Porter, R. (1997). *The Greatest Benefit to Mankind.* New York: Harper Collins.

Robert F. Kennedy, J. (2021). *The Real Anthony Fauci.* USA: Skyhorse.

Rose, L. (2012). *The Most Dangerous Superstition.* Larken Rose.

Rout, M. (2009, April 1). "Vioxx Maker Merck and Co Drew Up Doctor Hit List," ,. Retrieved from www.theaustralian.com.au/news/drug-company-drew-up-doctor-hit-list/story-e6frg6n6-1225693586492

Ruata, C. (1899, July 22). Vaccination in Italy. *The New York Medical Journal*, 188-189.

Rudden, J. (2019, October 30). *Statista*. Retrieved from statista.com: www.statista.com/statistics/200223/median-apartment-rent-in-the-us-since-1980/

Russell, J. F. (1906, February). Report of Fifty-Five Apparent Cures of Pulmonary Tuberculosis Occurring in Working People Who Were Treated at a Dispensary Without Interruption to Their Work. p. p. 9.

Salk, J., & Salk, D. (1977, March 4). *Science*.

Sarah Flood, M. K. (2018). *IPUMS CPS: Version 6.0.* Retrieved from IPUMS: https://www.doi.org/10.18128/D030.V6.0

Sawyer, W., & Wagner , P. (2020). *Mass Incarceration: The Whole Pie 2020.*

Schippers, M. C. (2020). For the Greater Good? The Devastating Ripple Effects of the Covid-19 Crisis. *frontiers in Psychology*.

Schmid, A. P. (n.d.). The Definition of Terrorism. In *The Routledge Handbook of Terrorism Research* (p. 39).

Segall, E. J. (n.d.). Yes, it's time to reform the Supreme Court but not for the wrong reasons.

Sifferlin, A. (2017, July 25). Men's Sperm Counts are Down Worldwide: Study. *TIME*.

Sigerist, H. E. (1943). *Civilization and Disease.* New York: Cornell University Press.

Speight, D. J. (2020). *Handbook of Gasification Technology; Science, Process, and Applications.* Hoboken, New Jersey, USA: Scrivener Publishing.

Statista Research Department. (2019, June 28). *Statista*. Retrieved from www.statista.com: www.statista.com/topics/768/cost-of-living/

Steele Global . (2020, December 18). *Exploring Circular Ownership in Compliance Investigations*. Retrieved from Steele : https://steeleglobal.com/exploring-circular-ownership-in-compliance-investigations/

Stewart, G. T. (1981). "Whooping Cough in Relation to Other Childhood Infections in 1977-9 in the United Kingdom,". *Journal of Epidemiology and Community Health, vol. 35*, p. 144.

Swisher, S. (2019, September 17). *STUDENTS SPEAK: THE RIGHT TO VOTE: A CONSTITUTIONAL GUARANTEE OR PRIVILEGE?* Retrieved from The Colleges of Law: https://www.collegesoflaw.edu/blog/2019/09/17/the-right-to-vote-a-constitutional-guarantee-or-privilege/

The Editorial Board. (2020, September 10). *Edward Snowden was right, the NSA has violated our rights*. Retrieved from OC Register: https://www.ocregister.com/2020/09/10/edward-snowden-was-right-the-nsa-has-violated-our-rights/

The Spectator. (1846). "The State of Ireland,". *The Spectator, vol. 19*, pp. pp.174-175.

The Venus Project. (n.d.). *The Venus Project*. Retrieved from The Venus Project: https://www.thevenusproject.com/resource-based-economy/

The World Bank. (2020). *DataBank World Bank Indicators* . Retrieved from Databank World Bank: https://databank.worldbank.org/reports.aspx?source=2&series=NY.GNP.MKTP.CD&country=

The World Bank. (2020). *GNI (current US$)*. Retrieved from Data World Bank : https://data.worldbank.org/indicator/NY.GNP.MKTP.CD?end=2020&start=1960&type=shaded&view=chart&year=2020

TheMindFool. (2019, 11 12). *TheMindFool*. Retrieved from TheMindFool: https://themindfool.com/how-to-understand-social-conditioning/#Social_Conditioning_Definition

Thoreau, H. D. (1849). *On the Duty of Civil Disobedience* .

Titus, J. (2020). Kicking People When They're Down. USA.
Titus, J. (2020, Aug 12). The Fed's Silent Takeover of the U.S. USA.
Tsao, S.-m., Hsu, C.-c., & Yin, M.-c. (2003, October). "Garlic Extract and Two Daily Diallyl Sulphides Inhibit Methicillin-Resistant Staphylococcus Aureus Infection in BALB/Ca Mice,". *Journal of Antimicrobial Chemotherapy*, p. p. 979.
UN Department of Economic and Social Affairs. (2018). Population of Urban Agglomerations with 300,000 Inhabitants or More in 2018, by country, 1950-2035. Retrieved from https://population.un.org/wup/Download/
United States Department of Justice. (2022, 1 5). *The United States Department of Justice*. Retrieved from The United States Department of Justice: https://www.justice.gov/crt/addressing-police-misconduct-laws-enforced-department-justice
United States Government, U. A. (2014). *FM 3-24/MCWP 3-33.5 Insurgencies and Countering Insurgencies.* USA: US Army.
University of Rijeka. (n.d.). *Maritime Law.* Retrieved from University of Maritime Studies: https://www.pfri.uniri.hr/bopri/documents/02_MaritimeLaw.pdf
US Census Bureau. (2021, July 1). *U.S. and World Population Clock.* Retrieved from United States Census Bureau: https://www.census.gov/popclock/world
usaspending.gov. (2021, September 30). *USA Spending*. Retrieved from USA Spending : usaspending.gov/agency/766
Velv W. Greene, P. M. (2001, August). Personal Hygiene and Life Expectancy Improvements Since 1850: Historic and Epidemiologic Associations. *American Journal of Infection Control*, 205.
Vespa, J., Medina, L., & Armstrong, D. M. (2020). *Demographic Turning Points for the United States: Population Projections for 2020 to 2060.* US Department Of Commerce. U.S. Census Bureau.
Werner, R. (2015, January 26). On Quantitive Easing and Central Banks. (E. Ade, Interviewer)
Werner, R. (2018, February 23). Today's Source of Money Creation. Zurich, Switzerland .
Whitehead, J. W. (2015). *Battlefield America: The War On The American People.* New York: SelectBooks, Inc.
whitehouse.gov. (n.d.). *whitehouse.gov.* Retrieved from whitehouse.gov: https://www.whitehouse.gov/about-the-white-house/the-constitution/
Wimmer, E. (2006, July 20). The Test Tube Synthesis of a Chemical Called Poliovirus: The Simple Synthesis of a Vrius Has Far-Reaching Societal Implications. *special issue, European Molecular Biology Organization Resport, 7*, S3-S9.
Wintemute, G. J. (2015, March). The Epidemiology of Firearm Violence in the Twenty-First Century United States. *Annual Review of Public Health.*
Wolf, N. (2012, February 29). *The NDAA: a clear and present danger to American liberty*. Retrieved from The Guardian: https://www.theguardian.com/commentisfree/cifamerica/2012/feb/29/ndaa-danger-american-liberty
Wolfe, C. (n.d.). *101 Things to Do 'Til the Revolution.*
ycharts. (2021, Sep 30). *US Gross National Income.* Retrieved from ycharts: https://ycharts.com/indicators/us_gross_national_income

EndNotes

[1] (Brinton, 1952)
[2] (Nader)
[3] (Kilcullen, 2013)
[4] (Bracken, 2019)
[5] (Nader)
[6] (Merriam-Webster, 2020)
[7] (Merriam-Webster, 2020)
[8] (Bassetti)
[9] (Bassetti)
[10] (Nader)
[11] (opensecrets.org, n.d.)
[12] (Rose, 2012)
[13] (Segall)
[14] (Bassetti)
[15] (U.S. Census Bureau)
[16] (Sawyer & Wagner , 2020)
[17] (Mauer)
[18] (Onyekwere)
[19] (Whitehead, 2015)
[20] (Kilcullen, 2013)
[21] (ACLU, 2014)
[22] (Kwet, 2020)
[23] (Kwet, 2020)
[24] (McMahon, 2020)
[25] (Whitehead, 2015)
[26] (Whitehead, 2015)
[27] (United States Department of Justice, 2022)
[28] (Whitehead, 2015)
[29] (Freeborn, 2018)
[30] (Merriam-Webster, 2022)
[31] (Barron's Dictionary of Banking Terms)
[32] (Cornell Law School, 2022)
[33] (University of Rijeka)
[34] (Whitehead, 2015)
[35] (Nader)
[36] (Falk, 2015)
[37] (Kilcullen, 2013)
[38] (UN Department of Economic and Social Affairs, 2018)
[39] (Mar, A History of Monetary Crimes, 1899)
[40] (Mar, The History of Money in America, 1899)
[41] (Mar, A History of Monetary Systems, 1895)
[42] (Mar, A History of Monetary Systems, 1895)
[43] (Oswald, 2014)
[44] (Werner, Today's Source of Money Creation, 2018)
[45] (Werner, Today's Source of Money Creation, 2018)
[46] (Griffin, 2012)
[47] (Bureau of Economic Analysis , 2021)
[48] (Bureau of Economic Analysis, 2010)
[49] (Dudley, 2020)

[50] (Titus, The Fed's Silent Takeover of the U.S., 2020)
[51] (Titus, Kicking People When They're Down, 2020)
[52] (Werner, On Quantitive Easing and Central Banks, 2015)
[53] (US Census Bureau, 2021)
[54] (The World Bank, 2020)
[55] (The World Bank, 2020)
[56] (ycharts, 2021)
[57] (Andrews, 2010)
[58] (Steele Global , 2020)
[59] (Steele Global , 2020)
[60] (Estulin, 2005)
[61] (DiLorenzo, 2017)
[62] (DiLorenzo, 2017)
[63] (DiLorenzo, 2017)
[64] (Rose, 2012)
[65] (Mitel, 2022)
[66] (Nader)
[67] (Aro, 2020)
[68] (Board, n.d.)
[69] (Statista Research Department, 2019)
[70] (New York Times Archives, 1973)
[71] (Rudden, 2019)
[72] (Bureau of the Census, Department of Commerce, 1971)
[73] (Sarah Flood, 2018)
[74] (in2013dollars, 2020)
[75] (Dr. Zalman, Dr. Hoffman, Dr. Gartzke, & Maj. Gen. Scales, 2018)
[76] (Dr. Zalman, Dr. Hoffman, Dr. Gartzke, & Maj. Gen. Scales, 2018)
[77] (Dr. Zalman, Dr. Hoffman, Dr. Gartzke, & Maj. Gen. Scales, 2018)
[78] (Dr. Zalman, Dr. Hoffman, Dr. Gartzke, & Maj. Gen. Scales, 2018)
[79] (Kilcullen, 2013)
[80] (The Editorial Board, 2020)
[81] (usaspending.gov, 2021)
[82] (Whitehead, 2015)
[83] (Whitehead, 2015)
[84] (Black, 2016)
[85] (Schmid)
[86] (Hannah Ritchie, 2013)
[87] (Curtin)
[88] (Corbett)
[89] (ACLU, 2022)
[90] (ACLU, 2022)
[91] (Barkley, 2021)
[92] (Wolf, 2012)
[93] (Boyd, 2021)
[94] (Gage)
[95] (Linklater, 2013)
[96] (Linklater, 2013)
[97] (Linklater, 2013)
[98] (Linklater, 2013)
[99] (Linklater, 2013)
[100] (Linklater, 2013)
[101] (Linklater, 2013)

[102] (Brinton, 1952)
[103] (Brinton, 1952)
[104] (Linklater, 2013)
[105] (Linklater, 2013)
[106] (Linklater, 2013)
[107] (Linklater, 2013)
[108] (Linklater, 2013)
[109] (Linklater, 2013)
[110] (Linklater, 2013)
[111] (Linklater, 2013)
[112] (Linklater, 2013)
[113] (Thoreau, 1849)
[114] (Noble, Plutocracy, 2015)
[115] (Oral Hygiene, 1911)
[116] (Bystrianyk & Humphries, 2015)
[117] (Frei)
[118] (Bystrianyk & Humphries, 2015)
[119] (Bystrianyk & Humphries, 2015)
[120] (Bystrianyk & Humphries, 2015)
[121] (Peabody, 1909)
[122] (Encyclopaedia Britannica, 1890)
[123] (Harmon, 1900)
[124] (Ruata, 1899)
[125] (Bystrianyk & Humphries, 2015)
[126] (Katzoff, 1920)
[127] (Bystrianyk & Humphries, 2015)
[128] (Millard, 1948)
[129] (Bystrianyk & Humphries, 2015)
[130] (New York Times, 1902)
[131] (Velv W. Greene, 2001)
[132] (Bystrianyk & Humphries, 2015)
[133] (Klenner, 1949)
[134] (Gordon, 2016)
[135] (McKinlay & McKinlay, summer 1977)
[136] (Pope, 1992)
[137] (Muphy & Topel, 2006)
[138] (Gordon, 2016)
[139] (Gordon, 2016)
[140] (Gordon, 2016)
[141] (Miller, 2005)
[142] (Bettmann, 1974)
[143] (Gordon, 2016)
[144] (Bettmann, 1974)
[145] (Ewbank & Preston, 1990)
[146] (Citizens Association of New York, 1865)
[147] (Bystrianyk & Humphries, 2015)
[148] (Porter, 1997)
[149] (Bystrianyk & Humphries, 2015)
[150] (Bystrianyk & Humphries, 2015)
[151] (Harvill, 2013)
[152] (Salk & Salk, 1977)
[153] (Bystrianyk & Humphries, 2015)
[154] (Bystrianyk & Humphries, 2015)

[155] (Bystrianyk & Humphries, 2015)
[156] (Bystrianyk & Humphries, 2015)
[157] (Bystrianyk & Humphries, 2015)
[158] (Bystrianyk & Humphries, 2015)
[159] (Bystrianyk & Humphries, 2015)
[160] (Bystrianyk & Humphries, 2015)
[161] (Bystrianyk & Humphries, 2015)
[162] (Bystrianyk & Humphries, 2015)
[163] (Stewart, 1981)
[164] (Goldman, Summer 2011)
[165] (Bystrianyk & Humphries, 2015)
[166] (Rout, 2009)
[167] (Bystrianyk & Humphries, 2015)
[168] (A. Casadevall et al., 2006)
[169] (Bystrianyk & Humphries, 2015)
[170] (Bystrianyk & Humphries, 2015)
[171] (Bystrianyk & Humphries, 2015)
[172] (The Spectator, 1846)
[173] (Porter, 1997)
[174] (Bystrianyk & Humphries, 2015)
[175] (Bystrianyk & Humphries, 2015)
[176] (Tsao, Hsu, & Yin, 2003)
[177] (Bystrianyk & Humphries, 2015)
[178] (Russell, 1906)
[179] (Bystrianyk & Humphries, 2015)
[180] (Merriam-Webster, 2022)
[181] (Merriam-Webster, 2022)
[182] (Robert F. Kennedy, 2021)
[183] (Aaron Kheriaty, 2021)
[184] (Schippers, 2020)
[185] (Merriam-Webster, 2022)
[186] (Micu, 2021)
[187] (Micu, 2021)
[188] (Micu, 2021)
[189] (Micu, 2021)
[190] (Carlo)
[191] (Sifferlin, 2017)
[192] (National Cancer Institute, 2020)
[193] (Hauter, 2012)
[194] (Hauter, 2012)
[195] (farmaid.org, n.d.)
[196] (farmaid.org, n.d.)
[197] (newrepublic.com, n.d.)
[198] (Fortuna)
[199] (Merriam-Webster.com, n.d.)
[200] (Kenton, 2019)
[201] (Morgan, 2018)
[202] (Morgan, 2018)
[203] (BP, 2019)
[204] (Speight, 2020)
[205] (Nader)
[206] (BP, 2019)
[207] (Speight, 2020)

[208] (Speight, 2020)
[209] (Speight, 2020)
[210] (Speight, 2020)
[211] (Speight, 2020)
[212] (Wolfe)
[213] (Gatto, 1992)
[214] (Gatto, 1992)
[215] (Gatto, 1992)
[216] (Haramein, 2000)
[217] (Merriam-Webster.com, n.d.)
[218] (Etymonline, n.d.)
[219] (Brinton, 1952)
[220] (Britannica.com, n.d.)
[221] (TheMindFool, 2019)
[222] (Britannica.com, n.d.)
[223] (Merriam-Webster, n.d.)
[224] (Azerrad, 2019)
[225] (Merriam-Webster, n.d.)
[226] (Etymonline, n.d.)
[227] (Peterson, 2019)
[228] (Hanus, 2009)
[229] (whitehouse.gov, n.d.)
[230] (Merriam-Webster, n.d.)
[231] (Mena)
[232] (Sigerist, 1943)
[233] (Bystrianyk & Humphries, 2015)
[234] (Child Liberation Foundation, 2022)
[235] (National Center for Victims of Crime, 2022)
[236] (Cooper, 2020)
[237] (Cooper, 2020)
[238] (Cooper, 2020)
[239] (Cooper, 2020)
[240] (Cooper, 2020)
[241] (Martino, 2010)
[242] (Martino, 2010)
[243] (Martino, 2010)
[244] (Bracken, 2019)
[245] (Wintemute, 2015)
[246] (Wintemute, 2015)
[247] (Bracken, 2019)
[248] (Whitehead, 2015)
[249] (Brinton, 1952)
[250] (Brinton, 1952)
[251] (Vespa, Medina, & Armstrong, 2020)
[252] (Martino, 2010)
[253] (Martino, 2010)
[254] (Martino, 2010)
[255] (Martino, 2010)
[256] (Kilcullen, 2013)
[257] (United States Government, 2014)
[258] (Rose, 2012)
[259] (The Venus Project, n.d.)

Made in the USA
Monee, IL
05 November 2026

67808958R00179